MEASURES OF POLITICAL ATTITUDES

John P. Robinson

Jerrold G. Rusk

Kendra B. Head

Survey Research Center

Institute for Social Research

September 1968

Library of Congress Number   68-65537

PREFACE

This volume is intended as a basic empirical reference work in the social sciences. It probably will be most useful for three quite different audiences:

1) Researchers in the social sciences, especially those carrying out survey work in political science, sociology, and psychology.

2) Students taking course work in research methods who may be interested in gaining familiarity with the tools of social scientists (as well as the obvious shortcomings of these tools).

3) Non-researchers in relevant content areas, such as political analysts, journalists, and social commentators (who may be even more interested in the major limitations of the tools of empirical social scientists).

The aim of this volume has been to include a complete list of relevant empirical instruments, their actual items and scoring instructions for them, and a comprehensive assessment of their strengths and weaknesses. Also, the hope has been that this work will help the reader to make his own judgments about the state-of-the-art in social research. The advanced scholar might well conclude that the authors have been only partially successful in achieving these goals. Yet, the important thing is that these goals be stated, stressed, and followed as much as possible and, as a result, serve as orientations for future compilations of this type.

The bulk of this work was supported by grant MH-10809-02 from the United States Public Health Service. However, had it not been for the generous extra support from the Inter-university Consortium for Political Research, and especially Professor Warren Miller, this volume would not have been completed and published.

Professor Philip Converse provided the general supervision and established the guidelines for this volume. The careful reader will also note much of the orientation to various topics is drawn from the many important contributions which Professor Converse has made to attitude research.

We also wish to express our appreciation to Professor Robert Lane, who originated the idea for this book. We are especially indebted to Lois Huang and Virginia Nye for their patient typing and retyping of unreadable manuscripts. We are also grateful to Deborah Linderman, Pamela Etzcorn, William Haney, Raburn Howland, and Nancy Robinson for their editing skills, which greatly enhanced the readability of this volume (even though their suggestions were not always followed).

John P. Robinson

Jerrold G. Rusk

Kendra B. Head

August 1968

CREDITS

HERBERT ABELSON. For permission to publish the Initiative Scale, and the Attitude toward Government Scale developed by the Opinion Research Corporation.

ROBERT AGGER. For permission to publish his Political Cynicism and Personal Cynicism Measures (co-authored with Goldstein and Pearl).

GABRIEL ALMOND. For permission to publish his Subjective Political Competence Scale, and Various Other Attitudes about the Political System(co-authored with Sidney Verba).

DEBABRATA BANERJEE. For permission to publish his Attitude toward Government Scale.

CHARLES BONJEAN. For permission to publish the Table of Contents to Sociological Measurement (co-authored with Hill and McLemore).

ANGUS CAMPBELL. For permission to publish his Domestic Social Welfare Scale, Internationalism Scale, Index of Issue Familiarity, Index of Political Participation, Political Involvement Scale, Issue Involvement Scale, and Issue Partisanship Scale (co-authored with Converse, Miller, Stokes, and Gurin).

RICHARD CENTERS. For permission to publish his Conservatism-Radicalism Battery.

BJORN CHRISTIANSEN. For permission to publish his International Reactions Scale and National Patriotism Scale.

DANIEL D. DAY. For permission to publish his Attitude Toward War Scale (co-authored with Quackenbush).

LAWRENCE DOMBROSE. For permission to publish his Ideological Militancy-Pacifism Scale (co-authored with Levinson).

HANS EYSENCK. For permission to publish his Radicalism-Conservatism Scale.

LEONARD FERGUSON. For permission to publish his Nationalism Scale.

J. GETZELS. For permission to publish his Paired Direct and Projective Questionnaires (co-authored with Walsh).

HARRY GRACE. For permission to publish his International Hostility Scale.

JOHN HAER. For permission to publish his Attitude toward Sources of Power Scale.

KENNETH HAMMOND. For permission to publish his Pro-Russia Error-Choice Test.

KENNETH HELFANT. For permission to publish his Hostility in International Relations Measure.

ELMER HINCKLEY. For permission to publish his Attitude toward the Negro Measure.

M. KENT JENNINGS. For permission to publish his Cosmopolitan Scale.

FRED KERLINGER. For permission to publish his Social Attitudes Scale.

ALBERT KUBANY. For permission to publish his Attitude toward Socialized Medicine Measure.

PAUL LAZARSFELD. For permission to publish his Public Affairs Opinion Leadership Measure (co-authored with Katz) and Opinion Leadership Measure (co-authored with Berelson and Gaudet).

THEODORE LENTZ. For permission to publish his C-R Opinionaire and Personage Admiration Measure.

DANIEL LEVINSON. For permission to publish his Internationalism-Nationalism Scale.

EDGAR LITT. For permission to publish his Attitude Dimensions of Political Norms.

DANIEL LUTZKER. For permission to publish his Internationalism Scale.

HERBERT MCCLOSKY. For permission to publish his Conservatism Scale, Democratic and Anti-Democratic Attitudes, and Isolationism Scale.

DONALD MATTHEWS. For permission to publish the measures used in Negroes and the New Southern Politics (co-authored with Prothro).

DELBERT MILLER. For permission to publish the Table of Contents to his Handbook of Research Design and Social Measurement.

JAMES MORGAN. For permission to publish his Concern with Progress Scale (co-authored with Sirageldin and Baerwaldt).

STUART OSKAMP. For permission to publish his Attitude toward United States and Russian Actions Measure.

W. ROBINSON. For permission to publish his Political Participation Measure.

EVERETT ROGERS. For permission to publish his Opinion Leadership Scale.

ELMO ROPER. For permission to publish his Political Activity Index (co-authored with Woodward).

DONALD SAMPSON. For permission to publish his World-Minded Attitudes Measure (co-authored with Smith).

M.A. SANAR. For permission to publish his Politico-Economic Radicalism-Conservatism Scale (co-authored with Pickard).

ROSALEA SCHONBAR. For permission to publish her Attitude toward Communists Measure.

ROBERT SCHULTZE. For permission to publish his Acquaintanceship Scale.

HOWARD SCHUMAN. For permission to publish his Prejudice and Rationality, and Identification with the Underdog Measures (co-authored with Harding).

WILLIAM SCOTT. For permission to publish his Policy Goals and Personal Values Measure.

GERTRUDE SELZNICK. For permission to publish her Ideological Agreement with Goldwater Measure (co-authored with Steinberg).

MARVIN SHAW. For permission to publish the Table of Contents to Scales for the Measurement of Attitudes (co-authored with Jack Wright).

PAUL SHEATSLEY. For permission to publish his Pro-Integration Scale.

BENJAMIN SHIMBERG. For permission to publish his Attitude toward World Affairs Measure.

ROSS STAGNER. For permission to publish his Nationalistic Attitude Changes Measure (co-authored with Osgood) and Attitude toward War Measure.

SAMUEL STOUFFER. For permission from Doubleday Publishing Company to print Stouffer's Willingness to Tolerate Nonconformists Scale and Perception of the Internal Communist Danger Measure.

JOHN WRIGHT. For permission to publish his Liberalism-Conservatism Scale (co-authored with Hicks).

LAWRENCE WRIGHTSMAN. For permission to publish his Dimensional Attitudes toward Negroes Measure and Interpretations of Government Policy Scale.

We were unable to locate or receive any reply from the following scale authors.

THEODOR ADORNO. For his Political-Economic Conservatism Scale and his Ethnocentrism Scale.

EMORY BOGARDUS. For his Social Distance Scale.

WILLIAM DOBRINER. For his Local-Cosmopolitan Scale.

THOMAS R. DYE. For his Local Cosmopolitan Scale.

G. HARTMANN. For his Liberalism-Conservatism Scale.

GWYNN NETTLER. For her Radicalism-Conservatism Scale.

LOIS NOBLE. For her Attitude toward Civil Liberties Measure.

SNELL PUTNEY. For his Attitude toward War Measure.

MORRIS ROSENBERG. For his Business-Minded and Socialism Planning Scale.

SIDNEY VERBA. For his Vietnam Policy Scale.

FRANK R. WESTIE. For his Prejudice toward Negroes Measure.

TABLE OF CONTENTS

Page

PREFACE   i

CREDITS   iii

CHAPTER

1. INTRODUCTION

    Background 1
    Contents of This Volume 3
    Evaluative Criteria 7

2. PUBLIC REACTION TO GOVERNMENT POLICIES (Alfred Hero)   23

    I.   Some General Trends
         Issues: Knowledge and Interest 24
         Attitudes on War 25
         Relations with the Communist World 28
         National Defense and Arms Control 29
         Foreign Aid and World Trade 31
         Civil Rights 33
         Economic and Welfare Issues 33
         Liberalism and Conservatism 35

    II. Some Comparative Trends
         Educational Groups 38
         Socio-Economic Status and Community of Residence 46
         Age 50
         Sex 52
         Religion 54
         Ethnic and Racial Groups 63
         Geographic Region 68
         Voting Behavior and Partisan Affiliation 73

3. LIBERALISM-CONSERVATISM   79

    1. Ideological Agreement with Goldwater (Selznick and Steinberg
        1966) 91
    2. Conservatism Scale (McClosky 1958) 94
    3. Social Attitudes Scales (Kerlinger 1963) 98
    4. Conservatism-Radicalism Battery (Centers 1949) 102
    5. Political-Economic Conservatism (PEC) Scale (Adorno et al.
        1950) 105
    6. Inventory of Social Attitudes (Eysenck 1947) 113
    7. Radicalism-Conservatism Scale (Nettler and Huffman 1957) . . . 116
    8. Liberalism-Conservatism Scale (Wright and Hicks 1966) 119
    9. Liberalism-Conservatism Scale (Kerr 1952) 123
    10. Liberalism-Conservatism Scale (Hartmann 1938) 126

Chapter 3 (continued)

11. C-R Opinionaire (Lentz 1935) 134
12. Personage Admiration (Lentz 1939) 141
13. Situation-Response Survey (Pace 1939) 142
14. Harper's Social Beliefs and Attitudes Test (Boldt and Stroud 1934) 145
15. Politico-Economic Radicalism-Conservatism (Sanai and Pickard 1949) 148
16. Radicalism-Conservatism and Social Mobility (Hetzler 1954) . . 151
17. Concern with Progress (Morgan, Sirageldin, and Baerwaldt 1966). 154

4. DEMOCRATIC PRINCIPLES   161

1. Willingness to Tolerate Nonconformists (Stouffer 1955) 163
2. Scale of Perception of Internal Communist Danger (Stouffer 1955) 167
3. Democratic and Anti-Democratic Attitudes (McClosky 1964) . . . 170
4. Attitude toward Democratic Principles (Prothro and Grigg 1960). 179
5. Attitude toward Communists (Schonbar 1949) 182
6. Attitude toward Civil Liberties (Noble and Noble 1954) 184

5. DOMESTIC GOVERNMENT POLICIES   187

1. Domestic Social Welfare Scale (Campbell et al. 1960). 191
2. Attitude toward Government (Opinion Research Corporation 1960). 193
3. Big Business-Minded Scale and Socialism-Planning Scale (Rosenberg 1957) 198
4. Attitude toward Socialized Medicine (Kubany 1953) 200
5. Attitude toward Government (Banerjee 1962) 202

6. RACIAL AND ETHNIC ATTITUDES   203

1. Prejudice and Rationality (Schuman and Harding 1964) 210
2. Identification with the Underdog (Schuman and Harding 1963) . . 223
3. Pro-Integration Scale (Sheatsley 1966) 236
4. Multifactor Racial Attitude Inventory (Woodmansee and Cook 1967) 240
5. Social Distance Scale (Bogardus 1959) 242
6. Ethnocentrism Scale (Adorno et al. 1950) 245
7. Racial Stereotype Index (Matthews and Prothro 1966) 258
8. Racial Identification Index (Matthews and Prothro 1966) 260
9. Community Race Relations Ratings (Matthews and Prothro 1966). . 262
10. Dimensional Attitude Measure toward Negroes (Wrightsman 1962) . 265
11. Prejudice toward Negroes (Westie 1953) 267
12. Paired Direct and Projective Questionnaires (Getzels and Walsh 1958) 270
13. Attitude toward the Negro (Hinckley 1932) 277

7. INTERNATIONAL AFFAIRS   279

    1. Foreign Policy Goals and Personal Values (Scott 1960) 287
    2. Isolationism Scale (McClosky 1967) 293
    3. Internationalism Scale (Campbell et al. 1960) 296
    4. Interpretations of Government Policy Scale (Wrightsman 1963) . 298
    5. World-Minded Attitudes (Sampson and Smith 1957) 302
    6. Internationalism-Nationalism Scale (Levinson 1951) 306
    7. Attitude toward United States and Russian Actions (Oskamp and
        Hartry 1965) 309
    8. Problems and Goals of the U.S. Government (Hefner and Robinson
        1964) 315
    9. Criteria for Foreign Aid (Hefner and Robinson 1964) 317
    10. Internationalism (Lutzker 1960) 321
    11. Attitudes toward World Affairs (Shimberg 1949) 326
    12. Pro-Russia Error-Choice Test (Hammond 1948) 329

8. HOSTILITY-RELATED NATIONAL ATTITUDES   331

    1. International Reactions Scale (Christiansen 1959) 339
    2. National Patriotism Scale (Christiansen 1959) 351
    3. International Hostility Inventory (Grace 1949) 353
    4. Attitudes toward War (Putney 1962) 360
    5. Vietnam Policy Scales (Verba et al. 1967) 366
    6. Ideological Militancy-Pacifism Scale (Dombrose and Levinson
        1950) 370
    7. Hostility in International Relations (Helfant 1952) 374
    8. Nationalism (Ferguson 1942) 377
    9. Nationalistic Attitude Changes (Stagner and Osgood 1946) . . . 380
    10. Attitude toward War (Day and Quackenbush 1942) 383
    11. Attitude toward War (Stagner 1942) 385

9. COMMUNITY-BASED POLITICAL ATTITUDES   389

    1. Community Attitude Scale (Bosworth 1954) 392
    2. Local-Cosmopolitan Scale (Dye 1966) 397
    3. Cosmopolitanism Scale (Jennings 1965) 400
    4. Localism-Cosmopolitanism Scale (Dobriner 1958) 403
    5. Acquaintanceship Scale (Schultze 1961) 406
    6. Attitude toward Sources of Power (Haer 1956) 408

10. POLITICAL INFORMATION   411

    1. Political Information Scale (Matthews and Prothro 1966) 413
    2. Information about Foreign Countries (Robinson 1967) 415
    3. Information about the Far East (Robinson 1967) 417
    4. Index of Issue Familiarity (Campbell et al. 1960) 419

11. POLITICAL PARTICIPATION   423

    1. Political Participation Scale (Matthews and Prothro 1966) . . . 427
    2. Political Activity Index (Woodward and Roper 1950) 431
    3. Index of Political Participation (Campbell et al. 1954) 433
    4. Political Participation (Robinson 1952) 434

Chapter 11 (continued)

    5.   Public Affairs Opinion Leadership (Katz and Lazarsfeld 1955). . 436
    6.   Opinion Leadership (Lazarsfeld, Berelson, and Gaudet 1944) . . 438
    7.   Opinion Leadership Scale (Rogers 1962) 439

12. ATTITUDES TOWARD THE POLITICAL PROCESS   441

    1.   Subjective Political Competence Scale (Almond and Verba 1963) . 446
    2.   Various Other Attitudes about the Political System (Almond
        and Verba 1963) 448
    3.   Index of Ratio of Support (McClosky et al. 1960) 453
    4.   Political Involvement (Campbell et al. 1960). 456
    5.   Political Efficacy (Campbell et al. 1954) 459
    6.   Sense of Citizen Duty (Campbell et al. 1954) 461
    7.   Extent of Issue Orientation (Campbell et al. 1954). 463
    8.   Issue Involvement (Campbell et al. 1954) 465
    9.   Issue Partisanship (Campbell et al. 1954) 467
   10. Overall Index of Psychological Readiness for Participation
        (Matthews and Prothro 1966) 468
   11. Sense of Civic Competence Index (Matthews and Prothro 1966) . . 471
   12. Party Image Score (Matthews and Prothro 1966) 473
   13. Attitude Dimensions of Political Norms (Litt 1963). 475
   14. Political Cynicism and Personal Cynicism (Agger, Goldstein,
        and Pearl 1961) 479

13. INDIVIDUAL QUESTIONS FROM SURVEY RESEARCH CENTER ELECTION STUDIES   483

    1.   Party Identification 495
    2.   Attitudes toward Government Principles 498
    3.   Domestic Policy 511
    4.   Civil Rights and Racial Attitudes 535
    5.   International Attitudes 560
    6.   War-Related Attitudes 576
    7.   Political Activity 591
    8.   Attitudes toward the Political Systems 626
    9.   Personality Variables 649

14. CONTENTS OF APPENDICES TO THIS VOLUME   671

    Table of Contents of Appendix A 673
    Table of Contents of Appendix B 677

15. CONTENTS OF RELATED VOLUMES   679

    Bonjean, Hill, and McLemore's Sociological Measurement 682
    Shaw and Wright's Scales for the Measurement of Attitudes . . . 685
    Miller's Handbook of Research Design and Social Measurement . . 694

INDEX OF NAMES   697

CHAPTER 1. INTRODUCTION

Background

The inspiration for this handbook comes from the pioneer efforts of Professor Robert Lane, a political scientist at Yale University. Professor Lane was disturbed, as many social scientists still are today, at the proliferation of empirical instruments in fields related to his area of interest. In the summer of 1958, he attempted to pull together those scales that would be of value to researchers in the field of political behavior, whose interests range from personality characteristics (e.g., neuroticism, authoritarianism) to occupational background (e.g., job satisfaction or status) to political attitudes (e.g., internationalism, conservatism). While Professor Lane was able initially to interest the National Institutes of Health to continue this research, previous commitments on his time prevented him from pursuing it further. Subsequently, the availability of personnel at the Survey Research Center ensured that this valuable work would be continued under the general supervision of Professor Philip Converse.

There exist, of course, many cogent reasons for such an undertaking. Empirical instruments are likely to appear under surprising book titles, in any one of 15 social science journals (and may appear in 20 others), in seldom circulated dissertations, from commercial publishers, as well as in the long undisturbed piles of manuscripts in the offices of social scientists. Surely this grapevine of information is inefficient for the interested researcher. One must stay in the same area of interest on a continuing basis for several years (and not enough social scientists can) to become aware of the empirical literature and instruments available. Often, the interdisciplinary investigator is interested in the relation of some variable, which he has heard of only casually, to his favorite area of interest. His job of combing the literature to pick a proper instrument consumes needlessly long hours that often ends only in a frustrating decision to forego measuring this or that characteristic. Worse still, he may resort to devising his own measure rapidly and adding to the already burdensome number of inadequately conceived instruments. In our search through the literature we found an unfortunate amount of replication of previous discoveries as well as an unawareness of related (and often better) research done in the same area.

Our searching procedure took us back through the earliest issues of Psychological Abstracts as well as the printed history through 1966 of the most likely periodical sources of psychological instruments (Journal of Abnormal and Social Psychology, Journal of Social Psychology, and the Journal of Applied Psychology) and sociological or political measures (Sociometry, American Sociological Review, Public Opinion Quarterly, and the American Political Science Review). Doctoral dissertations were combed by examining back issues of Dissertation Abstracts and we are grateful to University Micro-films of Ann Arbor for providing us with pertinent dissertations. Still, not all universities belong to this service; Harvard notably is not a member. Dissertation Abstracts is also relatively recent. Contact with the large variety of empirical research being done at the University of Michigan opened new leads and widened our search, as did conversations with expert researchers we were able to contact at the 1965 and 1966 annual meetings of the American Sociological Association and the American Psychological Association. These meetings also served to bring a number of other empirical instruments to our attention.

Our focus in the project has been in compiling attitude _scales_ (that is, series of items that are homogeneous in content) that are useful in a survey research rather than a laboratory setting. We have not attempted the gigantic and perhaps hopeless task of compiling single attitude items, except those that have been used in the Survey Research Center election studies (see Chapter 13). Many of these isolated items do tap important variables for purposes of analysis, but a complete compilation of them was beyond the scope of our project. In the following chapter, Alfred Hero has provided insight into some important trends in single attitude questions asked in national opinion polls.

There is one further body of attitude literature that we have chosen to ignore--that centered around the application of Osgood's _Semantic Differential_. An exhaustive bibliography of research applications of this technique, both in political and other areas, is given in Snider and Osgood (1968).

Although we attempted to be as thorough as possible in our searching procedure, we can make no claim that this volume contains every scale pertaining to our chapter headings. We do feel however that we have brought attention to the vast majority of higher-quality instruments available.

Contents of This Volume

A brief outline of the contents of the 15 chapters of this handbook may prove helpful to the reader. The remainder of this introductory chapter touches on the background of this project and lays out in brief detail the major criteria for scale construction which we have used in evaluating the 95 scales reviewed in this volume. These evaluative criteria fall into three groups:

1) Item construction criteria (sampling of relevant content, wording of items, and performing item analyses)

2) Response set criteria (controlling the spurious effects of acquiescence and social desirability on responses to items)

3) Psychometric criteria (representative sampling, presentation of proper normative data, test-retest reliability, item homogeneity, discrimination of known groups, cross-validation, and further statistical procedures).

Of course, to meet any one of these criteria does not alone determine the value of a scale. For example, one can construct a scale with high item homogeneity merely by including items which express the same idea in a number of different ways; again, one can ensure significant discrimination of known groups merely by sampling two groups so divergent that they would be unlikely to agree about any issue. For this reason, we recommend that the choice of a scale from this volume be placed as much as possible within a decision-theoretic framework, such as that outlined in Cronbach and Gleser (1965).

The second chapter contains a historical summary of public opinion on various domestic and international oriented political issues. This compilation of opinion poll and survey research materials was undertaken by Alfred Hero of the World Peace Foundation. Hero examines these materials in two ways--first, to ascertain the distribution of attitude patterns on these issues across time and, second, to discern the types of people who take differing stands on these issues over the last three decades. Among various types of people, especially as differentiated on socio-economic characteristics, there does seem to be differing support levels evidenced as well as differing amounts of information possessed on these issues. In essence, Chapter 2 is the first and only presentation of opinion data in a historical context from the first years of survey research to the present.

From this chapter we proceed to the ten chapters dealing with actual attitude scales. In Chapter 3, we first consider 15 scales dealing with the most frequently discussed political variable: liberalism-conservatism. Survey Research Center studies have found the variable to be considerably less useful in predicting mass political behavior than would be suggested in the literature from which the scales in Chapter 3 are derived. Most of the items in these scales are either too dated or too sophisticated to be applied currently to cross-section populations. We conclude this chapter with two scales treating more generalized orientations toward change; these measures, labelled "concern with progress" and "initiation," may be more realistic indices of orientations toward change in cross-section populations.

Chapter 4 contains measures of attitudes toward various principles of civil liberties, both with regard to general attitudes on the subject (e.g., toward statements contained in the Bill of Rights) and to specific attitudes as well (e.g., toward the exercise of these rights by particular groups such as communists or non-conformists). The reader may or may not be surprised to learn that general attitudes and specific attitudes in this area are often inconsistent and contradictory.

Chapters 5 and 6 refer to scales on domestic governmental policy. The center of concern in Chapter 5 is on those areas of governmental intervention in the economy, such as socialized medicine, ownership of utilities, and guaranteed employment. Chapter 6 is devoted to the area of race relations and racial attitudes which at the time of this writing comprised the nation's most pressing domestic problem. Even if the reader is not interested in the problem itself, we recommend that he examine the first two scales (by Schuman and Harding) in the chapter as examples of well constructed and methodologically sophisticated measuring instruments.

Chapters 7 and 8 are concerned with international affairs. The scales in the first of these two chapters deal with the more general attitudes in the area, such as the measurement of isolationism or the tapping of attitudes toward specific goals in foreign policy. Chapter 8 contains measures referring more directly to the idea of conflict or violence. Measuring instruments on hostility, nationalism, and militarism are included. Scott's <u>Foreign Policy Goals</u> scale in Chapter 7 and Christiansen's <u>International Reactions</u> scale in Chapter 8 are two examples of well-constructed instruments in the area of international relations.

Chapter 9 lists only six attitude scales relevant to studies of community politics. This is a disappointing commentary on the state of research in this area. Perhaps some measures either have eluded our search efforts or will be developed soon. The scales that are available deal with identifying the local power structure or designating community leaders and average citizens as either "local" or "cosmopolitan" in their orientation toward political affairs.

Chapters 10 and 11 depart somewhat from the attitudinal focus of this volume, but are concerned with such important variables--those of political information and participation--that it was deemed appropriate to include them. Research on the "political information" the electorate possesses has been rudimentary and piecemeal at best, but the results that have been obtained are startling enough to isolate "information" as a most fruitful variable for further research. The researcher may be surprised to find that few individuals in cross-section populations possess even the most elementary pieces of political information. He might also be surprised at their low levels of political participation, indices of which are given in Chapter 11. Also included in this chapter are measures of another variable that needs more research attention--opinion leadership.

In Chapter 12, a variety of measures of attitudes toward aspects of the political process are presented. Included in this category are instruments on political competence, political efficacy, political involvement, political cynicism, and sense of civic duty. These different measures have been applied in a variety of survey research contexts, from cross-national studies to studies in a single community.

Chapter 13 presents an extensive, if not exhaustive, listing of attitude questions asked in Survey Research Center election studies since 1952. These questions are grouped into one of nine sections, seven of which are analogous to titles of Chapter 3 through 12 (liberalism-conservatism, community attitudes, and information being the three categories omitted in Chapter 13). The two areas unique to Chapter 13 are party identification and personality. Each section contains the questions asked in one of these areas, the responses of the electorate to these questions, the correlations of these questions with each other, and the correlations of these questions with background variables (such as sex, age, education, etc.). The intercorrelations of many of these attitude variables with each other for the 1964 election study are presented in the introduction to Chapter 13.

Chapters 14 and 15 contain tables of contents for related works. Chapter 14 outlines the contents of Appendix A (Measures of Occupational Attitudes and Occupational Characteristics) and Appendix B (Measures of Personality) to the present volume, and Chapter 15 traces the contents of three similar compendia of measures produced by independent authors.

Evaluative Criteria

We have felt that there was more to our mission than a mere listing of the wide variety of potential instruments available. Likewise, our predecessors in this field (see the reviews of Miller, 1964, Shaw and Wright, 1967, and Bonjean, Hill, and McLemore, 1967, in Chapter 15) have taken care to include useful statistical data in their scale presentations. However, it is one thing to present statistical data and another thing to know what they mean. The casual reader or part-time researcher may find it difficult to interpret such statistical data when different authors use different statistical procedures. Thus, few researchers seem to know that a Guttman Reproducibility Coefficient of .91 may be equivalent to an inter-item correlation coefficient of .30, or that a test-retest reliability correlation of .50 may indicate higher reliability than a split-half reliability of .80. Nor are scale authors often disposed to point out the limitations of their instruments when they are writing articles for publication. Thus, many authors fail to alert the reader to the fact that they have used restricted samples, not guarded against response set, written items that were too complicated for most people to understand, failed to item analyze their scales before further analysis, or simply not covered adequately the totality of behaviors and attitudes relevant to the problem at hand. We have taken it upon ourselves, where possible, to make such liabilities clearly visible to the reader.

In addition, we have made some attempt to order the instruments in each section of this volume according to their probable future research utility and to their ability to meet certain desirable standards. Because scale write-ups were handled by a number of reviewers, however, the careful reader will notice some irregularities in the type and extent of critical comments made on each separate instrument. If there is a demand for further handbooks, we hope that this factor can be controlled in the future by collecting separate reviews, especially by skilled researchers in each area.

For now, where the experienced researcher may not agree with our assessments, he is free to supplement them with his own. But we hope he will be aware of a number of considerations that he must keep in mind, not only when deciding on which instrument to use, but also when evaluating his own scale(s). We trust that our assessment of each scale will not sway the less discriminating reader into making a choice more biased than he would have made anyway. Where possible we have tried to be fair, honest, consistent, and not overly demanding in our evaluations, and have tried to highlight the merits as well as the limitations of each instrument. As noted earlier, our evaluations are aimed more at the survey researcher than the laboratory experimenter. The evaluative criteria which we have chosen are listed in the order which may represent the ideal, but not absolute, chronological sequence in which attitude instruments should be constructed.

The first step for the scale builder, and the first criterion on which his work can be evaluated, is writing or finding items to include in the scale. It is usually assumed that the scale builder knows enough about the field to construct an instrument that will cover an important theoretical construct well enough to be useful to other researchers in the field. If it covers a construct for which instruments are already available, the author should demonstrate sound improvements over previous measures. There are three further preliminary considerations which represent the minimum that an adequately constructed scale ought to possess. These are:

> Proper Sampling of Content: Proper sampling is not easy to achieve, nor can exact rules be specified for ensuring that it is done properly (as critics of Guttman's phrase "universe of content" have been quick to point out). Nevertheless, there is little doubt of the critical nature of the sampling procedure in scale construction. Future research may better reveal the population of behaviors, objects, and feelings which ought to be covered in any attitude area, but some examples may suggest ways in which the interested researcher can provide better coverage in designing scales. Investigators of

the "authoritarian personality" lifted key sentiments expressed in small group conversations, personal interviews, and written remarks and transformed them into scale items; some of these items in fact consisted of direct verbatim quotations from such materials. In the job satisfaction area (covered in handbook Appendix A), we gave detailed consideration to the analysis from representative samples of responses to open-ended questions which ask the respondent, "What things do you like best (or don't you like) about your job?" We feel that these responses offer invaluable guidelines to the researcher both as to the universe of factors he should be covering and the probable weight that should be given to each factor. Other instruments in the job satisfaction area were built either on the basis of previous factor analytic work, or on responses to questions about critically satisfying or dissatisfying situations at work, or on both of these.

Difficult decisions remain to be made about the number of questions needed to cover each factor (probably a minimum of two in any lengthy instrument) but the important first step is to make sure that the waterfront has been covered.

Simplicity of Item Wording: One of the great advantages of securing verbatim comments from group discussions or open-ended questions (as people in advertising have apparently discovered) is that such attitudes are couched in language easily comprehended and recognized by respondents. One of the most obvious advantages of more recently constructed scales is that item wording has become far less stuffy, lofty, or idealistic. Even today, however, survey researchers still must adapt items developed from college samples for use on heterogeneous populations.[1]

There are other item wording practices that are, thankfully, going out of style as well: double-barrelled items which contain so many attitudes that it is hard to tell why the person agrees or disagrees with it (e.g., "The government should provide low-cost medical care because too many people are in poor health and doctors charge so much money"); items which are so vague they mean all things to all people ("Everybody should receive adequate medical care"); or items which depend on knowledge of little-known facts ("The government should provide for no more medical care than that implied in the Constitution"). Other considerations about writing items, such as negative vs. positive wording, will be covered under our discussion of response set.

Item Analysis: While item wording is something the investigator can manipulate to ensure coverage of attitudinal areas, there is no guarantee that respondents will reply to the items in the manner intended by the investigator. Item analysis is one of the most effi- cient methods whereby the investigator can check whether people are

---

[1] The process is often referred to as "farmerization," i.e., making items intelligible to the less sophisticated.

responding to the items in the manner intended. We have encountered too many instances in the literature where authors inadvertently assume that their a priori division of scale items corresponds to the way their respondents perceive these items.

There have been many methods of item analysis proposed, and, in fact, complex multidimensional analyses (described below under homogeneity, in our detailing of statistical procedures) can be seen as the ultimate item analytic procedure. The researcher need not go so far as factor analyzing his data to select items to be included or discarded, but an item intercorrelation matrix (on perhaps a small subsample or pretest sample) is certainly the most convenient basis of doing item analysis. If it is hypothesized that five items in a large battery of items (say those numbered 1, 2, 6, 12, and 17) comprise a scale of authoritarianism, then the majority of the ten inter-item correlations between these five items should be substantial. At the minimum they should be significant at the .05 level. While this minimum may seem liberal, it is in keeping with the degree to which items in the most reputable scales intercorrelate for heterogeneous populations (see Chapter 13). If items 1, 2, 12, and 17 intercorrelate substantially with each other but 6 does not correlate well with any of them, then item 6 should be discarded or rewritten.

Measuring the degree to which each of the five items correlates with some external criterion is a further valuable device for the selection of items. This is usually referred to as the item-validity method.

We learned one valuable lesson about writing items from a certain item analysis we performed. A previous study had uncovered four dimensions of value--authoritarianism, expression, individualism, and equalitarianism--and we wished to incorporate measures of these factors into a study of political attitudes. One individualism item--"It is the man who starts off bravely on his own who excites our admiration"--seemed in particular need of farmerization. Accordingly, the item was reworded, "We should all admire a man who starts out bravely on his own." Item analysis revealed this revised statement to be more closely associated with authoritarian items than with the other individualism items. It became clear that a seemingly logical wording change can unexpectedly alter the entire implication of an item.

Often a researcher does not have the benefit of pre-test groups in order to eliminate or revise unsatisfactory items. In such a case, the item-analysis phase of scale construction should be incorporated into the determination of the dimensionality, scalability, or homogeneity of the test items. This will ensure that there is empirical as well as theoretical rationale for combining the information contained in various items.

The second large area of evaluation is the concern that the scale builder has given to the avoidance of "response set" in the items. Response set refers to a tendency on the part of individuals to respond to attitude statements for reasons other than the content of the statements. Thus, a person who might want to appear agreeable and thus fail to disagree with any attitude statement is said to show an "agreement response set." Only through experience and by constant revision can the researcher insulate his scale from this potentially dangerous side effect. As a basic guard against response set, the researcher should try to make the scale as interesting and pleasant for the respondent as possible. If the respondent finds the instrument to be dull or unpleasant,there is a greater chance that he will try to speed through it as quickly as possible. It is in such a setting that the scale is most liable to response set contamination, such as indiscriminate agreement or checking off in a certain column.

There are two main sources of response set that are most difficult to control:

Acquiescence: Most of us have seen (or perhaps been) people whose attitudes change in accord with the situation. Such people are said to "acquiesce" in the presence of opposition from others. In the same way, some people are "yea-sayers," willing to go along with anything that sounds good, while others (perhaps optimists) are unwilling to look at the bad side of anything. These dispositions are thus reflected in people's responses to attitude questions. How then is it possible to separate their "real" attitudes from their personality dispositions?[2]

There are various levels of attack, all of which involve forsaking simple affirmative item format. The first involves at least an occasional switching of response alternatives between positive and negative. For simple "yes-no" alternatives, a few "no-yes" options should be inserted. Similarly, for the "strongly agree-agree-uncertain-disagree-strongly disagree" or Likert format, the five alternatives occasionally should be listed in the opposite order. This practice will offer some possibility of locating people who choose alternatives on the sole basis of the order in which they appear. It may also alert an overly casual respondent to think more about his answers.

---

[2] Rorer (1965) points out many relevant objections to attempting separation of the acquiescent response set from item content.

It is more difficult to vary the item wording from positive
to negative, as those who have tried to reverse authoritarianism
items have found. A logician can argue that the obverse of
"Obedience is an important thing for children to learn" is not
"Disobedience is an important thing for children to learn," and
the investigator is on shaky ground in assuming that a respondent
who agrees with both the first statement and the second is completely confused. Along the same line, the practice of inserting
a single word in order to reverse an item can produce some pretty
silly-sounding items, while changing one word in an unusual context
has produced items in which the ordinary respondent will not notice
a change. In sum, writing item reversals requires sensitivity.
The interested researcher would be well advised to check previous
competent work on the subject (Christie et al., 1958) before
undertaking such a task. However, the literature is still ambiguous as to the real value of item reversals (e.g., Wrightsman,
1966).

A third and more difficult, yet probably more effective,
approach concerns the construction of "forced-choice" items. Here
two (or more) replies to a question are listed and the respondent
is told to choose only one: "The most important thing for children
to learn is (obedience) (independence)." Equating the popularity
or "social desirability" of each alternative requires even more
intensive effort for both the scale constructor and the respondent.
Since the factor of social desirability is an important response set
variable in its own right, we give it individual attention next.

Social Desirability: In contrast to the theory that the
acquiescent person reveals a certain desire for subservience in
his willingness to go along with anything, Edwards (1957) has
proposed more positively that these people are just trying to
make a good impression. As yet research has been unable to determine clearly whether the overly high incidence of positive
correlation among questionnaire items is ultimately due more to
bias from acquiescence or to social desirability (Christie and
Lindauer, 1963). The methods of lessening social desirability
bias, in any event, usually involve the use of forced-choice items
in which the alternatives have been equated on the basis of social
desirability ratings. In more refined instruments, the items are
pretested on social desirability, and alternative-pairings (or
item-pairings) which do not prove to be equated are dropped or
revised.

One further method consists of using the respondent's score
on the Crowne-Marlowe social desirability scale as a correction
factor. Smith (1967) gives an explicit example of the mechanics
of this approach.

We have mentioned the major sources of response set contamination but
there are others of which the investigator should remain aware. One of the
more prevalent sources of contamination is the faking of responses according

to some preconceived image that the respondent wants to convey. On a job
satisfaction scale, for example, the respondent may try to avoid saying anything that might put his supervisor in a bad light or might involve a change
in work procedures. College students may be aware of a professor's hypothesized
relationship between two variables and try to answer so as to make this prediction work out or fail. Other undesirable variations of spurious response
patterns that the investigator might want to minimize can result from the
respondent's wanting (a) to appear too consistent, (b) to use few or many
categories in his replies, or (c) to choose extreme alternatives.

The third and final area of evaluation for each instrument is the various
statistical and psychometric procedures incorporated into its construction.
While each of these statistical considerations--sampling, norms, reliability,
homogeneity, and validation--is important, an inadequate performance on any
one of them does not render the scale worthless. Nevertheless, inadequate
concern with most of them certainly does indicate that the scale should be used
with reservation. Fortunately, scale constructors in the past few years appear
to have paid more heed to these considerations than did the vast majority of
their predecessors. Still, even today few scales rate optimally on all these
factors. It is very seldom indeed that one runs across scales which overcome
(or even attempt to overcome) the distortion due to restricted samples or
incomplete validation procedures.

We have chosen seven statistical standards which we hope cover the basic
requirements involved in the construction of competent scaling instruments.
These are:

> Representative Sample: In this day and age, it is hoped,
> researchers are aware of the fallacy of generalizing results from
> samples of college students[3] onto an older and much less well-
> educated general population. Significant differences are even

---

[3] Some statisticians contend that a sample of a single class should be
treated as having a sample size of one, not the number of students in the class.

likely to be found between freshmen and seniors, engineering and psychology students, and college A and college B so that one must be careful in expecting results from one class to hold for all college students. In the political attitude area, we shall see that there are great dangers in expecting findings from political elites to hold for typical citizens (or even in using scales developed on elites with such typical samples).

This is not meant to discourage researchers from improving the representativeness of whatever populations they do have available for study, but rather to caution them against implying that their findings hold for people not represented by their samples. Nor is it meant to imply that samples of college students are a useless basis on which to construct scales. In some areas (attitudes toward foreign affairs, for example), one might well argue that college exposure is probably the best single criterion of whether a person can truly appreciate the intricacies of the issues involved.

But an instrument constructed from replies of a random cross-section of all students in a university has much more to offer than the same instrument developed on students in a single class in psychology (even if there are many more students in the class than in the university sample). The prime consideration is the applicability of the scale and scale norms to respondents who are likely to use them in the future.

Normative Information: The adequacy of norms (e.g., mean scale scores, percent agreements, etc.) is obviously dependent on the adequacy of the sample. The absolute minimum of normative information, which should be available for the researcher to be aware of any differences between his sample and the sample on which the scale was developed, is the mean scale score and standard deviation for the sample on which the scale was constructed. There are further pieces of statistical data that are extremely useful: item means (or percent agreements) and standard deviations, median scores (if the scale scores are skewed), or more obscure statistics like the inter-quartile range.

Most helpful are means and standard deviations for certain well-defined groups (men or women, Catholics or Baptists) who have high or low scale scores. When such differences have been predicted, the results bear on the validity of the scale, which is discussed below. Validity, reliability, and homogeneity also constitute needed normative information, of course, and they are covered below in the detail required by their complexity.

Reliability (Test-Retest): Unfortunately, one of the most ambiguous terms in psychometrics is "reliability." There are at least three major entities to which the term can refer: (1) the correlation between the same person's score on the same items at two separate points in time; (2) the correlation between two different sets of items at the same time (called "parallel-forms"

if the items are presented in separate format, and "split-half"
if the items are all presented together); and (3) the correlation
between the scale items for all people who answer the items. The
latter two indices refer to the internal structure or homogeneity
of the scale items (the next criterion), while the former
indicates stability of a person's item responses over time. It
is unfortunate that test-retest measures, which require more effort
and sophistication on the part of the scale developer and show
lower reliability figures for his efforts, are available for so
few instruments in the literature. While the test-retest reliability level may be approximately estimated from indices of homogeneity, there is no substitute for the actual test-retest data.

Homogeneity: In addition to split-half, parallel forms, and
inter-item indices of the internal homogeneity of the test items,
there exist other measures of this desirable property. Some of
these item-test and internal consistency measures, as Scott (1960)
has shown, bear known statistical relationships with one another.
Included in this collection are certain indices of scalability for
Guttman items, although not the most often-used Coefficient of
Reproducibility. Even between such "radically" different procedures
as the traditional psychometric and Guttman cumulative, however,
there likely exist reasonably stable relationships between indices
based on inter-item, item-test, and total test characteristics; as
yet, however, these have not been charted. For now, the major
difference between the indices seems to lie in the researcher's
preference for large or small numbers. Inter-item correlations
and homogeneity indices based on Loevinger's concepts seldom
exceed .40; if one prefers larger numbers, a Reproducibility
Coefficient or split-half reliability coefficient computed on the
same data could easily exceed .90. Thus, since it seems at
present to be the only way of relating the various indices, one
is apparently forced to rely on the imperfect criterion of
statistical significance in order to evaluate instruments for
which different indices have been employed. To make the job even
more difficult, statistical distributions of these various indices
are not always available so that significance can be ascertained.

Of all the indices that have been proposed, however, probably
none combines simplicity with amount of information contained as
well as the inter-item correlation matrix. Computing Pearson r
correlation coefficients for more than five items is certainly a
time-consuming operation on a hand calculator. However, for the
researcher who does not have access to a computer that prints
out such a matrix, there are some simple rank-order correlation
formulas that can be calculated by hand in a few minutes, so that
even a ten-item scale inter-item correlation matrix can be put
together in a few hours. The job is too lengthy if there are too
many alternatives or over 100 subjects, but in the case of dichotomous items, the coefficients Y or γ (defined in a statistical
appendix to this chapter) can be easily calculated to determine
inter-item significance. These, however, constitute only rule-of-

thumb procedures for deciding whether a group of items deserves to be added together to form a scale or index. Similarly, the criterion of significance level is proposed only because it is a standard which remains fairly constant across the myriad of measures that are now, or have been, in vogue. Probably it is only the minimum to be expected before one can talk about a scale which can be reasonably called "homogeneous." Hopefully, more satisfactory norms may be proposed in the future.

When the number of items goes beyond ten, however, the inter-item matrix is indeed quite cumbersome to compute by hand calculator for any coefficient, and the researcher is well advised to look for a computer specialist and a correlation matrix program. Computers have the ability to generate 50 to 100 item intercorrelations in less than ten minutes, given a reasonably-sized sample. This does not work out to burdensome cost if the researcher has put much effort into his data collection. At this level of analysis (i.e., more than ten items), the researcher might as well proceed to invest in a factor analysis or cluster analysis of his data. This type of analysis will help him locate the groups of items that go together much faster than could be done by inspecting the correlation matrix.[4] There are many kinds of factor analysis programs and options; under most circumstances, however, the differences between them usually do not result in radical changes in the structure which is uncovered.

To say that factor analytic programs do not usually vary greatly in their output is not to imply that structures uncovered by factor analysis may not lead to serious ambiguities in the interpretation of data. There is one common type of attitudinal data arrangement in particular for which the factor structure seems indeterminant. This is the case where almost all the items are correlated from say .15 to .45. Sometimes only a single factor will emerge from such a matrix and sometimes a solution will be generated which more clearly reflects item differentiation on a series of factors. We have encountered one instance where an instrument--supposedly constructed carefully to reflect a single dimension of inner- vs. other-directedness, according to a forced-choice response format--was found when analyzed in Likert format to contain eight factors. Thus, one can offer no guarantee that inter-item significance will always yield unidimensional scales. Nor does it seem possible to offer any better advice or to recommend any competent practical literature on the inconsistencies into which factor analysis can lead one. On balance, however, one is further ahead performing such analyses than not doing so.

The length of this discussion clearly shows that we feel the determination of homogeneity to be a crucial step in scale construction. Only by these procedures can the analyst properly separate

---

[4] However, the researcher should not be deceived by what appear to be high factor loadings. Items having factor loadings which reach levels of .50 or .70 are equivalent to correlation coefficients of .25 and .49.

the apples, oranges, and coconuts from the salad of items he has put together. In a future volume we hope to be able to go into the detailed rationale for the conclusions and recommendations rather cursorily made in this section.

One final word of caution is in order: it is possible to devise a scale with very high internal consistency merely by writing the same item in a number of different ways. Sampling of item content then can be a crucial component in internal consistency.

Discrimination of Known Groups: This is where the value of a scale is truly tested--the aspect of validity. Nevertheless, group discrimination is not necessarily the most challenging hurdle to demonstrate validity. It is pretty hard to construct a liberalism-conservatism scale that will not show significant differences between John Birchers and Students for Democratic Society, or a religious attitude scale that will not separate Mormons from Jews or ministerial students from engineers. The more demanding hurdle is the ability of the scale scores to reliably single out those liberals or conservatives, agnostics or believers, in heterogeneous groups--or to predict which of them will demonstrate behavior congruent with their hypothesized attitudinal state. A still more definitive test is cross-validation, a test to which very few attitudes scales have been subjected.

Cross-Validation: A test of cross-validation requires two different samples and measures of some criterion variable on each sample. The question to be answered by the test is whether the combination of items for sample A that best correlates with the criterion variable in sample A will also work for sample B's criterion, and whether the best set of sample B items works on the sample A criterion. Note that the crux of the procedure involves picking (and, if necessary, weighting) the items from the sample A experience which work best on sample B.

An even more refined method, and probably the ultimate standard now available, is the multi-trait multi-method matrix as proposed by Campbell and Fiske (1959). The method requires more than one index of each of the several constructs (say x, y, and z) we want to measure by our instrument. It is best to include as many measures or indices of each construct as possible, as well as to measure for control purposes such variables as intelligence or agreement response set which could be at the root of any apparent relationship. In the resulting correlation matrix, the various indices of the single construct (say x) should correlate higher among themselves than any index of x correlates with any indices of y, z, or the control variables.

Needless to say, this comprises a gross oversimplification of the Campbell-Fiske method. The reader should peruse the authors' article thoroughly before attempting comparable analyses. It is worth noting that the authors find only a couple of personality scales which meet their conditions. To our knowledge, no attitude scales have as yet advanced the claim.

Other Procedures: Since there are many methods used in constructing scales beyond our recommended procedures, we should also note alternative methods that may be employed. Such alternatives may include special precautions taken to ensure better items, better testing conditions, or adequate validation--although at times the precautions have had the opposite effect from that intended.

One interesting procedure to which researchers have become increasingly attracted involves the use of positive and negative items. Sometimes, as we have noted, items intended as negative are responded to as negative correlates of positive items; in other instances, this does not work. A procedure which may provide valuable insights into the response patterns of the sample is the separation of the high and low scores on both the positive and negative scales. There are four groups to be examined: yea-sayers (who score high on both the negative and positive items), nay-sayers (who score low on both), assenters who score high on the positive items and low on the negatives, and the dissenters, who follow the opposite pattern. This division can be seen more clearly in the following diagram:

Positive Items

		Low	High
Negative Items	Low	Nay-sayers	Assenters
	High	Dissenters	Yea-sayers

A parallel analysis for Likert scales (or procedures which demand more than a simple dichotomous item response) is the separation of the group at the mean into those who are ambivalent (combining extreme positive responses with extreme negative responses) from those who fall in the middle by taking an extreme position on very few items.

In certain chapters of one of our other volumes, where a sufficient number of instruments to warrant comparison was present, we actually tried to rate each scale on the above twelve considerations. If these ratings prove helpful enough, it might be worthwhile compiling them for all the attitude scales in the future.

It is very important that the reader realize that even this extensive list of proposed criteria is not exhaustive. The actual choice of an instrument, where possible, should be dictated by decision-theoretic considerations. Thus, the increasing of homogeneity by adding questionnaire items needs to be balanced against corresponding increases in administrative analysis and cost (and against respondent fatigue and non-cooperation) before reaching a decision about how many attitude items to use. For assessing general levels of some attitude state (e.g., merely to separate believers from atheists), well-worded single items may do the job just as well as longer scales no matter how competently the scales are devised. For an excellent theoretical exposition of the decision-theoretic approach for psychometric problems Cronbach and Gleser (1965) is recommended. In this extended version of their earlier volume, the authors provide a number of relevant examples.

Appendices to this series will deal with (a) measures of occupational attitudes and characteristics and (b) authoritarianism, alienation, and other social-psychological values and attitudes. Resources permitting, a general sourcebook on attitude methodology will be produced. The general methodology report should be most valuable in making clear the rationale on which our instrument evaluation is based and in explaining why we feel the above factors to be the most crucial considerations out of vast numbers that have been proposed. For now, we highly recommend the American Psychological Association's publication (1966) as an invaluable guidebook for scale construction and evaluation.

STATISTICAL APPENDIX

COMPUTATION OF Y TO DETERMINE INTER-ITEM CORRELATION

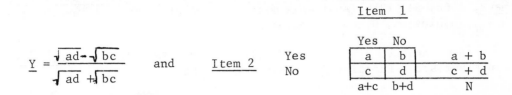

$$Y = \frac{\sqrt{ad} - \sqrt{bc}}{\sqrt{ad} + \sqrt{bc}}$$

and

Item 2

		Item 1		
		Yes	No	
Yes		a	b	a + b
No		c	d	c + d
		a+c	b+d	N

The significance of Y can be computed by calculating its standard error for the case where Y is hypothesized to be 0. Thus when Y exceeds

$$Y = \left(\frac{N - \sqrt{N}}{4} \right) \left(\frac{1}{(a+b) \quad (b+d) \quad (a+b) \quad (c+d)} \right)^{\frac{1}{2}}$$

by a factor of 2, the items are significantly related at the .05 level, and when it exceeds Y itself by a factor of 2.5 the items are related at the .01 level (assuming the number of respondents is greater than 30).

Goodman and Kruskal's (1959) gamma, γ , is a measure that can be called into use when the number of item alternatives is greater than 2. Approximate sampling distributions for this statistic have recently become available (Rosenthal, 1966). The reader may be interested to know that for the dichotomous case, gamma reduces to the formula for Y with the square root signs removed; hence, gamma tends to take on larger values than Y for the same data.

REFERENCES

American Psychological Association. Technical Recommendations for Psychological Tests and Diagnostic Methods, Psychological Bulletin Supplement, 1966, 51, #2. (Available from the APA at 1200 Seventeenth Street, N.W., Washington, D. C. 20036.)

Bonjean, C., Hill, R., and McLemore, S. Sociological Measurement. San Francisco: Chandler Publishing Co., 1968.

Campbell, D., and Fiske, D. "Convergent and Discriminant Validation by the Multi-trait Multi-method Matrix," Psychological Bulletin, 56, 1959, 81-105.

Christie, R. and Lindauer, F. "Personality Structure" Annual Review of Psychology, 1963, 14, 201-230.

Christie, R. et al. "Is the F Scale Irreversible?" Journal of Abnormal and Social Psychology, 1958, 56, 143-159.

Cronbach, L. and Gleser, Goldine. Psychological Tests and Personnel Decisions, Second Edition. Urbana: University of Illinois Press, 1965.

Edwards, A. The Social Desirability Variable in Personality Assessment and Research. New York: Dryden Press, 1957.

Miller, D. Handbook of Research Design and Social Measurement. New York: David McKay Co., 1964.

Rorer, L. "The Great Response Style Myth," Psychological Bulletin, 63 1965, 129-156.

Rosenthal, Irene. "Distribution of the Sample Version of the Measure of Association, Gamma," Journal of the American Statistical Association, 1966, 440-453.

Scott, W. "Measures of Test Homogeneity," Educational and Psychological Measurement, 20, 1960, 751-757.

Shaw, M. and Wright, J. Scales for the Measurement of Attitudes. New York: McGraw-Hill, 1967.

Smith, D. "Correcting for Social Desirability Response Sets in Opinion-Attitude Survey Research," Public Opinion Quarterly, 31, 1967, 87-94.

Snider, J. and Osgood, C. The Semantic Differential: A Sourcebook. Chicago: Adline Press, 1968.

Wrightsman, L. Characteristics of Positively-Scored and Negatively-Scored Items from Attitude Scales. Peabody Teachers' College (Nashville, Tennessee), 1966.

CHAPTER 2:   PUBLIC REACTION TO GOVERNMENT POLICY

Alfred Hero
World Peace Foundation

This chapter is a brief overview of the public's reactions to some of the important issues facing the U.S. government in the last three decades.[1] Attention will be focused mainly on foreign policy, although several controversial domestic questions will also be considered, largely for comparative purposes. A description of general trends in opinion among adult Americans as a group will be presented first, followed by an examination of comparative tendencies on these issues among the major demographic and political groupings.

The data upon which these trends of opinion are based come from various sources--most usually, the American Institute of Public Opinion (Gallup), Elmo Roper and Associates, the Fortune Poll, the National Opinion Research Center, and the Survey Research Center. Survey technology and sophistication among these organizations have improved over the years, making some of the earlier data less reliable than others in terms of their representativeness and validity. Many of the survey questions employed do not guard against contamination by agreement response set--the tendency, more prevalent among less educated respondents, to simply agree with attitude statements no matter what the content. Furthermore, it has been only recently that poll organizations have begun to control for the tendency among respondents to express views on issues about which they had thought little or had harbored feeble (if any) opinions prior to the interview.

However, the general picture of poll organizations has been one of competent

---

[1]An expanded and more comprehensive version of this paper, containing complete documentation and referencing, is available from the author at the World Peace Foundation, 20 Mount Vernon Street, Boston, Massachusetts, for $3.

study, planning, management, and administration. As a result, for the most part, one can conclude that their findings have been sufficiently representative to warrant the generalizations that follow.

I. Some General Trends

Issues: Knowledge and Interest

Data from the various polling organizations clearly show that the majority of Americans have paid relatively little or no attention to most international and national issues, and only relatively small minorities have possessed even rudimentary information about these issues. Such failure of knowledge and interest applies to both issue fronts, foreign and domestic.

In the area of foreign affairs, Americans have had little awareness of the nature and purpose of the reciprocal trade program, the Marshall Plan, or various later foreign aid programs. Majorities or large minorities of American citizens also have been unable to identify such leading international figures as Marshall Tito and the U.S. Secretary of State. Likewise, samples tested lacked information on such domestic issues as tax programs, farm policy, and even race relations.

Those who are knowledgeable about any one major issue or policy, whether foreign or domestic, usually are reasonably informed about most others. But such accurately informed persons are few--about 5 percent of the population--whereas the chronic "know nothings" have declined from roughly 35 percent in the 1930's to 15-20 percent in the late 1960's. On most of the questions discussed here, however, a third to as much as two-thirds of the samples may be typed as ignorant, apathetic, or both.

Many people who indicate an interest in an issue often know little, if anything, about it. Declared "interest" does not necessarily lead to seeking

of information. Those who have had both knowledge and interest in an international issue have tended to express more liberal opinions with regard to it
than the less informed and concerned. However, a major underlying factor in
this three-variable phenomenon has been another correlate--that of higher
education. This latter factor links up with possession of more information,
greater interest, and attitudes that are more liberal.

The rise in educational levels and wider public exposure to such stimuli
as the mass media have undoubtedly increased the number of people over the years
who hold knowledgeable and meaningful opinions on political issues. But one
factor has worked against this trend: the issues, at least in the public's
mind, seem more complicated today than they formerly did. This apparently
greater complexity tends to cause more anxieties and uncertainties and, hence,
a smaller percentage of citizens wishing to venture opinions. Even so, the
general trend has been for people to be more aware of, and informed about,
political matters in the contemporary time period than heretofore.

Attitudes on War

Most of the survey questions asked about world affairs prior to the
Japanese attack on Pearl Harbor concentrated on the public's reactions to the
threat of war and, later, actual war by the Axis against its neighbors. Early
attitudes portrayed Americans as being heavily isolationist. From 1937 through
1940, the predominant mood in the U.S. was that our involvement in any war
outside the Western Hemisphere would be a mistake. Consistent with this mood,
relatively few Americans thought that we should have entered the League of
Nations, or that our failure to have done so had any bearing on the troubles
in Europe.

Although the U.S. public wished to avoid involvement in the war, its sympathies always rested with the victims of the Axis aggression. Increasing majorities over the years hoped the bellicose behavior of the Axis nations would and could be effectively resisted by the Allied powers. This concern for the Allied powers, however, was partly one of self-interest, for many people thought that the U.S. would surely be attacked if the Allied forces were defeated. Still, Americans were not eager to enter the war on behalf of the Allies, since they believed that the Allied countries could defeat the enemy without U.S. help.

Majorities of American voters also opposed liberalization of terms on previous debts, further loans or credits, or other aids to the Western democracies until it became apparent that the Axis powers might win the war if such aid were not provided. Likewise, support for liberalization of the Neutrality Acts of 1935-1937 was not strong either. Few thought the existing laws placed the U.S. at a disadvantage in dealing with other countries in a wartime situation. After the Nazi attack on Poland, some of these attitudes changed, but still most Americans favored a fairly strict isolationist stance. Roosevelt barely achieved majority support for his "cash-and-carry" sales to belligerents, but large majorities still refused extension of credits to the Allies to purchase arms. Most people did not wish to extend any assistance which incurred substantial risk of involving this nation in the war.

Even the collapse of Allied resistance on the continent resulted in only a small increase in the number of Americans who were willing to enter the war on the side of Britain. The figure stood at about 13 percent favoring intervention, and this number did not increase much even at the height of the Battle of Britain. The attack on Russia, however, increased the support level to between 25-32 percent, and it stayed within that range until the attack on Pearl Harbor.

Support levels also increased in 1941 for the "Lend-Lease" program of

Franklin Roosevelt. People were beginning to feel, as expressed on the questionnaires of the day, that it was "more important to help Britain win" than to "keep
out of the war ourselves." By October of 1941, 70 percent of the public with
opinions considered it more important that Germany be defeated than that we stay
out of war, and 50 percent would ship goods to Britain on U.S. ships, convoyed
by the U.S. Navy, with orders to shoot German submarines on sight.

Openly expressed isolationist sentiments declined precipitously after
U.S. entry into the war. Only 15 percent in early 1943 said "after this war...
the U.S. should stay out of world affairs." This figure remained fairly constant
in the period from World War II to the Korean conflict. It increased to almost
a third of the public after the entry of Communist China into the Korean War,
but declined to 15-20 percent after the armistice. However, the extent of U.S.
involvement was questioned by considerably larger segments of the American
public, many maintaining that the U.S. should fight only in the Western Hemisphere, that it had "gone too far" in its foreign involvements, etc. However,
since the end of the Korean War, large majorities have wanted to "keep working
with our allies" and help them build up their military defenses.

With this increased post-war strength in internationally-oriented attitudes
came corresponding support for the United Nations as an international peace organization.[2] The U.N., and active U.S. participation in it, have been more widely
popular than virtually any other international institution or aspect of American
policy. Even during the height of the Korean War, when public support of the
U.N. was at its lowest level, the world organization was much more favorably

---

[2]For more detailed discussion of public attitudes toward the U.N., see
William A. Scott and Stephen B. Withey, The United States and the United Nations:
The Public View (New York: Carnegie Endowment for International Peace, 1958), and
Alfred O. Hero, Jr., "The American Public and the U.N., 1954-1966," The Journal
of Conflict Resolution, X (1966), pp. 436-475.

viewed than the League of Nations had ever been. Typically, even a considerable minority of self-declared isolationists and a small majority of neo-isolationists have favored American membership in this body.

Relations with the Communist World

Among our World War II allies, the U.S.S.R. was never as popular as Britain, or even the Free French, with the American public. Majorities of Americans opposed supplying arms and goods to Russia on the "Lend-Lease" plan prior to our formal entry into the war. But once the U.S. entered the war, the Soviet Union became more popular with Americans. In fact, the mood of Americans was quite optimistic toward that country in the latter years of the war.

The tables turned during the first year or so following the war. From 1946 through 1957, considerable majorities thought it unlikely or even impossible that the differences between the U.S. and the Soviet Union could be worked out peacefully through negotiation or other non-military means. The cold war had begun, in the public mind at least, by mid-1946. Many believed, in its early stages, that Russia wanted to rule the world and large numbers expected war with Russia or Communist countries in general within twenty-five years or less. Majorities of Americans favored "harder-line" U.S. policies toward the East than those then pursued by the government. They thought that trade should be terminated, that our own armed forces should be expanded, and that we should bomb Soviet cities with nuclear weapons if Communist armies attacked any other country.

These "hard-line" attitudes had their origin partly in the Korean conflict and the mood it generated. However, there was a marked bipolarization of opinion about Korea, some wanting to escalate the war and others to withdraw from it. Clear majorities preferred to escalate the conflict.

These "hard-line" attitudes gradually changed after the armistice in Korea and, particularly, during the second Eisenhower administration. The public anticipated war less and less. The new perception was of a Russia now less militarily adventurous, less bellicose, and more politically flexible. Exchanges of various sorts between the two nations were favored by most Americans. Majorities in the 1960's supported continued negotiations for arms controls, limitations of nuclear proliferation, expanded trade and cultural exchanges, and other non-military means of dealing with that country.

In the 1960's, however, a new threat in the public mind slowly replaced that of Russia, namely the spectre of Communist China which was now seen as the greater threat to world peace. The poll results revealed that a majority of Americans thought that in a military showdown between the U.S. and China, Russia would be on the side of the U.S. Coupled with this fear of China was a reaction against admitting it to membership in the U.N., although support levels in America gradually rose to 26 percent by 1967. Generally, Americans have softened their attitude only slightly in the last decade with regard to such topics as Chinese membership in the U.N., trading with that country, or negotiating with it in general. Yet, paradoxically, majorities have, in recent years, indicated a desire to improve relations with China, even to include it in the U.N., if our President felt its admission would in fact help improve mutual relations.

National Defense and Arms Control

The American people have expressed some concern over the years with the general defense establishment and security of our country. Most of the public has wanted the size of our armed forces at least maintained at current levels or increased. The proportion who would expand our military capabilities and funds needed for them has reached peaks during crisis periods.

This desire to increase our defense forces has had another aspect. A majority of people have believed that large armed forces are more likely to be a deterrent to war than a motivating force for war. The support of a large military establishment has led, as a consequence, to the public favoring the principle of military conscription. Since 1940, a majority of Americans have favored compulsory military service in peacetime.

The building of a large defense establishment is a prevailing American preference, but it has had isolationist tinges. Support for aid in arming our allies has never been as high as that for expending much larger resources on our own defenses. (In fact, many self-declared "isolationists" have been willing to pay higher taxes for the latter than for the former.) This does not mean that the U.S. public does not believe in the principle of collective security; clear majorities of people agree to such ideas as are embodied in the N.A.T.O. pact, but they want other countries to do their share commensurate with their own resources.

The emphasis on strong national defense and collective security has not diminished support for international control of arms, armed forces, and nuclear weapons. Fifty-nine to 73 percent of the samples between 1946 and 1956 have felt that the U.S. should be willing to reduce the size of its armed forces if others, especially the Soviets, agreed to do the same and if an effective enforcement system could be instituted. Majorities of the public have also favored the international control of nuclear weapons and nuclear energy, in preference to each country remaining free to make and to use whatever arsenals of mass destruction it wished. Such was the case not only when the U.S. had a nuclear monopoly but thereafter as well. In general, such attitudes prevailed even during the Korean War period and other crisis situations of the cold war era.

Two reservations have been placed by the American public on these general attitude preferences. For one thing, not many Americans (i.e., about 10 percent as late as 1959) have been optimistic about the U.S.S.R. permitting inspected control of its arms and nuclear systems. The general feeling has been that if the Soviets would not agree to such measures, most Americans would prefer to continue manufacturing and developing nuclear and other weapons. These attitudes could only be tempered by some international agreement on arms controls with effective enforcement or, at least, means of determining violations.

Foreign Aid and World Trade

From the time that programs were first established to feed the indigenous populations of North Africa, Italy, and other "liberated" or occupied areas during World War II, clear majorities of the public have supported the general ideal of aid for foreign peoples in need. Furthermore, support levels for administering aid have not wavered much in strength over the years since that time. The political difficulties in Congress over foreign aid programs in recent years cannot be attributed to any sizable drop in public support for the idea.[3]

However, the purposes and substance of aid have changed considerably since the shipment of food and other emergency supplies to the war-torn areas of the mid-forties. Large majorities have always approved the idea of sending food and other philanthropic relief to victims of man-made or natural catastrophies. Equally large numbers have favored technical assistance to less developed countries since its inception in 1949. Smaller segments of the public have approved of capital aid at prevailing levels and still fewer of military assistance. Except for a year or two, during the initial stages of the rearmament of Western Europe in 1949-51, military aid has been second in importance in the public mind to economic assistance, this being the very reverse of priorities

---

[3] Public attitudes in the U.S. toward foreign aid since the early 1950's are discussed in greater detail in Alfred O. Hero, Jr., "Foreign Aid and the American Public," Public Policy, XIV (1965), pp. 71-116.

usually assigned to the two forms of aid by Congress. Typically, only minorities have favored expanding the small proportion of our capital assistance channeled through multilateral organizations.

Public support for foreign aid has also fluctuated according to which countries were recipients. Those countries which have been our allies, or have been avowedly against Communism, have been much more favored than neutralist nations like Yugoslavia. With regard to geographic location, the non-Communist countries in Europe have fared better than those in other areas of the world. The conception of "foreign aid" by the public has remained rather simplistic-- it is most often seen in charitable terms, and next as an instrument in preventing the spread of Communism. Even as late as 1967 more people emphasized humanitarian than long-range developmental objectives.

Public awareness of the basic issues of foreign trade has been even less evident than awareness about most other major foreign policy concerns. Large minorities have neither cared nor known enough about tariffs, quotas, reciprocal trade agreements to express any opinions about these. People who have ventured such opinions have generally favored the idea of reciprocal liberalization of national trade barriers and the "most-favored-nation" concept. This attitude has been apparent since at least as early as the late 1930's with respect to Secretary Cordell Hull's trade policies. The key to public endorsement of such trade liberalization has been the qualification that it be reciprocated by other countries. Those inclining toward freer trade in the abstract, or favoring lower tariffs as a general idea, have never constituted a majority of those venturing opinions on the subject. Never have more than one in seventeen Americans favored the politically extreme proposal of simply doing away with tariffs and other U.S. trade restrictions.

Civil Rights

The public's attitudes on different aspects of the civil rights question have varied considerably over the years, although a moderate trend sympathetic to the Negro has been observed in the last few years. One indication of this trend has been the decline in the public's belief that Negroes are, as a race, biologically inferior. The number of people who have believed that gradual integration, both Northern and Southern, in schools, public accommodations, housing, etc.,was inevitable, likewise increased from a minority in the 1930's to over three-quarters of the public in the early 1960's.

Nevertheless, the public has changed most of its attitudes toward Negroes and civil rights quite slowly. Most federal action in this sphere has not been due to any enthusiastic majority support for it. Rather, the government has usually considered and favored such ideas before majorities of the public have; official action, in turn, has apparently resulted in shifts of both public behavior and expressed public attitudes. Thus, only minorities of American voters favored a federal anti-lynching bill, Truman's civil rights program, an F.E.P.C. law, and most of the civil rights legislation of the late 1950's and early 1960's at the time when they were being debated by Congress and the mass media. Even in the late 1960's many more people felt the federal government was pressing integration and civil rights "too fast" rather than "not fast enough"; majorities disapproved of enforcement of open housing, and even larger majorities thought that Negroes had on the whole been treated "fairly" in the United States. Given a free choice, most white Americans still preferred to live in a generally segregated rather than in a desegregated society.

Economic and Welfare Issues

Although specific federal domestic programs have varied in the support they have received, majorities of Americans have approved of federal intervention in the national economy and federal action for social welfare. Most of the New Deal was welcomed by a majority of the public. The concepts of Medicare and Medicaid were endorsed by most citizens long before they became law. Likewise, before they were ever federally implemented, such programs as regulation and prohibition of child labor, old age pensions, social security, public works, slum clearance, urban renewal, low-cost housing, federal responsibility for full employment and unemployment compensation, aid to education, veterans' benefits, assistance to depressed areas, anti-poverty legislation have been favored by clear majorities of those venturing opinions.

However, the numbers favoring such programs have been fewer when there was a question of increased taxes necessary for implementing them; even so, more have typically favored than opposed most such policies despite likely tax increases. Typically, whereas only minorities have supported U.S. foreign policy expenditures at prevailing or expanded levels--with the exception of national defense--majorities have either actively approved of the magnitude of resources voted to most domestic programs, or have felt that that magnitude should be increased.[4] Majorities have likewise approved "in general" of trade unions, and of the successive increases in the minimum wage permitted by the government since the mid-thirties. At no time during these three decades has more than a minority--an average of one American out of four--felt our federal government was doing "too much" for the people. Clear majorities have either supported the actual level of federal participation in the economy and in the welfare and lives of the citizenry, or have advocated expansion of such federal responsibility and action.

On the other hand, small majorities have felt their own taxes have been

---

[4]However, the number who supported aid to farmers declined from considerable majorities in the 1930's to less than half of those with opinions in the 1960's, a trend attributable primarily to the sharp reduction in the number of farmers.

too high, while much larger majorities have opposed increases in taxes in peacetime. Furthermore, although deficit financing and a growing national debt have been customary since the late thirties, more than half the public considered these practices undesirable as late as 1962. "Socialism," a "socialist economy," "socialized medicine," transformation of America into a "welfare state," and other "radical" concepts have also received consistently heavier opposition than support. Only during the Depression have small majorities favored nationalization of utilities, banks, interstate transportation, and other crucial industries. Majorities generally have felt such enterprises should remain under private ownership and control. Moreover, considerably more Americans have felt labor unions and their leaders have too much influence in the country and should be more strictly regulated than have felt similarly about "business" and private enterprise. Thus, the general picture seems to be one of most citizens approving of the specific welfare and economic programs of their national government, but opposing sharp shifts toward general or abstract socialist principles.

Liberalism and Conservatism

Terms like "liberalism" and "conservatism" have had little meaning to most voters; only minorities have adequately defined these terms with regard to politics, which suggests the lack of an all-embracing ideological structure or frame of reference within which specific issues and events are viewed. Many people indicate no preference between generally "liberal" and "conservative" policies or candidates when such questions have been posed. Those who have identified themselves in these terms have usually been more numerous on the conservative than on the liberal end of the attitude continuum.

Labels such as these have had varying issue connotations at different times, and among different groups at the same time. Labels themselves in fact have usually been more intimately associated with domestic economic and welfare questions than with most foreign issues. In the pre-war period self-identified liberals (especially outside the South) were at most only slightly more inclined to favor liberalization of the Neutrality Acts and more active U.S. participation in world affairs generally than were conservatives. Even views on Negroes and race relations had but a minor connection with foreign affairs issues. The public identified these terms mainly with the domestic New Deal program.

The Second World War resulted in some more intimate connection of the terms "liberal" and "conservative" in the public mind with foreign affairs. However, Americans who conceived of themselves as liberals were only 4 to 20 percentage points more favorable than were conservatives to cooperation with the U.N., the Marshall Plan, economic aid to neutralists, and most other international programs of this government during the first decade and a half following the war. Differences in views on some aspects of foreign policy between the two so-labelled groups increased somewhat during the Kennedy and Johnson administrations. But even during the mid- and late-1960's foreign policy differences between the two groups remained smaller than such differences over programs like aid to dependent children, the war against poverty, Medicare, urban renewal and federal aid to education. Correlations between self identification with these terms, and views on desegregation and civil rights, rose during the late 1950's and 1960's to about the same level as those terms with these other domestic issues.

People who have favored liberalized programs in one domestic field, such as assistance to dependent children, have tended to approve of liberalization of other domestic programs as well. Conversely, those who have opposed say expansion of social security coverage and benefits have been more inclined than those in favor of expansion to oppose aid to dependent children, unemployment benefits, federal involvement in public health and medical care. On the whole somewhat weaker, less stable, linkages have likewise been apparent among attitudes toward various aspects of foreign policy. In recent years racial desegregationists have come to hold more liberal views on most aspects of both internal and foreign policy than have segregationists. Even these interconnections, however, have been considerably weaker than has been the case among the small minority of intellectuals, political activists, and others more seriously interested in and aware of national and international issues.

But though there may be this tendency among the five percent of the most intellectually aware people, for liberals on domestic economic welfare policy to be libterals on foreign policy and for conservatives on domestic policy to be conservatives on foreign policy, such a correlation has hardly been apparent in the majority of the citizenry. New Dealers were at most only 10 percentage points more sympathetic to liberalized trade, U.S. cooperation with the League of Nations, or assistance to the opponents of the Axis before December 1941, than were opponents of the New Deal. The relationship between international and domestic economic and welfare policies rose only slightly under President Truman and declined to virtually zero by the end of the first Eisenhower administration. Consistency between liberal or conservative views in the two respective fields rose again gradually during John F. Kennedy's term in the White House; but as late as the 1964 election, relative liberals on a group of domestic issues other than race and civil liberties were at the very most only 20 percentage points more inclined than relative conservatives on these questions to favor non-military multilateral involvements in world affairs.

This inconsistency between views on domestic "bread and butter" type issues and foreign policy can be largely explained by the different biases toward the issues among major demographic, social and political groups in American society. It is to these phenomena that we now direct our attention.

II. Some Comparative Trends

Comparative distributions of attitudes among different demographic and social groups in America have varied from one issue to another. Whereas one sociological segment of the population may be more liberal about giving economic aid to nonaligned countries than another segment, the latter segment may be more likely to approve redistribution of wealth to the less affluent within the United States. However, save for a few exceptions, shifts and stabilities in opinion over the last generation and a half have been consistent within all major American groups. The exceptions have been more attributable to changes in the issue itself or in its connotations for the pertinent group than to major shifts in opinion within the group toward a relatively constant issue content.

Such findings do not necessarily imply that variables like education, socio-economic status, ethnic origin, age, sex, region, or political party preference are causal or explanatory factors in and of themselves. However, experiences and self-perceived interests of individuals in these various categories have been sufficiently different to result in significantly different views on a number of public issues.

Educational Groups

Better-educated groups--especially those who went to college--have been definitely more aware of and informed about virtually all national and inter-national issues than less-educated groups. The well-educated person has been more likely to declare an interest, offer his opinions, and react in a broader ideological context than his lower-educated counterpart. Similarly, his opinions have been more stable, firmly held, and consistent--particularly (but not only) in foreign affairs. The small minority which can be more than superficially or only partly misinformed about most major issues, has been concentrated in the college-educated.

The well-educated have usually learned of international and national developments first, and have also been much more likely to proceed to seek further information about them. If the issue remains an object of debate on the mass media for a considerable period, differences in awareness and knowledge of it tend to narrow somewhat between educational levels. Nevertheless, this tendency has been a relatively limited one. Large numbers of people, often majorities, below the national median of education attainment have had at most very foggy notions of such major issues as the Marshall Plan, technical assistance, N.A.T.O., and international trade, even after these have been important items of federal attention for years. Regardless of the so-called educationally uplifting effects of television and other mass communications since the Second World War, gaps between different educational background groups in knowledge have remained at least as wide in the 1960's as they were in the 1930's and early 1940's. Most of the increase in public understanding of these matters has been a result of the growth in the proportion of better-educated citizens in our population rather than of much improvement in comprehension among the grade school educated and high school dropouts.

Educational groups have also differed considerably in how they have perceived those questions which have come to their attention. The college-educated have been much more apt to consider particular issues or events in broader, more general, and more abstract contexts, as related to other issues and principles, and to objectives or styles of public policy; they have also been more apt to perceive practical implications of alternative policies--such as higher taxes. Grade schoolers, on the other hand, have tended much more to view each event of which they are aware in isolation from historical or other background factors and from longer-range implications.

Thus, attitudinal differences between educational groups have been smaller on issues in which cognitive or long-range considerations have been relatively unimportant, or in which humanitarian or charitable motivations have been especially salient. Also, education has had little relationship, not even negative, with support for programs with which the individual himself would receive some direct economic or other benefit. However, some types of issues, such as those which concern tolerance of ideas and groups different from one-self, have received considerably more liberal responses from the better educated than from their less educated counterparts. It is usually true for a given issue that the smaller the minority which harbors a particular liberal attitude, the more likely it is that the minority is concentrated among the college-educated. Occasionally a proposal for a particular liberal program has initially had only minority approval, but then gradually received majority support after it became law. In such instances the better educated have tended to be in the vanguard of the supporters, while an increasing number of the less educated came to approve of it after it went into effect and prestigious national figures and institutions had spoken out in its favor.

With some exceptions, education has been more closely related in the post-war era to support for international cooperation that to opinions on most liberal domestic programs other than civil rights and civil liberties. Prior to the war, when relatively isolationist thinking was the norm, college-educated citizens were for the most part only a dozen or fewer percentage points more favorable to actual or proposed international involvements among the totality of those citizens in favor of such involvements than among those who went no further than grade school. But since Pearl Harbor the few remaining patent isolationists have been highly concentrated among the latter. Similarly, the higher the educational level, the greater the willingness to accept compromises of U.S. sovereignty, and of its unilateral freedom to achieve mutual international objectives, reduction of tensions with foreign powers, and the like. Support for "utopian" proposals, such as world government, has been especially limited to those with college experience.

Level of education has had less impact on public attitudes toward the U.N. than on those toward some other international questions. Although slightly smaller minorities of better educated than less educated people have advocated U.S. withdrawal, overwhelming majorities of all groups have had generally favorable views of the world body and have approved of our continued membership. The better educated, though, have been less satisfied than the poorly educated with the U.N.'s performance, and are also less inclined to believe it has been or will be a major force in maintaining world peace--a perception undoubtedly more accurately related to the U.N.'s actual accomplishment, competence, and behavior.

The less-educated have consistently been more fatalistic and pessimistic about the future (both at home and abroad) and about the government's, and especially their own, ability to remedy problems that face them. Nonetheless, the educational groups did not differ much in their expectation of U.S. involvement in the Second World War or the probable length of that involvement. But trends on the expectation of war after 1946 did show some educational contrasts. The lower educational groups since that time have been consistently more pessimistic that another war was fairly imminent. Similarly, the educationally less privileged have been significantly less inclined to feel we could live peacefully with the U.S.S.R., that we could settle our disputes short of war, and that the Soviet Union would someday "make real peace with us."

The higher the level of education, the greater has been the willingness to engage in negotiation, conciliation, compromise, economic and cultural relations, and other non-military efforts to lower tensions with Communist states (as well as with other countries). In general, the search for other than military solutions--through arms control, economic aid, or otherwise--has been more characteristic of the better educated. Particularly has this been so with the lessening of cold war tensions during the last decade.

The decline in "hard-line" thinking vis-a-vis Eastern Europe and the U.S.S.R. has been clearly more evident at the upper educational levels. By the mid-1960's Communist China had replaced the U.S.S.R. as the greater long-run menace to world peace in the minds of the college experienced, whereas the Soviet Union maintained that unfavored position among large minorities of those who had never gone to high school. Only minorities of the least educated, contrasted with majorities of the most educated, thought the U.S.S.R. more likely to side with us rather than with China in case of war or major worsening of U.S. relations with China. In March 1967, 38 percent of the least educated versus 57 percent of the most educated believed that a war between the U.S. and China was "not very likely." College educated Americans have also been clearly more favorably disposed toward Chinese Communist membership in the U.N. and toward establishment of normal diplomatic relations with that country. Approval of the idea of so-called preventive or preemptive war against either Communist China, the U.S.S.R., or other Communist countries has likewise been largely concentrated among poorly educated citizens. Those who would expand or escalate local conventional military operations into broader conflicts, as in Korea or Vietnam, have likewise been disproportionately numerous among the less educated.

Education has been more intimately associated with attitudes toward some types of foreign aid than with others. Since the exchange of "overage" U.S. destroyers for British bases in 1940 and Lend-Lease shortly thereafter, support for military aid for allies and "friendly" countries has been less dependent on education than has approval of capital assistance. Although (except for

1949-1951) majorities at all educational levels have assigned higher priority to economic than to military aid, these majorities have been considerably larger near the upper end of the educational spectrum. Approval of capital assistance to allies, technical assistance, and charitable relief--even to Mainland China-- has had considerably less connection with education than has economic aid to nonaligned countries or to Yugoslavia or Poland. This is not surprising, given the greater antagonism to neutralism and to compromises with Communism at the lower educational levels. Similarly, support for U.S. commitments to aid pro- grams over several years rather than one fiscal year at a time, for channeling more economic assistance through international institutions, and for non-military aid at prevailing or increased magnitudes has been much less widespread among the lower educational categories.

Support for freer trade has been less dependent on education than has that for expansion and multilateralization of developmental assistance. Never- theless, majorities of grade schoolers with views have more or less consistently felt that U.S. tariffs and other trade barriers should be either kept at prevail- ing levels or increased, and that imports into this country should be held at current levels or reduced, whereas majorities of college-educated people have supported lower tariffs and expanded imports. However, educational differences have been smaller with respect to mutual reductions of trade barriers wherein foreign governments liberalize their restrictions in return for similar U.S. action.

Correlations of support for N.A.T.O. and other multilateral defense pacts (and for the stationing of U.S. military forces abroad) with level of education, although positive, have been normally lower than those relating education with approval of non-military approaches to alleviate the cold war. Education has had even less connection with approval of our own defense effort, i.e., the amounts of manpower and material resources devoted to our army, navy, air force, and nuclear armaments and their delivery systems. In fact, grade-school educated citizens have sometimes been somewhat more supportive of a strengthened defense establishment, including conscription, than have their college-experienced compatriots.

Still more diverse from one issue to the next have been relationships of education with attitudes toward domestic public policy. Endorsement of civil liberties, freedom of speech, and the like for such unpopular ideological groups as fascists, socialists, communists, atheists, and "beatniks" has been closely associated with education. Although the distribution of views on the Ku Klux Klan, lynchings, poll taxes, open housing, and biological equality of Negroes and whites has differed relatively little across the educational continuum, the college educated are twice as likely as those not reaching high school to have viewed interracial marriage as acceptable and to have said they would vote for a well qualified Negro for President. Whereas majorities of the former have approved of desegregation of public transportation, jobs, and schools, most grade schoolers have opposed such desegregation. College educated citizens have also been clearly the more cordial to peaceful civil rights demonstrations, the Civil Rights Act of 1964, and the general cause for racial equality.

Although educational differences have been quite limited with respect to opinions toward federal aid to education, the better educated have typically been somewhat more favorably disposed toward most types of federal aid to education than the less educated. However, since the Second War War, majorities of even the least schooled have favored most such programs about which they have heard anything.

On the other hand, education has had little or no bearing on views about federal expenditures on roads, dams, and most other public works, or about the general level of taxation (even including progressive income taxes). Prior to the Second World War better educated people were somewhat less favorably disposed toward labor unions than poorly educated citizens, undoubtedly due to the pre-dominance of the latter among union members. But since roughly 1945, educational groups have differed very little in this respect.

However, on most questions involving social welfare, domestic expenditures, and transfers of wealth from more to less prosperous citizens, better educated Americans have been clearly more conservative, or less liberal, than the educationally underprivileged. This phenomenon is, of course, primarily due to the rather close positive connections of education with income, standard of living, income tax bracket, and low likelihood of receipt of direct benefits from such programs. Educational and economic privilege versus underprivilege have been highly correlated with one another.

Thus, the higher the level of education, the more inclined has the citizenry been to oppose "federal spending" and deficit financing and to advocate reduction in the overall federal budget. College-educated Americans have been as much as three or more times as opposed as grade schoolers to such concepts as "the welfare state," "socialized medicine," and even Medicare and other less "radical" programs. Similarly, the former have been only approximately one half as ready as the latter to increase federal expenditures for veterans' benefits, farm subsidies, low-cost housing, old age pensions, and "social welfare, health, and social security." For three decades substantial majorities of college-educated people have opposed, while equally substantial majorities of grade schoolers have favored, successive increases in the minimum wage. Overall, the former were almost twice as inclined as the latter to hold unfavorable opinions of the New Deal in the late thirties and of the Great Society thirty years later. The higher the level of education, the more likely have Americans been to side with business against labor, to feel union rather than industrial leaders have too much influence in Washington, and to approve of open shops, right-to-work laws, and other concepts opposed by unions.

Socio-Economic Status and Community of Residence

Income, standard of living, and particularly occupation have been so closely linked with education that it is difficult to determine their impacts-- separate from those of differential education--on attitudes toward federal policy. It is not surprising, therefore, that correlations of income with in- terest, knowledge, attitudes, and other behavior toward public affairs have been for the most part in the same direction as those of education. Even more closely associated with education than income is type of occupation which--from most to least complex--has understandably more nearly paralleled education in its linkages with most public attitudes.

With specific reference to international affairs, education has been a more important factor in determining most choices than has either income or occupation. In very few instances have differences in information levels or attitudes on international relations been larger between the more and less affluent, or even between the professional-business and manual labor groups, than those between the college educated and grade schoolers. In fact, seldom have they been as large. When education has been held constant, income has had little bearing on most thinking about these matters. However, when income has been held constant, the better educated still have tended to be at least somewhat more liberal on world affairs.

However, despite the generalization that education is the more important variable in this area, socio-economic and occupational factors per se have been of some relevance. Higher-income Americans in each educational grouping have tended more to support such policies as economic aid to neutralists, freer trade, liberalized relations with Communist countries, and desegregation than have their lower-income counterparts. Business, professional, and even white collar groups in each educational category have also favored these items more than manual, particularly unskilled, workers. Moreover, the largely college-educated elite who have been particularly successful in their professions, business, regions, or communities (e.g., individuals in Who's Who) have on the whole been more disposed to such public policy alternatives than the general run of either college-educated or prosperous citizens. Farmers have either resembled the attitude patterns of manual workers or have been somewhat less informed and more conservative.

On very few international issues have differences related to size of community been as large as those between educational or occupational groupings. Rural people have been somewhat less well informed about national and international affairs (farm policy excepted) than small-town dwellers who, in turn, have been slightly less knowledgeable than inhabitants of medium sized and larger cities. But even informational differences between these groups have been smaller than those between occupational, socio-economic, or, especially, educational groups.

Attitudinal differences related to type of community on most international issues have been smaller still. Thus, very similar opinions prevailed before the Second World War among rural folk, small towners, and big city people on such matters as the League of Nations, the Neutrality Acts, and Lend Lease, whereas the more privileged occupational and economic groups held at least somewhat more liberal views on these questions than their less well-off compatriots. Although urbanites and suburbanites have become somewhat more liberal than rural and small-town Americans on certain international questions since 1945, such differences have been much smaller than popular lore and the utterances and roll-call votes of Congressmen from rural versus urban districts might suggest. On the other hand, the higher the occupational or economic status, the more widespread the support for economic aid, liberalization of relations with Communist regimes, and emphasis on conciliation, negotiation, and other non-military means in U.S. foreign policy in general.

However, as might be inferred from our discussion of the feeble relationships between education and views on the U.N., technical assistance, world relief, military aid, collective security, and the size of our own defense establishment, neither type of community, occupation, nor socio-economic status have had more than slight bearing on thinking about such issues. Although farmers should share less vested short-term interest in protectionism than many industrial groups, they have been less liberal on tariffs and trade since about the early fifties than have urbanites, even blue-collar workers.

In the domestic field, the more affluent elements, like the better educated, have voiced substantially more support for civil liberties, freedom of speech, and the like than have their less well-off compatriots. Nonetheless, socio-economic status among the U.S. population in general has had but slight connection with feelings about Negroes and race relations. The disproportionate number of Negroes in the lower socio-economic orders has tended to reduce the average level of racism there. However, lower-class whites have been more racist than more privileged whites. Smaller differences in racial views have separated rural and farming from urban, especially metropolitan, whites. But, again, none of these differences have been as large as those between educational groups.

However, the reverse has been the case with respect to most internal welfare and economic issues, other than aid to education. Income has been more closely connected with preferred domestic policy alternatives than occupation, community size, or even education. Perceived economic self-interest seems a

powerful determinant on such matters. The higher the income, the clearly more
conservative the attitudes, even when such factors as education are held constant.

Differences between the most affluent quarter and least well-off quarter
of the population on most New Deal measures were wide indeed, such that the
proportion in favor was frequently two to three times as great among the latter.
Such attitudinal divergencies between economic groups have declined in recent
decades, as more and more of the affluent came to accept federal intervention in
the national economy and society. But even in the 1960's the well-off have been
between one and a half and two times as apt to oppose expansion of welfare legislation and to advocate budget cutting as their relatively poor compatriots.
Moreover, whereas educational groups have differed relatively little in their
general approval of trade unions in recent years, the more affluent have remained
distinctly more hostile to them than have the lower economic orders. Furthermore,
although among the general population supporters of domestic welfare and related
programs have for the most part diverged hardly at all from opponents thereof in
their views on foreign policy, among the more affluent strata liberals on such
domestic questions have tended to be more supportive of multilateral world
cooperation than have conservatives on such issues.

Moreover, the rural-urban factor has had a more consistent bearing on such
domestic attitudes than on foreign-policy thinking. Aside from federal aid to
farmers, rural and farm folk have been at least somewhat more conservative on
virtually all such questions than urbanites, even when income has been held
constant. Country people have been more inclined than virtually all other major
demographic groups to advocate reduction of the federal budget and the national
debt and more stringent regulations of unions (and business) and to oppose expansion of federal aid to education (although rural schools need such aid more
than most), unemployment compensation, subsidized housing, public works, veterans'

benefits, and, in the mid-sixties, the Great Society program generally. Since at least 1937, farmers have been at least somewhat more likely to consider themselves conservatives than virtually all urban strata, including even the relatively well-off.

Age

Americans have not manifested much differentiation in their interest or even in their information in public affairs according to their respective ages-- even though the young have had more education. Young people in their twenties through the last three decades have, however, devoted somewhat less attention to international and national content in mass media and elsewhere than have their seniors. The most interested, attentive, and informed age groups have been those in their thirties, forties, and early fifties. The lower levels of awareness and concern among the older middle aged and aged than among these somewhat younger elements have been attributable primarily to the former's lower education. Among the college trained, concern and knowledge has gradually increased during the twenties and early thirties, reaching a rather stable plateau by the late thirties or early forties.

Differences among age groupings on foreign policy preferences have been somewhat more noticeable. Before and during World War II, the young disagreed with their seniors to some extent on the Neutrality Acts, Lend-Lease programs and other aid to the allies, entry into the war, and "peacetime" conscription. In each case, the younger groups were more inclined toward "conservative" or isolationist positions, which might have been motivated by their fear of being drafted if U.S. involvement in the European conflict became a reality. This impression is further suggested by the wider age differences among men than women on such questions. However, the age groups did not differ at all in their views on the desirability of expanding our armed forces, liberalized trade, or the need for a League of Nations.

After the war, the younger group came to accept the idea of peacetime conscription and an expensive military establishment to the same extent as their seniors. Even during the Vietnam war those in their twenties have been only somewhat (six or less percentage points) less favorably disposed to the draft than their seniors. Except on those matters wherein the issue of anti-communism was clearly salient, even the age groups at the extremes varied little during the first post-war decade. The older group was, however, more pessimistic about avoiding war and reaching peaceful settlements with the Communist powers and more inclined to prefer harder-line policies toward those governments than the ones then pursued by the U.S.

Attitudinal differences between the age groups with respect to world affairs appeared to widen somewhat following the mid-fifties, though not to the degree suggested by much of the press. Although to some extent due to the negative association of education with age, the college educated among the young were somewhat more liberal in both their international and domestic views than equally educated Americans in their late fifties and older. Such has been the case with respect to such varied issues as Chinese Communist membership in the U.N., negotiation rather than military escalation in Vietnam, foreign economic aid for nonaligned countries, negotiations, compromises, and economic and cultural exchanges with the U.S.S.R. and Eastern Europe, and freer trade. Age obviously has had some implications for more liberal world views, independent of education.

Age differences have likewise had some increased relevance in recent years to opinions on a number of domestic issues. Whereas Americans in their twenties were only slightly more liberal than oldsters in their thinking on race relations in the thirties, forties, and early fifties, by the sixties they were 8 to 26 percentage points more inclined to speed up the pace of integration, spend more federal money to improve the lots of Negroes, and vote for qualified Negroes for important political offices.

Except for old age pensions, Medicare, and other benefits coming primarily to older people, the elderly have also been somewhat more conservative than those in their twenties with regard to domestic welfare and economic policy. Thus, late middle aged and older citizens of the last decade or so have been 4 to 15 percentage points more inclined than those in their twenties to cut taxes and overall federal budgets, to regard poverty as due more to lack of individual effort than to social and economic circumstances, to oppose trade unions and the labor legislation favored by them, to disapprove of increased wage minimums, to disapprove of the Johnson anti-poverty and Great Society programs, and to view themselves as conservatives rather than liberals. Although age differences have had less connection with such views than income differences, the young have been at least somewhat more liberal on these domestic controversies even when such variables as income have been controlled.

Sex

Although the average education of the sexes has differed little, men have generally possessed more information on, been more interested in, and shown more willingness to express views on most aspects of public affairs than have women. However, when only those citizens venturing opinions have been considered, attitudinal differences between the sexes on most issues have been relatively small. Differences in opinion as well as in knowledge between the two sexes since the 1930's have tended to narrow, particularly among better educated seg-ments of the population. With few exceptions, opinion patterns have been asso-ciated with the same social and demographic factors among both sexes.

Insofar as they have advanced opinions, the sexes have not differed in their pre-war isolationist sentiments or in their post-war view that the U.S. should take a relatively active part in world affairs. Nor have the sexes varied consistently with respect to tariffs and trade, intercultural exchanges, stereotypes of foreigners, immigration, the League of Nations, and the U.N. The sexes were also equally likely to have sympathized with the victims of the Axis aggression in World War II. The sexes have also differed little in their impressions about the Communist world.

However, in the post-war period women have been slightly more likely to favor foreign non-military aid than have men--especially with regard to its humanitarian objectives. Larger differences between the sexes have pertained to attitudes on the use of military force and the implementation of policies regarded as risking U.S. involvement in war. Females were more likely to view our entry into the two world wars and the Korean and Vietnam conflicts as a mistake than were males. Women have been more likely to support U.S. withdrawals from wars already entered into and to be less receptive to the idea of "peacetime" conscription. Support for the defense establishment, military aid, and collective security arrangements has been less as well among the fair sex. Women have likewise been less disposed to accord the U.N. the means and authority to use force. Fear of war and hatred of it have been stronger themes in the thought of women than men.

The stronger humanitarian sentiments of women have carried over to the domestic scene as well. Since the 1930's they have been at least slightly more equalitarian than males with respect to most aspects of race relations. They have been similarly several percentage points more favorably disposed toward such programs as aid to dependent children, unemployment assistance, old age benefits, Medicare, anti-poverty programs, and "relief" generally.

Generally, however, women have not been more liberal than men, even in domestic areas. They have held a number of contradictory views. For example, their attitudes on fiscal policy, the national debt, and progressive taxation have been at least somewhat more conservative than those of men. Moreover, since the mid-thirties they have been less sympathetic to labor unions and labor legislation favored by them, including successive increases in the minimum wage. Finally, since early 1937, females have polled two to eight percentage points higher than men in their predilections to consider themselves conservatives rather than liberals and to say they would prefer a conservative political party or candidate over liberal ones.

Religion[5]

Throughout these three decades, Jews have been consistently more liberal than either Catholics, Protestants, or any other ethnic group on virtually all issues. The only exception to this pattern has been on the subject of race relations, in which Negroes in recent years have been more liberal than even Jews. On most questions, differences in levels of knowledge and in attitudes between Jews and other religious and ethnic groups have exceeded those among these other groups.

Whether or not Negroes have been included in the statistics, Catholics have been consistently more liberal than Protestants on most domestic issues-- Negro-white relations, the New Deal, social welfare, federal responsibility for full employment, Medicare, housing, trade unions, public works, and even federal aid to education. Southern white Protestants have tended to increase the average level of racist sentiment among Protestants, but even non-Southern

---

[5]Comparisons and trends mentioned in this section and the following section are discussed in detail in Alfred O. Hero, Jr., The Religious Factor and Foreign Policy (Baton Rouge: L.S.U. Press, forthcoming).

white Protestants have voiced at least somewhat more opposition to racial integration than have non-Southern white Catholics. Southern white Protestants have also been more segregationist than Southern white Catholics. The substantial differences between white Protestant and white Catholic racial attitudes seemed to widen somewhat in the sixties as pressures for desegregation accelerated, to the order of 6-28 percentage points depending on the aspect of civil rights in question. At least by the 1960's, Catholics significantly more than Protestants were apt to regard themselves as liberals rather than conservatives.

To some extent these religious differences were attributable in the pre-war period to the lower average income and socio-occupational status of most white Catholics as opposed to most white Protestants (at least outside the South) and to the larger proportion of Catholics affiliated with trade unions. But the average income of the two white religious groups in the late sixties is more nearly equal than it previously was, while the differences toward greater liberalism on these issues are at least as wide as they were before. Moreover, even when income and occupation are held constant, white Catholics have been more supportive of such social welfare programs than white Protestants. Well-to-do Catholics have thus favored them more than well-to-do Protestants; the former have also been more inclined to consider themselves Democrats and to vote for Democratic political candidates rather than view themselves as Republicans and vote for Republicans.

Although Catholics held generally more favorable views of their coreligionist, Senator Joseph McCarthy, than did Protestants, they have been no more apt than the latter to agree that the State Department, other federal governmental offices, or other "high places" have been significantly influenced or penetrated by Communists or other "subversives." Moreover, Catholics have not shown any greater inclination to exaggerate the number of Communists in America. Nor have the opinions of the two major Christian groups differed much with respect to free speech, freedom of the press, or other civil liberties.

The contrast between Catholic and Protestant views on foreign affairs has undergone a substantial transformation since the pre-war period. This phenomenon has undoubtedly been caused in part by the changed nature of the issues as well as by the change in the relative education and social and occupational roles of Catholics in American society. A probable third contributing factor is change within the Catholic Church itself.

Prior to our entry into the Second World War, white non-Southern Catholics were less informed about and somewhat less inclined to express views on most aspects of foreign policy than were white Protestants outside the South. Moreover, Catholics were distinctly less willing than Protestants to have the U.S. take an active role in most important international issues of the day. Although it is true that Catholics were more inclined to support Franco against the Loyalists, they displayed their more customary isolationist stance by not wanting to help the British, French, and Soviets against Germany and Italy before our formal entry into the war. They even manifested slightly greater willingness to let Japan control China rather than risk war to prevent her from doing so.

By the late 1940's, Catholics were at most only slightly less informed about most aspects of foreign relations than Protestants. Moreover, about equally large majorities of both Christian groups approved of a relatively active U.S. posture in international relations during the decade following the war. The proposed Bricker amendment was no more popular among Catholics than Protestants. During most of the initial post-war decade there was hardly any difference between Catholics' and Protestants' reactions to how well "the officials in Washington," "our government," the Secretary of State, or the like were handling our relations with other countries; this pattern remained true even during

Senator Joseph McCarthy's attacks on Executive officials in the early fifties. Although Catholics had been less enthusiastic than other religious groups about U.S. membership in or collaboration with the League of Nations, differences between the two Christian groups with respect to U.S. policies toward the U.N. during the initial decade and a half after the war were in most cases neither statistically significant nor consistent.

Few of the rather considerable pre-war differences in opinion between the two Christian groups with respect to foreign aid were apparent in regard to even early post-war aid programs. Similar majorities of both groups approved of the large shipments of food and other emergency relief to war-torn areas sent shortly after the war. The large loan to Britain in 1946 was only slightly less popular among Catholics than Protestants; the interreligious difference was smaller than it had been with respect to aiding Britain before 1942. Catholics were as inclined as Protestants to approve of both the Truman Doctrine and the Marshall Plan. Although Catholics were less enthusiastic than other Americans about sending military aid to the enemies of the Axis, in the late forties and early fifties military assistance to our allies in N.A.T.O. and other "friendly countries" was somewhat more popular among Catholics than Protestants. Catholics were likewise somewhat more favorably disposed than Protestants toward sending military supplies to Latin America, Nationalist China, and other parts of Asia.

These small differences between the two Christian groups with respect to military aid were associated with the tendency somewhat more prevalent among Catholics than Protestants of the initial post-war decade to anticipate war with the U.S.S.R. and to prefer a less compromising, more militarily based posture vis-a-vis that country. Conversely, the greater reluctance among Jews than among others prior to the Korean War to send military supplies was related to their more widespread optimism about avoiding war with the Soviet bloc, their more marked emphasis on economic and technical assistance to non-Communist countries, and their stronger proclivities toward negotiation and other non-military relationships with the Communist world. However, when the assault on South Korea led to a growth of fears of Communist attacks on their non-Communist neighbors, Jews became more favorably inclined toward military assistance than either Christian group.

During the early fifties Catholics were somewhat less inclined than Protestants to have heard of aid programs directed at the less developed world or to know much about them. But during the period 1949-1957, Catholics and Protestants were about equally predisposed to administering aid for "poorer countries," technical and economic assistance for "allies" and "friendly countries," military aid for Yugoslavia, and aid to less developed areas at prevailing or higher magnitudes. Although somewhat less inclined than Protestants, especially outside the South, to accord priority to economic over military aid, Catholics were slightly more likely to favor continuing "economic aid...to countries like India, which have not joined us against the Communists" as well as to "Communist countries like Poland which have rebelled against Russian control." Catholics also showed a greater proclivity to consider it "a good policy for the United States to try to help backward countries...raise their standard of living," to approve of channeling at least part of such assistance through the U.N., and to believe that such aid "helps the United States."

Nor did the two Christian groups differ much during the initial dozen or so years after V.J. Day with respect to tariffs and trade. Reactions of both to most foreign peoples were likewise similar. Even the more prevalent Catholic pre-war suspicions of the Protestant British and of their government had almost disappeared by the mid-1950's.

Catholics did, however, differ more or less consistently from Protestants during the early post-war period on the nature of the external Communist threat and how best to deal with it; nevertheless, these differences were small, typically only a few percentage points. Catholics were somewhat less likely to feel that the U.S.S.R. could "be trusted to cooperate with us," that it would change its policies and "make real peace with us," and that we could avoid a future war with it. Catholics were the most, and Jews the least, apt to believe our government "should be even firmer than we are today" with the Soviets, to oppose further compromises with them, to support the idea of "rolling back" Communism from Eastern Europe, and to oppose international control of atomic energy and weapons along with the proviso for the international inspection of the U.S. Conversely, Catholics were the least, and Jews the most, favorably disposed toward diplomatic negotiations, Summit discussions, continued membership of the Soviet Union in the U.N., and entry of Communist China into the world organization.

However, even these differences with respect to international Communism had declined or disappeared by the mid-fifties. By then the two Christian groups reacted about equally to proposed intercultural exchanges with Communist states, collective security arrangements to prevent Communist advances, and possible cooperative arrangements with Yugoslavia. They also voiced equivalent responses to the idea of an America taking the initiative for organizing a Summit conference with both Moscow and Peking in order to devise a solution to the problem of Quemoy and Matsu.

However, by the mid-1960's, Catholics had become at least somewhat more favorable to most forms of international cooperation than had Protestants, especially white Protestants. On successive surveys since 1962, Catholics have been an average of seven percentage points more inclined than Protestants to believe the U.N. was doing "a good job," six to ten percentage points more favorable to the idea of a standing U.N. emergency force, significantly more apt to feel that World War III would have been, and will continue to be, more likely without the U.N. They were also several percentage points more disposed to encourage U.N. intervention into the Vietnam issue.

Catholics have continued, as during the initial post-war decade, to be as supportive as Protestants of a strong U.S. defense establishment, of effective security arrangements with our allies, and of resistance to any Communist attack by military force, even at the risk of world nuclear war. Nevertheless, by the 1960's, Catholics, as well as Jews, were distinctly more optimistic than Protestants about avoiding such a war and reaching peaceful settlements of disputes with the Communist powers. The relative viewpoints of the two Christian groups on the international Communist problem of the early fifties and before had been reversed. During the sixties Catholics were more favorable to the partial nuclear test ban agreement, further compromises and negotiation for arms control, liberalized trade with the U.S.S.R., and broadened efforts generally to reduce cold war tensions.

By 1963, Catholics were also invariably eight or more percentage points more likely than Protestants to believe Communist China would be a greater long-run threat to world peace than the U.S.S.R. Nevertheless, since the fall of 1961, Catholics have been just as consistently (by 3 to 12 percent) more inclined than Protestants to favor Peking's admission to the U.N. and to "go along" with a majority of the U.N. on this matter.

In terms of economics, Catholics in the sixties have been no more favorably disposed than Protestants toward freer trade. On the other hand, they have become at least somewhat more approving of most types of aid to less developed countries and have been several percentage points more apt than Protestants to be "in general for foreign aid" and to favor giving economic "aid to other countries if they need help." Catholics have likewise recently been 3 to 8 percentage points more inclined than Protestants to support aid at its current or higher levels, to be willing to pay taxes to do so, to approve of the Peace Corps and other educational and technical assistance, and to feel "satisfied" with U.S. aid to "poor nations."

Catholics have been more favorably disposed than Protestants toward the Alliance for Progress and aid to Latin America in general, but not at the expense of assistance to Asia and Africa. They have, of course, been less willing than other groups to include birth control projects in aid, but the interreligious differences on even this loaded question have not been as large as might be expected; 31 percent of the Catholics versus 48 percent of the Protestants and 63 percent of Jews in early 1966 favored the inclusion of birth control programs.

Since 1936, Catholics have been more willing than Protestants, though not as willing as Jews, to expand or liberalize immigration into this country. However, differences between Catholics and Protestants seemed somewhat larger on the immigration issue in the mid-sixties than they did two decades before-- even where admitting non-Christians such as Jews and Orientals is in question.

Indications of degree of identification with religious institutions, such as frequency of church attendance, have never had much connection with attitudes toward national or international affairs. No consistent differences in attitudes on either international or national domestic issues have appeared between regular or frequent Protestant church-goers and Protestants who went to church less often or not at all. Among Catholics in the mid-sixties, those who frequently attended mass were slightly more liberal than less faithful Catholics on some domestic and international issues, but these differences were small and on numerous questions there were no differences at all.

Theological conservatives, fundamentalists, and persons of evangelical emphasis were, prior to our entry into World War II, at most only slightly more conservative about foreign policy than persons of a less literal--or more liberal--theological bent. The higher average education of the latter accounted for all or most of this small divergence. Fundamentalists have continued to be more segregationist, but this discrepancy can be attributed primarily to the combination of their lesser education, lower socio-economic and occupational status, and disproportionately large concentration in the South. Fundamentalists have remained somewhat more favorable to most transfers of wealth and services to the have-nots at home, a tendency again largely explained by their concentration among the less privileged economic groups.

By the 1960's, fundamentalists and members of denominations of that religious orientation were significantly less favorable than more theologically liberal, "social gospel" individuals and denominations toward economic aid to neutralist and Communist countries, trade with the latter, entry of Mainland China into the U.N., and, generally, efforts to relax tensions with the Communist and less developed worlds. Differences on these issues were at least somewhat wider than they had been between theological conservatives and theological liberals on the international issues of the pre-war period. However, these greater differences with respect to the same issues also occurred between the better and the less educated, the socio-economic classes, the occupational groups, and between rural and urban dwellers. These factors--education, class, occupation and region-- together with the relative shift of the heavily fundamentalist South on these questions, have undoubtedly been more important sources of recent changes in international attitudes than have religious considerations per se.

Ethnic and Racial Groups

Ethnic factors, together with the relative enthusiasm among Southern white Protestants for a more active foreign policy (see below), accounted for much of the difference between Catholics and Protestants with respect to some aspects of world affairs prior to December 1941. At that time Americans of Italian extraction--mainly Catholics--were the least inclined of white ethnic groups to favor most international commitments. German-Americans were almost as isolationist as Italian-Americans, while Irish-Americans were only somewhat more internationally disposed than German-Americans. Citizens of remote or, especially, more recent British or white British Commonwealth ancestry--mostly Protestants--were usually more apt than any of these three national groups to support active foreign involvements, especially aid to the Western allies against Germany and Italy. Sharing biases similar to those of Americans of British extraction were Scandinavian-Americans, non-Jewish Russian Americans, and persons whose parents or grandparents came from countries occupied by the Nazi or Fascist armies. After September 1, 1939, however, non-Jewish Polish-Americans, largely Catholics, were more inclined to aid Britain and France--even to the extent of America's entering the war herself--than were Protestants as a group. Moreover, German-American Protestants did not differ from German-American Catholics in their relative paucity of enthusiasm for aiding the opponents of the land of their ancestors. Irish-Americans were less willing to help the British, but they differed little from Protestants on how to deal with Japan, whether or not to sell munitions to China, and whether to extend Lend-Lease to the U.S.S.R. after the Nazi attack of June 22, 1941.

These ethnic differences had less pertinence to most post-war international issues than they had had in the struggles between their respective nations of origin prior to V.E. Day. Moreover, most ethnic identifications with the "old country" and, in the case of the Irish hostilities to Britain, seemed to have dissipated as the pre-war generations passed on and their offspring--less attached to the native lands of their ancestors--became adults. It is understandable that attitudinal differences between non-Jewish white ethnic groups with regard to most aspects of foreign policy were much smaller in the initial post-war decade than before; and, with the possible exception of Italian-Americans, they were almost non-existent by the 1960's. Italian-Americans seemed to continue to be somewhat less supportive of multilateral cooperation than most other ethnic groups even as late as 1965, although they diverged less then from national norms than they had earlier.

Ethnic differences on race relations have been mainly reflections of the location, education, and socio-occupational status of most members of the national groups in question. Anglo-Saxons and old-stock white Americans generally-- disproportionately rural, farmers, and Southerners--have been more segregationist than Irish, Germans, and other predominantly urban and non-Southern groups. Italians have tended to be somewhat more opposed to integration than the other mainly urban ethnic groups. Moreover, ethnic differences with respect to public welfare and related issues have been largely functions of the average family income of the groups in question.

Given the low average education and socio-economic-occupational status of Negroes, it is not surprising that they--as contrasted to whites--have been considerably less informed about, less interested in, less apt to ascribe im- portance to, and less inclined to hold opinions on, most international issues. It is generally true that the less well known the phenomenon is, the smaller the proportion of Negroes among those with some knowledge of it. These racial differences have narrowed over the years as the educational level of Negroes has gradually approached that of whites, but Negroes in the mid-sixties still lag behind whites by considerable margins in these regards.

The proportions of Negroes who have expressed opinions on foreign affairs have often been so much smaller than proportions among whites that it is often difficult to interpret interracial differences in views expressed. Negroes have frequently been less apt than whites to voice either approval or disapproval of particular policies. The most meaningful comparisons of the distributions of opinions between the two racial groups have been those statistics counting only individuals who expressed views.

Among those Americans who have ventured opinions, Negroes were substantially less inclined than whites to approve of pre-war American involvements such as membership in the League of Nations, liberalization of the Johnson and Neutrality Acts, Lend-Lease, and other assistance to the enemies of the Axis. Moreover, after 1945, the initial post-war loan to Britain, Truman Doctrine aid to Greece and Turkey, the Marshall Plan, N.A.T.O., the U.N., and most other bilateral or multilateral commitments of our government prior to the late 1950's, were like-wise less favorably received in the black than in the white communities.

These variations were to some extent related to the white race of Western Europeans and to the ethnic and cultural ties of white Americans with them. Nevertheless, prior to the late fifties, Negroes were on the whole also somewhat less supportive than whites of non-military aid to most less-developed recipients, at that time mainly in Asia. Even though Negroes were as favorably disposed as whites to sending military supplies to South Korea during the war there, and to the Arab Middle East under the Eisenhower Doctrine, the black community was less enthusiastic about according economic assistance to either area.

Throughout the early and mid-fifties as well, Negroes were less inclined than whites to assign relative importance to economic, as against military, aid. In April 1956, for instance, 78 percent of the Negroes versus 90 percent of the whites favored continuing technical assistance to improve agriculture and education in "backward countries,"; 84 percent versus 90 percent would "continue economic aid to countries that have agreed to stand with us against Communist aggression"; and 33 percent versus 48 percent would "continue economic aid to countries like India which have not joined us as allies against the Communists." The following fall 42 percent of the Negroes versus 60 percent of the whites approved of sending economic assistance to Poland, and two months later 59 percent contrasted with 68 percent felt Congress should appropriate approximately $4 billion for aid for the forthcoming fiscal year "as in recent years." Negroes were also less willing than white Americans to approve of President Eisenhower's unsuccessful proposal that at least part of our economic aid to less developed countries be placed on a longer term, more continuing, basis than was permitted by one-year Congressional authorizations.

However, by the end of the 1950's or the first year or so of the 1960's, most of these attitudinal (but not informational) differences, especially with regard to the less developed world, had disappeared. With the three concurrent developments--independence of most of Africa south of the Sahara, acceleration of Negro demands for equality at home, and assumption by a Democratic administration of control of U.S. foreign policy--the relative positions of the two races on foreign aid became reversed. By the mid-sixties, Negroes with views were more favorably inclined than whites toward most types of aid, and toward most other multilateral cooperation as well.

This wider support among Negroes than whites in recent years for economic assistance for underdeveloped, including neutralist, countries has not, however, implied any lessening approval of military aid; this phenomenon contradicts what some might have supposed from the recent attacks against U.S. military inter- vention by the left, more radical, wing of Negro civil rights leadership. In- stead, Negroes were slightly more favorable than whites toward military aid as well.

Negroes of the sixties remained distinctly less inclined than whites to ascribe importance to trade expansion, but those who harbored any views had by then become more liberal than whites about reduction of barriers to international commerce. Negroes had likewise become more favorably disposed than whites to liberalized immigration policies and to exchanges of people with other countries, even when Africa was not mentioned. They had also become several percentage points more inclined than whites with views to admit Peking to the U.N. and to "go along" with a General Assembly majority on this question.

Negroes possessing views have continued, to about the same extent as whites, to support a strong defense establishment, and they have remained slightly more likely than whites to anticipate another major war. However, by the mid-sixties, they were less inclined than whites to perceive domestic Communists as either a "great" or a "considerable" danger to our security; in fact, they were more apt to view them as being of no danger or not very much danger. Negroes have also been somewhat less supportive than whites of escalation of the Vietnamese war and more apt to advocate negotiation and compromise to settle it. In late 1964, 45 percent of the Negroes with views compared with only 35 percent of the whites felt U.S. farmers and businessmen should be permitted to do business in non-military items with Communist countries.

Since at least the New Deal, Negroes who have ventured opinions have been substantially more favorably disposed than whites to expansions of welfare programs--"relief," old age benefits, unemployment insurance, and so on. However, the black segment of the population has seemed to differ little on these matters, if at all, from white people with similarly low average income backgrounds. Negroes have, of course, been much more favorable to racial integration than whites, although considerable minorities of them a decade or more ago preferred, for one reason or another, a segregated social system. The proportions of Negroes preferring segregation have, however, declined substantially faster since the Second World War than have segregationist sentiments among whites.

Southern Negroes over the last thirty years have not only been significantly less well informed about national and international affairs than Northern ones, but also more conservative, isolationist and neo-isolationist, virtually regardless of the type of issue.

Geographic Region

The former Confederacy has historically been the most distinctive region of the country in its economy, culture, racial composition, and in other respects. The South has likewise differed more than any other region from the rest of the country in its views on certain aspects of public affairs.[6]

Southerners have been clearly less well informed, less interested, and less inclined to advance views than non-Southerners on virtually all the issues considered in this discussion. Although the large proportion of Negroes among the Southern population has lowered the average level of information, interest, and manifestation of opinions, Southern whites have also consistently lagged behind non-Southern whites in the same respects. In general, the more specialized or less generally known the information and the less widespread opinion throughout the country on an issue, the smaller the proportion of white Southerners among those Americans who have been informed or have expressed views on it.

The area of foreign affairs has had considerable attitudinal shift on the part of Southern white residents since the thirties. Prior to the Pearl Harbor attack, those white Southerners offering opinions to survey questions manifested a decidedly more internationalist or interventionist tendency than

---

[6]For more comprehensive discussions of these and other differences between the South and other regions, see Alfred O. Hero, Jr., The Southerner and World Affairs (Baton Rouge: L.S.U. Press, 1965).

other Americans; they showed more willingness than other regional groups to join the League of Nations, to expand trade and to lower tariffs, to liberalize the Neutrality Acts, and to aid the opponents of the Axis. But as the war came to a close, many of these regional differences began to disappear. Moreover, by the late 1950's and early 1960's, Southern whites were more disinclined than the rest of the country to favor economic aid to nonaligned countries (especially in Asia and Africa), to channel more such aid through international agencies, or to put more of it on a longer than one-year basis. However, Southern whites have remained at least as supportive as the rest of the country toward large defense budgets, collective security arrangements such as N.A.T.O., and foreign military aid. They were thus by the late fifties the most apt of regional groups to emphasize military means, and "hard-line" approaches generally, in our relations with Communist China and the U.S.S.R.

During the pre-war period, the populations of the Midwest and Plains states harbored the most isolationist views of the regions of the country. Second to the South, the Northeast was most interventionist. The Far West was less favorable to active U.S. participation in world affairs than the Northeast, but was more interventionist than the non-Southern areas in between.

These limited differences between regions outside the South had become greatly attenuated by the 1950's. Northeasterners of the 1960's were but half a dozen, or fewer, percentage points more willing than Midwesterners or any other non-Southern regional group to admit Communist China to the U.N. or to "go along" with a General Assembly majority to do so, to increase foreign aid or to maintain it at current levels, or to expand trade, encourage arms control negotiations, intercultural exchanges, or other efforts to reduce disagreements with Eastern Europe. Differences between residents of the Pacific Coast and those of the Northern interior on these questions were smaller still. By 1959-1967, the regions outside the South diverged hardly at all on defense policy, collective security, military aid, technical assistance, "Food for Peace," world trade, or other international matters. The Far West was at most only somewhat more inclined than the rest of the non-South to give the problems of East Asia priority over those of Europe, Africa, and Latin America.

Thus, the marked regional patterns in Congress on foreign policy seem little related to differences among Congressmen's regional constituencies after World War II. Congressmen from the Plains and Midwest have usually voted more conservatively on world issues than legislators from the Northeast and Pacific Coast. However, these regional patterns in Congress have been at most only marginally apparent among their respective voters.

The recent differences between the South (especially the white South) and other regions with respect to world affairs have been due in part to the impact of racial agitation and pressure for desegregation in the South. These pressures have also resulted in the South's further alienation from the federal government and its foreign policy, and in its greater sensitivity to racially related problems abroad. However, at least as important as domestic convulsion has been the changed nature of international relations itself: in particular, there has been the shift from giving aid to Britain and France in the pre-war period and to white, allied, industrialized Western Europe in the initial post-war years, to now administering aid to nonaligned, non-white, underdeveloped Asia and Africa. Also of some significance are the more recent efforts of our government to lessen its emphasis on military means for containing Communist regimes, and to work out agreements through negotiation, compromise, and other diplomatic approaches when possible.

Domestic issues have also resulted in differing opinions between the South and the North. The white South has, of course, diverged most from the rest of the country in its reactions to race relations. Although differences within

the South on this issue have been wide, even when Southern areas with few Negroes--
such as the mountains--have been excluded from the analysis, the gaps between the regions as a whole and the rest of the country have been large on most aspects of
racial change. For example, only 26 percent of Southern whites, contrasted with
50 percent of their Northern counterparts, approved of the proposed anti-lynch
law in 1940. In 1946 the former were similarly only one half as likely as the
latter to favor the ideas of F.E.P.C. Although Southern whites by the 1960's
were almost as convinced as Northern whites that integration would be inevitable,
the latter have remained several times more inclined to approve of it. The proportion of Northern whites favoring the various civil rights bills of the late
1950's and 1960's was typically at least twice as large when compared to the
white South. Even increasing education and urbanization of the South did not
greatly narrow these regional differences.

Southerners as a group, whether or not Negroes have been included, have
also been consistently less libertarian than their non-Southern compatriots
about freedom of speech and other civil liberties for communists, socialists,
atheists, and other "leftists," and for all those who do not conform to Southern
values. They have likewise, since at least the late thirties, been five to
thirteen percentage points less apt than non-Southerners to approve of labor
unions, strikes, and closed shops, and the size of these gaps has not changed much
by the sixties, even though the South has been increasingly unionized in these
last three decades. Southerners since the late thirties have likewise been an
average of six percentage points less favorably disposed than non-Southerners
both to the initial idea of establishing a minimum wage and then to its successive
increases.

Fear of agitation against the segregated system, together with the culturally
homogeneous and agrarian background of most of the South, largely account for its

lesser support of civil liberties for non-conformists. The relative paucity
of union members and the disproportionately large number of farmers and rural
and small-town folk in the region have been, to a considerable extent, responsible
for its more widespread disapproval of trade unions. Non-unionists and, especially,
farmers outside the South have been almost as critical of unions as their
Southern counterparts. The minimum wage has classically been perceived by many
in the South as applying mostly to urban workers in the North, with the result
of raising the costs of products which Southerners buy without significantly
raising their incomes.

The exacerbation of the race issue, however, seems primarily responsible
for shifts in Southern opinion on some other internal questions in recent years.
Although Southerners have always been about as opposed to higher taxes and as
inclined to feel their own federal income taxes have been too high as Northerners
have, their views on how these taxes should be spent on welfare and other
measures in America have been significantly affected by the race issue since
the mid-fifties.

In the late thirties and early forties, Southerners were more inclined to
consider themselves liberals rather than conservatives, and were also more
inclined to have favorable images of the programs of the New Deal than non-
Southerners. Southerners more than any other regional group felt that both
business and labor unions "should be regulated to a greater extent by the federal
government." Southerners were even at least several percentage points more
willing than others to have the federal government take over and run the railroads, the public utilities, and the banks.

But by the late fifties and sixties, Southern whites had become distinctly
more conservative than white Northerners on such issues as federal resources
devoted to social welfare, housing, public works, anti-poverty, and Great

Society programs generally. Similarly, by that time, whites in the South had become somewhat more apt than those elsewhere to regard themselves as conservatives rather than liberals.

Outside the South, Northeasterners have tended to be more liberal than Midwesterners and residents of the Great Plains with respect to civil rights. Inhabitants of the West Coast have for the most part been more equalitarian on this controversial question than compatriots in the Northern interior, but less so than Northeasterners. Plains and Midwestern people have understandably been six or more percentage points more favorable to expanded federal expenditures on agriculture than those in the Northeast and West. Although Northeasterners of the thirties and early forties were no more apt than Americans in the Northern interior, or than Westerners, to consider themselves liberals rather than conservatives, by the late fifties and sixties they were somewhat more so inclined. This development, like the reverse one in the South, seems largely attributable to the increasing civil rights connotations of these terms. But on most domestic economic and welfare issues, the several Northern regions have differed very little, if at all.

Voting Behavior and Partisan Affiliation

Voters have been better informed and more likely to express opinions on public affairs than those who have not voted in Presidential and Congressional contests. Voters have also been on the whole somewhat, and sometimes substantially, more supportive of active U.S. foreign involvements, particularly on issues in which support has been highly correlated with education. However, the reverse has been the case on most domestic economic and welfare issues-- non-voters have typically been more sympathetic to the New Deal, the Great Society, social security, pensions, unemployment benefits, "relief," Medicare, higher minimum wages, and the like. In general, the larger the voter turnout in an election, the less knowledgeable the electorate is likely to be, the more conservative its international views, and the more liberal its opinions on transfers of wealth and public expenditures at home. The explanation lies mainly in the higher average education and income of voters than non-voters.

Given their higher average education and social, occupational, and economic status, it is also understandable that Americans who have identified with the Republican Party and voted for its candidates have normally been somewhat better informed and more apt to advance opinions on public issues than their Democratic counterparts.

Republicans have been consistently more critical of trade unions, more favorable to right-to-work laws, more hostile to strikes, and more opposed to increases in the minimum wage. They have likewise been less sympathetic to federal regulation of business, high taxation, expansion of social security, unemployment benefits, aid to education and health, slum clearance and low cost housing, veterans' benefits, and even expensive farm programs. On most such questions other than public works, majorities of Democrats have normally approved of allocating prevailing or expanded resources to such programs, while majorities of Republicans have been opposed--revealing considerably larger partisan differences than those apparent with respect to issues of domestic race relations or foreign policy. Perceived self-interest in such redistributions of wealth is patently a more crucial determinant of partisan preference than views on either civil rights or foreign relations.

But even with respect to such bread-and-butter issues the magnitude of partisan differences has been significantly smaller when a Republican has been in the White House, or when a prominent Republican has been a leader in the program or proposal in question, than during a Democratic administration or when the Congressional leadership with respect to the issue has been largely Democratic.

Moreover, whereas Republicans and voters for Republican candidates have been considerably more apt than Democratic partisans to feel the national budget and debts have been too large and should be cut during Democratic administrations, during President Eisenhower's tenure the reverse was the case.

Such oscillations (depending on which party has controlled the Executive and which partisan figures have sponsored particular proposals) have been more marked in race relations, foreign affairs, and other areas which are not so directly linked with the differential economic self-interests of Republicans versus Democrats. Although Republicans have perhaps been fundamentally more conservative on some of these issues than Democrats, these partisan differences have been much smaller than might be assumed from the public stances of their partisan leaders in Congress and elsewhere.

It is true that expressed attitudes of Republicans on a few international issues have been slightly more conservative than those of Democrats even during the two Eisenhower terms. Since the late thirties Republicans and voters for their candidates have been 1 to 10 percentage points less favorably disposed than their Democratic counterparts to the Reciprocal Trade Agreements program, the Trade Expansion Act, the Kennedy Round negotiations, and liberalized trade relations generally. Although the partisan groups have not diverged much in their anticipation of another war, Republicans remained 2 to 8 percentage points less enthusiastic than Democrats, even during the Eisenhower years, to inter-cultural exchanges, visits by Soviet leaders to the U.S., and other such programs designed to reduce cold war tensions.

However, on a number of other foreign policy issues, partisan differences have been so small that Democrats have expressed somewhat more liberal views when a Democrat is in the White House, Republicans when one of them is President. Thus, prior to our entry into World War II, Democrats were more favorably disposed toward liberalizing the Johnson and Neutrality Acts and assisting the opponents of the Axis.

Partisan differences declined considerably after our entry into the war. For example, during the Truman administration, Republicans were about as apt as Democrats to label themselves as internationalists rather than isolationists and to advocate our taking an active part in world affairs. On a series of surveys of the period, Democrats were on the average only 6 percentage points more likely than Republicans to favor peacetime conscription and taxes and other sacrifices for expanded national defense. Partisan differences were even smaller, or were non-existent, with respect to N.A.T.O., the U.N., technical assistance to "backward" countries, multilateralization of such assistance, sending food to India, and helping South Korea repair its war damage. Moreover, Republicans and Dewey voters were actually somewhat more apt than their Democratic equivalents to favor the initial post-war loan to Britain, food shipments to war-torn areas, Truman Doctrine aid to Greece and Turkey, Marshall Plan and military aid to Western Europe, the amount of funds devoted to foreign aid generally, and, after the North Korean attack on South Korea, military aid to Asia and Yugoslavia. Republicans in the last year or so of Truman's administration were also slightly more inclined than Democrats to view economic aid as more important than military aid.

With the advent of the Eisenhower administration, relative international attitudes of the two partisan groups slowly shifted. By the time of his second four years in the White House, Americans who voted for Eisenhower or who viewed themselves as Republicans were at least slightly more favorably disposed than Stevenson voters or Democrats to most types of foreign aid, U.S. cooperation with the U.N. and N.A.T.O., and expansion of resources devoted to national defense.

However, during the Kennedy and Johnson administrations, these relative partisan opinions reversed once again. By the mid-sixties, Democrats and Kennedy voters were 2 to 13 percentage points more favorable than Republicans and Nixon voters to most types of aid, 4 to 5 percentage points more disposed to a U.N. emergency force, and 1 to 6 percentage points more willing to admit Peking to the U.N. Attitudinal differences between Johnson and Goldwater voters on such issues have been substantially larger.

Moreover, public approval of Democratic-sponsored measures by leading Republicans during a Democratic Presidency tends to eliminate or even reverse popular partisan differences. For example, Republicans expressed views somewhat more favorable than those of Democrats toward Lend-Lease and aid to Europe almost a decade later when informed that Wendell Willkie and Arthur Vandenberg, respectively, supported these programs.

Similar oscillations have transpired with respect to civil rights. Partisan groups differed not at all on the proposed federal anti-lynching law of 1940. Democrats and Truman voters were slightly more supportive of that President's civil rights proposals. But by the spring of 1955, for example, 64 percent of the Republicans contrasted with only 48 percent of the Democrats approved of the Supreme Court school desegregation decision of the previous May. However, under the administrations of Kennedy and Johnson, those who voted for these men, or considered themselves Democrats, became consistently more supportive of controversial civil rights bill, the pace of desegregation, etc.

Differences in the demographic composition of the two parties help to explain some of these findings. The lower average educational and socio-economic levels of Democrats and voters for their candidates tend to counteract any effects the more liberal national leadership might have on their opinions about world affairs and race relations. The disproportionate number of white Southerners in the Democratic fold has exerted a similar effect. But even when these factors are held constant, such as when Northern white Democrats are compared with Northern white Republicans of similar income and educational levels, partisan differences on these issues are certainly considerably smaller than those between the roll call votes of their respective Congressmen on the same matters.

CHAPTER 3: LIBERALISM-CONSERVATISM

The liberal-conservative dimension has intrigued scholars for years with its potential for explaining the variation in political attitudes of the populace. However, these hopes faded when encountered with research done on a mass level. Repeated samples of the national electorate by the Survey Research Center (Campbell et al, 1960; Converse, 1964) have convincingly demonstrated that no such organizing dimension or ideological structure exists for most citizens. Correlations between specific issue items were often low and when such congruence occurred, it was generally for other reasons than that of ideology (i.e., most usually a result of self-interest or group preference).

Research of this kind suggests that liberal-conservative scales and indices have limited utility when applied to large, cross-sectional samples. However, other research has pointed to the possible merit of these measures when administered to more "elite" segments of the population--such as political leaders and activists, strong party identifiers, and well-educated people in general. Many scales in this section were applied to one such elite group--the college student, who is far more likely to be knowledgeable, articulate, and politically sophisticated than the average citizen. Groups such as this generally have the information needed to organize political issues and events into a meaningful and consistent attitude system.

There are other limitations to these scales than just their being meaningful only to limited segments of the population. A large proportion of these scales were constructed many years ago. As a consequence, item content is often dated, referring to issues no longer of political relevance. Furthermore, a comprehensive review by Murphy and Likert (1938) of early studies of

liberalism-conservatism demonstrated that they had few consistent correlates--
the one apparent conclusion was that liberal-radical attitudes were somehow
associated with general feelings of dissatisfaction. Either the scales were
not tapping the dimension they were purporting to or (if they were considered
valid) they had little power to explain the variation in other attitude
dimensions.

The problem of scale restriction to elite populations suggests that
other dimensions might be more appropriate as research tools for the mass
electorate. The present authors feel that distinctions along the "modernism"
dimension might be more pervasive and relevant than the liberal-conservative
distinctions in cross-sectional samples. Accordingly, the reader might wish
to refer to the scale of Concern with Progress developed by Morgan and
associates which deals with this aspect of the liberal-conservative dimension.
Since this concept is most important in the study of underdeveloped countries,
we have also included references to empirical efforts to develop measures for
these populations. Measures developed by Lerner, Doob, Inkeles and Smith,
and Waisenan and Durlak will be summarized and referenced at the end of this
section.

The first sixteen scales in this section are presented in order of considered merit; the seventeenth scale taps the "modernism" dimension and is
included as a possible alternative to the liberal-conservative concept.

1. Ideological Agreement with Goldwater (Selznick and Steinberg 1966)
2. Conservatism Scale (McClosky 1958)
3. Social Attitudes Scales (Kerlinger 1963)
4. Conservatism-Radicalism Battery (Centers 1949)
5. Political-Economic Conservatism (PEC) Scale (Adorno et al. 1950)
6. Radicalism-Conservatism (Eysenck 1947)
7. The R-C (Radicalism-Conservatism) Scale (Nettler and Huffman 1957)
8. Liberalism-Conservatism Scale (Wright and Hicks 1966)
9. Liberalism-Conservatism Scale (Kerr 1952)
10. Liberalism-Conservatism Scale (Hartmann 1938)
11. C-R Opinionnaire (Lentz 1935)

12. Personage Admiration (Lentz 1939)
13. Situation-Response Survey (Pace 1939)
14. Harper's Social Beliefs and Attitudes Test (Boldt and Stroud 1934)
15. Politico-Economic Radicalism-Conservatism (Sanai and Pickard 1949)
16. Radicalism-Conservatism and Social Mobility (Hetzler 1954)
17. Concern with Progress (Morgan, Sirageldin, and Baerwaldt 1966)

The opinion of the present authors is that only the first five scales
are suitable for extensive use. The problems of datedness, overly sophisticated
wording, and inadequate meeting of psychometric criteria have made the remaining scales far less generally useful. This is not to deny their ability to
discriminate among some samples of college students or political elites, but
the precision and accuracy of this discrimination is felt to be less satisfactory than that of the first five measures.

The first scale was devised by Selznick and Steinberg and applied to a
national probability sample. It was found to have yielded an impressive correlation with vote intention for Goldwater in 1964, a correlation that would
undoubtedly have been less in an election in which the candidate's ideological
stance was not as obvious as it was in Goldwater's case. However, the scale,
in large part, did seem to be tapping pre-existing beliefs rather than those
induced by that particular campaign. One of the major findings when using the
scale in analysis work was that conservative beliefs did appear to affect
vote preference when a candidate clearly declared his agreement with those
beliefs. This association was strongest among those with strong ideological
beliefs, whereas the majority seemed to be reacting more to perceived group
self-interest and habitual party preference than to ideological convictions
in determining their voting choice. No evidence is given by the authors
regarding the homogeneity or reliability of the scale.

In contrast, another scale devised by McClosky showed little correlation
with either vote or party affiliation. It was designed not to measure agreement

with conservative political beliefs but rather a general attitudinal predisposition toward preference for the status quo and respect for the past. In many respects, some of the ideas for the item wordings go back as far as Edmund Burke and his philosophy of politics and society. One finding of the study was quite surprising--the lower-income people generally scored as more conservative than their higher socio-economic counterparts. This pattern was partly confounded by response set (i.e., the tendency of people to respond to the form rather than the content of the question), but, even when controls for this were imposed, the less affluent still appeared significantly more conservative. McClosky presents no reliability data for this scale and not a great deal of evidence in support of validity.

Unlike many scales developed in an academic setting, our third scale is composed of items worded in a relatively unsophisticated language. Although it has yet to be applied to large or representative cross-sectional samples or to satisfactorily demonstrate validity, Kerlinger has laid adequate groundwork for establishing his scale's homogeneity. He factor analyzed the scale results and found liberalism and conservatism to be isolated as two separate factors rather than as opposite ends of the same factor. The author was also responsible for drawing up an analogous scale for educational attitudes measuring the "progressivism-traditionalism" continuum earlier mentioned in this section.

The next scale, Centers' Conservatism-Radicalism Battery, is probably mistitled. Whereas it does isolate white-collar workers from blue collar ones, this could be expected since the item content has a strong labor vs. management orientation. The scale may capture something more general than this specific economic orientation, but it is difficult to verify such a claim. However, the scale does have some exceptional properties speaking well for its use-- such as simply worded items, fairly current item content, and strong evidence of homogeneity and unidimensionality.

Another measure that has received considerable attention is the PEC Scale by Adorno and others. Researchers contemplating use of this scale should become familiar with its history and the extensive critique of it provided in the Christie and Jahoda volume (1954). The scale was used to tap aspects of the general syndrome called "the authoritarian personality." Although necessary to their work, some of the items now seem dated and overly complicated. The major advantage of the scale is that it has been widely used and has generated certain results consistent with the authoritarian personality dimension, correlating especially well with ethnocentric attitudes.

The items in Eysenck's radicalism-conservatism (or R) scale seem somewhat dated and cumbersome. Moreover, they were developed for use with a British sample, and apparently a well-educated one as well. However, the 14 items in the scale do show substantial inter-item correlations (hence high scale homogeneity) and the author presents impressive data regarding known-groups validity. Seven of the items are worded in the radical direction and seven in the conservative direction allowing the possibility of controlling for response set.

The Nettler and Huffman R-C Scale is fairly recent and has very impressive evidence of validation by known groups. Test-retest reliability is also high. Although the items were used on a variety of non-college groups including business executives, political party workers, and union leaders, they do seem to require considerable sophistication for adequate comprehension by the rank-and-file. In an unusual application of the scale, R-C scores were correlated with scores on Maslow's Security Scale; it was found from this that conservatives and politically active radicals tended to be secure, while inactive radicals tended to be insecure.

Of the remaining scales, the instrument written by Wright and Hicks is the most recent. The items, developed on a sample of politically active college students, require such a high level of political sophistication that their use would be limited to comparable groups of students or to political elites. In addition, the evidence for homogeneity and validity is not completely convincing.

The items from Kerr's liberal-conservative scale also do not seem to be dated even though the measure was constructed some fifteen years ago. Kerr used simply worded items and did produce factors of interest from a factor analysis. However, neither the evidence for homogeneity nor validity is impressive.

One of the more interesting measures is Hartmann's liberal-conservative scale. Men of such repute as Norman Thomas and Earl Browder served as validational judges in preparing the scale for use with a national (but not cross-sectional) sample. In considering this measure for current use, however, it should be noted that, although the content of the items is general enough not to be dated, the specific wording of the items is certainly both dated and unsuited for rank-and-file samples.

Lentz's Conservatism-Radicalism Opinionnaire was considered one of the best measures of its time thirty years ago, and, indeed, it does boast parallel forms, reversed item wordings, impressive test-retest reliability, and several satisfactory validational studies. However, the scale was only administered to samples of college students since it required a high level of sophistication for adequate comprehension. As with Hartmann's scale, it is not so much the item content as the item wording that is dated.

Lentz also devised another measure, a Personage Admiration Test, which is worth noting both for its novel approach and for the interesting differences

that are found in the personage admirations of conservatives and radicals.
As might be expected, the list of names is quite dated. No evidence of
homogeneity or validity is presented.

The next scale, Pace's Situation Response Survey, is also quite dated.
Its importance lies in the fact that it is one of the few measures that deals
with the behavioral component of liberal-conservative attitudes. Convincing
evidence for validity is offered in that there was absolutely no overlap in
the scores of radical and conservative criterion groups. However, the items
seem long and complex, requiring a fair amount of knowledge on the part of the
subject. In addition, some of the items seem to tap more than one attitude
dimension.

Harper's Social Beliefs and Attitudes Test is the oldest of the scales
covered in this section. Not surprisingly, the items are overly complex and
express outdated sentiments. Unlike other instruments of its age, however,
this scale shows more than adequate concern with reliability and validity
in its construction.

The items in the Sanai and Pickard scale seem to preclude its use on
American rank-and-file respondents as they require a fairly high degree of
political sophistication to comprehend and were developed on upper middle-
class British respondents. The utility of the scale is made more questionable
by the scanty validational data. The liberal-conservative dimension could be,
in turn, more salient to British voters. In another study of the British
electorate, Trenaman and McQuail (1961) found a "traditional vs. radical"
component to be the largest factor emerging from electors' views of the
parties and candidates in the 1959 British national election. Unfortunately,
we were unable to clearly identify the specific steps or items that went into
the construction of their scales, making it impossible to describe and

evaluate them adequately in this volume.

One of the last scales mentioned above is Hetzler's <u>Radicalism-Conservatism</u> measure. This scale has two features of merit: it was applied to a cross-sectional sample and it appears to be a forerunner of the self-anchoring scale. The scale is brought into question, however, by the author's unvalidated assumption that a measure of "satisfaction/dissatisfaction with government" is a measure of "conservatism/radicalism." It was found that dissatisfaction, like conservatism, was higher in the lower social classes.

Still other liberal-conservative scales are mentioned in the literature, a few of which will be briefly considered here but not in the detailed scale profile descriptions which follow. Shaw and Wright (1967) present five such scales purporting to measure political ideology. The <u>Florida Scale of Civil Rights</u> is the most recent of these and is probably for this reason the most interesting and useful. Item wording is such as to qualify the scale mainly for use with the more literate segment of society, although it has been used to some extent outside of college classroom situations. Solid evidence for the validity of the scale is lacking. The Rundquist-Sletto scale of economic conservatism is over thirty years old, yet the items do not seem dated today. Test-retest correlations over a sixty day period were reported to be over .80, an impressive figure. The main problem with the Sanai scale is the same as with the Sanai-Pickard scale reviewed in this section--it was developed on and for British populations, especially selected segments of them. Newcomb's <u>PEP Scale</u> was developed on college students in 1939, and the items seem dated and complex; nevertheless, the .90 test-retest correlation between freshman and senior years of the students involved is quite high. Fifth and finally, the Edwards <u>Public Opinion Questionnaire</u> was developed on an even more limited college sample base. Although the items are not as dated as the PEP items, they would be difficult for those not exposed to college.

As noted above, we consider the modernism dimension more applicable to and useful on cross-sectional samples than the liberal-conservative distinction. One relevant and important measure that has been developed on a cross-section of the U.S. population is the Concern with Progress Scale by Morgan, Sira-geldin, and Baerwaldt. The scale consists of both behavioral and attitudinal components. Homogeneity, while not high, was statistically significant; in addition, some reasonable evidence for validity was reported. Many of the items have a built-in middle-class bias, which may explain why the scale correlates so highly with social class. However, the expectation that younger persons within each class level would show more "modernism" was confirmed.

The reader may also be interested in an Initiative Scale developed by the Opinion Research Corporation (1960), currently being revised and updated. For this reason, it is simply appended to the Concern with Progress Scale. The Initiative Scale consists of the following three groupings, each composed of about seven items:

1. Attention to the world (e.g., readership of printed media, travel)

2. Conversation with other people (e.g., politics, business conditions)

3. Activity in organizations (e.g., professional, business, church)

Scores on the Initiative Scale were found to be highly related to social class, as was true with the Concern with Progress Scale. While 40 percent of those initiating the above activities were found to come from the top sixth of the population as ranked by occupational prestige, only 11 percent were found among the bottom third of this population.

The reader will find four scales mentioned in Rogers (1962), a book which places heavy emphasis on the individual's belief in traditional or modern norms in a model of the diffusion of innovations. Three of these scales deal only with farmers, but the fourth is relevant to our more general purposes. This last measure was devised by Lerner (1958) and consists of the reactions of the individual to nine public issues. Lerner is interested in the number of "no-opinions" or "don't know" responses he receives from each individual. He assumes that the more "modern-oriented" the person the fewer of these responses he will give and vice-versa.

As yet unpublished is a multi-nation study of modernism done by the Harvard Project on the Sociocultural Aspects of Development (Inkeles and Smith 1966). A modernism scale was developed which utilized well over 100 items. When the results of the study are published, the scale will undoubtedly be a major contribution both to the measurement and to the understanding of modernism across societies.

Waisenan and Durlak (1967) present data indicating that in Costa Rica usage of the mass media is related to a modern view of the world. They found that respondents who reported higher use of the media also perceived themselves as more innovative, more favorable toward risk, planning, and birth control, more satisfied with national conditions, and more favorable toward high educational achievement for their children. Pure media usage would probably not reflect modernism in the United States, since in this country it is the least educated (and, hence, the least modern-oriented) segments of society who usually spend the most time watching television; however, attention to the printed media (i.e., newspapers and magazines) might prove to be an accurate indicator of modernism in America, as noted in Opinion Research Corporation Initiative Scale described just above.

Doob (1967) also has attempted to measure modernism by administering a collection of eighty Likert-type items to a number of African samples. Although these items are still in the developmental stage, Doob has already devised a noteworthy classification for them. He classifies the items into six response categories (e.g., modern, non-modern, mixed) and eight content categories (e.g., temporal orientation, patriotism, tribalism). His work is part of the continuing interest in and development of the "modernism-traditionalism" dimension in a wide variety of research situations and settings.

90

References:

Campbell, A. et al. The American Voter. New York: John Wiley, 1960.

Christie, R. and Jahoda, M. Studies in the Scope and Method of the
        Authoritarian Personality. Glencoe, Illinois: Free Press, 1954.

Converse, P. "The Nature of Belief Systems in Mass Publics," in D. Apter
        (ed.), Ideology and Discontent. New York: Free Press, 1964.

Doob, L. "Scales for Assaying Psychological Modernization in Africa,"
        Public Opinion Quarterly, 1967, XXXI, pp. 414-421.

Inkeles, A. and Smith, D. "A Comparative Measure of Attitudinal Modernity."
        Paper presented at the 1967 annual meetings of the American
        Sociological Association.

Lerner, D. The Passing of Traditional Society: Modernizing the Middle East.
        New York: Free Press, 1958.

Murphy, G. and Likert, R. Public Opinion and the Individual. New York:
        Harper, 1938.

Opinion Research Corporation. The Initiators. Princeton, New Jersey: ORC,
        1960.

Rogers, E. Diffusion of Innovations. New York: Free Press, 1962.

Shaw, M. and Wright, J. Scales for the Measurement of Attitudes. New York:
        McGraw Hill, 1967.

Trenaman, J. and McQuail, D. Television and the Political Image. London:
        Methuen and Lo, 1961.

Waisenan, F. and Durlak, J. "Mass Media Use, Information Source Evaluation,
        and Perceptions of Self and Nation," Public Opinion Quarterly, 1967,
        XXXI, pp. 399-407.

IDEOLOGICAL AGREEMENT WITH GOLDWATER (Selznick and Steinberg 1966)

Variable	This scale is intended to measure agreement with "ideological" tenets of conservative political belief expressed by Senator Goldwater in his campaign for the presidency in 1964.
Description	There are five items in the scale, two of them in agree-disagree and the other three in multiple choice format. One point is scored for each agreement with a response judged to correspond to agree with Goldwater's beliefs. Scores run from 0 (no agreement with Goldwater) to 5 (perfect agreement with Goldwater).
Sample	A national cross-sectional sample of about 2000 respondents was inter-viewed as part of a survey of religious attitudes. In the analysis of results, only the 1397 white respondents were considered, primarily because Negroes voted almost unanimously for Johnson. The interviews were conducted in the weeks prior to the 1964 election.
Reliability/ Homogeneity	No data bearing on reliability are presented.
Validity	A substantial correlation was found between scores on the index and vote for Goldwater. The percentage breakdown for each score is as follows:

% of Sample	Score	% Voting for Goldwater
19%	0	6%
24	1	18
21	2	34
16	3	56
13	4	64
7	5	87
100%		36%

Location	Selznick, Gertrude and Steinberg, Stephen. "Class and Ideology in the 1964 Election: A National Survey." Paper presented at the August 1966 Meeting of the American Sociological Association. Authors are from the Survey Research Center at the University of California (Berkeley).
Administration	The items should take no more than two or three minutes to administer. Average score for the white population was 3.0.
Results and Comments	Despite the dramatic increases in percentage vote for Goldwater with increasing ideological agreement with Goldwater (see results under Validity above), it should be noted that a portion of the great effects on vote were also due to differences in social class. Examine the following table:

Score/Class	Working	Middle	Upper
0-1	12%	13%	13%
2-4	32	50	64
5	86	85	85

It can be seen that only for the extreme scorers (0-1 and 5) did the effects of social class disappear.

The authors found that the effects of ideology also disappeared if the "conservative" person was in favor of medicare. When the scale was administered to a group of advanced undergraduate and graduate students taking a social psychology course at the University of Michigan, the senior author of this volume found the average score on this scale to be 1.3 (vs. 3.0 for the whole cross-section population). This is consistent with the expected liberal orientation of such a sample, of whom only 15 percent said they would have voted for Goldwater in 1964.

DISTRIBUTION OF RESPONSES ON ITEMS MEASURING IDEOLOGICAL
AGREEMENT WITH GOLDWATER[a]

(White voters only)

The Federal government is gradually taking away our basic freedoms.

AGREE	47%
Disagree	48%
Don't know	5%

In the past 25 years this country has moved dangerously close to Socialism.

AGREE	45%
Disagree	41%
Don't know	14%

Which of the statements on this card comes closest to expressing how you feel about the state of morals in this country at the present time?

THEY ARE PRETTY BAD, AND GETTING WORSE	42%
They are pretty bad, but getting better	13%
They are pretty good, but getting worse	21%
They are pretty good, and getting better	16%
Don't know, or the same as ever	8%

How great a danger do you feel that American Communists are to this country at the present time--a very great danger, a great danger, some danger, hardly any danger, or no danger?

A VERY GREAT DANGER	18%
A GREAT DANGER	23%
Some danger	39%
Hardly any danger	12%
No danger	5%
Don't know	3%

Do you feel the United States is losing power in the world or is it becoming more powerful? IF LOSING POWER: How much does this disturb you--a great deal, somewhat, or very little?

LOSING POWER AND DISTURBED A GREAT DEAL	15%
LOSING POWER AND DISTURBED SOMEWHAT	10%
Losing power and disturbed very little	5%
Becoming more powerful	41%
Staying the same	24%
Don't know	5%

---

[a] Responses in capital letters are considered in ideological agreement with Goldwater.

CONSERVATISM SCALE (McClosky 1958)

Variable	This scale attempts to measure the strength of general (not political) conservative belief in individuals and groups.
Description	The 12 agree-disagree items of the first form of the scale were selected from an initial pool of 43 items drawn from the works of conservative writers such as Edmund Burke. In a succeeding study, the items were reduced to nine, and the population was divided into scoring quartiles as follows: Extreme Conservatives, 7-9, Moderate Conservatives, 5-6, Moderate Liberals, 3-4, Liberals, 0-2.
Sample	The sample population for the scale construction stage was a general sample of 1200 persons in the vicinity of Minneapolis-St. Paul, Minnesota.
Reliability/ Homogeneity	No test-retest reliability was reported. The author states that his findings were replicated in three different studies, with different samples.
Validity	It was reported that 90 percent of a "validation group" consisting of 48 seniors or graduate students in a political theory class labeled subsets of items from the scale as conservative. High scorers on the conservatism scale also agreed with (non-scale) "conservative sentiments" far more frequently than did those who scored as liberal. In their 1956 study of a national cross-section of American voters, Campbell et al. (1960) found the scale to differentiate successfully between voters who had switched party loyalty. That is, Republicans who had formerly been Democrats scored as highly conservative while Democrats who had formerly been Republicans scored very low on the conservative scale. Nevertheless, the measure does not adequately predict party affiliation in the aggregate as mentioned in "Results and Comments" below.
Location	McClosky, Herbert, "Conservatism and Personality," _American Political Science Review_, 1958, <u>52</u>, pp. 27-45.
Administration	The scale was administered in an interview situation but could be used as a paper and pencil test, in which case estimated administration time is about seven minutes.
Results and Comments	The original measure proved to be subject to a severe problem of agreement response set, which is itself correlated with social status in the same direction as conservatism, although relations still held with controls for response set applied. Those scoring as strongly conservative proved, by comparison with the low scorers, to hold extremely conventional social attitudes, to be more responsive to naturalistic symbols, and to place greater emphasis upon duty, conformity and discipline, with controls instituted for education, occupation, socio-economic status, and possible agreement response set bias. High scorers were most frequently the uninformed and the

poorly educated, and significantly lower scorers in the author's measures of "awareness" and "intellectuality."

It was found that the correlations between conservatism and party affiliation and public issues tended to be low, a finding which was corroborated on a cross-national sample by Campbell et al. (1960). In this latter study, six of McClosky's items (reproduced below) were used with Likert-type response mode with no neutral point. It was also found that the scale did discriminate significantly between Republican and Democratic party elites and the "spectator" elites-- governalistic and academic. However, for the rank-and-file citizen, there is little or no connection between a person's stand on specific political and social issues, his party identification, his political behavior and his more general attitude toward change-- his conservative or liberal ideology. However the scale did a fairly good job of discriminating members of the public who had changed party identification from Democrat to Republican or from Republican to Democrat.

Photiadis and Biggar found the conservatism scale to be related to religious orthodoxy and extrinsic religious belief, as well as confirming many of the earlier correlates found by McClosky.

In a more recent study, Matthews and Prothro (1966) administered five McClosky items (starred below)--which met the Guttman scale criterion--to a large sample of southern Negroes and whites. It was found that 33 percent of the Negroes and only 19 percent of the whites sampled scored at the resistant end of the scale. Both Negroes and whites who favored change scored higher on the author's Political Participation Scale (see Chapter 11 on Political Activity), although the difference was greater for Negroes than for whites. The relationship persisted even when the effects of political interest and information were statistically controlled. It is interesting to note that while a sample of southern Negro college students were found to be much more favorable toward change than the adults sampled, over two thirds of the students scored on the "conservative" end of Campbell et al.'s Domestic Attitude Scale (see Chapter 5 on Attitude Toward Domestic Government Policy).

Reference

Campbell, A., Converse, P. E., Warren, W. E. and Stokes, D. E. The American Voter. New York: John Wiley and Sons, Inc., 1960, pp. 210-212.

Matthews, D. R. and Prothro, J. W. Negroes and the New Southern Politics. New York: Harcourt, Brace & World, 1966, p.526.

Photiadis, J. and Biggar, J. "Religiosity, Education and Ethnic Distance", American Journal of Sociology, 1962, 67, pp. 666-672.

CONSERVATISM SCALE

(First four items used in Campbell et al 1960 with distribution of replies of a national sample; starred items were used in Matthews and Prothro 1966.)

Agreement with each item indicates conservatism

		Strongly Agree	Agree	Disagree	Strongly Disagree
1.	I prefer the practical man anytime to the man of ideas.	40%	32	20	8
*2.	If you start trying to change things very much, you usually make them worse.	21	27	31	21
*3.	If something grows up after a long time, there will always be much wisdom to it.	33	34	22	11
*4	It's better to stick by what you have than to be trying new things you don't really know about.	31	20	30	19
*5.	We must respect the work of our forefathers and not think that we know better than they did.	23	26	30	21
*6.	A man doesn't really have much wisdom until he is well along in years.	23	23	30	24
7.	No matter how we like to talk about it, political authority really comes not from us, but from some higher power.				
8.	I'd want to know that something would really work before I'd be willing to take a chance on it.				
9.	All groups can live in harmony in this country without changing the system in any way.				

REVISED FORCED-CHOICE McCLOSKY ITEMS (SRC 1958)

Which of these types of people would you generally prefer--the practical man
or the man of ideas?

29%	1.	Man of ideas
4%	3.	Pro-con; it depends
67%	5.	Practical man

If something grows up over a long time do you think there is certain to be much
wisdom in it, or do you think sometimes it may get pretty old-fashioned?

49%	1.	Is old-fashioned
4%	3.	Pro-con; it depends
67%	5.	Much wisdom

Do you think it's always a good idea to look for new ways of doing things, or
do you think in some cases it's better to stick by what you have than to be
trying new things you don't really know about?

64%	1.	Look out for the new
3%	3.	Pro-con; it depends
33%	5.	Stick by what you have

Do you think we usually should respect the work of our forefathers and not
think that we know better than they did, or do you think that we must figure out
our problems for ourselves?

81%	1.	Figure out for selves
4%	3.	Pro-con; it depends
15%	5.	Respect forefathers

Do you think that a person has many worthwhile ideas whatever his age, or do
you feel that usually a man doesn't get to have much wisdom until he's well
along in years?

77%	1.	Ideas whatever age
1%	3.	Pro-con; it depends
22%	5.	Wisdom comes later

SOCIAL ATTITUDES SCALES (Kerlinger 1963)

Variable
This scale measures liberalism-conservatism on a number of issues for which this attitude dimension may be relevant, including private enterprise, education, and international relations.

Description
This is a 26-item Likert scale developed through a factor analysis of 40 items which, in turn, were pared down from an original pool of over 100 items. The analysis results produced four factors, two conservative and two liberal. The 13 highest loading liberal items and 13 highest loading conservative items were retained and make up the scale below.

Scoring is based on traditional Likert methods of assigning the individual the total sum of responses (+3 for strongly agree to -3 for strongly disagree) for each item. A higher score is indicative of liberalism or of conservatism, depending on which set of items is being summed.

Sample
The samples on which these scales were developed were 210 graduate students in education, 251 undergraduates, and 205 non-college respondents, with the main analysis being performed on the graduates in education and non-college respondents.

Reliability/
Homogeneity
Split-half reliabilities of .78 for the liberalism scale and .79 for the conservatism scale are reported for 168 unidentified students. No test-retest data are reported.

Validity
No evidence bearing directly on validity is reported.

Location
Shaw, M. and Wright, J. Scales for the Measurement of Attitudes. New York: McGraw-Hill, 1967, pp. 322-324 (taken from an unpublished paper by Kerlinger).

Administration
The scale can be completed in less than 20 minutes.

Results and
Comments
Probably the most interesting finding obtained with this scale is that liberalism and conservatism were isolated as separate factors in a factor analysis. The usual expectation is that they fall on separate ends of the same dimension or factor. Although it is not clear whether the original author recommends treating the items as two separate scales, it is our recommendation that they be so treated. For analysis purposes, then, at least four groups should be distinguished: the liberal ideologues (high on liberalism, low on conservatism), the conservative ideologues (low on liberalism, high on conservatism), yea-sayers (high on liberalism, high on conservatism), and nay-sayers (low on liberalism, low on conservatism).

Another interesting finding was that F-Scale (authoritarianism) items loaded highly on the conservatism factor, as did acquiescence items.

In a factor analysis of this scale, the author also constructed a comparable scale for educational attitudes, the two terms, labelled in this instance "progressivism-traditionalism" again fell into two separate dimensions rather than into opposite ends of the same dimension. Test-retest correlations over a three to four month period were around .70, and adequate evidence of validity was also reported.

Reference   Kerlinger, F. and Kaya, E. "The Construction and Factor Analytic Validation of Scales to Measure Attitudes toward Education," Education and Psychological Measurement, 1959, 19, pp. 13-29.

THE SOCIAL ATTITUDES SCALE

Given below are statements on various social problems about which we all have beliefs, opinion, and attitudes. We all think differently about each matter, and this scale is an attempt to let you express your beliefs and opinions. There are no right and wrong answers. Please respond to each of the items as follows:

Agree very strongly	+3	Disagree very strongly	-3
Agree strongly	+2	Disagree strongly	-2
Agree	+1	Disagree	-1

For example, if you agree very strongly with a statement, you would write +3 in the left margin beside the statement, but if you should happen to disagree with it, you would put -1 in front of it. Respond to each statement as best you can. Go rapidly but carefully. Do not spend too much time on any one statement; try to respond and then go on. Don't go back once you have marked a statement.

* 1 Individuals who are against churches and religions should not be allowed to teach in college.

  2 Large fortunes should be taxed fairly heavily over and above income taxes.

  3 Both public and private universities and colleges should get generous aid from both state and federal governments.

* 4 Science and society would both be better off if scientists took no part in politics.

  5 Society should be quicker to throw out old ideas and traditions and to adopt new thinking and customs.

  6 To ensure adequate care of the sick, we need to change radically the present system of privately controlled medical care.

* 7 If civilization is to survive, there must be a turning back to religion.

* 8 A first consideration in any society is the protection of property rights.

* 9 Government ownership and management of utilities leads to bureaucracy and inefficiency.

*10 If the United States takes part in any sort of world organization, we should be sure that we lose none of our power and influence.

 11 Funds for school construction should come from state and federal government loans at no interest or very low interest.

---

*
These are conservative items whose weights should be reserved for scoring purposes. All unmarked items are liberal.

*12 Inherited racial characteristics play more of a part in the achievement of individuals and groups than is generally known.

13 Federal Government aid for the construction of schools is long overdue, and should be instituted as a permanent policy.

14 Our present economic system should be reformed so that profits are replaced by reimbursements for useful work.

15 Public enterprises like railroads should not make profits; they are entitled to fares sufficient to enable them to pay only a fair interest on the actual cash capital they have invested.

*16 Government laws and regulations should be such as first to ensure the prosperity of business since the prosperity of all depends on the prosperity of business.

17 All individuals who are intellectually capable of benefiting from it should get college education, at public expense if necessary.

*18 The well-being of a nation depends mainly on its industry and business.

19 True democracy is limited in the United States because of the special privileges enjoyed by business and industry.

20 The gradual social ownership of industry needs to be encouraged if we are ever to cure some of the ills of our society.

*21 There are too many professors in our colleges and universities who are radical in their social and political beliefs.

*22 There should be no government interference with business and trade.

*23 Some sort of religious education should be given in public schools.

24 Unemployment insurance is an inalienable right of the working man.

*25 Individuals with the ability and foresight to earn and accumulate wealth should have the right to enjoy that wealth without government interference and regulations.

26 The United Nations should be whole-heartedly supported by all of us.

CONSERVATISM-RADICALISM BATTERY (Centers 1949)

Variable

Although this short scale purports to measure conservatism-radicalism, the items deal mostly with one's identification with the worker or with the employer.

Description

There are six items in the scale, five of which are in forced-choice and one in agree-disagree format. Individuals were grouped into five classes on the basis of their responses to these items:

Number of Conservative, Intermediate and Radical Replies

1.	Ultra-conservative	6-0-0,	5-1-0,	5-0-1		
2.	Conservative	4-2-0,	4-1-1,	4-0-2,	3-3-0,	3-2-1
4.	Radical	1-2-3,	0-3-3,	2-0-4,	1-1-4,	0-2-4
5.	Ultra Radical	1-0-5,	0-1-5,	0-0-6		
3.	Intermediate	All other combinations				

Conservative, radical and intermediate responses are indicated for each item in the scale below.

Sample

A national cross-sectional sample of 1100 white American adult males were interviewed in July, 1945. As in many surveys done in this period, the sample was overweighted with individuals in higher-status occupations. It was noted by Centers that since the interview was carried out two months before the surrender of Japan, a tendency toward maximum national solidarity should have prevailed during the interviewing period.

Reliability/ Homogeneity

Centers reports an inter-item tetrachoric correlation matrix in which all item pairs are significantly intercorrelated at the one percent level. The values range from .12 to .68, with an average of .36. Item-total score correlations run between .49 and .88, with an average of .70. For both measures, items 1 and 5 seemed to fit least well with the others. Case (1953) reports a coefficient of reproducibility of only .88 from a cross-section sample in the state of Washington. However, he trichotomized two of the items in scaling, which does lower values of this coefficient.

Validity

The striking differences between white-collar and blue-collar workers attest to the scale's basic validity in separating worker vs. employer identifiers, although this is not the same thing as radicalism-conservatism. Tetrachoric correlation between white vs. blue-collar occupation and scale values was .59, and between Dewey vs. Roosevelt vote in 1944 and scale values was .58. In percentage terms, about 50% of large and small business owners and managers scored as ultra-conservative vs. less than 5% of semi-skilled and skilled manual workers.

Location

Centers, R. The Psychology of Social Classes. Princeton, N.J.: Princeton University Press, 1949 (reprinted by Russell and Russell, New York, 1961).

Administration	Although the items were originally built for use in interview situations, they could easily be adapted for use in questionnaire format. They should take less than 5 minutes to answer. Note that item 3 needs to be updated or reworded.
Results and Comments	The claim that the scale measures conservatism-radicalism is certainly dubious in view of the item content. Nevertheless, the scale does a more-than-adequate job of discriminating between white and blue collar workers.
Reference	Case, H. "Guttman Scaling Applied to Centers' Conservatism-Radicalism Battery," <u>American Journal of Sociology</u>, 1953,<u>55</u>, pp. 556-563.

CONSERVATISM-RADICALISM BATTERY

1. Do you agree or disagree that America is truly a land of opportunity and that people get pretty much what is coming to them here?

         Agree (Con.)   Disagree (Rad.)   Don't Know (Int.)

2. Would you agree that everybody would be happier, more secure, and more pros- perous if the working people were given more power and influence in government, or would you say we would be better off if the working people had no more power than they have now?

         Agree (Rad.)   Disagree (Con.)   Don't Know (Int.)

3. As you know, during this war, many private businesses and industries have been taken over by government. Do you think wages and salaries would be fairer, jobs more steady, and that we would have fewer people out of work if the govern- ment took over and ran our mines, factories, and industries in the future, or do you think things would be better under private ownership?

         Better under government (Rad.)
         Better under private ownership (Con.)
         Other and don't know (Int.)

4. Which of these statements do you most agree with?

   1. The most important job for government is to make it certain that there are good opportunities for each person to get ahead on his own (Con.)

   2. The most important job for government is to guarantee every person a decent and steady job and standard of living (Rad.)

   3. Don't know (Int.)

5. In strikes and disputes between working people and employers do you usually side with the workers or with the employers?

         Workers (Rad.)   Employers (Con.)   Neither, don't know (Int.)

6. Do you think working people are fairly and squarely treated by their employers, or that employers sometimes take advantage of them?

   1. Fair treatment (Con.)
   2. Employers take advantage (Rad.)
   3. Don't know (Int.)

POLITICAL-ECONOMIC CONSERVATISM (PEC) SCALE (Adorno et al. 1950)

Variable

The PEC Scale was designed to give an estimate of the individual's general readiness to express conservative ideology. Items were constructed to reflect four underlying ideological trends which the authors believed to characterize conservatism and liberalism as contrasting approaches to political-economic problems.

A high score should indicate: 1) support of the status quo and particularly of business; 2) support of conservative values (practicality, financial success, morality, charity, etc.); 3) desire to maintain a balance of power in which business is dominant, labor subordinate, and the economic functions of government minimized; and 4) resistance to social change. Conversely, a low score was intended to reflect support of trends common to most left-of-center viewpoints: opposition to the status quo; a tendency to identify with labor and the "common man" and to oppose the power of business; and support for extension of the political and economic functions of government.

Description

The PEC Scale has three forms: Form 78, with 16 items, Form 60, with 14 items; and Form 45-40, with five items. All forms call for Likert-type item responses: slight, moderate, or strong agreement (marked +1, +2, or +3) and disagreement (marked -1, -2, or -3) with no neutral category. Form 78 contains 11 "conservative" items and five "liberal" items (reverse scored), Form 60 contains five "conservative" and nine "liberal" items; and Form 45-40, three "conservative" and two "liberal" items. Transformed scores on the scale range from 1 point for a -3 response to 7 points for a +3 response, with 4 points (neutral) assigned to omitted items. A person's score is the sum of his weighted responses.

Sample

The many different groups sampled are shown in the table on the following page. It should be noted that the subjects were mostly middle class Californians between the ages of 20 and 35 with an average of 12 years of schooling, with the non-college students generally members of voluntary organizations. The working class group selected probably was more "liberal" than most working class people.

The group chosen for validation consisted of 80 individuals selected equally from the highest and lowest quartiles on the Ethnocentrism Scale.

Reliability/
Homogeneity

Reliability of the first form (Form 78) of 16 items was reported to be .74 for 140 University of California Public Speaking Class women, .64 for 52 University of California Public Speaking Class men, .72 for 40 Extension Psychology Class women, and .81 for 63 professional women.

Reliability of the second form (Form 60) of 14 items was reported to be .73 for 47 University of Oregon Student women, .69 for 54 University of Oregon and University of California Student Women, .69 for

GROUPS FROM WHOM QUESTIONNAIRES WERE COLLECTED[a]

No. of
Cases

I. Form 78 (January to May, 1945)
    University of California Public Speaking Class Women 140
    University of California Public Speaking Class Men 52
    University of California Extension Psychology Class
      (adult women) 40
    Professional Women (public school teachers, social workers,
      public health nurses) (San Francisco area) 63

                                                   Total   295

II. Form 60 (Summer, 1945)
    University of Oregon Student Women 47
    University of Oregon and University of California Student
      Women 54
    University of Oregon and University of California Student
      Men 57
    Oregon Service Club Men (Kiwanis, Lions, Rotary Clubs)
      (Total questionnaire) 68
    Oregon Service Club Men (Form A only)[b] 60

                                                   Total   286

III. Forms 45 and 40 (November, 1945, to June, 1946)
    A. Form 45
        University of California Extension Testing Class (adult
          women) 59
        Psychiatric Clinic Patients (men and women) (Langley
          Porter Clinic of the University of California) 121
        San Quentin State Prison Inmates (men) 110

                                                   Total   243

    B. Both Forms 45 and 40
        Alameda School for Merchant Marine Officers (men) 343
        U.S. Employment Service Veterans (men) 106

                                                   Total   449

---

[a] In most cases each group taking the questionnaire was treated separately for statistical purposes, e.g., San Quentin Prison Inmates, Psychiatric Clinic Men. However, some groups were too small for this purpose and were therefore combined with other sociologically similar groups. When such combinations occurred, the composition of the overall group is indicated in the table.

[b] Form A included the scale for measuring potentially antidemocratic trends in the personality and half of the scale for measuring politico-economic conservatism.

C. Form 40
Working-Class Women:
   California Labor School   19
   United Electrical Workers Union (C.I.O.).   8
   Office Workers   11
   Longshoremen and Warehousemen (I.L.W.U.)
      (new members)   10
   Federal Housing Project Workers   5

                                               53

Working-Class Men:
   United Electrical Workers Union (C.I.O.) . 12
   California Labor School 15
   Longshoremen and Warehousemen (I.L.W.U.)
      (new members)   26
   United Seamen's Service   8

                                               61

Middle-Class Women:
   Parent-Teachers' Association 46
   California Labor School (middle-class
      members)   11
   Suburban Church Group   29
   Unitarian Church Group 15
   League of Women Voters 17
   Upper Middle-Class Women's Club   36

                                              154

Middle-Class Men:
   Parent-Teachers' Association 29
   California Labor School (middle-class
      members) 31
   California Labor School (middle-class
      members)   9

                                               69

California Service Club Men:
   Kiwanis Club 40
   Rotary Club 23

                                               63
George Washington University Women Students 132
Los Angeles Men (classes at University of California and
   University of Southern California, fraternity group,
   adult evening class, parents of students, radio writers
   group) 117
Los Angeles Women (same groupings as above)   130

                                 Total   779
                    Total Forms 45 and 40   1,518
                    Overall Total of All Forms 2,099

57 University of Oregon and University of California Student Men,
and .70 for 68 Oregon Service Club (Kiwanis, etc.) men.

Internal consistency of the five item PEC Scale is indicated by a
correlational analysis made on a group of 517 University of California
women students--a mean r of +.26 was found between each item and the
sum of the remaining items. The correlation among individual items
averaged .14. The highest correlation, between items 7 and 14, was
+.30, and there were three statistically insignificant correlations
with item 11. Reliability of the five item scale was not estimated.

The PEC Scale was developed with the intention of determining possible
psychological affinities between conservatism and ethnocentrism,
liberalism and anti-ethnocentrism. Scores on the PEC and E
(Ethnocentrism) Scales correlated most highly among the lower scorers
on the two scales, most notably with working class men and women
(r = .74 and .86), but most correlations were above .50.

Validity
:   The validity of the instrument was examined by two case studies and
    by the measure of agreement between the scale scores and the later
    responses to an intensive interview (semi-structured, projective
    questions) by selected subjects.

Administration
:   Estimated administration time is 16 minutes for Form 78; 14 minutes
    for Form 40, and five minutes for Form 45-40. Scoring requires
    simple summation of weighted responses to each question.

Location
:   Adorno, T. W., Frenkel-Brunswick, E., Levinson, D. J., and Sanford,
    R. N. The Authoritarian Personality. New York: Harper and Row, 1950.

Results and
Comments
:   Although the low reliability of the three forms of the PEC Scale
    precluded their use as measures of individual differences, significant
    differences in scale mean scores between groups did appear. On Form
    78, 63 professional women had significantly lower means than 140
    Public Speaking Class women, 52 PSC men, and 40 Extension Psychology
    Class women. On Form 60, 68 Service Club men had a significantly
    higher average mean than 101 University student women and 57 University
    student men (although great individual variability was present). On
    Form 45-40, 63 Service Club men and 110 San Quentin men obtained sig-
    nificantly higher PEC means than 191 University women, 212 Psychiatric
    Clinic patients, and 470 middle-class men and women, whose means in
    turn were significantly higher than a group of 114 working class men
    and women.

    There is some question whether the items of the PEC actually tap only
    one dimension, and whether the dimension is political-economic
    liberalism-conservatism. The probability that the scale taps more
    than one dimension is supported by the lack of internal consistency
    shown by the low reliabilities and the item analysis as well as an
    average item intercorrelation of .14.

    Hyman and Sheatsley (1954) point out that the validation procedure
    is weakened by the fact that the two sets of results--from scale scores

and interviews and ratings--were not independently derived, as the interviewers studied scale results beforehand and the raters were familiar with both the hypothesized relationships and the whole body of the interviews. They suggest that more appropriate validation criteria might be allegiance to or agreement with organizations representing an ideological position on the liberalism-conservatism dimension, such as the HUAC, ACLU, etc. Many of the items are clearly dated.

Close reading of the Hyman and Sheatsley article is strongly recommended for anyone thinking of using the PEC Scale or any of the other scales used in the original Authoritarian Personality investigation.

Reference   Hyman, H. and Sheatsley, P. "The Authoritarian Personality: A Methodological Critique" in Christie, R. and Jahoda, Marie (eds.), Studies in the Scope and Method of "The Authoritarian Personality." Glencoe, Illinois: Free Press, 1954.

THE AUTHORITARIAN PERSONALITY

INITIAL POLITICO-ECONOMIC CONSERVATISM SCALE (FORM 78)

1. A child should learn early in life the value of a dollar and the importance of ambition, efficiency, and determination.

5. Depressions are like occasional headaches and stomach aches; it's natural for even the healthiest society to have them once in a while.

8. Every adult should find time or money for some worthy service organization (charity, medical aid, etc.) as the best way of aiding his fellow man.

13. The businessman, the manufacturer, the practical man--these are of much greater value to society than the intellectual, the artist, the theorist.

15. The best way to solve social problems is to stick close to the middle of the road, to move slowly and to avoid extremes.

22. A political candidate, to be worth voting for, must first and foremost have a good character, one that will fight inefficiency, graft, and vice.

27. Young people sometimes get rebellious ideas, but as they grow up they ought to get over them and settle down.

*36. It is the responsibility of the entire society, through its government, to guarantee everyone adequate housing, income, and leisure.

*44. The only way to provide adequate medical care for the entire population is through some program of socialized medicine.

*52. It is essential after the war to maintain or increase the income taxes on corporations and wealthy individuals.

*61. In general, full economic security is harmful; most men wouldn't work if they didn't need the money for eating and living.

63. It is a fundamental American tradition that the individual must remain free of government interference, free to make money and spend it as he likes.

*68. Labor unions should become stronger by being politically active and by publishing labor newspapers to be read by the general public.

71. Whether one likes them or not, one has to admire men like Henry Ford or J. P. Morgan, who overcame all competition on the road to success.

*76. The government must play an even greater part in the economic and business life of the nation after the war than it has before.

78. Character, honesty, and ability will tell in the long run; most people get pretty much what they deserve.

---

*These six items are "liberal," the others are "conservative." A high score is given for agreement with the conservative items, disagreement with the liberal items.

SECOND FORM OF THE POLITICO-ECONOMIC CONSERVATISM SCALE (FORM 60)

*4. Labor unions should become stronger and have more influence generally.

*9. Most government controls over business should continue after the war.

13. Americans may not be perfect, but the American Way has brought us about as close as human beings can get to a perfect society.

*15. If America had more men like Henry Wallace in office, we would get along much better.

*20. The artist and the professor are of just as much value to society as the businessman and the manufacturer.

26. It would be dangerous for the U.S. to cooperate too closely with Russia.

27. The best political candidate to vote for is the one whose greatest interest is in fighting vice and graft.

*31. No one should be allowed to earn more than $25,000 a year.

*37. It is up to the government to make sure that everyone has a secure job and a good standard of living.

*43. The government should own and operate all public utilities (transportation, gas and electric, railroads, etc.).

*48. Depressions can be prevented by proper government planning.

*54. Poverty could be almost entirely done away with if we made certain basic changes in our social and economic system.

56. Men like Henry Ford or J. P. Morgan, who overcome all competition on the road to success, are models for all young people to admire and imitate.

60. In general, the best way of aiding our fellow men is to give time or money to some worthy charity.

---

*These nine items are "liberal," the other five are "conservative." A high score is given for agreement with the conservative items, disagreement with the liberal items.

THIRD FORM OF THE POLITICAL ECONOMIC CONSERVATISM SCALE (FORM 45-40)

*3. Labor unions should become stronger and have more influence generally.

7. America may not be perfect, but the American Way has brought us about as close as human beings can get to a perfect society.

*11. Most government controls over business should be continued even though the war is over.

14. Men like Henry Ford or J. P. Morgan, who overcame all competition on the road to success, are models for all young people to admire and imitate.

17. In general, full economic security is bad; most men wouldn't work if they didn't need the money for eating and living.

---

*These items are "liberal," the others are "conservative." A high score is given for agreement with the conservative items, disagreement with the liberal items.

INVENTORY OF SOCIAL ATTITUDES (Eysenck 1947)

Variable
This scale was constructed not as a measure of a specific personality variable but rather as an attempt to discern the primary dimensions underlying people's social attitudes and beliefs. Factor analysis yielded two basic dimensions which the author has labeled "radicalism-conservatism" and "tendermindedness-toughmindedness."

Description
The original scale was composed of 40 five-point Likert-type items chosen from a pool of 500 attitude items. All items in the literature which had been found by any method to be highly saturated on any factor were included in the pool. A factor analysis was carried out using Burt's Summation Method. The first factor, accounting for 18 percent of the variance, was labelled "radicalism-conservatism," and included 14 items which formed the R Scale (A similar "tendermindedness-toughmindedness" or T Scale was formed from the second factor which emerged. It accounted for an additional 8 percent of the variance).

One point was awarded for agreement with the response key and 0 for disagreement or a neutral answer resulting in a range of scores from 0 to 14, with high scores indicating radicalism. Seven items were keyed positively, and seven negatively.

Sample
This scale was administered to 750 subjects: 250 were conservatives, 250 liberals, and 250 socialists. They were matched for education, for sex and for age (over or under 30); all subjects were middle class, urban residents, and British.

Reliability
To measure reliability, the R Scale was evenly divided into subscales, R_1 and R_2: R_1R_2 (or split-half) correlation was .81 for the entire group, ranging from .63 for the conservative group to .73 for the socialists. Average inter-item correlation for the 14 items was about .34.

No test-retest reliabilities are reported.

Validity
Some evidence for the R factor can be formed by comparing the percent of Conservatives and Socialists agreeing with each item in Table 5. The differences in these percentages correlated .98 with item saturations on the R factor.

Location
Eysenck, H. Primary Social Attitudes: I the Organization and Measurement of Social Attitudes, International Journal of Opinion and Attitude Research, 1, #3, 1947. See also Eysenck, H. The Psychology of Politics. London, England: Routledge and Kegan Paul, 1954.

Administration
An estimated 10 minutes would be required to complete the scale.

The following average scores were obtained from the various population groups (Average Standard Deviation = 2.6).

Average scores on the R scale

Conser-vatives = 4.6	Males = 6.9	Under 30 = 6.9	University education = 7.4
Liberals = 6.3	Females = 6.7	Over 30 = 6.7	No university education = 6.1

Socialists = 9.4

Results and Comments

When the 24 subgroups of the sample are ordered according to average R score, old female non-university Conservatives are the least radical and young male university Socialists were the most radical. With one exception, the eight most conservative groups were Conservatives, and the eight most radical groups were Socialists. There were no significant differences among groups on the T factor except that females scored higher than males.

The author readily admits that some items are "double barreled." He argues, however, that the attitudes that are being measured are not rational, singular attitudes, but complex, irrational clusters of attitudes. He feels that items that capture the stereotyped attitudes indicated by the two factors are superior to simplified, logically defensible statements.

Eysenck's two factors (R and I) and his 40 items appear to be strongly related to the F Scale and other work in the area of Authoritarianism. The R and I scales correlated .12 with each other, conservatives being more tough-minded.

INVENTORY OF SOCIAL ATTITUDES
(C=Conservative items)

		C*	L	S	Factor Loading
3.	War is inherent in human nature. (C)	67%	57%	34%	-.51
6.	Our treatment of criminals is too harsh; we should try to cure not to punish them.	39	58	72	.57
8.	In the interests of peace, we must give up part of our national sovereignty.	32	60	76	.62
9.	Sunday-observance is old-fashioned, and should cease to govern our behavior.	36	44	68	.53
12.	Ultimately, private property should be abolished, and complete socialism introduced.	03	15	56	.68
17.	Marriages between white and colored people should be strongly discouraged. (C)	77	66	49	-.50
18.	Jews are as valuable, honest, and public-spirited citizens as any other group.	40	58	67	.55
26.	Crimes of violence should be punished by flogging. (C)	65	49	28	-.65
27.	The nationalization of the great industries is likely to lead to inefficiency, bureaucracy, and stagnation. (C)	86	58	16	-.72
28.	It it right and proper that religious education in schools should be compulsory. (C)	66	55	32	-.57
29.	Men and women have the right to find out whether they are sexually suited before marriage (e.g., by companionate marriage.)	35	40	62	.53
33.	The Jews have too much power and influence in this country. (C)	68	52	39	-.55
36.	The death penalty is barbaric, and should be abolished.	30	42	64	.60
39.	The Japanese are by nature a cruel people. (C)	58	37	19	-.65

* Percentages of Conservatives, Liberals and Socialists agreeing with each item.

THE R-C (RADICALISM-CONSERVATISM) SCALE (Nettler and Huffman 1957)

Variable	This scale is designed to measure radicalism-conservatism in political-economic opinion.
Description	The R-C Scale consists of 14 six-point Likert-type items. The authors state that the scale was constructed "by the usual item winnowing process" (described by Thurstone and Chave in their book, The Measurement of Attitude). The items were taken from many sources, including the writings of Eysenck, Centers and Adorno. The items are scored from 0 to 5, making the range of possible scores from 0 to 70. A high score indicates a high degree of conservatism.
Sample	The sample used in deriving the final scale is not described. In another study, the test was administered to 538 subjects. This group included 44 members of the Republican Central Committee of Los Angeles County, 14 workers in the Democratic Party headquarters in Santa Barbara, 15 members of the Socialist Party of California, 13 executives of the International Association of Machinists, seven officers of the International Hodcarriers and Building Laborers Union, ten executives of the International Ladies Garment Workers Union, 64 "miscellaneous" adults, and college students from the University of Southern California, Reed College, University of California at Santa Barbara, Stanford, and Santa Barbara College.
Reliability	The corrected split-half reliability on a two-week retest (sic) was .88 for a sample of 113 upper classmen and graduate students at Berkeley.
Validity	Attempts were made to validate the scale by comparing the scores of "known groups" of party workers. The mean score for 44 Republicans was 61.8 (standard deviation = 5.4); for 14 Democrats, 36.3 (sd = 4.0); and for 15 Socialists, 6.4 (sd = 4.6). These differences are in the expected direction and are significant beyond the .01 level.
	For the entire sample of 538, the distributions of scores on the R-C Scale by party affiliation were found to differ significantly from those expected by chance. As with the groups of party workers, Republican identifiers scored as conservatives, Socialist identifiers as radicals, with Democratic loyalists falling between these extremes of opinion.
	Subjects were also asked to rate themselves on an eight-point continuum ranging from very radical to very conservative. There was a significant association between attitude score and self-ratings.
Location	Nettler, G. and Huffman, J. "Political Opinion and Personal Security," Sociometry, 1957, 20. pp. 51-66.
Administration	This scale is self-administered, and can be completed in less than 10 minutes.

Results and Comments
: The following table presents the means and standard deviations for the different subgroups in the sample of 538.

Means and Standard Deviations of Political Opinion (R-C) and Security Scores (SI)
by Sample

Sample	N	R-C		S-I	
		$\bar{x}$	SD	$\bar{x}$	SD
Known Groups					
Republicans	44	61.8	5.4	4.2	3.6
Democrats	14	36.3	4.0	5.9	3.0
Socialists	15	6.4	4.6	5.3	3.2
Nonacademic Subjects					
Miscellaneous	64	49.5	13.1	5.4	4.7
Machinists	13	38.2	11.3	5.2	2.7
Hodcarriers	7	46.6	7.2	7.1	1.1
ILGWU	10	21.2	11.4	7.7	4.4
NCASP	1	12.0	—	13.0	—
College Students					
USC	76	44.9	12.5	5.1	3.7
Reed College	54	29.0	10.5	10.0	5.3
UC (Santa Barbara)	29	40.4	8.1	6.7	4.6
Stanford Univ.	170	48.4	10.1	5.7	4.3
Santa Barbara PN's	21	42.3	10.4	7.9	4.6
Santa Barbara Control	20	40.5	8.6	6.4	4.5
Total	538	37.0	9.0	6.8	3.8

The study for which the R-C Scale was designed represented an attempt to relate political-economic radicalism, measured by this scale, to "insecurity" measured by a 25-item subscale of the Maslow Security-Insecurity Inventory. A curvilinear association (Eta = .62) was found. The authors interpreted this result to mean that, in general, "secure" people tended to have conservative political-economic opinions, and "insecure" people tended to have radical opinions. However, radicals who were active in political groups also tended to be "secure."

Reference
: Nettler, G. and Huffman, J. "Political Opinion and Personal Security," Sociometry, 1957, 20. pp. 51-66.

1. Ultimately, private property in the instruments of production should be abolished and complete socialism introduced.

2. Profits of the great industries should be rigidly controlled by the Federal government.

3. The nationalization of the great industries is likely to lead to inefficiency, bureaucracy, and stagnation.

4. The reason that many advocate "free enterprise" is because it will enable them to continue exploiting the workers.

5. The traditional capitalistic system provides for the best possible distribution of wealth, human nature being what it is.

6. Labor unions should become stronger and have more influence generally.

7. The right to inherit wealth is a sound principle which provides a strong incentive for creative work.

8. In a socialist system the worker maintains his dignity and self-respect, while under capitalism he is just a tool or instrument to be exploited.

9. In general, full economic security is harmful; most men wouldn't work if they didn't need the money for eating and living.

10. No one should be allowed to earn more than $25,000 a year "take-home" income.

11. It is up to the government to make sure that everyone has a secure job and a good standard of living.

12. America may not be perfect, but the American way has brought us about as close as human beings can get to a perfect society.

13. Wages and salaries would be fairer, jobs more steady, and we would have fewer people out of work, if the government took over and ran our mines, factories, and industries.

14. The present arrangement for the distribution of wealth is altogether unsound.

LIBERALISM-CONSERVATISM SCALE (Wright and Hicks 1966)

Variable

This scale attempts to rank individuals along a dimension of political liberalism-conservatism.

Description

The scale was constructed by the Thurstone method of equal-appearing intervals. From an item pool of 358 statements of political attitudes, 23 agree-disagree items representing the entire attitude continuum and with the smallest standard deviation were selected for the scale. Range of scores for the validation sample was 3.87 to 6.39 for Young Democrats, and 4.10 to 7.07 for Young Republicans.

Sample

The construction sample was composed of 45 male and female members of an experimental psychology class at Wake Forest College. The validation sample consisted of male and female members of the Young Democrat (N = 80) and Young Republican (N = 35) organizations at Wake Forest College.

Reliability/
Homogeneity

Internal-consistency coefficient (corrected) was .79. The authors reported that the Guttman reproducibility score for the scale was .87, indicating quasi-scalability.

Validity

Validation criterion groups were political clubs actively engaged in the support of political candidates in the 1964 presidential campaign. "Because of the nature of the 1964 presidential campaign, issues, and candidates, the assumption that actively campaigning Republicans and Democrats represented conservative and liberal viewpoints, respectively, was considered unquestionable."

A point-biserial coefficient of correlation computed between political affiliations of the subjects and the mean of the scale items with which each of these subjects indicated agreement was .64.

Location

Wright, John H. and Hicks, Jack M. "Construction and Validation of a Thurstone Scale of Liberalism-Conservatism," Journal of Applied Psychology, 1966, 50, #1, pp. 9-12.

Administration

Estimated administration time is about 20 minutes.

Results and
Comments

Though 77 percent of the 80 Young Democrats placed themselves on the liberal end of the scale (mean score, 4.81), the Young Republicans failed to locate themselves at a point well within the conservative portion of the attitude continuum (mean score, 5.93).

The authors stated that the scale successfully differentiated the two validation groups. It appears, however, that the scale did not locate the groups well on an attitude continuum and would probably be less useful still in differentiating less politically active groups (let alone individuals) in a non-campaign, off-campus environment. Furthermore, the authors have made the empirically unproven assumption that domestic and foreign policy opinion is affected by the same attitude dimension. The low value of the Coefficient of Reproducibility also indicates the questionable claim for the scale's unidimensionality.

Finally, the items require a high degree of political familiarity (making them useful only to the politically involved and informed) and are likely to become dated in a short period of time.

THURSTONE SCALE VALUES AND STANDARD DEVIATIONS OF
THE TWENTY-THREE STATEMENTS OF THE
LIBERALISM-CONSERVATISM SCALE

We are interested in finding out how you feel about certain issues. Place a
plus (+) beside each of the following statements with which you agree and a
minus (-) beside the statements with which you disagree. Be sure to mark all of
the statements.

Attitude Statements	Scale Values	SD
1. All old people should be taken care of by the government.	2.30	0.88
2. The government should finance college education.	2.64	1.50
3. Government sponsored medical care for the aged is definitely desirable.	2.91	0.92
4. Efficient large-scale production necessitates government intervention.	3.11	1.12
5. It is the conern of the federal government to initiate, direct, and finance relief programs for poverty stricken areas.	3.26	0.94
6. The government should provide and create jobs to relieve the unemployment situation.	3.55	1.07
7. I favor increased federal aid to higher education.	3.84	1.02
8. T.V.A. is a very effective and beneficial program.	4.14	1.33
9. The NDEA is a good policy for educational improvement.	4.44	0.95
10. Labor unions play an essential role in American democracy.	4.84	1.52
11. I believe in a tax increase when justified.	5.36	1.19
12. I support legislative bills for a tax cut.	6.07	2.00
13. The U.S. is running a close second to Russia in technological achievements.	6.30	1.60
14. I am against parts of the Medicare Bill.	6.65	1.01
15. The national budget should be balanced.	6.97	1.15

16.	The federal government should attempt to cut its annual spending.	7.45	1.02
17.	I believe in less federal tax and more state tax.	7.98	0.99
18.	We should cut foreign aid in order to reduce our national debt.	8.05	0.90
19.	I favor a de-centralization of the federal government.	8.75	0.98
20.	The U.S. should withdraw from the U.N. because we bear the financial burden.	8.95	1.08
21.	Foreign aid spending should be abolished.	9.70	1.11
22.	Social security should be abolished.	10.07	0.82
23.	Isolation (complete) is the answer to our foreign policy.	10.50	0.98

LIBERALISM-CONSERVATISM (Kerr 1952)

Variable
This study used five scales to measure different dimensions of liberalism-conservatism, two of which are relevant here: (a) Political Liberalism, defined as an attitude favoring democratic processes throughout government, universal suffrage, citizen participation and responsibility for government, right of new political parties to rise spontaneously within the population, respect for and faith in elected representatives of the people, and applicability of these same characteristics to orderly international government; and (b) Economic Liberalism, defined as belief in support of economic policies which extend economic control by the state at the expense of economic freedom and initiative. The five different dimensions, of which the remaining three are religious, social, and aesthetic liberalism, are very similar to those introduced by Allport and Vernon (1931).

Description
The instrument consists of 76 Likert-type items which are divided into five subscales. The political subscale has 12 items, the economic 13, the religious 14, the social 12, and the aesthetic 25. All items are scaled on a five-point verbal continuum with five being the weight for the most liberal response. All unanswered items are scored as "undecided." A high total score indicates a high degree of liberalism. The score for each subscale is simply the sum of the numerical response values assigned to the items of that subscale.

No information about the construction of this scale or the source of the items is given.

Sample
A sample of 246 men from Tulane University served as subjects. The test was also administered to 251 Midwestern seminarians studying for the priesthood. No further information about the subjects is given.

Reliability/
Homogeneity
Split-half reliability coefficients for the five subscales (corrected) are political, .55, economic, .82, religious, .77, social, .95, and aesthetic, .88. The author does not state what group of subjects was used in computing these coefficients.

Validity
The author reported as evidence for validity of the scales that the subscales appeared to meet a criteria of relative factorial independence in two separate studies with an average tetrachoric intercorrelation among the five tests of -.17 for the 246 men and an average Pearsonian intercorrelation of .06 for the 251 seminarians. This has no bearing on validity despite the author's claim.

The religious liberalism-conservatism factor differed significantly between Catholics, Protestants, Jews and atheists. Economic liberalism was greater among Democrats than among Republicans. No further evidence for the validity of this scale was reported.

Location
Kerr, W. A. Manual of Instruction for Tulane Factors of Liberalism-Conservatism. Chicago: Psychometric Affiliates, 1955.

124

"Untangling the Liberalism-Conservatism Continuum," _Journal of Social Psychology_, 1952, _35_, pp. 111-125.

Administration

Estimated administration time is 30 minutes for the complete test, with 12 minutes for the Political Liberalism Scale and 13 minutes for the Economic Liberalism Scale. Scoring requires simple summation of the item codes.

Results and Comments

The Economic-Liberalism Scale appears more useful than the Political Liberalism Scale. The latter seems basically to consist of non-controversial democratic ideas (see Prothro and Grigg 1960, which is reported in Chapter 4). In addition, the items of this scale seem to cover too many aspects of political attitude. For a more thorough handling of this cluster of attitude variables, see McClosky (1958, 1964, which are reported in this chapter and in Chapter 4).

The following table presents arbitrary absolute standards for the interpretation of scores using conventional emotional stereotype labels.

	Polit.	Econ.	Relig.	Social	Aesth.
Radical	60-54	59-65	63-70	60-54	113-125
Liberal	43-53	46-58	49-62	43-53	88-112
Center	31-42	33-45	36-48	31-42	63-87
Conservative	19-30	20-32	22-35	19-30	38-62
Reactionary	12-18	13-19	14-21	12-18	25-37

References

Allport, Gordon W. and Vernon, P. E. "A Test for Personal Values," _Journal of Abnormal and Social Psychology_, 1931, _26_, pp. 31-48.

McClosky, Herbert. "Conservatism and Personality," _American Political Science Review_, 1958, _52_, pp. 27-45.

McClosky, Herbert. "Consensus and Ideology in American Politics," _American Political Science Review_, 1964, _58_, pp. 361-382.

Prothro, James W. and Grigg, Charles M. "Fundamental Principles of Democracy: Bases of Agreement and Disagreement," _Journal of Politics_, 1960, _22_, pp. 276-294.

Voor, J. J. "The Relationship Between the Religious Attitude and the Conservative-Radical Attitude among Seminarians Studying for the Catholic Priesthood." M. A. Thesis, Catholic University of America, Washington, D. C., February, 1953.

Sample Items

Respondents answer, "yes," "probably yes," "undecided," "probably no," or "no."

Political Scale

3. Should all able adults be permitted to vote?

6. Should the international world government have the right to overrule decisions of member nations?

7. Would the country be harmed by being governed permanently by a strong person chosen because of his good standing in some prominent organization?

9. Should you send your opinion on an important issue to your congressman?

Economic Scale

15. Should farmers be guaranteed a minimum annual income?

24. Should the government take over the ownership and operation of any national industry?

LIBERALISM-CONSERVATISM SCALE (Hartmann 1938)

Variable | This scale is designed to measure conservatism, defined as a "resistance to institutional change." The author describes the quality being measured as "a continuum ranging from the radical who favors the maximum degree of reconstruction in our social practices to the reactionary who is hostile to all modification save that which restores the conditions of an older day."

Description | The scale consists of 106 agree-disagree items. The items were first rated by liberals and conservatives prominent in American public life and then administered to a large sample of school teachers. An item analysis was performed to determine the ability of each item to discriminate between the highest and lowest scoring 27 percent of the sample.

One point is scored for each "liberal" response. Possible range of scores is 0 - 106, with the highest score indicating extreme liberalism.

Sample | The sample consisted of 3700 secondary school teachers drawn from every state in the union. The two criterion subgroups of this sample each contained 1000 subjects.

Reliability/ Homogeneity | The split-half reliability for the sample of 3700 is .94. No test-retest reliabilities are given.

Validity | No correlation coefficients between this scale and any independent measures of radicalism or conservatism are given. The only available datum pertaining to the validity of the scale is the agreement of the judges' ratings of the items. Among the ten radical judges were such men as the former editor of Nation, Earl Browder (former leader of the Communist Party in the United States), Upton Sinclair, and Norman Thomas. There was no disagreement among the judges on 72 of the 106 items, and 17 of the remaining items fell short of complete agreement by only one response. However, no correlations between judges' ratings (or the extent of agreement among judges) and the ability of each item to discriminate between the two subsamples were reported.

Location | Hartmann, G. "The Differential Validity of Items in a Liberalism-Conservatism Test," Journal of Social Psychology, 1938, 9, pp. 67-78.

Administration | Estimated administration time is about 50 minutes.

Results and Comments | Many pertinent factors about this scale are omitted by the author. The validity data are far from complete or conclusive. Although the agreement of the liberal judges is discussed at length, very little is said about the ratings of the conservative judges. Nonetheless, this study conducted in the mid-1930's is one of the largest-scale attempts to measure attitudes up to that time. For the most part, the items are dated, and their phrasing is certainly both sophisticated and quaint.

References   Hartmann, G. "Homogeneity of Opinion among Liberal Leaders," Public
                 Opinion Quarterly, 1937, 1, pp. 73-78.

                 Kilpatrick, W. H. (ed.) The Teacher and Society. New York: Appleton
                 Century, 1937 (Chapter 8).

LIBERALISM-CONSERVATISM SCALE

Items are listed in order of ability to discriminate between liberals and conservatives (the initial items giving best discrimination). The letters A or D refer to the "liberal" response to each question, with liberals agreeing with the A items and disagreeing with the D items.

1. The ideals of American education will be most readily obtained if we free business from restraint and continue our economic and political system essentially as it operated from 1920 to 1930. (D)

2. A system that has worked as well as capitalism has in this country for the last 150 years should not be changed now. (D)

3. For most people the opportunity to exercise beneficial personal initiative would be increased by life in a socialist state. (A)

4. No economic system can function efficiently without appealing to the desire for private profits. (D)

5. Although some persons take advantage of it for unworthy ends, at bottom our industry is organized on a fundamentally ethical basic. (D)

6. Classroom teachers should have a larger share in determining the major policies of their school. (A)

7. All banks and insurance companies should be run on a non-profit basis like the schools. (A)

8. An improved American nation will result from step-by-step advances in the socialization of the means of production and distribution. (A)

9. Genuine individual liberty will flourish under socialism as it never did before. (A)

10. The Federal government should provide to all classes of people opportunity for complete insurance against accident, sickness, unemployment, premature death, and old age. (A)

11. If we put capable honest men into office, most of our social problems would be solved. (D)

12. If the best possibilities of the American tradition are to be realized, a new social order qualitatively difficult from private capitalism must be built. (A)

13. Economic individualism is more appropriate to contemporary America than any proposed form of collectivism. (D)

14. In the interests of peace, the private manufacture of arms and ammunition must be abolished. (A)

15. Cheaper electric light and power could be had if the industry were owned and operated by governmental units. (A)

16. There is nothing fundamentally wrong with our society; all we need to do is to introduce a few reforms which will correct abuses and make some institutions more humane. (D)

17. The abolition of proverty in America is a technical impossibility. (D)

18. No person should be permitted to have an income of more than $25,000 a year until such time as the average wage earner receives at least $2,000 a year. (A)

19. The coal mines of the nation should be taken over by a public agency and run for the benefit of all the people. (A)

20. Our national health would suffer if physicians were made civil servants like the public-school teachers and placed on the government payroll. (D)

21. The behavior of the capitalists is doing more to discredit and undermine capitalism than all the activities of anti-capitalistic groups. (A)

22. Current social practices are fundamentally sound because they lead to the survival of the fittest. (D)

23. Production for use and present-day capitalism are incompatible systems. (A)

24. No government has a right to experiment with different social policies. (D)

25. Capitalism is immoral because it exploits the worker by failing to give him the full value of his productive labor. (A)

26. The formation of a comprehensive anit-capitalist Farmer-Labor political party in the United States would contribute greatly to our social progress. (A)

27. The largest possible amount of business competition is necessary to national welfare. (D)

28. Persons who wish to bring about a "New Social Order" make poorer teachers than those who adhere strictly to their own specialty. (D)

29. The greater the amount of governmental control over anything, the greater the increase in graft. (D)

30. More severe punishment of criminals will reduce crime. (D)

31. An average annual family income of approximately $4,000 could be obtained if the productive equipment of the nation were operated at full capacity. (A)

32. Aliens who criticize our Constitution should be sent out of this country. (D)

33. The exceptional wealth of the United States is the result of our continued loyalty to the capitalist system. (D)

34. If we had to choose between German Fascism and Russian Communism, I should prefer the former. (D)

35. Teachers have a moral obligation to remain rigorously neutral on all debatable issues, both in class and out. (D)

36. Compulsory military training in our schools and colleges is in harmony with our best educational ideals. (D)

37. Public business enterprises are always inefficient. (D)

38. The expenditure of public funds on behalf of the jobless should be entirely eliminated. (D)

39. Most of the undeisrable features of the newspapers, the movies, and the radio come from their being controlled by profit-making corporations. (A)

40. Complete academic freedom at all levels is essential if research and instruction in the social sciences are to prosper. (A)

41. Fascism is essentially a means of saving capitalism by abolishing political democracy. (A)

42. Transport service would deteriorate if all railroads were owned and managed by the Federal government or one of its agencies. (D)

43. Consumers cooperatives are detrimental to a country's prosperity. (D)

44. There is no such thing as a "class struggle" in American life today. (D)

45. Whenever great social needs require it, the ruling class will always be found willing to surrender some of its privileges in order to meet them. (D)

46. A general strike must be crushed at all costs. (D)

47. The United States Supreme Court should be deprived of its power to declare Acts of Congress unconstitutional. (A)

48. Higher income taxes on people with incomes of more than $10,000 a year should be levied immediately. (A)

49. War should be declared only after a popular referendum shows that a majority of the nation's voters favor such a step. (A)

50. The regular calling of conventions for the revisions of state and national constitutions at ten-year intervals would eliminate some of the evils of social lag. (A)

51. Teachers should affiliate with some genuine labor organization of their own choosing. (A)

52. The best way to secure decent homes for most of the people will be for the government to build them for its citizens on a large-scale basis. (A)

53. Adequate economic security for all is impossible under a laissez-faire system. (A)

54. Indoctrination by conservatives plays a smaller part in American schools today than radical propaganda. (D)

55. A satisfying life for the masses of people can be secured without introducing important economic changes. (D)

56. We need a Government Marketing Corporation empowered to buy and process farm products and to sell them here and abroad. (A)

57. The practice of birth control should be discouraged. (D)

58. Under the conditions of modern warfare, international and civil wars inevitably destroy more human and social values than they preserve or create. (A)

59. It is pedagogically unprofitable to discuss serious social problems with adolescent youngsters. (D)

60. Recipients of relief should be deprived of the right to vote as long as they are living on public charity. (D)

61. Our present tariffs are too low to prevent unfair foreign competition with domestic goods. (D)

62. The best form of society is one in which an intelligent and forceful elite rules over the stabilized masses. (D)

63. Efficiency and responsibility in government would be promoted by the uniform establishment of a one-chamber legislature. (A)

64. The legislative requirement of a special loyalty oath is a reflection on the integrity of the teaching profession. (A)

65. The initiative, referendum, and recall are perversions of sound democratic procedure. (D)

66. All schemes for economic betterment are bound to be wrecked by the fact that there is only a limited amount of money in the world. (D)

67. Contemporary school practice generally develops a fixity of outlook which hampers social readjustment. (A)

68. Jews are a menace to the integrity of American ideals. (D)

69. The less government the better. (D)

70. Most of the ten million or more unemployed will never again find steady work at good wages in a capitalist society. (A)

71. If we compare the Chamber of Commerce with the American Federation of Labor, we find that the former has been more helpful to the cause of public education. (D)

72. No school-teacher in active service should be permitted to be a candidate for political office on any party ticket. (D)

73. The school should cease trying to improve society. (D)

74. All social planning leads to human regimentation. (D)

75. "The greatest good of the greatest number" is the final test of the value of all community practice. (A)

76. A common international currency is desirable. (A)

77. Income and social usefulness are closely correlated at the present time. (D)

78. A classless society is desirable. (A)

79. America spends far too little upon her army and navy. (A)

80. The smooth functioning of a profit economy depends upon either natural or artificial scarcity. (A)

81. Capitalism can be abolished only through a violent seizure of power by anti-capitalists. (D)

82. The economic future for youth in 1936 is brighter than it ever was before. (D)

83. The average man will be happier in the year 2000 than he is in 1936. (A)

84. Trade unions do more harm than good to our industrial progress. (D)

85. Considering the present price level, no adult workman should be paid less than $100 monthly for his services if an adequate American standard of living is to be obtained. (A)

86. It is as difficult for a man of property to support basic social change as for a camel to go through the eye of a needle. (A)

87. All foreign trade should be a monopoly of the Federal government. (A)

88. The making of law is largely determined by the pressure of lobbies in Washington. (A)

89. A classless society is possible. (A)

90. A classroom teacher should make every effort to prevent his pupils from discovering his position on controversial issues. (D)

91. All school-teachers should be hired and promoted according to the merit system or universal Civil Service. (A)

92. Unless he is eager to combat the theories of social change, no person should be entrusted with the task of fitting the young for the responsibilities of citizenship. (D)

93. A policy of maximum international cooperation is morally superior to national isolation from world affairs. (A)

94. As the economic crisis lengthens and deepens, society tends to divide into two mutually-opposed sections. (A)

95. As soon as we create a high level of economic security for all, the finer arts and graces of living will blossom everywhere. (A)

96. Vital differences in public attitudes and beliefs exist between those who live on the returns of property investment and those who get their living by laboring with hand and brain. (A)

97. Free speech should be granted to everyone without exception. (A)

98. All farm mortgages should be assumed by the Federal Treasury at an interest rate not in excess of 1 per cent.

99. I believe that the U.S. is just as selfish as any other nation. (A)

100. Most labor trouble is due to the work of radical agitators. (D)

101. All human and social progress is an illusion. (D)

102. Free speech should be granted to all except to opponents of free speech. (D)

103. Wherever social ownership is substituted for private ownership, at least partial compensation for the value of the property transferred should be made. (A)

104. Education should develop among its beneficiaries a disposition to participate ethically and intelligently in the solution of social problems. (A)

105. The masses were happier 100 years ago than they are now. (D)

106. The spiritual leadership of the world, once held by America, is now held by Russia. (D)

C-R OPINIONAIRE (Lentz 1935)

Variable

This scale is designed to measure conservatism-radicalism on a continuum of attitude toward change.

Description

There are two forms of this scale, form J and form K, each consisting of 60 agree-disagree items of both conservative and radical orientation. A subject's numerical score is the total number of answers agreeing with the key. Added to this is half of the number of answers omitted for the total score. The range of possible scores is 0 to 60 with a high score indicating high conservatism.

Very little information is given about the construction of this measure or the source of the items. The scoring key was developed as follows: a small committee agreed tentatively on "trial items" which were administered to experimental groups. Each item was correlated with each subject's total score and discarded if it showed a negative or zero correlation. When the judgments of five advanced students on the items were compared to the statistically checked key, it was found that their judgments agreed 99 percent with the statistical correlations of items with total scores.

Sample

The percentile ratings and the reliability data are based on a sample of 580 college students, both male and female, otherwise undescribed.

Reliability/
Homogeneity

The correlation between forms J and K was .84. The predicted reliability (based on the Handy formula) for form J was .91, for form K was .84, and for form J and K combined was .94.

Validity

The authors state that the validity of this measure rests primarily on the validity of the scoring key. The high agreement of the committee of advanced students with the statistical analysis of the items is evidence for the validity of this key. Some further evidence for validity may be found in the data analysis information presented below. Fifty-six college students who were given one of the "preliminary forms" of the C-R Scale (no further information about these forms is given) were also asked to rate themselves as conservative, radical, or medium.

It was found that conservative or medium self-raters and those who had not changed their denomination had higher conservatism scores than the radical self-raters and those who had changed their church affiliation.

The same subjects were also asked if they had changed their church affiliation. Three hundred ninety-two subjects from five small denominational colleges on combined forms "J and K" were about 25 points higher than the mean scores of 187 subjects from two large midwestern universities.

Location	Lentz, Theodore F. and colleagues of the Attitude Research Laboratory, <u>C-R Opinionaire Test Manual</u>. St. Louis: Character Research Association, Dept. of Education, Washington University, 5th printing, 1950 (original printing, 1935).
Administration	Estimated administration time is 20 minutes.
Results and Comments	Many of the sentiments expressed in the items are dated, as is the wording generally. It has been used primarily on college student samples.
Reference	Handy, U. and Lentz, T. F. "Item Value and Test Reliability," <u>Journal of Educational Psychology</u>, 1934, <u>25</u>, pp. 703-708.

C-R OPINIONAIRE
Form J.

Here are some statements listed to see what people think about many questions. These are opinions, and each person will agree with some and disagree with others.

INSTRUCTIONS

If you <u>agree</u> more than you disagree with a statement, mark a plus (+
If you <u>disagree</u> more than you agree with a statement, mark a minus (—
<u>Be sure</u> to place either a <u>plus</u> or a <u>minus mark</u> to the left of each number.

* * * * * *

(1.   Three meals a day will always be the best general rule.
(2.   The metric system of weights and measures should be adopted instead of our present system.
(3.   Cleanliness is a more valuable human trait than curiosity.
(4.   We should celebrate Pasteur's birthday rather than Washington's, as he has done the world a greater service.
(5.   The proposal to change the present calendar to one having 13 months of 28 days is unsound.
(6.   Even in an ideal world there should be protective tariffs.
(7.   Our courts should be in the hands of sociologists rather than lawyers.
(8.   Not the young men, but the old men, should fight our wars.
(9.   In the Sunday School chiefly the Bible should be taught.
(10.   Socially-minded experts, rather than voters, should decide the policies of government.
(11.   Cat meat is out of the question for the human diet.
(12.   Conscience is an infallible guide.
(13.   The English and the Americans have the highest standards of morality.
(14.   Our universities should have as many research workers as teachers.
(15.   Ministers should preach more about immortality than about social justice.
(16.   A commission form of government would not be desirable for the nation.
(17.   Negroes should be permitted to attend educational institutions with whites.
(18.   People who are religious will be happier in the future life than will others.
(19.   Married women should not be allowed to teach in public schools.
(20.   Any science which conflicts with religious beliefs should be taught cautiously, if at all, in our schools.
(21.   It is more important to believe in God than to be unselfish.
(22.   Since the theory of evolution has been accepted by most scientists, it should be taught in our schools.
(23.   Skirts which do not come to the knee should not be worn by grown women.

(24.   Criminals should be treated like sick persons.

(25.   It is to be hoped that men will improve the comfort of their dress by abandoning or replacing the present necktie and collar.

(26.   Cremation is the best method of burial.

(27.   Conservative people are usually more intelligent than radical people.

(28.   Trial by jury has been, and always will be, the most effective way of securing justice.

(29.   Our spelling should be revised and simplified.

(30.   Capital punishment will some day be done away with.

(31.   The average person needs greater caution more than greater daring.

(32.   One is never justified in taking another's life, even when it would be a merciful act.

(33.   The Star-Spangled Banner is the most stirring in theme and noble in sentiment of national anthems.

(34.   At the age of 21, people should have the privilege of changing their given names.

(35.   The Bible is valuable primarily because it contains some of the world's best literature, and not because it is the word of God.

(36.   Race prejudice is, on the whole, beneficial as it keeps many undesirable foreigners from the country.

(37.   Democracy as practised in the United States is the best of all modern governments because it is most suited to the needs of modern times.

(38.   Freedom of teaching, that is, allowing teachers to teach what they think is the truth, is necessary for real education.

(39.   American civilization may some day be wiped out as was Roman civilization.

(40.   It is not probable that wood ever will be converted into humanly edible food.

(41.   The Japanese race is, on the whole, crafty and treacherous.

(42.   Children should be brought up to have higher respect for our ancestors (generally).

(43.   Radical agitators and propagandists should be allowed to speak publicly in parks and streets.

(44.   Telling a lie is worse than taking the name of God in vain.

(45.   National boundaries may some day become as truly obliterated as state lines have become in America during the past 150 years.

(46.   In college, students should be allowed to attend class as much or as little as they like.

(47.   Our present system of athletics in America is at fault in that it does not provide for mass participation.

(48.   The A.B. degree should continue to require four and only four years of work above the high school.

(49.   We should Europeanize our native Americans, as well as Americanize Europeans among ourselves.

(50.   We cannot say whether Christianity is sound or not because we have never practised it systematically.

(51.   Preaching is one of the most effective ways of teaching people to lead better lives.

(52.   Our present system of law, based upon outgrown conditions, should be replaced by a progressive system based upon the conditions of our present order.

(53.   We owe our progress to radically minded people rather than to the "middle of the road" folk.

(54.   Generally speaking, Americans are more intelligent and enterprising than people of most any other country.

(55.   The naval custom for a captain to stay with his ship until she sinks is out-moded, sentimental, and unnecessary.

(56.   It would not be possible to invent an ice cream which could be made merely by opening a tin can and exposing the contents to the air.

(57.   Deformed babes of whose permanent helplessness we can be sure, should be put to death at the outset.

(58.   Something more effective than our present brooms and mops and vacuum cleaners should be devised for cleaning our homes.

(59.   All children should have some sectarian religious training either on Sunday or week days.

(60.   Most members of the D.A.R. would repudiate as dangerous characters modern personalities equivalent to the progenitors through whom they claim membership in the organization.

* * * * * *

Form K.

(1.   The age of six is the logical time to start school.
(2.   Free Trade is economically unsound.
(3.   Any science which conflicts with religious beliefs should not be taught in our schools.
(4.   School boards are right in barring married women from teaching positions.
(5.   College or university professors should not put forth their own radical views in the class room.
(6.   A man should be a booster for his city to help it grow.
(7.   The present tendency among women to wear less clothing should be encouraged, especially in warm weather or climates.
(8.   The world needs a new religion.
(9.   Our responsibility to people of other races should be as great as our responsibility to our own race.
(10.   Science will never be able to create life.
(11.   Workers in industry should receive a part of the profits of their company in addition to their salary.
(12.   Women should have as much right to propose dates to men as men to women.
(13.   The ministry is a more noble calling than the law.
(14.   The ceremony of baptism is more than a symbolic rite of the church, and is essential for the spiritual welfare of the individual.
(15.   Church hymns should be revised to fit modern discovery.
(16.   Radical foreigners who wish to visit the United States should not be admitted.
(17.   Capital punishment will never be done away with.
(18.   Turkish people should not be admitted to our country as citizens.
(19.   The mind and spirit of man have kept pace with the rapid change in his material environment.
(20.   In case of war, men's wealth, as well as their lives, should be drafted so that no war debts exist after the war is over.
(21.   Censorship of speech, press and entertainment should be completely abolished.

(22. In presidential campaigns, the nominee receiving the second greatest number of votes should become the Vice-President, and the Vice-President given a more important role.

(23. No individual, even though he feels that life is not worth living, is justified in committing suicide.

(24. We should change our minds and policies progressively and constantly.

(25. Facilities should be increased for open forum discussions among the people where grievances against the existing social or political order could be voiced.

(26. Advertising is worthwhile because it increases purchasing power.

(27. Race prejudice is useful in that it prevents inter-marrying.

(28. Historic heroes should be 'debunked.'

(29. We should make our immigration restrictions with regard to the desirability of an individual, regardless of his nationality, and abolish the practise of a fixed quota for each nationality.

(30. As long as our captains of industry are as humane to their employees, and as long as wealthy people are as philanthropic as at present, there will be no need for socialism.

(31. All legislative bodies should be so constituted as to give representation to all groups in proportion to their voting strength (Republicans, Democrats, Socialists, Communists, Anarchists, etc.)

(32. All oil beneath the earth's surface should be common property of all men, and he who pumps it out should pay royalty to society as a whole, and not to any one man or group of men.

(33. Divorce by mutual consent would be a much better system than our present one.

(34. Aristocracies of worth should replace those of wealth or birth.

(35. Cremation should be made compulsory.

(36. Taxation should be used to mitigate the inequalities and to secure a greater socialization of wealth.

(37. The chivalry of women to men and of men to weaker (less intelligent, less informed) men is about as essential as the chivalry of men to women.

(38. World patriotism should be second to national patriotism.

(39. Faith healing is not miraculous, but always psychologically explainable.

(40. Most all men should wear neckties.

(41. There should be a definite and appreciable amount of compulsory military training.

(42. The Continental attitude towards mistresses is saner than ours.

(43. Much more energy should be expended in conserving what mankind does know, than in discovering what it does not know.

(44. If Russia demonstrates very clearly that communism is better than capitalism, then we should accept the former.

(45. It is bad for a married man to take another man's wife to the movies.

(46. "My country, may she always be right, but my country, right or wrong," is a good slogan.

(47. The best way to remedy the modern divorce situation would be to make the conditions of divorce more stringent, so that marriage would be considered in a more serious light.

(48. It would not be desirable to have a Chinese family move in next door.

(49. The presidential term of office of four years is as it should be.

(50. Well-trained elementary teachers should receive the same salary as well-trained high school teachers, if not more.

(51. It is not fitting that a statue of Einstein should occupy a niche in Dr. Fosdick's Riverside Drive Church.

(52. Modern fiction should be required to pass a board of censors before publication.

(53. The Government should own the water power sites and distribute the power.

(54. Children should be encouraged to choose, independently of parents and relatives, their own religion.

(55. Criminals retard our moral progress more than all other people combined.

(56. A marriage code should be in force in the United States, whereby the wife is not only given a right in the common property, but is made jointly responsible for the support of the family.

(57. Our national government should appropriate for the next twenty years at least 20 billion dollars for research work (chiefly in the social sciences of psychology, education, sociology, politics, and government).

(58. Science should endeavor to discover and develop a harmless liquor, retaining almost all the good features, but lacking the harmful ones, of alcoholic beverages.

(59. Football helps put a college on the map, and should be heartily supported by all the alumni.

(60. The United States should enter a world federation of nations.

PERSONAGE ADMIRATION (Lentz 1939)

Variable   An index constructed to discover the personage admiration of conservatives and radicals.

Description   This instrument was one of the 13 testing techniques incorporated into the Youth Expressionaire, a testing battery intended to determine significant correlates of "the trait of conservatism-radicalism," terms left (further) undefined in this reference. In the Personage Admiration test, subjects were confronted with 156 names (10 percent of which were fictitious) and asked to pick the six personally most admired and to cross out the unknowns.

Sample   Out of 409 high school graduates with a median age of 22 years, the 100 highest and 100 lowest scorers on a companion test, the C-R Opinionaire, were selected as the sample base for the Personage Admiration test.

Reliability/   No evidence of reliability is reported.
Homogeneity

Validity   No evidence of validity is reported.

Location   Lentz, Theodore F. "Personage Admiration and Other Correlates of Conservatism-Radicalism," Journal of Social Psychology, 1939, 10, pp. 81-93.

Administration   Estimated administration time is 15-20 minutes.

Results and   The author reports highly significant differences between preferences
Comments   of the "conservatives" and "radicals" selected by the Opinionaire. "Conservatives" preferred military leaders, athletes, financiers, industrialists and entertainers, while "radicals" preferred scientists, inventors and authors. "Conservatives" also apparently knew fewer names than "radicals" and more often tried to fake knowledge of the fictitious names. Sixty-eight of the "admired" names showed a frequency of choice difference of more than 14 percent between the "conservatives" and the "radicals."

Sample Items   "In each group of twelve personages, encircle the number preceding the six persons whom you most admire. Draw a line through those you do not know."

1. U. S. Grant	7. Walt Mason
2. Henry Ford	8. Charles Dickens
3. Al Jolson	9. Lawrence Tibbett
4. Herbert Hoover	10. Frances Perkins
5. James Dole	11. Earl Browder
6. Mae West	12. Nicholai Lenin

SITUATION-RESPONSE SURVEY (Pace 1939)

Variable

This instrument is designed to measure general social-political-economic liberalism and conservatism. The author defines liberalism as "agreement with or activities in harmony with the broad socio-economic objectives of the New Deal, Farmer-Labor, and Progressive parties, and with editorials and articles in The Nation and New Republic."

Conservatism in the scale means "agreement with the policies of the 'traditional Republican party' and with those currently classified as 'Liberty Leaguers' or 'economic royalists.'"

Description

The test consists of descriptions of 30 political and day-to-day situations on which nationally prominent liberals and conservatives differed, with from four to seven ways of reacting to the situation listed for each. The topics are those frequently discussed in political platforms and partisan speeches. Ten judges ranked the responses to the situations, leading to the elimination of five items from the original group of 43. A weight of 1 is assigned to the most conservative response, a weight of 2 to the next, etc., with the most radical response receiving the highest numerical value anywhere from 4 to 7, depending on the number of alternatives.

Total score is the average item score, and the range of possible scores is 1.00 to 5.34. A second form of the test was constructed in which five possible ways of reacting were listed for each situation.

Sample

The sample was comprised of 571 students from three colleges. The criterion validity samples were comprised of 25 "known radicals" (members of the Young Communist League, Trotskyites, Farmer-Laborites, liberal New Dealers) and 25 "known conservatives" (supporters of Landon in the 1936 election and members of a national fraternity, all of a comfortable economic background).

The second form of the test was administered to 253 "young people."

Reliability/
Homogeneity

The (corrected) odd-even reliability for the fully completed test ranged from .50 to .92, with an average of about .80. The second form of the instrument had an odd-even reliability of about .75.

No test-retest reliability was reported.

Validity

The ability of each item to discriminate between high and low quartiles of 100 cases drawn at random from one relatively homogeneous group was determined. Twenty-two items had significant discriminatory power at the .05 level, 14 of these items being significant at the .01 level as well.

The average score of the radical criterion group, 4.5 (range 3.2 to 5.1), was significantly higher than that of the conservative group, 2.8 (range 2.2 to 3.1).

On a group of 56 students, the test correlated .72 (corrected) with the Economic Conservatism section of the Rundquist-Sletto Scales for the Survey of Opinions (see the Introduction to this chapter for exact reference).

The second form of the test again discriminated significantly between "known radicals" and the rest of the sample.

Location	Pace, C. Robert. "A Situations Test to Measure Social-Political-Economic Attitudes," Journal of Social Psychology, 1939, 10, pp. 331-344.

Results and
Comments

The somewhat low odd-even reliability may result from the fact that the test calls for responses in diverse fields; in any case, the reliability of the test seems adequate for group measurement. The items of the second form of the test were not all as individually discriminating as those of the first form, but the two forms correlated .95.

In a subsequent study, Pace (1940) compared the results obtained from the Situation-Response Survey with a Survey of Opinions attempting to measure fundamentally the same liberal-conservative attitudes.

A sample of the items in the two scales is reproduced below. The sample was a group of 39 University of Minnesota students. All items in the two scales correspond and were designed to measure essentially the same attitude.

In the 1940 study, the correlation between the two scales was .89; the odd-even reliability (corrected) was .82 for the S-R Survey and .89 for the Opinion Survey. The S-R Survey, however, was found to discriminate better between the high and lower quartiles than the Opinion Survey. The distributions on the S-R Survey were significantly different from the distributions on the Opinion Survey for ten items (1,2,6,9,13,16,19,23,26, and 30). As the authors points out, in order to prove one test is more valid than the other, it would be necessary to observe students' behavior in actual life situations. It could also be argued that some of the items--notably 9 and 30--are not completely comparable. If the purpose of measurement is to predict specific behavior, the S-R Survey may be preferable. In reservation, it should be noted that administration of the S-R Survey is necessarily longer than the more simple Opinion Survey.

The form of measurement of the S-R Survey seems to be a forerunner to the Matthews-Prothro measure of Citizen Competence (see Chapter 12).

Reference

Pace, C. Robert. "Stated Behavior vs. Stated Opinions as Indicators of Social-Political-Economic Attitudes," Journal of Social Psychology, 1940, 11, pp. 369-381.

Sample Items   <u>Situation-Response Survey</u>

5. Suppose you belonged to some club or fraternity. Suppose, too,
    that there was a big strike going on in your city. The strikes
    claim that the employers have fired certain men for union
    activity, and refused to bargain with union representatives.
    The employers claim that they did not fire men for union activity
    and that the union does not represent a majority of the workers.
    Attempts to arbitrate have failed. Meanwhile 2 policemen and 6
    strikers have been injured. There has also been some property
    damage. If representatives from the employers came to your club
    or fraternity and asked you to help them in maintaining law and
    order, what would you do?

        . . . . a. Gladly go and help them.
        . . . . b. Not only go yourself but encourage others to
                    go also.
        . . . . c. Help them only if most of the others also do.
        . . . . d. Refuse to help them yourself even if most of
                    the others decide to go.
        . . . . e. Not only refuse to help them but try to
                    persuade others not to help them.
        . . . . f. Not only refuse to help them but try to
                    organize a group to help the strikes.

<u>Opinion-Survey</u>

5. When property damage and personal violence accompany labor
    strikes, citizens should help the employers and public officials
    maintain law and order.

                Agree   Disagree

HARPER'S SOCIAL BELIEFS AND ATTITUDES TEST (Boldt and Stroud 1934)

Note: Harper's original monograph, the source of this test, was not available. Reliability and validity data which Boldt and Stroud report from this original source together with the results from their own research are reported below.

Variable — This test was designed to measure conservatism-liberalism as expressed in "certain fundamental social beliefs and attitudes" including items on "government ownership, capital and labor, social problems, wealth and property rights, internationalism, politics and religion."

Description — The instrument is comprised of 71 items. Response choices were not given in this reference. A score of 71 represents the highest possible liberal score and a score of zero represents the highest possible conservative score.

Sample — The test was administered to 738 randomly selected students of the Kansas State Teachers College in 1933. The population contained 411 freshmen, 106 sophomores, 98 juniors, 103 seniors, and 20 graduate students.

Reliability/ Homogeneity — Test-retest reliability over a three-week interval was reported by the original author (i.e., Harper) to be .90.

Validity — Two tests of validity were reported to have been made by the author of the instrument. In the first, a group of "educators" was rated on a ten-point scale by "competent judges" as to conservatism-Liberalism on social questions. The median of the ratings correlated about .76, .13 with the scores actually made by the educators on the test. In the second instance, 47 judges rated the items as liberal or conservative, with an average agreement over all items of 98 percent.

Location — Boldt, W. J. and Stroud, J. B. "Changes in the Attitudes of College Students," Journal of Educational Psychology, 1934, 25, pp. 611-619.

Administration — Estimated administration time for the test with agree-disagree responses to the items is about 54 minutes.

Results and Comments — The average score was reported to be 45.9. It was found that the liberalism scores increased progressively with each succeeding level of college attainment, and that all inter-class differences were statistically highly significant. The difference between scores of students majoring or not majoring in the social sciences was reported to be statistically significant also. Among Juniors and Seniors, the number of hours of work taken in the social sciences were said to have shown a significant relationship to scores on the test, with the factor of number of years of college training held constant.

It should be noted that all the above relationships were observed among group rather than individual scores. The sample in this study revealed a tolerance of shibboleths (such as 'socialistic') in the items which is rarely found in American samples. The students reportedly turned in an unusual 56 percent agreement with the third item below, and 73 percent agreement with the ninth item.

Reference   Harper, Manly H. Social Beliefs and Attitudes of American Educators. Contributions to Education, No. 294, Teachers College, Columbia University.

Sample Items
(Liberal response
is in
parenthesis)

1. The development of the highest welfare of the country will require government ownership of the land. (Agree)

2. One should never allow his own experience and reason to lead him in ways that he knows are contrary to the teachings of the Bible. (Disagree)

3. Without directly teaching religion a teacher's influence in the public schools should always be definitely and positively favorable to the purposes and activities of our generally recognized religious organizations. (Disagree)

4. In the industries of this country proper opportunity and encouragement are usually given to laborers to progress from lower to higher positions of all grades of responsibility and reward. (Disagree)

5. Our educational forces should be directed toward a more thoroughly socialistic order of society. (Agree)

6. The power of huge fortunes in this country endangers democracy. (Agree)

7. Reproduction should be made impossible, by segregation or by surgical operation, for all those below certain low standards of physical and mental fitness. (Disagree)

8. Licenses to teach in the public schools should be refused to persons believing in socialism. (Disagree)

9. Among the poor, many more individuals fall short of highest satisfaction on account of too many desires than on account of lack of income. (Disagree)

10. If any facts should be found favorable to socialism they should be omitted from histories written for high school use. (Disagree)

11. As a rule, the laborer in this country has as favorable an opportunity to obtain a fair price for his labor as his employer has to obtain a fair price for the goods which the laborer produces. (Agree)

Sample Items
(continued)

12. Many more industries and parts of industries should be owned and operated cooperatively by the producers (all the workers) themselves. (Agree)

13. No school, college, or university should teach anything that is found to result in its students doubting or questioning the Bible as containing the word of God. (Disagree)

14. The government should provide to all classes of people opportunity for insurance at cost against accident, sickness, premature death, and old age. (Agree)

15. The man whose vacant lots in a thiriving city increase many fold in value because the city's homes and business grow up around those lots, should, in justice, be required to repay in taxes a large part of the unearned profits to the city that created the increased values. (Agree)

POLITICO-ECONOMIC RADICALISM-CONSERVATISM (Sanai and Pickard 1949)

Variable	This instrument purports to be a measure of politico-economic radicalism, a term which the authors leave undefined.
Description	A factor analysis was performed on responses to a questionnaire of 20 seven-point Likert-type items on different aspects of politico-economic opinion, and the twelve items most highly saturated with the first general factor, considered to be a factor of "radicalism," were used as a test of "radicalism." Source of the 20 items was reported to be the previous literature and suggestions from colleagues and students. Range of scores for the twelve-item test was 0-12, as all agreements were scored as "1" and all others responses (marked 0, -1, -2, -3) were scored as "0."
Sample	The test construction population was a group of 250 British university, W.E.A. (sic) and teachers' college students.
	The experimental population consisted of 70 upper middle-class students in a private London teachers' college, ranging in age from 19 to 24.
Reliability/ Homogeneity	The split-half reliability of the twelve-item test was .86, corrected by the Spearman-Brown formula. No test-retest reliability was reported.
Validity	The authors remarked that the designation of the first general factor as "radicalism" was "not quite satisfactory." A correlation of .25 was observed between "radicalism" and intelligence. No significant correlations were found between "radicalism" and any of seven "temperamental traits" as investigated by the Rorschach Test.
Location	Sanai, M. and Pickard, P. H. "The Relation between Politico-Economic Radicalism and Certain Traits of Personality," Journal of Social Psychology, 1949, 30, pp. 217-227.
Administration	Estimated administration time is about twelve minutes. Scoring requires sample summation of dichotomized scoring codes.
Results and Comments	This instrument is insufficiently validated. The items require sophisticated respondents, appear suitable only for British respondents, and are also somewhat dated.

POLITICO-ECONOMIC ATTITUDES

Below are 20 questions which represent widely held opinions on various political questions. They are chosen in such a way that most people are likely to agree with some and disagree with others.

    You are requested to observe the following Rule of Markings:

In the left hand margin before the statement put:

+3 When you are in complete agreement with the statement.
+2 When, on the whole, you agree with the statement.
+1 When you are in doubt, but if forced to choose, will agree with the statement.
 0 When you are totally unable to decide.
-1 When you are in doubt, if forced to choose, will disagree with the statement.
-2 When, on the whole, you disagree with the statement.
-3 When you are in complete disagreement with the statement.

Your answers will be kept secret. Please answer carefully and frankly.

1 Industries such as electricity, mines and railways should be owned and operated by the State--not for private profit.

*2 If 10 percent of the population owns 90 percent of the country's wealth it is because the most able rise to the top.

3 In practice the rich and the poor are not equal before the law.

4 Slumps and unemployment are inevitable consequences of capitalism.

5 It is clearly unfair that some people should acquire large incomes, not through any work of their own, but by inheritance.

6 But for the controls which the Labor Government maintained there would have been economic chaos in this country.

*7 Socialism leads to too much bureaucracy.

*8 Capitalism is a misleading term in Britain now that the majority of the population have invested savings or buy their own homes.

9 Many of the errors in our foreign policy are due to the diplomatic service being drawn so exclusively from the "Upper Class."

10 Before any satisfactory measure of social progress can be achieved the working class must exercise a temporary dictatorship.

*11 British Governments have so far aligned themselves in foreign countries with reactionary elements.

*12 It is not possible to put democratic principles into practice owing to wide differences in innate intelligence between individuals.

13 Stable peace will only be possible in a Socialist world.

14 Capitalism is immoral because it exploits the worker by failing to give him the full value of his productive labor.

15 In the present state of capitalist societies genuine social progress is impossible without the aid of revolution.

16 In capitalist countries the economic system impels the capitalists and the workers into irreconcilable conflict with one another.

17 All large scale means of production and distribution must be owned and operated by the State.

18 In the interest of peace we must give up a large part of our national sovereignty.

19 Unrestricted freedom of discussion on every topic is desirable in the press, in literature, on the stage, etc.
20 In a capitalist country, like the United States for example, it is really big business that controls the state, not the people at large.

---

* These are conservative statements and must be reversed for purposes of scoring.

RADICALISM-CONSERVATISM AND SOCIAL MOBILITY (Hetzler 1954)

Variable

This study attempted to measure radicalism-conservatism with scales of "felt" satisfaction with the city's government, industries, and general economic opportunities and to measure social mobility with a scale of degree of "felt" mobility of social position over a twelve-year period.

Description

The instrument for each variable consisted of a foot-long profile scale with two reference points: one end was marked, "The person with the highest (e.g., satisfaction with city government) in your town," and the opposite end was marked, "The person with the lowest (e.g., satisfaction with city government) in your town." Each respondent was asked to indicate his own opposition on the three scales.

The measure of social mobility was derived from the differences between similar scales of present (1952) social position and of position in 1940.

Sample

The population sample was a random sample of 300 (persons) from Washington Court House, Ohio, in 1952.

Reliability/
  Homogeneity

A pre-test performed with 45 university undergraduates yielded a test-retest correlation coefficient of .91. The inter-test period was not reported.

Validity

No data bearing on validity are reported.

Location

Hetzler, Stanley A. "Radicalism-Conservatism and Social Mobility," Social Forces, 1954, 33, #2, pp.161-166.

Results and
  Comments

In general, the lower status occupational groups were less satisfied with city government, industries and economic opportunity than the upper status groups. Very little difference in social mobility among the occupational status groups was noted. No correlations between the "social mobility" and "radicalism-conservatism" measures were reported, leaving the author's question about this relation still unsolved. Furthermore the use of the three satisfaction scales as a basis for assumptions about attitudes of "radicalism-conservatism" remains questionable.

The assumption of numerical comparability of subjective ratings and individual conceptions of the relative position of unmarked intervals is a controversial procedure. The author also attempted to measure "intensity" on the same rating scales by arranging responses in units from 0 to 11, letting 6 represent the zero point in intensity, and deriving positive and negative measures of intensity from the direction and degree to which unit medians varied from the zero point.

The scales are similar in many respects to the self-anchoring scale developed by Kilpatrick and Cantril (1960).

152

Reference   Kilpatrick, F. P. and Cantril, Hadley. "Self-anchoring Scaling: A Measure of Individuals' Unique Reality Worlds," _Journal of Individual Psychology_, 1960, 16, #2, pp.158-173.

RADICALISM-CONSERVATISM

Place an "x" at the spot of each of the following lines indicating where you stand on the issue in question.

The person with the highest
satisfaction with city
government in your town.

The person with the highest
satisfaction with industries
in your town.

The person with the highest
satisfaction with general
economic opportunities in
your town.

The person with the lowest
satisfaction with city
government in your town.

The person with the lowest
satisfaction with industries
in your town.

The person with the lowest
satisfaction with general
economic opportunities in
your town.

CONCERN WITH PROGRESS (Morgan, Sirageldin, and Baerwaldt 1966)

Variable   The index of concern with progress is designed to measure progressive attitudes and behavior as part of "a modernism syndrome."

Description   Ten sets of interview schedule items which seemed to express a common theme of modernism were intercorrelated to check for unidimensionality. The following four sets of items intercorrelated at a highly significant level and seemed to form a meaningful composite:

1. Achievement orientation (9 items)
2. Receptivity to change (four subindices with 1,2,3, and 6 items)
3. Ambition and aspiration (8 items)
4. Planning and time horizon (6 items)

Potential scores for the items range from 0 (low concern with progress) to 37 (high concern) but actual scores ranged from 3 to 30, with a mean of 15.3. The scores were approximately normally distributed as follows:

Score	Percent of family heads
3-6	3%
7-9	11
10-11	11
12-13	12
14-16	21
17-18	14
19-20	12
21-24	13
25-30	3
	100%

Sample   The 2214 adult respondents, who were personally interviewed by the Survey Research Center during January and February of 1965, were a national cross-section sample of family heads living in households.

Reliability/   Average inter-scale correlation was .18, .26 if the fourth index of
  Homogeneity planning and time horizon is excluded. All of the correlations, while low, are highly significant statistically.

No test-retest data are reported.

Validity   Average correlation of the four subsets of items making up the total index with reported use of new products was .17, again highly significant. However, the reported use of new products is itself incorporated into the scale.

Location   Morgan, J., Sirageldin, I. and Baerwaldt, N. Productive Americans. Ann Arbor, Michigan: Survey Research Center, 1966.

Results and
Comments

Many of the items in the index (especially those dealing with use of new products) would seem to have a built-in social status component.

Concern with progress was highest among the 24 percent of the sample who were under 55 years old and who had some education beyond high school (mean score = 19.3) and lowest among the 16 percent of the sample who were over 55 and had not finished high school (mean score = 9.9). Individual experience with success appears to lead to more concern with progress.

Concern with progress was highly related to an Index of Social Participation (average tau-beta = .22), which, of course, is also related to age and education. Four sets of items significantly related to the index of concern with progress but not included in the final index were (1) caution and risk avoidance, (2) mobility behavior, (3) sense of personal effectiveness, and (4) mobility experience.

Two variables which unexpectedly did not correlate with the index were (1) attitude toward mother's working, and (2) closeness of family ties.

A similar scale, called the Initiative Scale, was developed from interviews given to a cross-sectional American sample by the Opinion Research Corporation; see the reference given in the introduction to this section for more information about this scale.

CONCERN WITH PROGRESS

1. Achievement Orientation

Head of family has sent, is sending, or will send children to a four-year college and expects them to get a degree (only for families where total family income is under $10,000)

Head of family ranked chances for advancement are good first or second among six job characteristics

Head of family ranked the work is important, gives a feeling of accomplishment first or second among six job characteristics

Head of family believes that he falls short of what he could do

Head of family took more than forty hours of courses in 1964

Head of family desires to get better at his sports or hobbies

Head of family's income aspirations are realistic but positive

Nonself-employed head of family thinks it is important to make changes in his work

Head of family admires those who try difficult things for their initiative

2. Receptivity to Change

Use a steam iron

Use an electric frying pan

Use a gasoline credit card

Use a coin-operated dry-cleaning machine

Have seat belts in the car

Bought car new rather than used

Head of family approves without qualification the addition of fluoride to water

At least some of family have had polio vaccine

Head thinks that the program to try to land a man on the moon is good

"Would you say you try new products when they first come out, or do you wait until others have tried them first, or what?"

"Some people say that most new things are just a way to get us to spend more money. Others feel that most new things are really improvements. How do you feel?"

"Do you like to keep things running smoothly or are you more interested in trying new things in your work?" (R is self-employed)

"How important is it to you to have some chance to make changes in your work?" (R is not self-employed)

3. Ambition and Aspiration

Head of family expects to send children to college

Head of family expects to provide financial aid to parents or other relatives within next 20 years

Head of family ranks high income first or second among 6 job characteristics

Head of family took courses to increase his economic skills

Family would like to buy some new things or replace some things

Family would like a new home or would like to make additions or repairs to present home

Head of family would like to work more hours if paid for it

Head of family would like to be earning at least $1000 more five years from now than earning now

4. Planning and Time Horizon

Head of family has money set aside to pay for his children's college education

Head of family has no children under 18, or has children who will not go to college

Family planned its most recent vacation more than one month in advance

Family never takes vacations

Head of family is retired, or less than 35 years old

Head of family knows when he will retire

5. <u>Social Participation Index</u>

    Head of family took a vacation in 1964

    Head of family attends religious services regularly or often

    Family eats at restaurants at least once every 2 weeks

    Wife did more than 40 hours of volunteer work in 1964

    Head of family did more than 40 hours of volunteer work in 1964

    Head of family participates in sports or hobbies

    Head of family is strong Republican or strong Democrat

SUPPLEMENTARY SCALE

SELF-ADMINISTERED INITIATIVE SCALE
(OPINION RESEARCH CORPORATION, PRINCETON, N.J.)

(Draw a circle around the numbers on each question that comes closest to your opinion.)

B.10.   Please check all of the following that you do quite a bit of in your free time.

1 Travel
2 Visit or entertain friends or relatives
3 Read daily newspapers
4 Participate in sports
5 Watch sports events
6 Read weekly news magazines
7 Read magazines, like LIFE, LOOK, POST, etc.
8 Hobbies like woodworking, photography, etc.

1 Listen to the radio
2 Read business or professional journals
3 Watch television
4 Work in the yard or garden
5 Go to the movies
6 Listen to music
7 Attend plays, opera or ballet
8 Read books
9 Others_____
                    Explain

B.11.   When you get together with other people, which several of the following things are you likely to talk about?

1 Your work
2 Religion
3 Political affairs
4 World affairs
5 Your family
6 Business conditions

1 National problems
2 Sports
3 Music, art, etc.
4 Community problems
5 Government policies
6 Labor union matters
7 Others_____
                    Explain

B.12.   Are you very active in any of the following types of organizations? Check all those in which you are very active.

1 Professional association
2 Church or religious group or club
3 Political organization
4 Service club such as Rotary, Lions, Junior League
5 Sports club like a country club, golf club, swimming, sports club, etc.
6 Labor union or organization

7 Fraternal or veteran's organization such as Elks, Legion, etc.
8 Civic or local association such as school board, community association, etc.
9 Drama, arts, or cultural group, etc.
X Business association
Y Others_____
                    Explain
0 None of these

To obtain this measure an experimental set of questions (see the preceding questionnaire) covered the types of activities to which the respondent devoted substantial attention. Items receiving positive scores were:

Read weekly news magazines*
Read daily newspapers*
Read business or professional journals*
Read books
Read magazines like LIFE, LOOK, POST, etc.
Travel
Attend plays, opera or ballet

Talk to other people about:

Political affairs
World affairs
Community problems
Government policies
Labor union matters
Business conditions
National problems

"Very active" in following types of organizations:

Professional association
Church or religious group or club
Political organization
Service club such as Rotary, Lions, Junior League
Labor union or organization
Fraternal or veteran's organization
Civic or local association
Business association

---

*Actual weighting scores 1 point for each item selected, except for those with asterisks above, which are scored 2 points. Weighting was based on examination of the Image data for closeness of association of items with level of education and with voting frequency. (Image data are discussed in the ORC monograph The Initiators 1960).

CHAPTER 4:   DEMOCRATIC PRINCIPLES

The scales reviewed in this section provide intriguing evidence

of the non-ideological nature of American attitudes toward democratic principles

and the specific instances of their application. Americans, especially the less

affluent, have been found to be intolerant of specific groups (such as deviants

and nonconformists) and in specific situations. At the same time almost all

Americans have still professed belief in the general principles of democracy

and tolerance. The expected socio-economic correlates of such inconsistencies

in attitudes have also been evident. Findings such as these were taken from

the studies using the following scales. These scales are listed according to

our opinion of their merit.

1. Willingness to Tolerate Nonconformists (Stouffer 1955)
2. Scale of Perception of the Internal Communist Danger
    (Stouffer 1955)
3. Democratic and Anti-Democratic Attitudes (McClosky 1964)
4. Attitudes toward Democratic Principles (Prothro and Grigg 1960)
5. Attitude toward Communists (Schonbar 1949)
6. Attitude toward Civil Liberties (Noble and Noble 1954)

The first scales listed were devised by Stouffer and were constructed

with far greater concern for methodological correctness than any of the other

four measures. Both scales have high reproducibility values, .96 and .94,

respectively, although these coefficients were attained by using the "contrived

technique" which gives rather generous estimates of homogeneity. Stouffer's

scales also correlated well with certain socio-economic and psychological

traits, showing the usual intolerance of nonconformists and Communists among

the less educated, the elderly, and those holding "conformist" attitudes. Both

scales were administered to large cross-sectional samples.

McClosky's scale of democratic attitudes was also developed on a national sample and, in addition, has been applied to large samples of Democratic and Republican leaders. Data on validity and reliability are as yet incomplete, although the findings are generally consistent with those of Stouffer and of Prothro and Grigg. The study includes a noteworthy effort to control for agreement response set.

The scale by Prothro and Grigg on democratic attitudes is one of the most interesting presented here. It includes items on both abstract and specific democratic principles concerning majority rule and minority rights. The authors find little consensus of opinion among respondents between the specific and the abstract. However, the scale is somewhat brought into question since no evidence of its reliability or validity is presented. Also, the samples exposed to the scale were from two college towns, with a highly disproportionate number of well-educated citizens, thereby limiting the study's level of generalization.

The most interesting aspect of Schonbar's <u>Attitude toward Communists</u> scale is the findings resulting from its use. The sample of female college students generally had low anti-Communism scores on the scale. A negative correlation also existed between anti-Communist feelings and amount of general political information possessed by those sampled. These findings might be explained, in part, by the fact that the study was conducted prior to the advent of a salient and pervasive "cold war" between America and the Communist nations. Reliability, validity, and sample selection were far from adequate for this scale.

The same low ratings on psychometric considerations must be given the Noble and Noble scale. In this case, however, the nature of major findings—that students were nearly unanimous in their defense of civil rights—is not as interesting as Schonbar's findings.

WILLINGNESS TO TOLERATE NONCONFORMISTS (Stouffer 1955)

Variable   This scale attempts to measure the degree of willingness to tolerate
                  nonconformists such as Socialists, atheists, or Communists,
                  or suspected nonconformists such as people whose loyalty
                  has been criticized. It does not attempt to measure intolerance in
                  general.

Description   This Guttman-type scale is composed of 15 modified forced choice
                  items comprising five sets of three items each. Scores ranged from
                  5, tolerant on all subtests, to 0, tolerant on none. The dichoto-
                  mization of responses for each item is reproduced below.

Sample   The main sample was composed of two national cross-section samples
                  with a total N of 4939. Fourteen kinds of community leaders were
                  selected from a national cross-section sample of 123 cities of 1,000
                  to 150,000 population. A total 1533 interviews were completed with
                  community leaders.

Reliability/   The coefficient of reproducibility was .96, possibly artificially
  Homogeneity   inflated by use of the "contrived technique."

Validity   No direct tests for validity were reported, although those classified
                  as "conformists," "authoritarians", and "rigid categorizers" by other
                  single-question measures were shown to be less tolerant of noncon-
                  formists, as were rural, Southern, and female respondents.

Location   Stouffer, Samuel A., Communism, Conformity, and Civil Liberties.
                  Garden City, New York: Doubleday & Company, Inc., 1955, pp. 262-266.

Administration   The items should take less than 10 minutes to complete. The distri-
                  bution of scores into the six types was as follows.

		Cross-section	Leaders
Group 5 4	More tolerant	31%	66%
3 2	In-between	50%	29%
1 Group 0	Less tolerant	19%	5%

Results and   It was found that community leaders in each of the 14 categories
  Comments   tended to become more tolerant than the rest of the population
                 sampled. Increasing age was clearly inversely related to tolerance,
                 while education was positively related. Those classified as "con-
                 formists," were shown to be less tolerant of nonconformists, as were
                 rural, Southern, and female respondents.

                 An updating of some of these findings, with the variable of educa-
                 tional background controlled, is given in Alford and Scoble (1968).

164

Reference   Alford, R. and Scoble, H. "Community Leadership, Education, and
               Political Behavior," <u>American Sociological Review</u>, 1968, <u>33</u>, pp.
               259-272.

WILLINGNESS TO TOLERATE NONCONFORMISTS

GROUP 5   (Most tolerant: + answers to at least 2 out of these 3 items and
            2 out of 3 + answers to each of the remaining four groups)

Now, I should like to ask you some questions about a man who admits he is a
Communist.
Suppose this admitted Communist wants to make a speech in your community.
Should he be allowed to speak, or not?

              + Yes   - No   - Don't know

Suppose he wrote a book which is in your public library. Somebody in your
community suggests the book should be removed from the library. Would you
favor removing it, or not?

              - Favor   + Not favor   - Don't know

Suppose this admitted Communist is a radio singer. Should he be fired, or not?

              - Should be fired   + Not be fired   - Don't know

GROUP 4   (+ answers to at least 2 out of these 3 items and 2 out of 3 + answers
            to each of the remaining three groups)

Should an admitted Communist be put in jail, or not?

              - Yes   + No   - Don't know

There are always some people whose ideas are considered bad or dangerous by other
people. For instance, somebody who is against all churches and religion.
If such a person wanted to make a speech in your city (town, community) against
churches and religion, should he be allowed to speak, or not?

              + Yes   - No   - Don't know

If some people in your community suggested that a book he wrote against churches
and religion should be taken out of your public library, would you favor removing
this book, or not?

              - Yes   + No   - Don't know

GROUP 3   (+ answers to at least 2 out of these 3 items and 2 out of 3 + answers
            to each of the remaining two groups)

Now suppose the radio program he (an admitted Communist) is in advertises a brand
of soap. Somebody in your community suggests you stop buying that soap. Would
you stop, or not?

              - Would stop   + Would not stop   - Don't know

Or consider a person who favored government ownership of all the railroads and all big industries.
If this person wanted to make a speech in your community favoring government ownership of all the railroads and big industries, should he be allowed to speak, or not?

+ Yes   - No   - Don't know

If some people in your community suggested that a book he wrote favoring government ownership should be taken out of your public library, would you favor removing the book, or not?

- Yes   + No   - Don't know

GROUP 2   (+ answers to at least 2 out of 3 of the following items and 2 out of 3 of the next group)

Now I would like you to think of another person. A man whose loyalty had been questioned before a Congressional committee, but who swears under oath he has never been a Communist.
Suppose he is teaching in a college or university. Should he be fired, or not?

- Yes   + No   - Don't know

Should he be allowed to make a speech in your community, or not?

+ Yes   - No   - Don't know

Suppose this man is a high school teacher. Should he be fired, or not?

- Yes   + No   - Don't know

GROUP 1   (+ answers to only 2 out of 3 of the following--with respect to a man whose loyalty has been questioned but who swears he is not a Communist)

Suppose he has been working in a defense plant. Should he be fired, or not?

- Yes   + No   + Don't know

Suppose he is a clerk in a store. Should he be fired, or not?

- Yes   + No   + Don't know

Suppose he wrote a book which is in your public library. Somebody in your community suggests the book should be removed from the library. Would you favor removing it, or not?

- Favor   + Not favor   + Don't know

GROUP 0   (The least tolerant group. Fail to qualify in any of the groups above)
            (Do not give answers scored + in any of the groups above)

SCALE OF PERCEPTION OF INTERNAL COMMUNIST DANGER (Stouffer 1955)

Variable   This scale attempts to measure how severe people perceive the
                    Communist threat to the internal structure of American society.

Description   This Guttman-type scale is composed of 11 multiple-choice items,
                    which comprise five scalar steps. Scores range from 5 (tolerant
                    on all subtests) to 0 (tolerant on none). The dichotomization of
                    responses for each item is reproduced below.

Sample   The main sample was composed of two national cross-section samples
                    with a total N of 4939. Fourteen kinds of community leaders were
                    selected from a national cross-section sample of 123 cities of
                    1,000 to 150,000 population. A total 1533 interviews were completed
                    with community leaders.

Reliability/   The coefficient of reproducibility was .94, possibly high due to the
  Homogeneity   use of the "contrived technique."

Validity   No tests for validity were reported.

Location   Stouffer, Samuel A. Communism, Conformity, and Civil Liberties.
                    Garden City, New York: Doubleday & Company, Inc., 1955, pp. 266-268.

Administration   Items should take less than 10 minutes to complete. Distribution of
                    scale scores was as follows:

Scores		Cross-section
4 or 5	Great threat	30%
2 or 3	In-between	51%
0 or 1	Little threat	19%

Results and   In general, it was found that tolerance of nonconformists was lower
  Comments   when the internal Communist threat was perceived as great, and
                    higher when it was conceived as small.

                    Perception of threat appeared to have a curvilinear relationship
                    with the person's education. Perception of Communist threat was
                    somewhat related to tolerance of nonconformists at each educational
                    level, but education was clearly related to the capability of being
                    relatively tolerant in spite of perception of great internal
                    Communist danger. In this category fell such groups as community
                    leaders, Northerners, younger males, the more interested, and the
                    better informed.

168

SCALE OF PERCEPTION OF THE INTERNAL COMMUNIST DANGER

GROUP 5 (+ reply to this question and to those in the next four groups)

Do you think there are any Communists teaching in American public schools, or not?
IF ANY YES ANSWER: How much danger is there that these Communists in public
schools can hurt the country--a great danger, some danger, not much danger, or
no danger?

    + Great   - Some   - Not much   - None   - Don't know

GROUP 4 (+ reply to this question and to those in the next three groups)

Do you think there might be any Communists with the American Government now,
or not? IF ANY YES ANSWER: How much danger is there that these Communists
within the Government can hurt the country--a great danger, some danger, not
much danger, or no danger?

    + Great   - Some   - Not much   - None   - Don't know

GROUP 3 (+ reply to this question and to those in the next two groups)

How great a danger do you feel that American Communists are to this country at
the present time--a very great danger, a great danger, some danger, hardly any
danger, or no danger?

    + A very great danger   + A great danger   - Some danger
    - Hardly any danger   - No danger   - Don't know

GROUP 2 (+ reply to this question and to those in the next group)

Do you think there are any Communists teaching in American colleges and universities now, or not?
IF YES: If you had to guess, how many would you think--just a few, or hundreds,
or thousands?

    Yes, a few   Yes, hundreds   Yes, thousands   Yes, don't know how many
    - No, don't think there are any   + Don't know if there are any

OR, IF ANY YES ANSWER: How much danger is there that the Communists in colleges
and universities can hurt the country--a great danger, some danger, not much
danger, or no danger?

    + Great   + Some   - Not much   - None   + Don't know

GROUP 1 (+ reply to this item only)

Do you think there are any Communists working in key defense plants, or not?
IF YES: If you had to guess, how many would you think--just a few, or hundreds,
or thousands?

     Yes, a few   Yes, hundreds   Yes, thousands   Yes, don't know how many

    - No, don't think there are any   + Don't know if there are any

OR, IF ANY YES ANSWERS: How much danger is there the Communists working in key
defense plants can hurt the country--a great danger, some danger, not much
danger, or no danger?

    + Great   + Some   - Not much   - None   + Don't know

GROUP 0 (Do not give answers scored + in any of the groups above)

DEMOCRATIC AND ANTI-DEMOCRATIC ATTITUDES (McClosky 1964)

Variable	This is a study of popular and elite consensus about American democratic ideology, where "consensus" was defined as a state of concurrence around certain values.
Description	Agree-disagree items for assessing the following values were constructed:

1) "Rules of the Game," with emphasis on fair play, respect for legal procedures, and consideration for the rights of others (12 items)

2) "Support for General Statements of Free Speech and Opinion" (8 items)

3) "Support for Specific Applications of Free Speech and Procedure Rights" (9 items)

4) "Belief in Equality"; broken down into political, social and ethnic, and economic equality (15 items)

5) "Political Cynicism," defined as a feeling that the system will not govern justly and for the common good (14 items)

6) "Sense of Political Futility"; defined as a feeling that one cannot reach and influence the system (7 items)

Scores were categorized for comparative purposes into "high," "medium," and "low," each category comprising a third of the popular distribution on the scale in question.

Sample	There were two population groups sampled: (1) Leaders, drawn from the 1956 Democratic (1788) and Republican (1232) national convention delegates; (2) Followers, a national cross-section sample (N=1481).
Reliability/ Homogeneity	Test-retest reliability was not reported. Some Guttman reproducibility coefficients, which bear on homogeneity, were apparently calculated although they were not reported.
Validity	The author reported that each of the scales had been independently validated either by empirical validation procedures employing appropriate criterion groups, or by a modified Guttman reproducibility procedure supplemented, in some instances, by a "face validity" procedure utilizing item rating by experts.

To control for agreement "response-set," each respondent was scored on a scale of contradictory item pairs. The relationships tested were controlled for crucial demographic variables as well. The author reports that the introduction of these factors did not change the direction of the findings, although it sometimes affected the magnitude of the scores.

Location	McClosky, Herbert. "Consensus and Ideology in American Politics," _American Political Science Review_, 1964, <u>58</u>, pp. 361-382.
Administration	Estimated administration time for the scales is between ten and fifteen minutes for each scale, depending on length. Scoring requires simple summation of the number of "agree" responses.
Results and Comments	More specific information on the criterion-related validity of these scales would have been helpful in evaluating this instrument.

On the "Rules of the Game" scale, Leaders were found to score higher than Followers. (This relationship was reported to have been reversed on the author's related scales of "Faith in Direct Action," "Willingness to Flout Rules of Political Integrity," and "Totalitarianism.")

On the two scales concerning attitude toward free speech, Leaders exhibited stronger support for the general statement than Followers, and also were more consistent in applying such general principles to specific instances.

Responses to the "Belief in Equality" scale indicated respondent ambivalence in that they were inconsistent among the three subscales. It seems probable that this instrument tapped several conflicting attitudes.

Analysis of responses to the "Political Cynicism" scale also reveals ambivalence. It is impossible to say how much the sample's distrust in government <u>per</u> <u>se</u> colored the pattern of "cynical" responses, but a strong majority of respondents did not question the <u>legitimacy</u> of the system. Leaders were found to score lower than followers on this scale and on the related scale of "Pessimism."

On the "Sense of Political Futility" scale, many more Followers than Leaders scored high. Followers also scored lower on the related scale of "Social Responsibility."

RULES OF THE GAME

Items	Political Influentials (N=3020)	General Electorate (N=1484)
	% Agree	
There are times when it almost seems better for the people to take the law into their own hands rather than wait for the machinery of government to act.	13.3	26.9
The majority has the right to abolish minorities if it wants to.	6.8	28.4
We might as well make up our minds that in order to make the world free a lot of innocent people will have to suffer.	27.2	41.6
If congressional committees stuck strictly to the rules and gave every witness his rights they would never succeed in exposing the many dangerous subversions they have turned up.	24.7	47.4
I don't mind a politician's methods if he manages to get the right things done.	25.6	42.4
Almost any unfairness or brutality may have to be justified when some good purpose is being carried out.	13.3	32.8
Politicians have to cut a few corners if they are going to get anywhere.	29.4	43.2
People ought to be allowed to vote even if they can't do so intelligently.	65.6	47.6
To bring about great changes for the benefit of mankind often requires cruelty and even ruthlessness.	19.4	31.3
Very few politicians have clean records, so why get excited about the mud slinging that sometimes goes on?	14.8	38.1
It's all right to get around the law if you don't actually break it.	21.2	30.2
The true American way of life is disappearing so fast that we may have use force to save it.	12.8	34.6

FREE SPEECH AND OPINION SCALE

Items	Political Influentials (N=3020)	General Electorate (N=1484)
	% Agree	
People who hate our way of life should still have a chance to talk and be heard.	86.9	81.8
No matter what a person's political beliefs are, he is entitled to the same legal rights and protections as anyone else.	96.4	94.3
I believe in free speech for all no matter what their views might be.	89.4	88.9
Nobody has a right to tell another person what he should and should not read.	81.4	88.7
You can't really be sure whether an opinion is true or not unless people are free to argue against it.	94.9	90.8
Unless there is freedom for many points of view to be presented, there is little chance that the truth can ever be known.	90.6	85.2
I would not trust any person or group to decide what opinions can be freely expressed and what must be silenced.	79.1	64.6
Freedom of conscience should mean freedom to be an atheist as well as freedom to worship in the church of one's choice.	87.8	77.0

SPECIFIC APPLICATIONS OF FREE SPEECH (AND PROCEDURAL RIGHTS) SCALE

Items	Political Influentials (N=3020)	General Electorate (N=1484)
	% Agree	
Freedom does not give anyone the right to teach foreign ideas in our schools.	45.5	56.7
A man ought not to be allowed to speak if he doesn't know what he's talking about.	17.3	36.7
A book that contains wrong political views cannot be a good book and does not deserve to be published.	17.9	50.3
When the country is in great danger we may have to force people to testify against themselves even if it violates their rights.	28.5	36.3
No matter what crime a person is accused of, he should never be convicted unless he has been given the right to face and question his accusers.	90.1	88.1
If a person is convicted of a crime by illegal evidence, he should be set free and the evidence thrown out of court.	79.6	66.1
If someone is suspected of treason or other serious crimes, he shouldn't be allowed to be let out on bail.	33.3	68.9
A person who hides behind the laws when he is questioned about his actions doesn't deserve much consideration.	55.9	75.7
Dealing with dangerous enemies like the Communists, we can't afford to depend on the courts, the laws and their slow and unreliable methods.	7.4	25.5

BELIEF IN EQUALITY SCALE

Items	Political Influentials (N=3020)	General Electorate (N=1484)
	% Agree	

Political Equality

The main trouble with democracy is that most people don't really know what's best for them.	40.8	58.0
Few people really know what is in their own best interest in the long run.	42.6	61.1
"Issues" and arguments" are beyond the understanding of most voters	37.5	62.3
Most people don't have enough sense to pick their own leaders wisely.	28.0	47.8
It will always be necessary to have a few strong, able people actually running everything.	42.5	56.2

Social and Ethnic Equality

We have to teach children that all men are created equal but almost everyone knows that some are better than others.	54.7	58.3
Just as is true of fine race horses, some breeds of people are just naturally better than others.	46.0	46.3
Regardless of what some people say, there are certain races in the world that just won't mix with Americans.	37.2	50.4
When it comes to the things that count most, all races are certainly not equal	45.3	49.0
The trouble with letting certain minority groups into a nice neighborhood is that they gradually give it their own atmosphere.	49.8	57.7

Economic Equality

Labor does not get its fair share of what it produces.	20.8	44.8
Every person should have a good house, even if the government has to build it for him.	14.9	28.2

Belief in Equality Scale (cont'd)

Items	Political Influencials (N=3020)	General Electorate (N=1484)
	% Agree	
Economic Equality (cont'd)		
I think the government should give a person work if he can't find another job.	23.5	47.3
The government ought to make sure that everyone has a good standard of living.	34.4	55.9
There will always be poverty, so people might as well get used to the idea.	40.4	59.4

CYNICISM TOWARD GOVERNMENT AND POLITICS SCALE

Items	Political Influentials (N=3020)	General Electorate (N=1484)
	% Agree	
Most politicians are looking out for themselves above all else.	36.3	54.3
Both major parties in this country are controlled by the wealthy and are run for their benefit.	7.9	32.1
Many politicians are bought off by some private interest.	43.0	65.3
I avoid dealing with public officials as much as I can.	7.8	39.3
Most politicians can be trusted to do what they think is best for the country.	77.1	58.9
I usually have confidence that the government will do what is right.	81.6	89.6
The people who really "run" the country do not even get known to the voters.	40.2	60.5
The laws of this country are supposed to benefit all of us equally, but the fact is that they're almost all "rich-man's laws."	8.4	33.3
No matter what the people think, a few people will always run things anyway.	30.0	53.8
Most politicians don't seem to me to really mean what they say.	24.7	55.1
There is practically no connection between what a politician says and what he will do once he gets elected.	21.4	54.0
A poor man doesn't have the chance he deserves in the law courts.	20.3	42.9
Most political parties care only about winning elections and nothing more.	28.3	46.2
All politics is controlled by political bosses.	15.6	45.9

SENSE OF POLITICAL FUTILITY SCALE

Items	Political Influentials (N=3020)	General Electorate (N=1484)
	% Agree	
It's no use worrying my head about public affairs; I can't do anything about them anyhow.	2.3	20.5
The people who really "run" the country do not even get known to the voters.	40.2	60.5
I feel that my political leaders hardly care what people like myself think or want.	10.9	39.0
Nothing I ever do seems to have any effect upon what happens in politics	8.4	61.5
Political parties are so big that the average member hasn't got much to say about what goes on.	37.8	67.5
There doesn't seem to be much connection between what I want and what my representative does.	24.0	43.7
It seems to me that whoever you vote for, things go on pretty much the same.	21.1	51.3

ATTITUDE TOWARD DEMOCRATIC PRINCIPLES (Prothro and Grigg 1960)

Variable
This scale attempted to measure the amount of consensus on abstract and specific democratic principles based on majority rule and minority rights.

Description
The instrument is composed of 15 agree-disagree items: five principles stated in abstract terms and ten specific applications of these principles. Since perfect consensus is 100 percent agreement, only agreement of over 75 percent was held to be closer to consensus than to discord. An "agree" response to items 5, 6, 7, and 8 and a "disagree" response to the other 11 items were coded as democratic.

The specific propositions were expressly designed to embody the principles of majority rule and minority rights in such a clear fashion that a "correct" or "democratic" response could be deduced from endorsements of the general principles.

Sample
A random sample of registered voters was drawn from Ann Arbor, Michigan (N = 144), and Tallahassee, Florida (N = 100). Although the communities chosen were skewed in over-representing the more highly educated, they did permit a detailed comparison of the highly educated with the poorly educated.

Reliability/
Homogeneity
No homogeneity or test-retest reliability are reported.

Validity
No data bearing directly on validity are reported.

Administration
If the instrument were given as a paper and pencil test, estimated administration time would be about 15 minutes.

Location
Prothro, James W. and Grigg, Charles M. "Fundamental Principles of Democracy: Bases of Agreement and Disagreement," Journal of Politics, 1960, 22, pp. 276-294.

Results and
Comments
It was found that while responses to the abstract principles neared perfect consensus, the response pattern was closer to discord on six of the ten specific propositions in Ann Arbor, and on eight of the ten in Tallahassee. In addition, it was found that about half of the statements elicited the "wrong" (undemocratic) answers.

Of the demographic variables, education was found to have the greatest effect on responses, even with community and income controlled (excepting Southern responses to race-related questions). Even among respondents with high education, however, there was meaningful consensus on only three of the ten specific statements (3, 7, and 9) and that consensus occurred only in the Ann Arbor sample. While the authors' expressed intent was to test the proposition that consensus on "democracy" exists in the United States, this instrument might be useful in comparing consistency in attitude toward democratic propositions in different groups. It does not attempt to tap a unitary attitude, but rather attempts to give a basis for analyzing the systematic inter-group variance in consensus on democratic opinions.

DEMOCRATIC PRINCIPLES

(Do you agree or disagree with the following statements?)

(PRINCIPLE OF DEMOCRACY ITSELF)

1. Democracy is the best form of government.

(PRINCIPLE OF MAJORITY RULE)

2. Public officials should be chosen by majority vote.
3. Every citizen should have an equal chance to influence government policy.

(PRINCIPLE OF MINORITY RIGHTS)

4. The minority should be free to criticize majority decisions.
5. People in the minority should be free to try to win majority support for their opinions.

From these general statements, the following specific embodiments of the principles of democracy were derived.

(PRINCIPLE OF MAJORITY RULE IN SPECIFIC TERMS)

6. In a city referendum, only people who are well informed about the problem being voted on should be allowed to vote.
7. In a city referendum deciding on tax-supported undertakings, only tax-payers should be allowed to vote.
8. If a Negro were legally elected mayor of this city, the white people should not allow him to take office.
9. If a Communist were legally elected mayor of this city, the people should not allow him to take office.
10. A professional organization like the AMA (the American Medical Association) has a right to try to increase the influence of doctors by getting them to vote as a bloc in elections.
11. If a person wanted to make a speech in this city against churches and religion, he should be allowed to speak.
12. If a person wanted to make a speech in this city favoring government ownership of all the railroads and big industries, he should be allowed to speak.
13. If an admitted Communist wanted to make a speech in this city favoring Communism, he should be allowed to speak.
14. A Negro should not be allowed to run for mayor of this city.
15. A Communist should not be allowed to run for mayor of this city.

ATTITUDE TOWARD COMMUNISTS (Schonbar 1949)

Variable	This instrument attempts to produce an estimate of anti-Communist sentiment in two ways--by measuring the extent of the attitude by placing it in conflict with civil liberties, and by measuring the intensity of the attitude by asking the subjects to estimate the relative threat of Communism in the United States.
Description	The instrument consists of four, five-point Likert-type items. Range of scores was 1 to 5, with high score indicating high anti-Communism. Subjects were also administered seven true-false and one multiple choice information questions.
Sample	The experimental population consisted of 157 students in a small female liberal arts college, being 80 percent Republican and 73 percent Protestant (Episcopal and Presbyterian).
Reliability/ Homogeneity	No data on homogeneity or test-retest reliability were reported.
Validity	No specific tests of validity were reported.
Location	Schonbar, Rosalea Ann. "Students' Attitudes toward Communists: 1. The Relation between Intensity of Attitude and Amount of Information," Journal of Psychology, 1949, 27, pp. 55-71.
Administration	Estimated administration time is about 4 minutes. Scoring requires averaging of item scores.
Results and Comments	It was found that most subjects did not have a strong anti-Communist attitude. Though the correlation between anti-Communist attitude and information scores was negative and low, it was found that students in government courses had significantly higher scores than the others. The lowest scoring groups on the anti-Communist scale also had significantly higher information scores than the highest scorers on the scale. As the reliability and validity of this instrument were never established, and as the items are somewhat dated, the scale's continued utility is diminished.

COMMUNISM SCALE

All of the statements below have something to do with Communism in the United States. Follow the instructions given for each section, and give each question careful thought before answering. Do not omit any item.

Section I: Encircle the word or words following each statement which most accurately describe how you feel about the statement.

1. Communists should not be allowed to hold jobs in private industry.

   Strongly   Agree   Indifferent   Disagree   Strongly
    Agree   Disagree

2. Communists should not be allowed to hold jobs in government service.

   Strongly   Agree   Indifferent   Disagree   Strongly
    Agree   Disagree

3. Combatting Communism in the United States is the most serious domestic task facing our country today.

   Strongly   Agree   Indifferent   Disagree   Strongly
    Agree   disagree

4. Living in a Fascist state would be preferable to living in a Communist state.

   Strongly   Agree   Indifferent   Disagree   Strongly
    Agree   Disagree

ATTITUDE TOWARD CIVIL LIBERTIES (Noble and Noble 1954)

Variable	The purpose of this study was to investigate the attitude of college students toward the protection of civil liberties and to see what effect "totalitarian aggression" (Communism) might have had upon these attitudes.
Description	The instrument is composed of 20 statements, each dealing with a separate civil liberties issue, and each to be answered either "agree," "disagree," or "no opinion." An "agree" answer to items 1, 3, 6, 7, 9, 12, 15, 17, and 18 and a "disagree" answer to the remaining items indicated support of a civil liberties position and was given a score of 1. Source of many of the statements was a leaflet published by the American Civil Liberties Union.
Sample	The sample population was 195 students in architecture, engineering, home economics, and art for commerce and industry at a professional and technical school in the New York Metropolitan area.
Reliability/ Homogeneity	No test-retest reliability was reported.
Validity	No criterion-related validity tests were reported.
Location	Noble, Lois A. and Noble, Ransom E. "A Study of the Attitudes of College Students toward Civil Rights," Journal of Social Psychology, 1954, 42, pp. 289-297.
Administration	Estimated administration time, about 20 minutes. Scoring requires simple summation of item scores.
Results and Comments	Differences in scores between different curricula groups were never significant beyond the .10 level. The authors state that the issues on which the statements are based are controversial and that they scored as libertarian responses which indicated the greatest amount of personal freedom, the strictest separation of church and state, or the widest opportunity for minority groups. The evidence presented for the validity of this instrument is far from convincing.

CIVIL LIBERTIES SCALE

1. Communists should have the same right to make public speeches as the members of other political parties.

   Agree   Disagree   No opinion

2. Government authorities should be allowed to ban books and movies which they consider harmful to the public interest.

3. Public school time should not be set aside for the teaching of sectarian religion.

4. State universities would be justified in limiting enrollment by members of racial and religious groups in proportion to their percentage of the state's population.

5. Communists should not be allowed to hold government jobs.

6. Personal ability alone should determine an applicant's right to a job regardless of his race, religion, or national origin.

7. Poll taxes, white primaries, and other devices sometimes used to restrict the right to vote are never justified.

8. Residents of a neighborhood should be entitled to prevent members of any particular racial or religious group from living there.

9. Trade unions should not be entitled to restrict their membership on the basis of color, religion, or national origin.

10. Parochial schools should be included in government financial aid to education.

11. Communists should not be allowed to teach in schools and colleges.

12. Tests of government employees' loyalty should be required only in jobs where national security is involved.

13. Communist-dominated organizations should not be allowed to furnish bail for prisoners.

14. Movies, plays, and books should be suppressed if they present an offensive characterization of a particular racial or religious group.

15. Private housing developments which receive state assistance should not have the right to refuse tenants on the basis of color, religion, or national origin.

16. Law enforcement officials should have the right to listen in on private telephone conversations whenever in their judgment it is necessary for carrying on their work.

17. Teachers should not be required to sign special non-communist loyalty oaths.

18. Government employees accused of disloyalty should have the right to know their accusers and to cross-examine them.

19. The Communist party should be made illegal in the United States.

20. Fraternities and sororities are justified in using race, religion, or national origin as qualifications for membership.

CHAPTER 5: DOMESTIC GOVERNMENT POLICIES

The five attitude measures reviewed in this section are concerned with feelings toward the exercise of federal power, especially the intervention of government into previously private sectors of society. While the attitudes being measured doubtlessly overlap with the "liberal-conservative" dimension examined in a previous section, the specific nature of their item content justified placing them in a separate section. They are listed below in rough order of merit:

1. Domestic Social Welfare Scale (Campbell et al. 1960)
2. Attitudes toward Government (Opinion Research Corporation 1960)
3. Big Business-Minded Scale and Socialism-Planning Scale (Rosenberg 1957)
4. Attitude toward Socialized Medicine (Kubany 1953)
5. Attitude toward Government (Banerjee 1962)

The first scale was devised by the Survey Research Center and administered to a national cross-sectional sample. In constructing the scale, an analysis of responses to it showed that attitudes toward social welfare issues were determined more by self-interest than by ideological constraint or political party preference. The items included in the scale were and are current in topic and scope, except for the fourth item which might have become dated with the institution of Medicare. Basic data on the scale's validity have yet to be collected.

The Opinion Research Corporation scale on domestic government policy also has the advantage of having been constructed on a national probability sample. Full psychometric data are not yet available for this scale since it was developed mainly for commercial and not for scholarly purposes. Evidence for homogeneity does seem adequate, however. The items in the scale cover much the same range of issues as the previous scale, and in both surveys, greatest public support was noted for government action on education and least support for such action in the electric power and housing industries. The job guarantee and medical care items drew support between these extremes in both studies, but their relative popularity was reversed.

Rosenberg devised two scales in this area. One attempts to measure an attitude of business self-interest on social welfare issues; the other is concerned with tapping feelings toward government planning or receptivity to "socialist" measures. Both scales have as their focus the student population, necessitating a simplification of wording and design for their use on cross-sectional samples. Findings of the study show that ideological support of "socialist" measures and opposition to business are determinants of one's reluctance to enter the business field as a career. The evidence bearing on validity is unusual and intriguing.

Kubany's socialized medicine scale is more interesting in terms of its unusual methodology than in terms of its substantive findings. The scale is based on the error-choice method which presents two equally wrong alternatives on a given question to the respondent. The assumption is that the respondent will unknowingly indicate his attitudinal bias on the item by the particular wrong answer that he chooses. Apparently, this method worked for Kubany on college samples--his validational evidence showed that criterion groups were almost completely separated by scores on the measure. Items from the scale would, however, have to be simplified for use on any cross-sectional sample. We should also add that the error-choice method can and has elicited adverse reactions from respondents when informed of its purpose after administration of the test.

Banerjee's scale of government attitudes seems to be applicable only to citizens' attitudes toward the government of India. Many items may already be dated. The sample base and reliability seem adequate, although further data on responses need to be reported.

The main focus in this section has been on attitudes toward actual or intended domestic public policy, although a few scales have also included attitude items on big business and big labor. While we recognize that attitudes toward the latter non-governmental institutions probably bear on political attitudes, we have considered measures of such attitudes to be beyond the scope of this volume. The reader interested in attitudes toward big business is referred to a study done by Fisher and Withey (1951) at the Survey Research Center in 1950. This study examines a number of important aspects of the public's perception of "big business", such as its beneficial and adverse effects and how people define the term itself.

In our Appendix A to this volume (Robinson et al. 1968) we reviewed a series of other measures dealing with labor-management relations in which the labor-business-government dimension became salient. Probably the most relevant measure taking into account this triad of items was Kornhauser's Index of Pro-Labor Orientation (1964) which was composed of the following four sub-indices of pro-labor feelings:

1) Identification with working class views
2) Attitudes toward government help
3) Attitudes toward business and industry
4) Attitudes toward labor and industry

Many of the items in the index were based on open-ended interview questions. In the study, they revealed some interesting relationships with the standard background and socio-economic variables. Quantitative estimates of reliability and validity were not reported by the author.

190

References:

Fisher, B. and Withey, S. Big-Business as the People See It. Ann Arbor,
    Michigan: Survey Research Center, 1951.

Kornhauser, A. Mental Health of the Industrial Worker. New York: John
    Wiley, 1965.

Robinson, J., Athanasiou, R. and Head, K. B. Measures of Occupational Attitudes
    and Occupational Characteristics. Ann Arbor, Michigan: Survey Research
    Center, 1968.

DOMESTIC SOCIAL WELFARE SCALE (Campbell et al. 1960)

Variable   This scale attempts to rank persons along a continuum of attitudes on
                    the desirability of governmental action in areas of domestic social
                    welfare.

Description   Out of ten social welfare items included in the Survey Research
                    Center's 1956 voting study, five were found to form a Guttman scale,
                    meeting the criteria described in Campbell et al., 1954. The 5-point
                    Likert responses were dichotomized in scoring. Assigned scores ran
                    from 1 to 6 (from low support of active role for government to high
                    support of active role) and unique scale scores ran from 0 to 31.
                    The items are reproduced below in order from "easiest" to "hardest."

Sample   The sample population was a representative national sample of citizens
                    of voting age living in private households. The number of pre-election
                    respondents was 1929; of these, only 1286 gave answers that could
                    reasonably be scaled.

Reliability/   The instrument demonstrated its unidimensionality by meeting the
   Homogeneity   Guttman criteria with a plus percentage ratio of .80. Although
                    authors presented no test-retest reliability data from the 1956
                    study, Converse (1964) reports two year test-retest correlations
                    running from .28 for the housing and power item to .41 for fair
                    employment practices.

Validity   No tests of validity were reported, but information bearing on validity
                    is reported under "Results" below.

Location   Campbell, Angus, Converse, Philip E., Miller, Warren E., Stokes,
                    Donald E. The American Voter. New York: John Wiley & Sons, 1960,
                    pp. 194-208.

Administration   The scale could be administered as a paper and pencil test with an
                    estimated administration time of under five minutes.

Results and   The authors concluded that in most cases the social welfare scale
  Comments   tapped an attitude of self-interest rather than of ideology. They
                    found that differences in attitude attributable to party affiliation,
                    although statistically significant, were considerably smaller than
                    these differences correlated with socio-economic status. The authors
                    also noted that those respondents who advocated the enlargement of
                    public services often did not support a correlative tax policy: only
                    about one-fifth of the respondents were ideologically consistent in
                    this area. Again, incongruent opinion cleavages appeared in the
                    independence of responses on restraint of business from responses to
                    the government job-guarantee question. Such partisan differences on
                    social welfare attitudes as did exist were shown to be dependent on
                    extent of political involvement.

                    The scale thus does not claim to rank persons along an abstract

192

liberal-conservative continuum, but it successfully differentiates among those more or less in favor of governmental action in the areas covered by the questions.

References   Campbell, Angus, Gurin, Gerald, and Miller, Warren E. The Voter Decides. Evanston, Illinois: Row Peterson & Co., 1954, pp. 187-189.

Converse, P. "The Nature of Belief Systems in Mass Publics" in Apter, D., Ideology and Discontent. New York: Free Press, 1964.

Instrument

1. If cities and towns around the country need help to build more schools, the government in Washington ought to give them the money they need.

    Strongly   Not sure;   Strongly
    Agree   Agree   it depends   Disagree   Disagree

2. If Negroes are not getting fair treatment in jobs and housing, the government in Washington should see to it that they do.

3. The government in Washington ought to see to it that everybody who wants to work can find a job.

4. The government ought to help people get doctors and hospital care at low cost.

5. The government should leave things like electric power and housing for private businessmen to handle.

ATTITUDE TOWARD GOVERNMENT (OPINION RESEARCH CORPORATION 1960)

Variable	This scale measures a person's attitudes toward federal involvement in social welfare. It was administered in conjunction with scales of attitudes toward big business and the value of labor unions.
Description	This six item scale requires the respondent to indicate whether the government should do "a great deal," "fair amount," "very little" or "nothing" about each issue. The respondent was also asked how intensely he felt about his attitudes in this area. Details on the construction of the scale were not given.
Sample	The sample was a national probability sample, but the size of the sample was not given.
Reliability/ Homogeneity	A coefficient of reproducibility of .90 was reported for the government scale, .92 for the business scale and .93 for the labor union scale.
	No test-retest data were reported.
Validity	No data bearing directly on validity were reported.
Location	The Initiators. Princeton, New Jersey: Opinion Research Corporation, 1960, pp. T-4 to T-7.
Administration	The items were part of an interview schedule and should take less than 10 minutes to administer.
Results and Comments	Although exact scoring details were not given, the following distribution of scores for the general public were reported. Whether scores across the three scales are exactly comparable is not known.

	Business	Labor Union	Government
Very favorable	10%	8%	18%
Mostly favorable	17	23	13
Moderate attitude	15	26	23
Mostly unfavorable	27	22	19
Very unfavorable	18	14	23
	87%	93%	96%

The following comparison shows "initiators" (that minority of the public who are most involved and show most initiative) to be located in the extremes of opinion distribution in terms both of scale score and of intensity of feeling. (See the reference to this initiation scale in Chapter 3.)

	Business		Labor Union		Government	
	Pro	Anti	Pro	Anti	Pro	Anti
Initiators	13%	12%	11%	11%	11%	27%
General Public	5	7	8	7	8	9

The percentage of public support for government intervention (including responses of "great deal" plus "fair amount") ranged from 31 percent for operating essential industries to 81 percent for aiding education, with controlling business profits, providing medical insurance, guaranteeing farm prices, and guaranteeing jobs in ascending order of support in between.

It was concluded that:
1) there was broad public support for government action in both the public and private spheres of activity;
2) people overwhelmingly accepted the essential nature of large companies but relatively few defended large company concentration of power;
3) like companies, unions were accepted as essential, but few people defended unlimited power for unions.

ATTITUDES TOWARD GOVERNMENT, LARGE COMPANIES AND LABOR UNIONS

(Questions are listed along with the percent response in ascending order in the most favorable category.)

I. Support for Government Activity

	Total Public
How much would you like to see the federal government do on each of the following:	

Owning and operating essential industries.

Great deal or fair amount	31%
Very little or nothing	51
No opinion	18

Controlling how much profit a large company can make.

Great deal or fair amount	42%
Very little or nothing	39
No opinion	19

Providing medical insurance for doctor and hospital bills.

Great deal or fair amount	59%
Very little or nothing	32
No opinion	9

Guaranteeing the prices farmers get for their products.

Great deal or fair amount	61%
Very little or nothing	28
No opinion	11

Guaranteeing a job to everyone able to work.

Great deal or fair amount	67%
Very little or nothing	26
No opinion	7

Giving financial aid to local and state education.

Great deal or fair amount	81%
Very little or nothing	12
No opinion	7

II. Large Company Series

Total
Public

In many of our largest industries, one or two
companies have too much control of the industry.

Disagree	20%
Agree	57
No opinion	23

There's too much power concentrated in the hands of
a few large companies for the good of the nation.

Disagree	24%
Agree	53
No opinion	23

As they grow bigger, companies usually get cold
and impersonal in their relations with people.

Disagree	27%
Agree	55
No opinion	18

For the good of the country, many of our largest
companies ought to be broken up into smaller
companies.

Disagree	37%
Agree	38
No opinion	25

The profits of large companies help make things
better for everyone who buys their products or
services.

Agree	60%
Disagree	21
No opinion	19

Large companies are essential for the nation's
growth and expansion.

Agree	82%
Disagree	7
No opinion	11

III.   Labor Union Series

Like companies, unions are accepted as essential, but note
that questions dealing with labor union power do not find
very many in the public defending unlimited power for unions.

Total
Public

The government should do a lot more to regulate
the activities of labor unions.

Disagree	15%
Agree	67
No opinion	18

Labor unions have become too big and powerful
for the good of the country.

Disagree	27%
Agree	55
No opinion	18

The gains that labor unions have made for their
members have been at the expense of other groups
in this country.

Disagree	32%
Agree	37
No opinion	31

The gains that labor unions win for their members
help make the country more prosperous.

Agree	56%
Disagree	24
No opinion	20

The gains that workers have made in this country
are chiefly due to labor unions.

Agree	66%
Disagree	17
No opinion	17

Labor unions are very necessary to protect the
workingman.

Agree	73%
Disagree	15
No opinion	12

BIG-BUSINESS-MINDED SCALE AND SOCIALISM-PLANNING SCALE (Rosenberg 1957)

Variable	The Big-Business-Minded (BBM) Scale attempts to measure an attitude of business self-interest on various socio-economic and political issues. The Socialism-Planning (SP) Scale is concerned with measuring an attitude toward government planning or receptivity to socialist measures.
Description	The Big-Business-Minded Scale consists of seven modified agree-disagree items; positive responses indicate an "attitude of business self-interest." The Socialism-Planning Scale is made up of five modified agree-disagree items, with negative responses indicating favorableness to Socialism-planning. Both instruments formed Guttman scales in the present study, according to the author.
Sample	The population sample was a group of 2758 Cornell students in 1950. Respondents were divided into Reluctant-, Willing-, and Non-Businessmen. The first category included those who expected to enter business but did not want to, the second, those who both expected and wanted to enter business, and third, those who neither expected nor wanted to enter business.
Reliability/ Homogeneity	No test-retest reliability was reported. The reproducibility coefficients of these scales were not reported.
Validity	On the Big-Business-Minded Scale, it was found that many fewer "Reluctants" scored high than did the "Willings," or even the "Non-Businessmen." Similarly, on the Socialism-Planning Scale, the "Reluctants" scored significantly higher (at the .01 level) than the "Willings."
Location	Rosenberg, Morris. Occupations and Values. Glencoe, Illinois: The Free Press, 1967, pp. 114-116.
Administration	Estimated administration time for the Big-Business-Minded Scale is about five minutes, and for the Socialism-Planning Scale, about three minutes. Scoring is accomplished by summation of item scores.
Results and Comments	The author concluded that ideological opposition to business-- disagreement with big business views on social welfare--was a factor conducive to reluctance to enter the field.
	Insufficient information was reported about the two scales to determine their reliability or unidimensionality according to Guttman criteria. Further reliability and validity studies would be required before the generally good face validity of the scales could be documented. Item wording would have to be simplified for use with representative or non-college populations.

Instrument

Do you agree or disagree with the following statements.

Big Business Minded Scale

Philosophies of Government:
1. The best government is the one which governs least.
2. Democracy depends fundamentally on the existence of free business enterprise.

Business and Labor:
3. If there is no ceiling on business profits, there is a better chance to develop better products at lower cost.

Right of Private Employers to Hire and Fire:
4. The individual employer should sacrifice this privilege for the social welfare.

Right to a Free College Education for People Who Meet Requirements:
5. Taxes are high enough now.

Right to Free Medical Care:
6. Would lead to higher taxes and our taxes are high enough.

Privileges of Ideal Government:
7. Unrestricted right of any employer to hire and fire his own employees.

Socialism-Planning Scale

Philosophies of Government:
1. The best government is the one which governs least.
2. Government planning almost inevitably results in the loss of essential liberties and freedom.
3. The "welfare state" tends to destroy individual initiative.
4. Individual liberties and justice under law are not possible in socialist countries.

Right to Free Medical Care:
5. People might learn to rely on the government for everything.

ATTITUDE TOWARD SOCIALIZED MEDICINE (Kubany 1953)

Variable	This instrument attempts indirectly to measure attitudes on National Health Insurance or socialized medicine through the use of the error-choice method.
Description	The test originally was composed of 50 items, 22 of which were genuinely informational, or factual in nature, and the remainder of which were error-choice, or nonfactual. The number of error-choice items in this study was reduced to 18 after an item validity test. The correct answer to the nonfactual items is midway between the two choices. The test was scored so that all the error-choice items would be on the same key, with those scoring most favorable to National Health Insurance having a high score, and those scoring least favorable (or, opposed) having a low score.
Sample	The two validation group samples were 59 third-year medical students at the University of Pittsburgh Medical School opposed to socialized medicine and 42 first or second-year students in the graduate school of Social Work at the same University presumed to be in favor of socialized medicine.
Reliability/ Homogeneity	The odd-even reliability coefficient computed for the error-choice items was found to be .87.
Validity	The validation groups were scored by a general criterion, a positive expression of bias determined by response to a direct question asked at the end of the inventory.
	The validity of each item was determined by Phi coefficient and those below +.33 were eliminated. It was found that the test differentiated the two populations almost completely. The social work students averaged 14.6 pro-NHI responses, while the medical students averaged only 5.9 favorable responses. A dichotomized grouping of individual scores above or below the general mean of 9.6 indicated that the instrument was highly favorable for individual prediction.
Location	Kubany, Albert J. "A Validation Study of the Error-Choice Technique Using Attitudes on National Health Insurance," _Educational and Psychological Measurement_, 1953, 13, pp. 157-163.
Administration	Estimated administration time for the 40-item test is about 30 minutes. Scoring requires simple summation of item codes.
Results and Comments	The author feels the inventory to be "quite capable of predicting individual degrees of attitude as being either in favor of, or opposed to National Health Insurance." It was found that the amount of information a respondent possessed about NHI (as measured by the number of information items correct) had no relation to attitude ($R = -.03$).

The instrument seems satisfactorily reliable and valid for this sample but should be tested on representative samples before its predictive validity could be assumed. That the error-choice method of attitude testing, apparently quite effective, has not been widely adopted is reputedly due mainly to subjects' post-test ire upon learning of the nature of the test.

Sample Items

Sample "Error-Choice" Items from the Information Inventory

Item 18   The fact that medical progress has moved from Germany and Austria (previous centers of post-graduate medical education) to the United States is due mainly to
(a) These areas adopting some form of socialized medicine
(b) Ravages of wars on their own soil and other more significant causes than (a) above.
Correct Answer: unavailable

Item 39   Of the total recorded physical defects listed as causes for rejection during World War II, what percentage could have been prevented and/or corrected?
(a) 25-30 percent
(b) 15-20 percent
Correct answer: 20-25 percent

Sample Actual Information Item

Item 1   Which of the following diseases currently has the highest death rate?
(a) Cancer
(b) Heart disease
Correct answer: Heart disease

ATTITUDE TOWARD GOVERNMENT (Banerjee 1962)

Variable	Although the author defines the attitude object, "Government," in universal terms as "a body of people who implement or operate some social controls with respect to some organized and regulated institutions of society like law, education, marriage and so on," items were designed to express the specific domestic and foreign policies and programs of the then Government of India.
Description	The final form of the scale consists of 20 five-point Likert-type items, ten positively and ten negatively stated. Items were selected from a 50-item pool on the basis of ability to discriminate between high and low scorers. The 50 items had been selected from a much larger item pool by ten "experienced judges" and 20 undergraduates. Possible range of scores is 20-100.
Sample	The scale construction sample was a random sample of 200 adults (above 16 years) of varying educational, marital and employment status.
Reliability/ Homogeneity	First half vs. second half and odd vs. even reliabilities (corrected) obtained on the same sample were reported to be .78 and .84, respectively.
Validity	No criterion-related validity tests were undertaken. The scale's sole claim to validity rests on the judgments of the "expert" judges.
Administration	Estimated administration time is 20 minutes. Scoring requires simple summation of item scores, which range from 1 to 5.
Location	Banerjee, Debabrata. "Development of Scales for Measuring Attitudes towards Government, Morality, Religion and Society," Indian Journal of Psychology, 1962, 37 (3), pp. 137-142.
Results and Comments	This scale needs to be more sufficiently validated. The items would seem to tap an attitude toward the Indian Government rather than toward "Government" in general, and are, therefore, limited to use on Indians and in addition are possibly dated. A study of response patterns controlled for political party differences would have enhanced the value of the study.

Sample Items	1. All the Government laws are constituted for the benefit of the rich.
	7. The five year plans are really the steps to national progress.
	16. The government's Refugee Rehabilitation cannot be supported.

CHAPTER 6: RACIAL AND ETHNIC ATTITUDES

The number of actual scales collected in the important area of race-related attitudes falls short of our original expectations. Most of the work has been done with single item questions asked by the pollsters, such as Gallup and Harris (see, for example, Brink and Harris 1967). Trends on these questions through 1963 have been well summarized by Schwartz (1966), who found that attitudes toward Negroes have become more favorable over the last twenty-five years. This favorable trend was most marked on questions dealing with normative matters such as equal job opportunity, somewhat less so on items pertaining to Negro characteristics such as intelligence, and least on inquiries on current social issues like open housing.

The following scales constitute the universe of attitude measures found in this area. They are listed in approximate order of merit.

1) Prejudice and Rationality (Schuman and Harding 1964)
2) Identification with the Underdog (Schuman and Harding 1963)
3) Pro-integration Scale (Sheatsley 1966)
4) Multifactor Racial Attitude Inventory (Woodmansee and Cook 1967)
5) Social Distance Scale (Bogardus 1956)
6) Ethnocentrism Scale (Adorno et al. 1950)
7) Racial Stereotype Index (Matthews and Prothro 1966)
8) Race Identification Index (Matthews and Prothro 1966)
9) Community Race Relations Ratings (Matthews and Prothro 1966)
10) Dimensional Attitudes toward Negroes (Wrightsman 1962)
11) Prejudice toward Negroes (Westie 1953)
12) Paired Direct and Projective Questionnaires (Getzels and Walsh 1958)
13) Attitude toward the Negro (Hinckley 1932)

The first two scales by Schuman and Harding are noteworthy both for their methodological construction and for the substantive findings resulting from their application. Both scales show considerable concern with evidence of reliability and validity that is not often seen in the literature. The two measures also depart in welcome ways from the familiar agree-disagree, Likert, or other rating scale item formats which are so susceptible to contamination from agreement response set. The difference in item format has resulted in scale reliabilities which may seem low (especially for the <u>Reactions</u> <u>Scale</u>) in comparison with conventional scale reliabilities. In terms of substantive content, some interesting findings have emerged. The <u>Rationality</u> <u>Scale</u> indicated that while people in a Boston sample did have irrational attitudes about race and ethnic relations, they tended to have many more irrational notions that are <u>favorable</u> to minority groups than are unfavorable. The <u>Reaction</u> <u>Scale</u> demonstrates that women are no more sympathetic to the underdog than are men, and that least feeling of sympathy was evident among the lower-educated and elderly segments of the sample. Detailed clinical interviews with some of the respondents also revealed further aspects of meaning accorded to the scale items which led to a better interpretation of the resulting scale scores.

The scale by Sheatsley has an advantage over the Schuman-Harding measures in having been applied to a national cross-sectional sample of white Americans. The eight items in the scale are simple and straightforward and use a variety of item formats. Although the author claims the scale conforms to the Guttman scalogram pattern, he does not indicate the quantitative extent of such conformity. Direct evidence of validity is missing, although the scale does intercorrelate highly with other attitude measures and also shows Southerners to be much less oriented toward integration than respondents from other regions. Sheatsley's article (1966) also contains a valuable and up-to-date review of trends in white attitudes toward Negroes.

The Woodmansee and Cook <u>Inventory</u> separates attitudes toward Negroes into ten factors. Although the authors treat these factors as ten independent dimensions (and six of the ten scales do show high <u>internal</u> consistency), almost all of the scales intercorrelate significantly, if not strongly. This means that the <u>Inventory</u> may be more unidimensional than multidimensional, despite

the fact that the scales were constructed from a multidimensional analysis.
Nevertheless, the authors present solid evidence for the essential validity
of each of the scales. The Inventory has yet to be applied to cross-section
samples of the public; it would appear that many of the items might be
inappropriate for such purposes.

The Bogardus Social Distance Scale is one of the oldest attitude measures
of social research. It is concerned with the "social distance" the respondent
perceives between himself and members of Negro and other ethnic groups. Data
from cross-sectional samples need to be collected on this instrument to see
if it has the unidimensional properties of a Guttman scale as has often been
assumed. Despite the possibility and some research already indicating such,
there has been recent evidence that the concept of "social distance" has
multidimensional properties in some contexts (Triandis and Triandis 1967).
Further work needs to be done to ascertain what dimensional properties the
scale assumes in a variety of research situations.

The Ethnocentrism or E Scale which emerged from the study of "the
authoritarian personality" is, of course, one of the best known and most widely
used measures in social science research. Its intent is to tap attitudes
toward Negroes and other minority groups, especially the imagery and stereotypes associated with such groups. One of the main problems of the scale is
its possible contamination by agreement response set. This problem and many
other points about the scale are mentioned in Hyman and Sheatsley's excellent
methodological critique (1954) which is recommended reading for anyone contemplating the use of this measure. Evidence for the internal reliability
and validity of the scale is adequate (although bias from response set enters
here as well), but evidence of test-retest reliability and external validity
is lacking. On the whole, however, the scale remains quite relevant for
social research.

The next three scales were used in Matthews and Prothro's study of Southern people. Thus far, the data published on these scales refer only to Southern Negroes, although both whites and Negroes were interviewed. Probably the most interesting of the three measures is the <u>Racial</u> <u>Stereotype</u> <u>Index</u> which was subsequently found to discriminate between participating and non-participating Negroes in the 1967 Detroit riots. Matthews and Prothro also reported some important findings with this scale. Standard reliability and validity data have yet to be presented by the authors. The same is true of the other two scales reviewed here, the <u>Racial</u> <u>Identification</u> <u>Scale</u> and the <u>Community</u> <u>Race</u> <u>Relations</u> <u>Ratings</u>. The identification scale is directly comparable to the questions asked in the Survey Research Center's 1956 and 1960 election studies (described in Chapter 13); the race relations ratings employed the self-anchoring scale technique. All three scales are of interest more for the data results obtained from their use than for their psychometric characteristics.

Like the Matthews-Prothro measures, the Wrightsman scale is distinguished less by its contribution to the attitude scale literature than by the nature of the results obtained. Wrightsman's major conclusion was that prejudice was composed of at least two components: cognitive and affective. This finding agrees with the earlier research of Schuman and Harding. In further work on the subject, Wrightsman, together with Cook (1965), conducted a most comprehensive methodological study in racial attitudes (using, unfortunately, only female Southern college students as a sample). A total of seventy-eight attitude scales were administered to each subject and then factor-analyzed. Of the eleven factors that emerged, only one, "the positive attitude toward people" factor, successfully predicted lower prejudice over time.

The Getzels-Walsh and Westie scales used by Wrightsman to measure "cognitive" and "affective" dimensions of prejudice may also be of interest. The Westie measure is based on the respondent's differential reactions to Negroes and whites in the same occupation, while the Getzels-Walsh instrument is a projective sentence completion task. The Westie scale is composed of four subscales (residential, position, physical, and interpersonal), all of which have fairly high test-retest reliability. Although the results obtained with the scale are interesting, direct evidence bearing on its validity is missing. Only data bearing indirectly on the reliability and validity of the Getzels-Walsh measure is presented, but the technique used in the scale could be valuable for the investigator interested in indirect ways of measuring prejudice.

The last scale reviewed is by Hinckley and has been in existence about as long as Bogardus' scale. It is concerned with feelings of Negro racial inferiority and attitudes on civil rights for the Negro. The scale's most noteworthy use has been as a foil for the Hovland-Sherif development of their notion of the assimilation-contrast phenomenon. Reliability and validity are in evidence, although the items are, of course, dated and phrased in rather quaint language. This is one of few scales in the attitude measurement literature for which parallel forms are available.

Numerous other scales dealing with race do exist in the literature, although they are mainly of historical or specialized interest. Shaw and Wright (1967) report on six of these that are not treated here. The most interesting of the six is the one used by Steckler (1957) to tap the stereotyped attitudes of Negro students; this scale was found to correlate significantly with anti-white attitudes and authoritarian feelings.

Of the remaining five scales, four were constructed prior to 1941. Thurstone's attitude scale has been used far less in the literature than those of Hinckley and Bogardus, although the items do not seem as dated as those in Hinckley's scale. The same advantage is found in Rosander's measure which, laudably, introduces a behavioral component into the scale items. Likert's scale of attitudes toward Negroes, on the other hand, is extremely dated. Ford's measure is not really an attitude scale but is designed rather to describe the types of contacts (both community and personal) that the respondent has had with Negroes.

Finally, the most recent scale presented by Shaw and Wright is Kagan and Downey's <u>Social Situation Questionnaire</u>. This measure deals with discriminatory behavior toward Negroes in a variety of situations with three types of individuals--peers, authorities, and strangers. Although the scale was developed on a restricted teen-age sample, evidence for homogeneity and validity seemed more than adequate. Most of the scale items are restricted in use to this age group.

It is possible that Komorita's <u>Segregation Scale</u> (1963) may also be of interest. The available reference gave no information on reliability, validity, or item content.

An excellent psychological exposition of the subject of prejudice is given in Allport (1954); for a more sociological interpretation, we recommend Bettleheim and Janowitz (1964).

References:

Allport, G., <u>The Nature of Prejudice</u>, New York: Beacon, 1954.

Bettleheim, B. and Janowitz, M., <u>Social Change and Prejudice</u>, New York: Free Press, 1964.

Brink, W. and Harris, L., <u>Black and White</u>. New York: Simon and Schuster, 1967.

Hyman, H. and Sheatsley, P., "The Authoritarian Personality: A Methodological Critique," in R. Christie and M. Jahoda (eds.), <u>Studies in the Method and Scope of the Authoritarian Personality</u>, Glencoe: Free Press, 1954.

Komorita, S., "Attitude Content, Intensity, and Neutral Point on a Direct Scale," <u>Journal of Social Psychology</u>, 1963, 61, 327-334.

Schwartz, M., <u>Trends in White Attitudes toward Negroes</u>, Chicago: National Opinion Research Center, 1966.

Shaw, M. and Wright, J., <u>Scales for the Measurement of Attitudes</u>, New York: McGraw-Hill, 1967.

Steckler, G., "Authoritarian Ideology in Negro College Students," <u>Journal of Abnormal and Social Psychology</u>, 1957, <u>54</u>, pp. 396-399.

Triandis, H. and Triandis, L., "Some Studies of Social Distance" in M. Fishbein (ed.) <u>Readings in Attitude Theory and Measurement</u>, New York: Wiley, 1967.

Wrightsman, L. and Cook, S., "Factor Analysis and Attitude Change." Paper presented at the 1965 annual meeting of the Southeastern Psychological Convention.

PREJUDICE AND RATIONALITY (Schuman and Harding 1964)

Variable   The scale attempts to measure both the respondent's prejudice toward
                    three minority groups (Negroes, Jews and "others") and the rationality
                    with which these views are held.

Description   The questionnaire consists of 48 pairs of generalizations concerning
                    ethnic groups in 24 of which the more pro-group response is more
                    "rational" than the other alternative and in the other 24 the anti-
                    group response is more "rational". Hence two scales are generated,
                    one of Irrational "Pro" attitudes and the other of Irrational "Anti"
                    attitudes. For analysis purposes, the authors grouped the scorers
                    into four categories (numbers indicate the number in the Boston
                    sample qualifying for each group):

                                                    Irrational Pro

                                            Low   High

                                | Rationalist | Irrational Pro (N=104) |
                    Low | (N=14) | |
Irrational Anti |-----------------------|---------------------------|
                    High | Irrational Anti | Confused (N=70) |
                                | (N=33) | |

The low-high dividing line in each scale was the score (here 48)
which indicates the respondent answers half the items in the rational
direction and half in the irrational direction. Since the respondent
indicates not only his choice but also how sure he feels about his
choice, the range of scores for each item is as follows:

                    Rational answers = 1
                    No answer = 2
                    Irrational answer (not very sure) = 3
                    Irrational answer (moderately sure) = 4
                    Irrational answer (very sure) = 5

Total scores for both the Irrational Pro and the Irrational Anti
items thus run between 24 (most rational) and 120 (most irrational).
On the Irrational Anti scale, mean score was 50 (standard deviation
= 16) for Boston adults and 47 (sd = 14) for the college sample; on
the Irrational Pro scale, the means were 60 (sd=15) for the Boston
sample and 53 (sd=13) for the college sample.

Sample   A heterogeneous quota sample of 229 Boston adults and a sample of
                    112 girls from a Northern Catholic college completed the questionnaire.

Reliability/   Corrected split-half reliabilities for the Boston adults were .84
  Homogeneity   for the Irrational Anti scale and .78 for the Irrational Pro scale.
                    For the college sample, the figures were .81 and .76 respectively.
                    No test-retest data were reported.

Validity	The authors found that scale scores for items dealing with each of the three minority groups intercorrelated at about the same relatively high level, indicating a general pattern of prejudice non-prejudice toward all minority groups.

The Pro-Anti correlations were -.47 for the Boston sample and -.61 for the college sample.

Average correlations between the Anti scale and six other measures of prejudice and ethnocentrism was .61 for the Boston sample and .54 for the college sample; for the Pro scale, the values were much lower, .37 for the Boston sample and .37 for the college sample. The authors attribute these differential findings to the correlation between prejudice and rationality itself.

Correlation with a seventh measure (the Reactions Questionnaire described as the next scale in this section) was much lower, although still substantial and in the expected direction.

The "rationality" of each item was pre-tested by three noted and "rational" social scientists.

Location	Schuman, H. and Harding, J. "Prejudice and the norm of rationality" Sociometry, 1964, 27, pp.353-371.

Administration	Approximate administration time is not given by the author but should require between 15 and 35 minutes. Rational answers to the items below are in parenthesis.

Results and Comments	The authors note that the reaction of "love-prejudice" was far more prevalent than the reaction of "hate-prejudice", as indicated by the fact that among the irrational replies there were many more favorable to the minority groups than unfavorable. There were three times as many among the sample.

Rationality is, of course, highly related to educational attainment. Eight of the 18 college graduates in the sample scored as "rational" and none as "confused", while none of the 85 respondents who had not finished high school scored as rational, and almost half scored as "confused". The nature of the scoring then would make it very difficult for an average American to be considered rational. When questionnaire together with a scale of values was administered to a random sample of Radcliffe College students it was found that the Rationals tended to score high on economic and theoretical values and Irrational Pros on aesthetic and social values. Students in the sciences were more Rational; those in humanities more Irrational Pro.

Detailed and informal interviews with 15 of the Boston respondents yielded interesting insights into the meaning and functioning of various scale scores. The authors' remarks on the interviews should be read by anyone contemplating use of the scale, as should their argument on item construction.

A SURVEY ON GROUPS

You will find on the next pages some pairs of statements. You are to choose the statement in each pair that seems in your own judgment to be the more correct of the two. (You do not have to decide whether any statement is completely correct or completely incorrect, but only which of the two statements seems to you the more correct of the two.)

Show your choice for each pair by the following two steps:

1. First, circle the letter (either A or B) of the statement that you think is the more correct one.

2. Then circle the one phrase ("Not very sure," "Moderately sure," or "Very sure") that best tells how sure you feel that the statement you have chosen is the more correct of the two.

For example, the first pair of statements below deals with American Indians. Read both statements. Circle the letter of the statement that you think is the more correct one. Then circle the phrase that best indicates how sure you feel.

CIRCLE HOW SURE
YOU FEEL OF   CIRCLE
YOUR CHOICE   A or B

1. _____

IA   Not very sure   (A)   Some American Indians are definitely much
                                 superior in intelligence to some white
      Moderately sure   people

      Very sure   B   Few if any American Indians are really
                                 superior in intelligence to any white
                                 people
_____

Now go ahead and do the other pairs in the same way. Please be sure to answer all the pairs.

CIRCLE HOW SURE
YOU FEEL OF   CIRCLE
YOUR CHOICE   A or B

2. _____

IP   Not very sure   A   American Jewish groups rarely, if ever attempt
                               to influence our country's policies toward
     Moderately sure   other nations.

     Very sure   (B) American Jewish groups sometimes work behind
                               the scenes to influence, or even pressure, our
                               government's policies with regard to other
                               nations.

3. _____

IP   Not very sure   (A) The percentage of children born to unmarried
                               mothers is higher among Negroes than among
     Moderately sure   white people.

     Very sure   B   The percentage of children born to unmarried
                               mothers among Negroes is about the same as among
                               white people.

4. _____

IA   Not very sure   A   While every group has a right to get ahead, the
                               Jews are a little too apt to disregard the
     Moderately sure   rights and possessions of other people.

     Very sure   (B) Jews and Christians are pretty much alike in
                               their regard for the rights and possessions of
                               other people.

5. _____

IP   Not very sure   (A) Mexican-American children in this country are
                               at a lower educational level, on the average,
     Moderately sure   than other American children.

     Very sure   B   Mexican-American children in this country are
                               at about the same educational level, on the
                               average, as other American children.

6. _____

IA   Not very sure   A   It is a fairly well-established fact that
                               Negroes have a less pleasant body odor than
     Moderately sure   white people.

     Very sure   (B) It is doubtful that there is much difference
                               in body odor between Negroes and whites.

214

CIRCLE HOW SURE
YOU FEEL OF CIRCLE
YOUR CHOICE A or B

7. _____

IP Not very sure   A   Japanese-Americans rarely try to outdo their
                              business rivals.
    Moderately sure
                        (B)   The success of Japanese-Americans has fre-
    Very sure   quently meant hardship for their white American
                              business rivals.

8. _____

IP Not very sure   (A)   There are more Jews in well-paid professions,
                              like law and medicine, than their percentage
    Moderately sure   in the country would lead one to expect.

    Very sure   B   There are probably no more Jews in highly paid
                              professions, like law and medicine, than their
                              percentage in the country would lead one to
                              expect.

9. _____

IP Not very sure   A   Although Negroes may be behind white people in
                              some areas of achievement, there is definite-
    Moderately sure   ly no difference between the two races in basic
                              intelligence
    Very sure
                        (B)   We cannot rule out the possibility that Negroes
                              as a group average below white people in
                              intelligence.

10. _____

IA Not very sure   A   The problem with letting so many Puerto Ricans
                              into this country is that most members of that
    Moderately sure   group are not capable of really learning
                              American customs and ideals.
    Very sure
                        (B)   It is likely that there are many Puerto Ricans
                              who live up to American ideals better than the
                              average white American who has been here much
                              longer.

11. _____

IA Not very sure   (A)   Very little of the heavy industry in the United
                              States is controlled by persons of Jewish
    Moderately sure   descent.

    Very sure   B   About half the heavy industry (steel, machine
                              tools, etc.) in the United States is controlled
                              directly or indirectly by Jews and about half
                              by non-Jews.

12. _____

IA   Not very sure   (A)   A great number of Negroes in this country have some white ancestry.

     Moderately sure

     Very sure   B   Except in a few cases, most Negroes in this country are still of pure African ancestry.

13. _____

IP   Not very sure   A   There is really no difference in the time or type of holidays celebrated by Jews and other Americans.

     Moderately sure

     Very sure   (B)   Jewish people sometimes take off holidays while other Americans are hard at work.

14. _____

     Not very sure   (A)   There may be some truth in the image of the Puerto Rican in this country as a little less ambitious and hard-working on the average, than many other groups.

     Moderately sure

     Very sure

                    B   Puerto Ricans in the United States have certainly demonstrated that they are as ambitious and hard-working as any racial or national group in the country.

15. _____

IA   Not very sure   A   Negroes should be given every opportunity to get ahead, but they could never be capable of holding the top leadership positions in a country like ours.

     Moderately sure

     Very sure

                 (B)   Some of the ablest and most intelligent people in the United States today are Negroes.

16. _____

IA   Not very sure   (A)   The abilities of highly-educated Mexicans in this country are more like those of highly-educated white Americans than like those of little educated Mexican-Americans.

     Moderately sure

     Very sure

                 B   The abilities of highly-educated Mexicans in this country are more like those of other Mexican-Americans than like those of highly-educated white Americans.

CIRCLE HOW SURE
YOU FEEL OF   CIRCLE
YOUR CHOICE   A or B

17. _____

IP   Not very sure   A   If there were complete equality of opportunity
                                tomorrow, American Indians would almost imme-
      Moderately sure   diately show themselves equal to whites in job
                                skills and in most other areas.
      Very sure
                           (B)   Even if there were complete equality of treat-
                                ment tomorrow, there would still be a sizeable
                                gap between whites and American Indians in job
                                skills and in many other areas.

18. _____

IA   Not very sure   (A)   Christians may not like to consider it, but it
                                is possible that Jewish lawyers are more honest,
      Moderately sure   on the average, than Christian lawyers.

      Very sure   B   While some Jewish lawyers are quite honest, the
                                average Jewish lawyer is not as honest as the
                                average Christian lawyer.

19. _____

IP   Not very sure   (A)   When a Negro family moves into an all-white
                                neighborhood, it sometimes leads to serious
      Moderately sure   disturbance.

      Very sure   B   The moving of a single, respectable Negro
                                family into an all-white neighborhood never
                                really leads to serious disturbances.

20. _____

IA   Not very sure   A   While there are no doubt a few exceptions, in
                                general Jews tend to be especially clannish
      Moderately sure   (keep to their own group) almost from birth.

      Very sure   (B)   Jews are probably no more clannish than many
                                other national or religious groups.

21. _____

IA   Not very sure   A   Perhaps because of their traditions, Orientals
                                tend to be just a little sneaky in most of
      Moderately sure   their dealings in this country, though of
                                course there are some exceptions.
      Very sure
                           (B)   There are Orientals in this country today who
                                are more honest and open-dealing than the
                                typical white American.

CIRCLE HOW SURE
YOU FEEL OF   CIRCLE
YOUR CHOICE   A or B

22. _____

IP   Not very sure   A   Some Negroes are clean and some are dirty, but
                                the average Negro does not differ in any way
      Moderately sure   in his personal habits from the average white
                                person in the United States.
      Very sure

                           (B)   One must admit that many Negroes in this coun-
                                try do not live up to the standards of cleanli-
                                ness usually expected among better educated
                                people.

23. _____

IP   Not very sure   (A)   Relatively few Jews in the United States have
                                known what it's like to work with their hands
      Moderately sure   as farmers, as the American pioneers did.

      Very sure   B   Jews are spread quite evenly through all types
                                of occupations in our country.

24. _____

IA   Not very sure   (A)   It is certainly possible for mixed Negro-white
                                housing areas to have as high property values
      Moderately sure   as all-white areas.

      Very sure   B   When Negroes move into good white neighbor-
                                hoods, property values are sure to drop.

25. _____

IP   Not very sure   A   Some Jews are rich and some are poor, but the
                                average income of Jews is the same as that of
      Moderately sure   other national and religious group in America.

      Very sure   (B)   Jews, on the average, make more money than the
                                majority of national and religious groups in
                                our country.

26. _____

IA   Not very sure   A   It is hard to understand all the reasons, but
                                whites and Negroes can never get along well
      Moderately sure   with one another if they mix and mingle too
                                closely.
      Very sure

                           (B)   When whites and Negroes mix together closely--
                                by living on the same block, eating and enter-
                                taining in one another's homes, and so forth--
                                their relations may well improve greatly.

218

27. _____

IA   Not very sure   A   While there are a few exceptions, even the more
                                 successful Mexican-Americans tend to remain
      Moderately sure   slightly dirty and unkempt.

      Very sure   (B)   There is probably no difference between the
                                 cleanliness of Mexican-Americans and other
                                 Americans of the same educational level.

28. _____

IA   Not very sure   (A)   On the average, Jews are probably as honest
                                 as most other groups in America.
      Moderately sure
                            B   On the average, there is something just a
      Very sure   little less honest about Jews then about most
                                  Americans.

29. _____

IA   Not very sure   (A)   Almost all Japanese Americans in this country
                                 are loyal citizens of the United States.
      Moderately sure
                            B   One thing so many Japanese Americans seem to
      Very sure   have in common is a tendency to put their loy-
                                  alty to Japan ahead of their loyalty to the
                                  United States.

30. _____

IA   Not very sure   (A)   Physical characteristics of Negroes, such as
                                 dark skins or woolly hair, do not necessarily
      Moderately sure   indicate anything about mental or moral traits.

      Very sure   B   The typical Negroid features--dark skin, broad
                                 nose, woolly hair--are probably related to the
                                 more primitive nature of the Negro.

31. _____

IP   Not very sure   A   The difficulties between American Indians and
                                 others in this country have nothing to do with
      Moderately sure   drunkenness, disease, or ignorance among the
                                 Indians.
      Very sure
                           (B)   Many white people would accept American Indians
                                 more easily if there were less drunkenness,
                                 disease, and ignorance among them.

CIRCLE HOW SURE
YOU FEEL OF   CIRCLE
YOUR CHOICE   A or B

32. _____

IP   Not very sure   (A) The percentage of Jews who have gotten into
                              influential positions in the motion picture and
      Moderately sure   television industries is greater than the per-
                              centage of Jews in the general population.
      Very sure
                         B   The percentage of Jews with influence in the
                              motion picture and television industries is no
                              greater than would be expected on the basis of
                              the number of Jews in the general population.

33. _____

IP   Not very sure   (A) The percentage of Negroes convicted of murder
                              is higher than the percentage of white people
      Moderately sure   convicted of murder.

      Very sure   B   The percentage of whites who commit murder is
                              about the same as the percentage of Negroes
                              who commit murder.

34. _____

IA   Not very sure   A   In general, the Jews in the United States tend
                              to use their power more selfishly than do most
      Moderately sure   other groups.

      Very sure   (B) The Jews in the United States do not tend to
                              use their power more selfishly than do most
                              other groups.

35. _____

IP   Not very sure   A   Only a few extreme white people are against
                              equal treatment for Negroes in restaurants,
      Moderately sure   hotels and similar places.

      Very sure   (B) Negroes sometimes try to enter stores, hotels,
                              and restaurants where they are just not welcome.

36. _____

IP   Not very sure   (A) It must be admitted that in large cities of the
                              United States, there is a higher percentage of
      Moderately sure   delinquency and crime among Puerto Rican youth
                              than among native-born white youth.
      Very sure
                         B   In large cities of the United States, there is
                              the same rate of delinquency and crime among
                              Puerto Rican youth as among native-born youth.

220

37. _____

IA   Not very sure   (A)   In general, Negroes who have openly opposed
                                segregation in the South have shown unusual
      Moderately sure   self-restraint and courage.

      Very sure   B   It takes no special virtue for Negroes to
                                oppose segregation openly in the South.

38. _____

IA   Not very sure   A   Most of the biggest industries in America are
                                controlled by persons of at least some Jewish
      Moderately sure   background.

      Very sure   (B)   Jews do not control most of the biggest
                                American industries.

39. _____

IP   Not very sure   A   Scientists have shown that there is no differ-
                                ence in intelligence between American Indians
      Moderately sure   and white people in this country.

      Very sure   (B)   It is possible that there is some difference
                                in intelligence between the average white
                                person and the average American Indian.

40. _____

IP   Not very sure   A   Because they have felt intolerance against
                                themselves, Negroes tend to show much less
      Moderately sure   intolerance toward other groups than do most
                                people
      Very sure
                          (B)   If Negroes were to have dominant political
                                power in this country, they might well show
                                real intolerance toward white people.

41. _____

IP   Not very sure   (A)   It is pretty certain that some Jews in this
                                country have been draft-dodgers from the mili-
      Moderately sure   tary service that is required of American youth.

      Very sure   B   It may not be widely known, but far more Jewish
                                men have volunteered for the military services
                                than one would expect on the basis of their
                                percentage in the population as a whole.

CIRCLE HOW SURE
YOU FEEL OF   CIRCLE
YOUR CHOICE   A or B

42. _____

IA   Not very sure   A   One of the main characteristics of Puerto
                              Ricans in the United States is their sexual
      Moderately sure   looseness and immorality.

      Very sure   (B) The sexual standards of many Puerto Ricans
                              are as high as those of other Americans.

43. _____

IA   Not very sure   A   Considering all the circumstances, race rela-
                              tions in the United States have always been
      Moderately sure   pretty good.

      Very sure   (B) In all sections of the United States, Negores
                              are denied opportunities for many good jobs
                              and promotions that are given to white people.

44. _____

IA   Not very sure   (A) Jews have little real control over the American
                              money system, in spite of the wealth of some
      Moderately sure   individual Jews.

      Very sure   B   Jewish power and control over the American
                              money system is far out of proportion to the
                              number of Jews in the total population.

45. _____

IP   Not very sure   (A) Chinese workers in this country have often made
                              things hard for other workers by their willing-
      Moderately sure   ness to take low wages.

      Very sure   B   Chinese in this country have rarely been will-
                              ing to work for lower wages than other Ameri-
                              cans.

46. _____

IP   Not very sure   (A) Racial integration in housing, recreation, and
                              similar areas of life may well lead to more
      Moderately sure   Negro-white intermarriage and mixed-blood
                              children.
      Very sure

                         B   Racial integration in housing, recreation, and
                              similar areas of life has nothing to do with
                              the rate of intermarriage between Negroes and
                              whites.

222

47. _____

IA   Not very sure   (A)   Many Puerto Ricans are quite intelligent--
                                above the average for the white population of
     Moderately sure   the United States.

     Very sure   B   Some Puerto Ricans may be very capable, but
                                the group as a whole is unfortunately much
                                less capable and intelligent than the white
                                American population.

48. _____

IP   Not very sure   A   Jews are not at all different in business
                                matters from other Americans.
     Moderately sure
                          (B)   There may be some truth to the image of Jews,
     Very sure   on the average, as shrewder in business
                                matters than non-Jews.

IDENTIFICATION WITH THE UNDERDOG (Schuman and Harding 1963)

Variable   This scale attempts to measure "sympathetic identification with the underdog", the underdog in this case being a member of a minority group.

Description   The scale consists of 11 short and simple stories for which the respondent has to describe how a minority group member is likely to react in a difficult social situation with one or more majority group member(s). After each story, the respondent is given four alternative ways in which the minority group member is likely to react. Of these four alternatives, only one is characteristized by immediate sympathetic identification, the other three alternatives indicating difference, agnosticism, and interpretation of the situation as beneficial for the minority group member.

A respondent scores one point if he chooses the sympathetic alternative, three points if he chooses any of the other three alternatives, and two points if he chooses two or no alternatives. Total scores thus run from 11 (total sympathy) to 33 (total lack of sympathy). Two additional control items (numbered 3 and 7 below) were included to disrupt the appearance of a repeated mechanical trend in the items.

Sample   A heterogeneous quota sample of 229 adults in Boston comprised the main standardization sample. The representatives of the sample is limited both by its character and by the fact that nearly 60% of the respondents were Catholic.

In addition, samples of 52 Southern college students, 183 Northern Catholic college students, and 47 students taking a Harvard race relations course were used as "known groups" to validate the scale.

Reliability/   Split-half reliability (corrected) for the Boston sample was .76, Homogeneity   while for the homogeneous Catholic college sample it was .62. The other college samples having higher reliability.

A test-retest reliability coefficient (rho) of .80 was obtained on a small college group (30 students) over a one month interval.

Validity   A quarter of the Southern students, half of the Northern Catholic students and three-quarters of the Harvard race relations class took a position of "sympathy with the underdog" (total score of 22 or under), results which were strongly in line with expectations.

Correlations between "lack of sympathy" and three measures of prejudice varied between .29 and .43 for the Boston sample and between .14 and .44 for the college sample. When corrections for the number of items and scale reliability were taken into account the authors considered the correlations too weak to indicate synonymity of "sympathy" and prejudice although the two were definitely related.

The highest correlations obtained were with the Social Problems Questionnaire, a 13-item measure of willingness to discriminate against minority
groups. This scale is reproduced at the end of the description of the
present scale.

Location   Schuman, H. and Harding, J. "Sympathetic Identification with the
Underdog", Public Opinion Quarterly, 1963, 27, pp. 230-241.

Administration   Estimates of time required to complete the questionnaire were not
reported, although it would seem too difficult to complete in less
than 10 minutes. Contrary to the author's expectations that the
items would be too obvious to respondents, they turned out to be
"difficult". Median score on the test for the Boston adults was 25,
indicating the sympathic reply was chosen in 7 of the 11 stories.
Scores were approximately normally distributed, although 20 percent
were at the non-sympathetic extreme (scores 31-33) and seven percent
at the sympathetic extreme (scores 11-13).

Results and
Comments
Although there were definite correlations of scale scores with education and age (the more sympathetic being younger and better educated),
analysis of these two demographic factors revealed that the strength
of the correlations was mainly due to a certain population group.
Of those respondents older than 50, with less than a high school education,
only 5% scored as sympathetic.

Surprisingly, almost no sex differences appeared in degree of sympathy
in the cross-section sample, although there was a slight tendency
(as expected) in the college sample for women to be more sympathetic.
Correlation between "lack of sympathy" and ten-item F-scale was .24
for the Boston sample and -.07 and .36 in the two Northern college
samples.

The authors also give a valuable clinical description of 15 of their
Boston respondents who were interviewed informally and at length
several months after the questionnaire was administered. Several of
the intricacies of interpreting the scale scores came out of these
interviews, something to be kept in mind by those planning to use
the scale.

IDENTIFICATION WITH THE UNDERDOG

How do different groups react in typical situations? Below are some situations involving various groups. After each situation four possible choices are given. Put a check (√) next to the choice that you feel is the best answer to the question asked for each situation. Leave the other three choices blank.

This is a questionnaire rather than a test: your own personal opinion is the best way to answer each question. This questionnaire takes only about eight minutes to complete. Do not sign your name.

SYMPATHETIC REACTIONS ARE NOTED BY AN ASTERISK *. ITEMS 3 AND 7 ARE NOT SCORED.

1. A colored man born in New England goes South for the first time and sees in a Mississippi bus station two waiting rooms, one for colored and one for whites. How do you think he would be likely to react to this?

   _____ (a) He probably thinks it is a good thing at present, since it prevents trouble from arising.

   _____ (b) He may notice it at first, but after a while he probably gets used to it and it doesn't make much difference to him.

   * (c) He very likely feels hurt by it, and perhaps angry.

   _____ (d) It is hard to know exactly how he would react to such a situation, though with more information one might be able to tell.

2. A Jewish men walking through a store hears one woman say to another, "That Betty, she's always trying to Jew the sales price down." What do you suppose the Jewish man's reaction is likely to be?

   * (a) Underneath he doesn't like what he has overheard.

   _____ (b) Very likely the comment goes in one ear and out the other.

   _____ (c) It is difficult for a non-Jew to know exactly how a Jewish person would react to this.

   _____ (d) If he is interested at all, it might be in several things -- for example, in knowing who was such a good bargainer or what was on sale.

3. A Chinese couple opens a Chinese restaurant in a large American city. The restaurant is quite successful, but often customers mispronounce the names of Chinese foods when ordering meals. How would Chinese owners be most likely to react to this?

_____ (a) They would feel hurt that their customers do not take the trouble to learn to pronounce Chinese words correctly.

_____ (b) They would understand why Americans are likely to have trouble with a language like Chinese that they have never studied.

_____ (c) Without talking to the Chinese couple about the matter, it is impossible to know how they would react.

_____ (d) Probably the Chinese couple never even notices such mistakes in pronounciation by Americans.

4. A colored man who is working on a construction gang is always called "boy" or "Black Sambo" by the Superintendent, whereas the white workers doing the same job are called by their actual first names. How is the colored man likely to react to this?

_____ (a) It probably makes little difference, since over the years he is likely to have become used to it.

_*_ (b) He probably resents it and may even hate the Superintendent for talking to him in this way.

_____ (c) He may well regard it as a friendly, informal way of speaking to him, especially if the Superintendent is generally a nice person.

_____ (d) The story does not give enough information to tell how he would react in this particular case.

5. A Jewish person reads that some teen-age boys have painted anti-Jewish slogans on a Jewish clothing store. What is his reaction likely to be?

_____ (a) One cannot judge fairly without knowing more about the particular Jewish person and his make-up.

_____ (b) Unless it was a store that he owned or traded in, he would probably not pay too much attention to the incident.

_____ (c) He probably regards it as a harmless boyish prank, something the boys will grow out of in time.

_*_ (d) He takes this seriously and doesn't like it at all.

6. Two Chinese girls get jobs in a large American business office. The white girls in the office are polite, but do not want to become too friendly with them. What is the reaction of the Chinese girls likely to be?

____ (a) They might prefer it this way, since they have each other as friends and would rather not mix too much with white people.

____ (b) Probably it makes little difference if the job is good in all other ways.

____ (c) The Chinese are so different in some of their customs that it would be difficult for a person who is not Chinese to figure out exactly what they would think.

__*__ (d) They would almost certainly feel sad or angry or both.

7. A Jewish boy graduates from his religious school. A Christian family that lives down the block hears of this and decides to send a small gift to the Jewish boy. What will be the Jewish family's most likely reaction when the gift arrives from the Christian family?

____ (a) The Jewish parents probably will not like having Christians try to take part in what is usually just a Jewish occasion.

____ (b) Since it will be only one of a number of gifts received by the boy, the Jewish family will take little or no notice of it.

____ (c) The Jewish parents will very likely consider this a nice act by the Christian family and will be pleased.

____ (d) The Jewish parents will probably be a little suspicious and wonder just what is in the mind of the Christian family in sending the gift.

8. A Puerto Rican in New York is trying to find an apartment and goes to an attractive apartment building. The agent meets him, and explains that he would like to rent to him but that the tenants wouldn't like having a Puerto Rican in the building. The agent suggests another very good build-ing that specializes in apartments for non-whites. How do you think the Puerto Rican is likely to react to this?

____ (a) He will probably appreciate the agent's help in recommending another good building.

____ (b) It is not easy to know what such a person would really think.

__*__ (c) He may well be sad to learn that the people in the building don't want to live near him.

____ (d) Very likely he would think nothing special of it, but just keep on looking until he finds a good place that takes Puerto Ricans.

9. A group of colored teen-agers decide to picket and "sit in" at a drug store where coloreds are not allowed to sit at the same part of the soda counter as whites. What is the most likely reason for their acting in this way?

  _*_ (a) They strongly dislike the drug store's policy and want to get it changed.

  ____ (b) They are probably out on a lark, doing this mostly because it seems exciting.

  ____ (c) The average white person in a different city cannot really understand the situation completely.

  ____ (d) It is likely they are being put up to this by some radical organization.

10. The daily newspaper carries a story describing how a certain club in another city refused to admit a woman to membership because of her Japanese ancestry. How do you think Japanese readers of the newspaper are likely to react when they read the story?

  ____ (a) The Japanese are so different that it is hard for a person who hasn't really studied them to know for sure how they would react.

  _*_ (b) They might very much resent having a Japanese person treated in this way.

  ____ (c) They would probably read the article with interest, but not worry over it if the people in the other city were not known personally to them.

  ____ (d) They would probably think that the woman was wrong in trying to join a white club in the first place when there are plenty of fine Japanese clubs.

11. The white school board in a community builds two new schools and fixes the school lines so that almost all the colored children go to one new school and all the white children to the other new school. How do you suppose most of the Negroes in the community would react to this?

  ____ (a) While there are some exceptions, many Negroes are mainly concerned with getting money for food, rent, and other things, and so do not have too much interest in the matter of schools one way or the other.

  ____ (b) Every community is different, and it is almost impossible for someone not living there to know enough about the situation to judge.

  _*_ (c) The average Negro mother or father would not like what the school board has done about drawing school lines.

_____ (d) The average Negro parent would simply be pleased to have a
            new school for their children, especially if it were equal to
            the white school in every way.

12. A Jewish couple is out for a drive in the country, and they pass a fine
     private club. The club has a sign out front describing the advantages of
     membership in the club, and at the bottom it says "Membership reserved
     for Christians only." How do you think the Jewish couple is likely to
     react to this?

     __*__ (a) It makes them unhappy to realize that they are not wanted in
                the club.

     _____ (b) They might think that they could easily join a Jewish club
                with twice the advantages of the club they are passing.

     _____ (c) It is hard for a Christian to know for certain just how
                Jewish people react to a sign of this sort.

     _____ (d) They may read the sign quickly, but probably wouldn't think
                much of it for very long.

13. A well-dressed colored man answers a "Home for Sale" advertisement in
     the newspaper. It happens that the home is in an all-white neighborhood.
     Despite the fact that the real estate agent clearly doesn't want to sell
     the home to him, the colored man asks to fill out an application to buy
     it and to leave a deposit. What is most likely the colored man's real
     reason for this action?

     _____ (a) He may have connections with a business group or some other
                kind of group that is trying to scare white owners into sell-
                ing their homes at lower prices.

     __*__ (b) He probably thinks it is a good house for his family at the
                price and convenient to his work.

     _____ (c) Probably he is well-meaning enough, but just hasn't realized
                that the neighborhood is completely white and wants to stay
                white.

     _____ (d) It is impossible to know in this case whether the colored
                person is simply making a mistake, or has some scheme in the
                back of his mind--only a careful investigation of his real
                motives could answer the question.

SOCIAL PROBLEMS QUESTIONNAIRE

(This supplementary scale was found to correlate highly with the Identifica-tion Scale. It was designed by Harding and Schuman to measure willingness to discriminate and has reported reliabilities of .93 in the heterogeneous Boston sample and .82 in the homogeneous college sample.)

In this part of the questionnaire you will find a number of stories, followed by questions. Answer all the questions in the way YOU think is best. After each question you will find five possible answers:

(YES)   yes   ?   no   NO

If you are sure that your answer to a question is "yes," then put a circle around the YES. Like this:

YES   (yes)   ?   no   NO

If you think that your answer to a question is "yes," but you have some doubts about it, then put a circle around the yes. Like this:

YES   yes   ?   no   (NO)

If you are sure that your answer is "no," then put a circle around the NO. Like this:

YES   yes   ?   (no)   NO

If you simply cannot make up your mind whether your answer is "yes" or "no," then put a circle around the question mark. But try to use the question mark as little as possible.

YES   yes   (?)   no   NO

There are three questions after each story. Be sure to answer ALL the questions.

1. An elderly Negro entered a Chicago barbershop. Before he could sit down, the head barber said: "I'm sorry, we can't give you a haircut. It takes special clippers and experience which none of our barbers have. There's a place across the street that specializes in haircuts for Negroes, and I'm sure they'd be glad to serve you."

   a. Should the head barber have been willing
      to give the Negro a haircut?   YES yes ? no NO

   b. Is it all right for some barbershops to
      refuse to serve Negroes?   YES yes ? no NO

   c. Would you mind going to a barbershop
      that refused to serve Negroes?   YES yes ? no NO

2. Mr. and Mrs. Levy wanted to spend two weeks at a summer resort in New England which some Christian friends had recommended. They wrote for a reservation, but the manager replied that he was sorry but he could not make one for them. He recommended two other nearby resorts which he said usually took Christian and Jewish families in about equal numbers.

   a. Was it all right for the resort manager
      to refuse to make a reservation for
      a Jewish couple?   YES yes ? no NO

   b. Should the Levys' Christian friends pro-
      test to the manager of the summer resort,
      when they learn he has refused to make
      a reservation for the Levys?   YES yes ? no NO

   c. Should there be a law requiring summer
      resorts always to rent cottages to the
      first person who applies?   YES yes ? no NO

3. In a town in Southern California, Mexican and white children are sent to different public schools. The school authorities say that most of the Mexican children read and understand English so poorly that nearly all of them would have to be in special classes anyway. Also they report that in towns where Mexican and white children are placed in the same schools, fights between the two groups are very frequent.

   a. Is it a good idea to have separate
      schools for Mexican and white children?   YES yes ? no NO

   b. Should the school authorities try placing
      Mexican and white children in the same
      schools, in spite of the danger of fights
      and other problems?   YES yes ? no NO

   c. If the parents of a white child do not
      want him assigned to a school with a lot
      of Mexican children, should they be able
      to transfer him to an all-white public
      school?   YES yes ? no NO

4. A Negro girl who had just got a job in San Francisco was looking for a place to live in an all-white neighborhood. She went to see several people who had advertised rooms for rent, but all of them suggested she find a room in a Negro neighborhood instead. They were always pleasant to her, but said that renting to her would make it hard for them to rent their other rooms. Finally she found a landlady in the white neighborhood, Mrs. Williamson, who agreed to take her.

   a. If you had been Mrs. Williamson, would
      you have rented to the Negro girl?   YES   yes   ?   no   NO

   b. Should the other landladies in the
      neighborhood have been willing to
      rent to the Negro girl?   YES   yes   ?   no   NO

   c. Is it unfair to the white roomers to
      let a Negro move in?   YES   yes   ?   no   NO

5. In a large Western city there has been for many years an informal group called the Businessmen's Luncheon Club. None of the members is Jewish. Recently one of the members proposed they add to the group a Jew who was head buyer for one of the larger clothing stores. A majority of the members voted against this. The president of the club said: "I think Mr. Rothman is a fine person, but I don't think we should add him to the Luncheon Club. This has always been a small, closely knit private group; and if we took in Mr. Rothman we would soon need to admit every Jewish businessman in town who wanted to join."

   a. If you had been a member of the club,
      would you have objected to the
      president's statement?   YES   yes   ?   no   NO

   b. If the club does admit Jewish members,
      should it be a little more careful in
      picking them than in picking non-Jews?   YES   yes   ?   no   NO

   c. Should business and professional clubs
      admit members without paying any atten-
      tion to whether the new members are Jewish?   YES   yes   ?   no   NO

6. Mr. Ramirez, a Puerto Rican, was looking for an apartment in a New York City suburb. He went into a real estate office which had a list of apartments in the window, and asked about one of the places that was listed. The clerk told him that this apartment was in a private house in a white neighborhood, and the owner would not rent to Puerto Ricans. Also, the white neighbors would probably reject Puerto Ricans and make life unhappy for them. However, he suggested several other apartments elsewhere at about the same rent which he thought would be just as satisfactory.

   a. Should the owner of the house be willing to
      rent to Puerto Ricans, regardless of what
      the neighbors think?   YES   yes   ?   no   NO

b. Should there be a law requiring landlords
always to rent to the first one applying? YES yes ? no NO

c. Is it better to keep people such as Puerto
Ricans in one section of a city, to avoid
tensions and trouble? YES yes ? no NO

7. A Jewish boy graduated from a famous Northern engineering college, where
he specialized in industrial design. After graduation he applied for a
job with a Northern manufacturer, and the personnel manager told him:
"I'd hire you except for one thing. The three men you would have to
work with most closely--the plant manager, the accountant, and the head
of the drafting room--all have strong feelings about Jews. If you were
going to work down in the plant, I'd never give your religion a thought;
but at the level of top management any serious friction can ruin an
organization."

a. Was it all right for the personnel manager
to refuse to hire the Jewish engineer to
avoid friction with the other employees? YES yes ? no NO

b. Should the personnel manager have asked
the other men how they would feel about
working with a Jewish engineer, and then
made his decision on the basis of their
wishes? YES yes ? no NO

c. Should employers hire men for top management jobs without paying any attention to
whether they are Christian or Jewish YES yes ? no NO

8. Arthur Brady was a Negro lawyer in a town near Boston. He wanted to join
the local tennis club so he could play on their courts. He knew that a
new member had to be recommended by an old member, so he asked a friend
of his who belonged to the club if he would recommend him. The friend
said: "I'm terribly sorry, but I can't. The tennis club has always had
a policy of not admitting Negroes. A proposal to change it was brought
up at the last membership meeting, but it was voted down overwhelmingly."

a. Is it all right for a private tennis
club to refuse to admit Negroes? YES yes ? no NO

b. Should Mr. Brady's friend try to get the
club to change its rules so that he
could be admitted? YES yes ? no NO

c. Is it a good idea to have separate tennis
clubs, bowling leagues, and so on, for
whites and Negroes? YES yes ? no NO

234

9. In a factory in California, Japanese immigrants were working for less
money than native Americans doing similar jobs. When the white workers
joined a union they demanded that all employees be treated the same,
regardless of where they came from. The owner of the factory replied
that Japanese did not mind working for lower wages, because they were
already being paid twice as much as they were used to in Japan. He added
if the Japanese workers' wages were raised, it would only encourage more
of them to come to the United States and take jobs away from white workers.

    a. Was the owner right in paying lower wages
to the Japanese workers?   YES yes ? no NO

    b. Should the Japanese be kept out of better-
paying jobs when native Americans are idle?   YES yes ? no NO

    c. If you worked at the same job as a Japanese,
would you want him to be paid the same?   YES yes ? no NO

10. Richard Jenkins lived in a very nice Los Angeles suburb. All the families
in the neighborhood were Christian and most of them had lived there for
many years. When Mr. Jenkins learned that his company was going to trans-
fer him to another city, he put his house up for sale and soon had an
offer from a Jewish businessman. Several of his friends and neighbors
were very upset and called on him to ask him not to sell his house to a
Jewish person.

    a. Should Mr. Jenkins disregard the wishes
of his friends and neighbors and sell his
house to the Jewish businessman if this
man offers him a higher price than anyone
else?   YES yes ? no NO

    b. If you owned a house in an all-Christian
neighborhood, would you be just as willing to sell your house to a Jew as to
anyone else?   YES yes ? no NO

    c. In general, is it better for Christians
not to sell their houses to Jews, so long
as there is good housing available for
Jews in their own neighborhoods?   YES yes ? no NO

11. One Monday night a group of youngsters, all of Mexican background, decided
to go roller skating at a public rink in downtown Los Angeles. When
they arrived at the rink, they found that they could not get in. The
ticket agent pointed to a sign which read: MEXICAN NIGHT *** WEDNESDAY.
He explained that on Wednesdays they had a special program of Latin-
American music, and on that night the Mexican kids could have as much
fun as they liked without bothering the skating rink's regular customers.

a. Is it all right for a public skating rink
   to have special programs on certain
   evenings mainly intended for Mexican
   youngsters?   YES   yes   ?   no   NO

b. Is it a good idea to keep Mexicans out of
   a roller skating rink on all but certain
   evenings?   YES   yes   ?   no   NO

c. Would the Mexicans have any ground for
   complaint if the rink was given over to
   them every second night?   YES   yes   ?   no   NO

12. In a large factory just outside Cincinnati, Ohio, there was need for a
    new foreman in one department. Both a white man and a Negro were
    eligible for the job in terms of training, but the Negro had been working
    in that department for a longer time. After serious thought, the
    Personnel Department picked the white man for the job, but also saw to
    it that the Negro received an equal raise in salary, though he did not
    get a promotion in duties. The Personnel manager explained to the Negro
    that since many of the workers were from the south and not used to having
    a Negro over them, it might seriously damage the harmony and productivity
    of the plant if a Negro were made foreman.

    a. Was it wrong for the Personnel manager
       to pick the white man for the job of
       foreman, assuming the reasons for his
       decision were really the ones he gave?   YES   yes   ?   no   NO

    b. Should the Negro accept the raise in
       salary and not attempt to become
       foreman?   YES   yes   ?   no   NO

    c. If you worked in a factory, would you
       object to having a Negro put over you
       as foreman?   YES   yes   ?   no   NO

PRO-INTEGRATION SCALE (Sheatsley 1966)

Variable	This scale is designed to measure racial attitudes of whites in terms of willingness to allow Negroes to take part in various types of activities.
Description	This is an eight-item Guttman scale, composed of two Likert items, three agree-disagree items, two forced choice and one multiple choice item. One point is given for each item answered in the pro-integration direction; the total scores thus run from 0 (no pro-integration responses) to 8 (all pro-integration responses). The average score for white Americans was 4.3, with those in the North scoring 5.0 and those in the South 2.5.
	Further breakdowns for various demographic background factors are given in the left-hand table on the following page. It can be seen that residents of Middle Atlantic and Pacific states are more pro-integrationist, as are residents of large cities, those who have the most integrated schools, those who never lived in the South, those under 25, Jews, those with moderate to strong (but not very strong) religious beliefs, and those with more formal education, higher income and higher status occupations.
Sample	A national cross-section sample of between 1250 and 1500 white adults took part in the survey, which was conducted by the National Opinion Research Center in December 1963.
Reliability/ Homogeneity	Although the author claims this is a Guttman scale, he presents no figures to indicate how high a coefficient was obtained. (Judging from the items and the correlations from similar Survey Research Center questions, it should be adequate, however). No test-retest data are reported.
Validity	No data bearing directly on validity are reported, although the differences in scale scores between Southerners and non-Southerners are as expected. Further evidence for validity is found in the right hand table on the following page, in which substantial differences are apparent between individuals at various attitude questions about the civil rights movement. The effects are far more apparent for items B through H than for items A, I and J.
Location	Sheatsley, P. "White attitudes toward the Negro", _Daedalus_ 1966, _95_, pp. 217-238.
Administration	It should take between 3 and 10 minutes to complete the scale.
Results and Comments	In constrast to the responses to the 1964 Survey Research Center questions (see the next chapter) better educated Southerners were more in favor of integration. Included in the author's article is valuable, interesting and recent trend data on a number of other racial attitude questions.

MEAN SCORES ON PRO-INTEGRATION SCALE
(White Population, U.S.A., December 1963)

	North	South			North	South
TOTAL	4.97	2.54				

A. By Region:

	North	South
New England	5.03	--
Middle Atlantic . . .	5.47	--
East North Central. .	4.61	--
West North Central. .	4.37	--
South Atlantic. . . .	--	2.53
East South Central. .	--	1.89
West South Central. .	--	2.70
Mountain.	4.33	--
Pacific	5.43	--

B. By Population Size:

	North	South
10 largest M.A.'s . .	5.33	a
All other M.A.'s. . .	4.97	2.65
Urban counties. . . .	5.04	1.36
Rural counties. . . .	4.23	2.70

C. By Number of Negroes in Public Schools:

	North	South
No Negroes.	4.62	2.29
A few Negroes	5.01	2.80
Considerable number .	5.49	a

D. By Prior Residence:

	North	South
Formerly lived in South	4.80	--
Never lived in South	5.05	--
Formerly lived in North	--	3.22
Never lived in North	--	1.97

E. By Sex:

	North	South
Male.	4.91	2.57
Female.	5.03	2.51

F. By Age Group:

	North	South
Under 25	5.70	2.76
25-44.	5.34	2.86
45-64.	4.71	2.33
65-up.	4.07	2.10

G. By Religion:

	North	South
Protestant	4.75	2.38
Catholic	5.18	3.41
Jewish	6.44	a

H. By Strength of Religious Belief:

	North	South
Very strong.	5.00	2.34
Strong.	5.15	2.86
Moderate	4.87	2.53
Not strong	4.30	2.37

I. By Educational Level:

	North	South
8 years or less. . . .	3.88	1.70
9-12 years (H.S.). . .	5.01	2.71
Attended college . . .	5.96	3.54

J. By Family Income:

	North	South
Under $5,000	4.36	2.20
$5,000-7,499	5.24	2.75
$7,500-9,999	5.26	2.78
$10,000 or over. . . .	5.56	3.41

K. By Occupation:

	North	South
Professional	6.08	4.31
Proprietors, managers.	5.09	2.79
Clerical, sales. . . .	4.96	2.98
Skilled.	4.96	2.04
Semi-skilled	4.90	2.04
Unskilled.	4.73	1.82
Farm	3.86	2.87

[a] Insufficient cases to justify reliable answers.

WHITE ATTITUDES TOWARD NEGRO PROTEST MOVEMENT IN NORTH AND SOUTH,
AND BY SCORES ON PRO-INTEGRATION SCALE, DECEMBER 1963

			Pro-Integration Scale Scores			
			0-2 (High Seg.)	3-4 (Mod. Seg.)	5-6 (Mod. Int.)	7-8 (High Int.)
Per Cent Who Say:	North	South				
A. Most Negroes feel strongly about						
The right to vote	80%	77%	79%	76%	84%	79%
Right to hold same jobs as white people.	84	81	76	84	85	89
Right to use same parks, hotels, restaurants.	84	80	67	82	83	90
Right to send children to same schools as whites.	63	35	45	51	59	66
Right to live in white neighborhoods	45	33	42	39	42	44
Right to marry white people	10	8	13	9	7	10
Having a separate area of U.S. set aside for Negroes.	5	3	7	6	4	2
B. The Negro protest movement has been generally violent rather than peaceful	47%	63%	78%	50%	47%	30%
C. Demonstrations have hurt rather than helped the Negro cause.	43%	60%	71%	52%	45%	24%
D. Generally disapprove of actions Negroes have taken to obtain civil rights	59%	78%	89%	73%	62%	33%
E. Negro groups are asking for too much	37%	55%	74%	45%	31%	16%
F. "Others" are really behind the Negro protest movement	39%	52%	56%	46%	43%	24%
Communists are behind it	21	27	30	26	22	12
G. Problem of Negro rights should be left to states rather than federal government	34%	59%	57%	45%	36%	24%
H. Negro-white relations will always be a problem for U.S.	42%	49%	61%	52%	36%	26%
*I. Self or family have been affected favorably by integration	4%	1%	—%	2%	4%	7%
Have been affected unfavorably . . .	9	11	16	14	4	3
Have not been affected	87	83	82	83	91	87
J. Are around Negroes:						
Almost every day.	29%	39%	33%	28%	31%	35%
Less often than that.	45	52	45	47	46	51
Never around Negroes.	26	9	22	25	23	14

*Percentages do not always add to 100 per cent. Omitted are a small group who answered vaguely or irrelevantly.

GUTTMAN SCALE OF PRO-INTEGRATION SENTIMENTS
(Percentages figures are those giving starred response)

82%   1. Do you think
       *a) Negroes should have as good a chance as white people to get
            any kind of job
       or b) White people should have the first chance at any kind of job

77%   2. Generally speaking, do you think there should be separate sections
       for Negroes in street cars and buses?
       *a) No   b) Yes

71%   3. Do you think Negroes should have the right to use the same parks,
       restaurants and hotels as white people?
       a) No   *b) Yes

63%   4. Do you think white students and Negro students should go to
       *a) The same schools
       or b) Separate schools

49%   5. How strongly would you object if a member of your family wanted to
       bring a Negro friend home to dinner?
       a) Quite a bit
       b) Somewhat
       *c) Not at all

44%   6. White people have a right to keep Negroes out of their neighborhoods
       if they want to, and Negroes should respect that right.
       a) Agree strongly
       b) Agree slightly
       *c) Disagree slightly
       *d) Disagree strongly

36%   7. Do you think there should be laws against marriage between Negroes
       and whites?
       *a) No   b) Yes

27%   8. Negroes shouldn't push themselves where they're not wanted
       a) Agree strongly
       b) Agree slightly
       *c) Disagree slightly
       *d) Disagree strongly

MULTIFACTOR RACIAL ATTITUDE INVENTORY (Woodmansee and Cook 1967)

Variable	This instrument consists of ten separate subscales of various attitudes toward Negroes.
Description	The ten subscales emerged from factor and cluster analyses of responses to a large battery of attitude items about Negroes. The ten subscales have ten items each and are labelled as followed.

      1) Integration-segregation policy (.84)
      2) Acceptance in close personal relationships (.91)
      3) Negro inferiority (.68)
      4) Negro superiority (.71)
      5) Ease in inter-racial contacts (.74)
      6) Derogatory beliefs (.70)
      7) Local autonomy (.86)
      8) Private rights (.89)
      9) Acceptance in status-superior relations (.87)
   10) Gradualism (.86)

Internal consistency coefficients (Cronbach's coefficient alpha) are given in the parentheses above.

Sample	Preliminary construction of the scales were based on two samples: one of 593 white college students from Northeast, Midwest and Border South, and the other of 609 white college students from the Midwest and Border South. The students ranged from students in introductory psychology courses to members of pro- or anti-Negro campus organizations. The final validation sample consisted of 630 white college students from schools in two Border South cities and two western states. About half of these students belonged to groups having specified attitudes toward Negroes and these formed the four criterion groups.
Reliability/ Homogeneity	The average coefficient alpha for the ten scales was .81, with the values for individual scales given above under "Description". No test-retest data are reported.
Validity	The four criterion groups (ordered from most pro-Negro to most anti-Negro groups) were ordered on each of the ten scales exactly as predicted in 15 of 20 possible comparisons and on the 5 that did not fit only one group was out of line. All 20 comparisons differed significantly at the .01 level on the F-test.
Location	Woodmansee, J. and Cook, S. "Dimensions of Racial Attitudes: Their Identification and Measurement", Journal of Personality and Social Psychology, 1967, 7, pp. 240-250.
Administration	Items are apparently in simple agree-disagree format. The 100 items should be completed in 30-50 minutes.

Results and Comments	The authors interpret their findings as indicating that the tripartite division of attitudes into cognitive, affective and conative components did not hold up.

The ten scales are obviously not independent. Excluding the Negro superiority scale from the matrix, the average inter-scale correlation is .47 with some scales intercorrelating well over .60. This indicates that the scales could be treated as unidimensional and that a single summary score might be useful.

The average correlation of each scale with Schuman and Harding's measure of Identification with the Underdog (described earlier in this section) was .16, which is significant but low.

Sample Items

(This instrument came to our attention too late to be fully documented here. The entire Inventory is available from American Documentation Institute at the Library of Congress in Washington. It is available as document 9584 from the ADI Auxiliary Publications Project).

The items below represent one example from each of the scales.

1. The Negro should be afforded equal rights through integration.

2. I would not take a Negro to eat with me in a restaurant where I was well known.

3. Many Negroes should receive a better education than they are now getting, but the emphasis should be on training them for jobs rather than preparing them for college.

4. I think that Negroes have a kind of quiet courage which few whites have.

5. I would probably feel somewhat self-conscious dancing with a Negro in a public place.

6. Although social equality of the races may be the democratic way, a good many Negroes are not yet ready to practice the self-control that goes along with it.

7. Even though we all adopt racial integration sooner or later, the people of each community should be allowed to decide when they are ready for it.

8. A hotel owner ought to have the right to decide for himself whether he is going to rent rooms to Negro guests.

9. If I were being interviewed for a job, I would not mind at all being evaluated by a Negro personnel director.

10. Gradual desegregation is a mistake because it just gives people a chance to cause further delay.

SOCIAL DISTANCE SCALE (Bogardus 1959)

Variable

This scale attempts to measure the social "distance" the respondent perceives between himself and members of different national, racial or other groups by reference to the type of interaction with group members in which the respondent is willing to engage.

Description

The respondent is given a list of nationalities or races and asked to indicate the number of "steps" he would move toward the members of each group. The lowest step (or longest distance) is "would exclude from my country"; the next step is "would accept as visitors only to my country"; the highest step (or shortest distance) is "to close kinship by marriage".

Sample

A sample of 2053 selected persons in the United States in 1956 gave the ratings which are discussed below.

Reliability/
  Homogeneity

Hartley and Hartley (1952) report split-half reliability coefficients at .90 or above.

Validity

Various data bearing on validity are reported in the original source.

Location

Bogardus, E. Social Distance. Yellow Springs, Ohio: Antioch Press, 1959.

Administration

The scale should take less than two minutes to administer for the first group being rated and far less time for each succeeding group. The average scale ratings for 30 nationalities obtained from the sample of 2053 Americans was 2.08. Negroes rated 27th on the list at 2.74, with only Mexicans, Indians (from India) and Koreans being rated lower. Scores for other nationalities were as follows: White Americans, 1.08 (1st); English, 1.23 (3rd); Jews, 2.15 (16th); Russians, 2.56 (24th); Chinese, 2.68 (25th); and Japanese, 2.70 (26th).

Results and
  Comments

The social distance scale is perhaps the most appropriate application of the Guttman scaling model in the attitude literature, as the "steps" of social distance conform to common everyday behavioral expectations of most individuals in society. There is some evidence, however, that the social distance scales do not always conform to unidmensionality (Triandis 1967).

The senior author of the present volume investigated feelings of social distance from various groups, including sex criminals. It was found that the usual scalar steps were not observed in feelings toward sex criminals: people were willing to admit sex criminals to close kinship or to their clubs but were not willing to have them as neighbors.

Cross-cultural data on how difference nationalities view each other are given in Buchanan and Cantril (1954).

References

Bogardus, E. <u>Immigration and Race Attitudes</u> Boston: Heath, 1928.

Buchanan, W. and Cantril, H. <u>How Nations See Each Other</u> Urbana: University of Illinois Press, 1954.

Hartley, E. and Hartley, Ruth <u>Fundamentals of Social Psychology</u> New York: Knopf 1952, pp. 431-443.

Triandis, H. "Exploratory factor analyses of the behavioral component of social attitudes", M. Fishbein (ed.) <u>Readings in Attitude Theory and Measurement</u> New York: Wiley, 1967.

SOCIAL DISTANCE SCALE

1. Remember to give your <u>first feeling reactions</u> in every case.

2. Give your reactions to each race as a <u>group</u>. Do not give your reactions to the best or to the worst members that you have known, but think of the picture or stereotype that you have of the whole race.

3. Put a cross after each race in as many of the rows as your feelings dictate.

Category	English	Poles	Negroes	Chinese	Etc.
1. To close kinship by marriage.					
2. To my club as personal chums.					
3. To my street as neighbors.					
4. To employment in my occupation.					
5. To citizenship in my country.					
6. As visitors only to my country.					
7. Would exclude from my country.					

THE E(ETHNOCENTRISM) SCALE (Adorno et al. 1950)

Variable   This scale was designed to measure ethnocentrism, which was conceived as an ideological system pertaining to groups and group relations and referring to general cultural narrowness.

Description   The E Scale consists of 3 subscales: Negro, Minorities, and Patriotism. The "Negro" subscale deals with the Negro stereotype and Negro-white relations. The "Minorities" subscale deals with the negative opinions and imagery directed to many minority groups (excluding Negroes and Jews) in America. The "Patriotism" subscale deals with jingoistic attitudes in which America is regarded the superior "in-group" and other nations are viewed as inferior "out-groups". The authors prefer to use the term "pseudo-patriotism" rather than patriotism to describe these attitudes.

All items are negatively stated Likert-type items with which the subject expresses his agreement or disagreement on a +3 to -3 scale with the neutral point excluded. An individuals total score is computed by adding +4 to each response and then summing the item scores. A high score indicates a high degree of ethnocentrism.

There are five forms of this scale. The original form consists of 34 items: 12 Negro, 12 Minorities, and 10 Patriotism. The items on this scale, unlike many scale items, were not selected from an "item pool" by item analysis. The authors, when composing the items, tried to make each "maximally rich in ideas" and to keep duplication at a minimum. Item analysis yielded an average discriminatory power (D.P.) of 2.97 for the 34 items. Five D.P.'s were over 4.0, 13 were between 3.0 and 3.9, ten were between 2.0 and 2.9, three were between 1.0 and 1.9, and three were less than 1.0. The average D.P. for the Negro subscale was 3.00, for the Minorities subscale 2.87, and for the Patriotism subscale, 3.07.

The second form, form 78, consisted of 14 items: four Negro, four Patriotism and six Minorities; ten of these items were retained from the original scale on the bases of statistical adequacy and richness of content of the items. In some cases, the wording was changed. Four new items were added. Item analysis yielded a mean D.P. of 2.90 for the 14 items. Two D.P.'s were over 4.0, five were between 3.0 and 3.9, six were between 2.0 and 2.9, and one was below 2.0.

The third form, form 60, which included the authors' A-S (Anti-Semitism) Scale as well, consisted of 12 items: four A-S items, three Negro items, and five Minorities and Patriotism items. Item analysis yielded a mean D.P. of 3.30 for the 12 items. Two D.P.'s were above 4.0, six were between 3.0 and 3.9, three were between 2.0 and 2.9, and one was below 2.0 (1.80).

The fourth and fifth forms of the E Scale, forms 45 and 40, consisted of ten and five items, respectively. Form 45 was the same as form 60 with two items eliminated. The purpose of this reduction was to make the test short enough to administer to large and diverse groups of people. Form 40 was the same as form 45 with the five items pertaining to Jews eliminated. Item analysis yielded a mean D.P. of 3.89 for form 45, with four D.P.'s above 4.0, five between 3.0 and 3.9, and one of 2.99. Form 40 had a mean D.P. of 4.88 with three D.P.'s over 5.0 and two between 4.0 and 4.9.

The author's suggested final form of the E Scale contains 20 items: six A-S items, six Negro items, and eight Minorities and Patriotism items.

Sample

The original form of the E Scale was administered to 144 women students in introductory psychology at the University of California. Form 78 was administered to 4 groups:

```
Group A -- University of California Public Speaking Class
           Women - - - - - - - - - - - - - - - - - - - - -140
Group B -- University of California Public Speaking Class
           Men - - - - - - - - - - - - - - - - - - - - - - 51
Group C -- University of California Extension Psychology
           Class Women - - - - - - - - - - - - - - - - - - 40
Group D -- University of California Professional
           Women - - - - - - - - - - - - - - - - - - - - - 63
```

Total N for form 78   295

Form 60 was administered to the following groups:

```
Group   I -- University of Oregon Student Women  - - - - - 47
Group  II -- University of Oregon and University of
             California Student Women  - - - - - - - - - 54
Group III -- University of Oregon and University of
             California Student Men  - - - - - - - - - - 57
Group  IV -- Oregon Service Club Men - - - - - - - - - - 68
```

Total N for form 60   226

Form 45 was administered to the following groups:

```
Group   I -- Extension Testing Class Women - - - - - - - - 59
Group  II -- San Quentin Men Prisoners - - - - - - - - - -110
Group III -- Psychiatric Clinic Women - - - - - - - - - - 71
Group  IV -- Psychiatric Clinic Men  - - - - - - - - - - 50
Group   V -- Working-Class Men and Women - - - - - - - - 50
Group XIV -- Employment Service Men Veterans - - - - - - 51
Group  XV -- Maritime School Men - - - - - - - - - - - -179
```

Total N for form 45   570

Form 40 was administered to the following groups:

```
Group    VI -- George Washington University Women - - - -   132
Group   VII -- California Service Club Men  - - - - - - -    63
Group  VIII -- Middle-Class Men - - - - - - - - - - - - -    69
Group    IX -- Middle-Class Women - - - - - - - - - - - -   154
Group     X -- Work-Class Men                               61
Group    XI -- Working-Class Women - - - - - - - - - - -     53
Group   XII -- Los Angeles Men - - - - - - - - - - - - -    117
Group  XIII -- Los Angeles Women  - - - - - - - - - - - -   130
Group   XIV -- Employer Service Men Veterans  - - - - - -    55
Group    XV -- Maritime School Men - - - - - - - - - - - -  164
```

Total N for form 40   988

Reliability No test-retest data were reported.

All following reliabilities are split-half estimates based on the samples cited above. By using the Spearman-Brown formula, the split half reliability of the original form (total scale) was .91. The reliability of the Negro subscale was .91, the Minorities, .82, the Patriotism, .80.

The following table of raw correlation coefficients presents the intercorrelations among subscales and the total scale

	Negro	Minorities	Patriotism	Total E
Negro		.74	.76	.90
Minorities			.83	.91
Patriotism				.92

The split half reliability for form 78 for all the groups receiving this form was .80. The reliability for group A was .80, for group B, .74; for group C, .80; and for group D, .88.

The split half reliability for form 60 for all the groups receiving this form was .86. The reliability for group I was .88, for group II, .88; for group III, .86; for group IV, .82.

The reliability coefficients for form 45 were computed from the five A-S item vs. the five non A-S items. The reliability for groups I-V receiving this form was .79. Group I had a reliability of .82; group II, .65, group III, .84; group IV, .75; group V, .91; group XIV, .86; and group XV, .73. No reliability coefficients were computed for form 40.

248

Validity

The most direct evidence for the validity of this scale is obtained by comparing the response of only two subjects, Mack and Larry, who were given extensive interviews. In these interviews, Mack "...exhibited in a clear-cut fashion all of the trends which... are most characteristic of ethnocentrism." Larry, on the other hand, "...makes every effort to place himself squarely on the side of democratic internationalism and social equality for minorities". On form 78 of the E Scale, Mack's mean score per item was 5.3 while Larry's was 1.8. On this form, the group mean was 3.3.

The remaining evidence for validity is on internal rather than external criteria. The original 34-item E Scale correlated .80 with the original form of the Anti-Semitism Scale. For all the groups taking form 78, the E Scale correlated .59 with the Political Economic Conservatism Scale. For all the groups taking form 60, the E Scale correlated .52 with the PEC Scale. The E Scale correlated .51 with the PEC Scale for all the groups taking form 45. The E Scale correlated .66 with the PEC Scale for all groups taking form 40. For those groups taking form 40 and 45, the E Scale correlated .47 with the PEC Scale. The over-all E-F Scale correlation for the groups taking form 78 was .65. For the groups taking form 45, the over-all E-F correlation was .73. The over-all E-F corelation for form 40 was .77. The E-F correlation over-all forms was .73.

Location·

Adorno, T., et al., The Authoritarian Personality, New York: Harper, 1950.

Administration

The time required to complete the E Scale depends on the form given, allowing an estimated 30 seconds per item. Item mean scores rather than total scores are used for comparisons. The item mean score is computed by summing the corrected item scores and then dividing the sum by the number of items.

Results and Comments

Before using the E Scale or any of the authors' scales constructed for their study of the Authoritarian Personality, the reader should consult Hyman and Sheatsley's (1954) comprehensive critique of this work.

The mean score per item for the subjects taking the original E Scale was 3.17. The mean for all the groups taking form 78 was 3.29, with group means ranging from 2.72 to 3.68. For form 60, the over-all group mean was 3.30 with single group means ranging from 2.96 to 3.33. The mean for groups I-V taking form 45 was 3.74 with group means ranging from 3.34 to 4.61. Groups VI-XIII taking form 40 had an over-all mean of 3.90, with group means ranging from 3.64 to 4.31. It is interesting to note that very few of these item means exceed or even reach the neutral point 4.00. There are two possible explanations of these results: perhaps the American population as a whole is slightly less ethnocentric than the neutral point, or perhaps this result is the effect of the unrepresentativeness of the sample. Evidence for the latter explanation is found in examination of the sample used in computing each mean. The means for form 45 and form 40 come closer to the neutral point than the means for the other forms. Forms 45 and 40 were administered to larger and more varied groups of the American population than were the other forms.

The high correlation coefficients among the three subscales (which, if corrected, would all be .9 or over) suggest that the authors' notion of a variable such as "ethnocentricity", which is postulated to be the focal point for attitudes toward a variety of issues and groups, is not entirely unfounded. Further evidence for such a variable is found in the correlations between the A-S Scale and the subscales of the E Scale. Corrected correlation coefficients are Anti-Semitism/Negro subscale .91, Anti-Semitism/Minorities subscale -.82, and Anti-Semitism/Patriotism subscale -.80.

The authors studied ethnocentrism in relation to religious affiliation. Mean Anti-Semitism and E scores for all members of large denominations were close to the neutral point with variabilities almost as great as the variability in the total sample. Subjects professing some religious affiliation expressed more prejudice than those not professing church affiliation. Those who never attended church obtained lower E scores than those who did attend. An open-ended questionnaire revealed that objective factors such as church attendance were less related to prejudice than certain psychological trends apparent in the way the subject accepted or rejected religion (conventionalism, authoritarianism, submission, etc.).

Reference   Hyman, H. and Sheatsley, P. "The Authoritarian Personality: A Methodological Critique", R. Christie and M. Jahoda (eds.) Studies in the Method and Scope of the Authoritarian Personality, Glencoe, Illinois: Free Press, 1954.

ETHNOCENTRISM SCALE (Suggested Final Form)

The following statements refer to opinions regarding a number of social groups and issues, about which some people agree and others disagree. Please mark each statement in the left-hand margin according to your agreement or disagreement as follows:

+1: slight support, agreement   -1: slight opposition, disagreement
+2: moderate support, agreement   -2: moderate opposition, disagreement
+3: strong support, agreement   -3: strong opposition, disagreement

Jews

1) One trouble with Jewish businessmen is that they stick together and prevent other people from having a fair chance in competition.

2) I can hardly imagine myself marrying a Jew.

3) There may be a few exceptions, but in general Jews are pretty much alike.

4) The trouble with letting Jews into a nice neighborhood is that they gradually give it a typical Jewish atmosphere.

5) To end prejudice against Jews, the first step it for the Jews to try sincerely to get rid of their harmful and irritating faults.

6) There is something different and strange about Jews; it's hard to tell what they are thinking and planning, and what makes them tick.

Negroes

1) Negroes have their rights, but it is best to keep them in their own districts and schools and to prevent too much contact with whites.

2) It would be a mistake ever to have Negroes for foremen and leaders over whites.

3) Negro musicians may sometimes be as good as white musicians, but it is a mistake to have mixed Negro-white bands.

4) Manual labor and unskilled jobs seem to fit the Negro mentality and ability better than more skilled or responsible work.

5) The people who raise all the talk about putting Negroes on the same level as whites are mostly radical agitators trying to stir up conflicts.

6) Most Negroes would become overbearing and disagreeable if not kept in their place.

251

Other Minorities and Patriotism

1) Zootsuiters prove that when people of their type have too much money and freedom, they just take advantage and cause trouble.

2) The worst danger to real Americanism during the last 50 years has come from foreign ideas and agitators.

3) Now that a new world organization is set up, America must be sure that she loses none of her independence and complete power as a sovereign nation.

4) Certain religious sects who refuse to salute the flag should be forced to conform to such patriotic action, or else be abolished.

5) Filipinos are all right in their place, but they carry it too far when they dress lavishly and go around with white girls.

6) America may not be perfect, but the American Way has brought us about as close as human beings can get to a perfect society.

7) It is only natural and right for each person to think that his family is better than any other.

8) The best guarantee of our national security is for America to have the biggest army and navy in the world and the secret of the atom bomb.

EARLIER ETHNOCENTRISM SCALES

Subscale

Ethnocentrism   1) The many political parties tend to confuse national issues, add to the expense of elections, and raise unnecessary agitation. For this and other reasons, it would be best if all political parties except the two major ones were abolished.

Negro   2) If there are enough Negroes who want to attend dances at a local dance hall featuring a colored band, a good way to arrange this would be to have one all-Negro night, and then the whites could dance in peace the rest of the time.

Patriotism   3) Patriotism and loyalty are the first and most important requirements of a good citizen.

Ethnocentrism   4) Certain religious sects whose beliefs do not permit them to salute the flag should be forced to conform to such patriotic action, or else be abolished.

Negro   5) The Negroes would solve many of their social problems by not being so irresponsible, lazy, and ignorant.

Ethnocentrism   6) Any group or social movement which contains many foreigners should be watched with suspicion and, whenever possible, be investigated by the FBI.

Patriotism   7) There will always be superior and inferior nations in the world and, in the interests of all concerned, it is best that the superior ones be in control of world affairs.

Negro   8) Negro musicians are sometimes as good as white musicians at swing music and jazz, but it is a mistake to have mixed Negro-white bands.

Ethnocentrism   9) Although women are necessary in the armed forces and in industry, they should be returned to their proper place in the home as soon as the war is over.

Patriotism   10) Minor forms of military training, obedience, and discipline, such as drill, marching, and simple commands, should be made part of the elementary school educational program.

Negro   11) It would be a mistake to have Negroes for foremen and leaders over whites.

Patriotism   12) The main threat to American institutions during this century has come from the infiltration of foreign ideas, doctrines, and agitators.

Patriotism	13)	Present treatment of conscientious objectors, draft evaders, and enemy aliens is too lenient and mollycoddling. If a person won't fight for his country, he deserves a lot worse than just prison or a work camp.
Negro	14)	Negroes may have a part to play in white civilization, but it is best to keep them in their own districts and schools and to prevent too much intermixing with whites.
Ethnocentrism	15)	One main difficulty with allowing the entire population to participate fully in government affairs (voting, jobs, etc.) is that such a large percentage is innately deficient and incapable.
Negro	16)	Manual labor and menial jobs seem to fit the Negro mentality and ability better than more skilled or responsible work.
Ethnocentrism	17)	It is a mistake to allow any Japanese to leave internment camps and enter the army where they would be free to commit sabotage.
Patriotism	18)	In view of the present national emergency, it is highly important to limit responsible government jobs to native, white Christian Americans.
Negro	19)	In a community of 1000 whites and 50 Negroes, a drunken Negro shoots and kills an officer who is trying to arrest him. The white population should immediately drive all the Negroes out of town.
Patriotism	20)	European refugees may be in need, but it would be a big mistake to lower our immigration quotas and allow them to flood the country.
Ethnocentrism	21)	The many faults, and the general inability to get along, of the Oklahomans ("Okies") who have recently flooded California, prove that we ought to send them back where they came from as soon as conditions permit.
Negro	22)	The people who raise all the talk about putting Negroes on the same level as whites and giving them the same privileges are mostly radical agitators trying to stir up conflicts.
Patriotism	23)	It has become clear that the Germans and Japanese are racially war-minded and power-seeking, and the only guarantee of future peace is to wipe out most of them and to keep the rest under careful control.
Ethnocentrism	24)	A large-scale system of sterilization would be one good way of breeding out criminals and other undesirable elements in our society and so raise its general standards and living conditions.
Negro	25)	An occasional lynching in the South is a good thing because there is a large percentage of Negroes in many communities and they need a scare once in a while to prevent them from starting riots and disturbances.

Patriotism	26)	Mexico can never advance to the standards of living and civilization of the U.S., due mainly to the innate dirtiness, laziness, and general backwardness of Mexicans.
Ethnocentrism	27)	Filipinos are all right in their place, but they carry it too far when they dress lavishly, buy good cars, and go around with white girls.
Negro	28)	It would be best to limit Negroes to grammar and trade school education since more schooling just gives them ambitions and desires which they are unable to fulfill in white competition.
Ethnocentrism	29)	Zoot suiters demonstrate that inferior groups, when they are given too much freedom, and money, just misuse their privileges and create disturbances.
Ethnocentrism	30)	The most vicious, irresponsible, and racketeering unions are, in most cases, those having largely foreigners for leaders.
Negro	31)	There is something inherently primitive and uncivilized in the Negro, as shown in his music and his extreme aggressiveness.
Ethnocentrism	32)	We are spending too much money for the pampering of criminals and the insane, and for the education of inherently incapable people.
Patriotism	33)	There will always be wars because, for one thing, there will always be races who ruthlessly try to grab more than their share.
Negro	34)	Most Negroes would become officious, overbearing, and disagreeable if not kept in their place.

Second form   Form 78

4) All forms of racial and religious discrimination should be made illegal and punishable.

7) Zootsuiters demonstrate that inferior groups, when they are given too much freedom and money, just misuse their privileges and create disturbances.

18) The main threat to basic American institutions during this century has come from foreign ideas, doctrines, and agitators.

25) If and when a new world organization is set up, America must be sure that she loses none of her independence and full sovereignty as a separate nation.

29) Negroes have their rights, but it is best to keep them in their own districts and schools and to prevent too much contact with whites.

34) Women if they work at all, should take the most feminine positions such as nursing, secretarial work, or child care.

37) If Negroes live poorly, it's because they are just naturally lazy, ignorant, and without self-control.

41) America may not be perfect, but the American Way has brought us about as close as human beings can get to a perfect society.

45) It would be a mistake to have Negroes for foremen and leaders over whites.

48) The only full guarantee of future peace is to wipe out as many as possible of the Germans and Japs, and to keep the rest under strict control.

51) Most of our social problems would be solved if the immoral, corrupt, and defective people could somehow be removed from the scene.

54) One main difficulty with allowing the entire population to participate fully in government affairs is that such a large percentage is innately deficient and incapable.

57) The people who raise all the talk about putting Negroes on the same level as whites are mostly radical agitators trying to stir up trouble.

64) Citizen or not, no Jap should be allowed to return to California.

Third Form   Form 60

3)   Zoot suiters prove that when people of their type have too much money
     and freedom, they just take advantage and cause trouble.

8)   One trouble with Jewish businessmen is that they stick together and
     prevent other people from having a fair chance at competition.

14) Negroes have their rights, but it is best to keep them in their own
     districts and schools and to prevent too much contact with whites.

21) I can hardly imagine myself marrying a Jew.

28) It would be a mistake ever to have Negroes for foremen and leaders over
     whites.

33) If and when a new world organization is set up, America must be sure
     that she loses none of her independence and complete power in matters
     that affect this country.

38) There may be a few exceptions, but in general, Jews are pretty much alike.

42) If Negroes live poorly, it's mainly because they are naturally lazy,
     ignorant, and without self-control.

47) The trouble with letting Jews into a nice neighborhood is that they
     gradually give us a typical Jewish atmosphere.

51) The worst danger to real Americanism during the last 50 years has come
     from foreign agitators and ideas.

55) Citizen or not, no Jap should be allowed to return to California.

59) For the good of all, the Oklahomans ("Okies") who recently flooded
     California ought to be sent back home as soon as possible.

Fourth Form   Forms 45 and 40

5) Zootsuiters prove that when people of their type have too much money and freedom, they just take advantage and cause trouble.

10) Negroes have their rights, but it is best to keep them in their own districts and schools and to prevent too much contact with whites.

15) The worst danger to real Americanism during the last 50 years has come from foreign ideas and agitators.

20) It would be a mistake ever to have Negroes for foremen and leaders over whites.

24) One trouble with Jewish businessmen is that they stick together and prevent other people from having a fair chance in competition.

28) I can hardly imagine myself marrying a Jew.

32) If Negroes live poorly, it's mainly because they are naturally lazy, ignorant, and without self-control.

36) There may be a few exceptions, but in general, Jews are pretty much alike.

40) The trouble with letting Jews into a nice neighborhood is that they gradually give it a typical Jewish atmosphere.

45) If and when a new world organization is set up, America must be sure that she loses none of her independence and complete power in matters affect this country.

RACIAL STEREOTYPE INDEX (Matthews and Prothro 1966)

Variable	This simple instrument attempts to determine whether the respondent holds the opinion that certain characteristics of whites and/or Negroes are racially determined.
Description	Four questions were asked each respondent about his views of the Negro and white races. A response favorable to whites was scored as a +1; a response favorable to Negroes was scored as a -1; responses indicating no racial difference were counted as 0. The sum of a respondent's item scores is his Index score, which thus can range from +4 (strongly pro-white) through 0 (all races are the same) to -4 (strongly pro-Negro).
Sample	The sample to which this measure was administered is described in the Political Participation Scale write-up, in Chapter 11. Data have been reported only for the Negro sample.
Reliability	No reliability data were reported.
Validity	No data bearing on validity are reported.
Location	Matthews, D. R. and Prothro, J. W., Negroes and the New Southern Politics New York: Harcourt, Brace & World, 1966.
Results and Comments	It was found that Southern Negroes tended to be relatively free of racial bias, and that most of the biased sample possessed a sense of racial inferiority rather than superiority. An apparent strong effect of racial attitudes on the higher levels of political participation was reduced to insignificance by controlling for political interest. The authors concluded that feelings of racial inadequacy did not seem appreciably to reduce Negro voting rates, but they did diminish the frequency with which Negroes participated beyond the voting stage.
	These items and similar other stereotype items were administered to a random sample of Detroiters living in the riot areas of July 1967 (Meyer 1967). They were found to discriminate significantly between riot participants and non-participants, with the participants expressing much greater feelings of Negro superiority. The senior author of this volume asked these questions of University of Michigan undergraduate psychology students and found their answers to be essentially neutral in contrast to responses of both participant and non-participant Detroit Negroes, which were decidedly pro-Negro. It is uncertain whether the opinions tapped by the stereotype questions are stable or are affected by external events.
Reference	Meyer, P., A Survey of Attitudes of Detroit Negroes After the Riot of 1967 Detroit: Detroit Free Press, 1967.

RACIAL STEREOTYPE INDEX

(Numbers below refer to location in the three questionnaires used.)

Negro Student	White Adult	Negro Adult	
62	74	84	On the whole, do you think white people are smarter than Negroes, Negroes are smarter than white people, or that they are about the same?
63	75	85	In general, do you think white people behave better than Negroes, Negroes behave better than white people, or that they are about the same?
64	76	86	By and large, do you think white people are more dependable than Negroes, Negroes are more dependable than white people, or that they are about the same?
65	77	87	On the whole, do you think white people try to get ahead more than Negroes, Negroes try to get ahead more than white people, or that they are about the same?

RACIAL IDENTIFICATION SCALES (Matthews and Prothro 1966)

Variable

A simple Race Identification Index was constructed from coded responses to SRC questions about interest and perceived closeness to other individuals in similar social groupings.

Description

Items and coding categories are reproduced on the following page. Scores range from 0 to 3, with high score indicating high level of identification.

Sample

The sample is described in the author's PPS scale write-up in Chapter 11 of the present volume.

Reliability

No reliability information was given for this rough Index.

Validity

No data bearing on validity are reported.

Location

Matthews, D. R. and Prothro, J. W., Negroes and the New Southern Politics, New York: Harcourt, Brace and World, 1966.

Results and Comments

It was found that identification with other Negroes was so strong among Negro Southerners sampled that no significant difference existed in its frequency among students and adults. College-educated Negro adults expressed somewhat more interest in the fate of other Negroes than did the college students. College students in turn expressed more interest than did the Southern Negro adults in general.

No information was given on the pattern of responses to questions on identification with other Southerners, which were asked of white respondents.

For distribution of responses of national samples of Negroes over several years, see Chapter 13 of the volume.

NEGRO IDENTIFICATION WITH OTHER NEGROES

1. Some Negroes feel they have a lot in common with other Negroes, but others we talk to don't feel this way so much. How about you? Would you say you feel pretty close to Negroes in general or that you don't feel much closer to them than you do to other people?

2. How much interest would you say you have in how Negroes as a whole are getting along in this country? Do you have a good deal of interest in it, some interest, or not much interest at all?

WHITE IDENTIFICATION WITH THE SOUTH

1. Some people in the South feel they have a lot in common with other southerners; but others we talk to don't feel this way so much. How about you? Would you say that you feel pretty close to southerners in general or that you don't feel much closer to them than you do to other people?

2. How much interest would you say you have in how southerners as a whole are getting along in this country? Do you have a good deal of interest in it, some interest, or not much interest at all?

INDEX SCORE	Reply to Question 1	Question 2
3	Feel pretty close	Good deal of interest
2	Feel pretty close	Some interest
	Feel pretty close	DK
	Feel pretty close	NA
	Can't decide	Good deal of interest
	DK	Good deal of interest
	NA	Good deal of interest
1	Feel pretty close	Not much interested at all
	Not closer than to others	Good deal of interest
	Not closer than to others	Some interest
0	Not closer than to others	Not much interest at all
	Can't decide	Not much interest at all
	DK	Not much interest at all
	Not closer than to others	NA
	Not closer than to others	DK
	NA	Not much interest at all

COMMUNITY RACE RELATIONS RATINGS (Matthews and Prothro 1966)

Variable

This is a "self-anchoring" scale employing as end points the respondent's own conception of the "best" and "worst" in race relations, thus tapping as well the respondent's sense of relative deprivation.

Description

With a ten-step "ladder" scale as a reference, respondents were asked to evaluate their community's race relations today, five years ago, and in the future, relative to their own conceptions of the best and the worst in race relations (points 10 and 1 respectively on the ladder). Respondents were also asked to locate six other communities on the rating scale.

A sample of southern Negro college students were asked to evaluate in the same manner race relations in the South as a whole.

Sample

The various samples to whom this measure was administered are described in the review of the authors' Political Participation Scale (Chapter 11). Data have been reported only for the Negro portion and not for the white portion of the samples.

Reliability/ Homogeneity

No reliability information was reported.

Validity

No tests of validity were reported.

Administration

This scale was administered as part of a long interview schedule but possibly could be converted for pencil-and-paper test use.

Location

Matthews, D. and Prothro, J. W. Negroes and the New Southern Politics, New York: Harcourt, Brace & World, 1966. p. 525.

Results and Comments

While the modal rating of the local community for whites was 10 (best possible), for Negroes the modal rating was 5. Fifteen percent of the Negroes gave "10" ratings, while only one quarter gave low ratings.

The authors found that political participation as measured by the Political Participation Scale was lowest at the two extremes on the ratings--among those Negroes either highly satisfied or highly dissatisfied. Participation was found to be significantly higher between the two extremes, an effect that was independent of level of information. Higher participants also were those who felt well off relative to five of the six other communities (the exception was New York) and those who expected improved race relations in the future, regardless of present rating.

The modal rating given by Negro college students was 4.5, with fewer extreme ratings than in the cross-section sample. The authors found that students with the greatest sense of discontent tended to be more active in the protest movement than were the relatively content, and that the activists felt relatively fortunate when comparing their lot to that of other Negroes in the South.

Reference   Kilpatrick, F. P. and Cantril, Hadley "Self-anchoring scaling, a measure of individuals' unique reality worlds," *Journal of Individual Psychology*, 1960, 16, pp. 158-173.

264

COMMUNITY RACE RELATIONS RATINGS
(Numbers refer to place in the questionnaire)

Negro Student	White Adult	Negro Adult	
	80	90	(Hand the ladder card 1 to respondent) Here is a picture of a ladder. Suppose we say that at the top of the ladder (point to the top) is the very best, the really perfect, kind of race relations you have just described. At the very bottom is the very worst kind of race relations. (picture of ten-step scale) Where on this ladder (move finger rapidly up and down ladder) would you put ____ (local community)--that is, where you are living now? (circle step number on R's card)
	81	91	Now think of race relations here in _____(local community) five years ago. Where on this ladder would you put the race relations of _____(local community) five years ago?
	82	92	Thinking now of future race relations here in _____ (local community), where on the ladder do you expect the race relations of _____ (local community) to be five years from now?
	83	93	Now, let's think about some other places. Where on the ladder would you put the race relations of (indicate comments, if any)
	83a	93a	_____ New York?
	83b	93b	_____ Little Rock?
	83c	93c	_____ Chicago?
	83d	93d	_____ Atlanta?
	83e	93e	_____ A small town in Mississippi?
	83f	93f	_____ A small city in Ohio?
68			Where on this ladder (move finger rapidly up and down ladder) would you put the South today--that is, the South as a whole right now? (circle step number on R's card)
69			Now think of race relations in the South five years ago. Where on this ladder would you put the race relations of the South as a whole five years ago?
70			Thinking now of future race relations in the South, where on the ladder do you expect the race relations of the South as a whole to be five years from now?
71			Now, let's think about some specific places. Where on the ladder would you put the race relations of (Indicate comments, if any)
71a 71b to g			_____ the town or place where you grew up? same as 83 and 93a through f, above.

DIMENSIONAL ATTITUDE MEASURE TOWARD NEGROES (Wrightsman 1962)

Variable This study essayed an examination of the hypothesized three dimensions of racial prejudice.

Description Attitudes of Southern whites toward Negroes are used as an example of minority group prejudice, which the author believes to have three dimensions: cognitive, affective, and conative. Three independent tests were used to assess these dimensions.

The cognitive dimension was loosely defined as beliefs and perceptions about minority groups. This dimension was measured by asking each subject to rate eight imaginary persons (two races: Negro and white, paired with four occupations: doctor, bookkeeper, student, and ditchdigger) on each of 15 personality characteristics on semantic differential scales. Of these 15, six were stereotyped: intelligent vs. unintelligent, etc. The ratings, 120 in all, were expressed on a 1 to 7 semantic differential rating scale with high numbers indicating favorable characteristics. A subjects' final score was the difference between this Negro and white rating for the four occupations on the six stereotyped characteristics.

The affective dimension was described as being one's "feeling" toward the minority group, that is, liking and accepting them. Getzel's and Walsh's Paired Direct and Projective Questions test was used to assess this dimension. (See the following scale descriptions)

The conative dimension was defined as the individual's policy orientation concerning treatment and privileges of the minority groups. This dimension was measured by the Summated Differences Technique (the Westie social distance measure, described on the following pages), in which subject's prejudice score is a function of differences in his responses to whites and Negroes in the same occupation. Items were added which assessed social distance desired from the Negro in different social situations such as community participation, residential, etc.

Sample The subjects were 100 white college students (33 male and 67 female) from five colleges in Nashville, Tennessee.

Reliability/ Test-retest reliabilities for 27 subjects tested after an interval
 Homogeneity of one to three months were: Stereotype of Negroes, .69; PDPQ (first person), .83; PDPQ (third person) .68; and Westie Prejudice Scale, .95. No data on internal consistency or homogeneity were given.

Validity Data bearing indirectly on validity are presented below under Results and Comments.

Location Wrightsman, L. "Dimensionalization of Attitudes Toward the Negro," Psychological Reports, 1962, 11. pp. 439ff.

Results and
Comments   The following intercorrelations were reported: Negro Stereotyping
and PDPQ (first person), .49; Negro Stereotyping and PDPQ (third
person), .40; Negro Stereotyping and Westie Prejudice Scale .58;
PDPQ (first person) and Westie Prejudice Scale, .80; PDPQ (third
person) and Westie Prejudice Scale, .61. The author's prediction
that the PDPQ and the Prejudice Scale would correlate better with
each other than either would with the Negro Stereotyping Scale was
upheld. The author concluded that it is helpful to think of prejudice
as being composed of two dimensions: the cognitive (objective facts
and beliefs), and the affective.

It is worth noting that the three measures used employed different
measurement techniques. Previous attempts to measure different
dimensions of prejudice may have resulted in spuriously high correlations between these dimensions caused by using the same measurement
techniques.

References   Getzels, J. and Walsh, J. J., "The Method of Paired Direct and Projective Questionnaires in the Study of Attitude Structure and
Socialization," Psychology Monographs, 1958, 72, #1, whole #454.

Westie, F. "A Technique for the Measurement of Race Attitudes,"
American Sociological Review, 1953, 18, pp. 73-78.

Sample Items   Negro doctor

    1. Unintelligent __ __ __ __ __ __ __ Intelligent

    2. Strong   __ __ __ __ __ __ __ Weak
            .
            .
            .
            .
    15. Bad   __ __ __ __ __ __ __ Good

Repeat same rating procedure for: white doctor, Negro bookkeeper,
white bookkeeper, Negro student, white student, Negro ditchdigger,
white ditchdigger

Westie and Getzels-Walsh measures are described in the following
scale write-ups.

PREJUDICE TOWARD NEGROES (Westie 1953)

Variable	Prejudice toward Negroes is measured by the summation of differences in responses to social distance scales which refer to Negroes and the whites in identical occupational positions.
Description	There are a total of four scales in this instrument. The <u>Residential Scale</u> measures the degree of residential proximity the respondent will permit the attitude object; the <u>Position Scale</u> measures the extent to which the respondent is willing to have the attitude object occupy positions of prestige and power in the community; the <u>Interpersonal-Physical Scale</u> measures the degree to which respondents are averse to physical association with the attitude object; the <u>Interpersonal Social Scale</u> measures the degree of proximity permitted the attitude object in interpersonal interaction.

The six-item scales were designed to measure social distance toward Negroes and toward whites in eight occupations (doctor, lawyer, big-business executive, banker, owner-manager of a small store, bookkeeper, machine generator, and ditch digger) and toward the average Negro man and the average white man. A five point response system was used, with responses scored 0 for no difference in response to a white and Negro in a particular occupation (e.g., the person who reacts the same way to a white lawyer and a Negro lawyer in a particular situation) to 4 for the maximum possible difference (e.g., the person who <u>strongly agrees</u> that he would be willing to have a white lawyer live across the street from him but who <u>strongly disagrees</u> to having a Negro lawyer live across the street). Scale scores for each of the four scales thus range from 0 to 24. Each item has equal weight.

Two panels of judges were used to eliminate ambiguous items and to rank the original universe of 161 items according to 11 categories of favorableness so that the final scale items selected would be fairly evenly distributed along the proximity-distance continuum. Using four scales of six items each and substituting the two races in combination with eight occupations into the items produced a total of 432 scale items.

Sample	The "judging" samples consisted of 36 advanced graduate students and faculty members in sociology and psychology at Ohio State University and of 149 undergraduate students in sociology classes at Ohio State. The reliability sample was 99 Indiana University undergraduate students.

A sample of 174 white male adults living in Indianapolis in blocks without Negro population was also used.

Reliability/ Homogeneity	Test-retest reliability coefficients for the four scales with time interval of five weeks were as follows: Residential, .95; Position, .95; Physical, .80; Interpersonal, .87. The reliability of all four scores combined was .96.

Westie in Bonjean et al. (1967) reports a later study which found a lower test-retest figure of .80, still a very respectable figure.

Items selected for the scale were those whose Q value (semi-inter-quartile range) were no larger than the average for all items on both panels, and whose differences in median placement by the two panels were no greater than 1.00. |
Validity	No evidence directly pertaining to validity was reported.
Location	Westie, F. R. "A Technique for the Measurement of Race Attitudes," American Sociological Review, 1953, 18, pp. 73-78.
Administration	Administration time was not reported.
Results and Comments	The author found evidence of a systematic relationship between socio-economic status and prejudice: the higher the socioeconomic status, the less the prejudice, "a finding which in general met acceptable standards of statistical significance".

Respondents were found to be most rigid on their responses in the areas of Interpersonal Physical Distance and Residential Distance, and least rigid regarding Position Distance and Interpersonal Social Distance. In general, social distance was least where both the Negro on the scale and the whites had high socioeconomic status and greatest where both Negro and white had low socioeconomic status. More detailed results of the author's study can be found in Westie (1952) and some sugges-tions for updating the scale are given by Westie in Bonjean et al. (1967), pp.160-162.

The author noted his concern with possible response set bias problems, which he attempted to obviate by means of "a rather elaborate schedule-assembly design" with random distribution among the subjects of questionnaires containing randomly distributed items. |
| References | Westie, F. R. "Negro-White Status Differentiates and Social Distance" American Sociological Review, 1952, 17, pp. 550-558.

Bonjean, C., Hill, R. and McLemore, S. Sociological Measurement. San Francisco: Chandler Publishing Co., 1967. |

NEGRO PREJUDICE SCALE

Residential Scale

I believe I would be willing to have a Negro (lawyer, doctor etc.) . . . .

   1. live in the same apartment building I live in

	Strongly Agree	Agree	Undecided	Disagree	Strongly Disagree

   2. live across the street from me
   3. live in my neighborhood
   4. live in my end of town
   5. live in my town
   6. live in my country

Positional Scale

I believe I would be willing to have a Negro (lawyer, doctor etc.) . . . .

   1. as president of the United States
   2. as U.S. Congressman from my district
   3. as a councilman on my city's council
   4. as head of the local community chest drive
   5. as a member of a Red Cross Committee in my town
   6. as a member of a national patriotic organization

Physical Scale

   1. use the same towel that I use
   2. swim in the same pool as I do
   3. have his hair cut by the same barber who cuts mine
   4. try on clothes at the store where I buy my clothes
   5. ride in a crowded elevator I am in
   6. use lending library books I also borrow

Interpersonal Scale

   1. as a close personal friend
   2. as a dinner guest in my home
   3. as a person I might often visit with
   4. as an acquaintance
   5. as someone I might say hello to
   6. as someone I might see on the street

PAIRED DIRECT AND PROJECTIVE QUESTIONNAIRES (PDPQ) (Getzels and Walsh 1958)

Variable
This instrument is an indirect measure of attitudes toward Negroes, using sentence-completion items.

Description
Methodologically, the PDPQ employs sentence-completion-type questions in direct (first person) and projective (third person) response format to the same objects of inquiry. Using the Negro as a "social conflicted object of inquiry", the authors predicted that there would be a sizeable discrepancy between projective and direct responses involving the expression of favorable or unfavorable attitudes toward the Negro. The 10 third-person incomplete sentences dealing with Negroes administered directly as an "intelligence test". The 10 first-person incomplete sentences were administered as part of a 40 item questionnaire of personal and social attitudes.

A subject's score on both the projective instrument and the direct instrument is the number of negative responses given to the "Negro items". A discrepancy score was provided by the proportion of negative responses to the projective instrument which were reversed on non-negative responses to the direct questionnaire.

Sample
Subjects were described as a class of 48 freshmen and sophomores in a women's college in New England.

Reliability/
Homogeneity
No inter-item or test-retest data on reliability are reported.

Interscorer reliability was checked by correlating the scores assigned 20 tests by original scores with these assigned by two independent scores; average interscorer reliability was .95 and the lowest was .91.

Validity
No data bearing directly on validity are reported.

Location
Getzels, J. W. and Walsh, J. J. "The Method of Paired Direct and Projective Questionnaires in the Study of Attitude Structure and Socialization'," Psychological Monographs, 1958, 72, p.454.

Administration
Estimated administration time for the two instruments is less than an hour apiece.

Results and
Comments
As predicted, responses that were positive on the projective test only rarely were changed to negative responses on the direct test, while negative responses on the projective test were frequently (72% of the cases) changed to positive responses on the direct test. Eight of the ten items yielded chi-square values for discrepancies of responses that were significant beyond the .01 level.

Also as predicted, the distribution of negative projective scores approximated normality (model score, 7), while the distribution of negative direct scores tended toward a J curve (modal score, 0).

Some of the <u>PDPQ</u> items were subsequently used by Wrightsman (1962) to tap the affective dimension of prejudice.

Reference   Wrightsman, L. "Dimensionalization of attitudes toward the Negro" <u>Psychological Reports</u>, 1962, <u>11</u>, p.439.

PAIRED DIRECT AND PROJECTIVE QUESTIONNAIRES
(Racial Questions Noted with an Asterisk *)

PROJECTIVE QUESTIONNAIRE
The Merrill-Brown Verbal Intelligence Test
FORM II F

This is a test of how fast you can think. Complete each of the following sentences so that it makes the best sense possible. You may use either a word or a phrase, although a phrase is preferable. Since you will have only a limited time, work quickly. In most cases the best way to answer the test is to put down the first thing that comes to your mind.

Example:
The unfinished sentence: "When Ann scored the goal, she . . . . " may be finished by adding "felt good" or "won the game" or "told her friend" or "wanted to score another" or something like that.

The score you get depends on how quickly you finish the sentences. Work Fast. Do Not Skip Any Sentences.

THIS IS A SPEED TEST. WORK FAST. DO NOT SKIP ANY SENTENCES.

1. The thing Mary liked to do best in her spare time was . . . .

2. After Florence finished talking she thought that she . . . .

3. Barbara thinks most politicans are . . . .

4. When Joan thought the job was too much for her, she . . . .

5. What Dot disliked most about her family was . . . .

*6. When Alice saw Negroes moving in next door, she . . . .

7. When they asked Elizabeth to be in charge, she. . . . .

8. Ruth sometimes thought her father was . . . .

9. When Marge heard she would have to join a union in her new job, she . . . .

10. Kate often thinks of herself as a . . . .

11. When Anne's new friend said she was against God, Anne . . . .

*12. When they put a Negro forelady over her, Enda . . . .

13. The reason Lillian tried to get ahead was . . . .

14. Nancy believes most people think of her as . . . .

15. When they tried to get Margaret to be like her mother, she . . . .

16. When Janet had something to say and others were around, she. . . . .

*17. When Jane saw the doctor they were trying to give her was a Negro she. . . .

18. According to Irene, if a person remains poor it is because . . . .

19. When they asked Louise what nations the U.S. could trust, she said . . . . .

20. Like most girls, Betty sometimes thinks her family is . . . .

21. Most jobs with responsibility made Nora feel . . . .

22. From past experience, Gail felt most people were . . . .

*23. When Jean saw her younger sister dancing with a Negro, she . . . .

24. When Connie was asked whether she could ever see herself voting Socialist, she said . . . .

25. Above all else, Mary wished her father were . . . .

26. When the man running for mayor admitted he did not believe in God, Joan decided . . . .

27. After Madeleine finished the test she thought that she . . . .

28. If Ruth's mother could change things she would try to . . . .

29. When Alice saw others doing better than she, Alice. . . . .

*30. When Janice discovered the school she was planning to enter was half Negro, she . . . .

31. Jane feels most people who meet her for the first time think she is . . . .

32. Betty thinks the things that make a person work hardest are . . . .

33. Dorothy believed most labor leaders are . . . .

34. As between mother's and father's ways Liz usually chose. . . . .

*35. When her favorite beauty shop began being used by Negroes, Barbara . . . . .

36. Lillian feels most persons hold high public office are . . . .

37. Rosalind sometimes thought her father . . . .

38. Edith often felt like . . . .

39. When told she would have to do the whole thing by herself, Ruth . . . .

40. Peggy feels most people don't reach their goals because of . . . .

*41. When Negroes began being admitted to the club, Ethel decided. . . . .

42. Joan believes her family thinks she is . . . .

43. If Marge had any children, the one thing she would surely do for them is . . . .

44. When Nan thought the odds were against her, she . . . .

45. Dot would do anything in order to be . . . .

*46. When the boss began hiring many Negroes, Evelyn . . . .

47. Estelle's feeling about most labor unions was that they . . . .

48. If Jean's father could change, Jean would want him to be . . . .

49. Mary believes most Russians want . . . .

50. From past experience, no matter what others thought, Peg herself knew that she . . . .

*51. When they put a Negro to work next to her, Gail decided . . . .

52. Working with others all the time made Jane . . . .

53. When she was asked her opinion of public ownership, Kate said . . . .

54. Joan's fondest ambition was to become a . . . .

55. Every time they didn't invite Betty to the party, she . . . .

*56. When Edith saw a Negro and a white involved in the accident, she naturally blamed the . . . .

57. When she found out the candidate belonged to a different religion, Ruth decided. . . . .

58. Before the game started Alice felt her side would . . . .

59. If there is one group in the U.S. that can't be trusted, Isobel thought it was . . . .

<u>DIRECT QUESTIONNAIRE</u>

THE PERSONAL AND SOCIAL ATTITUDES RECORD
For the Use of Schools, Colleges and Records Offices
FORM III M-F

    The office would like to have in its files a record of your personal and social attitudes--that is, your attitudes toward politics, responsibility, parents, minority groups, race prejudice, etc.
    Complete each of the statements by writing in what best applies in your case.
    Consider each statement carefully. There is no time limit. What you write in will represent the record of your personal and social attitudes.

DO NOT SKIP ANY SENTENCES.

1.   When I think the job is too much for me, I tend to . . . .

2.   I think most politicians are . . . .

3.   If I heard I would have to join a union in a new job, I would . . . .

*4. If I saw Negroes moving in next door, I would . . . .

5.   When I am asked to be in charge, I generally tend to . . . .

6.   The reason I try to get ahead is that I want to . . . .

*7. If I saw the doctor they were trying to give me was a Negro, I would . . . . .

8.   Most jobs with responsibility make me feel . . . .

9.   If I have something to say and others are around, I . . . .

*10. If I saw my younger sister dancing with a Negro, I would--(If you don't have a younger sister, answer as if you did.) . . . .

11. If I were asked whether I could ever see myself voting Socialist, I would say . . . .

12. After I finish a test I usually think that I have . . . .

13. If the man running for mayor admitted he did not believe in God, I would decide . . . .

14. I believe most people think of me as . . . .

15. I believe most labor leaders are . . . .

*16. If I discovered the school I was planning to enter was half Negro, I would . . . .

17. As between mother's and father's ways, I choose . . . .

18. According to me, if a person remains poor it is because . . . .

*19. If the boss began hiring many Negroes, I would . . . .

20. If I had any children, the one thing I would surely do for them is . . . .

21. I often feel like . . . .

22. When I am asked my opinion of public ownership, I say . . . .

*23. If I see a Negro and a white involved in an accident, I naturally blame the . . . .

24. When I see others doing better than I, I . . . .

25. Every time they don't invite me to the party, I tend . . . .

26. If I found out the candidate belongs to a different religion, I would decide . . . .

*27. If they put a Negro to work next to me, I would . . . .

28. Working with others all the time makes me . . . .

29. From past experience, I feel most people are . . . .

30. I feel most persons holding high public office are . . . .

31. When I am told I have to do the whole thing by myself . . . .

32. My feeling about most labor unions is that they are . . . .

*33. If my favorite beauty shop began being used by Negroes, I would . . . . . .

34. If they tried to get me to be like Mother, I would . . . .

35. If a new friend of mine said she was against God, I would . . . .

*36. If they put a Negro forelady over me, I would . . . .

37. When I think the odds are against me, I tend to . . . .

38. I often think of myself as . . . .

*39. If Negroes began being admitted to the club, I would decide . . . .

40. I sometimes think my father is . . . .

ATTITUDE TOWARD THE NEGRO (Hinckley 1932)

Variable — This scale is intended to measure both feelings of Negro racial inferiority and attitudes on civil rights for the Negro.

Description — This Thurstone scale is one of the earliest scales of attitude toward Negroes and consequently is the most widely used. Of the two parallel forms of the scale that were developed, only the first is reproduced here. As is usual with Thurstone scales, respondents need only express agreement or disagreement with the items, which have been assigned scale values by judgments of experts. The respondent's score is the average scale value of those items with which he agrees. The higher the scale value the more favorable the attitude toward Negroes. The lowest scale value is 0.0, the highest 10.6.

Sample — About 900 college students (both Negro and white) served as the original respondents.

Reliability/
Homogeneity — The parallel-forms reliability of the two forms of the scale has been found to vary between .62 and .78. Thurstone Q-values for all items were between 1.8 and 4.0.

Validity — The scale has been found to discriminate satisfactorily between Southern and Northern college students. High correlations between the scale and measures of prejudice and anti-Negro behavior are reported in Shaw and Wright (1967).

Location — Hinckley, E. "The Influence of Individual Opinion on Construction of an Attitude Scale," Journal of Social Psychology, 1932, 3, pp.283-296.

The scale is copyrighted by the Journal Press, Provincetown, Mass.

Administration — One form of the scale should be able to be administered in less than 10 minutes. The second form of this scale can be found in Shaw and Wright (1967).

Results and
Comments — As might be expected with a 35-year-old scale, some of the items are outdated; the wording of the items is also replete with highly sophisticated terms. A comprehensive bibliography on the use of this scale as well as attempts to update it can be found in the Shaw-Wright reference. A very important reference omitted by these authors is Hovland and Sherif (1952), in which is described the principle of assimilation-contrast. According to this principle, the judge's own attitude severely affects the scale value he gives to items in the Thurstone procedure. For example, both pro-Negro and Negro judges see items judged as "neutral" by neutral judges as highly unfavorable to Negroes.

References — Shaw, M. and Wright, J., Scales for the Measurement of Attitudes. New York: McGraw-Hill, 1967.

Hovland, C. and Sherif, M. "Judgmental Phenomena and Scales of Attitude Measurement: Item Displacement in Thurstone Scales", Journal of Abnormal and Social Psychology, 1952, 47, pp.822-832.

ATTITUDE TOWARD THE NEGRO

(Thurstone scale values are given following each item in parentheses.
The items below comprise Form A of the scale. A parallel form B can
be found in the Shaw and Wright volume.)

Please indicate your own attitude by a check mark when you agree and
by a cross when you disagree.

1. The difference between the black and white races is not one of
   mere degree, but of kind.   (4.9)

2. The educated Negro is less of a burden on the courts and is less
   likely to become a dependent or a defective than the educated
   white man.   (8.9)

3. No Negro should hold an office of trust, honor, or profit. (2.3)

4. The Negro should not be simply the doormat of American civilization.   (7.2)

5. I place the Negro on the same social basis as I would a mule.
                                                                (0.0)

6. The Negro should be given the same educational advantages as the
   white man.   (9.6)

7. I am not at all interested in how the Negro rates socially.(5.7)

8. Inherently, the Negro and the white man are equal.   (10.3)

9. The inability of the Negroes to develop outstanding leaders
   dooms them to a low level in society.   (3.5)

10. No Negro has the slightest right to resent, or even question the
    illegal killing of one of his race.   (1.1)

11. After you have educated the Negro to the level of the white man,
    there will still be an impassable gulf between them.   (4.2)

12. The Negro is fully capable of social equality with the white man,
    but he should not be so recognized until he is better trained.
                                                                (8.3)

13. The Negro is by no means fit for social equality with the common-
    est white people.   (1.8)

14. I would not patronize a hotel that accommodates Negroes.   (2.9)

15. It is possible for the white and Negro races to be brothers in
    Christ without becoming brothers-in-law.   (6.6)

16. The Negro should have the advantage of all social benefits of the
    white man but be limited to his own race in the practice thereof.
                                                                (7.7)

CHAPTER 7: INTERNATIONAL AFFAIRS

The measures in this section deal with general attitudes toward various foreign policy goals and with a corresponding cosmopolitan or parochial view of foreign affairs. Those measures which focus on war attitudes or which have overtones of hostility or patriotism are considered in the next section. However, in some cases, the distinctions in the subject matter of various scales are not clear in this regard, necessitating somewhat arbitrary placement into either this chapter or the next one.

The scales presented in this section are again placed in rough order according to our estimate of their merit and utility. They are:

1) Foreign Policy Goals and Personal Values (Scott 1960)
2) Isolationism Scale (McClosky 1967)
3) Internationalism Scale (Campbell et al. 1960)
4) Interpretations of Government Policy Scale (Wrightsman 1963)
5) World-Minded Attitudes (Sampson and Smith 1957)
6) Internationalism-Nationalism (IN) Scale (Levinson 1951)
7) Attitude toward U. S. and Russian Actions (Oskamp and Hartry 1965)
8) Problems and Goals of the U. S. Government (Hefner and Robinson 1964)
9) Criteria for Foreign Aid (Hefner and Robinson 1964)
10) Internationalism (Lutzker 1960)
11) Attitude toward World Affairs (Shimberg 1949)
12) Pro-Russia Error-Choice Test (Hammond 1948)

The first instrument by Scott included scales of eight distinct goals in foreign policy, such as pacifism, humanitarianism, and independence. The author also constructed eight scales of personal values which correspond to each of these foreign policy goals. The intent of the research design was to examine the extent to which foreign policy goals and personal values were interrelated. Only one of the pairings failed to intercorrelate significantly. The average correlation for the pairs of scales was moderate in value--approximately .28. While this fact does not constitute a strong case for validity, the scales do have more than adequate internal consistency and can be controlled statistically for response set. The scales have only been applied to a college student population from which it was found that foreign policy goals seemed to form two clusters of competitive and cooperative behavior. Attempts to link interpersonal and international attitudes have also been made by Grace and Christiansen; since their measures are concerned specifically with hostility, they will be reviewed in the next Chapter.

Another study by McClosky applied an _Isolationism Scale_ both to a national cross-sectional sample and to a sample of delegates to the 1956 Republican and Democratic conventions. The author's claims of reliability and validity of the measure seem more than satisfactory, although he does not present any quantitative estimates of these two criteria. Nevertheless, McClosky shows that the scale has predictable relationships with an amazing variety of attitudinal, personality, and background factors. An interesting empirical distinction is made between "pacifist" and "jingoist" isolationists. The results are shown to hold when controlled for agreement response set, although many of the scale items would seem to require a sophistication beyond the capability of the average citizen.

The _Internationalism Scale_ of the Survey Research Center was also applied to a national cross-sectional sample of the electorate. Consisting of four items, it shows adequate but not impressive homogeneity and test-retest reliability. The relatively low coefficients may be more a reflection of the amorphous nature of the general public's attitudes on international affairs than of the complexity or lack of quality of the items themselves. The most interesting characteristic of this scale is its correlation with other political attitudes and behavior. Those showing an internationalist orientation and mood tended to be involved in the political process and informed on political matters.

The scale by Wrightsman focuses on the respondent's interpretation of governmental foreign policy along a "soft-headed/hard-headed" dimension. The items require some sophistication on the part of the respondents, but could probably be administered to non-college samples as well. Since the items are in forced-choice format, they are not subject to agreement response set. The scale's basic validity has yet to be supported by empirical evidence.

Unlike most of the above scales, Sampson and Smith's World-Minded Attitude Scale is one that appears quite often in the literature. This Likert-type scale has noteworthy split-half and test-retest reliability values and more than adequate evidence of validity. The items are relatively simple and straightforward and are phrased both positively and negatively to reduce (and possibly control for) the possibility of agreement-response set. In reservation, it should be noted that the scale has only been used on populations of college students.

Levinson's Internationalism-Nationalism Scale was developed in conjunction with the measures designed to examine "the authoritarian personality." In line with this study's theoretical framework, internationalist-oriented attitudes were found to be negatively associated with the main characteristics of "the authoritarian personality"--traditional family orientation, religious traditionalism, religious conventionalism, and political-economic conservatism. No further evidence of validity was reported. Split-half and test-retest reliability coefficients were quite high. Item wording is somewhat complex and might make the scale difficult to administer outside of the college setting which has been its only focus to date. Three of the twelve scale items are reversed, assuring some control over agreement response set.

The study by Oskamp and Hartry probed attitudes toward actions of the United States and Russia in foreign policy. Scale results revealed the existence

of a double standard in people's attitudes--a given set of actions and policies
was approved when the U.S. used them but condemned when the Russian government
did so. This anomaly was especially marked in attitudes toward hostile
international actions, the major factor of the fifty diplomatic actions listed
by the authors. The differences in attitude uncovered by these items was
generally quite impressive. More information should be gathered on the basic
validity and reliability of this scale. Since the scale was administered
only to college students, considerable rewording of items would probably be
warranted if the sampling base was extended to mass populations.

The next two measures are somewhat different than the earlier ones.
Hefner and Robinson have asked members of a Detroit sample to respond to and
rank order various sets of problems, goals, and other criteria pertaining to
foreign policy and, in particular, foreign aid decisions of the American
government. Although analysis work has not yet been completed, some interesting
preliminary findings can be stated. Analysis of one of the measures shows
that people tend to rank domestic issues and problems higher in importance
than foreign-oriented ones, although the better-educated reveal more of a
tendency to react in the opposite fashion. The other measure demonstrates that
though people are generally in favor of the foreign aid program they do have
definite criteria in mind for how the funds are to be dispensed. The amount of
aid a country receives is perceived as being influenced most by how carefully
and judiciously it will use the funds and whether it has a strong internal
Communist movement which could threaten the existing government. Since
both of these measures involved self-ranking by respondents, no standard
reliability and homogeneity indices are applicable. Test-retest figures
have yet to be calculated, and no attempt has been made to establish the
validity of these scales. The items are probably too complicated to expect

replies of high validity or reliability to be manifested by cross-sectional samples.

Another aspect of this study and probably the most important was the probing of respondents' judgments of the similarity of various countries in the world (see Robinson and Hefner 1967). Respondents were told to use their own criteria in making judgments of similarity and to choose which three of sixteen countries were "most similar" to one particular country. The same task was repeated for each of the seventeen countries used in the study. Multidimensional analysis of the similarity judgments produced "mappings" of the countries in relation to each other. The two most important dimensions which emerged from the separate judgment mappings of the general public (the Detroit sample mentioned earlier), and in Figure 2, judgments of 150 academic experts in international relations from the University of Michigan. It can be seen that the political distinction between capitalist and communist countries was the primary dimension for the public sample, while economic development was more critical for academic experts. These interpretations were validated against respondent ratings of important factors and against multiple regression analysis of ratings of country characteristics. As of now, use of these data seems valid for group analysis but not for individual analyses. The four main factors in order of apparent importance for the two sample groups are as follows:

Public	Academic
Communism	Development
Development	Culture (Spanish influence)
Culture (Spanish influence)	Communism
Culture (Europe vs. Asia)	Culture (Africa vs. Asia)

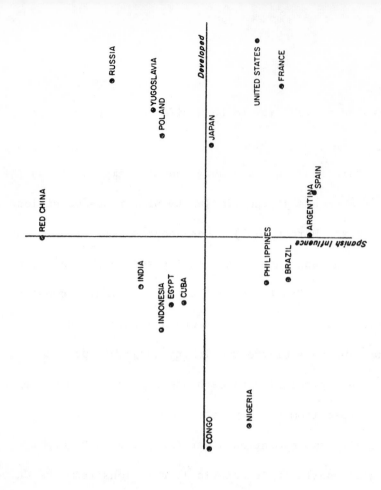

FIGURE 2

COUNTRY POSITIONS (FOR FIRST TWO DIMENSIONS)
DETERMINED BY SMALLEST SPACE ANALYSIS: ACADEMIC SAMPLE

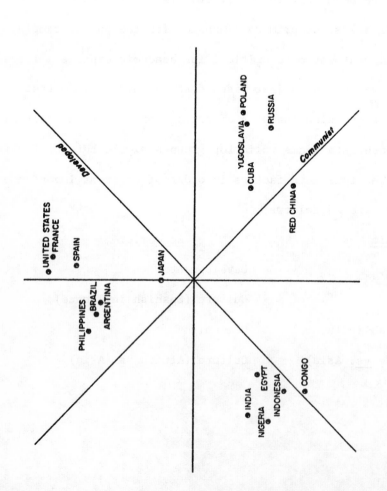

FIGURE 1

COUNTRY POSITIONS (FOR FIRST TWO DIMENSIONS)
DETERMINED BY SMALLEST SPACE ANALYSIS: PUBLIC SAMPLE

These results highlight the nature of the large differences between public and academic descriptions of the world and interpretations of the aims of our country's foreign policy. Using additional data, Robinson and Hefner (1968) found that students at the University of Michigan who shared the academic perceptions of the world were more opposed to the Vietnam War and more likely to feel that the United States was "too hard" in its relations with Communist countries than were students who shared the public's view of the world.

Of the remaining three scales in this section, Lutzker used a large number of Likert-type questions to delineate a possible internationalist dimension. He found intriguing evidence for the validity of his scale in a mock "prisoner's dilemma" game which stressed the alternatives of cooperative or competitive behavior. Internationalist-oriented respondents were found to be more cooperative than isolationist-oriented respondents. Unfortunately, available references did not contain even sample items so that we are unable to reproduce them here. Also, evidence of reliability and validity were not included in the published reports.

Shimberg's set of items on Attitudes toward World Affairs was administered to a large sample of high school students. Both information and opinion items were used in the study, but only the former were included in the scale construction. Well-informed students were found to be more optimistic, more cosmopolitan, and more in favor of private enterprise. Information on reliability and validity was not reported in the study. Most of the items also appear to be quite dated.

The last scale in this section, Hammond's error-choice test of Attitudes toward Russia, also suffers from the problem of datedness. However, as mentioned in an earlier section, the "error-choice" method is of interest

because of its particular approach to the measurement of attitudes. The
method has been successful in separating criterion groups on a number of
attitude issues and the Attitudes toward Russia Scale was no exception to
this established pattern. The scale, however, has only been administered
to limited samples.

For the reader interested in pursuing the topic of international
relations measures still further, an interesting summary of research findings in the area is presented by Atkinson (1967).

References:

Atkinson, T. A Propositional Inventory of Empirical Work Involving Foreign
 Affairs and National Security Attitudes, 1960-1966: A Non-Evaluative
 Review. Oak Ridge, Tennessee: Oak Ridge National Laboratory, Oct.
 1967 (ORNL-TM-2028).

Robinson, J. and Hefner, R. "Multidimensional Differences in Public and
 Academic Perceptions of Countries," Journal of Personality and Social
 Psychology, I, pp. 251-259.

Robinson, J. and Hefner, R. "Perceptual Maps of the World," Public Opinion
 Quarterly, Summer 1968, 32, pp.273-280.

FOREIGN POLICY GOALS AND PERSONAL VALUES (Scott 1960)

Variable	This instrument attempts to assess the amount of correlation between conceptions of ideal relations among people and corresponding conceptions of ideal relations among nations.
Description	Eight different possible goals of United States foreign policy are represented by scales which assess the degree to which subjects advocate each goal by presenting response choices of: "should be a goal," "should not be a goal," or "depends on the situation." The ideals for interpersonal relations are embodied in corresponding rates of "personal values."

There were 38 foreign policy items and 41 personal value items. All items were scored dichotomously with neutral and negative responses not distinguished. Items as listed below are arranged approximately in order of cumulative difficulty (or unpopularity), from easy to hard (or popular to unpopular).

Sample	The sample population was comprised of 218 subjects from a large state university, representing 90 percent of a random sample.
Reliability/ Homogeneity	Scale reliabilities were estimated from Kuder-Richardson Formula 20; the mean reliability for foreign policy goals was about .56 (for personal value scales it was about .61). The author remarks that the shortness of the scales produced reliabilities too low to be sensitive to individual differences but sufficient to generate the predicted correlations between paired scales. Average inter-item phi correlation over all international scales was .23, varying between .15 for pacifism and .42 for religiousness (for personal values the average phi was .24). Average Loevinger value for these scales was .40, varying between .30 for pacifism and .58 for religiousness (average for personal values was .37).
Validity	No direct tests for validity are reported.
Location	Scott, William A. "International Ideology and Interpersonal Ideology," Public Opinion Quarterly, Vol. 24 (Fall, 1960), pp. 419-435.
Administration	Administration time for the questionnaire was 45 minutes. All items were scored dichotomously, with checks in the second and third columns (either the "depends" or negative response) not distinguished.
Results and Comments	Mean correlations between corresponding personal values and advocated international goals was .28, varying between .09 for independence and .68 for religiousness. To attempt to eliminate response set contamination, the author compared correlations between corresponding pairs of value goals to correlations between noncorresponding pairs. It was found that for six of the predicted value-goal pairs the predicted correlations were significantly larger than the nonpredicted ones. The two value-goal pairs for which this relationship did not hold were humanitarianism and independence.

Foreign policy goals intercorrelations showed two major clusters which the author called the ideologies of "international cooperation" and "international competitiveness." The author concluded that these clusters did not agree very closely with clusters of correlation among the personal values--so that the general international ideologies did not reflect directly the ideologies of interpersonal relations. However, inspection of Scott's intercorrelation matrix of personal values indicates self-control, kindness, social skills, religiousness, and loyalty did form a reasonably stable cluster that might reflect the cooperative dimension that Scott found for the foreign policy goals. Only further research can show whether this conjecture is valid.

The question inevitably must arise of whether the personal values and policy goals are really comparable; the data for some scale pairings (especially intellectualism-cultural development and loyalty-nationalism) does call the assumption of comparability into question.

Initial pairings of international goals and personal values depended on the author's judgment. He remarks that relationships could not be artificially inflated by errors in judgment because of the separate development of the instruments for each of the values and goals.

The scales are well-constructed and reflect a sophistication in and concern with methodology unfortunately lacking in most social science instruments and research.

Two sets of measures by Grace and Christiansen also have dealt with the relation between international and interpersonal attitudes, but since they are concerned mainly with hostility, they are described in the next section.

SCALES OF FOREIGN POLICY GOALS
AND
SCALES OF PERSONAL VALUES

Introduction to Foreign Policy Statements:

Following is a list of statements that have been made on the subject of what should be the goals of U.S. foreign policy. You may find some of them agreeable, some not. Please put a check in the appropriate column, according to whether you think it should be a goal of U.S. foreign policy, should not be a goal, or depends on the situation whether or not it should be a goal of U.S. foreign policy.

Should
Be a Goal   Depends   Should Not
Be a Goal

_____   _____   _____

Introduction to Personal Value Statements:

Please read over the following statements, and for each one indicate (by a check in the appropriate space) whether it is something you always admire in other people, or something you always dislike, or something that depends on the situation whether you admire it or not.

Always   Depends on   Always
admire   situation   Dislike

_____   _____   _____

(Foreign policy items were administered first, in the order indicated by the IBM card column numbers listed below. Then, after some intervening questions, the personal value items appeared, in the order indicated. Here the corresponding scales appear together and, within each, items are arranged approximately in order of difficulty, from easy to hard. All items were scored dichotomously, with checks in the second and third columns not distinguished.)

IBM
Column   Item

1. a. Self-control (Personal Value)
        41   Practicing self-control.
        26   Always being patient with people.
        60   Replying to anger with gentleness.
        33   Never losing one's temper, no matter what the reason.
        79   Not expressing anger, even when you have a reason for doing so.
    b. Pacifism (Foreign Policy)
        35   Avoiding hasty, intemperate acts toward other nations.
        38   Not letting other nations goad us into war.
        68   Aiming at complete disarmament of all nations, including our own.
        72   Promising not to use the most destructive weapons, like the hydrogen bomb, in wars.

IBM
Column   Item

2. a. Intellectualism (Personal Value)
    62 Having a keen interest in international, national, and local affairs.
    18 Having a strong intellectual curiosity.
    36 Developing an appreciation of the fine arts--music, drama, literature, and ballet.
    75 Having an active interest in all things scholarly.
    67 Being an intellectual.
  b. Cultural Development (Foreign Policy)
    27 Working to raise the level of education all over the world.
    30 Trying to encourage world-wide cultural development.
    63 Putting our emphasis on basic research, to increase man's understanding of the universe.
    51 Concentrating on cultural achievement, rather than putting so much into national defense.

3. a. Kindness to People (Personal Value)
    45 Being kind to people, even if they do things contrary to one's beliefs.
    63 Helping another person feel more secure, even if you don't like him.
    68 Helping another achieve his own goals, even if it might interfere with your own.
    54 Turning the other cheek, and forgiving others when they harm you.
  b. Humanitarianism (Foreign Policy)
    77 Helping underdeveloped countries to advance.
    44 Working to rehabilitate conquered nations after a war.
    60 Extending a helping hand to all countries that are friendly toward us.
    50 Helping to improve living conditions in nations, even if they are against us.
    32 Going out of our way to lend a helping hand to all countries.
    53 Trying to raise the status of other nations, even though it hurts our own position.

4. a. Social Skills (Personal Value)
    46 Being well mannered and behaving properly in social situations.
    64 Dressing and acting in a way that is appropriate to the occasion.
    69 Being able to get people to cooperate with you.
    20 Being able to get along with all kinds of people, whether or not they are worthwhile.
    38 Being poised, gracious, and charming under all circumstances.
    42 Being the person in the house who is the most popular with the opposite sex.
  b. Coexistence (Foreign Policy)
    62 Adopting a policy of peaceful coexistence toward all nations.
    55 Trying to get other nations to like us.
    66 Trying to be friendly toward all countries, even if we don't like their policies
    74 Being as friendly toward our enemies as we are toward our allies.

```
IBM
Column                 Item
```

5. a. Religiousness (Personal Value)
- 25 Being devout in one's religious faith.
- 50 Always living one's religion in his daily life.
- 32 Always attending church regularly and faithfully.
- 74 Avoiding the physical pleasures that are prohibited in the Bible.
- 59 Encouraging others to attend church and lead religious lives.

    b. Religiousness (Foreign Policy)
- 28 Abiding by the laws of God in our dealings with other nations.
- 40 Praying for divine guidance in our international policies.
- 58 Opening international conferences with a prayer for their successful outcome.
- 52 Showing our devotion to religious principles in the conduct of foreign affairs.
- 67 Teaching all nations to follow religious principles.
- 73 Seeking in the Bible for direction of our foreign policies.

6. a. Independence (Personal Value)
- 27 (Reverse) Conforming to the requirements of any situation and doing what is expected of one.
- 35 Being outspoken and frank in expressing one's likes and dislikes.
- 44 Thinking and acting freely, without social restraints, and encouraging others to do likewise.
- 61 Being independent, original, nonconformist, different from other people.
- 28 (Reverse) Working and living in harmony with other people.

    b. Independence (Foreign Policy)
- 45 Doing what we know is right, even if others object.
- 75 Doing what we feel is right, in world affairs, regardless of what others think.
- 42 Taking care of our own problems, without depending on others.
- 48 Staying neutral in fights between other nations.

7. a. Status (Personal Value)
- 23 Being respected by people who are themselves worthwhile.
- 57 Showing great leadership qualities.
- 40 Having the ability to lead others.
- 76 Gaining recognition for one's achievements.
- 49. Being in a position to direct and mold others' lives.

    b. Power (Foreign Policy)
- 65 Developing our leadership potential in this country, so that other nations will want to follow us.
- 43 Striving to maintain this country's position of power among nations.
- 70 Being able to get other nations to cooperate with our foreign policies.
- 34 Keeping the United States the leader of the world.
- 57 Trying to get other nations to imitate our way of life.

IBM
Column   Item

8. a. Loyalty (Personal Value)

21 Defending the honor of one's house whenever it is unfairly criticized.

70 Working hard to improve the prestige and status of one's group.

34 Helping organize group activities.

55 Doing all one can to build up the prestige of the organization.

47 Treating an attack on one's group like an attack on oneself.

51 Concealing most of one's dislikes or disagreements with fellow members of the organization.

b. Nationalism (Foreign Policy)

61 Working to advance our national interests in world affairs.

59 Doing all we can to build up the international prestige of the United States.

71 Considering ourselves as Americans first, internationalists second.

31 Putting the interests of this nation first in all international negotiations.

37 Treating any slanderous attack on our institutions as a threat to the country.

ISOLATIONISM SCALE (McClosky 1967)

Variable	This scale measures isolationism, "a sense of disengagement from other nations, accompanied often by the conviction that American interests differ from and are incompatible with those of the rest of the world."
Description	There are a total of nine items (empirically reduced from a larger number of items) in the scale, which are apparently given in agree-disagree format. An agree response to each item adds one point to the person's degree of isolationism. Those scoring 0-2 are categorized as nonisolationists, 3-5 as middle isolationists and 6-9 as isolationists.

Average scores on the scale for various groups in this study (broken down on a measure of their degree of articulateness) were as follows:

Articulateness	Democratic Leaders	Republican Leaders	Democratic Followers	Republican Followers
High	1.9	3.0	2.5	2.7
Medium	3.5	4.6	4.5	4.6
Low	5.2	6.1	5.9	5.9

Sample	The sample was interviewed in the middle and late 1950's and consisted of:

a) A national cross-section of 1484 Americans interviewed by the Gallup Poll (AIPO).
b) A total of 3020 Democratic and Republican party leaders (all delegates and alternates to the 1956 national conventions) interviewed by mail.

In addition the scale was applied to a cross-section of 1082 residents of Minnesota.

Reliability/ Homogeneity	The author claims that the scales met established tests of reliability (modified Guttman reproducibility), although he presents no quantitative estimates nor test-retest data.
Validity	The author claims that, while no data on criterion group validity were collected, the scale satisfied construct validity evaluation in that theoretical expectations confirmed to actual results (see below). The items met face validity assessments of experts and were based on sentiments expressed by active isolationist groups.

Isolationism scores were found to correlate positively with measures of the following:

1) General Personality Traits: Misanthropy, authoritarianism, distrust of people, ethnocentrism, political cynicism, dissatisfaction with self and manifest anxiety.

2) <u>Social Orientation</u>: Alienation, lack of organizational participation, lack of efficacy, lack of political activism.

3) <u>Indices of Lack of Information</u>: Educational level, information level and political awareness.

4) <u>Foreign Issue Opinions</u>: Domestic conservatism, low defense spending, low foreign aid spending, anti-UN feelings and belligerency.

5) <u>Cognitive Orientation</u>: Intolerance of ambiguity, rigidity, simplicity, extremity.

Location   McClosky, H. "Personality and Attitude Correlates of Foreign Policy Orientation," in J. Rosenau (ed.), <u>Domestic Sources of Foreign Policy</u>. New York: The Free Press, 1967.

Results and Comments   The author concludes that "isolationism is a complex attitude that can be arrived at by different routes and understood in different ways." The general results summarized under validity held when the scale was corrected for agreement response set. Expected differences between Democrats and Republicans held for the party leaders but not the rank and file.

The author also shows some interesting differences between "pacifist" isolationists and "jingoist" isolationists.

ISOLATIONISM SCALE

The best market for American goods is right here at home.

    Agree   Disagree   Don't know

We almost have to restrict the amount of goods we let into this country because labor is so cheap in most other nations.

Most of the countries which have gotten economic help from America end up resenting what we have done for them.

These foreign wars America has been in are just part of the old quarrels Europeans have been having among themselves for centuries.

The federal government should be prevented from giving away any more of our wealth to foreign governments.

In spite of all the claims to the contrary, America can defend herself, as she has always done, without the aid of our so-called allies.

George Washington's advice to stay out of agreements with foreign powers is just as wise now as it was when he was alive.

By belonging to the UN we are running the danger of losing our constitutional right to control our own affairs.

Anytime American boys are found fighting on foreign shores, it is doubtful that the war is one that the United States should really be in.

INTERNATIONALISM SCALE (Campbell et al. 1960)

Variable

This scale attempts to rank persons along an attitude continuum on the desirable degree of United States intervention in international affairs.

Description

Out of six foreign issue questions included in SRC's 1956 voting study interview schedule, four were found to form a Guttman scale, meeting the criteria described in Campbell (1954). The items are five-point Likert type. Assigned scores run from 1 to 5, from isolationist to internationalist, and unique scale scores run from 00 to 15. The items are reproduced here in order from the "easiest" to the "hardest" in terms of a cumulative scale.

Sample

The sample population was a representative national sample of citizens of voting age living in private households. The number of pre-election respondents was 1929; only 1286 could be adequately represented on the scale.

Reliability/
Homogeneity

The scale had a Plus Percentage Ratio of .79, indicating satisfactory unidimensionality in the Guttman sense. Test-retest correlations on individual items over a two-year period were between .30 and .40. Average inter-item correlation was .22.

Validity

No direct test of validity is available.

Location

Campbell, Angus, Converse, Philip E., Miller, Warren E., Stokes, Donald E. The American Voter. New York: John Wiley & Sons, 1960, pp. 194-208.

Administration

The scale could be administered as a paper and pencil test, in which case estimated administration time is under four minutes.

Results and
Comments

The authors found no relationship between scale positions of individuals on the domestic and foreign attitude dimensions, or between the Internationalism Scale and party identification. A high score on the Internationalism Scale was correlated with political involvement, issue familiarity, and with high political efficacy. With involvement controlled, there was no systematic variation in position on the scale as a function of education. But the authors found that only one fifth of the respondents were ideologically consistent in this area to the extent of simultaneously supporting aid to poorer countries and believing taxes ought not to be cut.

References

Campbell, A., Gurin, G. and Miller, W. E. The Voter Decides. Evanston, Ill.: Row, Peterson and Co., 1954.

Key, V. O., Jr. Public Opinion and American Democracy. New York: Alfred Knopf, 1961, p. 562.

INTERNATIONALISM SCALE

1. This country would be better off if we just stayed home and did not concern ourself with problems in other parts of the world.

   Strongly Agree   Agree   Can't Decide   Disagree   Strongly Disagree

2. The United States should give economic help to the poorer countries of the world even if they can't pay for it.

3. The United States should keep soldiers overseas where they can help countries that are against Communism.

4. The United States should give help to foreign countries even if they are not as much against Communism as we are.

INTERPRETATIONS OF GOVERNMENT POLICY SCALE (Wrightsman 1963)

Variable
To categorize interpretations of the government's motives, the author suggests the "soft-headed" vs. "hard-headed" dimension. The "soft-headed" person is defined as an idealist who sees our country as ethical and unselfish with its actions influenced more by moral principles than by expediency. The "hard-headed" person is defined as a cold realist who sees the government as basically selfish and power oriented, and who is both cynical about motives behind foreign aid and "almost paranoid" in his perception of the Russians as a constant threat.

Description
The final form of the scale consists of 10 of 16 original statements of United States' policies, each with a "soft-headed" and a "hard-headed" interpretation of the reasons behind the policy. Subjects were instructed to choose the reason they thought was nearer the real reasons for the government's policy. Order of choices was randomly varied to control for response set. "Soft-headed" responses were scored as one point; "hard-headed" responses and omissions as no points, making the possible range of scores 0-10. Mean scores were 4.0 for males and 4.5 for females.

Sample
The item analysis sample was composed of 101 male and 92 female college students at three colleges in the South and Midwest.

Reliability/
Homogeneity
The split-half reliability (corrected) of the 10 item scale was reported to be .55 for the males and .63 for the females, or .60 overall. The 16 items were subjected to two item analyses, one for male and one for females. Each group was divided into high, medium and low groups on the basis of summated scores, and a 2 x 3 chi-square test of independence was performed on each item. The male subjects did not differ significantly (at the .05 level) on items 4, 8, 9 and 14, and responses of the female subjects added items 5 and 16 to the reject list.

Validity
No evidence of validity is reported.

Administration
Estimated administration time is about 12 minutes. Scoring requires simple summation of item scores.

Location
Wrightsman, Lawrence S., Jr. "A Scale for Assessing Interpretations of Motives Behind Our Government's Policies," Peabody Papers in Human Development, 1963, 1 (1). Requests for further information on this scale should be addressed to the author at:

> George Peabody College for Teachers
> Division of Human Development
> Nashville 5, Tennessee

Results and
Comments
Some evidence for validity would be helpful.

INTERPRETATIONS-OF-GOVERNMENT-POLICY SCALES

Directions: Why do our government and its leaders act in the ways they do?
The following set of statements attempts to assess your opinion
of why our government has adopted certain policies. Notice
that for each statement, there are two possible reasons for the
government policy, marked "A" and "B". You are to decide which
reason you think is nearer the real reason for the government's
policy. Place the letter (A or B) of your choice in the blank
by the statement. Since these are opinions, there is no right
or wrong answer. If you have any questions, ask the test-
administrator.

_____ 1. The main reason our government helps the underdeveloped
countries of Africa is that:
A. It is our responsibility as a Christian nation to try
to improve the standard of living of less fortunate
countries.
B. If we don't help these countries, the Communists will
take them over and they will end up in an enemy camp.

_____ 2. Much of our policy toward Russia is based on:
A. The belief of our leaders that Russia wants to attack
us as soon as the time is ripe.
B. The belief of our leaders that Russia does not want war
any more than we do.

_____ 3. Our leaders are confident about our eventual triumph over
Russia because:
A. They know that Communism is evil and that it will not
succeed.
B. They know that we have the better of it in goods, man-
power, and know-how.

(Rejected) 4. If our leaders knew for sure that they could attack Russia
and Red China and destroy them without loss of American
life or destruction of American property.
A. They would attack.
B. They would not attack.

(Rejected) 5. The purpose of American missile bases in countries surrounding Russia (such as Turkey, Greece, and Iran) is:
A. To protect the peoples of these countries from attack
by Russia.
B. To aid us in a quick retaliation if Russia attacks us,
and to serve as an offensive weapon if we decide to
attack Russia first.

_____ 6. The reason why we keep American troops within the city of
West Berlin is:
A. If we didn't, the million citizens of West Berlin would
fall under Communist domination.

300

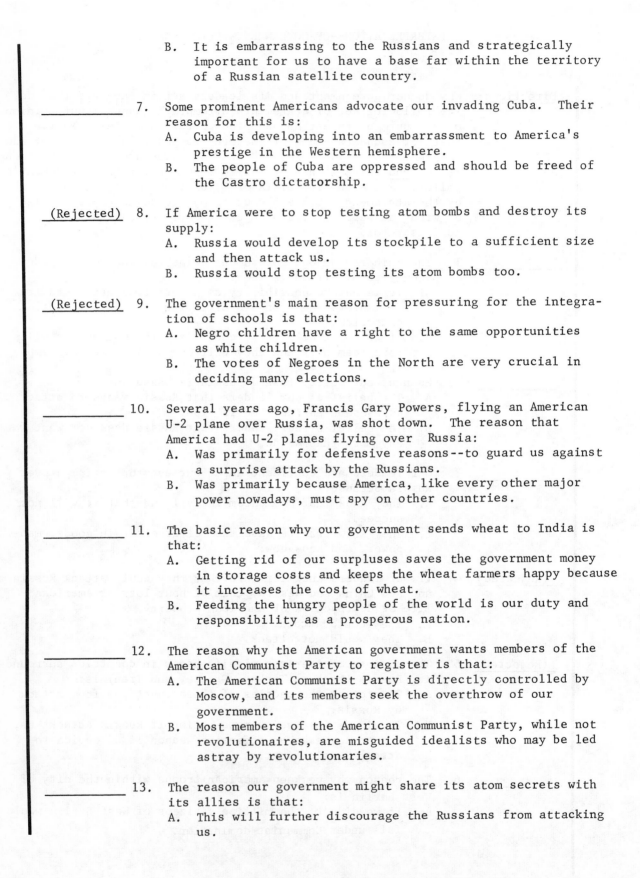

B. It is embarrassing to the Russians and strategically
important for us to have a base far within the territory
of a Russian satellite country.

_____ 7. Some prominent Americans advocate our invading Cuba. Their
reason for this is:
A. Cuba is developing into an embarrassment to America's
prestige in the Western hemisphere.
B. The people of Cuba are oppressed and should be freed of
the Castro dictatorship.

(Rejected) 8. If America were to stop testing atom bombs and destroy its
supply:
A. Russia would develop its stockpile to a sufficient size
and then attack us.
B. Russia would stop testing its atom bombs too.

(Rejected) 9. The government's main reason for pressuring for the integration of schools is that:
A. Negro children have a right to the same opportunities
as white children.
B. The votes of Negroes in the North are very crucial in
deciding many elections.

_____ 10. Several years ago, Francis Gary Powers, flying an American
U-2 plane over Russia, was shot down. The reason that
America had U-2 planes flying over Russia:
A. Was primarily for defensive reasons--to guard us against
a surprise attack by the Russians.
B. Was primarily because America, like every other major
power nowadays, must spy on other countries.

_____ 11. The basic reason why our government sends wheat to India is
that:
A. Getting rid of our surpluses saves the government money
in storage costs and keeps the wheat farmers happy because
it increases the cost of wheat.
B. Feeding the hungry people of the world is our duty and
responsibility as a prosperous nation.

_____ 12. The reason why the American government wants members of the
American Communist Party to register is that:
A. The American Communist Party is directly controlled by
Moscow, and its members seek the overthrow of our
government.
B. Most members of the American Communist Party, while not
revolutionaires, are misguided idealists who may be led
astray by revolutionaries.

_____ 13. The reason our government might share its atom secrets with
its allies is that:
A. This will further discourage the Russians from attacking
us.

        B. It is our duty to treat our allies like we would like them to treat us, to share our benefits with them.

(Rejected) 14. The reason we no longer send U-2 planes over Russia is that:
        A. It is immoral to spy, even in today's international affairs.
        B. We are afraid of getting caught and precipitating another crisis.

_____ 15. The U.S. government's aid in the development and rearming of West Germany:
        A. Is motivated by our national spirit of forgiveness and our willingness to give a former enemy a chance to get back on its feet.
        B. Is basically done to protect ourselves--to give ourselves an extra buffer state between us and the Russians.

(Rejected) 16. When asked why Russia has refrained from greater military aggression, our leaders would reply that:
        A. Russia is afraid of our superior military strength.
        B. Russia really does not want to go to war more than we do.

WORLD-MINDED ATTITUDES (Sampson and Smith 1957)

Variable   This scale is concerned with world-mindedness, that is, with an
                  international frame of reference rather than with knowledge about
                  or interest in international affairs.

Description   The following subscales are represented:

                      1. Religion (Items 1, 9, 17, 25)
                      2. Immigration (2, 10, 18, 26)
                      3. Government (3, 11, 19, 27)
                      4. Economics (4, 12, 20, 28)
                      5. Patriotism (5, 13, 21, 29)
                      6. Race (6, 14, 22, 30)
                      7. Education (7, 15, 23, 31)
                      8. War (8, 16, 24, 32)

                  The instrument is composed of a total of 32 six-point Likert-type
                  items selected to be neither statements of fact nor topical in ref-
                  erence. Items included in the scale were those out of an original
                  60 statements which differentiated two scale points or more between
                  the highest and the lowest 10 percent of the scores.

                  Sixteen of the items are pro-world-minded, 16 are anti-world-minded;
                  each of eight dimensions of the world-minded attitude are represented
                  by four items, as listed above.

Sample   The population sample is described only as 120 university students.

Reliability/   Based on an analysis of the responses of 56 college students, the
  Homogeneity   odd-even product-moment correlation was .87 (corrected). A test-
                  retest reliability check with 33 students over a one month interval
                  yielded a product moment correlation of .93. The reliability of the
                  sub-scales is not mentioned.

Validity   In a "known group" validity test, the authors found the mean score
                  on the World-mindedness Scale for a group of 192 student tourists to
                  be 123.7 as compared to a mean score of 155.8 for a group of 25 students
                  selected by the Quaker International Voluntary Service as having a
                  world-minded frame of reference. A separate set of two similar groups
                  showed mean scores of 125.8 and 148.2, respectively. Predictive validity
                  was demonstrated by the fact that the 19 most world-minded and least
                  ethnocentric subjects from the above study personally corresponded with
                  a significantly greater number of persons in Europe, were more likely
                  to belong to organizations with primarily international interests, and
                  scored lower on Adorno et al.'s E and PEC Scales and on Riecken's
                  D Scale than did the least world-minded, most ethnocentric subjects.

Location   Sampson, D. L. and Smith, H. P. "A Scale to Measure World-minded
                  Attitudes," Journal of Social Psychology, 1957, 45, pp. 99-106.

Administration	Estimated administration time for the scale is 32 minutes. Scoring requires summation of item codes.
Results and Comments	Using a sample of 223 secondary school and college students, the authors found the World-mindedness Scale to be negatively associated with an 11-item form of the Ethnocentrism Scale (-.71), with a ten-item PEC Scale (-.53), with an 11-item F Scale (-.46), and with eight of 15 items on Riecken's (1952) Democracy Scale (-.29).

Research use of the scale shows commendable concern and good criterion-related, known group, and predictive validity, as well as more than adequate reliability.

Subsequent replications of this study have proven the scale to be useful. See Garrison (1961) and Paul (1966), below.

References	Adorno, T., et al. The Authoritarian Personality. New York: Harper, 1950.

Garrison, Karl C. "Worldminded Attitudes of College Students in a Southern University," Journal of Social Psychology, 1961, 54, pp. 147-153.

Paul, Satinder K. "Worldminded Attitudes of Panjab University Students," Journal of Social Psychology, 1966, 69, pp. 33-37.

Riecken, H. W., Jr. The Volunteer Work Camp: A Psychological Evaluation. Cambridge: Addison, Wesley, 1952.

WORLDMINDEDNESS SCALE

The items in the Worldmindedness Scale are as follows with world-minded attitudes marked with a W:

1. Our country should have the right to prohibit certain racial and religious groups from entering it to live.

2. Immigrants should not be permitted to come into our country if they compete with our own workers.

3. It would be a dangerous procedure if every person in the world had equal rights which were guaranteed by an international charter.

(W) 4. All prices for exported food and manufactured goods should be set by an international trade committee.

(W) 5. Our country is probably no better than many others.

6. Race prejudice may be a good thing for us because it keeps many undesirable foreigners from coming into this country.

7. It would be a mistake for us to encourage certain racial groups to become well educated because they might use their knowledge against us.

8. We should be willing to fight for our country without questioning whether it is right or wrong.

9. Foreigners are particularly obnoxious because of their religious beliefs.

10. Immigration should be controlled by an international organization rather than by each country on its own.

(W) 11. We ought to have a world government to guarantee the welfare of all nations irrespective of the rights of any one.

12. Our country should not cooperate in any international trade agreements which attempt to better world economic conditions at our expense.

(W) 13. It would be better to be a citizen of the world than of any particular country.

(W) 14. Our responsibility to people of other races ought to be as great as our responsibility to people of our own race.

(W) 15. An international committee on education should have full control over what is taught in all countries about history and politics.

16. Our country should refuse to cooperate in a total disarmament program even if some other nations agreed to it.

17. It would be dangerous for our country to make international agreements with nations whose religious beliefs are antagonistic to ours.

(W) 18. Any healthy individual, regardless of race or religion, should be allowed to live wherever he wants to in the world.

19. Our country should not participate in any international organization which requires that we give up any of our national rights or freedom of action.

(W) 20. If necessary, we ought to be willing to lower our standard of living to cooperate with other countries in getting an equal standard for every person in the world.

21. We should strive for loyalty to our country before we can afford to consider world brotherhood.

22. Some races ought to be considered naturally less intelligent than ours.

(W) 23. Our schools should teach the history of the whole world rather than of our own country.

(W) 24. An international police force ought to be the only group in the world allowed to have armaments.

25. It would be dangerous for us to guarantee by international agreement that every person in the world should have complete religious freedom.

(W) 26. Our country should permit the immigration of foreign peoples even if it lowers our standard of living.

(W) 27. All national governments ought to be abolished and replaced by one central world government.

28. It would not be wise for us to agree that working conditions in all countries should be subject to international control.

29. Patriotism should be a primary aim of education so our children will believe our country is the best in the world.

(W) 30. It would be a good idea if all the races were to intermarry until there was only one race in the world.

(W) 31. We should teach our children to uphold the welfare of all people everywhere even though it may be against the best interests of our own country.

(W) 32. War should never be justifiable even if it is the only way to protect our national rights and honor.

INTERNATIONALISM-NATIONALISM (IN) SCALE (Levinson 1951)

Variable

This scale attempts to provide a measure of nationalism with items dealing with controversial issues current at the time of its development (1951) such as United States role in the UN, emphasis on military versus economic aid to other countries, and choice of allies in the cold war.

Description

The instrument consists of 12 items scored on a 1-7 scale, with higher scores indicating agreement with "nationalistic" items and disagreement with "internationalistic" items. The total scale score is the average item score times 10, with possible range of scores 10-70. Three of the items take an "internationalist" position and the other nine take a "nationalist" position.

Sample

The population sample consisted of 84 graduate students and undergraduates attending Harvard summer school education and social relations classes in 1951. Mean score for the sample was 31.8 with a standard deviation of 12.5 and a range of 10-64.

Reliability/ Homogeneity

The split-half reliability was .86, and the test-retest correlation for one education class was .90 after an interval of six weeks. All 12 items discriminated beyond the one percent level between top and bottom scores.

Validity

No direct tests for validity are reported, although the correlations with other scales are as the author predicted.

Location

Levinson, Daniel J. "Authoritarian Personality and Foreign Policy," Journal of Conflict Resolution, 1957, 1, pp. 37-47.

Administration

Estimated administration time is 12 minutes.

Results and Comments

The following correlations of the IN Scale with scales measuring personality variables were reported:

.77 with a 16-item Ethnocentrism Scale; .65 with the author's Traditional Family Ideology Scale; .52 with Lichtenberg's Religious Conventionalism Scale; .34 with the Political Economic Conservatism Scale.

The author stated that the high correlations provided evidence that foreign policy orientation is part of a broader ideological context reflecting an autocratic approach to the world. It was also found that Republicans in the sample had a significantly higher mean IN score than the Democrats or Independents.

In a study of attitude changes among 172 students enrolled in undergraduate international relations and foreign policy courses, Singer combined the IN items with Sampson and Smith's Worldmindedness Scale to form the Cosmopolitan (COS) Scale. The (corrected) inter-scale reliabilities were .70 before the courses and .59 after. It was found that the mean score for the entire population became significantly more pro-cosmopolitan (at the .001 level). Again, no direct test for validity was reported although the high correlation with the <u>WM Scale</u> gives some support for the attitude dimension being tapped. It would seem desirable to have more than three of the items in the internationalist direction.

Reference   Singer, J. D. "Cosmopolitan Attitudes and International Relations Courses: Some Tentative Correlations," <u>Journal of Politics</u>, 1965, <u>27</u>, pp. 318-338.

THE INTERNATIONALISM-NATIONALISM (IN) SCALE

Item [*]		Mean [+]	D.P. [++]
1 . . .	We need more leaders like MacArthur, who have the morals and the strength to put our national honor above appeasement	3.1	4.2
2 . . .	If it weren't for Russia and her satellites, the world would be headed toward peace and prosperity by now	3.4	3.5
3 [*] . . .	In the long run, it would be to our best interest as a nation to spend less money for military purposes and more money for education, housing, and other social improvements	2.6	2.2
4 . . .	The immigration of foreigners to this country should be kept down so that we can provide for Americans first	3.4	3.8
5 . . .	The only way peace can be maintained is to keep America so powerful and well armed that no other nation will dare to attack us	3.2	4.1
6 [*] . . .	Our best policy in China would be to forget about Chiang Kai-shek and to work for a coalition between the Communists and the "center" parties	4.8	3.1
7 . . .	If the United Nations doesn't show more signs of getting tough with Russia soon, America must be prepared to carry on the fight by itself	3.4	3.3
8 . . .	While we should give military aid to countries which are prepared to fight our enemies, we ought to cut down on foreign economic help, or else the other countries will just play us for a sucker	3.3	3.2
9 . . .	In these troubled times, if we are to be strong and united against our common enemy, we must have more laws and safeguards against the spreading of dangerous ideas	3.0	3.8
10 [*] . . .	One main trouble with American foreign policy today is that there is too much concern with military force and too little concern with political negotiation and economic reconstruction	3.0	2.4
11 . . .	In view of America's moral and material superiority, it is only right that we should have the biggest say in deciding United Nations policy	2.4	2.8
12 . . .	The first principle of our foreign policy should be to join forces with any country, even if it is not very democratic, just as long as it is strongly anti-communist	2.8	2.4

---

[*] Items marked with an asterisk take an "internationalist" position as here defined; the others represent a "nationalist" position.

[+] Responses are scored on a 1-7 scale; 7 points are given for strong agreement on the nationalistic items and for strong disagreement on the internationalistic items.

[++] The "D.P." is the "Discriminatory Power" of an item, i.e., its ability to discriminate between high and low scores on the total scale. It is obtained by subtracting the item mean earned by the low group (bottom quarter of the total-scale distribution) from the mean of the high group (top quarter). All D.P.'s are significantly greater than zero (at beyond the 1 percent level of confidence).

ATTITUDE TOWARD U.S. AND RUSSIAN ACTIONS (Oskamp and Hartry 1965)

Variable	A factor analysis was performed to examine an hypothesized equivalent double standard of evaluation of United States and Russian actions in international affairs.
Description	The instrument consists of statements of 50 identical actions taken recently by the United States and Russia, administered in two forms identical in wording except for substitution of the terms "U.S." for "Russian," and "Head of the Russian government" for "President of the United States." Response mode was a Likert scale of favorability from +3 to -3 with no neutral point. Item scores were transformed to a scale ranging from 0 to 6.
Sample	The population sample was composed of the 320 members of the freshman class of a small, coeducational, liberal arts college with a fairly diversified student body. A random group of approximately 1/4 of the subjects took only the U.S. Form, 1/4 took only the Russian Form, 1/4 took the U.S. Form first and the Russian Form second, and 1/4 took the Russian Form first and the U.S. Form second.
Reliability/ Homogeneity	The resulting orthogonal factors were: "warlike or hostile actions," the first factor for both Russia and the United States; "free access to information," "peaceful statements and conciliatory behavior," "non-military disapproval," the second, third, and fourth United States factors; and "statements of peaceful intentions," "technical advancement and assistance to other nations," and "non-military competition and cold-war intransigence," the second, third, and fourth Russian factors.

No test-retest reliability was reported. |
Validity	No test validity was reported.
Location	Oskamp, Stuart and Hartry, Arlene. "A Factor-Analytic Study of the Double Standard in Attitudes toward U.S. and Russian Actions," Claremont Graduate School: paper presented at the American Psychological Association meeting in Chicago, September 4, 1965.
Administration	Estimated administration time for each form is about 50 minutes.
Results and Comments	On the United States Form, Factor I accounted for 31 percent of the variance, Factor II added 20 percent, Factor III seven percent, and Factor IV four and a half percent. On the Russian Form, the figures were: Factor I, 45 percent; Factor II, 14 percent; Factor III, five and a half percent; Factor IV, four and a half percent.

For both United States and Russian items, a similar first factor of warlike or hostile action emerged, but the three smaller factors for the two nations showed little overlap. As predicted, a double standard was clearly evident, especially on the first factor: the United States |

actions were almost always rated favorably, while the identical
Russian actions were usually evaluated unfavorably.

A two-sided presentation of information (taking both forms of the
questionnaire) produced more neutral attitudes, particularly less
favorable attitudes toward United States' warlike or disapproving
actions toward other nations. The authors noted that this effect
has never been tested on a non-student population.

MEAN ATTITUDE SCORES ON U.S. AND RUSSIAN FORMS
FOR SUBJECTS TAKING EACH FORM FIRST OR ONLY

(Items are ordered in terms of U.S.-Russian differences)

	Item (worded as on U.S. form)	U.S. Mean (N=158)	Russian Mean (N=162)	Diff.
13.	The U.S. has established rocket bases close to the borders of Russia	4.66	.51	4.15
7.	The U.S. has carried on a blockade to prevent shipment of goods from entering a nearby area.	4.91	.81	4.10
31.	Some Russian citizens have fled from their country and been given refuge in the U.S.	5.18	1.25	3.93
28.	The U.S. has warned another nation that it runs the risk of retaliation if it allows its territory to be used for Russian missile bases.	4.97	1.13	3.84
36.	The U.S. supports regular propaganda broadcasts beamed at nations on the other side of the "iron curtain".	5.06	1.31	3.75
3.	The U.S. has sent supplies and military help to one faction in the civil war in Laos.	4.64	.96	3.68
49.	U.S. leaders have repeatedly said that the U.S. system of government will inevitably win in a peaceful competition with the Russian system.	4.78	1.12	3.66
20.	Leaders of the U.S. government have frequently called for "liberation of the captive peoples" in nations allied with Russia.	4.80	1.28	3.52
24.	The U.S. has intercepted and interfered with Russian transportation to a foreign area.	4.12	.64	3.48
50.	The President of the U.S. has said that the U.S. resumption of nuclear tests was necessary for the safety of the country.	4.72	1.24	3.48
1.	The U.S. has increased its military budget markedly in the last few years.	4.40	1.09	3.31
33.	The U.S. has stated that it was compelled to resume nuclear testing by the actions of Russia.	4.21	.95	3.26
38.	The U.S. has provided military training and military assistance to smaller nations.	4.92	1.70	3.22
45.	The U.S. maintains armed forces of about 2,500,000 men.	4.61	1.47	3.14

| | U.S.
Mean
($\underline{N}$=158) | Russian
Mean
($\underline{N}$=162) | Diff. |
Item (worded as on U.S. form)			
47. The U.S. has threatened to engage in nuclear war if Russia carried out certain acts, such as attacking a third country.	4.17	1.09	3.08
32. The U.S. government has accused Russian foreign policy of being "imperialistic".	4.40	1.43	2.97
17. The U.S. has stockpiled more than enough nuclear warheads to kill all the citizens of Russia.	3.47	.59	2.88
25. Recently the U.S. has rejected a Russian proposal for another moratorium on nuclear testing.	3.84	1.01	2.83
2. U.S. planes have flown over parts of Russia.	3.87	1.12	2.75
12. The U.S. government has aided groups which were attempting to overthrow the governments of other countries.	3.45	.72	2.73
14. The U.S. still has troops in some areas taken in World War II and has refused other nations' requests to remove its forces from these areas.	3.45	.75	2.70
42. The U.S. has often refused to compromise on important points in international negotiations.	3.90	1.22	2.68
6. The U.S. has closed large areas of the country to travel by Russian diplomats.	3.63	1.06	2.57
19. A few years ago the President of the U.S. indicated that the U.S. would feel free to resume nuclear testing after the expiration of the existing test moratorium.	3.42	.95	2.47
41. The U.S. has used economic sanctions against other nations.	3.57	1.21	2.36
27. The U.S. has offered many scholarships to students from the underdeveloped countries of Asia and Africa to come for study in the U.S.	5.52	3.18	2.34
30. The head of the U.S. government has publicly denied any intentions to conquer the territories of other nations.	4.72	2.45	2.27
10. The U.S. spends about half of its total national budget for military purposes.	3.15	.93	2.22

Item (worded as on U.S. form)	U.S. Mean (N=158)	Russian Mean (N=162)	Diff.
18. The U.S. government has sometimes lied in attempts to conceal its actions in international events.	2.67	.59	2.08
9. The U.S. has frequently stated that its armaments are for defensive purposes and will not be used in a "first strike" against Russia.	4.62	2.69	1.93
23. The President of the U.S. has publicly pledged U.S. support for the neutrality and independence of Laos.	4.90	3.08	1.82
46. The U.S. has sent extensive aid and technical assistance to the underdeveloped nations.	4.99	3.27	1.72
39. The U.S. has often displayed disapproval of the opinions and policies of smaller nations.	3.63	1.97	1.66
8. The U.S. has accomplished great scientific and technical feats in its exploration of space.	5.65	4.15	1.50
11. The U.S. has made several proposals concerning East-West disarmament.	4.72	3.25	1.47
4. In several countries the U.S. has supported dictatorial leaders who suppressed the freedoms of their citizens.	1.88	.48	1.40
48. The U.S. has put itself on record as favoring general and complete disarmament.	4.75	3.54	1.21
40. The U.S. government has frequently misled its citizens about events and conditions in its allied nations which are governed by dictatorial regimes.	1.70	.84	.86
22. The President of the U.S. made a personal appearance at the United Nations to present his country's viewpoint on international affairs.	5.27	4.42	.85
5. The U.S. has sent great musicians and other artists to perform in countries on the other side of the "iron curtain".	5.53	4.95	.58
26. The U.S. recently signed a treaty reserving the continent of Antarctica exclusively for peaceful purposes.	5.42	4.89	.53

Item (worded as on U.S. form)	U.S. Mean (N=158)	Russian Mean (N=162)	Diff.
44. A personal interview with the head of the Russian government has been widely reported in the U.S. press.	4.92	4.42	.50**
37. U.S. scientists have made great contributions to advanced areas of medical research.	5.68	5.21	.47
29. U.S. diplomatic personnel in foreign countries have been accused of spying and espionage.	2.18	1.92	.26[a]
15. The U.S. has handed back to Russia a convicted Soviet intelligence agent in exchange for the return to the U.S. of a convicted American intelligence agent.	4.38	4.22	.16[a]
16. The performances of several U.S. musicians have been highly acclaimed by Russian audiences.	5.51	5.39	.12[a]
43. The U.S. government has recently made it easier for tourists, students, and professional delegations from Russia to visit the U.S.	4.88	4.94	-.06[a]
35. There have been many incidents of racial and religious persecution in the U.S.	1.24	1.32	-.08[a]
21. The U.S. has accepted certain Russian proposals concerning inspection of disarmament procedures.	4.03	4.48	-.45*
34. On some occasions the U.S. government has refrained from aiding rebellions in countries on the other side of the "iron curtain".	3.38	3.99	-.61**

Note: Scale from 0-6; 0 indicates "strongly unfavorable", 6 indicates "strongly favorable". Ns for some items vary slightly (U.S. N=153 - 158; Russian N=156 - 162). All differences are significant at the .001 level unless indicated otherwise.

** Significant at the .01 level.

* Significant at the .05 level.

[a] Not significant.

PROBLEMS AND GOALS OF THE U.S. GOVERNMENT (Hefner and Robinson 1964)

Variable

These two scales attempt to determine whether a respondent gives higher priority to national or international governmental goals and problems.

Description

Respondents are given a list of seven problems facing the government and asked to rank order them in terms of their importance. The procedure is repeated for the importance of goals facing the government. Three of the problems are domestic, and four international, while five of the goals are international, and only two domestic.

Sample

A probability cross-section sample of 558 Detroit area adults was personally interviewed in early 1964. Response rate was just over 80 percent.

Reliability/
Homogeneity

No data bearing on reliability are available.

Validity

Although data bearing directly on validity are available, some indirect evidence is presented under "Results and Comments."

Location

Data are as yet unpublished but were collected jointly by the Detroit Area Study and the Conflict Resolution Center of the University of Michigan.

Administration

It took the respondent about five minutes to rank order each set of problems or goals.

Results and
Comments

It was found that while 40 percent of college graduates said that international problems were more important, less than 20 percent of those with less than a high school education did. When the items were asked of a sample of 150 academic experts about international affairs at the University of Michigan (Robinson and Hefner 1967), 77 percent of them placed greater emphasis on international problems. The question on foreign goals was not asked of the academic experts.

Thus far, only the items dealing with aid to underdeveloped countries have been analyzed in any detail. As might be predicted from the results reported above, "helping underdeveloped countries" was ranked by the total sample as lowest in importance among both problems and goals, but was ranked considerably higher by the better educated whites in the sample. Better educated Negroes, on the other hand, thought such aid even less important than did the less educated of either race. Younger people and men thought the problem more important than older people and women.

RANKINGS GIVEN BY A CROSS-SECTION OF DETROIT ADULTS TO:

a) Problems Facing the U.S. Government

		% of First Choices	Average Rank
1.	Controlling or cutting down the supply of military weapons in the world	5%	4.8
2.	Handling problems with the Russians and other Communist countries	20%	3.5
3.	Finding jobs for Americans who are out of work	28%	3.0
4.	Handling racial problems in the United States	24%	3.0
5.	Helping the underdeveloped countries of South America, Asia, and Africa	4%	5.3
6.	Reducing taxes for our citizens	6%	4.4
7.	Getting the United Nations to work effectively	11%	4.0

b) Goals of the U.S. Government

		% of First Choices	Average Rank
1.	Improve our economy and standard of living	8%	4.8
2.	Win friends and allies among other countries	10%	4.5
3.	Prevent war	30%	3.3
4.	Be prepared to defend our country against possible aggression	13%	3.7
5.	Show other countries the value of democracy by practicing it here at home	20%	3.4
6.	Prevent the spread of communism in free countries	13%	3.8
7.	Help other countries grow and develop	6%	4.5

CRITERIA FOR FOREIGN AID (Hefner and Robinson 1964)

Variable These items deal separately with attitudes on three criteria for assignment of foreign aid: whether the U.S. should give more or less aid than it has, what things people in underdeveloped countries really need, and what are the most important factors bearing on how much foreign aid is given.

Description While the "amount" of aid question is a simple forced choice item, the "what underdeveloped countries need" item has ten response choices; the "factors determining amount of foreign aid" item list has seven choices. Respondents ranked the five most important things that underdeveloped countries need and the four most important factors in giving foreign aid.

Sample A probability cross-section sample of 558 Detroit area adults was interviewed in early 1964.

Reliability/ Homogeneity No data bearing on reliability are available.

Validity No data bearing on validity are available.

Location Data are as yet unpublished but were collected jointly by the Detroit Area Study and the Conflict Resolution Center of the University of Michigan.

Administration All three tasks took respondents about 10 minutes.

Results and Comments The public split down the middle on the question of more or less foreign aid: 26 percent favored more aid, 25 percent favored less and 43 percent volunteered the response "the same"; 6 percent gave no answer. Support for more aid was highest among the young and among those in professional and business occupations, but lowest among Jews and non-church attenders. On the other hand, 89 percent of the sample of academic experts at the University of Michigan (see previous scale write-up) favored increased aid.

Regarding the things that underdeveloped countries need, the more personalized factors of food for the people, good leaders, desire for improvement, and more schools were perceived as more important than system economic needs such as modern farming methods, factories, more equitable distribution of wealth, and highways or communication lines. The better-educated placed relatively more emphasis on leaders and relatively less emphasis on schools and religious faith. Regarding the factors to be considered in giving aid, careful use of the money was considered most important, followed by the amount of Communist threat, and the determination of the people in the country to be helped. The democratic structure of government was named as the least important concern.

Follow-up questions revealed that the major objections to foreign aid were that there were too many poor people in our country already and that the money was likely to be misspent.

RESPONSES OF THE DETROIT PUBLIC TO QUESTIONS ABOUT FOREIGN AID

Should the United States do more than it has, or less than it has to help these (underdeveloped) countries develop?

More	26%
Less	25%
Same	43%
Don't know	6%

Of course there are many things that the underdeveloped countries do not have. Which of the following are things they <u>don't have</u> now, and <u>really need</u>? First, what is their biggest need?

		% of First Choices	Average Rank
a)	Highways, airports, communication lines etc.	3%	7.1
b)	Good political leaders, administrators and public opinion	20	4.1
c)	Well-fed and healthy people	32	3.9
d)	Religious faith	8	5.7
e)	Modern farming methods	5	6.0
f)	Schools and teachers	10	4.1
g)	Engineers, scientists, technicians, etc.	3	6.0
h)	A fair share of the country's land and wealth for everybody	3	6.9
i)	Factories and equipment	1	6.6
j)	The desire to improve themselves	15	4.6
		100%	5.5

Here are some things which the United States government might consider when deciding whether or not to send aid to a foreign country. Which one do you feel is the most important--the one that should be given greatest weight in reaching the decision?

		% of First Choices	Average Rank
a)	How friendly the government is to the United States	12%	4.3
b)	How strong the Communist threat to the foreign government is	19	3.8
c)	How democratic the government of the foreign country is	5	4.7
d)	How carefully the aid funds will be used by the foreign country	26	3.0
e)	How poor the people in the foreign country are	11	4.3
f)	How hard working and willing to do their part the people are	15	3.7
g)	Whether the aid will help or hinder the American economy	12	4.2
		100%	4.0

INTERNATIONALISM (Lutzker 1960)

Variable	In this scale, an internationalist is defined as one who trusts other nations, is willing to cooperate with them, perceives international agencies (such as the United Nations) as deterrents of war, and considers international tensions reducible by mediation. The isolationist is defined as one who demands national strength in lieu of international mediation and does not encourage commerce or transactions with other nations.
Description	The instrument consists of 36 six-point Likert-type items with no neutral choice. Internationalistic attitude is indicated by positive replies to 17 items and negative replies to 19 items. Response choices are scored 1-3 and 5-7, with high score indicating internationalism. Possible range of scale scores is 36-252. Sources for 20 of the items were Murphy and Likert (1938) and Adorno et al. (1950). The remaining items were constructed by the author.
Sample	The sample population was a group of 484 students in introductory psychology classes at Ohio State University. Range of scores was 62 to 228, with a mean score of 193.2 and standard deviation of 21.6.
Reliability/ Homogeneity	No test-retest reliability was reported, nor any other data on reliability.
Validity	No data directly pertaining to validity are reported, although some indirect evidence is presented under "Results and Comments."
Location	Lutzker, Daniel R. "Internationalism as a Predictor of Cooperative Behavior," Journal of Conflict Resolution, 1960, 4 (4), pp. 426-430.
Administration	Estimated administration time is 36 minutes. Scoring requires simple summation of item scores.
Results and Comments	This scale was administered to isolate high and low scorers to be used as criterion groups in a study of cooperative behavior in a "prisoner's dilemma" (non-zero-sum) game. High scorers, or those having an attitude of internationalism, were predicted to have a general attitude of trust and thus to be more likely to make a cooperative choice in the game. It was found that the "internationalists" were not more cooperative than a control group but were more persistent in seeking cooperation. The "isolationists," however, were significantly less cooperative and more competitive than either the "internationalists" ($p < .01$) or the control group ($p = .002$). In a later similar study, McClintock et al. (1963) also found significant differences in the number of cooperative choices of high and low scorers (controlled for six) on the Internationalism Scale.

322

References

McClintock, C. G., Harrison, A., Strand, S. and Gullo, P. "Internationalism-Isolationism, Strategy of the Other Player and Two-Person Game Behavior," Journal of Abnormal and Social Psychology, 1963, 67, pp. 631-635.

Murphy, G. and Likert, R. Public Opinion and the Individual. New York: Harper and Bros., 1938.

Adorno, T. W., Frenkel-Brunswick, E., Levinson, D. J. and Sanford, R. N. The Authoritarian Personality. New York: Harper & Row, 1950.

INTERNATIONALISM
(A Survey of Political Opinions)

You are being asked to participate in a survey of opinions on political topics. Below, you will find a list of statements. Each statement is followed by six "reactions": "disagree strongly," "disagree moderately," "disagree mildly," "agree mildly," "agree moderately," and "agree strongly." You are to read each statement and then <u>encircle</u> the words which best describe your reaction to it. For example, if the statement read:

"People who make up questionnaires should be shot."

Disagree	Disagree	Disagree	Agree	Agree	Agree
Strongly	Moderately	Mildly	Mildly	Moderately	Strongly

You would respond by drawing a circle around the alternative above which best describes your own reactions to the statement.

Remember, read each statement carefully before responding and be sure to do <u>all</u> of the items.

1. The United States should take more of its problems to the U.N. than it has been doing.

Disagree	Disagree	Disagree	Agree	Agree	Agree
Strongly	Moderately	Mildly	Mildly	Moderately	Strongly

2. There will always be wars because, for one thing, there will always be races who ruthlessly try to grab more than their share.

3. Sending food and badly needed supplies to other nations will do more to maintain stable international relations than will our present policy of increasing our military strength.

4. Whereas some people feel that they are citizens of the world, that they belong to mankind and not to any one nation, a true American always feels that his primary allegiance is to his own country.

5. Only a show of military strength can prevent the Russians and Chinese Communists from trying to gain world domination.

6. Underdeveloped areas should be helped through U.N. agencies like the World Health Organization and UNESCO.

7. The United Nations should be abandoned as unworkable.

8. All military training should be abolished.

9. The United Nations should be strengthened by giving it control of the armed forces of all the member nations.

10. We need compulsory universal military training to keep our country strong and safe from attack.

11. European refugees may be in need, but it would be a big mistake to lower our immigration barriers and allow them to flood the country.

12. We should have a World Government with the power to make laws which would be binding to all its member nations.

13. The United States should recognize the Chinese Communist government.

14. It would be a good idea if all nations gave up the production of military weapons.

15. The best way to insure peace is to keep the United States stronger than any other nation in the world.

16. We should be willing to let American investments in foreign countries be lost if the only other alternative is war.

17. The stars and stripes is the only flag, national or international, to which we should give allegiance.

18. The United States should be willing to provide the United Nations with troops to act, along with troops of other countries, as an international police force.

19. We should cooperate fully with smaller democracies and should not regard ourselves as their leaders.

20. It is an idle dream to expect to abolish war.

21. The United States should not trade with any communist country.

22. The United States should concentrate upon keeping itself strong and should not get involved in the affairs of other countries.

23. We should be willing to fight for our country whether it is in the right or in the wrong.

24. A person who loves his fellow man should refuse to engage in any war, no matter how serious the consequences to his country may be.

25. The idea of a World Government as the future hope of international peace should be viewed with suspicion.

26. Any form of international government is impossible.

27. In the interest of permanent peace, we should be willing to settle absolutely all differences with other nations within the framework of a World Government.

28. Any group or social movement which contains many foreigners should be watched with suspicion and, whenever possible, be investigated by the FBI.

29. If an international police force is established, the United States should retain a large army and navy anyway so that we can be certain of having military forces when we need them.

30. Patriotism and loyalty are the first and most important requirements of a good citizen.

31. The United Nations deserves our whole-hearted support in its efforts to settle international disputes.

32. The main threat to basic American institutions during this century has come from the infiltration of foreign ideas, doctrines, and agitators.

33. Every effort should be made to reach an understanding with the Soviet Union and Communist China so that friendly relations can be established and maintained.

34. We must strive for loyalty to our country before we can afford to consider world brotherhood.

35. In the interests of humanity, America's doors should be opened wide to immigrants from all nations and current restrictive quotas should be abolished.

36. The United States should rely on world organization and collective security rather than atomic stockpiles as a deterrent to potential aggressors.

ATTITUDES TOWARD WORLD AFFAIRS (Shimberg 1949)

Variable
In a study of the relationship between information and attitude, the
instrument consisted of information questions dealing with atomic
energy and the United Nations, and opinion questions measuring the
attitudes of young people toward certain international problems:
war-expectancy, the A-bomb, world government, universal military
training, and war with Russia.

Description
There were four multiple choice information questions and 16 agree-
undecided-disagree opinion questions. Those who answered correctly
three or four information questions were scored as well-informed, while
those who answered correctly one or no information questions were
scored as poorly-informed. Opinion items were not formed into a scale.

Sample
The instrument was administered to about 10,000 high school juniors
and seniors by their teachers in 1947. For analysis purposes, the well
and poorly informed were divided into two groups of 129 students matched
on sex, geographical region, urban-rural residence, socio-economic
status and political party preference.

Reliability/
  Homogeneity
Test-retest reliability are not reported.

Validity
No tests for validity are reported.

Location
Shimberg, B. "Information and Attitude Toward World Affairs,"
Journal of Educational Psychology, 1949, 40, pp. 206-222.

Administration
Estimated administration time is four minutes for the information
questions and 12 minutes for the opinion questions.

Results and
  Comments
Significant differences were found between the two information groups
on all but the twelfth question. The well-informed group appeared to
the author to be more optimistic, more internationally-minded, more
aware of the implications of events, and less given to emotional
solutions to international problems. They were also more in favor
of private enterprise. Most of the items are somewhat dated.

WORLD AFFAIRS ITEMS

INFORMATION ITEMS   (Correct items underlined)

1. By an act of Congress, who has control over U.S. atomic energy
    at the present time?
    The Military Forces -- A Civilian Commission -- Private Industry -- DK

2. Who is the present director of the U.S. Atomic Energy Commission?
    Bernard Baruch -- Leslie Groves -- David Lilienthal -- DK

3. Do or do not most scientists think the U.S. will be able to work
    out an effective defense against the atomic bomb?
    Do -- DK -- Do not

4. Do all nations or only a certain few have the veto power in the
    U.N.?
    All nations -- DK -- A certain few

ATTITUDE ITEMS

1. Do you or do you not expect the United States to fight in another
    war within five years?
    Do -- ? -- Do not

2. Do you or do you not expect the United States to fight in another
    war within the next twenty-five years?
    Do -- ? -- Do not

3. Some people have said that all raw materials and plants for making
    atomic power in all countries, including the United States, should
    be put under the direct control of an international atomic
    authority. Do you or do you not approve of such a plan?
    Do -- ? -- Do not

4. The United States is still making atomic bombs. Do you or do you
    not approve of this?
    Do -- ? -- Do not

5. If all the nations except Russia could agree on a plan to control
    atomic energy under the United Nations, would you or would you not
    favor adopting such a plan without Russia?
    Would -- ? -- Would not

6. Do you or do you not believe that all nations should form a world
    organization with power to use an international police force
    against any nation, including the United States, which tried to
    start a war?
    Do -- ? -- Do not

7. Should the development of atomic energy in the United States for
    peaceful use be carried on by private industry or by the government?
    Private -- ? -- Government

8. Some people believe that because of changes in warfare brought
    about by the atomic bomb, we no longer need a large standing army.
    Do you agree or disagree?
    Agree -- ? -- Disagree

9. Do you or do you not think that the United Nations should be
    strengthened to make it a world government with power to control
    the armed forces of all nations, including those of the United
    States?
    Do -- ? -- Do not

10. Should or should not some military training be given to all
    able-bodied young men?
    Should -- ? -- Should not

11. Under no circumstances should the United States go to war against
    the Russians.
    Agree -- ? -- Disagree

12. If the Russians attack United States territory, should we or
    should we not go to war against them?
    Should -- ? -- Should not

13. If the Russians get control of any country in Latin America,
    should we or should we not go to war against them?
    Should -- ? -- Should not

14. If the Russians refuse to withdraw their occupation troops from
    Germany after the other allies have agreed upon a peace treaty
    with Germany, should we or should we not drive the Russians out
    by force?
    Should -- ? -- Should not

15. If we found out that the Russians were making atomic bombs of their
    own, should we or should we not go to war against them?
    Should -- ? -- Should not

16. Should we or should we not go to war against the Russians right now?
    Should -- ? -- Should not

PRO-RUSSIA ERROR-CHOICE TEST (Hammond 1948)

Variable	The instrument attempts to measure the extent of pro-Russia attitude by direction and amount of systematic error in a "non-factual" information test.

Description   The test consists of 20 factual and 20 non-factual forced-choice items. Among the latter, one series of eight questions offers alternate answers for which the facts are indeterminable. In this study, the 20 "factual" or straight information items were used to disguise the test and were interspersed among the 20 "non-factual" items. A priori determined positive (or pro-) systematic errors were given a score value of 1 on each item; negative errors, no value. Selection of items was based primarily on "the writer's hunch."

To check for attitude test "set," the instrument was also administered to a different sample with the non-factual items separated from the factual items and presented as an attitude test (called ATT-INFO). A control group from the same sample was given the original test (called INFO).

Sample   The experimental validation groups consisted of the following:

1. Pro-Russia bias group, consisting of 18 adults employed by a major labor organization in clerical and semi-professional positions, and

2. Anti-Russia bias group, consisting of two businessmen's luncheon clubs, one made up of 23 middle-aged businessmen making over $10,000 a year, and one composed of 19 younger businessmen. A third experimental population was a group of 144 students in an elementary psychology class.

Reliability/ Homogeneity   Split-half reliability (corrected) was .87 on the Russia questionnaire. The reliability sample consisted of ten cases from the union group, 40 from the two business groups, and a random sample of ten of the college students.

The reliability (corrected) on the ATT-INFO test for the sample of students was .51.

Validity   In this "known group" validity test, the mean errors in the pro-Russia and anti-Russia groups were found significantly different (at the .05 level) in the direction predicted, i.e., the pro-Russia group gave more incorrect pro-Russia opinions.

Location   Hammond, Kenneth R. "Measuring Attitudes by Error-Choice: An Indirect Method," Journal of Abnormal and Social Psychology, 1948, 43, pp.38-47.

Administration   Estimated administration time for each of the tests is about 30 minutes. Scoring requires simple summation of response codes.

Results and
Comments

The items appeared to discriminate fairly well between the known groups, and the reliability coefficient on the INFO form was high. The author suggests that the reliability coefficient on the ATT-INFO form was probably lowered by the affect produced by the subjects attempting control. Attitude test "set" apparently was successfully controlled for.

The author offers the following suggestions for improvement:

-- If the items were preselected by content or symbolic analysis, the errors might provide a clue as to the prevailing set of "factual" justifications which a sample is using.

-- The more disguised the test, of course, the better.

-- Tests constructed with four error-choices to provide for intensity of error might prove useful for scaling items.

-- Factual items can provide evidence of amount of information possessed by the subject so that the amount of error-choice should be meaningful.

Subjects' anger at the disguised nature of this type of attitude test reportedly has limited its adoption. Its nature also prevents the expression of a truly neutral or uncommitted attitude.

Sample Items

"NON-FACTUAL" QUESTIONS FROM THE "INFORMATION" TEST

(44) Molotov is known in diplomatic circles for his manners.
    (1) excellent
    (2) poor

(54) There (is) / (is not) freedom of religion in Russia.

(66) In most countries surrounding Russia where Communists are now in the government they have been (1) duly elected (2) appointed by Moscow.

CHAPTER 8: HOSTILITY-RELATED INTERNATIONAL ATTITUDES

The eleven   scales presented in this section vary widely in content and
format. Half were constructed during World War II and only two as recently
as the present decade. Some of the instruments are based on complex psychological constructs, but most are composed of relatively straightforward questions. In rough order of estimated merit and utility, the eleven   scales
considered in this section are as follows:

1. International Reactions (IR) Scale (Christiansen 1959)
2. National Patriotism (NP) Scale (Christiansen 1959)
3. International Hostility Scale (Grace 1949)
4. Attitude toward War (Putney 1962)
5. Vietnam Policy Scale (Verba et al. 1967)
6. Ideological Militancy-Pacifism (IMP) Scale (Dombrose and Levinson
    1950)
7. Hostility in International Relations (Helfant 1952)
8. Nationalism (Ferguson 1942)
9. Nationalistic Attitude Changes (Stagner and Osgood 1946)
10. Attitude toward War (Day and Quackenbush 1942)
11. Attitude toward War (Stagner 1942)

Of the measures in this section, Christiansen's International Relations
(IR) Scale is probably based on the most elegant theoretical assumptions and
is the result of the most impressive quantitative methodology. Results
obtained with this scale correspond to the author's complex set of initial
hypotheses. The forced-choice format of the scale rules out agreement response
set tendencies. There are, however, two possible limitations of the scale.
First, it was constructed for use on Norwegian citizens. Second, its
forced-choice format, though discouraging response set, contributes a greater
element of complexity for the respondents. Overall, the scale's merits far
outweigh its limitations, and its author is to be commended for his sophisticated use of theory and method.

A second scale by Christiansen, the <u>National Patriotism (NP) Scale</u>, is a short, simple, and more straightforward Likert-type measure. It shows hypothesized correlations with certain components of his first scale on international relations. However, a wide heterogeneity in scale content is suggested by the low value of the item-test correlations. Data on the scale's validity are unclear.

A third scale on international hostility was devised by Grace for American respondents. It is extremely similar in theoretical orientation to Christiansen's first scale. Many of Grace's findings, however, seem to be different from those of Christiansen. He did not find similar reactions to international and everyday situations except for one reaction. In that particular case, a laissez-faire reaction was seen to be generalized across a variety of situations and was the most popular response as well for most of them. The items in Grace's scale seem dated today (especially those which refer to China), but they are in a simpler format than Christiansen's items. It is difficult to accurately assess the author's claims of reliability and validity.

The <u>Putney Pacifism Scale</u> has the dual advantage of having been administered to students at sixteen different colleges and of being the only scale in this section to have been used recently. It would be interesting to see these items repeated on today's undergraduate students. Internal consistency of the scale seems satisfactory, and the moderate to high correlations with the author's other scales argue well for its basic validity. Although the scale is short, some of the items would require simplification for use on cross-sectional samples.

The Verba et al. scale is a very well constructed instrument on a national sample, but it is limited to specifics of the Vietnam War. It is for this reason that we have not placed it higher on our list. Information on the scale's basic validity is still lacking, but reliability and normative data are quite satisfactory.

The Militancy-Pacifism Scale of Dombrose and Levinson was used in a study of "the authoritarian personality." Most of its items required some political sophistication on the part of the respondents. The scale showed evidence of solid construction in terms of internal consistency of items and the use of reversed wordings on some of the questions. As the authors predicted, their scale correlated well with the F (Fascism), E (Ethnocentrism), and PEC (Political-Economic-Conservatism) Scales, offering some indirect evidence on the validity of the scale.

Helfant's Hostility Scale also attempts to tap attitudes of militancy in foreign relations. It has the advantage of having been asked of both high school students and their parents. Evidence for homogeneity and validity seems at least adequate, and the items are simply worded and are balanced to reduce the effects of agreement response set.

Of the four World War II (or earlier) scales, Ferguson's Nationalism Scale seems the least dated and the best worded. The two forms of this scale correlate .79, indicating adequate internal consistency. In addition, the scale has evidence of "known group validity" (especially in relation to measures used by Stagner and Thompson).

A scale devised by Stagner and Osgood on nationalist attitudes has at least two interesting features. It was a precursor to Osgood's famed "semantic differential measure," and it was administered to the same sample both before and after American entry into World War II. Test-retest reliability figures are quite high. The little evidence for validity that is reported is also convincing.

A thirteen item scale on <u>Attitudes toward War</u> was developed and administered by Day and Quackenbush just prior to the (official) start of World War II. The most interesting feature of this scale was its distinction between various types of wars (defensive, cooperative, and aggressive). Internal consistency of items was high, but no evidence of validity was reported.

Another World War II scale by Stagner is marred by dated phrasing of items as well as by dated item content. Some evidence for validity was presented, but internal consistency coefficients for the <u>Attitude toward War Scale</u> varied widely for different samples. The fact that scale scores were collected on the same people before and after the war enhances the instrument's historical interest.

We encountered two other World War II vintage scales, one by Miller (1941) and the other by Gristle (1940). However these two scales were so badly dated that we considered them practically useless for current research purposes.

All of the above scales suffer from one basic liability--none of them have been administered to mass cross-sectional populations. For this reason, some attention should be given to the structure of public attitudes on war. Some studies have asked a limited number of such attitude questions which might be useful information in this context. These questions have the added advantage of having been asked repeatedly over the years, so that both general trends over time and the effects of specific world events can be ascertained.

One question of continuing relevance was tapped in a series of civil defense studies conducted by the Survey Research Center between 1952 and 1961 (Withey 1962). It asked the respondent to assess the likelihood of the United States being involved in another major world war. Percentage distributions of such expectations are given below for the sample of each study.

	April 1952	March 1954	June 1956	Oct-Nov 1961
Very likely	17%	23%	17%	10%
Likely	36	24	21	23
Maybe, pro-con	9	9	21	18
Unlikely	21	25	23	22
Very unlikely	1	6	8	13
Don't know	12	9	13	13
No answer	4	4	1	1
	100%	100%	100%	100%

A general trend toward a lowered expectation of world war involvement can be noted over this time period. However, the situation changes when the percentage distributions are analyzed within the years of the studies. In such circumstances, the proportion thinking a major world war is likely exceeds the proportion thinking in the opposite vein in each study year except 1961. Another interesting feature of the table is the increasing number of respondents giving "maybe" or "pro-con" (i.e., ambivalent) answers to this question over time.

Interpretation of these data is confounded by the fact that the early readings were taken during the Korean War. However, similar questions used by the National Opinion Research Corporation (NORC) from 1952 to 1954 also showed that expectations of United States involvement in a world war were on the decline. Figure 1 places the effect of the Korean conflict on these expectations in proper perspective--it shows that the SRC and NORC data points in the 1952-1954 time span do not represent a ceiling of world war expectations, but rather a leveling-off period from the peaks imposed by the earlier years of the Korean War, especially the years in which the heaviest fighting took place. A more extensive discussion of these and other related data can be found in Scott and Withey (1958) and Hero (1966).

336

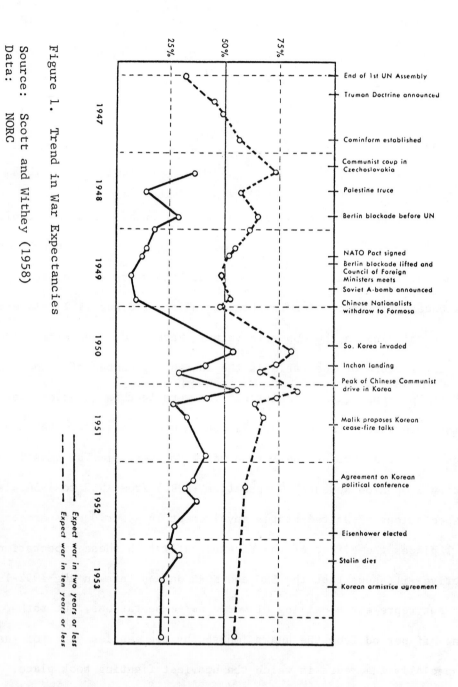

Figure 1.   Trend in War Expectancies

Source: Scott and Withey (1958)
Data: NORC

End of 1st UN Assembly

Truman Doctrine announced

Cominform established

Communist coup in
Czechoslovakia

Palestine truce

Berlin blockade before UN

NATO Pact signed

Berlin blockade lifted and
Council of Foreign
Ministers meets

Soviet A-bomb announced

Chinese Nationalists
withdraw to Formosa

So. Korea invaded

Inchon landing

Peak of Chinese Communist
drive in Korea

Malik proposes Korean
cease-fire talks

Agreement on Korean
political conference

Eisenhower elected

Stalin dies

Korean armistice agreement

25%

50%

75%

1947

1948

1949

1950

1951

1952

1953

Expect war in two years or less

Expect war in ten years or less

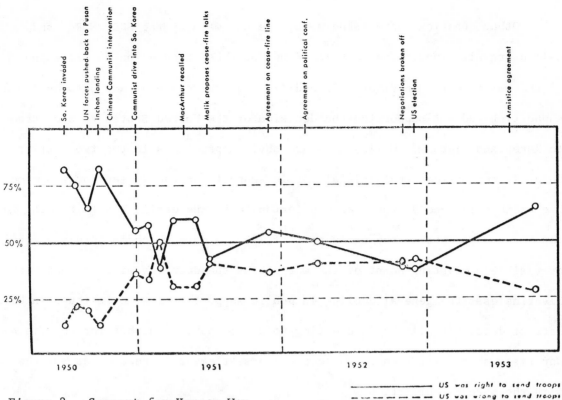

Figure 2. Support for Korean War

Source: Scott and Withey (1958)
Data: SRC, NORC, Gallup

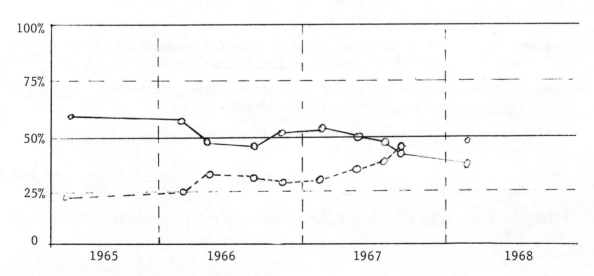

Figure 3. Support for Vietnam War

Source: Gallup Organization (AIPO)
Data: Gallup

_____ US did not make mistake in
          sending troops to Vietnam

- - - - - -US made a mistake in sending
          troops to Vietnam

Other questions were asked about the two wars by the SRC, NORC, and Gallup organizations. The most important of these focused on public support of the war effort. In Figures II and III, comparisons are made between those supporting and not supporting the decision of the United States to send troops to Korea and Vietnam. While there are obvious parallels in the two sets of data, it can be seen that initial public support for the Korean War was much higher than for the Vietnam War. Unfortunately, the earliest data reading for the Vietnam War was in the early part of 1965, a date which is hardly as obvious or visible a starting point of the war as was the open invasion of South Korea. Nevertheless, the general decline in public support over time is found in both sets of data. It will be interesting to see if public support for the Vietnam War rises sharply as soon as an acceptable settlement is reached as was the case with the Korean conflict.

References:

Gallup Opinion Index. Princeton, New Jersey: Gallup International, Inc., Report 29, November 1967.

Gristle, Murray. "The Construction of a Scale for Measuring Attitude toward Militarism-Pacifism," Journal of Social Psychology, 1940, 11, pp.383-39.

Hero, A. "The American Public and the United Nations, 1954-1966," Journal of Conflict Resolution, 1966, 10, pp.436-475.

Miller, D. C. "The Measurement of National Morale," American Sociological Review, 1941, 6, pp.482-498.

Scott, W. and Withey, S. The United States and the United Nations. New York: Manhattan Publishing Co., 1958.

Withey, S. The U.S. and the U.S.S.R. Ann Arbor: Survey Research Center, 1962.

INTERNATIONAL REACTIONS (IR) SCALE (Christiansen 1959)

Variable   This instrument yields scores on six separate types of reactions
to a series of international situations. Of particular interest
is the tendency to assign blame to others in a threat-oriented
fashion (E).

Description   A total of 40 international situations are described, for each of
which are listed six possible alternative responses. The six responses
fall into each of the cells in the following matrix:

	Threat-oriented	Problem-oriented
Outwardly directed	E	e
Inwardly directed	I	i
Passive directed	M	m

The individual makes both a first and a second choice, which are
weighted two and one, respectively.

Sample   The original sample was composed of a total of 103 applicants to Oslo
Military Academy and 64 applicants to Oslo Naval Academy of an average
age of 23, ranging from 20 to 30. Respondents were interviewed in the
late summer of 1952.

Reliability/   Reliability coefficients (Hoyt's analysis of variance measure Λ_{tt})
Homogeneity   for the six scales are as follows:

E (.81)   e (.75)
I (.70)   i (.69)
M (.72)   m (.72)

These values are in general higher than those obtained for parallel
scales of everyday situations (see the ER Scale below).

No test-retest data are reported.

Validity   No data bearing directly on validity are reported, although the correlation for scores on the IR Scale and parallel scores on reactions to
everyday situations (the ER Scale) are as follows:

E (.42)   e (.19)
I (.44)   i (.15)
M (.08)   m (.30)

Location   Christiansen, B. Attitudes toward Foreign Affairs as a Function of
Personality. Oslo, Norway: Oslo University Press, 1959.

Administration   Administration time was not reported, nor was the method of scoring.
The distribution of mean scores is as follows, with high scores
indicating higher frequency of choice:

E (16.6)   e (37.8)
I (8.7)   i (39.7)
M (9.2)   m (7.7)

**Results and
Comments**

The .42 correlation between the E scores on the Everyday Reactions (ER) Scale and the E score on the International Reactions (IR) Scale jumped from .23 for the least nationalistic third of the sample to .62 for the most nationalistic third. This indicates the importance of the felt salience of the attitude object (here the nation) in the expected generalization from everyday to international situations. The correlation between E and i scales scores on the IR Scale and the author's scale of National Patriotism were .29 and -.33 respectively. This indicates a high tendency for nationalistic individuals to prefer aggressive reactions to international situations, as one might expect.

The Everyday Reactions (ER) Scale, which also has 40 items, yielded the following distribution:

E (18.9)   e (19.9)
I (16.7)   i (23.0)
M (16.4)   m (24.8)

It can be seen that the everyday situations elicited more E, I and M reactions and fewer e and i reactions than the international situations.

A sample item from the ER scale is as follows:

21. A friend absent-mindedly puts a lighted cigarette on your table and burns a large hole in the cloth and on the tabletop. In which of the following ways would you be likely to react?

(a) Reproach him, tell him to look what he is doing another time. (E)
(b) Ask him to compensate for the damage or see that it is repaired. (e)
(c) Be annoyed with myself for not having paid more attention. (I)
(d) Be sorry for my friend, offer to fix myself. (i)
(e) Say it was just an accident, such things can happen to anybody. (M)
(f) Take it calmly. (m)

Reference

Hoyt, C. "Test Reliability Estimated by Analysis of Variance," Psychometrika, 1941, 6, 1953-1960.

INSTRUCTIONS

In what follows you will be presented with a series of international situations. You are to state what should be done in these imagined situations. After each situation are listed six alternative reactions. You are asked to give two answers for each situation: in which of the ways listed you would most prefer and next most prefer Norway to react. Your answers are not to be written in this booklet, but on a special answer sheet. Put a circle round the letters on the sheet which stand for those alternative responses to each individual situation which you think best cover the reactions you prefer. Here is an example:

    100. most prefer   a (b) c   d   e   f
          next most prefer   a   b (c) d   e   f

In this case (situation 100) the alternative response "b" would stand for the reaction amongst those listed which you would most prefer, and "c" for your second preference.

There is no time limit, but it is important to work rapidly. Sometimes you will probably feel uncertain as to what you should answer. In that case don't stop, but choose the alternative which first strikes you as best. Avoid reflections concerning your responses and try to work as continuously as possible.

Don't say what you think Norway would actually do, but what we ought to do in the following situations.

1. India demands that all Norwegian missionaries leave the country immediately.
    How would you prefer Norway to react?
    a) Demand a satisfactory explanation, turn the matter over to the United
        Nations. (e)
    b) Introduce restrictions on Indians who wish to live in Norway. (E)
    c) Blame the activities of Norwegian missions which have made the Indian
        action necessary. (I)
    d) Offer to withdraw the missionaries at once. (i)
    e) Take it calmly, these matters can be settled amicably. (m)
    f) Decide that there is nothing to be done about it; the Indians must
        naturally decide on matters affecting their own country. (M)

2. The United States demands that Norwegian shipping stop all freight transport
    to Communist China.
    How would you prefer Norway to react?
    a) Blame the Norwegian shipowners who have been carrying on such traffic.
    b) Demand an explanation, if necessary send the matter to an international
        forum.
    c) Refuse to agree to the demand, ask the United States to attend to her
        own affairs and not meddle in ours.
    d) Take the whole thing calmly, the matter is bound to be settled after a
        while.
    e) Start investigations to find out what would best serve Norwegian intersts.
    f) Feel that we were in a difficult situation, with nobody to blame.

3. Russian nationals who have lived in Norway for some time tell Russian newspapers that they have been submitted to unpleasant cross-examination by the
Norwegian police, and that the attitude of the Norwegian people has on the
whole been unfriendly.
How would you prefer Norway to react?
a) Take it calmly, wait and see.
b) Offer to investigate the complaints and put matters right.
c) Answer in the same vein, protest.
d) Demand more exact information.
e) Blame the Norwegian people and the behavior of the police.
f) Do nothing about it, unfriendly people can be found in any country.

4. Leading politicians in Germany demand that the Norwegian occupation force
return home immediately.
How would you prefer Norway to react?
a) Offer to consider recalling the brigade.
b) Tell the Germans we will not put up with taking orders from them.
c) Blame ourselves for not having recalled the brigade earlier.
d) Take it calmly, wait and see.
e) Protest, turn the case over to a forum of the Western allies.
f) Do nothing about it, no one can be blamed for wanting to be master
in his own country.

5. Finland has decided that Norwegian tourists shall not be permitted to visit
the country.
How would you prefer Norway to react?
a) Do the same in return, bar Finnish tourists from Norway.
b) Do nothing about it, all nations have the right to close their frontiers.
c) Take it calmly, it should be possible to settle such a question amicably.
d) Demand an explanation immediately.
e) Investigate the reason, suggest discussions.
f) Get irritated at the Norwegian tourists who have given cause for the
Finnish decision.

6. The United States demands to control Norwegian air and naval bases.
How would you prefer Norway to react?
a) Offer to negotiate.
b) Reject the demand immediately, reproach the United States for its
imperialistic tendencies.
c) Protest, turn the matter over to an international forum.
d) Reproach ourselves for having made such a demand possible.
e) Take it calmly, wait and see.
f) Not reproach anyone; the United States' motives must be good.

7. A spokesman for an Indonesian delegation on a visit to Norway maintains that
the delegation has been given bad treatment by Norwegian ships and hotels.
How would you prefer Norway to react?
a) Ask the Indonesians to stay home if they are not satisfied with Norwegian
conditions.
b) Blame Norwegian tourist organizations for discrimination.
c) Do nothing; unfriendly people can be found in all countries.
d) Wait and see, hope that the Indonesians' impressions of Norwegian conditions will improve in time.
e) Offer to help the Indonesians to see the best we have.
f) Ask the Indonesians for a more detailed explanation.

8. A Norwegian legation in French North Africa has been blown up after Norway voted against taking up the question of the country's independence at the United Nations' General Assembly.
   How would you prefer Norway to react?
   a) Blame ourselves for our attitude at the General Assembly.
   b) Demand compensation, and an investigation of the matter.
   c) Demand that those responsible be punished, threaten to break off diplomatic relations with the country if a similar incident occurs again.
   d) Take it calmly, leave the matter to the authorities in North Africa for the time being.
   e) Build a new legation; one has to allow for such happenings in North Africa.
   f) Revise our attitude towards colonial peoples, offer our support in future.

9. The United States threatens to cut off all economic and military aid to Norway if Norway does not immediately put a stop to all trade relations with the Soviet Union.
   How would you prefer Norway to react?
   a) Demand an explanation, turn over the case to an international organization.
   b) Investigate the consequences, offer to negotiate.
   c) Blame ourselves for having made such a request possible.
   d) Assert our independence, accuse the United States of dictatorial tendencies.
   e) Do nothing; the United States is no worse than other great powers.
   f) Wait and see, don't do anything rash.

10. Czechoslovakia has begun an extensive propaganda campaign against Norway over several short wave radio stations.
    How would you prefer Norway to react?
    a) Get the United Nations or some other international organization to take the matter up.
    b) Do nothing; all large nations carry on radio propaganda.
    c) Start jamming, or do the same thing.
    d) Take it calmly, wait and see.
    e) Wonder whether there is anything in the Czechoslovakian propaganda.
    f) Invite Czechoslovakian broadcasters to Norway to get to know the country.

11. A Norwegian citizen has been arrested and imprisoned in Germany for no reason.
    How would you prefer Norway to react?
    a) Demand compensation on behalf of the man.
    b) Wait and see, avoid rash action.
    c) Suggest that the case be investigated by representatives of both countries.
    d) Wonder what the Norwegian could have done to cause the German police to interfere.
    e) Take it calmly, any nation's police can make mistakes.
    f) Demand to have him returned, undertake reprisals.

12. Some Eskimos have accused Norwegian hunters of undermining the basis of their existence by excessive hunting of seals and other arctic animals.
    How would you prefer Norway to react?
    a) Offer to investigate the matter, offer compensation.
    b) Protest, Norwegian hunters also have the right to their existence.
    c) Blame ourselves for having given cause for such a protest.

    d) Turn the matter over to the International Court of Justice, maintain that the hunting takes place in international territory.

    e) Not blame anyone, hunting conditions have probably been bad for all concerned.

    f) Take it calmly, these matters can be settled amicably.

13. Norwegian citizens are refused entry visas to the United States.
How would you prefer Norway to react?
    a) Do nothing about it; each nation has the right to decide who it wants.
    b) Refuse permission to American citizens to visit Norway.
    c) Wait and see, there are plenty of other places to go to.
    d) Demand a statement as to why the United States refuses entry visas to Norwegian citizens.
    e) Blame the Norwegian police who issue passports to all kinds of people.
    f) Take the initiative in getting information as to how the matter is handled by the American authorities.

14. The Nazi party has begun to make itself felt again politically in the Norwegian zone of occupation in Germany.
How would you prefer Norway to react?
    a) Do nothing about it; wait and see.
    b) Not get mixed up in it; the Germans must be allowed to have whatever parties they want.
    c) Protest, appeal to the Bonn government.
    d) Forbid the Nazi party to hold public meetings, reproach the Germans who are again allowing themselves to be attracted by this party.
    e) Offer the Germany authorities help in reforming social conditions in the occupation zone.
    f) Blame ourselves for not having taken strong action sooner.

15. Russia demands that the price of bread corn exported to Norway be doubled.
How would you prefer Norway to react?
    a) Stop these imports or multiply the prices of goods we export to the Soviet Union.
    b) Demand other goods from the Soviet Union correspondingly reduced in price.
    c) Be irritated with ourselves for having entered into trade treaties with the Soviet Union.
    d) Do nothing; the Soviet Union has the right to decide what prices it wants.
    e) Offer the Soviet Union more Norwegian goods, propose discussions.
    f) Wait and see, and do nothing rash.

16. The NATO authorities in Paris have reproached Norway for maintaining too high a standard of living and for not investing large enough sums in military preparations.
How would you prefer Norway to react?
    a) Ask the authorities to stop meddling in Norwegian affairs.
    b) Invite observers to Norway to investigate the matter.
    c) Reproach ourselves for not having invested more in military preparations.
    d) Take the complaints calmly, wait and see.
    e) Do nothing about it, the authorities must know what is necessary.
    f) Demand reasons and concrete proof.

17. Swedish shrimp fishers keep fishing far into Norwegian waters, driving out Norwegian fishermen.
    How would you prefer Norway to react?
    a) Blame ourselves for not having sufficient patrol ships to prevent such fishing.
    b) Try to get the Swedish fishermen punished, threaten them with being shot at.
    c) Do nothing, the Swedish fishermen probably didn't realize they were fishing in Norwegian waters.
    d) Demand compensation, protest.
    e) Take it calmly, the matter is bound to settle itself after a time.
    f) Take the initiative in getting the matter discussed with the Swedish authorities, offer to mark the boundary better.

18. American tourists in Norway write in American newspapers that Norwegian citizens generally behave in an unfriendly fashion and that the Norwegian police are often tactless.
    How would you prefer Norway to react?
    a) Be irritated at the behaviour of the Norwegian public and police who have given such an impression.
    b) Do nothing about it; it is not easy for foreigners to understand the Norwegian temperament.
    c) The Americans are doubtless to blame themselves; ask them to behave more tactfully when they come to this country.
    d) Investigate the matter, start a campaign for better service.
    e) Take it calmly, such things are soon forgotten.
    f) Demand more exact information.

19. Czechoslovakia has asked all Norwegian citizens to leave the country.
    How would you prefer Norway to react?
    a) Break off all relations with Czechoslovakia and make a similar demand here.
    b) Demand the reason, send the case to the United Nations.
    c) Offer to see to it that all Norwegian citizens come home.
    d) Wonder what Norwegians have done in Czechoslovakia since they have been asked to leave.
    e) Do nothing about it: the Czechoslovakians have the right to make decisions in their own country.
    f) Reflect that these things always turn out all right if only one shows enough patience.

20. The Soviet Union demands the use of ice-free harbors in North Norway.
    How would you prefer Norway to react?
    a) Mobilize, send military units to defend the north.
    b) Demand a further explanation, send the case to an international organization.
    c) Find out why the Soviet Union wants to use the harbors, offer to discuss the matter.
    d) Take it calmly, wait and see.
    e) Not blame anyone; all nations should have the opportunity of leasing fuelling berths in Norwegian harbors.
    f) Blame ourselves for not having allowed the Soviet Union to do this earlier.

21. The United Nations has charged Norway with not taking enough refugees from Central Europe.
    How would you prefer Norway to react?
    a) Offer to investigate the matter, if necessary try to rectify it.
    b) Tell the United Nations that it is our own business; point to the small amount other countries have done for the refugees.
    c) Take the whole thing calmly, avoid hasty action.
    d) Demand more detailed reasons and further discussion.
    e) Blame ourselves for having given grounds for such a charge.
    f) Feel that it is important to think of the refugees, but that Norway has limited resources.

22. A Norwegian tanker has been sunk by Viet-Minh forces off French Indo-China.
    How would you prefer Norway to react?
    a) Do nothing about it; one has to expect such things in time of war.
    b) Blame ourselves for not having armed our merchant vessels sailing in such waters.
    c) Demand compensation; bring the case before an international forum.
    d) See to it that the Viet-Minh forces are severely punished.
    e) Support the building of a new ship
    f) Feel that nothing can be done about it as long as the war lasts; wait and see.

23. Norwegian citizens residing in Russia are not allowed freedom of travel.
    How would you prefer Norway to react?
    a) Prevent Russian citizens in Norway from moving about freely.
    b) Do nothing, the Russians have the right to decide in their own country.
    c) Protest, demand an explanation.
    d) Blame ourselves for having provoked the Russian travel restrictions.
    e) Try to arrange talks with the Russian authorities.
    f) Do nothing hasty, wait and see.

24. The United States demands the right to carry out air manoeuvres over Norwegian territory.
    How would you prefer Norway to react?
    a) Tell the United States that we will not be dictated to by them.
    b) Turn the matter over to the North Atlantic Council.
    c) Do nothing about it; the United States has the right to demand this.
    d) Offer to discuss the matter with the U.S.
    e) Wait and see; avoid taking hasty action.
    f) Blame ourselves for having given occasion for such a demand.

25. Sweden threatens to stop all imports of fertilizers from Norway. Fertilizers are our most important export to Sweden.
    How would you prefer Norway to react?
    a) Take it calmly, wait and see.
    b) Try to develop an export market somewhere else.
    c) Threaten Sweden with reprisals, by stopping imports of goods which Sweden wishes to sell us.
    d) Demand an explanation.
    e) Blame ourselves for not having found more stable customers for our fertilizer exports.
    f) Do nothing about it; Sweden must decide herself where she wants to get her fertilizers from.

26. A Russian radio station starts jamming Norwegian wave-lengths used for broadcasting to Norwegians abroad.
    How would you prefer Norway to react?
    a) Take the matter calmly; wait and see. (m)
    b) Protest and retaliate on Russian broadcasts in Norwegian. (E)
    c) Change the wavelength. (i)
    d) Demand an explanation and bring the matter before an international forum. (e)
    e) Wonder what reasons the Russians might have for disturbing these broadcasts. (I)
    f) Do nothing; such things can be due to pure accident. (M)

27. The United States demands that the rental charges for American films be increased by 200%
    How would you prefer Norway to react?
    a) Protest, stop importing American films.
    b) Do nothing about it; all prices have risen and the United States has the right to decide itself what prices it wants to charge.
    c) Let the matter rest, wait and see.
    d) Accept the demand; reduce our income by abolishing duty on American films.
    e) Blame ourselves for having become so dependent on American films.
    f) Demand a further explanation, try to contact other countries importing American films.

28. The Chinese Communist government has confiscated the property of Norwegian missionaries and categorically refused Norway any kind of compensation.
    How would you prefer Norway to react?
    a) Break off all relations with Communist China, undertake reprisals.
    b) Demand compensation, send the matter to the United Nations.
    c) Do nothing about it; the Chinese are masters in their own country.
    d) Let the matter rest until China's international status is clarified.
    e) Blame the Norwegian missionaries for having incurred the ill-will of the Chinese.
    f) Offer China aid on a non-missionary basis.

29. Canada has started intense radio propaganda against Norway.
    How would you prefer Norway to react?
    a) Invite Canadian radio broadcasters to come to Norway to get to know the country.
    b) Do the same thing against Canada.
    c) Do nothing, all large nations carry on radio propaganda.
    d) Send the matter to the United Nations or some other international forum.
    e) Take it calmly, wait and see.
    f) Wonder whether we have irritated the Canadians in some way since they have started this propaganda.

30. German war toys are being exported to Norway again and sold extensively all over the country.
    How would you prefer Norway to react?
    a) Demand that such trade be stopped; blame the Germans for producing such toys again.
    b) Do nothing about it; German toys are of a high standard and Germany has to export.

    c) Take it calmly, wait and see.
    d) Blame ourselves for not providing ourselves with good Norwegian toys.
    e) Demand a very high import duty on German toys.
    f) Try to increase the production of Norwegian toys.

31.   The Norwegian standard of living has been seriously threatened by England's reduction of the prices she is willing to pay for Norwegian paper and pulp. How would you prefer Norway to react?
    a) Blame ourselves for having linked our export trade so one-sidedly with England.
    b) Do nothing about it; England has the right to decide how much she wants to give for her imports.
    c) Take the matter calmly, wait and see how other export countries will react.
    d) Demand an explanation; bring the matter before an international organization.
    e) Try to develop export markets elsewhere.
    f) Undertake reprisals, reduce the prices we are willing to pay for English exports.

32.   Russia protests against the removal of Russian war graves in North Norway. How would you prefer Norway to react?
    a) Try to persuade the Russians that it is necessary to move them; initiate discussions.
    b) Continue moving them; tell the Russians that the graves in Norway are none of their business.
    c) Blame ourselves for having started moving the graves without first having discussed the matter thoroughly with the Soviet authorities.
    d) Take it calmly; it should be possible to come to an agreement about such a matter.
    e) Demand that the Soviet authorities pay for the upkeep of the graves if they insist that they remain spread about in many different places.
    f) Do nothing we might be blamed for later; the case can be understood both from the Norwegian and the Russian point of view.

33.   English trawlers have repeatedly violated Norwegian fishing boundaries and fished in Norwegian waters.
    How would you prefer Norway to react?
    a) Confiscate the trawlers and punish their captains severely.
    b) Develop a warning system which would make it possible for the English trawlers to be informed when they cross the fishing boundary.
    c) Demand compensation; refer the case to the Hague International Court.
    d) Do nothing about it; the English trawlers couldn't have realized that they had crossed the boundary.
    e) Blame ourselves because we don't have an efficient patrol system.
    f) Take the matter calmly.

34.   The Soviet Union asks Norwegian ships to refrain from transporting military material to Chiang Kai-shek's government on Formosa.
    How would you prefer Norway to react?
    a) Remember that the Soviet demand is understandable, but Norwegian interests must be respected.
    b) Try to find out what Norway's best interests are.

c) Take the matter calmly; it is bound to be settled when China's international status is clarified.
d) Refuse to meet to the request, ask the Soviet authorities to mind their own business and to stop sending us requests of this kind.
e) Demand a further explanation.
f) Blame the Norwegian shipowners who have been carrying on this traffic.

35. Spain has decided that Norwegian diplomats are to be allowed very limited freedom of movement.
How would you prefer Norway to react?
a) Do nothing hasty; wait and see.
b) Try to institute discussions with the Spanish authorities.
c) Blame ourselves for having been unfriendly towards Spain.
d) Protest, demand an explanation, seek the support of other nations.
e) Do nothing, the Spaniards must decide for themselves in their own country.
f) Institute the same restrictions for Spanish diplomats in Norway.

36. Switzerland has started intense propaganda within the continent of Europe against Norway as a tourist country.
How would you prefer Norway to react?
a) Answer in the same coin, start propaganda against Switzerland.
b) Do nothing about it; Switzerland has more to offer tourists than we have.
c) Blame ourselves for having neglected our tourist propaganda with the results that the Swiss arguments cannot be rejected.
d) Take the initiative in getting the matter discussed with the Swiss authorities.
e) Protest, send the case to an international forum.
f) Take it calmly; other things matter more than propaganda in competition for the tourist trade.

37. Western Germany has instituted very strict trade restrictions against Norway on the basis of our trading activities with Eastern Germany.
How would you prefer Norway to react?
a) Investigate the matter; try to find out what will best serve Norwegian interests.
b) Institute the same trade restrictions against Western Germany.

    c) Demand an explanation; get the matter discussed in an international organization.

    d) Take it calmly; wait and see.

    e) Blame ourselves for our trade with Eastern Germany.

    f) Do nothing about it; no one can prevent Western Germany from instituting what trade restrictions she wants.

38. British military planes have been observed at a great height over several towns in North Norway.
How would you prefer Norway to react?

    a) Protest, demand an explanation.

    b) Take it calmly; wait and see.

    c) Try to chase them away; if necessary shoot them down.

    d) Do nothing about it; it was most likely due to a mistake in navigation.

    e) Blame ourselves for our inefficient warning system.

    f) Take the initiative in getting the matter investigated in cooperation with the British authorities.

39. Egypt refuses to allow Norwegian ships to call at Egyptian ports because the ships are being used to transport weapons and military material to Israel.
How would you prefer Norway to react?

    a) Try to take reprisals; stop calling at Egyptian ports.

    b) Blame ourselves for having carried on contraband activities.

    c) Demand proof, send the matter to the United Nations.

    d) Take it calmly; these always turn out all right in time.

    e) Do nothing about it; Egypt can decide herself what ships she will permit to call at her ports.

    f) Allow Egypt to inspect the Norwegian ships which call at Egyptian ports.

40. A Norwegian diplomat has been wrongfully arrested and accused of spying in Iran.
How would you prefer Norway to react?

    a) Blame ourselves for having sent diplomats to the country when conditions are so uncertain.

    b) Demand that the diplomat be handed over; take reprisals.

    c) Take it calmly; the police of any nation can make mistakes.

    d) Demand compensation; try to get Iran to put the matter right.

    e) Wait and see, hope the matter will be cleared up after a while.

    f) Offer to help Iran to investigate the case.

NATIONAL PATRIOTISM (NP) SCALE (Christiansen 1959)

Variable	This scale is designed to detect a tendency "to see one's own nation as superior to humanity."
Description	This is a nine-item Likert scale with the five response alternatives running from strong agreement (1), to moderate agreement (2), to slight agreement (3), to moderate disagreement (4), to strong disagreement (5). Possible scale scores thus ran from 9 (low patriotism) to 45 (high patriotism). Two of the nine items (items 1 and 5) have reversed wording.

National loyalty is measured in relation to

a) National subgroups, by items 3 and 5
b) Supra-national organizations, by items 4 and 7
c) National outgroups, by items 1 and 6 and
d) Humanity as a whole, by items 2, 8 and 9

Sample	The sample consisted of 159 of the 1967 Oslo military students described as the sample in the preceding IR Scale write-up.
Reliability/ Homogeneity	Hoyt's r_{tt} (see the IR Scale) for the scale was .54. No test-retest data are reported. Item analyses revealed that items 2, 4, and 9 (two of these are "humanity" items) had the highest correlations with total scale scores and that items 1 and 5 had the lowest.
Validity	While no data bearing directly on validity are reported, the author reported the actual occurrence of an hypothesized relation between national patriotism and the E score on his IR Scale (see previous scale write-up).

The NP Scale correlated only .07 with a scale of national idealization, in line with the author's expectations.

Location	Christiansen, B. Attitudes toward Foreign Affairs as a Function of Personality. Oslo: Oslo University Press, 1959.
Administration	Estimated administration time is about five minutes. Average NP Scale score for this military sample was 27.4 (s.d. = 4.6), with scores ranging from 16 to 40.
Results and Comments	The author felt that the very low correlation between his NI Scale and the NP Scale was the result of the confounding of feelings of national idealization with ordinary feelings of satisfaction with one's country.

PATRIOTISM SCALE

1. No duties are more important than duties toward one's own country.

    1. Strongly   2. Moderately   3. Slightly   4. Moderately   5. Strongly
       Agree   Agree   Agree   Disagree   Disagree

2. Norway's frontiers should be open to all those who wish to settle in Norway.

3. When a national government is incompetent, the use of force to remove it can be justified.

4. Norway ought to be willing to give up its independence and submit to the authority of a United States of the World.

5. One should always show greater loyalty to the King and the government than to a national political party.

6. All human beings are equally important. No Norwegian is of more value than any person from any other country.

7. Norway ought to support the establishment of a World Government that could solve international disputes by force.

8. The defense of Norway can never justify the taking of another human life.

9. One should show greater loyalty towards humanity than towards Norway as a nation.

INTERNATIONAL HOSTILITY INVENTORY (Grace 1949)

Variable	This instrument is designed to examine hostile responses to international situations having the United States as a referent.
Description	The instrument consists of 35 short statements of situations, each offering four categories of response choices: autohostile, laissez-faire, verbal heterohostile, and direct heterohostile. The inventory items were chosen from an original 60 by three judges. The instrument is one-third of a hostility inventory; measures of hostility in everyday situations and in professional (teaching) situations completed the inventory. Response choices were adapted from the responses of 60 students to prior administration of the inventory items in open-ended format.
Sample	The sample was comprised of 210 graduate students in education at Teachers College, Columbia University, with an average age of 31.
Reliability/ Homogeneity	After an item analysis, the author discarded as unreliable the eight items for which the ratio of scores of the highest 20 percent to the scores of the lowest 20 percent was less than 2:1 or for which the ratio was higher in favor of the lowest 20 percent. Since a correlation technique of determining reliability was deemed unapplicable to the inventory, the chi-square and the determination of the significance of difference between means were used on the odd-even scores. A significant difference between odd and even responses was found in the autohostile and verbal heterohostile categories.
Validity	The items administered as the final inventory were agreed upon unanimously by the three judges. No further evidence of validity was presented.
Administration	Estimated administration time is about 30 minutes.
Location	Grace, H. A. "A Study of the Expression of Hostility in Everyday, Professional, and International Verbal Situations," Ph.D. thesis, Columbia University, 1949.
Results and Comments	It was found that in all response categories except laissez-faire, the international responses were opposite to the everyday and the professional. The author suggested that the international situations elicited more specific responses than the everyday and professional situations. There was found to be a high significance of difference among the categories of hostility. The three fields of behavior were not significantly different and so appeared to be sub-fields of a general field of human social behavior.
	It was found that Republicans, Protestants, and Roman Catholics in the sample tended to express more heterohostility in the international field than the everyday and professional fields, while progressive,

second-generation Americans, and veterans tended to express auto-hostility in the international field. Non-religious persons tended to show very little direct heterohostility in the international field.

Laissez-faire behavior tended to be the most general response in all fields.

An example of an "everyday" item is:

1. While you are all dressed up a car splashes mud over you.
   Which one of the following would you feel most like doing:
   a. Swearing at the driver
   b. Blaming myself for having stood too close to the curb
   c. Throwing something at the car
   d. Feeling that such things happen now and then

An example of a "professional" item is:

3. Some of the students in your class keep passing notes to one another.
   Which one of the following would you feel most like doing:
   a. Finding out why they are bored with my class
   b. Demanding an explanation from them
   c. I wouldn't mind at all
   d. Sending all of them to the principal's office.

355

SITUATIONAL INVENTORY

2. Panama asks for direct control of the Panama Canal. Which one of the following would you feel most like doing:

   a. Letting the United Nations handle it
   b. Sending American troops to Panama to hold the Panama Canal
   c. Backing Panama, we should not be there
   d. Refusing the request flatly

5. During a revolt in China a United States citizen has been killed. Which one of the following would you feel most like doing:

   a. Sending a sharp note to China demanding indemnity
   b. Keeping our citizens out of China
   c. So what, ignore it
   d. Killing a Chinese in return

9. An American friend of yours announces his engagement to a Japanese girl. Which one of the following would you feel most like doing:

   a. Feeling that that is his business
   b. Telling him he is a fool
   c. Not allowing him to leave Japan with her
   d. Wondering what is wrong with American girls

11. An American is arrested by the Polish police for being a spy. Which one of the following would you feel most like doing:

   a. Condemning the United States for spying on a friendly nation
   b. Demanding his release
   c. Arresting some Poles here
   d. Nothing, that's the chance he takes

14. German toys are sent to the United States for sale here. Which one of the following would you feel most like doing:

   a. Sending them back to Germany
   b. Feeling so what, that's their business
   c. Buying them in preference to American toys to help Germany reconstruct
   d. Protesting their sale here

16. An English diplomat asks the United States to take a large number of displaced persons into the country immediately. Which one of the following would you feel most like doing:

   a. Taking no notice of it
   b. Cutting off the loan to Britain
   c. Protesting his statement
   d. Asking my Congressman to back the proposal

17. The United Nations asks for the end of racial discrimination in the world, including the United States. Which one of the following would you feel most like doing:

    a. Boycotting the United Nations
    b. Telling the United Nations that it is out of their province
    c. Feeling that what they say doesn't matter
    d. Supporting the resolution whole-heartedly

22. An American citizen is captured by bandits in China. Which one of the following would you feel most like doing:

    a. Writing Congress to get all Americans out of "trouble" areas
    b. Feeling that if he takes the chances, then he'll have to take the consequences
    c. Demanding that the bandits release him
    d. Sending United States troops to gain his release

25. A newspaper reports that American troops are being sent to the Mediterranean Sea area to set up a naval and air base. Which one of the following would you feel most like doing:

    a. Feeling angry at Europe for not being able to patrol its own areas
    b. Sending more troops to be sure it is held
    c. Protesting to the United States government and demanding the return of the troops
    d. So what, let it go

27. Chinese students in Peking demonstrate for the removal of American troops from China. Which one of the following would you feel most like doing:

    a. Removing all of the American troops
    b. Mowing the Chinese down
    c. Letting the incident blow over
    d. Protesting to the Chinese government about the demonstration

29. Mexican laborers in the United States protest about their mistreatment by Americans. Which one of the following would you feel most like doing:

    a. Feeling that that's their business
    b. Censuring the Americans and telling them to provide better for the Mexicans
    c. Protesting to our immigration officials about letting them into the country
    d. Sending the Mexicans home

32. The government of Siam, which is supported by the United States, is suddenly overthrown. Which one of the following would you feel most like doing:

    a. Protesting any interference of the United States in Siam's affairs
    b. Sending United States troops to restore the government
    c. Sending financial aid to the ex-government and harboring its members
    d. Letting the Siamese handle the situation

36. A new branch of the Nazi Party is begun in the American Zone in Germany.
Which one of the following would you feel most like doing:

    a. Warning the Germans about this
    b. Shooting the leaders
    c. Recognizing it as a natural reaction to the American forces there
    d. Letting the Germans handle it themselves

40. The United States has taken under its control the Pacific Islands which
were captured from Japan, but China protests this action. Which one of the
following would you feel most like doing:

    a. Letting the United Nations handle it
    b. Sending American troops to protect the islands
    c. Protesting to the United States government and demanding that we give
       up the islands
    d. Telling China that she is in no position to protest our actions

45. A Czechoslovakian delegate to the United Nations accuses the United States
of warmongering. Which one of the following would you feel most like doing:

    a. Throwing him out of the room
    b. Admitting that the charge has some truth in it
    c. Demanding a formal retraction of the statement
    d. Ignoring him, this happens all the time

48. A French government official states that since scientists from all over the
world helped to make atomic energy possible, the United States should tell
the world of the atomic bomb's secrets. Which one of the following would
you feel most like doing:

    a. Telling him that he is all wet
    b. So what, the matter is not that important
    c. Having our secret service keep an eye on the French official
    d. Agreeing with him and demanding that the United States release any
       secrets it has

50. While coming out of a foreign country you are detained at the border with
passport difficulty. Which one of the following would you feel most like
doing:

    a. That's the chance you have to take
    b. Preventing that country from getting a United States loan
    c. Making sure that I check everything next time
    d. Protesting the delay to the United States consul

54. Spokesmen for Puerto Rico demand that the United States give them voting
privileges in Congress. Which one of the following would you feel most
like doing:

    a. Blaming Congress for not having given them the vote already
    b. Throwing these spokesmen in jail
    c. Refusing the request
    d. Ignoring them

56. In occupied Japan Japanese workers go on strike for higher wages and shorter hours. Which one of the following would you feel most like doing:

   a. Throwing them in jail
   b. Letting the Japanese handle the problem
   c. Writing to Congress to see that the Japanese get their demands
   d. Telling them to shut up and produce more

61. In the United Nations, the Scandinavian countries demand that the "Big Five" give up the veto power. Which one of the following would you feel most like doing:

   a. Vetoing the proposal
   b. Sending a note to the United States government urging it to abolish the veto
   c. Letting the United Nations fight it out
   d. Telling them they are crazy

63. An American embassy in the Arab lands is bombed after the United States supports the Jews at the United Nations. Which one of the following would you feel most like doing:

   a. Demanding that the United States change its policy toward the Arabs
   b. Feeling that this is natural
   c. Demanding that the Arabs apologize and pay for the damages
   d. Bombing the Arabs

64. Leading Austrians ask that all the occupation troops be withdrawn from the country. Which one of the following would you feel most like doing:

   a. Sending more United States troops to Austria
   b. Nothing, that's their business
   c. Telling the Austrians that we won the war and so we'll make the decisions
   d. Petitioning the United States government for withdrawal of our troops

66. After a revolution in Latin America, the new government asks that all foreign investors leave. Which one of the following would you feel most like doing:

   a. Urging that the American interests get out
   b. Threatening to cut our relations with them
   c. Sending American troops to back our interests
   d. Letting the United Nations settle it

72. While being returned to Japan by the American government many Japanese have died aboard ship. Which one of the following would you feel most like doing:

   a. Throwing the Japs overboard
   b. Writing to Congress condemning the American government
   c. Telling the Japs to use their own ships
   d. Feeling that such things cannot be avoided

74. The British government places a heavy tax on American films. Which one of the following would you feel most like doing:

   a. Banning British films
   b. Lowering the United States tax on British films to help them out
   c. Letting the governments settle it themselves
   d. Demanding that the British cut the tax

76. The Chinese demand that all foreign investors leave the country and turn their business over to the Chinese. Which one of the following would you feel most like doing:

   a. Insisting that all Americans leave China
   b. Protesting to China and demanding reparations
   c. Referring China to the United Nations
   d. Sending American troops to back our interests

81. In Trieste the Yugoslavs protest American interference on the side of the Italians. Which one of the following would you feel most like doing:

   a. Telling the Yugoslavs to mind their own business
   b. Condemning our government for backing one side against the other
   c. Letting them take care of it themselves
   d. Sending troops to Trieste to back our policy

85. In the Palestine fighting an American oil pipe-line is broken and much American money lost. Which one of the following would you feel most like doing:

   a. Demanding that the United States turn the pipe-line over to the Palestinians
   b. Writing it off as profit and loss
   c. Suing the guilty persons for damages
   d. Demanding formal apologies from the guilty persons

88. Latin American delegates in the United Nations demand that the United States ask permission to explore the South Pole. Which one of the following would you feel most like doing:

   a. Supporting the Latin Americans' request
   b. Sending American troops to hold the South Pole
   c. Telling the Latin Americans to mind their own business
   d. It makes no difference to me anyway

90. India asks that all American missionaries leave the country. Which one of the following would you feel most like doing:

   a. Sending the Indians here back to India
   b. Petitioning for the withdrawal of all American missions from India
   c. Demanding an "open door" policy in India
   d. Feeling it is too far away to worry about

ATTITUDES TOWARD WAR (Putney 1962)

Variable — This study attempts to measure the extent of anti-war sentiment among American college and university students and to illuminate the factors associated with their acceptance or rejection of war.

Description — The four scales used are as follows:

a) Pacifism Scale, where pacifism is defined as "a tendency to regard war as inherently unacceptable in the modern world."

b) Level of Provocation Scale, measuring the degree of provocation deemed necessary to justify the United States' use of nuclear weapons against our enemy.

c) Maximum Fatalities Scale, measuring the number of tolerable fatilities to be incurred in pursuing a nuclear war.

d) Nuclear Information Scale, measuring knowledge of nuclear weapons.

The Pacifism Scale is a Guttman scale of seven, 5-point Likert-type items. "Disagree" responses to items 1, 3, and 7, and "agree" responses to the remaining items were coded as Pacifistic. The Provocation Scale consists of a single Guttman-type item of seven responses, which, however, did not meet normal Guttman scale criteria. Lower estimates on the Fatalities Scale were considered more pacifistic. The Nuclear Information Scale is a Guttman scale consisting of six true-false items.

Sample — The population sample consisted of 1100 students in 16 American colleges and universities in 1961, being mostly undergraduates, 58 percent male and 55 percent lower classmen. The author cautioned against generalizing the results to all American college students, since the sampling involves the selection of classes rather than individuals.

Reliability/ Homogeneity — The coefficient of reproducibility for the Pacifism Scale was .91. Since the Rep. for the Provocation Scale was artificially inflated by the distribution of answers to the first two items and last two items, two of the items were eliminated. The recomputed Rep. for the shortened scale was .97.

Items 5, 6, 7, and 8 of Kaufman's (1957) Status Concern Scale were also administered to the sample. The Rep. for this abbreviated scale was .93.

No estimates of test-retest reliability were reported.

Validity	No tests for validity were reported.
Location	Putney, Snell. "Some Factors Associated with Student Acceptance or Rejection of War," _American Sociological Review_, 1962, <u>27</u>, pp. 655-667.
Administration	Estimated administration time for the <u>Pacifism Scale</u> is about seven minutes, for the <u>Provocation and Fatalities Scales</u>, about seven minutes each, and for the <u>Information Scale</u>, about five minutes.
Results and Comments	It was found that the three acceptance measures were related significantly (average association was about .44) but not highly enough to suggest complete unidimensionality. The pattern of responses to the three acceptance measures was ambivalent, with females scoring consistently more pacifistic. It was found that acceptance of war tended to be positively associated with an informed image of war, with the personal reality of war (living in likely target areas) and with "involvement in society," as indicated by a low score on the abbreviated <u>SC</u> scale.
Reference	Kaufman, Walter C. "Status, Authoritarianism and Anti-Semitism," _American Journal of Sociology_, 1957, <u>62</u>, pp. 379-382.

PACIFISM SCALE

	Percentage of Students Who Agree or Mostly Agree with the Item as Worded		
	Males	Females	Total
*1. The U.S. must be willing to run any risk of war which may be necessary to prevent the spread of Communism.	78	64	72
2. If disarmament negotiations are not successful, the U.S. should begin a gradual program of unilateral disarmament--i.e., disarm whether other countries do or not.	4	9	6
*3. Pacifist demonstrations--picketing missile bases, peace walks, etc.--are harmful to the best interest of the American people.	50	37	44
4. The U.S. has no moral right to carry its struggle against Communism to the point of risking the destruction of the human race.	30	40	34
5. It is contrary to my moral principles to participate in war and the killing of other people	15	20	17
6. The real enemy today is no longer Communism but rather war itself.	26	37	31
*7. Pacifism is simply not a practical philosophy in the world today.	60	45	54
Number of cases.	(697)	(502)	(1199)

* Reverse scoring items on Pacifism Scale.

LEVEL OF PROVOCATION

	Percentage of Students Who Believe Nuclear Weapons Should Be Used Against Enemy		
	Males	Females	Total
1. Present circumstances ("pre-emptive war")	3	2	3
2. Communists attempt to take over in any other country, however small	11	4	8
3. Communists interfere with important rights of the U.S., such as access to Berlin	29	20	25
4. Communists attack an ally of the U.S. with conventional weapons	33	16	26
5. Communists attack the U.S. with conventional weapons	53	32	44
6. Communists attack an ally of the U.S. with nuclear weapons	90	75	84
7. Communists attack the U.S. with nuclear weapons	96	95	95
Number of cases	(694)	(497)	(1191)

MAXIMUM FATALITIES SCALE

Question:

*" Suppose the Soviet Union makes a nuclear attack on our European allies but announces that it will attack the U.S. only in self-defense. The U.S. can use its nuclear weapons at once on the Soviets and suffer their reprisal, or hold off unless they actually attack the U.S. Scientific and military advisers give the President an estimate of U.S. casualties from the Soviet reprisal if he orders an immediate attack. If you were the President, would you order the attack given each of the following estimates of U.S. casualties?"

(Highest Level of American Fatalities Considered Tolerable)	Percentage of Students		
	Males	Females	Total
1. 100% of population killed (180 million)	17	8	13
2. 75 to 100% of population killed (135-180 million)	7	2	5
3. 50 to 75% of population killed (90-135 million)	12	6	10
4. 25 to 50% of population killed (45-90 million)	19	15	18
5. 10 to 25% of population killed (18-45 million)	18	20	19
6. 1 to 10% of population (2-18 million)	10	18	13
7. Less than 1% of population killed (less than 2 million)	17	31	22
TOTAL	100	100	100
Number of cases	(674)	(449)	(1123)

NUCLEAR INFORMATION SCALE

1. The primary materials used in the atomic bombs
   dropped in Japan were derived from uranium. (T)

2. A 20-megaton bomb has the destructive force of
   about twenty-thousand tons of TNT. (F)

3. The neutron bomb would result in less property
   damage than the hydrogen bomb. (T)

4. A "fire storm" is the initial flash of an atomic
   explosion. (F)

5. Strontium 90 concentrates in the blood like iron
   and quickly causes death. (F)

6. The bomb dropped on Hiroshima had a power of
   approximately 20 kilotons. (T)

VIETNAM POLICY SCALES (Verba et al. 1967)

Variable	These scales tap public support for various escalation and de-escalation policies with regard to Vietnam.
Description	There are two separate scales: one for escalation and one for de-escalation. Each is composed of responses to eight agree-disagree type questions, scale scores thus running from 0 to 8. Distribution of scores was as follows.

Score	Escalation	De-escalation
0 (Low)	10%	2%
1	11	6
2	11	14
3	12	20
4	12	22
5	11	13
6	11	9
7	6	3
8 (High)	16	11
	100%	100%
Average	3.9 (S.D. = 2.5)	3.8 (S.D. = 1.9)

Sample	A national cross-section sample of 1495 adults was administered this scale in late February and early March 1966.
Reliability/ Homogeneity	Coefficients of reproducibility were "in excess of .90" and coefficients of scalability "in excess of .60" for the two scales. Scale scores differed from chance at .001 levels.
	Scale scores were apparently determined by adding the number of "approve" items together rather than treating the items as a true Guttman scale (this does not make the scale any less valid or useful). No test-retest data are reported.
Validity	No data reporting directly on validity are reported. Correlation between the two scales is -.37, which is well short of what one would expect from two scales measuring opposite ends of the same dimension. This probably reflects (as the authors point out) the lack of a coherent war ideology among people rather than any basic fault in the scale itself.
Location	Verba, Sidney, et al. "Public Opinion and the War in Vietnam," American Political Science Review, June 1967, LXI, pp. 317-333.
Administration	The items could be easily revised for use in questionnaires, rather than their original interview format. It should take no more than 10-15 minutes to complete both scales.

Results and
Comments

Negroes, women, and the less informed were more in favor of de-escalation and opposed to escalation of the war. Those in favor of escalation were willing to pay the costs of the increased war effort, being willing to forego spending for welfare measures ($r = .30$) and willing to undergo wartime measures ($r = .37$).

Little difference was found between "activists" and "non-activists," at least as indexed by that 16 percent who said that they had ever written letters to public officials or newspapers.

The authors note an interesting convergence between public and congressional opinion on Vietnam.

VIETNAM ESCALATION SCALE

1. There is talk these days about a number of different actions we might have to take at home and abroad if we are to continue the fighting in Vietnam. I'd like to know whether you approve or disapprove of doing the following in order to continue fighting?

    c) Having 200,000 American troops in South Vietnam (61% approve)

    d) Bombing military targets in North Vietnam (77% approve)

    e) Having half a million troops in South Vietnam (45% approve)

2. Would you favor or oppose continuing the fighting in Vietnam if it meant ...

	% Favoring
a) Fighting the Chinese Army in Vietnam?	56%
b) Fighting a ground war in China itself	32%
c) Fighting an atomic war with China?	29%
d) Fighting an atomic war with Russia?	22%
e) All out mobilization of American men in the armed forces?	40%

VIETNAM DE-ESCALATION SCALE

3. A number of different steps have been proposed to end the present fighting in South Vietnam. Would you approve or disapprove of the following actions to end the fighting?

% Approving

a) Forming a new government in which the Viet Cong took some part — 52%

b) Holding free elections in South Vietnam even if the Viet Cong might win — 54%

c) Getting the United Nations or some neutral countries to negotiate a truce, with each side holding the territory it now holds — 69%

d) Gradually withdrawing our troops and letting the South Vietnamese work out their own problems — 39%

4. If it meant eventual control of South Vietnam by the Viet Cong, would you approve of ending the fighting now? — 28%

5. Would you approve of ending the fighting in South Vietnam even if it meant the eventual loss of independence of other nations like Laos and Thailand? — 13%

6. Would you be in favor of American negotiations with the Viet Cong if they were willing to negotiate? — 88%

7. If President Johnson were to announce tomorrow that we were going to withdraw from Vietnam and let the Communists take over, would you approve or disapprove? — 15%

IDEOLOGICAL MILITANCY-PACIFISM (IMP) SCALE (Dombrose and Levinson 1950)

Variable	This scale attempts to measure individual preference for "pacifistic" as compared with "militant" modes of realization of democratic values.
Description	Out of an original 32 five-point Likert-type items, 28 were included in the scale after item analysis. Source of the items was the literature of liberal political and religious groups, newspapers, and discussions. The items were designed to imply an acceptance in some degree of certain basic beliefs and values of "democratic ideology" (anti-ethnocentrism). Seven items deal with problems of group relations, 19 with solutions to political-economic problems, and two with ethical beliefs. Agreement with items indicated preference for a pacifistic program of action, except for seven statements for which scoring was reversed. Range of average item scores on the five-point scoring scale of the IMP was 1.1 to 3.9.
Sample	The initial sample of 100 was comprised of social workers, college students, and college administrators who were administered the E Scale to obtain the experimental group of 40 subjects characterized by rejection of ethnocentrism. Range of E Scale scores (seven point scoring) for this group was 1.0 - 2.9, the E Scale is described in Chapter 6.
Reliability/ Homogeneity	The split-half reliability (corrected) was .90. No test-retest reliability was reported.
Validity	No direct tests for the validity of this measure were reported.
Location	Dombrose, Lawrence A. and Levinson, Daniel J. "Ideological 'Militancy' and 'Pacifism' in Democratic Individuals," Journal of Social Psychology, 1950, 32, pp. 101-113.
Administration	Estimated administration time is about 28 minutes. Scoring requires averaging of item scores.
Results and Comments	In line with their initial hypothesis, the authors conclude from the high correlation of IMP scores with E scores that those who strongly reject ethnocentrism tend toward militancy in their programs of action for the realization of democratic values, whereas those who moderately reject ethnocentrism tend toward pacifistic programs of action.

Reported correlation between scores on the E scale and scores on IMP was .74, and between scores on the PEC (see Chapter 3) and IMP was .52 (correlation between E and PEC for this sample was .62).

It was found that the IMP scores correlated with F Scale scores .67, and .38, with E and PEC scores partialled out (significant beyond the five percent level). The most militant quartile scored an average 1.9, and the most pacifistic quartile scored an average 3.4 on the seven-point scale. It was proposed that differences in personality exist between the militant lows and the pacifistic lows. |

The authors suggest that the most pacifistic quartile may be unable to feel intensely about an issue, but they concede that, with two exceptions, the items lacked statements which directly stated vital pacifistic values.

The seven reversed items were judged to guard successfully against negative response set.

IMP SCALE

This is an experimental study of how people feel about some social issues. Your personal opinion on the statements below is wanted. There are no right and wrong answers and every viewpoint has many supporters.

Mark an X through the number in the left margin according to whether you agree, are uncertain, or disagree about each statement. Please mark every one. Read each statement carefully.

+2: I AGREE PRETTY MUCH   -2: I DISAGREE PRETTY MUCH
+1: I AGREE A LITTLE   -1: I DISAGREE A LITTLE
              0: UNCERTAIN

+2 +1 0 -1 -2   (1) Most race hatred would end if the Golden Rule of "Do unto others what you would want others to do unto you" were taught in every school.

+2 +1 0 -1 -2   (2) If labor and capital would sit down and intelligently discuss their problems they could reach a satisfactory compromise.

+2 +1 0 -1 -2   (3) There is a lot of truth to what some reformers and communists say but things aren't really as bad as they make them out to be.

+2 +1 0 -1 -2   (4) The more intelligent and educated a person the less prejudice he has.

*+2 +1 0 -1 -2 (5) One can be democratic and believe in free speech and still deny fascists the right to speak and hold meetings.

*+2 +1 0 -1 -2 (6) Every possible means, including laws, should be used now to give equal social status and rights to Negroes and other groups.

+2 +1 0 -1 -2   (7) Our two parties--Democratic and Republican--correct the mistakes of each other and thereby preserve our democracy.

+2 +1 0 -1 -2   (8) Politicians being what they are it's highly improbable that we'll ever achieve any of the utopias some individuals believe in.

+2 +1 0 -1 -2   (9) "Turn the other cheek" is still a good rule for living.

+2 +1 0 -1 -2   (10) Prices will come down if we allow the economic laws of supply and demand to make themselves felt.

+2 +1 0 -1 -2   (11) There is a middle ground for intelligent people between the conflicting ideologies of Right and Left.

+2 +1 0 -1 -2   (12) Picketing a fascist meeting defeats its purpose because it serves to advertise the meeting and causes more people to attend.

+2 +1 0 -1 -2   (13) It is best for society as a whole to raise the social status of Negroes by means of a slow, gradual process extending over many generations.

+2 +1 0 -1 -2   (14) If we could find a way to curb a few grasping selfish business men our economic system would work all right.

+2 +1 0 -1 -2   (15) International tension is largely the result of lack of knowledge of other people and nations.

+2 +1 0 -1 -2 (16) Negroes should be given equal political and economic rights, but intermarriage is definitely undesirable.

+2 +1 0 -1 -2 (17) Voters' opinions should not be forced on Congress by means of petitions and letters, because these matters should be handled through the regular channels of government.

*+2 +1 0 -1 -2 (18) The present difference between the Republicans and the Democrats is very minor and we need a party which will really represent the people.

*+2 +1 0 -1 -2 (19) More government controls over business are needed as a first step in preventing an economic crisis.

+2 +1 0 -1 -2 (20) There are two sides to every question and both must constantly be given equal consideration.

+2 +1 0 -1 -2 (21) Labor unions go too far when a boss can't fire his own workers.

+2 +1 0 -1 -2 (22) Communism is a leftist version of rightist fascism.

*+2 +1 0 -1 -2 (23) The passage of laws and energetic government action are an important step in fighting racial and religious discrimination.

*+2 +1 0 -1 -2 (24) The differences between labor and capital are not capable of being compromised; either one or the other will win out.

*+2 +1 0 -1 -2 (25) Sometimes things get so bad that instead of replacing Democrats by Republicans and vice versa, it might be a good idea to change our economic or political system.

+2 +1 0 -1 -2 (26) It doesn't do much good opposing anti-Jewish remarks; you only get into pointless arguments.

+2 +1 0 -1 -2 (27) Getting angry and complaining to elected officials about the high cost of living and the lack of housing is a waste of time because it doesn't accomplish anything.

+2 +1 0 -1 -2 (28) Laws limiting the power of unions are just as necessary as laws designated to prevent abuses by big business.

---

*These seven items are militant; the others are pacifistic.

HOSTILITY IN INTERNATIONAL RELATIONS (Helfant 1952)

Variable	This scale is designed mainly to measure an attitude of hostility in international relations in terms of criticism of foreign nations or peoples, and of approval of a more militant stand in international relations.
Description	This is a 16-item Likert scale, composed of eight items in favor of a more hostile stance, and eight in favor of an open or friendly stance. With the respondent stating his reaction to each item on a five-point scale, scores vary between 16 (very friendly) and 80 (very hostile).
Sample	The sample consisted of 166 seniors and their parents at Teaneck High School in Teaneck, New Jersey, a suburb of New York.
Reliability/ Homogeneity	Corrected split-half reliabilities were .84 for the student sample, .71 for the mothers, and .81 for the fathers.
Validity	Scale scores were found to correlate at .70 with students' self-ratings of their attitude toward international relations.
Location	Helfant, K. "Parents' Attitudes Versus Adolescent Sociopolitical Attitudes," Psychological Monographs, 1952, 66, pp. 1-23. Whole No. 345.
Administration	The scale should take about 10 minutes to administer.
Results and Comments	The scale is simply written and has the advantage of having been asked of both students and their parents.

OPINIONS AND BELIEFS ABOUT INTERNATIONAL RELATIONS

DIRECTIONS: Indicate your feeling about each statement by putting a check (√) in the appropriate column. Be sure to put a check after every statement.

	Strongly Agree	Agree	Don't Know	Dis- agree	Strongly Disagree
1. In my opinion, the United States should give up trying to be on friendly terms with other countries.	1	2	3	4	5
*2. I think that if the United States is friendly toward other countries they are not as likely to be aggressive toward us.	5	4	3	2	1
3. In my opinion, only foolish dreamers believe that international friendliness can accomplish anything in the modern world.	1	2	3	4	5
*4. I feel that in international relations it is just plain common sense to "love they neighbor as thyself".	5	4	3	2	1
*5. I believe that the U.S. should send food and materials to any country that needs them.	5	4	3	2	1
6. In my opinion, we shouldn't risk our happiness and well-being by getting involved with other countries.	1	2	3	4	5
7. I think that helping foreign countries is a waste of money.	1	2	3	4	5
*8. In my opinion, international good will is essential to the welfare of the United States.	5	4	3	2	1
9. It is my belief that we should get even with any country that tries to take advantage of the United States.	1	2	3	4	5
10. I feel that we can't have "peace on earth, good will to men," because other nations are not of good will.	1	2	3	4	5

	Strongly Agree	Agree	Don't Know	Dis-agree	Strongly Disagree
*11. I think that being friendly with other countries will do more good than harm.	5	4	3	2	1
*12. It is my feeling that we should try to help all nations, whether we get anything special out of it or not.	5	4	3	2	1
13. I think that other countries are always getting us into wars.	1	2	3	4	5
*14. I think that being friendly with other nations is a real help in solving international problems.	5	4	3	2	1
15. It is my belief that other nations are often plotting against us.	1	2	3	4	5
*16. In my opinion, all sensible people believe in trying to be friendly with other countries.	5	4	3	2	1

---

*Items marked with an asterisk express a favorable attitude toward internationalism, whereas other items express a favorable attitude toward nationalism. Scoring weights are given after each item but of course are not present when the scale is administered.

NATIONALISM (Ferguson 1942)

Variable

The scale attempts to measure an attitude of "nationalism," as the author calls a primary factor which emerged from the factor analysis of data from scales measuring attitudes toward law, censorship, patriotism, and Communism.

Description

The scale consists of 64 items. Response mode is some sort of agree-disagree format but was not described in detail. The weight for each item was determined according to Thompson's (1939) procedure. An individual's score is the algebraic sum of the values of the statements with which he agrees. High score indicates nationalism.

Sample

The sample was not described.

Reliability/
Homogeneity

A parallel focus reliability coefficient of .79 was reported. No test-retest data are reported.

Validity

One hundred fifty-eight subjects, who were classified as "nationalistic" and "internationalistic" on Stagner et al.'s Survey of Opinion on Methods of Preventing War, were administered the Nationalism Scale. It was found that for every Survey item, the "nationalistic" response group scored higher on the Nationalism Scale than did the "inter-nationalistic" response group. The scale was also found to have a validity of .90 according to Thompson's (1939) procedure, but this refers to an internal rather than an external criterion.

Location

Ferguson, L. W. "The Isolation and Measurement of Nationalism," Journal of Social Psychology, 1942, 16, pp. 215-228.

Administration

Estimated administration time is 48-64 minutes.

Results and
Comments

The scale items are not as dated as most scales of this vintage.

References

Stagner, R., et al. "A Survey of Public Opinion on the Prevention of War," Journal of Social Psychology, 1942, 16, pp. 109-130.

Thompson, G. A. The Factoral Analysis of Human Ability. New York: Houghton-Mifflin, 1939, pp. XVI-326.

NATIONALISM SCALE (FORM A)

Circle the number of each item with which you agree.

1. People should be allowed to make their own distinctions between good and bad.
2. It is only the ignorant and incompetent that want communism.
3. There is no room in the United States for people who find fault with this country.
4. Censorship is needed because most people are unable to judge for themselves.
5. The communists are on the right road.
6. Censorship is a good thing on the whole although it is often abused.
7. The whole world must be converted to communism.
8. The United States is closer to being an ideal country than any other nation has ever been.
9. Nobody has any right to dictate to me what I shall read.
10. Communists should have the same rights as other people.
11. When I see so much corruption in the government of my country I can't support it wholeheartedly.
12. I doubt if censorship is wise.
13. I'm for my country, right or wrong.
14. Censorship is a gross violation of our constitutional rights.
15. We have too many laws.
16. If a man has the vision and the ability to acquire property, he ought to be allowed to enjoy it himself.
17. Let the Reds stay in Russia where they belong.
18. This is in every way the greatest nation in the world.
19. Censorship is effective in raising moral and aesthetic standards.
20. In the long run law and justice are synonymous.
21. The communists are the most destructive element in our civilization.
22. The law is often the refuge of the scoundrel.
23. Censorship is a very difficult problem, and I am not sure how far I think it should go.
24. Some parts of the communist program are entirely sensible and practicable.
25. I believe that the United States is just as selfish as any other nation.
27. Most of the communistic doctrines are false.
28. The sanctity of the law should be taught in all schools.
29. Everything that is printed for publication should first be examined by government censors.
30. The individual who refuses to obey the law is a menace to civilization.
31. The law is the true embodiment of eternal justice.
32. Censorship might be warranted if we could get reasonable censors.

NATIONALISM SCALE (FORM B)

Circle the number of each item with which you agree.

1. In America there is rightly no room for Old World sentimental idealism.
2. Censorship is absurd because no two people agree about morality.
3. A truly free people must be allowed to choose their own reading and entertainment.
4. Workers can hardly be blamed for advocating communism.
5. Foreign nations have done some very fine things, but it takes America to do things in a big way.
6. Communists are too visionary for a practical world.
7. Share-and-share-alike sounds well, but it won't work.
8. We should be openminded about communism.
9. I think the American people are the finest in the world.
10. Censorship can never be justified in a free country.
11. Give Russia another twenty years or so and you'll see that communism can be made to work.
12. The law represents the wisdom of the ages.
13. Common sense keeps me from being too enthusiastic about the United States.
14. The communists are a menace to this nation and to the world in general.
15. Men are not all equal before the law.
16. What we need is more and better censorship.
17. Morality is produced by self control, not by censorship.
18. The hatred of the United States by foreign countries is caused mostly by envy of our greatness.
19. Police are justified in shooting down communists.
20. Censorship is a good thing if there isn't too much of it.
21. Communism would destroy the family and the home.
22. The law is more than the enactments of Congress: it is a sacred insitution.
23. I don't know much about other countries but I'm satisfied with the United States.
24. The communist is too radical and extreme in his views.
25. More people would favor communism if they only knew something about it.
26. I prefer to be a citizen of the world than of any country.
27. The theory of censorship is sound, but censors make a mess of it.
28. I can accept the leadership of foreign countries in many fields.
29. The whole communistic scheme is unsound.
30. The less one tampers with the law, the better.
31. It is too early to judge communism by its results in Russia.
32. Censorship protects those who lack judgment or experience to choose for themselves.

NATIONALISTIC ATTITUDE CHANGES (Stagner and Osgood 1946)

Variable This instrument was devised in an attempt to measure the impact of war on a nationalistic attitude by quantifying evaluative judgments.

Description The final form of the instrument (Form IV) was comprised of 65 seven-point gradient scales (an early form of Osgood's semantic differential) on which the subject was asked to make discriminations as to the degree to which a given concept (Russians, neutrality) manifests either of a pair of polar qualities (noble-bestial, strong-weak). There were 16 concepts (eight "nationalities" and eight "policies") and 16 gradients, and each concept was paired with each gradient.

Sample The main sample of "about 50" was drawn from different cross-sectional groups of students at Dartmouth College between April of 1940 and March of 1942. Supplementary adult samples were drawn from the membership of various voluntary organizations.

Reliability/ Homogeneity The test-retest reliability for the different groups over different time intervals varies from a high of .94 on Form IV for the same group over a six-week period to a low of .75 for two different groups over a 59-week period.

Validity The authors report that "no ultimate criterion of validity is available" but that their data "agree with the Gallup poll, and ... correspond to reasonable predictions based on objective events." Some indication of validity may be seen in the fact that veterans' groups' gradient scores on "Americans" were so polarized in the nationalist direction that they did not overlap with students' scores.

Administration Reported time of administration to student samples was 3 to 10 minutes. Adults reportedly found the procedure more difficult than did students, especially the retesting.

Location Stagner, Ross and Osgood, Charles E. "Impact of War on a Nationalistic Frame of Reference: I. Changes in General Approval and Qualitative Patterning of Certain Stereotypes," Journal of Social Psychology, 1946, 24, pp. 187-215.

Results and Comments The authors felt that the gradients located attitudes toward the concepts on a general "approval-disapproval" dimension. It was found that as concepts were changing locus on the approval dimension over time, the uniformity of judgments on the specific gradients generally diminished--a loss of internal consistency of the stereotype.

It was reported in comparison of scores made before and after the United States entered World War II, that polarization on nationalistic terms jumped markedly; that is, judgments became more unanimous and more nationalistic. Judgments on nationalities remained relatively stable, but judgments on policies and ideas were very different. It was found that most "nationalities" stereotypes were little changed by United States entry into the war, but that the "English" stereotype changed markedly as they became allies (less "strong," much more "honest").

NATIONALIST ATTITUDE SCALE

Sample Item   1. Russians   kind ___: ___: ___: ___: ___: ___: ___ cruel

List of Concepts and Scales Used (each concept is rated on each scale)

Form 1

Concepts	Scale
Russians	Kind--cruel
Socialists	Noble--bestial
Americans	Strong--weak
Foreigners	Tolerant--intolerant
Frenchmen	Christian--anti-Christian
Pacifists	Fair--unfair
Germans	Honest--dishonest
Englishmen	Happy--sad

Form 2

Concepts	Scale
Human Being	Wise--foolish
Patriot	Brave--cowardly
Big Navy	Idealistic--realistic
Soldier	Noble--bestial
Isolation	Valuable--worthless
Dictator	Strong--weak
Fighting	Happy--sad
Conscientious Objector	High--low

Form 3

Concepts	Scale
100% Americanism	Wise--foolish
National Self-Defense	Brave--cowardly
League of Nations	Idealistic--realistic
War	Noble--bestial
Neutrality	Valuable--worthless
Dictatorship	Strong--weak
Pacifism	Happy--sad
Big Army	High--low

ATTITUDE TOWARD WAR (Day and Quackenbush 1942)

Variable	This instrument attempts to measure the difference in attitude toward war when it is defensive (for the purpose of the defending the United States in case of attack), cooperative (in cooperation with the democratic countries of Europe for the defense of democracy), or aggressive (for the purpose of gaining more territory).
Description	The final form of the scale is comprised of 13 agree-disagree items on war in general, each of which is to be answered with reference to defensive, cooperative, or aggressive war.
	The scale was constructed by the Thurstone method of equal-appearing intervals: 50 judges (faculty, graduate students, college seniors) classified 28 statements into nine groups according to degrees of attitude.
	An individual score is the average of the scale values endorsed by the informant. Low values indicated favorable attitudes and high values unfavorable attitudes toward war. Items' scale values ranged from 0.2 to 8.5,
Sample	The sample was a group of 326 male students at the University of Mississippi in 1938-1939.
Reliability/ Homogeneity	Split-half reliability (corrected) was reported to be .87 for defensive war, .88 for cooperative war, and .80 for aggressive war.
Validity	No data on validity were reported.
Location	Day, D. and Quackenbush, O. F. "Attitudes Toward Defensive, Cooperative, and Aggressive War," Journal of Social Psychology, 1942, 16, pp. 11-20.
Results and Comments	It was found that, as a whole, the students were strongly in favor of a defensive war (average score, 2.1), slightly in favor of cooperative war (average score, 4.2), and slightly unfavorable to aggressive war (average score, 5.1). The significance of findings on the comparative scores of small groups of different student majors was not presented.
	This instrument seems to have been fairly well constructed, and could be of interest to students of social change.

ATTITUDE TOWARD WAR

This is a study of attitudes toward war. Below you will find a
number of statements expressing various degrees of attitudes toward
war or tendencies to act in case of war.

In expressing your agreement or disagreement with the statements,
please put yourself in three possible situations. First, imagine
that the United States had declared a Defensive War (war for the
purpose of defending the United States in case of an attack).
Please indicate in the first parenthesis your agreement, disagreement,
and doubt. Put a check mark (√) if you agree with the statement,
put a minus sign (-) if you disagree with the statement, and a
question mark (?) if you are in doubt about the statement.

Second, imagine that the United States has declared a Cooperative
War (war in cooperation with the democratic countries of Europe
for the defense of democracy). Go over the statements again and
indicate in the second parenthesis your agreement, disagreement,
and doubt in a similar way.

Third, imagine that the United States has declared an Aggressive War
(war for the purpose of gaining more territory). Read the statements
again and indicate in the third parenthesis your agreement, disagreement, and doubt by a similar method.

( ) ( ) ( ) 1. I would support my country even against my convictions.

( ) ( ) ( ) 2. I would immediately attempt to find some technicality
on which to evade going to war.

( ) ( ) ( ) 3. I would immediately go to war and would do everything
in my power to influence others to do the same.

( ) ( ) ( ) 4. I would rather be called a coward than go to war.

( ) ( ) ( ) 5. I would offer my services in whatever capacity I can.

( ) ( ) ( ) 6. I would not only refuse to participate in any way in
war but also attempt to influence public opinion
against war.

( ) ( ) ( ) 7. I would take part in war only to avoid social ostracism.

( ) ( ) ( ) 8. I would not go to war unless I were drafted.

( ) ( ) ( ) 9. If possible, I would wait a month or two before I
would enlist.

( ) ( ) ( ) 10. I would go to war only if my friends went to war.

( ) ( ) ( ) 11. I would refuse to participate in any way in war.

( ) ( ) ( ) 12. I would disregard any possible exemptions and enlist
immediately.

( ) ( ) ( ) 13. I would not enlist but would give whatever financial
aid I could.

ATTITUDE TOWARD WAR (Stagner 1942)

Variable   This scale attempts to measure attitude toward war as an institution.

Description   The short form of the scale consists of 15 of the 27 items which com-
                    prised the original long form. In a variation of the Thurstone scale
                    construction technique, items were rated by judges instructed to
                    apply "absolute judgments" on a five-point scale in which 5 represented
                    a rating of most favorable to war, and 1   a rating of least favorable
                    to war.

                    Subjects indicate agreement with an item by marking it with a check.
                    A score is the mean of scale values of checked items. Possible range
                    of scores is 1.2 - 4.8, with higher scores indicating the more
                    favorable attitude toward war.

Sample   The judges were described as five graduate and undergraduate classes
                    with a total of 125 students. The evaluation sample consisted of
                    four groups of 265 adult men, 191 adult women, 229 college men, and
                    181 college women, who were administered the scale in 1938.

Reliability/   A corrected split-half reliability coefficient of .58 was reported
  Homogeneity   for the short form of the scale as tested on a group of 100 college
                    men, but see "Results and Comments" below for later and more encourag-
                    ing data.

Validity   In one test of validity by known groups, it was found that military
                    training groups and veterans groups scored significantly higher than
                    men with no military training. In another known groups validity test,
                    differences in responses of the Dartmouth students and 27 members of
                    the Young People's Socialist League were highly significant.

Administration   Estimated administration time is about 20 minutes for the long form
                    and about 11 minutes for the short form. Scoring requires summation
                    and averaging of item values.

Location   Stagner, Ross. "Some Factors Related to Attitude toward War, 1938,"
                    Journal of Social Psychology, S.P.S.S.I. Bulletin, 1942, 16,
                    pp. 131-142.

Results and   In this study, the reliability of the short form of the scale is
  Comments   rather low. There also appeared to be a consistency between mili-
                    taristic attitude and expressed willingness to fight in war but, as
                    the author points out, expression of willingness is verbal, not behav-
                    ioral evidence.

                    The author administered the short form of the Attitude Toward War Scale
                    again in the fall of 1940, with five responses per item instead of two
                    and with differential item weights eliminated. The sample was 157
                    students at Dartmouth College, and the test-retest reliability

(corrected) was .83 on 93 students, with an inter-test interval of one month. Eighteen months later, after the United States had entered the war, a retest on 50 of the subjects produced a test-retest coefficient of .40.

Reference   Stagner, Ross. "Studies of Aggressive Social Attitudes:
I. Measurement and Interrelation of Selected Attitudes;
II. Changes from Peace to War," Journal of Social Psychology,
1946, 24, pp. 187-215.

ATTITUDE TOWARD WAR

Consider each of the statements below. Regardless of your own opinion, mark it as to whether you consider it to be favorable to war or to peace. Let 5 be the statements most favorable to war, and 1 those most favorable to peace. If a statement is somewhat favorable to war, mark it 4. If somewhat favorable to peace, mark it 2. If a statement is not favorable to either, mark it 3. Be sure not to consider your own agreement or disagreement, but just the question, Does this statement indicate an attitude favoring war or peace?

Item	Median rating	Range of scoring Means	Value
*1. War brings out the best qualities in men.	4.76	0.51	—
2. War is often the only means of preserving the national honor.	4.24	0.33	7
3. The desirable results of war have not received the attention they deserve.	4.24	0.32	7
4. There can be no progress without war.	4.67	0.38	7
5. War is the only way to right tremendous wrongs.	4.72	0.30	8
6. Patriotism demands that the citizens of a nation participate in any war.	4.26	0.20	7
*7. The United States has never fought an unjust war.	4.10	0.34	6
8. The United States should always be armed to the limit of its treaty rights.	4.10	0.26	6
*9. War is necessary to avoid overpopulation of nations.	4.62	0.30	7
*10. The Biblical command against killing does not apply to warfare.	4.19	0.37	6
*11. Nations should pay high honor to their military leaders.	4.05	0.38	6
*12. College students should be trained in times of peace to assume military duties.	3.90	0.33	6
*13. Modern warfare provides a glorious adventure for men not afraid of danger.	4.52	0.40	7
14. Under some conditions, war is necessary to maintain justice.	3.76	0.36	6
15. Although war is terrible, it has some value.	3.81	0.31	6
16. Defensive war is justified but other wars are not.	3.48	0.49	5
*17. We should abolish military armaments for offensive purposes.	1.97	0.53	—
*18. The average citizen can do nothing to oppose war.	3.29	0.82	—
19. Those who profit by war profit by the preparations for war.	2.33	0.47	3
*20. We expect war to endanger life and property rather than protect it.	1.72	0.52	—

21.	The benefits of war rarely pay for its loses even for the victor.	1.72	0.42	2
22.	There is no conceivable justification for war.	1.24	0.34	1
23.	War is a futile struggle resulting in self-destruction.	1.45	0.29	1
24.	The evils of war are greater than any possible benefits.	1.32	0.47	1
*25.	International disputes should be settled without war.	1.48	0.47	1
*26.	War breeds disrespect for human life.	1.36	0.59	—
*27.	It is good judgment to sacrifice certain rights in order to prevent war.	1.43	0.63	—

*Starred items were omitted in the short form.

CHAPTER 9:   COMMUNITY-BASED POLITICAL ATTITUDES

The six scales in this section represent a disappointingly small collection for such an important and interesting area of research. Hopefully, more and better instruments in this area will be developed in the near future. Of the five scales considered in this section, three deal with the "local-cosmopolitan" differentiation first noted by Merton (1949)[*], and the other three touch on different subjects. The six scales are reviewed below as follows:

1. Community Attitude Scale (Bosworth 1954)
2. Local-Cosmopolitan Scale (Dye 1966)
3. Cosmopolitan Scale (Jennings 1965)
4. Local-Cosmopolitan Scale (Dobriner 1958)
5. Acquaintanceship Scale (Schultze 1961)
6. Attitude toward Sources of Power (Haer 1956)

The first scale by Bosworth is designed to measure how progressive the attitudes of people in a given community are toward such matters as living conditions, education, and various community programs. The sixty items that comprise the scale were empirically selected from a larger initial pool of items. Reliability of the scale is high, and evidence for validity seems more than satisfactory.

Dye's scale is one of the three measures on the "local-cosmopolitan" distinction. It consists of five items, some of which seem to use overly complicated phrasing. Evidence for validity and reliability is more than adequate. While the scale was applied to a sample of the public, it was unfortunately part of a mailed questionnaire, which may have elicited a biased sample.

---

[*]Two scales by Marvick and Slesinger that deal with this dimension in the occupational domain are reviewed in Appendix A on occupational measures.

The Jennings' scale of Cosmopolitanism is one of the few attitude measures we have encountered which is based on Coombs' (1964) unfolding model. In this instance the fit of the data to the model was not exact. Nevertheless, results with the scale bore out predictions: people scoring as cosmopolitans tended to be politically aware and interested. Jennings also presents some interesting differences between students and their parents on the cosmopolitanism dimension.

The scale by Dobriner was part of an admittedly exploratory investigation into some of Merton's original findings with regard to the "local-cosmopolitan" dimension. Satisfactory evidence for the scale's basic validity is presented. The author's evidence of reliability is unclear; such evidence is especially important for this scale since the item content appears quite heterogeneous. Items are all worded in the same direction and, hence, subject to response set tendencies.

The Acquaintanceship Scale by Schultze is a simple sociometric device which attempts to measure the closeness of relationships between the respondent and various power groups in the community. Evidence of reliability and validity is difficult to evaluate for this scale because of the nature and purpose of its construction.

The last scale, by Haer, attempts to assess the degree to which one favors or does not favor certain sources of community power. One or possibly two items of this five item scale are quite inapplicable for residents of most communities, and the other items have a strong flavor of alienation or political inefficacy. While the scale shows satisfactory, if not large, internal consistency, no evidence for validity is presented. In addition, the scale items seem susceptible to agreement response set.

Miller (1964) reviews three further measures which may be of interest to readers of this section. Fessler's Community Solidarity Index (1952) was developed for use in small rural communities, although the items are well-written and seem just as applicable to larger communities. Evidence for the scale's reliability and validity is uncelar. The Community Rating Schedule (1952) is a simple and probably worthwhile instrument for comparative community studies, although no empirical data on the scale are presented. Finally, Miller's own Community Scorecard (1964) measures the degree to which the individual himself participates in community services. No empirical data on this scale are reported.

For further methods of measuring community variables, see Gibbs (1961), Jonassen (1959), and Shevky and Bell (1955).

References:

"Community Rating Schedule," Adult Leadership. New York: State Citizens Council, October, 1952.

Coombs, C.H. A Theory of Data. New York: John Wiley and Sons, 1964.

Fessler, D. "The Development of a Scale for Measuring Community Solidarity," Rural Sociology, 17, pp.144-152.

Gibbs, J. (ed.) Urban Research Methods. Princeton, New Jersey: Van Nostrand, 1961.

Jonassen, C. The Measurement of Community Dimensions and Elements. Columbus, Ohio: Center for Educational Administration, Ohio State University Press, 1959.

Merton, R. "Patterns of Influence," in P. Lazarsfeld and F. Stanton (eds.) Communications Research, 1948-49. New York: Harper and Brothers, 1949.

Miller, D. Handbook of Research Design and Social Measurement. New York: David McKay, 1964.

Shevky, E. and Bell, W. Social Area Analysis. Stanford: Stanford University Press, 1955.

COMMUNITY ATTITUDE SCALE (Bosworth 1954)

Variable	This scale is designed to measure the person's degree of progressive attitudes on community life in such areas as community improvement, living conditions, and business.
Description	The scale consists of 60 Likert-type five alternative items which were found to be most discriminating from an original pool of over 300 items.

The scale is divided into three subsets of 20 items each:

1) Community Integration
2) Community Services
3) Civic Responsibilities

Sample	The sample consisted of a random sample of 300 householders selected from a test city of 50,000 population. Response rate was 80 percent.
Reliability/ Homogeneity	A Kuder-Richardson reliability coefficient of .88 is reported; comparable figures for the subscales are .70 for Integration, .68 for services and .66 for Responsibilities. Average inter-subscale correlation was .65.

No test-retest data are reported.

Validity	Difference in score of progressive and unprogressive groups was found to be significant at the .025 level. Progressive individuals were also found to be more likely to vote for a sewer extension plan.
Location	Bosworth, C. A Study of the Development and the Validation of a Measure of Citizens' Attitudes toward Progress and Game Variables Related Thereto Ph.D. dissertation, University of Michigan, 1954. Available from University Microfilms No. 11,251.
Administration	It appears that the scale would take 15 to 30 minutes to complete. We were unable to ascertain how the items are to be scored, although obviously not all of the items are worded in the same direction.
Results and Comments	As expected, better educated persons were more progressive. The variable under study seems an important one and the items do show good wording and high homogeneity even though item content seems quite heterogeneous.

COMMUNITY ATTITUDE SCALE

(Community Services Subscale)

	Strongly Agree	Agree	?	Disagree	Strongly Disagree
1. The school should stick to the 3 R's and forget about most of the other courses being offered today.					
2. Most communities are good enough as they are without starting any new community improvement programs.					
3. Every community should encourage more music and lecture programs.					
4. This used to be a better community to live in.					
5. Long term progress is more important than immediate benefits.					
6. We have too many organizations for doing good in the community.					
7. The home and the church should have all the responsibility for preparing young people for marriage and parenthood.					
8. The responsibility for older people should be confined to themselves and their families instead of the community.					
9. Communities have too many youth programs.					
10. Schools are good enough as they are in most communities.					
11. Too much time is usually spent on the planning phases of community projects.					
12. Adult education should be an essential part of the local school program.					
13. Only the doctors should have the responsibility for the health program in the community.					
14. Mental illness is not a responsibility for the whole community.					
15. A modern community should have the services of social agencies.					

394

(Community Services Subscale cont'd)

16. The spiritual needs of the citizens are adequately met by the churches. ___ ___ ___ ___ ___

17. In order to grow, a community must provide additional recreation facilities. ___ ___ ___ ___ ___

18. In general, church members are better citizens. ___ ___ ___ ___ ___

19. The social needs of the citizens are the responsibility of themselves and their families and not of the community. ___ ___ ___ ___ ___

20. Churches should be expanded and located in accordance with population growth. ___ ___ ___ ___ ___

(Community Integration Subscale)

21. No community improvement program should be carried on that is injurious to a business. ___ ___ ___ ___ ___

22. Industrial development should include the interest in assisting local industry. ___ ___ ___ ___ ___

23. The first and major responsibility of each citizen should be to earn dollars for his own pocket. ___ ___ ___ ___ ___

24. More industry in town lowers the living standards. ___ ___ ___ ___ ___

25. The responsibility of citizens who are not actively participating in a community improvement program is to criticize those who are active. ___ ___ ___ ___ ___

26. What is good for the community is good for me. ___ ___ ___ ___ ___

27. Each one should handle his own business as he pleases and let the other businessmen handle theirs as they please ___ ___ ___ ___ ___

28. A strong Chamber of Commerce is beneficial to any community. ___ ___ ___ ___ ___

29. Leaders of the Chamber of Commerce are against the welfare of the majority of the citizens in the community. ___ ___ ___ ___ ___

30. A community would get along better if each one would mind his own business and others take care of theirs. ___ ___ ___ ___ ___

	Strongly Agree	Agree	?	Disagree	Strongly Disagree

(Community Integration Subscale Cont'd)

31. Members of any community organization should be expected to attend only those meetings that affect him personally.

32. Each of us can make real progress only when the group as a whole makes progress.

33. The person who pays no attention to the complaints of the persons working for him is a poor citizen.

34. It would be better if we would have the farmer look after his own business and we look after ours.

35. All unions are full of Communists.

36. The good citizens encourage the widespread circulation of all news including that which may be unfavorable to them and their organizations.

37. The good citizen should help minority groups with their problems.

38. The farmer has too prominent a place in our society.

39. A citizen should join only those organizations that will promote his own interests.

40. Everyone is out for himself at the expense of everyone else.

(Civic Responsibilities Subscale)

41. Busy people should not have the responsibility for civic programs.

42. The main responsibility for keeping the community clean is up to the city officials.

43. Community improvements are fine if they don't increase taxes.

44. The younger element have too much to say about our community affairs.

45. A progressive community must provide adequate parking facilities.

46. Government officials should get public sentiment before acting on major municipal projects.

396

(Civic Responsibilities Subscale cont'd)

	Strongly Agree	Agree	?	Disagree	Strongly Disagree

47. A good citizen should be willing to assume leadership in a civic improvement organization.

48. Progress can best be accomplished by having only a few people involved.

49. Community improvement should be the concern of only a few leaders in the community.

50. A community would be better if less people would spend time on community improvement projects.

51. Only those who have the most time should assume the responsibility for civic programs.

52. Living conditions in a community should be improved.

53. A good citizen should sign petitions for community improvement.

54. Improving slum areas is a waste of money.

55. The police force should be especially strict with outsiders.

56. The paved streets and roads in most communities are good enough.

57. The sewage system of a community must be expanded as it grows even though it is necessary to increase taxes.

58. Some people just want to live in slum areas.

59. The main problem we face is high taxes.

60. Modern methods and equipment should be provided for all phases of city government.

LOCAL-COSMOPOLITAN SCALE (Dye 1966)

Variable — This instrument attempts to identify an individual as a "local" or a "cosmopolitan" according to the scale of social environment in which he sees himself.

Description — Items were cumulatively intended to identify persons whose scale of social experience is limited, whose primary interest and involvement are in local rather than in national or international affairs, who perceive themselves primarily as members of a local community rather than as members of larger social organizations, and who identify with and allocate respect toward individuals with local, rather than national, reputations.

The five 6-point Likert-type items were distributed at random throughout a mailed questionnaire. Agreement with each item was interpreted as a localistic response, and scores on the scale ranged from 30 (most localistic) to 5 (least localistic).

Sample — The sample population of 340 residents and 105 elected public officials was drawn from 16 surburban municipalities in the Philadelphia metropolitan area. The municipalities were selected as to social types (six upper, five middle, five lower) using occupational and educational characteristics as criteria. Respondents returning the mailed interviews were probably biased toward interest in politics.

Reliability/ Homogeneity — The reliability of the item was tested by an item analysis called the Likert Discriminatory Power Technique (1938). Each of the five items discriminated significantly between respondents in the highest and lowest quartiles on the scale.

Validity — The relevance of the attitude tapped by the scale to local-cosmopolitan policy choices was tested by comparison of scale scores to answers to a short opinion poll involving three recurring metropolitan issues: governmental integration, public support of mass transit operations, and discriminatory zoning.

These "opinion poll" items are also reproduced below. With community social rank held constant the data showed that the local-cosmopolitan dimension was significantly and independently related to the three issues in the poll: significantly more cosmopolitans than locals were in favor of improving mass transit and area-wide government, and were against discriminatory zoning.

Location — Dye, T. R. "The Local-Cosmopolitan Dimension and the Study of Urban Politics," Social Forces, 1966, 41 (3), pp. 239-246.

Administration — Estimated administration time is about five minutes. Scoring requires simple summation of item scores.

Results and Comments — It was found that localism was inversely related to status: the mean of residents from upper-ranked municipalities was 16.3 as compared

398

to means of 17.2 and 19.3 for residents of middle and lower ranked municipalities, respectively. This relationship held for individual respondents as well.

In each social type of community, leaders possessed significantly higher localistic mean scores than their constituents, even though the leadership mean varied consistently with social rank.

To guard against sampling bias, returns were grouped by social rank of municipality and inferences from those grouped returns were made only to the specific sub-population represented.

This instrument seems to be a simple and direct method for identifying the local-cosmopolitan attitude dimension in groups and individuals. This scale is liable to agreement response set, especially in lower socio-economic status communities, which might somewhat account for this group's higher localism scores.

The author warns that the multidimensional nature of most political issues precludes any conclusion that high status communities will respond to political issues in a more socially responsible fashion.

Reference

Murphy, G. and Likert, R.   Public Opinion and the Individual. New York: Harper, 1938.

LOCAL-COSMOPOLITAN SCALE

1. The most rewarding organizations a person can belong to are local clubs and associations rather than large nation-wide organizations.

| Strongly Disagree | Disagree | Slightly Disagree | Slightly Agree | Agree | Strongly Agree |

2. Despite all the newspaper and TV coverage, national and international happenings rarely seem as interesting as events that occur right in the local community in which one lives.

3. No doubt many newcomers to the community are capable people; but when it comes to choosing a person for a responsible position in the community, I prefer a man whose family is well established in the community.

4. Big cities may have their place but the local community is the backbone of America.

5. I have greater respect for a man who is well-established in his local community than a man who is widely known in his field but who has no local roots.

Opinion Poll Items

1. Would you favor your local or country government spending tax money to improve mass transit (railroad, bus, and trolley service) in your area?

    Yes   No   Don't know

2. If you could be convinced that joining many small boroughs and townships into an area-wide government would save money and help keep taxes down, would you favor such a change?

3. Do you favor using zoning laws to keep out of your community the type of people who usually build cheaper houses on smaller lots?

COSMOPOLITANISM SCALE (Jennings 1965)

Variable   This instrument attempts to tap individuals' orientations toward multiple levels of government.

Description   The scale consists of a simple rank ordering of the degree to which an individual follows local, state, national, or international affairs.

These four items can be rank ordered in any one of 24 ways. Only seven of these orderings however fit Coomb's (1964) criterion of a unidimensional scale. These orderings from most cosmopolitan (1) to least cosmopolitan (7) are as follows:

Ordering	% of Population
1) International-National-State-Local	21
2) National-International-State-Local	33
3) National-State-International-Local	18
4) State-National-International-Local	17
5) State-National-Local-International	5
6) State-Local-National-International	3
7) Local-State-National-International	3
	100%

Actually only 53% of the sample gave the above seven orderings, the remaining 17 orderings being assigned to the most similar acceptable ordering (thus International-National-Local-State and National-International-Local-State were given the same code as ordering 2).

Sample   The sample consisted of 1669 seniors selected to represent a national cross-section of high-school seniors in the United States. The interviews were conducted in the spring of 1965 with a response rate of 97%.

Reliability/   No data bearing directly on the internal structure of the scale are
Homogeneity   reported, although as noted above 53% of the sample gave one of the seven acceptable response patterns.

An alternative scale ordering running from Local-International-National-State to State-National-International-Local resulted in 66% of the students fitting the scale.

Validity   Cosmopolitanism was found to be moderately related to political knowledge (gamma=.35), and notably related to interest about the United Nations. These relations held when controlled for three other variables to which cosmopolitanism is related--general concern with public affairs, student grade average, and mother's educational level.

Location   Jennings, M. Kent. "Pre-adult Orientations to Multiple Systems of Government," paper prepared for Midwest Conference of Political Scientists, April 1966 (Paper available from the author at the Survey Research Center).

Administration | The items should be able to be administered in less than three minutes. The following total distribution of ranking was obtained:

Rank of how closely followed	Level of Affairs				
	Inter-national	National	State	Local	
First	39%	44	6	11	100%
Second	26%	38	18	18	100%
Third	16%	14	45	25	100%
Fourth	19%	3	32	46	100%

Results and Comments

The relatively high proportion of response patterns that did not fit the model and the fact that an alternative scale ordering fit the data better suggests that more than one dimension is needed to account for the data.

When compared with their parents, students were found to voice much greater relative interest in international affairs. Thus, while over half the students scored 1 or 2 on the cosmopolitan end of the scale, less than a third of their parents did.

Students in the South proved less cosmopolitan than students in other geographical regions, as did students who had experienced more permanent residency. No differences were found between urban and rural dwellers or between boys and girls.

Reference

Coombs, C. A Theory of Data New York: Wiley, 1964.

COSMOPOLITANISM SCALE

Screening Question:

Some people seem to think about what's going on in government most of the
time, whether there's an election on or not. Others aren't that interested.
Would you say you follow what's going on in government most of the time, some
of the time, only now and then, or hardly at all?

Rank Order Data Sequence   (Not asked of those giving the "hardly at all" response to
the previous question)

Which one do you follow most closely -- international affairs, national
affairs, state affairs, or local affairs?

Which one do you follow least (interviewer reads the three remaining
levels)?

Of the other two, (interviewer reads the two remaining levels) which
one do you follow most closely?

(The residual level occupies the third rank.)

LOCALISM-COSMOPOLITANISM (L-C) SCALE (Dobriner 1958)

Variable | This scale attempts to measure the extent to which a suburban indivi-dual has internalized the characteristic cosmopolitan orientation of urban society.

Description | The scale consists of ten 6-point Likert type items without a zero point. Items were taken from substantive findings of Robert K. Merton's Rovere study (1949).

Sample | Sample population was composed of 275 residents of Huntington Village, Long Island. There were two population groups: 128 "old timers," or locals of 10 or more years residence, and 147 "newcomers," or new suburbanites.

Reliability/ Homogeneity | The author remarked that reliability of the scale was "checked primitively" by comparing for consistency the scores of "selected groups of college students and.... similar groups."

Validity | The content validity of the scale was checked primarily by a "logical validation" of the continuum largely as indicated by Merton's find-ings.

The PEC scale of Adorno, et al., (1950) was included in the question-naire to determine whether the L-C dimension was different from a liberal-conservative orientation. It was found that oldtimers scored 4.7 points higher on the "local" end of the scale than newcomers in terms of median L-C Scale scores; in contrast, oldtimers scored only .8 points higher on median PEC Scale scores (the PEC scale is described in Chapter 3).

Location | Dobriner, W. "Local and Cosmopolitan as Contemporary Suburban Character Types," in Dobriner, William M. (ed.), The Suburban Community New York: G. P. Putnam's Sons, 1958, pp.132-43.

Administration | Estimated administration time is about ten minutes. Scoring simply requires subtracting the total "minus" score from the total "plus" score for each subject.

Results and Comments | The stated purposes of this study were purely exploratory. The scale seems to be useful in being able to differentiate between levels of localism-cosmopolitanism in the predicted direction among locals and suburbanites. A cross tabulation of age, sex, and income status failed to reveal that any of those variables were highly associated with localism or cosmopolitanism, but showed that education and possibly occupation were associated with the dimension. The author remarks that the possibility remains that occupation or education may be a greater determinant of localism or cosmopolitanism than is mere involvement in urban social relations. The number of subjects was too small to compare L-C scores with SES held constant.

One intervening variable, which the author called "out-group," produced atypical findings: there was little variation in L-C scores among

404

Catholic and Jewish professional oldtimers and newcomers, suggesting that a person's original status may prevent him from identifying with the dominant social structure.

References   Merton, Robert K. "Patterns of Influence: A Study of Interpersonal Influence and of Communications Behavior in a Social Community," in Lazarsfeld, Paul F. and Stanton, Frank N. (eds.). Communications Research 1948-1949. New York: Harper and Brothers, 1949.

Adorno, T. W., Frenkel-Brunswick, (eds.) Levinson, Daniel J., and Sanford, R. Nevitt. Authoritarian Personality. New York: Harper and Brothers, 1950, p. 169. (Note: Item #3 in the short PEC Scale was changed by Dobriner to read as follows: "In order to protect the health of the nation the Congress should pass a law in which the Federal Government would contribute to our medical bills.")

L-C SCALE

Directions: Respondents were instructed to indicate the extent of
their agreement or disagreement with each of the statements below by marking the statement on a six-point
scale from +3 to -3.

1. National and international happenings rarely seem as interesting
and important as events that occur right in the local community
in which one lives.

2. Generally speaking, news commentators on radio or TV who give
personal interpretations of the news and human interest stories
are more worth listening to than commentators who just give the
news straight.

3. National and international events are important largely because
of the way they effect Huntington as a community.

4. Many personal relationships and contacts with other people in the
local community are essential in life today.

5. The most rewarding organizations a person can belong to are local
organizations serving local needs.

6. Huntington is one of the finest communities in the United States.

7. Meeting and knowing many people is extremely important in establishing myself in the community.

8. Big cities may have their place, but when you get right down to
it, the local community is the backbone of America.

9. Huntington's weekly newspapers are extremely important in order
to know what's going on.

10. News about Huntington is generally more interesting than national
and international news.

ACQUAINTANCESHIP SCALE (Schultze 1961)

Variable	This scale is a simple device for eliciting a respondent's perception of the closeness of his relationship to other respondents, with the purpose in this study of measuring the degree of familiarity among different power groups in a community.
Description	In a city of 20,000, each member of two power groups (described below) was asked to indicate on a nine-point scale the extent of his acquaintanceship with each of the others in the power categories. The names of all individuals were alphabetically arranged, thus mixing the groups. Perceived closeness of relationship was measured by composite mean selection scores.
Sample	The sample population was composed of the following elites: 18 "public leaders," consisting of those persons most frequently nominated by 153 (83%) of the heads of white adult voluntary association as influential persons, and 17 "economic dominants," consisting of those persons who occupied the foremost occupational positions in the community's dominant economic units, both local-firm and absentee-firm.
Reliability/ Homogeneity	The author reports that he found the scale to be "pretty reliable" by comparing the reciprocal scores of the various elites. The average difference in mean scores within each of the four paired comparisons was .10 (range of scores was 1.00 to 9.00).
Validity	Although no evidence for validity is reported, adequate validational criteria do not readily come to mind.
Location	Schultze, O. "The bifurcation of power in a satellite city," in Janowitz, Morris (ed.), Community Political Systems, Glencoe, Illinois: The Free Press, 1961, p. 51.
Administration	Amount of time required for administration of this instrument depends on the number of individuals each respondent must place on the scale. It is estimated that less than one minute could be required for each rank ordering.
Results and Comments	This instrument appears to be simple, direct method for eliciting perceived closeness of relationship among respondents. The close similarity of compared reciprocal scores indicates its utility in this context.

PUBLIC LEADER-ECONOMIC DOMINANT
ACQUANITANCESHIP SCALE: MEAN SELECTION SCORES

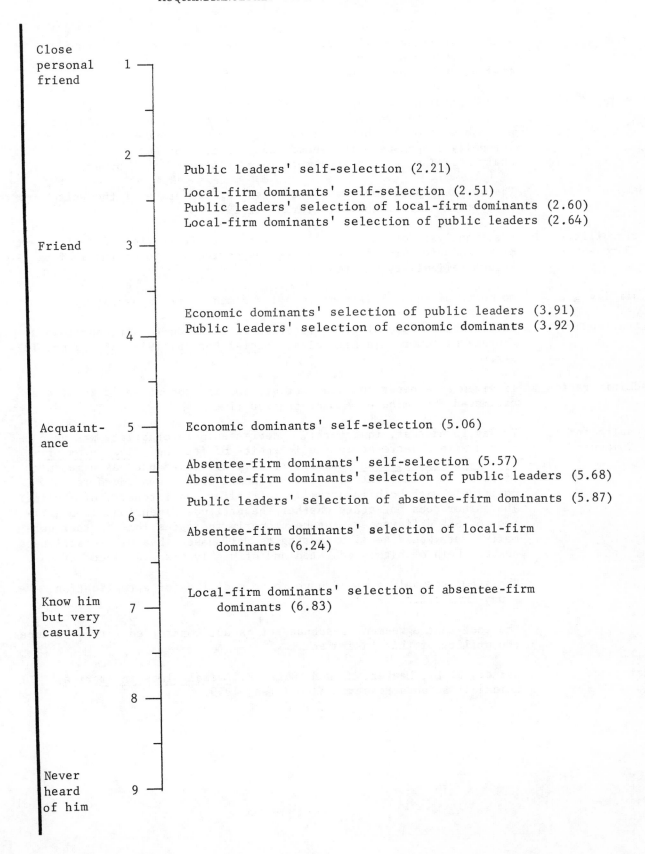

ATTITUDE TOWARD SOURCES OF POWER (Haer 1956)

Variable	This scale attempts to measure the degree of reported favorability toward sources of community power and the degree of intensity of feeling accompanying such belief.
Description	This instrument is composed of five items requiring "agree," "undecided," or "disagree" responses. After each item, respondents were asked how strongly they felt about the item response. Opinion and intensity responses were ranked independently by Guttman scale analysis. The two rankings were then related to each other.
Sample	The sample population was 320 adults representative of the white population of Tallahassee, Florida in 1953.
Reliability/ Homogeneity	Scale analysis of the content and intensity items yielded coefficients of reproducibility of .90 and .92 respectively. No estimate of test-retest reliability was reported.
Validity	No tests of the validity of this instrument were reported.
Location	Haer, John L. "Social Stratification in Relation to Attitude toward Sources of Power in a Community," Social Forces, 1956, 35, 2, pp. 137-142.
Administration	If given as a paper and pencil test, the instrument would require an estimated five minutes administration time.
Results and Comments	It was found that, in general, a decrease in favorability was associated with a decrease in the intensity of feeling. The Index of Status Characteristics (Warner, et al., 1949) was used as a measure of socio-economic status. Socio-economic status was found to vary positively with both favorability of belief and intensity of feeling. The author does not state whether the attitude dimension is an artifact of SES differences, but he properly indicates that further normative data would be illuminating as Tallahassee has disproportionate numbers both of highly educated and of highly disadvantaged persons.
	The items themselves would have to be modified for a replication study in a different city.
	The fact that agreement response-set is not controlled further reduces the utility of this instrument.
Reference	Warner, W. L., Meeker, M. and Eels, K. Social Class in America. Chicago: Science Research Associates, 1949.

ATTITUDE TOWARD SOURCES OF POWER

1. The civic organizations like the Lions, J. C.'s and others in Tallahassee have too much to say about affairs in the city. (Agree--undecided--disagree)

   How strongly do you feel about this? (Very strongly--somewhat strongly--not at all strongly)

2. The officials of the state government have too much to say about the running of the city. (Tallahassee is the capital city of Florida) (Agree--undecided--disagree)

   How strongly do you feel about this? (Very strongly--somewhat strongly--not at all strongly)

3. The ordinary citizen of Tallahassee doesn't have a chance to say much about how things are run. (Agree--undecided--disagree)

   How strongly do you feel about this? (Very strongly--somewhat strongly--not at all strongly)

4. The local courts are sometimes unfair to the little man. (Agree--undecided--disagree)

   How strongly do you feel about this? (Very strongly--somewhat strongly--not at all strongly)

5. The businessmen in this community have too much influence over how things are run. (Agree--undecided--disagree)

   How strongly do you feel about this? (Very strongly--somewhat strongly--not at all strongly)

CHAPTER 10:   POLITICAL INFORMATION

Four scales dealing with knowledge of political and social factors are

presented in this section:

1.   Political Information Scale (Matthews and Prothro 1966)
2.   Information about Foreign Countries (Robinson 1967)
3.   Information about the Far East (Robinson 1967)
4.   Index of Issue Familiarity (Campbell et al. 1960)

There is no evidence of validity presented for any of these scales,

unless the substantial correlations between education and information scale

scores are taken as a criterion of validity. On only one of the scales, the

Robinson Foreign Countries Scale, is any information on reliability given and

here the inter-item correlations are low, though statistically significant. Two

of the scales, the first two, are highly loaded with "school knowledge" type

questions which might seem inappropriate or irrelevant to the average person.

The Political Information Scale by Matthews and Prothro was applied to

cross-sectional samples of Negroes and whites living in the South. The questions

composing the scale were concerned with such "domestic" information as the name

of the state governor and the length of his term. Analysis results showed that

the information scale was more highly related to political activity than was

education itself. Also, at each level of schooling, whites were observed to

possess more of such political information than were Negroes.

Robinson's Foreign Countries Scale is made up of three sets of items

which deal with a particular country's form of government, geographic location,

and development of atomic weapons. The questions were asked of a cross-section

of Detroit adults. Robinson also constructed an information scale on Far East

countries based on questions asked of a national cross-sectional sample. The

questions involved seem more dated than those in the first scale. Both scales appear to be highly related to usage of the mass media (for news content purposes).

Unlike the three previous measures, the Survey Research Center's Index of Issue Familiarity was not based on the respondent's knowledge of certain facts or events but rather on whether he expressed an opinion, knowledgeable or not, on various political issues. The sample used was a representative cross-section of the national population. The same items were used in the Center's Index of Intensity.

Numerous other political information questions have been asked of cross-sectional populations. The reader will find data on specific questions in Erskine (1962, 1963, 1963), Lane and Sears (1964), and Robinson (1967).

References:

Erskine, Hazel. "The Polls," Public Opinion Quarterly, #4, 1962; #1, 1963, #4, 1963.

Lane, R. and Sears, D. Public Opinion. Englewood Cliffs, N.J.: Prentice Hall, 1964. (Chapter 6)

Robinson, J. Public Information about World Affairs. Ann Arbor, Mich.: Survey Research Center, 1967.

POLITICAL INFORMATION SCALE (Matthews and Prothro 1966)

Variable
: This instrument consists of seven factual questions intended to provide a rough measure of the individual's level of political information.

Description
: Included are items requiring political knowledge on the federal level (F.D.R.'s party affiliation, number of Supreme Court Justices, last two states entering the United States, length of term of a United States Senator), on the state level (name and length of term of Respondent's state governor), and on the county level (county seat of Respondent's county). The score consists of the number of correct answers given by each respondent. A score of 6-7 was called "high," 3-5 "medium" and 0-2 "low."

Sample
: The sample to which this measure was given is described in the PPS write-up in Chapter 11.

The Political Information Scale was part of a large study of Southern Negro political participation conducted in the spring of 1961.

Reliability/ Homogeneity
: No data on reliability are reported.

Validity
: No direct data bearing on validity are reported although higher information scores were obtained by those with more education.

Location
: Matthews, D. R. and Prothro, J. W. Negroes and the New Southern Politics. New York: Harcourt, Brace & World, 1966.

Results and Comments
: The authors found that at every level of schooling except the very highest, Negroes had less political information than whites. They also found that even at the highest levels, information far outweighed schooling as a factor predictive of political activity (as measured on their PPS measure described in Chapter 11), regardless of level of political interest.

Among southern Negro college students, who was asked only the federal level items, the authors found that students who had been active in the Civil Rights protest movement answered more questions correctly (an average 2.3 out of 4) than the inactive students (average score, 1.9).

The scale might have to be modified for use outside the South, in sections where the county is a less important political boundary. The item on Alaska and Hawaii might also be replaced by one on a topic currently in the news.

414

POLITICAL INFORMATION SCALE
The numbers below refer to question location in interviews with
(A) Negro Students, (B) White Adults and (C) Negro Adults

% Correct

Negro	White	(A)	(B)	(C)	
57	87	91	101	113	Now, I'd like to ask you a few questions that you may or may not be able to answer. Do you happen to recall whether President Franklin Roosevelt was a Republican or a Democrat? (Which?)
68	90		102	114	Who is the governor of _____ (this state) now?
65	67		103	115	About how long a term does the governor serve?
65	89		104	116	What's the county seat of _____ County (County R lives in)?
8	20	92	105	117	About how many years does a United States Senator serve?
8	21	93	106	118	Do you happen to know about how many members there are on the United States Supreme Court? How many?
35	79	94	107		What were the last two states to come into the United States?

INFORMATION ABOUT FOREIGN COUNTRIES (Robinson 1967)

Variable	This is a series of questions dealing with a person's knowledge of certain characteristics about foreign countries.
Description	The scale consists of 16 items, five dealing with whether certain countries have Communist governments, five dealing with countries which are in Africa, and six dealing with countries which have developed and tested their own atomic weapons. One point is given for each correct answer, one subtracted for each incorrect answer and no points are given for a "don't know" response. Scores can thus run from -17 (all items incorrect) to +17 (all items correct).
Sample	The sample consisted of a representative cross-section of Detroit adults interviewed in early 1964. Their average score was 7.0.
Reliability/ Homogeneity	Average item-test correlation was .37, .41 if the 15th question (on England) is excluded. Average inter-item correlation was .13, .15 if the England question is excluded.
Validity	No direct evidence of validity is reported but the scale did correlate highly with educational background.
Location	Robinson, J. Public Information about World Affairs. Ann Arbor: Survey Research Center, 1967.
Results and Comments	Degree of education was the major correlate of scores on this measure. When education was controlled for, men answered correctly about 3.5 more questions than did women. Persons who scored higher on the quiz also were more likely to report that they used the mass media for news.

INFORMATION ABOUT FOREIGN COUNTRIES

Now we have three short questions about some things you might not hear about from the newspapers or TV.

(Percent of the Detroit sample with correct answers are given in parentheses.)

1) First of all, which of these countries have communist governments and which do not?

	Correct Answer	(% Correct)
Egypt	Non-Communist	(61%)
Poland	Communist	(70%)
Spain	Non-Communist	(65%)
Mainland China	Communist	(70%)
India	Non-communist	(64%)

2) Very good, now which of these countries are located in Africa? Again name all the African countries on the list.

	Correct Answer	(% Correct)
Ecuador	Not Africa	(64%)
Ghana	Africa	(63%)
Afghanistan	Not Africa	(34%)
Mongolia	Not Africa	(51%)
Morocco	Africa	(45%)

3) Finally which of these countries have developed and tested their own atomic weapons?

	Correct Answer	(% Correct)
West Germany	Has not	(62%)
Algeria	Has not	(76%)
France	Has	(60%)
Japan	Has not	(66%)
England	Has	(52%)
Russia	Has	(95%)

INFORMATION ABOUT THE FAR EAST (Robinson 1967)

Variable
The four questions in this measure deal with basic public awareness of Red China, Taiwan, Vietnam and differential U.S. relations with China and Russia.

Description
The respondent scores one point for each item answered correctly and no points for an incorrect answer. The range of scores thus runs from 0 (least informed) to 4 (most informed).

If a person did not know that China was a Communist country, he was not asked whether he knew about the Chinese government in Taiwan. Hence, the total score was not made up of independent items.

Sample
The sample consisted of a representative national sample of 1429 American adults interviewed in the spring of 1964.

Reliability/
Homogeneity
No data on reliability are reported.

Validity
No direct evidence of validity is available, but the scale did correlate highly with the respondent's educational background.

Location
Robinson, J. Public Information about World Affairs. Ann Arbor: Survey Research Center, 1967.

The original data came from Patchen, M. The American Public's View of U.S. Policy toward China. New York: Council on Foreign Relations, 1964.

Results and
Comments
Amount of formal education was the major correlate of scores on this short information quiz. When education was controlled for, men, older people, whites and non-Southerners were found to score significantly higher on the questions than women, younger people, Negroes and Southerners. Scores on this quiz would undoubtedly be somewhat higher if applied currently to the same type of sample.

Robinson notes that those types of individuals who are best informed are most likely to attend to mass media sources of information.

INFORMATION ABOUT THE FAR EAST

1. Do you happen to know what kind of government most of China has
   right now -- whether it's Democratic, Communist, or what?

   Answer: Communist (72% answered correctly)

2. (Asked only of those who had the correct answer to 1)
   Have you happened to hear anything about another Chinese government besides the Communist one?

   Answer: Yes (43% answered correctly: 60% of those who answered
           the first question correctly)

3. Do you happen to know whether the United States has been treating
   Russia and China the same up to now, or whether we've been treating them differently?

   Answer: Differently (65% answered correctly)

4. Have you happened to hear anything about the fighting in Vietnam?

   Answer: Yes (74% answered correctly)

INDEX OF ISSUE FAMILIARITY (Campbell et al. 1960)

Variable
: This Index ranks people on their willingness to express an opinion on 16 issue propositions and on their willingness to express a judgment on government performance with respect to those issues, in order to arrive at a measure of public familiarity with the issues.

Description
: A person who passed both requirements (i.e., expressed an opinion and a judgment) on an issue was regarded as "familiar" with the question, and given one point, for a possible total of 16. The issue questions upon which the Index was based were included in SRC's 1956 voting study interview schedule.

On each issue, a respondent was asked whether he had an opinion and then whether the government should or should not act in accordance with the proposed statement (a five-point Likert-type question). Respondents who expressed an opinion were later asked, on each issue proposition, whether the government was going too far, doing less than it should or doing just about right. A respondent could either reply that he hadn't heard what the government was doing, or he could express an opinion.

Sample
: The sample population was a representative national sample of the electorate. The number of pre-election respondents of whom these items were asked was 1929. The study was done in the early fall of 1956.

Reliability/
Homogeneity
: No information on reliability was reported.

Validity
: The authors presented no specific tests of validity.

Location
: Campbell, Angus, Converse, Philip E., Miller, Warren E., Stokes, Donald E. The American Voter. New York: John Wiley & Sons, 1960, pp. 171-176.

Administration
: This instrument could probably be administered in about 10-20 minutes. Additional attitudinal data on those people who express opinions are available to the analyst.

Results and
Comments
: The authors remark that the list of propositions included most of the better known issues and that the Index might overstate average familiarity with specific issues. They emphasized that "familiarity" refers not to accuracy of opinions but to the existence of an opinion that is given some sort of political meaning by its possessor.

About one third of the respondents ranked at the lowest extreme on the Index. More familiarity was found with the general issues than with the more specific ones, especially in the area of foreign policy. The list of issues still has current relevancy.

These items were also the basis of an index devised to supply a quantitative measure of intensity, or strength of opinion, on a given issue. The Index of Intensity is a measure of the relative frequency of strong statements of policy position as opposed to milder expressions of feeling.

The relevant sample were those of the SRC 1956 cross-sectional voting sample who qualified in terms of the cognitive and evaluative components of the Index of Issue Familiarity.

The utility of the index was shown in its application to race-related issue questions. The variation in opinion showed heightened intensity of opinion among those experiencing a threat to values of a type generally held in their population.

ISSUE FAMILIARITY

Around election time people talk about different things that our government in Washington is doing or should be doing. Now I would like to talk to you about some of the things that our government might do. Of course different things are important to different people, so we don't expect everyone to have an opinion about all of these.

12. I would like you to look at this card as I read each question and tell me how you feel about the question. If you don't have an opinion, just tell me that; if you do have an opinion, choose one of the other answers.

12a. "The government ought to cut taxes even if it means putting off some important things that need to be done."

Now, would you say you have an opinion on this or not?

            Yes   No

(IF "NO," GO ON TO Q. 12b)
(IF "YES"): Do you agree that the government should do this or do you think the government should not do it?

    1. Agree strongly; government definitely should
    2. Agree but not very strongly
    3. Not sure; it depends
    4. Disagree but not very strongly
    5. Disagree strongly; government definitely should not
    6. Don't know

(On the schedule this list of alternatives was repeated for each issue proposition.)

12b. "The government in Washington ought to see to it that everybody who wants to work can find a job."

12c. "This country would be better off if we just stayed home and did not concern ourselves with problems in other parts of the world."

12d. "The government ought to help people get doctors and hospital care at low cost."

12e. "The United States should give economic help to the poorer countries of the world even if they can't pay for it."

12f. "If Negroes are not getting fair treatment in jobs and housing, the government in Washington should see to it that they do."

12g. "The government ought to see to it that big business corporations don't have much say about how the government is run."

12h. "The best way for this country to deal with Russia and Communist China is to act just as tough as they do."

12i.   "If cities and towns around the country need help to build more schools, the government in Washington ought to give them the money they need."

12j.   "The United States should keep soldiers overseas where they can help countries that are against communism."

12k.   "The government should leave things like electric power and housing for private businessmen to handle."

12l.   "The government ought to see to it that labor unions don't have much say about how the government is run."

12m.   "The United States should be willing to go more than half-way in being friendly with the other countries of the world."

12n.   "The government ought to fire any government worker who is accused of being a communist even though they can't prove it."

12o.   "The United States should give help to foreign countries even if they are not as much against communism as we are."

12p.   "The government in Washington should stay out of the question of whether white and colored children go to the same school."

CHAPTER 11:   POLITICAL PARTICIPATION

Unlike the scales of earlier sections, the ones presented here consist of behavioral rather than attitudinal items. The first four scales are concerned with the more usual, general types of political activity--such as voting, giving money to the parties, campaigning for given candidates, and attending political rallies.   The last three scales tap a much more specific form of political participation--that of opinion leadership, especially at campaign time. The names of these scales are listed below in the order in which they will be reviewed:

1. Political Participation (PPS) Scale (Matthews and Prothro 1966)
2. Political Activity Index (Woodward and Roper 1950)
3. Index of Political Participation (Campbell et al. 1954)
4. Political Participation (Robinson 1952)
5. Public Affairs Opinion Leadership (Katz and Lazarsfeld 1955)
6. Opinion Leadership (Lazarsfeld, Berelson, and Gaudet 1944)
7. Opinion Leadership Scale (Rogers 1962)

The four scales on general political activity share certain methodological characteristics. First, they reveal similar item content, presumably because the range of possible types of political activity can take only quite limited form. Second, they rate high on tests of internal consistency of items, reflecting the fact that behavioral items usually show a greater tendency to intercorrelate than do attitudinal items. Third, all scales have been tested on representative, cross-sectional samples--the Woodward-Roper and Survey Research Center measures on a national basis, the Matthews-Prothro scale in the South only, and the Robinson scale in Erie County, Ohio. At the present time, Sidney Verba at Stanford University is analyzing data on political activism from four countries and this research promises the possibility that cross-national activism scales may be developed.

Information on the validity and reliability of the measures in this chapter is, in general, meager or absent. While this may at first seem surprising, it must be remembered that the cost and time involved in collecting the auxiliary information needed to establish the validity of behavioral reports is a formidable obstacle for most researchers. Also, a standard belief in social science circles has been that the validity testing of behavioral measures is far less crucial than establishing relations of attitudinal measures to corresponding activities. It is somewhat paradoxical that the very measures which are generally not tested for validity often turn out to be the criteria that determine whether a given attitude scale is valid or not.

The first of the measures to be reviewed is the Matthews-Prothro <u>Political Participation Scale</u>. Of all the measures, it is the one that conforms most closely to the ideal Guttman scale model. The scale is composed of activity items on such subjects as voting, talking politics, and holding party or public office. The authors also discuss the pattern of errors found in the scale analysis. It is interesting to note that the scale contains more "Guttman errors" for Negroes than for whites and that, even with status controlled, Negroes come out less active than whites.

The Woodward-Roper <u>Political Activity Index</u> consists of seven items, weighted so that the possible range of scores is between zero and twelve. The activity items are quite similar to those in the Matthews-Prothro measure. The findings show that only ten percent of the national sample scored "high" (i.e., a score of six or better) on the activity index.

The participation index of the Survey Research Center has only three scale scores, although it is based on five questions. In this case, 27 percent of the sample scored "high" on the scale. It was also found that scores on the index correlated well with three attitudinal measures that one would expect to be related to political participation.

The last general activity scale by Robinson is based on data from the classic Erie County voting study (described below). It is the one measure reviewed here which definitely indicates, according to the author's own tests, a marked departure from a unidimensional model of political participation. Nevertheless, the twelve items that Robinson examined do intercorrelate positively and most intercorrelated significantly as well. Many readers may find Robinson's factor analysis of his scale items interesting and his distinction between "spectator," "partisan," and "citizen" types of items to be quite useful.

The interested reader should consult Milbrath (1965) for a more comprehensive review of the structure and correlates of political participation. The items dealing with political activity from the SRC election studies, reviewed in Chapter 13, should also be helpful in this regard.

The final three scales in this section measure opinion leadership as a form of political activity. Measurement in this area has often followed the direct survey research technique, although some indirect methods of measurement such as the sociometric approach or the rating systems of key informants have also been used. Researchers interested in these alternate methods of coping with the measurement problem should consult the references in Rogers (1962). Rogers reports statistically significant, though not large, correlations between the three methods of measuring opinion leadership.

Katz and Lazarsfeld have probably devised the best scale of opinion leadership to date. It consists of three items--specific instances of possible opinion leadership at two points in time and a general evaluation of one's own leadership in this regard for the second time point. The questions on specific instances of such leadership show a fairly low correlation between the two points in time, but the combination of these specific items reveals a substantial association with the general evaluation item. The scale as developed was applied only to cross-sectional samples of women. The authors' evidence for the validity of the scale was commendable. They demonstrated that those evaluating themselves as influential in conversation were considered by other individuals to have had influence in the specific instances of record. Parallel scales on opinion leadership were also constructed by the authors in other areas than that of politics--those of marketing, fashion, and movies. Finally, the reader might find the description of the Abelson and Rugg adaptation of one of the scale items interesting--the item correlated quite highly with general political and civic participation.

The first opinion leadership measure was used by Lazarsfeld, Berelson, and Gaudet in Erie County, Ohio, in 1940. The scale was composed of only two items, for which no intercorrelation value was presented. The instrument was used on a cross-sectional sample, but in this case both men and women were included. Opinion leadership was found to be highly related to other forms of political participation and to agree with interviewers' assessments of the respondents' opinion leadership.

The last scale by Rogers focuses its attention on opinion leadership in relation to the adoption of new farm practices by farmers. Although the scale items seem restricted in scope at first glance, in reality, they could easily be adapted for use in other research settings. Reliability and validity data are adequate but not striking.

Reference:

Milbrath, L. Political Participation. Chicago: Rand McNally, 1965.

Rogers, E. The Diffusion of Innovations. New York: The Free Press, 1962.

POLITICAL PARTICIPATION (PPS) SCALE (Matthews and Prothro 1966)

Variable   This instrument attempts to measure extent of political participation
            on a cumulative scale of participation behavior.

Description   On this Guttman-style scale, the "hardest" form of political partici-
               pation is holding party of public office, which is combined with having
               membership in political groups to form scale Type V. This is followed
               by taking part in electoral campaigns, Type IV; voting, Type III;
               talking politics, Type II; and none of the above, Type I. Respondents
               were dichotomized into those who had ever engaged in any of these
               activities and those who had not. The scale steps are coded responses
               to about 15 questions which were part of a long interview schedule.

Sample   The main sample was composed of a representative cross section of
          citizens of voting age living in private households in the 11 states
          of the former Confederacy, drawn by SRC's stratified and multistage
          probability sampling techniques. Negroes were sampled at about three
          times their actual proportion of the region's population to produce
          approximately equal numbers of whites and Negroes, bringing the total
          Negro N to 618, the white N being 694. Supplementary representative
          county samples of about 50 to 100 each white and Negro citizens were
          drawn for four community studies.

          An additional sample of 264 Southern Negro college students was drawn,
          the students being a representative cross section of Negro students
          from Southern homes working toward degrees at accredited, predominantly
          Negro institutions of higher learning in the 11 states of the former
          Confederacy.

Reliability/   The coefficient of reproducibility was reported to be .98 for whites
  Homogeneity   and .95 for Negroes. The authors note that scale errors were not
                randomly distributed between the items but tended to cluster at the
                "voting" stage for Negroes and the "talking" stage for whites, and
                that the proportion of Negroes assigned to Types IV and V despite
                errors were 42 and 41 percent, respectively.

Validity   No tests for the validity of this behavior-based measure are reported.

Location   Matthews, D. R. and Prothro, J. W. Negroes and the New Southern
            Politics. New York: Harcourt, Brace & World, 1966.

Administration   The questions used to determine a respondent's scale type were part
                  of an interview schedule but could be converted to a paper and pencil
                  test; in the latter case, estimated administration time is about 15
                  minutes.

Results and   Probably the most marked result of the comparison of white and Negro
  Comments   PPS scores was that, while white scores approximated a normal-distribution
               curve, Negro PPS scores formed a strongly bimodal curve with peaks at
               scale Types II and IV. This curve was found to exist only in the Deep

South and not in the Peripheral South--an effect independent of sex, age, income, education, occupation of Respondent and of head of household.

The authors also found that the Southern Negro of their sample became more politically active the longer his experience at participation, regardless of the age at which he first registered.

The relationship of PPS scores to 11 other measures used in the study are covered in other Matthews-Prothro write-ups in this volume, but it is interesting to note that of the demographic variables, income was found to have the strongest independent effect on Negro PPS scores.

When the authors reconstructed PPS scores of Southern Negroes with the Negroes having the same educational, income, and occupational distributions as whites, it was found that although the peculiar bimodal distribution of Negro PPS scores was eliminated, Negro political activity comparable to that of whites was not produced. In contrast, Negro political interest was found to exceed that of whites at every educational level but one.

POLITICAL PARTICIPATION SCALE

Numbers below refer to location in the questionnaire for
(A) Negro Students, (B) White Adults and (C) Negro Adults

(A)   (B)   (C)
(on political discussion)

1		1	When you talk with your friends, do you ever talk about public problems--that is, what's happening in the country or in this community? Do you ever talk about public problems with any of the following people?
	2a	2a	Your family?
	2c	2c	People where you work?
		2f	Negro community leaders--such as club or church leaders?
	2e		Community leaders such as club or church leaders?
	3		Do you ever talk about public problems with any colored people?
		3	Do you ever talk about public problems with any white people?
	4	4	Do you ever talk about public problems with government officials or people in politics, I mean Democratic or Republican leaders?
	9	9	Have you ever talked to people to try to get them to vote for or against any candidate?

430

(A)   (B)   (C)
(on voting)
        27   30   What about you? Have you ever voted?

(on campaign participation)
        6   6   Have you ever given any money or bought tickets or anything to help
                        someone who was trying to win an election?

        7   7   Have you ever gone to any political meetings, rallies, barbecues,
                        fish fries, or things like that in connection with an election?

        8   8   Have you ever done any work to help a candidate in his campaign?

(on office holding and political memberships)
        5   5   Have you ever held an office in a political party or been elected
                        or appointed to a government job?
        5a   5a   (If yes) What office or job was that?

        11   11   Do you belong to any clubs or groups like these (show card 1)
                        _____ labor union (like AFL-CIO or a carpenters' union)
                        _____ political club or group (like Young Democrats, Young Republicans,
                               or a political organization)
                        _____ organizations concerned with race relations (like Human
                               Relations Council, NAACP, voters' leagues)
                        _____ fraternal organizations or lodges (like the Masons, Knights of
                               Pythias, or Knights of Columbus)
                        _____ PTA (that is, Parent-Teachers Association)
                        _____ business, professional, or civic groups (like the Kiwanis or
                               Lions clubs)
                        _____ farm group (like Farm Bureau)
                        _____ a church or church-connected group
                        _____ other
                        _____ none

        11a   11a   (If "yes" to any of above) Which is that?

POLITICAL ACTIVITY INDEX (Woodward and Roper 1950)

Variable	This index attempts to classify individuals in terms of the amount of political activity in which they engage, specifically referring to political activity in channels of possible influence on legislators and government officials.
Description	The instrument is composed of seven items concerned with voting, being a member of potential pressure group, communicating with legislators, participating in political party activity, and habitually talking politics. Possible range of scores is 0-12, with points given for reported frequency of activity in addition to a simple positive response.
Sample	The items were first tested in a pilot study with a national sample of 500 respondents; after revision, items were administered to a representative national cross-section of 8000 respondents.
Reliability/ Homogeneity	The authors report "partial but not perfect" inter-item correlation.
Validity	No tests for validity are reported. The authors warn that the responses are probably inflated somewhat by the natural tendency of people to exaggerate their own activity a bit when they are questioned by an interviewer.
Location	Woodward, Julian L. and Roper, Elmo. "Political Activity of American Citizens, <u>American Political Science Review</u>, 1950, <u>44</u>, pp. 872-885.
Administration	If the index were administered as a paper and pencil test, estimated administration time would be under seven minutes. Scoring requires simple summing of response codes.
Results and Comments	It was found that only about ten percent of the sample could be classed as politically active (a score of 6 or better).

POLITICAL ACTIVITY INDEX

Question Number	
1	Do you happen to belong to any organizations that sometimes take a stand on housing, better government, school problems, or other public issues? (If "yes") What organizations?

* * * * * * *

| 2a | When you get together with your friends would you say that you discuss public issues like government regulation of business, labor unions, taxes, and farm programs frequently, occasionally, or never? |

and

| 2b | (If "frequently" or "occasionally") Which of the statements on this card best describes the part you yourself take in these discussions with your friends? |

    (1) Even though I have my own opinions, I usually just listen
    (2) Mostly I listen, but once in a while I express my opinions.
    (3) I take an equal share in the conversation.
    (4) I do more than just hold up my end in the conversation; I usually try to convince others that I am right.

* * * * * * *

| 3 | Have you ever written or talked to your Congressman or Senator or other public officials to let them know what you would like them to do on a public issue you were interested in? |

and

| 4 | In the last four years have you worked for the election of any political candidate by doing things like distributing circulars or leaflets, making speeches, or calling on voters? |

* * * * * * *

| 5 | Have you attended any meetings in the last four years at which political speeches were made? |

* * * * * * *

| 6 | In the last four years have you contributed money to a political party or to a candidate for a political office? |

* * * * * * *

| 7 | Probably you can't remember exactly, but about how many times do you think you have gone to the polls and voted during the last four years? |

INDEX OF POLITICAL PARTICIPATION (Campbell et al. 1954)

Variable	This scale was designed as a "crude, but serviceable" index of the level of political activity in the national electorate.
Description	The three levels of political activity in the index include:

    1) High (voting and other participation)
    2) Medium (voting only)
    3) Low (did not vote, even though involved in other participation)

Sample	The sample was a national cross-section of 1614 Americans interviewed after the 1952 election. Slightly over a quarter (27 percent) of this sample scored "high," 47 percent scored "medium" and 26 percent scored "low."
Reliability/ Homogeneity	No reliability data are reported, although participation in each of the non-voting forms of activity was noticeably higher among voters than non-voters.
Validity	No direct data on validity are reported. This variable itself is usually considered a criterion for validity. The index was found to be highly related to three political attitudinal measures described in the next chapter: Sense of Political Efficacy, Sense of Citizen Duty, and Issue Involvement.
Location	Campbell, Angus, Gurin, Gerald, and Miller, Warren E. The Voter Decides. Evanston, Ill.: Row, Peterson, 1954.
Administration	The items should take no more than 3-5 minutes to answer.

Instrument	1. In talking to people about the election, we find that a lot of people weren't able to vote because they weren't registered or they were sick or they just didn't have time. How about you, did you vote this time?

           Yes   No

2. Did you give any money, or buy tickets, or anything, to help the campaign for one of the parties or candidates?

3. Did you go to any political meetings, rallies, dinners, or things like that?

4. Did you do any other work for one of the parties or candidates?

5. Did you talk to any people to try to show them why they should vote for one of the parties or candidates?

POLITICAL PARTICIPATION (Robinson 1952)

Variable

This study is an attempt to determine the dimensions of psychological involvement in a political campaign, such as knowledge, media usage and conversation.

Description

A factor analysis was performed on the intercorrelations of 12 behavior items used in the Lazarsfeld, Berelson, Gaudet (1948) study of the 1940 presidential campaign in Erie County, Ohio. The author states that the 12 activities constitute a denotative definition of psychological involvement in a political campaign. Three major factors were found, which the author names: (1) role of spectator; (2) role of citizen (primary concern being how to vote); and (3) role of partisan (primary concern being the election of his candidate).

It was found generally that "spectators" gave positive responses only to items 3-9, "citizens" gave positive responses only to items 1 and 2, while "partisans" gave positive responses to items 9-12.

Sample

The sample consisted of a cross-section of 600 citizens in Erie County, Ohio during the 1940 electoral campaign.

Reliability/ Homogeneity

Average inter-item correlation of the 7 spectator items was .33. Average inter-item correlation of the 4 partisan items was .21. The two citizen items intercorrelated .52.

No test-retest data are reported.

Validity

The fact that the items in both of the spectator and the partisan sets of items did correlate with self-rated interest and vote (item 1 and 2) may be taken as some evidence of validity.

Location

Robinson, W. "The National Structure of Political Participation," American Sociological Review, 1952, 17, pp. 151-156.

Administration

The items should take less than five minutes to answer. They would have to be updated with respect to candidates and mass media.

Results and Comments

This three dimensional division of political activity could be a useful distinction in the analysis of participation data.

Reference

Lazarsfeld, Paul, Berelson, Bernard and Gaudet, Hazel. The People's Choice. New York: Columbia University Press, 1944.

Instrument   Behavior Items

1. The respondent's self-rating on interest.
2. Voting.
3. Listening to the Democratic Convention on the radio.
4. Listening to the Republican Convention on the radio.
5. Reading about the Democratic Convention in the newspaper.
6. Reading about the Republican Convention in the newspaper.
7. Knowing who Henry A. Wallace is.
8. Knowing who Wendell Willkie is.
9. Listening to political speeches on the radio.
10. Trying to convince someone about candidates or issues.
11. Having one's advice asked about candidates or issues.
12. Doing active political work.

Inter-item Correlation Matrix (Pearson coefficients; decimal points omitted)

	1	2	3	4	5	6	7	8	9	10	11	12
1	X	52	35	28	30	27	35	24	37	33	17	22
2		X	22	22	24	20	26	17	26	00	10	10
3			X	47	37	28	40	20	39	27	14	14
4				X	27	40	33	22	41	14	17	10
5					X	48	42	24	28	24	14	10
6						X	37	32	30	22	14	10
7							X	17	33	17	14	17
8								X	22	20	00	10
9									X	24	20	25
10										X	17	17
11											X	22
12												X

PUBLIC AFFAIRS OPINION LEADERSHIP (Katz and Lazarsfeld 1955)

Variable
These items reflect the degree to which persons feel they influence the opinions of others about public affairs.

Description
The scale consisted of only three items, one of which (a specific question), was repeated on two separate occasions two months apart. The general question was asked only on the second interview.

From the two questions the following typology was constructed.

	Specific		
	2-time Adviser (June & Aug.)	1-time Adviser (June or Aug.)	Did not give Advice either time
General			
More likely (or same) to give advice	1	3	5
Less likely to give advice	2	4	6

After analysis of the background and attitudinal characteristics of individuals in these six groups, it was decided that the most appropriate dichotomy was as follows: Opinion leaders (1,2,3) and Non-leaders (4,5,6).

Sample
The sample consisted of a random cross-section of 800 women over 16 years of age in Decatur, Illinois. The women were interviewed in June and August of 1945.

Reliability/ Homogeneity
Rogers (1962) reports that the data presented by Katz and Lazarsfeld (pp. 375-376) show a split-half (actually inter-item) correlation of .49 and a test-retest reliability of .15 for the repeated question (i.e., the first or specific question).

Validity
Interviews were conducted with people whom the respondent specifically either reported influencing or being influenced by. In subsequent interviews with those people specified by the respondent two-thirds of them confirmed the influence attempt, and only ten percent denied the attempt. The remaining quarter could not recall the situation.

The above data refers to influence attempts in all of the other influence areas (see below) examined in the study. Little difference was found in the confirmation of data from "influentials" and "influencees."

Location
Katz, E. and Lazarsfeld, P. Personal Influence. Glencoe, Ill.: The Free Press, 1955.

Results and Comments
Unlike the other influence areas, stage in the life-cycle made little difference in whether a woman was an opinion-leader or not. Social status and "gregariousness" (indexed by belonging to organizations and contact with friends) were found to be the major determinants of opinion leadership. Opinion leaders read significantly more magazines and books than non-leaders. Parallel opinion-leadership questions were asked in the areas of marketing, fashion and movies. Rogers (1962) reports that reliability figures for fashion leaders were higher than for public affairs: split-half .56 and test-retest .24.

Abelson and Rugg (1958) modified the second (general) question and applied it to a national probability sample of 1059 American business-men. About a quarter of the sample said "more likely" and another quarter said "about the same." Those who said "more likely" were twice as likely to be highly involved in civic and political activities as those who said "about the same" and over three times as likely to be involved as those who said "less likely."

References
Rogers, E. Diffusion of Innovations. New York: The Free Press, 1962.

Abelson, H. and Rugg, W. "Self-designated Influentiality and Activity," Public Opinion Quarterly, 1958, 22, 566-567.

Instrument
1. Have you recently been asked your advice about what one should think about social or political opinion?
   (Asked in both June and August)

2. Compared with other women belonging to your circle of friends, are you more or less likely than any of them to be asked for your advice on what one should think about social or political opinions?
   (Asked only in August)

OPINION LEADERSHIP (Lazarsfeld, Berelson, and Gaudet 1944)

Variable

This short index reflects an aspect of the degree of interest and articulateness about public issues.

Description

The scale consists of two items. A person who answers "yes" to both of them is designated as an opinion leader. In all, 21 percent of the sample in question qualified as opinion leaders, the remaining 79 percent being called followers.

Sample

The sample consisted of a random cross-section of 3000 adults (every fourth household) in Erie County, Ohio. From these, four groups of 600 were selected by stratified sampling. Three of these groups were interviewed only once during the election period, and the remaining "main panel" was interviewed seven times during the campaign.

The results below refer to the whole sample.

Reliability/
Homogeneity

No data on reliability are reported. Robinson (see previous scale description in this chapter) reports that the two items correlate at .17.

Validity

No data bearing directly on validity are reported. However, the authors report that "in all respects, the opinion leaders demonstrated greater political alertness," e.g., 61 percent of the leaders vs. 24 percent of the followers said they had a great deal of interest in the election and followed the campaign more closely in each of the mass media.

The question replies were also found to correspond with interviewer impressions of the respondents' opinion leadership.

Location

Lazarsfeld, Paul, Berelson, Bernard, and Gaudet, H. The People's Choice. New York: Columbia University Press, 1944.

Results and
Comments

Opinion leaders were found in all social strata, although highest among sales workers (44 percent) and skilled and professional workers (35 percent) and lowest among farmers (15 percent) and housewives (13 percent).

Instrument

1. Have you tried to convince anyone of your political ideas recently?
   Yes   No

2. Has anyone asked your advice on a political question recently?
   Yes   No

OPINION LEADERSHIP SCALE (Rogers 1962)

Variable	This scale attempts to identify farm opinion leaders, or "individuals who are influential in approving or disapproving new ideas."
Description	This scale consists of six items, devised for use with farmers. Scores run from 0 (no leadership) to 6 (high leadership).
Sample	The sample consisted of a state-wide random area sample of 104 farm operators in Ohio in the middle 1950's.
Reliability/ Homogeneity	A split-half reliability of .70 and coefficient of reproducibility of .91 are reported for these items.
	No test-retest reliability figures are given.
Validity	Correlation of scores on this scale with sociometric choices of opinion leadership was .23. The author feels that this low figure may be due to the crude nature of the sociometric data. In later studies, correlations of .41 and .30 were reported along with a correlation of .64 between scale scores and the ratings of key informants.
Location	Rogers, E. Diffusion of Innovations. New York: The Free Press, 1962.
Results and Comments	Rogers presents his findings with this scale along with a far larger variety of studies on opinion leadership. These are far too complex to summarize here.

440

OPINION LEADERSHIP SCALE
(Opinion leader responses are noted with an asterisk*)

1. During the past six months have you told anyone about some new farming practice?

   *Yes   No   Don't know

2. Compared with your circle of friends

   * (a) are you more, or
     (b) are you less likely

   to be asked for advice about new farming practices?

3. Thinking back to your last discussion about some new farm practices

   * (a) Were you asked for your opinion of the new practice, or
     (b) Did you ask someone else?

4. When you and your friends discuss new ideas about farm practices, what part do you play?

     (a) Mainly listen, or
   * (b) Try to convince them of your ideas?

5. Which of these happens more often

   * (a) Do you tell your neighbors about some new farm practice?
     (b) Do they tell you about a new practice?

6. Do you have the feeling that you are generally regarded by your friends as a good source of advice about new farm practices?

   * Yes   No   Don't know

CHAPTER 12: ATTITUDES TOWARD THE POLITICAL PROCESS

The scales in this section are all of rather recent origin and are fairly uniform in overall quality. The authors of the various scales have, in many instances, borrowed the ideas and methods of each other as aids in designing their own measures. For these reasons, there has been no attempt to list the scales in order of quality or utility. Rather, a decision has been made to review the scales in terms of the breadth of sample coverage involved in the various studies. This decision would prompt a consideration of Almond and Verba's multi-nation study first, followed by McClosky and the Survey Research Center's national ones, and finally end the presentation with the Southern sample of Matthews and Prothro and the more localized or community samples of Litt and Agger.

The names of the various scales to be reviewed are as follows:

1. Subjective Political Competence Scale (Almond and Verba 1963)
2. Various Other Attitudes about the Political System (Almond and Verba 1963)
3. Index of Ratio of Support (McClosky et al. 1960)
4. Political Involvement (Campbell et al. 1960)
5. Political Efficacy (Campbell et al. 1954)
6. Sense of Citizen Duty (Campbell et al. 1954)
7. Extent of Issue Orientation (Campbell et al. 1954)
8. Issue Involvement (Campbell et al. 1954)
9. Issue Partisanship (Campbell et al. 1954)
10. Overall Index of Psychological Readiness for Participation (Matthews and Prothro 1960)
11. Sense of Civic Competence Index (Matthews & Prothro 1966)
12. Party Image Score (Matthews and Prothro 1966)
13. Attitude Dimensions of Political Norms (Litt 1963)
14. Political Cynicism and Personal Cynicism (Agger, Goldstein, and Pearl 1961)

The first scale by Almond and Verba purports to measure a person's sub-jective political competence. In many respects, it resembles the Political Efficacy Scale of the Survey Research Center, but it differs from the latter in having a stronger behavioral orientation and a more local governmental flavor. Internal consistency of the scale seems to vary widely across countries, but the scale's record of consistent correlations with such other behavior as political discussion and communication, and with such attitudes as pride and other positive feelings about one's political system, does much to justify the scale's basic claim of validity.

The numerous other measures developed by Almond and Verba in their five nation study contain too few items to warrant detailed review here and are accordingly examined only briefly and as a group. The areas covered by the measures are political cognitions (which include items on the impact of government on daily life, exposure to politics, political information, and range of political opinion), output affect, political communication, sense of civic obligation, and voting satisfaction.

The Index of Support by McClosky has the advantage of having been applied to national samples of both political party leaders and the public. It attempts to tap basic attitudes toward various governmental issues and, hence, the degree of support toward the political process in these areas. Evidence for the validity of the scale is impressive, particularly data showing the different emphasis on concern over issues between the party elite and mass samples. No reliability figures are reported.

The scale of Political Involvement by the Survey Research Center is composed of three single items and two other separate scales--the scales of Political Efficacy and Sense of Citizen Duty. The intent of this measure is to assess the respondent's general interest in politics and his more personal involvement in the current election campaigns. Internal consistency of the scale seems high. The scale also does an impressive job of predicting turnout. The two scales included in the measure are also important in their own right and will be discussed next.

The Political Efficacy Scale was developed by the Survey Research Center prior to the one on political involvement. As noted before, it measures a person's subjective competence in politics, especially with regard to one's feeling of playing an important role in telling the government how things should be run. Internal consistency of the scale is adequate. Evidence for the scale's essential validity can be found in its high correlations with political participation questions and with the act of voting itself.

The Sense of Citizen Duty Scale, also developed earlier than the one on political involvement, is composed of four items. Internal consistency of the items seems high, although scale scores may be subject to agreement response set (as may also be the case with the efficacy scale above). The measure attempts to pinpoint one's sense of civic obligation, one's feeling that he ought to participate in the political process regardless of whether his perceptions of this activity are seen as effective or not. Scores on this measure correlated strongly with political participation scores. A closer examination of the correlations between the scale items themselves can be found in Chapter 13.

The following three scales--Issue Orientation, Issue Involvement, and Issue Partisanship--were also developed by the Survey Research Center. The scale on issue involvement has been used primarily for building the orientation and partisanship scales. The latter two measures attempt to capture the respondent's involvement with issues, the partisan ways in which he perceives them, and the degree to which he takes a partisan attitude on them. Quantitative data on the reliability or homogeneity of these measures are available only for the basic scale on issue involvement. However, there is more than adequate evidence for the validity of the other two scales; the orientation scale was highly related to political participation and the partisanship scale was strongly associated with one's presidential vote.

Matthews and Prothro's <u>Readiness for Participation Index</u> is an omnibus measure which takes into account eight separate psychological variables (mainly attitudinal) related to political outlook. The scale was constructed only for Negroes, although only three of the items would not be applicable if one wished to use the scale with white samples. The scale's intent is to ascertain a person's psychological predisposition toward participating in the political system. No evidence on the reliability of the scale is presented, but evidence on its validity is more than adequate--the scale accounting for about 40 percent of the variance in Negro political activity in the South.

The <u>Civic Competence Index</u> by Matthews and Prothro is one of the measures making up their larger <u>Readiness for Participation Index</u>. The items are similar to those employed by Almond and Verba in the <u>Political Competence Scale</u> discussed earlier. No evidence of reliability was given for the Matthews-Prothro measure. The fact that political participation was positively related to feelings of civic competence provides some evidence of measurement validity.

Matthews and Prothro's <u>Party Image Score</u> is an entirely independent measure. It consists of four simple open-ended questions about the political parties, almost identical to those typically used in Survey Research Center election studies. The scale touches general perceptions of the good and bad points of the two major political parties. Higher party image scores were found among people who were generally politically active. Positive Republican image scores increased markedly among Southern whites and Democratic image scores increased dramatically among Negroes over the three year period prior to the Johnson-Goldwater election year of 1964.

Litt's <u>Attitude Dimensions</u> consists of three original measures and reformulations of two other instruments--the SRC <u>Political Efficacy Scale</u> and the Prothro-Grigg <u>Democratic Creeds Index</u>. Each of the five measures was used as a separate index rather than being combined to form an overall index of a single attitudinal dimension. The topics of the five indices ranged from democratic principles to political functions. Internal consistency figures for the five measures were not high; in addition, the author presented no evidence for validity or information on the intercorrelation of the five measures. However, interesting differences in scale scores were reported among the various groups which comprised the study's sample base.

The last scales were developed by Agger, Goldstein, and Pearl and pertain to feelings of cynicism. These authors probed for feelings of both Personal Cynicism and Political Cynicism and found the two scales to be related. Evidence of reliability and validity were given and seemed adequate.

SUBJECTIVE POLITICAL COMPETENCE SCALE (Almond and Verba 1963)

Variable	This scale attempts to measure belief in the efficacy of one's own political action in local government.
Description	The five items of this instrument were treated as forming six-step Guttman scales for United States, English, German and Italian samples with dichotomized positive and negative responses. Range of scores is 0-5, with 5 representing the highest degree of subjective competence. Mexican respondents were assigned scores based on the simple arithmetic sum of their responses, since those answering negatively to item 2 were not asked item 3.
	In this study, respondents scoring 4-5 were grouped as "high," 2-3 as "medium," and 0-1 as "low."
Sample	The population samples were careful national cross-section samples of about 1000 of which completed interviews numbered in the United States, 970; in Great Britain, 937; in Germany, 955; in Italy, 955; and in Mexico, 1008.
Reliability/ Homogeneity	The coefficients of reproducibility for the four countries whose data were treated as forming Guttman scales were: United States, .92; Great Britain, .93; Germany, .90; and Italy, .87. Menzel's (1953) coefficients of scalability for the four countries were: United States, .80; Great Britain, .71; Germany, .90; and Italy, .87.
Validity	It was found that with education controlled, in every nation, those scoring high on subjective competence were more likely to expose themselves to political communications, to engage in political discussion, and to be partisan activists. In terms of attitudes, competence was correlated with feeling satisfaction with one's vote, believing that the local government improves things (except in Mexico), expressing price in one's political system (except in Germany and Italy), feeling election campaigning is good, and believing that the ordinary man has an obligation to be a participating citizen.
Location	Almond, G. A. and Verba, S. The Civic Culture. Princeton, New Jersey: Princeton University Press, 1963.
Administration	The items were administered in an interview situation and would probably have to be modified for use as a pencil and paper test. Scaling was accomplished by Guttman analysis, with the "minimum error" criterion and the "distribution of perfect types" criterion used to assign imperfect scale types to scale positions.
Results and Comments	For further study of the effect of this attitude dimension on political participation, see Matthews and Prothro (1966).

References   Matthews and Prothro. The Negro and the New Southern Politics.
New York: Harcourt, Brace & World, 1966.

Menzel, Herbert. "A New Coefficient for Scalogram Analysis,"
Public Opinion Quarterly, 1953, 17, pp. 268-280.

POLITICAL COMPETENCE

1. How about the local issues in this town or part of the country?
   How well do you understand them? (This question was asked as a
   follow-up question to the following two questions: "Some people
   say that politics and government are so complicated that the
   average man cannot really understand what is going on. In
   general, do you agree or disagree with that?" and "How well do you
   think you understand the important national and international
   issues facing this country?")

2. Suppose a regulation were being considered by (most local
   governmental unit specified by interviewer) that you considered
   very unjust or harmful. What do you think you could do?

3. If such a case arose, how likely is it that you would actually
   do something about it?

4. If you made an effort to change this regulation, how likely is
   it that you would succeed?

5. Have you ever done anything to try to influence a local
   regulation?

VARIOUS OTHER ATTITUDES TOWARD THE POLITICAL SYSTEM (Almond and Verba 1963)

In The Civic Culture, Almond and Verba presented a number of attitude "measures" for purposes of cross-national comparison which were comprised of straightforward questions whose responses were not intended to form scales. These measures depend for their validity primarily on inherent "face validity," but in some instances different groups' responses to the items provide evidence that the measures did tap the hypothesized attitude dimension. Presented below are brief descriptions of the different measures of political attitudes employed in the five-nation study, followed by a summary of a few of the findings reported by the author. Further information on these measures was not reported.

I. Political Cognition:

(1) Impact of Government on Daily Life
(2) Exposure to Politics
(3) Political Information
(4) Range of Political Opinion Index

The first of these measures, Impact of Government, attempted to discover how much importance was attributed to national and local government in each of the five countries studied: the United States, Great Britain, Germany, Italy and Mexico. Exposure to Politics attempted to measure the minimal degree of political involvement: following political and governmental affairs, and following political campaigns. Responses to these two questions were grouped into a rough index: low = two negative responses; medium = one positive, one negative response; high = two positive responses. Some evidence of the validity of this simple measure was provided by the similarity in the national pattern of responses to these items and to questions on following reports of public affairs in the various mass media.

The Political Information measure is based on ability to identify the national leaders of the principal parties in each country and to name cabinet offices or departments at the national level of government. The authors cautioned that since the governmental and party structures of the five countries differed, these limited quantitative measures were not strictly comparable. The cross-national comparisons of proportions of the populations who scored at the extremes (low, no correct information; high, four or more names or ministries) were felt to be fairly reliable, however.

The Range of Political Opinion Index is a measure of readiness to express political opinion. It is based on the frequency with which respondents expressed opinions on a series of six general political attitude questions. In this, the index is similar to the Campbell et al. Index of Issue Familiarity (Chapter 10).

It was found that in four of the countries studied, an overwhelming number of respondents who scored high on Exposure to Politics also attributed significance to both their national and local governments. In Mexico, however, 56 percent of high scorers on Exposure attribute significance to neither their national nor local government. Awareness of government significance and exposure ("civic cognition") are both strongly correlated with education. It was found that in all the countries except Italy, persons who score low in information still score high in the expression of opinions. Mexico had the largest percent of these respondents, dubbed "civic aspirants."

II. Output Affect

This measure was intended to discover what qualities respondents imputed to the executive side of government by questions on expectations of how they would be treated by government officials and by police. It was found that respondents in Great Britain and the United States had the most confidence in the fairness of their officials, and respondents in Italy the least.

III. Political Communication

This measure of minimal active political participation was comprised of a question on frequency of talking politics with other people (never or sometimes), together with the interviewer's assessment of the respondent's willingness to discuss politics, i.e., to reveal how he voted in the last national elections and to report his usual local vote. Two thirds of the Italian and Mexican respondents reported they did not talk politics, but Germany and Italy returned the most respondents who refused to report their vote.

IV. Sense of Civic Obligation

This single-question measure attempted to assess the extent to which the respondent felt one should participate in his community. It was found that the percent of people who say that the ordinary man should be active in his community rises with education and occupational level in all countries except in Italy, where few of the professional and managerial class feel a sense of civic obligation.

V. Satisfaction with Voting Participation

This single-question measure was designed to ascertain the feelings evoked by voting itself: satisfaction, annoyance, fulfilling a duty, or no feelings at all. The measure attempted to tap the citizen's attitude toward the most basic role in the "input structure" of participatory government. A feeling of satisfaction was revealed to be associated with high levels of subjective political competence.

I-1. IMPACT OF GOVERNMENT ON DAILY LIFE

Thinking now about the national government (in Washington, London, Bonn, Rome, Mexico City), about how much effect do you think its activities, the laws passed and so on, have on your day-to-day life? Do they have a great effect, some effect, or none?

Now take the local government. About how much effect do you think its activities have on your day-to-day life? Do they have a great effect, some effect, or none?

I-2. EXPOSURE TO POLITICAL COMMUNICATION

Do you follow the accounts of political and governmental affairs? Would you say you follow them regularly, from time to time, or never?

What about the campaigning that goes on at the time of a national election-- do you pay much attention to what goes on, just a little, or none at all?

I-3.   POLITICAL INFORMATION

1. We are also interested in how well known the national leaders of the various political parties are in the country. Could you name three leaders of the _____ party? Could you name three leaders of the _____ party? Could you tell me the name of a leader from the _____ party?

2. When a new Prime Minister (or President) comes into office, one of the first things he must do is appoint people to cabinet positions and ministries. Could you tell me what some of these cabinet positions are? Can you name any others? (Continue up to five cabinet positions)

I-4. RANGE OF POLITICAL OPINION INDEX

1. One sometimes hears that some people or groups have so much influence on the way the government is run that the interests of the majority are ignored. Do you agree or disagree that there are such groups?

2. We know that the ordinary person has many problems that take his time. In view of this, what part do you think the ordinary person ought to play in the community affairs of his town or district?

3. People speak of the obligations that they owe to their country. In your opinion, what are the obligations that every man owes to his country?

4. Some people say that campaigning is needed so the public can judge candidates and issues. Others say that it causes so much bitterness and is so unreliable that we'd be better off without it. What do you think--is it needed or would we be better off without it?

5. The _____ party now controls the government. Do you think that its policies and activities would ever seriously endanger the country's welfare? Do you think that this probably <u>would</u> happen, that it <u>might</u> happen, or that it probably <u>wouldn't</u> happen?

6. Let me ask you about some other parties that might someday take control of the government. If the _____ (chief opposition party) were to take control of the government, how likely is it that it would endanger the country's welfare. Do you think that this would <u>probably</u> happen, that it <u>might</u> happen or that it probably <u>wouldn't</u> happen?

II. OUTPUT AFFECT

Suppose there were some question that you had to take to a government office--for example, a tax question or housing regulation. Do you think you would be given equal treatment--I mean, would you be treated as well as anyone else?

If you explained your point of view to the officials, what effect do you think it would have? Would they give your point of view serious consideration, would they pay only a little attention, or would they ignore what you had to say?

III. POLITICAL COMMUNICATION

What about talking about public affairs to other people? Do you do that nearly every day, once a week, from time to time, or never?

(INTERVIEWER RATING)
Articulateness of respondent

IV. SENSE OF CIVIC OBLIGATION

We know that the ordinary person has many problems that take his time. In view of this, what part do you think the ordinary person ought to play in the local affairs of his town or district?

V. SATISFACTION WITH VOTING PARTICIPATION

Which one of these statements comes closest to describing your feelings when you go to the polls to cast your ballot?

I get a feeling of satisfaction out of it
I do it only because it is my duty
I feel annoyed, it's a waste of time
I don't feel anything in particular

INDEX OF RATIO OF SUPPORT (McClosky et al. 1960)

Variable

This index was designed to measure whether a particular group predominantly favors or opposes the issue in question, and how strongly it does so. It was hypothesized that the leaders of the two parties would differ on issues more sharply than their followers would.

Description

Respondents were asked their attitudes on 24 important national issues, and were also asked to state whether they believed support for each issue would be "increased," "decreased," or "remain as is." The weights assigned to each response were: 1.0, 0.0, and 0.5, respectively. Ratio-of-support score for any given sample is in effect a mean score of the item with a possible range of 0 to 1.0. In general, the scores can be taken to approximate the following over-all positions: .00 to .25--strongly wish to reduce support; .26 to .45--wish to reduce support; .46 to .55--satisfied with the status quo; .56 to .75--wish to increase support; and .76 to 1.00--strongly wish to increase support.

The issues can be grouped into five broad headings: Public Ownership, Government Regulation of the Economy, Equalitarianism and Human Welfare, Tax Policy, and Foreign Policy.

Sample

There were two population groups sampled:

1) Leaders, drawn from Democratic (1788) and Republican (1232) national convention delegates:

and

2) Followers, a national cross-section sample of 1484.

Reliability/
Homogeneity

No reliability figures are reported.

Validity

Party disagreements were generally consistent with differences turned up by studies of Congressional roll calls (Turner, 1961).

Location

McClosky, H., Hoffman, P., and O'Hara, R. "Issue Conflict and Consensus Among Party Leaders and Followers," American Political Science Review, 1960, 54, pp. 406-427.

Administration

Estimated administration time is about 25 minutes. Scoring requires aggregation and averaging of scores.

Results and
Comments

It was found that the leaders of the two parties differed significantly on 23 of the 24 issues listed and were separated on 15 of these issues by .18 or more ratio points. In strong contrast, the followers differed significantly on only seven out of 24 issues; there was no difference in ratio scores larger than .14, and on the majority of issues the disparity was smaller than .05.

Insofar as they differed at all, the followers tended to divide in a

454

pattern similar to that shown by the leaders, the correlation between
their rank orders being .72. But only in the differential trust they
expressed toward business and labor are the two sets of followers
widely separated. Republican followers disagreed far more with their
own leaders than with the leaders of the Democratic party. There was
also no consistent connection between inter-party conflict and intra-
party cohesion. It was clear that party differentiation among followers
did not depend heavily upon ideological considerations.

The authors warned that the validity of item content was current
(1957-1958) and limited to specific issues although the issues seem
just as relevant today. The form of the issue questions precluded
gathering data on degree of political knowledge and intensity, a
limitation somewhat offset by controls for education and SES in
comparisons of leaders with followers.

The authors felt that the accuracy of the reflection of the stage of
party opinion was not biased by the anonymous nature of collection.

Reference   Turner, Julius. Party and Constituency: Pressures on Congress.
The Johns Hopkins University Studies in Historical and Political
Science Series, LXIX, #1 (1951).

RATIO-OF-SUPPORT INDEX

Do you think that government support for _____ should be increased, decreased or remain the same?

Public Ownership Issues

1. Public Ownership of Natural Resources
2. Public Control of Atomic Energy

Government Regulation of the Economy Issues

3. Level of Farm Price Support
4. Government Regulation of Business
5. Regulation of Public Utilities
6. Enforcement of Anti-Monopoly Laws
7. Regulation of Trade Unions
8. Level of Tariffs
9. Restrictions on Credit

Equalitarian and Human Welfare Issues

10. Federal Aid to Education
11. Slum Clearance and Public Housing
12. Social Security Benefits
13. Minimum Wages
14. Enforcement of Integration
15. Immigration into United States

Tax Policy Issues

16. Corporate Income Tax
17. Tax on Large Incomes
18. Tax on Business
19. Tax on Middle Incomes
20. Tax on Small Incomes

Foreign Policy Issues

21. Reliance on the United Nations
22. American Participation in Military Alliances
23. Foreign Aid
24. Defense Spending

POLITICAL INVOLVEMENT (Campbell et al. 1960)

Variable
:   This scale attempts to measure the individual's characteristic degree of interest and involvement in political affairs, a dimension which the authors postulate remains stable for the same person through successive election campaigns. The instrument includes measures intended to tap two sorts of attitudes that describe the individual's orientation to a specific election and two additional attitudes that characterize his orientation to politics and elections more generally.

Description
:   The nine-interval scale was formed by a linear combination (not further specified) of measures of Intensity of Partisan Preference, Interest in the Campaign, Concern Over the Election Outcome, Sense of Citizen Duty, and Sense of Political Efficacy. The first two components of the scale, Intensity of Partisan Preference and Interest in the Campaign, were derived from responses to two, three-point Likert-type questions. The third component was derived from responses to a simple Likert-type question coded on a five point scale from least to most care. The last two components came from cumulative scales reviewed in the following scale write-ups.

Sample
:   The sample population was a representative national sample of citizens of voting age living in private households. The number of pre-election respondents was 1929.

Reliability/
Homogeneity
:   No test-retest reliability was presented. Except for Intensity of Partisan Preference, all measures, treated as quantitative scales, were examined by factor analysis. A principal component was found that could account for half the variance of the several measures across SRC's 1952 and 1956 samples. The mean loadings of the form measures with the principal component was about .70 for both years indicating that inter-item correlations were in the .40 to .50 range.

Validity
:   Behavioral evidence for the validity of this measure may be seen in comparisons of voting turnout. (Intensity of Partisan Preference was included among the component variables so that their combined power to account for voting turnout behavior might be compared directly with that of Intensity of Partisan Preference alone.) It was found that the rate of voting turnout increased steadily with political involvement and differed by more than 75 percent from one extreme to the other, whereas the proportions voting at the extremes of low and high intensity of partisan preference alone differed by less than half this much.

Location
:   Campbell, Angus, Converse, Philip E., Miller, Warren E., Stokes, Donald E. The American Voter. New York: John Wiley & Sons, Inc., 1960, pp. 101-107.

Administration   This instrument conceivably could be administered as a pencil and paper test, in which case estimated administration time would be less than 12 minutes.

The distribution of scores on the scale was as follows:

1) (Low)	2%	6)		26%
2)	3%	7)		26%
3)	4%	8)		16%
4)	6%	9) (High)		3%
5)	14%			

Results and Comments

The authors state that involvement and education are most probably functionally related, as they found a substantial association between the two, regardless of geographical location and with the other status dimensions controlled. When the Interest and Concern questions alone were used as an index of political involvement, it was found that partisan differences on social welfare attitudes were dependent on current political involvement.

POLITICAL INVOLVEMENT

1. Intensity of Partisan Preference

We would like to know how strongly you felt about the importance of voting in this election.

Would you say you cared a great deal whether or not you voted, cared somewhat, or didn't care too much this time?

2. Interest in the Campaign

Some people don't pay much attention to the political campaigns. How about you? Would you say that you have been very much interested, somewhat interested, or not much interested in following the political campaigns so far this year?

3. Concern over the Election Outcome

Generally speaking, would you say that you personally care a good deal which party wins the presidential election this fall, or that you don't care very much which party wins.

4. Sense of Political Efficacy

(See following review)

5. Sense of Citizen Duty

(See following review)

POLITICAL EFFICACY (Campbell et al. 1954)

Variable	Sense of political efficacy is defined as "the feeling that political and social change is possible, and that the individual citizen can play a part in bringing about this change." The authors predicted that the variable would be positively related to their Index of Political Participation. (See Chapter 11)
Description	Five items designed to produce the scale were part of SRC's interview schedule for the 1952 election study. "Disagree" responses to items 1, 3, 4 and 5 and an "agree" response to item 2 were coded as "efficacious." Scores range from 0 (low) to 4 (high).
Sample	The sample population was a representative cross-section of 1614 citizens of voting age living in private households in the United States, chosen by area probability sampling methods in early fall 1952.
Reliability/ Homogeneity	No test-retest reliability was reported. Guttman scale analysis resulted in an over-all coefficient of reproducibility of .92 with a range of error of 6 to 8 percent for four of the individual items. When the second item, with 10.8 percent error was dropped because of its ambiguity, the recomputed Rep was .94.
Validity	The correlation of the Political Efficacy Scale with the Index of Political Participation indicated that the higher one's sense of political efficacy, the higher the level of his participation in the 1952 election.
Location	Campbell, Angus, Gurin, Gerald and Miller, Warren E. The Voter Decides. Evanston, Ill.: Row Peterson & Co., 1954, pp. 187-189.
Administration	Originally part of an interview schedule, this instrument could be administered as a paper and pencil test, in which case estimated administration time would be under five minutes. To convert the response patterns into scale types, the authors used minimum error assignment wherever possible and Henry's (1950) distribution of perfect types for the "ambiguous" response patterns.
Results and Comments	The socio-economic status variables, income, occupation and education, were highly positively related to the Efficacy Scale, with men scoring higher than women, Negroes scoring lower than whites, and those in the South lower than people from the other three regions of the country. Sense of political efficacy increased directly with population density. The relationship between political efficacy and political participation held even when controlled for eight demographic variables. It was found, however, that there was less spread between extreme scores on the Political Efficacy Scale among those respondents with the highest

socioeconomic status than there was among those of lower education and lower income. The authors concluded that other factors than the sense of political efficacy might have greater relevance to political participation for the people of upper economic status.

References   Henry, Andrew F. "A Method of Classifying Non-scale Response Patterns in a Guttman Scale," <u>Public Opinion Quarterly</u>, (Spring 1952), <u>16</u>, pp. 94-106.

POLITICAL EFFICACY SCALE

1. I don't think public officials care much about what people like me think.

         Agree   Disagree

2. The way people vote is the main thing that decides how things are run in this country.

3. Voting is the only way that people like me can have any say about how the government runs things.

4. People like me don't have any say about what the government does.

5. Sometimes politics and government seems so complicated that a person like me can't really understand what's going on.

SENSE OF CITIZEN DUTY (Campbell et al. 1954)

Variable

Sense of citizen duty is defined as the feeling that one (and others) ought to participate in the political process, regardless of whether such political activity is seen as worthwhile or efficacious. The variable was predicted to be positively related to the authors' Index of Political Participation.

Description

The scale is comprised of four agree-disagree items forming a five-point (0-4) Guttman scale. Negative responses to all items were coded as indicating a sense of civic duty.

Sample

The sample population was a representative cross-section of citizens of voting age living in private households in the United States, chosen by the area probability sampling method. The total N of 2021 was interviewed in the fall of 1952.

Reliability/ Homogeneity

No test-retest reliability are reported. The Coefficient of Reproducibility was .96, with a maximum error of 5 percent, giving a Plus Percentage Ratio (see previous scale description) of .77.

Validity

The Index of Citizen Duty was found to be positively correlated with the Index of Political Participation. The range of Participation Index scores was from +17 for highest Citizen Duty scores to -69 for the lowest, with no reversals among intervening scale types.

Location

Campbell, Angus, Gurin, Gerald, and Miller, Warren E. The Voter Decides. Evanston, Ill.: Row Peterson & Co., 1954, pp. 194-199.

Administration

The instrument formed part of an interview schedule, but could be administered as a paper and pencil test, in which case estimated administration time is under four minutes.

Guttman scale analysis was performed using Ford's IBM sorter technique. Response patterns were assigned to scale types according to minimum error assignment wherever possible, and according to Henry's distribution of perfect types for the "ambiguous" response patterns (see previous scale description).

Results and Comments

The Index appeared to be related to every demographic variable except sex and age. The relationship between Citizen Duty and Political Participation persisted when eight demographic variables were held constant, but in several crucial categories there were too few cases to permit the computation of a reliable participation index. The items are susceptible to agreement response set since they are all phrased in the same direction.

CITIZEN DUTY SCALE

1. It isn't so important to vote when you know your party doesn't have a chance to win.

2. A good many local elections aren't important enough to bother with.

3. So many other people vote in the national elections that it doesn't matter much to me whether I vote or not.

4. If a person doesn't care how an election comes out he shouldn't vote it.

EXTENT OF ISSUE ORIENTATION (Campbell et al. 1954)

Variable
This measure is designed to combine two components of a person's issue orientation: amount of issue involvement and sensitivity to party differences.

Description
The empirical construction of this five point scale from the two components was as follows:

Amount of Issue Involvement

		High	Medium	Low
	High	1	2	3
Sensitivity to Party Differences	Medium	2	3	4
	Low	3	4	5

The Sensitivity Index is built on the basis of whether the individual perceives differences between the two major parties on two of the items making up the Involvement Index: social welfare and foreign involvement. If the individual perceives party differences on one or both of these issues he scores high on sensitivity; if he sees one difference and doesn't know about the other or if he sees the parties as same, he scores medium; and if he gives one same and one don't know, or two don't know replies, he scores low.

The Issue Involvement Scale is described in the following write-up.

About five percent of the population could not be classified on the scale.

Sample
The sample consisted of a national cross-section of 1614 Americans interviewed before the 1952 election.

Reliability/ Homogeneity
No reliability figures are presented.

Validity
Scale scores were highly related to degree of political participation. While 46 percent of those high in issue orientation had "high" political participation, only 7 percent scoring low had high participation.

Location
Campbell, Angus, Gurin, Gerald, and Miller Warren E. The Voter Decides. Evanston, Ill.: Row, Peterson & Co., 1954.

Administration
The components of this scale should take about 10 minutes to complete.

464

Results and
Comments

The national sample to which this scale was applied divided itself
as follows on the scale:

High issue orientation	1)	25%
	2)	23%
	3)	21%
	4)	14%
Low issue orientation	5)	12%

ISSUE ORIENTATION

Party Sensitivity Index

i) Some people think the national government should do more in
trying to deal with such problems as unemployment, education,
housing, and so on. Others think that the government is already
doing too much. On the whole, would you say that what the government has done has been about right, too much, or not enough.

ii) Some people think that since the end of the last world war this
country has gone too far in concerning itself with problems in
other parts of the world. How do you feel about this?

Immediately following the response to each of these two issue questions,
the people being interviewed were asked, "Now how do you think the two
parties feel about this question--do you think there are any differences
between the Democratic and Republican parties on this issue, or would
you say they feel the same?" The responses to these questions about
party differences were categorized in five groups: (a) Democrats will
(go further) (do more) than the Republican; (b) both parties have the
same position; (c) Republicans will go further (do more) than the
Democrats; (d) I don't know the parties' positions on the question;
and (e) not ascertained.

Amount of Issue Involvement (see following scale description)

ISSUE INVOLVEMENT (Campbell et al. 1954)

Variable

These two measures indicate the amount and direction of individual support or rejection of the present administration's position on some political issues.

Description

On seven political attitude questions asked in SRC's 1952 election study, responses were coded as supporting the Democratic administration's policy (D), as opposing this policy (R), or as indicating no partisan commitment (?). Of the seven questions, four were chosen on the basis of their relation to political participation and presidential preference to make up the issue involvement measure:

1) Government Social Welfare Activity
2) Taft-Hartley Labor Law Revision
3) U. S. Foreign Involvement
4) U. S. China Policy

The remaining three items (which consist of two questions on Korea and one on fair employment) were excluded either for being of too recent origin or for being based mainly on regional rather than national political distinctions.

The Amount of Issue Involvement measure is a three point scale constructed as follows:

High Involvement : "?" answers to one or none of the four items
Medium Involvement: "?" answers to two of the four items
Low Involvement   : "?" answers to three or four of the four items.

Half of the national population were rated "high," 31 percent "medium" and 19 percent "low" on this measure.

The Direction of Issue Involvement measure is a scale of five steps, running from completely Democratic to completely Republican orientation:

			% of Population
Democrat (no conflict)	:	DDDD, DDD?, DD??, D???	22%
Democrat (conflict)	:	DDDR, DDR?	16
Neither	:	DDRR, DD??, ????	24
Republican (conflict)	:	RRRD, RRD?	17
Republican (no conflict):		RRRR, RRR?, RR??, R???	21
			100%

Sample

The sample consisted of a national cross-section of 1614 Americans interviewed in the period prior to election day 1952.

Reliability/ Homogeneity

No data on the reliability of the scale are reported.

Validity   Since the items were selected on the basis of their relation to
                criterion measures, they have a built-in validity component.

                The Amount of Issue Involvement measure was built from relations with
                political participation.

                The Direction of Issue Involvement measure was built from relations
                with presidential preference.

Location   Campbell, Angus, Gurin, Gerald, and Miller, Warren E. The Voter
                Decides. Evanston, Ill.: Row, Peterson & Co., 1954.

Administration The items should take about 10 minutes to administer.

Results and   Outside of the results described under Validity the authors used
   Comments   these scales mainly to construct the two further indices described
                previously in this section.

ISSUE INVOLVEMENT

Governmental Social Welfare Activity

"Some people think the national government should do more in trying to
deal with such problems as unemployment, education, housing, and so on.
Others think that the government is already doing too much. On the
whole, would you say that what the government has done has been about
right, too much, or not enough?"

Taft-Hartley Labor Law Revision

"Have you heard anything about the Taft-Hartley Law? (If Yes) How
do you feel about it--do you think it's all right as it is, do you
think it should be changed in any way, or don't you have any feelings
about it? (If should be changed) Do you think the law should be
changed just a little, changed quite a bit, or do you think it should
be completely repealed?"

U. S. Foreign Involvement

"Some people think that since the end of the last world war this country
has gone too far in concerning itself with problems in other parts of
the world. How do you feel about this?"

U. S. China Policy

"Some people feel that it was our government's fault that China went
Communistic--others say there was nothing that we could do to stop it.
How do you feel about this?"

ISSUE PARTISANSHIP (Campbell et al. 1954)

Variable
This measure is designed to tap the degree to which a person takes a partisan view of political issues.

Description
The empirical construction of this five point scale from the following two components was as follows:

		Direction of Issue Involvement				
		Democrat	Weak Democrat	Non Partisan	Weak Republican	Republican
Sensitivity to Party Differences	High	1	2	3	4	5
	Medium	2	2	3	4	4
	Low	2	3	3	3	4

The Sensitivity Index and the Direction of Issue Involvement are described in the previous two scale reviews. The national sample to which this index was applied was distributed as follows on the index (five percent were not classified):

Democrat	1)	7%
	2)	26%
	3)	28%
	4)	25%
Republican	5)	9%

Sample
The sample consisted of a national cross-section of 1614 Americans interviewed before the 1952 election.

Reliability/ Homogeneity
No data on reliability are reported.

Validity
As hypothesized, the index was highly related to presidential choice, with 86 percent of those on the Republican end of the scale voting for Eisenhower as opposed to 17 percent of those at the Democratic end of the side.

Location
Campbell, Angus, Gurin, Gerald, and Miller, Warren E. The Voter Decides. Evanston, Ill.: Row, Peterson & Co., 1954.

Administration
It should take about ten minutes to administer the scale.

Results and Comments
It was found that those respondents scoring at the extremes of the scale had higher rates of political participation than those respondents scoring in the middle, at values 2, 3, 4.

It was also concluded that variations in the amount of issue involvement did not affect the finding that conflict in issue partisanship was related to lowered political partisanship.

OVERALL INDEX OF PSYCHOLOGICAL READINESS FOR PARTICIPATION
(Matthews and Prothro 1966)

Variable   The authors call this index a rough overall measure of psychological
                    predisposition toward political participation.

Description   Five of eight psychological attributes were combined into a single
                    index using arbitrarily assigned weights, in order to measure the
                    collective influence of the psychological characteristics of Southern
                    Negroes on their political participation. Five of the attributes,
                    as measured by instruments covered elsewhere in the scale write-ups,
                    are as follows: Political Information, Chapter 10, Sense of Civic
                    Competence, Chapter 12, Sense of Deprivation (from Race Relations
                    Ratings in Chapter 6), Sense of Racial Inferiority/Superiority (from
                    Racial Stereotype Index, Chapter 6), and Attitude toward Change (McClosky
                    Chapter 3).   Two of the remaining attributes were single-question
                    indices: Political Interest and Awareness of Local Racial Incidents.
                    Strength of Partisanship was measured by the standard questions and
                    coding procedures of the Survey Research Center of the University of
                    Michigan (see previous scale reviews in this chapter).

                    The weighting of the responses and the wording of the two single-
                    question indices are given below. Summing these weights for each
                    respondent yields a composite score theoretically ranging from 0
                    (no psychological influences associated with participation) to 16 (all
                    eight psychological factors strongly in support of participation).

Sample   The sample to whom this composite index was administered is described
                    in the authors' PPS write-up in Chapter 11.

Reliability/   No reliability figures are reported.
  Homogeneity

Validity   Using a causal model analysis developed by Blalock (1964) and a path
                    coefficient analysis, as developed by Boudon (1965) the authors
                    determined the direction of causation and the number of operative
                    paths of direct causal relationships. The overall explanatory power
                    of the authors' model was sufficient to account for about 50 percent
                    of the variance in the political activities of Negroes throughout the
                    South.

                    Coefficients of contingency (Tschuprow's "T") were calculated to
                    indicate the extent of association between psychological characteristics
                    and participation with scores ranging from 0 (absolutely no association)
                    to 1 (the characteristic completely predicts PPS). Political Partisan-
                    ship, Interest, and Information were shown to be the three most important
                    variables for Negro participation, followed by the Sense of Civic
                    Competence.

Administration	The different measures comprising the Index were developed for use in an interview situation, and would probably require modification before they could be used as a paper and pencil test.
Location	Matthews, D.R. and Prothro, J.W. <u>Negroes and the New Southern Politics</u>. New York: Harcourt, Brace & World, 1966, p. 527.
Results and Comments	It was found that all phases of political participation were influenced by Negro attitudes and cognitions. Community social and economic characteristics directly affected the social and economic attributes of individual Southern Negroes and the community political system, which in turn directly affect Negro attitudes and cognitions.

Coefficients of contingency (Tschuprow's "T") were calculated to indicate the extent of association between psychological characteristics and participation by scores ranging from 0 (absolutely no association) to 1 (the characteristic completely predicts PPS). Political partisanship, interest, and information were shown to be the three most important variables for Negro participation, followed by sense of civic competence.

It was found that all Negroes with a score of 11 or more on the Index had voted or had participated at an even higher level (half were PPS Type V), while Negroes scoring 1 or 0 were almost all PPS types I and II. (See Chapter 11 for definition of these scores.)

References	Blalock, Hubert M. <u>Causal Inferences in Nonexperimental Research</u>. Chapel Hill, N.C.: University of North Carolina Press, 1964.

Boudon, Rayman. "A Method of Linear Causal Analysis: Dependence Analysis: <u>American Sociological Review</u>, 1965, <u>30</u>, pp. 365-374.

READINESS FOR PARTICIPATION

Single-Question Indices

(Political Interest)

    10   Generally speaking, how interested are you in politics--a great deal, somewhat, or not much at all?

(Awareness of Local Racial Incidents)

    68   Have you ever heard of anything happening to Negroes around here who have voted or taken some other part in politics or public affairs?

Weighting of Responses   (see the authors' Political Participation Scale described in Chapter 11 for exact question wording)

	2	1	0
Strength of partisanship	Strong	Weak	Leaners, Independents, Apoliticals, DK,NA,RA *
Political interest	Great deal	Somewhat	Not much, DK, NA, RA
Political information	6-7 correct	3-5 correct	0-2 correct, DK,NA,RA
Sense of civic competence	3 definite actions	1-2 definite actions	0 definite actions, DK, NA, RA
Sense of deprivation	Community ratings of 3-4	Community ratings of 5-6	Community ratings of 1-2,9-12, DK, NA, RA
Sense of racial inferiority/superiority	Negroes better	No difference	Whites better, DK,NA,RA
Attitude toward change	Types I-II	Types III-IV	Types V-VI, DK,RA,NA
Awareness of local intimidation	Heard scare stories about protest movement	Heard no stories	Heard other scare stories

* DK = Don't know
  NA = Not ascertained
  RA = Respondent absent

SENSE OF CIVIC COMPETENCE INDEX (Matthews and Prothro 1966)

Variable	This index attempts to measure an attitude which has been defined by Almond and Verba in The Civic Culture as a belief in the efficacy of one's own political action, consisting of (1) a belief that public officials can be and are influenced by ordinary citizens, (2) some knowledge about how to proceed in making this influence felt, and (3) sufficient self-confidence to try to put this knowledge to work at appropriate times and places.
Description	Each respondent was presented with five hypothetical problems and then asked if he would "do anything about it, or would you figure there wasn't much you could do?" The number of times a respondent "definitely could take action" in three of these situations was counted as a rough index of subjective competence. Scores range from 0 (no action in any case) to 3 (action in all three cases).
Sample	The sample to whom the index was administered was a group of 618 adult Southern Negroes further described in the authors' Political Participation Scale (PPS) described in Chapter 11.
Reliability/ Homogeneity	No reliability information was given for this instrument.
Validity	Although no data directly bearing on validity were reported, the authors found that political participation as measured by the PPS increased significantly as the Negroes' subjective civic competence increased--an effect which was independent of the effects of political information and interest. They duly note that causality cannot be inferred.
Administration	This index was administered as a part of a long interview schedule and would have to be modified for use as a paper and pencil test.
Location	Matthews, D. R. and Prothro, J. W. Negroes and the New Southern Politics. New York: Harcourt, Brace & World, 1966, p. 526.
Results and Comments	Although no direct measures of reliability or validity of this index were offered, both the careful and extensive research underlying its formulation and the unusual item format, which should hold the interest of the respondent, suggest that further study use would prove fruitful. Additional questions following each of the five problems were designed to probe whether the respondent would talk to other people about the problem, and who these people would be.
Reference	Almond, G. and Verba, S. The Civic Culture. Princeton, N. J.: Princeton University Press, 1963.

SENSE OF CIVIC COMPETENCE INDEX

Now, I would like to describe some things that sometimes happen to people. Then I'll ask you: If you were faced with this problem, would you do anything about it or would you not bother with it?

20   First, let's imagine you have a child going to a school where there is nobody to help the children get across the street. The crossing is dangerous, and one day a child is hit by a car. You think that somebody should be put there to help the children. Do you think you would do anything about it, or figure that there wasn't much you could do?

        * Would do   Wasn't much you could do

21   Let's say you have a close friend who gets in trouble somehow with the police. You feel he hasn't done anything wrong. Would you try to do anything about it, or would you stay out of it?

        * Do anything   Stay out

23   What if some friends of yours needed help pretty bad. The man is out of work and the children are hungry. Would you do anything about it, or would you figure there wasn't much you could do?

        * Do anything   Wasn't much you could do

Items not used in forming the Index

22   What if you aren't treated right at some white store. Would you do anything about it, or would you figure there wasn't much you could do?

        Do anything   Wasn't much you could do

24   What if you decided that the white school closest to where you live is much better than the Negro school. Would you want your children to go there, even if they were among the first few Negroes to attend the school?

Would you do anything about it, or would you figure there wasn't much you could do?

        Do anything   Wasn't much you could do

PARTY IMAGE SCORE (Matthews and Prothro 1966)

Variable

This score is meant to reflect a person's attitudes toward the Republican and Democratic parties, independent of actual party identification.

Description

The Party Image Score is comprised of the total number of favorable and unfavorable remarks elicited from a respondent by questions on his likes and dislikes concerning the Republican and Democratic parties. The items are standard SRC election study items, but in this study responses were taken as a measure of cognitive "richness" of the respondent's picture of partisan realities. Remarks favorable to Democrats and remarks unfavorable to Republicans were scored as +1; remarks favorable to Republicans and remarks unfavorable to Democrats were scored as -1. Scores ranged from +8 to -8.

Sample

The Party Image Score items were part of a large study of Southern Negro political participation conducted in the spring of 1961. The sample to whom this measure was administered is described in the PPS write-up in Chapter 11.

Reliability/
Homogeneity

No measures of reliability are reported.

Validity

The authors found that those who had high party image scores tended to participate at rather high levels whether they were partisans or not.

Location

Matthews, D. R. and Prothro, J. W. Negroes and the New Southern Politics. New York: Harcourt, Brace & World, 1966.

Results and
Comments

Apparently a simple index of partisan sentiment, the Party Image Score may be revealed as a potentially powerful research tool. Especially in cases where voters declare weak party identification, the authors suggest that the Party Image Score may be more useful than actual party identification for an understanding of changing voting behavior. Using Survey Research Center 1964 election study data in comparison with their own data, the authors found that at the expense of mildly pro-Democratic images, the number of Southern whites with strongly pro-Republican party images doubled between 1961 and 1964, from 9 to 18 percent, an effect which agreed with the unusual Southern white vote for Goldwater.

Again, concomitant with the nearly solid Southern Negro vote for Johnson, the proportion of Southern Negroes with strongly Democratic images more than doubled, from 24 to 52 percent. In addition, the authors found a steady increase of about 10 percentage points in the proportion of Negroes with pro-Democratic images, regardless of party identification.

The authors point out that though the Index counts each expression of party attitude equally, in fact some party attitudes are more closely related to presidential voting than others. A deeper analysis of the content of the responses to the open-ended questions might reveal more ultimately useful information as it could filter out remarks reflecting transitory issues and personalities of the campaign.

For a more thorough review and analysis of how responses to these questions have changed over the national scene over the years, see Stokes (1966).

Reference   Stokes, Donald E. "Some Dynamic Elements of Contests for the Presidency," American Political Science Review, March 1966, pp. 19-28.

PARTY IMAGE SCORE

I'd like to ask you what you think are the good and bad points about the Democratic and Republican parties. Is there anything in particular that you like about the Democratic party? (What is that?)

Is there anything in particular that you don't like about the Democratic party? (What is that?)

Is there anything in particular that you like about the Republican Party? (What is that?)

Is there anything in particular that you don't like about the Republican Party? (What is that?)

ATTITUDE DIMENSIONS OF POLITICAL NORMS (Litt 1963)

Variable   These five measures tap a variety of attitudes toward the political
                  system and deal mainly with citizen participation in the political
                  process.

Description   In a study of political indoctrination in civic education classes in
                  different communities, the following attitude indices were used:
                  (a) "The Democratic Creed," or attitude toward the rights of citizens
                  and minorities to attempt to influence governmental policy through
                  non-tyrannical procedures; (b) "Political Chauvinism," or attitude
                  toward nationalistic glorification of the American political system;
                  (c) "Political Activity" or sense of political efficacy, cynicism,
                  and participation; (d) "Political Process," or sense of the influen-
                  tial nature of power and influence activities; (e) "Political Function"
                  or attitude toward politics as a means toward conflict resolution.

                  The five indices consist of five-point Likert-type items, and are
                  composed of 4, 4, 6, 5 and 4 items respectively. Source of the items
                  for the first index was Prothro and Grigg (1960) and sources for the
                  third index were Campbell et al. (1954) and Agger et al. (1961); the
                  remaining indices were constructed by the author.

                  Respondents who were community leaders were also asked if each state-
                  ment in the indices should be included in their community's civic edu-
                  cation program. Respondents drawn from classes and control groups
                  were interviewed before and after a semester course in civic
                  education.

Sample   The sample population groups were drawn from each of three communities;
                  one upper-middle-class with much political activity; one lower middle-
                  class with moderate political activity, and one working-class with
                  little political activity. Of the first population group, the
                  "potential civic and educational influentials," 66 were interviewed
                  in the first community, 57 in the second, and 63 in the third. The
                  second population group consisted of a civic education class in each
                  community together with matched control groups.

Reliability/   The reported reproducibility coefficients for the five indices, in
  Homogeneity   the order listed above, is as follows: (a) .91, (b) .93, (c) .85,
                  (d) .87, (e) .92.

Validity   The first and the third indices were based on earlier studies in
                  which some validity was already indicated, but no specific evidence
                  of validity of the remaining indices is reported in this reference.

Location   Litt, E. "Civic Education, Norms, and Political Indoctrination,"
                  American Sociological Review, 1963, 28, pp. 69-75.

Administration   Estimated administration time for the five indices is under 25
                  minutes.

476

Results and
Comments

It was found that students in the civic education classes were more likely to endorse parts of the democratic creed and less likely to hold characteristic political sentiments than the control groups. None of the three classes was more likely to favor political participation than the controls, and only in the upper-class community did students score high on the Political Function Scale.

The indices constructed for this study have yet to be adequately validated, and the reliability coefficients are not terribly high.

References

Agger, R., Goldstein, M., and Pearl, S. "Political Cynicism: Measurement and Meaning," The Journal of Politics, 23 (1961), pp.477-506.

Campbell, A., Gurin, G., and Miller, W. The Voter Decides, Evanston: Row-Peterson, 1954, pp. 187-204.

Prothro, J., and Grigg, C. "Fundamental Principles of Democracy: Bases of Agreement", Journal of Politics, 1960, 22, pp.276-294.

DIMENSIONS OF POLITICAL NORMS

1. The Democratic Creed: (Coefficient of Reproducibility=.911)

    Every citizen should have an equal chance to influence government policy.
       Strongly   Strongly
          Agree   Agree   Undecided   Disagree   Disagree

    Democracy is the best form of government.

    The minority should be free to criticize government decision.

    (Adopted from a scale of James Prothro and Charles Grigg appearing in
     "Fundamental Principles of Democracy: Bases of Agreement", Journal of
     Politics, 1960, 22, pp.276-294.)

2. Political Chauvinism: (CR=.932)

    The American political system is a model that foreigners would do well to
    copy.

    The founding fathers created a blessed and unique republic when they gave
    us the constitution.

    Americans are more democratic than any other people.

    American political institutions are the best in the world.

    (Index constructed for this study).

3. Political Activity: (CR=.847)

    It is not very important to vote in local elections.

    It is very important to vote even when so many other people vote in an
    election.

    Public officials do care what people like me think.

    Given the complexity of issues and political organizations there is little
    an individual can do to make effective changes in the political system.

    People like me do not have any say about what the government does.

    Politics is often corrupt and the interests of the underworld are looked
    after by some public officials.

    (Adapted from the civic duty and sense of political effectiveness measures of
     the Michigan Survey Research Center, and Agger's index of political cynicism.
     See Angus Campbell, Gerald Gurin, and Warren E. Miller, The Voter Decides,
     Evanston: Row-Peterson, 1954, pp.187-204, and Robert E. Agger, Marshall N.
     Goldstein, and Stanley A. Pearl, "Political Cynicism: Measurement and

Meaning," The Journal of Politics, 23 (1961), pp. 477-506.

4. Political Process: (CR=.873)

    The use of political power is crucial in public affairs.

    Many political decisions are made by a minority of political activists who seek to secure the agreement of the majority to the decisions.

    Politics is basically a conflict in which groups and individuals compete for things of value.

    Differences of race, class, and income are important considerations in many political issues.

    Governmental institutions cannot operate without politicians.

    (Index constructed for this study).

5. Political Function: (CR=.919).

    Politics should settle social and other disagreements as its major function.

    Since different groups seek favorable treatment, politics is the vehicle for bargaining among these competing claims.

    Politics is not a means of insuring complete harmony, but a way of arriving at temporary agreements about policies within agreed-upon rules.

    The politician is the key broker among competing claims made within society.

    (Index constructed for this study).

POLITICAL CYNICISM AND PERSONAL CYNICISM (Agger, Goldstein,and Pearl 1961)

Variable	The scale of political cynicism attempts to measure the extent to which one is contemptuously distrustful of politicians and the political process. The scale of personal cynicism is intended to assess one's views of human nature in general.
Description	The measure of Political Cynicism is a Guttman-type scale consisting of six modified Likert items. "Agree" responses were coded as cynical, except for Item 6, which was reversed. Scores ranged from 0 to 6 and items were dichotomized as follows: between (a) and (b) for items 1 and 6; between (b) and (c) for items 2 and 3; between (c) and (d) for items 4 and 5. The Personal Cynicism Scale is a Guttman type scale composed of four modified forced-choice items drawn from Christie's (circa 1959) Mach Scale.
Sample	The sample population consisted of 779 returned mailback interviews out of a random sample of 1230 drawn from an industrial working-class community of 20,000 and a white collar, middle-class community of 50,000 in Oregon. A second sample population was a group of 250 party activists from the same area.
Reliability/ Homogeneity	The Kuder-Richardson coefficient of reliability for the Political Cynicism scale was .62 and .25 for the Personal Cynicism scale. The coefficient of reproducibility for the Political Cynicism scale was .94 and .92 for the Personal Cynicism scale.
Validity	It was found that the more politically impotent (as measured by Campbell et al.'s Political Efficacy Scale), were considerably more politically cynical than the more potent, even with educational level and response set controlled. At the middle and upper levels of the social structure, political cynicism was seen to exert an independent negative effect on the levels of political discussion (see "Results and Comments") with friends, and also on political discussion with party activists.
Location	Agger, R. E., Goldstein, M. N. and Pearl, S. A. "Political Cynicism: Measurement and Meaning," Journal of Politics, 1961, 23, pp. 477-506.
Administration	Estimated administration time for the Political Cynicism Scale is six minutes and for the Personal Cynicism Scale, four minutes.
Results and Comments	To test the relationship between political cynicism and political participation, a measure was devised which consisted of two questions on the level of political discussion both with friends and with party activists. To guard against the bias of response set, a four-item scale of contradictory statements was devised and each respondent's score set as a control.

480

References   Campbell, Angus, Gurin, Gerald and Miller, Warren E. <u>The Voter</u>
<u>Decides</u>. Evanston, Ill.: Row, Peterson & Co., 1954.

Christie, Richard. "A Quantification of Machiavelli" (Unpublished
memorandum, Department of Social Psychology, Columbia University
Circa 1959).

PERSONAL CYNICISM

1. Barnum was very wrong when he said that there's a sucker born
  every minute.

2. Generally speaking, men won't work hard unless they are forced
  to do so.

3. It is safest to assume that all people have a vicious streak and
  it will come out when they are given a chance.

4. The biggest difference between most criminals and other people
  is that criminals are stupid enough to get caught.

POLITICAL CYNICISM ITEMS AND RESPONSE SET ITEMS

	Agree Strongly (a)	Agree Somewhat (b)	Agree Slightly (c)	Disagree Slightly (d)	Disagree Somewhat (e)	Disagree Strongly (f)	No Answer	Total*
1. In order to get nominated, most candidates for political office have to make basic compromises and undesirable commitments.	11%	17	18	14	18	16	6	= 100%
2. Politicians spend most of their time getting re-elected or reappointed	11%	15	19	18	22	10	4	= 99%
3. Money is the most important factor influencing public policies.	17%	23	20	12	16	7	3	= 98%
4. A large number of city and county politicians are political hacks.	8%	14	19	16	20	12	10	= 99%
5. People are very frequently manipulated by politicians.	6%	25	29	9	14	7	11	= 101%
6. Politicians represent the general interest more frequently than they represent special interests.	9%	27	22	18	12	6	6	= 100%

*The total N is 7793

CHAPTER 13

ELECTION STUDIES OF THE SURVEY RESEARCH CENTER

This chapter presents the political attitude questions asked in the
SRC election studies from 1952 through 1966 and their particular patterns of
response. The materials for each of these studies were collected from
representative cross-sectional samples of the United States selected on a
strict probability basis. Respondents were interviewed after the election
in Congressional election years and both before and after the election in
presidential year studies. For the 1956, 1958, and 1960 studies, interviews
were taken in all three years with the same members of a nationwide panel.
The total number of respondents for each of the studies is as follows:

Year of Study	Pre-Election	Post-Election
1952	1799	385
1954	No study	No study
1956	1929	1762
1958	No study	1822*
1960	1954	1954*
1962	No study	1297
1964	1571	1450
1966	No study	1291

The attitude questions asked these respondents are grouped into different sections of this chapter according to the following substantive content
categories: party identification, government principles, domestic policy,
civil rights, international attitudes, war-related attitudes, political

---

*This number is weighted to represent a valid cross-sectional sample.
The actual number of respondents for 1958 and 1960 are 1450 and 1181,
respectively.

activity, political system, and personality variables. Included within each section is the wording of each relevant question, a listing of code categories for responses to the question, and the corresponding percentage breakdown of the national sample giving each type of response. In some cases, two-part questions were asked about the same subject--the first to ascertain if the respondent had an opinion on the issue and the other to ascertain what that opinion was. (Those who did not indicate an interest in the issue were, of course, not asked the second question.) Percentage distributions of both the total sample and the sample of opinion holders were computed from these types of questions.

Tables are also presented in each section of this chapter to show the relation of the attitude measures (and certain other variables pertaining to political activity) to such factors as sex, race, education, age, income, and party identification. In this way, one can gauge in a rather rudimentary fashion the types of people who favor or oppose certain issues or who locate themselves in different positions on given attitude continuums.

Most of this kind of analysis focuses on presidential election data because the 1966 materials are not yet available for general use and the 1958 materials are from a panel which had been asked the same questions in both 1956 and 1960. Much attention is given in this introduction to the analysis of the 1964 election material, partly because it is the most recent presidential study and partly because of the nature of the questions asked. Several indices, constructed in this study from individual questions, are then correlated with the respondent's demographic information.

Included in each section are tables which show the intercorrelation values of the opinion items. In some instances, these values are substantial, and, in most cases, they indicate that a reasonable degree of homogeneity exists among given sets of items, justifying treatment of the questions as essentially unidimensional in nature. For this reason, the replies of separate questions are often added together to form a single index or scale. The resultant measures are then used in several analysis contexts in this chapter.

The correlation coefficients used in the tables are the Pearson product-moment and tau-beta varieties, most usually the former. Justification for the use of either rests on the assumption that the variables involved can be conceived of as having at least ordinal properties of measurement. Interchangeability in the discussion of the two statistics is not unwarranted either since their values correspond quite closely throughout the correlation range for the same sets of data (unless the marginals are heavily skewed in nature). Most of the values in the table are found in the lower end of the correlational range, but this should not lead one to suspect that they are generally not statistically significant at high confidence levels. One must remember that statistical significance at even the one percent level of confidence can be obtained with correlations over .10 in value because of the large sample sizes of the SRC studies. The reader will find many values greater than this figure, but few that exceed .50 and almost none over .70. Such is the nature of survey research data and the strength of relationships therein.

There are several different pieces of information about the nature of a relationship between variables which can be gained by looking only at a correlation coefficient. The first one, that of statistical significance, has already been noted. Any correlation value exceeding .10 (with over 1000 respondents) generally denotes that a bivariate relationship is beyond that expected as the product of chance factors involved in the sampling aspects of the study. One can also observe the absolute strength of a given relationship within the bounds of the correlational range (0.0 to 1.0) and thereby attach to it its due importance in some theoretical or substantive sense.

Another descriptive item in the analysis is the positive or negative direction of the relationship. All coefficients in the tables are computed from the standard SRC code systems of the variables involved (unless otherwise noted in the text). Hence, the reader has only to see how the replies are coded to understand what the signs of the correlations mean in substantive terms.

It is noteworthy that a low correlation value may disguise an important finding, as witness the tremendous Negro preference for Johnson in 1964 for which the correlation between race and vote was only -.05. Furthermore, curvilinear relations might exist in the data (as between age and income) and be substantively important but not be reflected by a coefficient based on assumptions of linear relations between variables.

There are pitfalls, of course, in trying to interpret data by using a single parameter such as the correlation coefficient. Such coefficients should serve, however, to guide the reader through the major findings with respect to each variable. It is not suggested that analyses end with these correlations; rather, they are meant to give the potential investigator a certain feeling about what kinds of things each attitude question seems to tap and what types of people favor or oppose a particular attitude position. In this way, they serve as potential springboards for new ideas and analytic plans.

The correlation statistic is a good first guide through the data, but only a guide. The next step of understanding the meaning of relationships

in a correlation table is a more difficult undertaking. Rarely do two variables relate to each other without the influence of other factors, which are
themselves correlated to the variables in question and often to each other as
well. In the present case, many of the demographic (i.e., independent) variables used here are intercorrelated. This means that correlations of attitudes
with a single background variable are often not independent of such correlations with other background factors. Table 1 shows some substantial intercorrelations among the various pairings of background factors. For instance,
the associations between party identification and vote and between education
and income are distinguished by their size in relation to the rest of the
correlation coefficients in Table 1. Looking at the correlations among all
four variables, one can see that Republican identifiers and voters are more
likely to be better-educated, wealthier, white, and older than Democratic
identifiers and voters. Because of these (and other) intercorrelations, the
reader would expect the correlations between political attitudes and these background variables to show essentially the same pattern of relationships. This
turns out to be the case for quite a variety of attitude measures.

Other intercorrelational patterns are noticeable in the table. Education and income reveal much the same relation to such variables as race, age,
and community size--Negroes, older people, and rural residents being less
educated and earning less than whites, the young, and urban dwellers. The
correlations of sex with education and income indicate that women have (or
estimate) lower total household incomes than men, although women appear only
slightly less educated than men. (The first of the two findings might be
explainable, in part, as a function of having a larger number of low-earning
single women than single men in the samples.) Of the six intercorrelations
among the four remaining variables (race, sex, community size, and age), only

TABLE 1: INTERCORRELATION OF BACKGROUND VARIABLES

	Sex	Race	Education	Income	Age	Community Size	Party Identification	Actual Vote
1952 Sex	X							
1952 Race	.02	X						
1952 Education	.01	-.11	X					
1952 Income	-.13	-.15	.45	X				
1952 Age	-.00	-.03	-.25	-.20	X			
1952 Community Size	-.04	-.03	-.12	-.21	.03	X		
1952 Party Identification	.00	-.07	.18	.16	.10	-.04	X	
1952 Actual Vote	-.01	-.03	.15	.08	.07	.05	.65	X
1956 Sex	X							
1956 Race	.03	X						
1956 Education	-.01	-.12	X					
1956 Income	-.13	-.14	.47	X				
1956 Age	-.07	-.06	-.29	-.27	X			
1956 Community Size	-.02	-.11	-.08	-.12	.03	X		
1956 Party Identification	.03	-.11	.13	.12	.08	.02	X	
1956 Actual Vote	.06	-.10	.08	.04	.02	.01	.67	X
1960 Sex	X							
1960 Race	.00	X						
1960 Education	.08	-.16	X					
1960 Income	-.11	-.23	.46	X				
1960 Age	-.04	-.04	-.29	-.36	X			
1960 Community Size	.01	-.16	-.06	-.08	-.05	X		
1960 Party Identification	-.02	-.12	.15	.07	.07	.01	X	
1960 Actual Vote	.06	-.10	.08	.04	.02	.01	.67	X
1964 Sex	X							
1964 Race	.06	X						
1964 Education	-.03	-.11	X					
1964 Income	-.12	-.14	.46	X				
1964 Age	.01	-.08	-.27	-.32	X			
1964 Community Size	.01	-.16	-.15	-.18	.07	X		
1964 Party Identification	-.01	-.10	.22	.14	.04	.03	X	
1964 Actual Vote	-.03	-.05	.15	.06	.06	.04	.55	X

Note: Values in the table are Pearson product-moment correlation coefficients. Correlations were performed on standard SRC code systems for these variables unless otherwise noted in the text.

one merits attention--the correlation between race and community size, which points to the tendency of Negroes to live in the larger urban communities. There is also some tendency for Negro respondents to be younger than whites.

The correlation tables on attitude items are also better understood if the reader has an initial idea of how these items cluster together and how these resulting clusters relate to each other and to the above mentioned background factors. In Table 2, attitudinal material from the 1964 election study is presented as an outline to the type of relationships the reader will find discussed more thoroughly in the sections that follow. The reader will learn in later sections how some of the indices in Table 2 were actually constructed.

Attitude questions on various subjects are examined in Table 2-- on the basic domestic and foreign policies of the day, on feelings toward government in general and political activity in particular, and even on non-political, personality-oriented characteristics and configurations. The 1964 study was selected for this examination on the basis of its being the most recent study in which a large number of attitude and issue areas are covered and in which indices of so many attitude areas can be constructed.

On some of the basic political questions of the day, evidence for a moderate clustering of attitudinal variables into "liberal" and "conservative" camps can be found in the upper left quadrant of Table 2. The pattern of correlation among the items reveals that people favoring international contact also tend to support racial integration and governmental intervention in domestic affairs. These people are also more sympathetic to labor unions and the Democratic Party than are those people characterized by an isolationist attitude configuration. Other attitudes and feelings also distinguish the two groups of respondents. Liberal-oriented individuals appear to trust

TABLE 2: INTERCORRELATION OF ATTITUDE, BEHAVIOR, AND BACKGROUND VARIABLES
FOR THE 1964 ELECTORATE

	Political Attitudes				Personality Variables				Political Process			Political Activity	
	Int	Intg	Dom	L-C	Nost	PCm	St-M	TrPp	TrG	GovA	PEff	Part	Info
International Attitudes	X												
Racial Integration	.25	X											
Increased Domestic Policies	.17	.37	X										
Liberal-Conservative Organization	.34	.27	.29	X									
Nostalgia	-.13	-.11	-.03	-.12	X								
Personal Competence	-.05	.00	-.10	-.12	-.10	X							
Strong-Mindedness	-.04	-.06	-.06	-.07	-.01	.14	X						
Trust in People	.10	.10	.05	.09	-.14	.28	.01	X					
Trust in Government	.32	.23	.08	.23	-.25	.11	-.01	.24	X				
Government Attention	.25	.22	.05	.11	-.19	.13	.00	.23	.33	X			
Political Efficacy	.13	.18	-.06	-.08	-.06	.20	.17	.25	.13	.27	X		
Political Participation	-.13	.02	-.10	-.21	.02	.12	-.17	.13	-.13	.09	.25	X	
Information about Congress	.00	-.07	-.09	-.19	.00	.18	-.15	.24	-.05	.16	.25	.29	X
Background Variables													
Sex	-.04	.05	.01	.06	.09	-.09	-.11	.03	.01	-.01	-.07	-.05	-.15
Race	.03	.22	.19	.13	-.08	-.09	-.03	-.12	.06	.04	-.08	-.06	-.14
Education	-.01	.11	-.12	-.21	-.02	.22	.15	.28	-.01	.18	.43	.32	.31
Income	.02	.03	-.14	-.16	-.08	.21	.07	.22	.02	.17	.31	.22	.26
Age	-.11	-.13	-.05	-.05	.10	.00	-.05	-.04	-.11	-.12	-.16	-.05	.02
Community Size	-.07	-.02	-.10	-.08	.05	.10	.03	.08	.01	.02	.07	.06	.06
Party Identification	-.27	-.08	-.20	-.57	.13	.15	.03	.10	-.20	-.10	-.09	.18	.13
Johnson-Goldwater	-.44	-.32	-.28	-.62	.13	.04	.06	.00	-.30	-.17	-.01	.20	.10

Note: Values in the table are Pearson product-moment correlation coefficients. Each attitude and behavior scale in the table is constructed so that higher scores reflect more of the characteristic in question. Thus, higher scores on "Internationalism Attitudes" are given to respondents who give more internationalist responses. The positive correlation of .25 between Internationalist Attitudes and Racial Integration indicates that higher scores on the first variable are associated with higher scores on the second.

government more and believe it to be more responsive to the people than do those individuals with a conservative orientation toward politics. However, only the "internationalists" and "integrationists" within the large group of liberal respondents exhibit feelings of political efficacy discernibly greater than the conservatives. With the exception of the "integrationists," the group possessing liberal opinions reports more political activity than do those holding opposing opinions. The former group also feels more personally competent and is more likely to trust people.

At the bottom of Table 2, a preliminary sketch is given of how the background variables relate to these clusters of attitudes. The correlations which appear in most instances are not surprising. The cluster of liberal attitudes is characteristic of Johnson supporters, Democratic party identifiers, young people, and urbanites. Negroes take a more liberal position than whites in all issue areas except that of internationalism. People in the higher educational and income levels also have some tendency to support liberal domestic policies and liberal groups as well.

The personality variables in Table 2 do not show the degree of clustering characteristic of the political attitude items. Only one noteworthy exception exists to disrupt this pattern. The trust in people and personal competence measures are substantially correlated and do show the same pattern of relationships with other variables. People who achieve high scores on these personality variables are likely to have corresponding feelings of trust in government, political efficacy, and belief in governmental responsiveness to the public. They are also possessors of more information about Congress and report more political activity than lower scorers on these measures. At first glance, it would seem that the people thus identified have a general personality syndrome of competence and trust which is manifested in several specific areas of life, one of which, according to these data, is surely the political arena. Other indications of this general syndrome are provided by the demographic variable information--the personally competent and trusting are seen to be better-educated and wealthier in background than the less competent. These people are also of white origin and live in areas of low population density. However, the syndrome is not as consistent on other attributes, such as sex, vote choice, and party identification. Women and men, Goldwater and Johnson backers, and Democratic and Republican loyalists do not show the same pattern of relationships with the two personality variables, thereby indicating that these background factors have a more flexible and less integrated position vis-a-vis any such personality syndrome.

The remaining two personality variables, nostalgia and strong-mindedness, are unrelated to each other although they show consistent, if low, positive correlations with a conservative pattern of political views. Highly nostalgic persons admit to a low trust in government and to the feeling that the government is basically not attentive to public demands. Such people are most usually found among the older, Republican, and white segments of the sample. Women and low income individuals also feel a strong affinity to earlier times. The major correlates of strong-mindedness, on the other hand, appear to be reported political participation, feelings of political efficacy, and educational level. Men also report greater feelings of strong-mindedness than do women.

Attitude measures of the political process comprise the third group of measures presented in Table 2. The three main measures in this area do inter-correlate significantly. They show that people who feel politically effica-cious are favorably disposed toward the government and think it is responsive to the people and their needs. These variables also show some relation to other attitudinal variables. Especially striking is the consistent degree to which these variables relate to the trust in people and personal competence measures. The politically efficacious and trusting individual also tends to take a consistently "liberal" position on international and racial issues. Such an individual is likely to be older than the less confident respondents.

Other correlates with these political process attitudes are also noticeable. Trust in government is linked to weak feelings of nostalgia, low levels of political participation, and identification with the Democratic Party. Feelings of government responsiveness are related to low nostalgia levels but are associated with greater levels of political participation. Confidence in government responsiveness to public demands is also found among the better-educated, higher income, younger, and Democratic respondents. Feelings of political efficacy are more likely among those respondents who are nostalgic, strong-minded, well-informed, well-educated, wealthy, and elderly.

The final variables covered in the table, political participation and information about Congress, are significantly related to each other and show very similar patterns of relations with the other variables in the table. The politically active and informed individual has less favorable attitudes toward government intervention in domestic problems and is more likely to identify with the Republican Party than the politically inactive, uninformed respondent. Such an individual feels personally competent, strong-minded, and trusting of people as well as politically efficacious. The active and informed person most often is white and male and has high levels of educational and financial attainment. (The correlations between education and the other variables are virtually identical with those of information level.) The politically active (but not the informed) individual is noticeably not an internationalist in orientation, nor is he one who trusts government to any great extent.

This concludes a cursory look at the pattern of correlations obtained from the 1964 electorate sample. It points to some interesting relations in the data and suggests some ways in which one can and should interpret these relationships in this and later sections of this chapter. A single piece of information conveyed by the correlation statistic is only a first indication of the descriptive trends in the data. Researchers should use this material as background information in planning more detailed investigation of the data. For others not so inclined, the data presentations offer information about some of the basic findings of voting studies which can be quite interesting in their own right.

Before proceeding to the separate sections into which actual SRC questions are divided, one important historical and methodological factor must be taken into account. Most of the SRC attitude questions asked prior to 1964 were written in straightforward Likert format or agree-disagree format. Research evidence, both at SRC and elsewhere, indicates that this item format is especially liable to agreement response set (discussed in Chapter 1 and mentioned periodically as a weakness of particular attitude scales in Chapters 3 through 12). Thus, any implication that such attitude questions can be unambiguously interpreted as reflecting the actual division of public sentiment on the issue is unwarranted. This is especially true of questions in the Domestic Policy section which are in the form "The government should intervene ...... Do you agree or disagree?"

Based on their research experience, SRC began a transition to phrasing attitude questions in forced-choice format in 1958. In the 1964 study, the transition was practically complete. This necessary methodological gain, however, had to be won at the expense of losing question comparability over time, a loss about which we remark many times in the rest of this chapter.

PARTY IDENTIFICATION

In this section, we briefly examine probably the most important attitude variable in the field of political behavior--party identification. As is noted in Table 1 of the previous section, this measure is by far the best predictor of a respondent's voting behavior. The two-part question used to tap party identification in SRC surveys is listed in the following table along with the distribution of replies to the question.

The distribution has, of course, been quite stable over the seven readings between 1952 and 1966. The proportion of Democrats has varied between 43 and 51 percent, Republicans between 23 and 30 percent, and Independents between 15 and 28 percent. The latest figure for Independents does appear to signify a true shift; Gallup (1967) figures indicate much the same trend. While Democratic party identifiers outnumber Republican identifiers almost two to one (and among Independents the Democratic "leaners" usually outnumber the Republican "leaners"), election results are much closer than this division of identification would indicate. Converse (1966) has examined this apparent paradox more fully within the framework of his "normal vote" concept. Because Republican identifiers are much more likely to turn out to vote than Democratic identifiers, the normal vote is around 54 percent Democratic to 46 percent Republican. This division of the vote, of course, assumes little visible difference between particular candidates. Highly visible differences between candidates have been noted on the basis of personality (which worked in favor of President Eisenhower in 1952 and 1956), religion (which worked against President Kennedy in 1960), or unpopular policy stands (which worked against Senator Goldwater in 1964).

Converse (1964) has found that not only was the distribution of party

Table 1: The Distribution of Party Identification in the United States, 1952-1966

Question: "Generally speaking, do you usually think of yourself as a Republican, a Democrat, an Independent, or what? (IF REPUBLICAN OR DEMOCRAT) Would you call yourself a strong (R)(D) or a not very strong (R)(D)? (IF INDEPENDENT) Do you think of yourself as closer to the Republican or Democratic Party?"

	Oct. 1952	Sep. 1953	Oct. 1954	Apr. 1956	Oct. 1956	Nov. 1957	Oct. 1958	Oct. 1960	Oct. 1961	May 1962	Nov. 1962	May 1963	Jan. 1964	May 1964	Oct. 1964	Mar. 1965	Nov. 1966
Democrat																	
Strong	22%	22%	22%	19%	21%	21%	23%	21%	26%	25%	23%	22%	23%	24%	26%	25%	18%
Weak	25	23	25	24	23	26	24	25	21	25	23	27	27	22	25	25	27
Independent																	
Democrat	10	8	9	6	7	7	7	8	9	7	8	6	9	7	9	9	9
Independent	5	4	7	3	9	8	8	8	10	9	8	9	10	10	8	9	12
Republican	7	6	6	6	8	6	4	7	5	4	6	5	6	5	6	4	7
Republican																	
Weak	14	15	14	18	14	16	16	13	13	15	16	16	14	17	13	13	15
Strong	13	15	13	14	15	10	13	14	11	11	12	12	9	11	11	12	10
Apolitical, Don't know	4	7	4	10	3	6	5	4	5	4	4	3	2	4	2	3	2
Total	100%	100%	100%	100%	100%	100%	100%	100%	100%	100%	100%	100%	100%	100%	100%	100%	100%
Number of Cases	1614	1023	1139	1731	1772	1488	1269	3021	1474	1269	1289	1301	1489	1465	1571	2195	1291

Source (October, 1952, Q.28, Deck 4, Col.9; Oct., 1956, Q.22, Card 4, Col.9; ", 1960, Q.36, Card 5, Col.38; Oct.,1964, Q.51, Deck 6, Col.11)

identification stable over time for the population as a whole, but that this was also the case for the individual citizen. Interview materials collected from a "panel" of the same 1150 respondents in 1956, 1958, and 1960 provide clear documentation of this point. The correlation of a person's position on the seven-point party identification scale between 1956 and 1960 (as computed across the entire population of 1150 respondents) is .72, an extremely high figure for survey research data.

Further evidence and discussion of the import of the party identification variable is given in Chapters 6 and 7 of Campbell et al. (1960). Strong identifiers were found to be more politically active and to defect less from party loyalties than weak identifiers in particular elections. Identification predicts quite well how individuals will generally react to the parties, their candidates, and their platforms. Identification is highly dependent on the party identification of one's parents but distinct generational changes are noticeable, with younger people more likely to be independent and, if they do make a choice of parties, to prefer the Democratic party and to hold less strong allegiances to the party of their choice.

More recent examination of the effects of the party identification variable is given in Chapters 2-8 of Campbell et al. (1966).

References:

Campbell, A. et al. The American Voter. New York: Wiley, 1960.

Campbell, A. et al. Elections and the Political Order. New York: Wiley, 1966.

Converse, P. "The Nature of Belief Systems in Mass Publics" in D. Apter (ed.), Ideology and Discontent. New York: Free Press, 1964.

Converse, P. "The Concept of a Normal Vote" in A. Campbell et al. (eds.), Elections and the Political Order. New York: Wiley, 1966.

Gallup Opinion Index. Princeton, New Jersey: Gallup International, Inc., November, 1967.

ATTITUDES TOWARD GOVERNMENT PRINCIPLES

In this section, questions of diverse content have been included which deal with attitudes toward government principles and one of the principal bodies of government which decides on questions of this nature. Specifically, the three sets of SRC items which are covered here are as follows:

1. Attitudes toward firing suspected Communists in government (1956)

2. Attitudes toward prayer in public schools (1964, 1966)

3. Attitudes toward the Supreme Court and some of the issues with which it is concerned (1966)

The first question involves the firing of suspected Communists from their governmental posts without necessarily having any concrete proof for this action-- a topic that received considerable attention in "the McCarthy period" and aftermath. Respondents having an opinion on this matter were more inclined not to have the government dismiss its employees under such circumstances, 67 percent believing this versus 25 percent taking a contrary opinion, with 8 percent showing more ambivalence to the question. Of all respondents, however, 16 percent did not have any opinion on the subject.

A search into the background characteristics of the opinion-holders revealed that the better-educated, higher income, and younger people were most likely to disapprove of firing these people. The finding is not unique to SRC samples--the Stouffer study described earlier in this volume presents similar findings. Tolerance of one's legal rights and freedoms and of the need for due process of law increases as one moves up the socio-economic and educational ladders.

In 1964, the controversial question of saying prayers in school received much publicity. The relation of church and state was prominent in any

TABLE 1: CORRELATION OF GOVERNMENT PRINCIPLE QUESTIONS WITH BACKGROUND VARIABLES

	Sex	Race	Education	Income	Age	Community Size	Party Identification	Actual Vote
1956 Communists in Government	-.07	-.01	.16	.13	-.13	-.04	.01	-.04
1964 Prayer in the Schools	-.10	.00	.09	.06	-.08	-.07	-.01	-.03

Note: Values in the table are Pearson product-moment correlation coefficients. Correlations were performed on standard SRC code systems for these variables unless otherwise noted in the text.

resolution of the question, and the settlement of the matter eventually rested with the U.S. Supreme Court. Respondents were asked in 1964 and 1966 how they felt about the issue, and the predominant response was that schools should be allowed to start each day with a prayer. There were few who did not venture an opinion on this matter.

Correlational analysis on this issue area revealed a significant difference in attitude between the sexes, a background factor not usually separating holders of particular political attitudes. It was discovered that women were more likely than men to be in favor of allowing prayer in the public schools. It was also found that the better educated were more likely to oppose prayer in public schools, and that older people and rural residents showed some tendency to favor it. Obvious implications of varying degrees of socialization into religious patterns, especially according to sex and role definitions and the presence or absence of some countervailing exposure to secularism (as with higher education), are being registered here as notable influences on opinions.

The last set of questions concerns the respondent's perception and evaluation of the Supreme Court and the actions it has taken or possibly will take on important matters of public life, much in the vein of the earlier-mentioned "school prayer case." Most of the questions on this branch of government were confined to the 1966 election study, which is not yet in a state permitting correlational analysis. However, information is available on the percentage distribution of key questions as a guide to the electorate's knowledge of the Court and feelings toward some of the issues with which it is concerned.

The data distributions from the study indicate that a large percentage of the sample (35 percent) did not know the main job of the Supreme Court in 1966. Of those who did, a majority (62 percent) thought this branch of government did its job well, and many (42 percent) believed no favoritism was registered for specific groups in court decisions. But, paradoxically, other questions showed a different public mood toward the court--more people were seen to trust Congress than the Court (despite the heritage and prestige associated with the latter body through the popular lore) and some felt the court got too mixed up in politics, perhaps another expression of this possible lack of trust. However, on these items as well, a large proportion of the people did not give an opinion, probably indicating a real lack of information or concern with the Supreme Court and what it does.

The public's view of issues identified with possible Supreme Court action showed that about 50 percent approved of open housing and about 70 percent opposed the newsstand sale of "indecent" magazines. In both issue areas, most respondents indicated they would not change their opinion to that of the Court if the two conflicted and about half of them would think less of the Court for adopting an opposing viewpoint. These preliminary findings might suggest a lowering public evaluation of the Court as a result of their taking unpopular stands on these issues (and, perhaps, on others as well).

COMMUNISTS IN GOVERNMENT

"The government ought to fire any government worker who is accused of being a Communist even though they don't prove it." Now, would you say you have an opinion on this or not? (IF YES) Do you agree that the government should do this or do you think the government should not do it?

		1956	
		% Total	(% with Opinion)
1.	Agree strongly	14%	(17%)
2.	Agree but not very strongly	7	(8)
3.	Not sure; it depends	7	(8)
4.	Disagree but not very strongly	13	(16)
5.	Disagree strongly	43	(51)
9.	DK	1	--
0.	No opinion	15	--
		100%	(100%)

(Source: 1956, Q. 12n, deck 3)

PRAYER IN SCHOOLS

"Some people think the public schools should be allowed to start each day with a prayer. Others feel that religion does not belong in the public schools but should be taken care of by the family and the church." Have you been interested enough in this to favor one side over the other? (IF YES) Which do you think:

	1964		1966	
	% Total	(% with Opinion)	% Total	(% with Opinion)
1. (YES) Schools should be allowed to start each day with a prayer	75%	(80%)	75%	(81%)
3. (YES) Other. Depends. Both boxes checked	3	(4)	4	(4)
5. (YES) Religion does not belong in the schools	15	(16)	13	(15)
8. DK	1	--	1	--
0. No interest	6	--	7	--
	100%	(100%)	100%	(100%)

(Source: 1964, Q.19-19a, deck 4; 1966, Q. A4-A4a, deck 1.)

PRAYERS IN THE SCHOOLS RECODED TO INCORPORATE CERTAINTY OF POSITION

	1964	
	% Total	(% with Opinion)
1. Favors prayers in the schools and mind made up	73%	(78%)
2. Favors prayers in the schools and has some doubts or NA certainty of position	2	(2)
3. Other. Depends. Both boxes checked in question of prayers in schools	3	(4)
4. Against prayers in schools and has some doubts or NA certainty of position	1	(2)
5. Against prayers in the schools and mind made up	14	(14)
8. DK	1	--
0. No interest	6	--
	100%	(100%)

(Source: 1964, Q. 19-19b, deck 4.)

SUPREME COURT

1. How well do you think the Supreme Court does this job ("main job in the government"): <u>very well</u> or <u>not very well</u>?

	1966	
	% Total	(% with Opinion)
1. Very well	35%	(62%)
3. Pro-con; well in some ways and not well in others	1	(1)
5. Not very well	15	(27)
7. It depends	6	(10)
8. DK	8	--
0. Inap., R does not know main job of Supreme Court	35	--
	100%	(100%)

(Source: 1966, Q.C39a, deck 4.)

2. Some people think that the Supreme Court gets too mixed up in politics. Others don't feel that way. How about you? Do you think the Supreme Court gets too mixed up in politics or not?

	1966
1. Yes	27%
5. No	31
7. It depends	3
8. DK	39
	100%

2a. (IF YES OR NO) Do you feel strongly about that or not so strongly?

	1966
1. Strongly	55%
5. Not so strongly	44
8. DK	1
	100%

(Source: 1966, Q.C40-C40a, deck 4.)

506

3. Sometimes people tell us they trust the Supreme Court more than Congress. Others disagree with that. Which do you trust more, the Supreme Court or Congress?

		1966
1.	Supreme Court	26%
2.	Congress	34
3.	Both	2
5.	Neither	1
7.	It depends	5
8.	DK	32
		100%

3a. (IF ANSWERS "SUPREME COURT" OR "CONGRESS") Do you feel strongly about that or not so strongly.

		1966
1.	Strongly	57%
5.	Not so strongly	43
8.	DK	0
		100%

(Source: 1966, Q.C41-C41a, deck 4.)

4. Do you think that in its decisions the Supreme Court favors any particular group or groups in this country?

		1966
1.	Yes	20%
5.	No	47
7.	It depends	1
8.	DK	32
		100%

(Source: 1966, Q.C42 deck 4.)

5. In talking with people, they sometimes tell us things that I'd like your opinion about. Some people say that Negroes should be allowed to live in any part of town they want to. How do you feel? Should Negroes be allowed to live in any part of town they want to, or not?

		1966
1.	Should be allowed	49%
2.	Should be allowed, qualified	1

5. (cont'd)

4.	Should not be allowed, qualified	0
5.	Should not be allowed	32
7.	It depends	13
8.	DK	5
		100%

5a. (IF SHOULD OR SHOULD NOT BE ALLOWED) Do you feel strongly about that or not so strongly?

		1966
1.	Strongly	72%
5.	Not strongly	28
8.	DK	*
		100%

5b. (IF SHOULD BE ALLOWED) Now suppose the Supreme Court of the United States decided that Negroes do <u>not</u> have the right to live in any part of town they want to. Would that change your feelings about where Negroes should be allowed to live? (IF NECESSARY) How's that?

		1966
1.	(YES) Would change to accept court's judgment	5%
3.	Pro-con; depends; it might	1
5.	(NO) Would not change feelings; would keep own opinion	93
7.	Other	0
8.	DK	1
		100%

5c. (IF SHOULD BE ALLOWED) Would that change your feelings any toward the Supreme Court? (IF NECESSARY) How's that?

		1966
1.	(YES) Would think less of Court; would be disappointed in Court; Court would be wrong	51%
3.	Pro-con; depends; it might	2
5.	(NO) Would maintain same opinion of Court	41
6.	(NO) Couldn't think less of Court than do now	4
7.	Other	*
8.	DK	2
		100%

508

5d. (IF SHOULD NOT BE ALLOWED) Now suppose the Supreme Court of the United States decided that Negroes <u>do</u> have the right to live in any part of town they want to. Would that change your feeling any about where Negroes should be allowed to live? (IF NECESSARY) How's that?

	1966
1. (YES) Would change to accept Court's judgment	3%
3. Pro-con; depends; it might	1
5. (NO) Would not change feelings; would keep own opinion	95
7. Other	0
8. DK	1
	100%

5e. (IF SHOULD NOT BE ALLOWED) Would that change your feelings any toward the Supreme Court? (IF NECESSARY) How's that?

	1966
1. (YES) Would think less of Court; would be disappointed in Court; Court would be wrong	40%
3. Pro-con; depends; it might	3
5. (NO) Would maintain same opinion of Court	50
6. (NO) Couldn't think less of Court than do now	3
7. Other	0
8. DK	4
	100%

(Source: 1966, Q.C43, C43b and C43e, C43c, C43d, C43f C43g, deck 4.)

6. Some say that a newsstand should be allowed to sell any kind of magazine to adults even if it is what many people call indecent. How about you? Do you think newsstands should be allowed to sell such magazines or not?

	1966
1. Should be allowed	21%
2. Should be allowed, qualified	1
4. Should not be allowed, qualified	*
5. Should not be allowed	69
7. It depends	3
8. DK	6
	100%

6a.   (IF SHOULD OR SHOULD NOT BE ALLOWED) Do you feel strongly about this or not so strongly?

		1966
1.	Strongly	82%
5.	Not strongly	18
8.	DK	0
		100%

6b.   (IF SHOULD BE ALLOWED) Suppose that the Supreme Court decided that a newsstand does <u>not</u> have the right to sell indecent magazines to adults, would that change your feelings about selling this kind of magazine? (IF NECESSARY) How's that?

		1966
1.	(YES) Would change to accept Court's judgment	12%
3.	Pro-con; depends; it might	3
5.	(NO) Would not change feelings; would keep own opinion	84
7.	Other	0
8.	DK	1
		100%

6c.   (IF SHOULD BE ALLOWED) Would that change your feelings any about the Supreme Court? (IF NECESSARY) How's that?

		1966
1.	(YES) Would think less of Court; would be disappointed in Court; Court would be wrong	28%
3.	Pro-con; depends; it might	1
5.	(NO) Would maintain same opinion of court	65
6.	(NO) Couldn't think less of Court than do now	4
7.	Other	1
8.	DK	1
		100%

6d.   (IF SHOULD NOT BE ALLOWED) Suppose that the Supreme Court decided that a newsstand <u>does</u> have the right to sell indecent magazines to adults, would that change your feelings about selling this kind of magazine? (IF NECESSARY) How's that?

6d.   (Cont'd)

		1966
1.	(YES) Would change to accept Court's judgment	3%
3.	Pro-con; depends; it might	1
5.	(NO) Would not change feelings; would keep own opinion	96
7.	Other	*
8.	DK	*
		100%

6e.   (IF SHOULD NOT BE ALLOWED) Would that change your feelings any about the Supreme Court?

		1966
1.	(YES) Would think less of Court; would be disappointed in Court; Court would be wrong	48%
3.	Pro-con; depends; it might	2
5.	(NO) Would maintain same opinion of Court	44
6.	(NO) Couldn't think less of Court than do now	3
7.	Other	*
8.	DK	3
		100%

(Source: 1966, Q.C44, C44b and C44e, C44c, C44d, C44f C44g, deck 4.)

7.   Now I want to ask you about the justice of the Supreme Court in Washington. Do you happen to know the names of any of the justices? (IF NECESSARY) Who? any others?

		1966
1.	One	23%
2.	Two	13
3.	Three	9
4.	Four	3
5.	Five	1
6.	Six	1
7.	Seven	*
8.	Eight or nine	*
0.	None, DK	50
		100%

(Source: 1966, Q.C45, deck 4.)

Key: * = Less than 1%

DOMESTIC POLICY

All of the election studies have included some questions on actual or proposed domestic policies of the federal government. The studies in presidential election years have considered this area a major part of the questionnaire and have concentrated especially on those issue areas most closely associated with the concept and ideology of "the social welfare state." In this section, the attitudes resulting from responses to these questions will be discussed in four separate clusters, some of which appear to comprise quite homogeneous sets of items. The four different clusters of attitudes are as follows: (1) government intervention in education, medical care, and guaranteed employment; (2) government ownership of electric power and housing; (3) government regulation of the influence of big business and big labor; and (4) government policy toward such miscellaneous items as taxation and aid to parochial schools.

The first cluster of attitude questions involves the central concept of "government assistance" in various areas common to the social welfare ideology. The respondent is asked whether he favors such matters as government help in building schools, providing medical care at low cost, and guaranteeing a job to everyone who wants one. The pattern of responses to these questions shows very strong tendencies toward unidimensionality. Within this attitude cluster, however, support for the individual issues has not remained completely constant over the years. For instance, the samples have indicated a generally declining acceptance rate of government help in education over the years. For the questions on medical care and guaranteed employment, the general trend has shown increasing acceptance of governmental intervention. However, the interpretation of these trendlines must take into consideration the fact that the three issue questions have been worded differently in some of the studies, possibly influencing to some degree the resulting distribution of responses.

In most of the election studies, government aid in these three areas has consistently received its chief support from those low education and income groups that would most benefit from such policies. The correlations with these background variables are among the largest in the table, ranging in value from .14 to .41 with an average value of .29 for education and .22 for income. The rationale explaining these figures can also be used to understand the consistent support of Negroes, Democratic Party identifiers, Democratic voters, rural residents, and the elderly for these policies. The correlations are lower here, but, nevertheless, indicate the general type of people associated with the social welfare ideology. The mean correlation values for these groups are: race, -.15; party identification, .20; vote, .23; community size, .10; and age, -.07.

A different method was used in the 1964 study to compare the effects of these background variables on domestic policy. Six issue areas were combined into an index of governmental intervention rather than being treated separately in the analysis. The justification for construction of the index, and the assumption of unidimensionality as well, rested on the fairly substantial intercorrelation of the six items. Once the index was constructed, a simple scoring system was used, giving a value of "1" for each favorable response to governmental intervention and a value of "5" for the opposite reaction. Addition of the scores produced a potential range of values from six (favoring governmental intervention on all six questions) to thirty (opposed to such action in all areas). The scores were then converted to a

TABLE 1: CORRELATION OF DOMESTIC POLICY QUESTIONS WITH BACKGROUND VARIABLES

	Sex	Race	Education	Income	Age	Community Size	Party Identification	Actual Vote
1956 Aid to Education	-.06	-.10	.22	.14	.02	.08	.13	.11
1956 Medical Care	.00	-.13	.34	.26	-.08	.03	.24	.25
1956 Guaranteed Employment	-.04	-.12	.33	.25	-.08	.06	.18	.15
1956 Power & Housing	-.02	.03	-.02	-.02	-.12	-.04	-.23	-.26
1956 Labor Unions	.02	.08	.01	-.01	-.08	-.08	-.12	-.15
1956 Big Business	.05	-.04	.17	.12	-.03	-.04	.16	.13
1956 Cut Taxes	-.06	-.14	.26	.22	-.14	.03	.13	.07
1960 Aid to Education	-.07	-.20	.19	.15	-.03	.15	.26	.29
1960 Medical Care	-.06	-.21	.35	.30	-.13	.10	.21	.26
1960 Guaranteed Employment	-.08	-.19	.26	.21	-.09	.20	.14	.29
1960 Power & Housing	-.01	.10	-.04	.01	-.05	.01	-.21	-.26
1960 Labor Unions	-.09	.13	-.07	.04	-.11	-.06	-.14	-.21
1960 Aid to Education	.01	-.10	.20	.16	-.02	NA	.18	NA
1960 Medical Care	.01	-.16	.41	.25	-.17	NA	.26	NA
1960 Aid to Parochial Schools	.01	-.10	.21	.15	-.01	NA	.12	NA
1964 Aid to Education								
1964 Medical Care								
1964 Guaranteed Employment ⎫	-.01	-.19	.12	.14	.05	.10	.20	.28
1964 Power ⎬ Governmental Intervention Index								
1964 Government Power ⎭								
1964 Open Accommodations								

Note: Values in the table are Pearson product-moment correlation coefficients. Correlations were performed on standard SRC code systems for these variables unless otherwise noted in the text.

NA--data not calculated

TABLE 2: INTERCORRELATION OF DOMESTIC POLICY QUESTIONS

	ED	MC	GE	PH	LU	BB	CT
1956 Aid to Education	X						
1956 Medical Care	.31	X					
1956 Guaranteed Employment	.33	.44	X				
1956 Power & Housing	-.12	-.22	-.11	X			
1956 Labor Unions	-.04	-.11	-.05	.15	X		
1956 Big Business	.12	.15	.13	-.08	.27	X	
1956 Cut Taxes	.11	.23	.20	-.01	-.02	.11	X

	ED	MC	GE	PH	LU
1960 Aid to Education	X				
1960 Medical Care	.41	X			
1960 Guaranteed Employment	.47	.47	X		
1960 Power and Housing	-.14	-.16	-.12	X	
1960 Labor Unions	-.13	-.12	-.11	.04	X

	ED	MC	PA
1962 Aid to Education	X		
1962 Medical Care	.36	X	
1962 Aid to Parochial Schools	.13	.18	X

	ED	MC	GE	PP	GP	OA
1964 Aid to Education	X					
1964 Medical Care	.33	X				
1964 Guaranteed Employment	.27	.36	X			
1964 Power Plants	.31	.25	.26	X		
1964 Government Power	.25	.27	.24	.25	X	
1964 Open Accommodations	.21	.20	.15	.22	.32	X

Note: Values in the table are Pearson product-moment correlation coefficients (except in 1964 where tau-beta is used). Correlations were performed on standard SRC code systems for these variables unless otherwise noted in the text.

nine-point index as noted below, with the resulting percentage distributions by categories:

Index Score	Original Score	% of Sample
1 (Favor)	6-10	3%
2	11-13	9
3	14-15	13
4	16-17	18
5	18	13
6	19-20	18
7	21-22	16
8	23-25	7
9 (Oppose)	26-30	3
		100%

A quick glance at the resulting correlations of the index with the respondent's demographic background revealed much the same story as the earlier analysis above (the correlation of the scale with other attitude domains is given in the introductory section). Intervention-oriented people were once again found among the lower education and income groups, Democratic identifiers, Democratic voters, Negroes, and rural dwellers. The relative position of correlation values, however, was somewhat different from the earlier studies, with vote, party identification, and race emerging as more prominent explanatory variables than education or income in 1964. Age showed little discriminatory power, even less than earlier, and the variable of sex demonstrated no importance as an analytic factor.

The second broad area of government intervention and involvement concerns ownership of housing and electric power. In three election studies (1956, 1958, and 1960), these two subjects were combined into a single question, forcing the respondent to evaluate them as a package. In 1964, the basic question was changed considerably and only asked about the respondent's reaction to the federal ownership of power plants. Despite this and other instances of question rewording, the attitude distributions for these studies remained remarkably constant from 1956 to 1964. The range for the period was from 29 percent to 32 percent voicing approval for federal housing and power, with 31 percent favoring the single item of federal power plants in 1964.

The issue of government involvement in power plants and housing did not show the strong relations with education and income (and their correlates) that the issues of government intervention in education, medicine, and employment did. Government involvement in electric power and housing was opposed most vigorously by those with Republican leanings. The correlations with party identification and party vote were among the strongest in the table, their mean values being .22 and .26, respectively. Negroes evinced somewhat greater approval of the federal role in both fields than whites, presumably being more influenced by the "housing" aspect of the question. Older age groups showed some reaction to the federal role in 1956. Obviously, some groups who would most benefit from the cheaper housing and power favored continued federal action, although the low correlations with income and education qualify the strength and importance of this argument.

The third area of government involvement examined by the SRC election studies was quite different in content and purpose from those previously discussed under the rubric of social welfare ideas. It involved government regulation of the influence of big business and big labor interests--but regulation only of such influences on the operation of government itself. The electorate overwhelmingly agreed that government should restrain business and labor from trying to dictate how the country should be run. The way in which the questions were worded undoubtedly was a factor contributing to this reaction against the two economic concerns. In regard to labor unions, 67 percent voiced disapproval of union influence on government in 1956 and 72 percent followed suit in the 1960 study. Big business as an institution fared no better, with 70 percent of the 1956 sample believing that it should not have much say in how government ran things. Not surprisingly, the Democrats were most opposed to big business influence, and the Republicans reciprocated by being most opposed to labor union influence. Other groups who opposed union influence included the elderly and the whites. The less educated and the poor seemed to disapprove of big business influence. The standard socio-economic profile of the respondent and his corresponding party affiliation were, in general, seen as adequate predictors of attitude formation toward these two economic institutions.

Finally, the electorate has been asked its opinion on a number of miscellaneous aspects of governmental policy. The question of whether taxes should be cut has been raised. The 1956 sample generally did not favor cutting taxes--55 percent voicing this opinion in contrast to the 32 percent taking the opposing view. It may seem paradoxical, but the support that did exist for a tax cut came from those segments of the population most in favor of social welfare ideas. The less educated, the poor, the elderly, and the Negroes numbered among the supporters of a tax cut. While these individuals wanted the government to provide social welfare services, they did not favor the means necessary to help pay for them.

The question of federal aid to parochial schools was asked in the 1962 and 1964 election studies. Those with an opinion on the subject split fairly evenly in both studies, 55 percent favoring it in 1962 and 44 percent supporting it in 1964. The 11 percent difference in support between the two years might be due, in part, to the different wordings of the question. Response patterns to this issue were practically identical to those elicited by the question on general federal aid to education, with the better educated, higher income, Republican, and white segments of society being most opposed to it.

Except for the last few election years (especially 1964), the SRC samples have generally approved of government involvement in most social welfare (as well as other) areas. As noted in the introductory remarks to this chapter, however, questions used in the earlier studies were subject to agreement response set. The format of these questions may well have been biased in a pro-intervention direction.

Moreover, a question on governmental power in the 1964 and 1966 studies indicated that the people were accepting such involvement with some qualifications and, indeed, some fears. When asked to evaluate whether government was getting too strong for the good of the country and the individual person, SRC samples showed an increasing tendency to be alarmed about this condition. In 1964, 44 percent feared the government was getting too powerful, 37 percent of whom were steadfast in their opinion. In 1966, even more people thought this way--56 percent in all. Unfortunately, no comparable questions exist in earlier election studies for an adequate trend analysis of this subject. The current data merely indicate that the extent of present government activity is viewed with some apprehension and qualification by a large proportion of the electorate.

ATTITUDE TOWARD GOVERNMENT AID TO EDUCATION

1. "If cities and towns around the country need help to build more schools, the government in Washington ought to give them the money they need." Do you have an opinion on this or not? (IF YES) Do you think that the government should do this? (Do you agree that the government should do this or do you think the government should not do it? -- 1956)

| | | 1956 | | 1958 | | 1960 | |
		% Total	(% with Opinion)	% Total	(% with Opinion)	% Total	(% with Opinion)
1.	Agree strongly	48%	(53%)	46%	(51%)	38%	(43%)
2.	Agree but not very strongly	20	(22)	17	(19)	16	(18)
3.	Not sure; it depends	9	(9)	6	(7)	10	(11)
4.	Disagree but not very strongly	5	(6)	7	(8)	8	(9)
5.	Disagree strongly	9	(10)	14	(15)	17	(19)
9.	DK	1	--	1	--	2	--
0.	No opinion	8	--	9	--	9	--
		100%	(100%)	100%	(100%)	100%	(100%)

(Source: 1956, Q.12i, deck 3; 1958, Q.14a, deck 3; 1960, Q.20-20a, deck 4.)

2. "If cities and towns around the country need help to build more schools, the government in Washington ought to give them the money they need." Do you have an opinion on this or not? (IF YES) Do you agree that the government should do this or do you think the government should not do it?

| | | 1962 | |
		% Total	(% with Opinion)
1.	Agree	58%	(65%)
2.	Not sure; it depends	5	(5)
5.	Disagree	27	(30)
8.	DK	*	--
0.	No opinion	10	--
		100%	(100%)

(Source: 1962, Q.45-45a, deck 14)

3. "Some people think the government in Washington should help towns and cities provide education for grade and high school children. Others think this should be handled by the states and local communities." Have you been interested enough in this to favor one side over the other? (IF YES) Which are you in favor of:

		1964	
		% Total	(% with Opinion)
1. (YES)	Getting help from government in Washington	31%	(38%)
3. (YES)	Other. Depends. Both boxes checked	5	(6)
5. (YES)	Handling it at the state and local level	46	(56)
8.	DK	2	--
0.	No interest	16	--
		100%	(100%)

(Source: 1964, Q.15-15a, deck 4.)

FEDERAL AID TO EDUCATION RECODED TO INCORPORATE CERTAINTY OF POSITION

	1964	
	% Total	(% with Opinion)
1. Favors federal aid and mind is made up	26%	(31%)
2. Favors federal aid and has some doubts or NA certainty of position	5	(7)
3. Other. Depends. Both boxes checked on question of aid	5	(6)
4. Favors handling at the local level and has some doubts or NA certainty of position	8	(10)
5. Favors handling at local level and mind is made up	38	(46)
8. DK	2	--
0. No interest	16	--
	100%	(100%)

(Source: 1964, Q.15-15b, deck 4.)

ATTITUDE TOWARD GOVERNMENT MEDICAL CARE

1. "The government ought to help people get doctors and hospital care at low cost."
   Do you have an opinion on this or not? (IF YES) Do you think the government
   should do this? (Do you agree that the government should do this or do you
   think the government should not do it?--1956)

		1956		1960	
		% Total	(% with Opinion)	% Total	(% with Opinion)
1.	Agree strongly	39%	(44%)	49%	(54%)
2.	Agree but not very strongly	15	(17)	11	(12)
3.	Not sure; it depends	8	(9)	12	(13)
4.	Disagree but not very strongly	8	(9)	5	(6)
5.	Disagree strongly	18	(21)	14	(15)
9.	DK	1	--	1	--
0.	No opinion	11	--	8	--
		100%	(100%)	100%	(100%)

(Source: 1956, Q.12d, deck 3; 1960, Q.24-24a, deck 4.)

2. "The government ought to help people get doctors and hospital care at low cost."
   Do you have an opinion on this or not? (IF YES) Do you agree that the government
   should do this or do you think the government should not do it?

		1962	
		% Total	(% with Opinion)
1.	Yes	50%	(58%)
2.	Yes, qualified	7	(8)
3.	Yes, for the aged; "medicare"	2	(3)
4.	No, qualified	2	(2)
5.	No	22	(26)
6.	No, except for aged or "medicare"	*	(*)
7.	Yes, for those who need it; for those financially unable	2	(3)
8.	DK	*	--
0.	Inap. (No, DK, or NA to opinion question)	15	--
		100%	(100%)

(Source: 1962, Q.46-46a, deck 14.)

3. "Some say the government in Washington ought to help people get doctors and
    hospital care at low cost, others say the government should not get into this."
    Have you been interested enough in this to favor one side over the other?
    (IF YES) What is your position? Should the government in Washington:

		1964	
		%	(% with
		Total	Opinion)
1.	(YES) Help people get doctors and hospital care at low cost	50%	(59%)
3.	(YES) Other. Depends. Both boxes checked	6	(7)
5.	(YES) Stay out of this	28	(34)
8.	DK	3	--
0.	No interest	13	--
		100%	(100%)

(Source: 1964, Q.17-17a, deck 4.)

MEDICARE RECODED TO INCORPORATE CERTAINTY OF POSITION

		1964	
		%	(% with
		Total	Opinion)
1.	Favors medicare and mind made up	45%	(53%)
2.	Favors medicare and has some doubts or NA certainty of position	5	(6)
3.	Other. Depends. Both boxes checked on question of medicare	6	(7)
4.	Against medicare and has some doubts or NA certainty of position	3	(4)
5.	Against medicare and mind made up	25	(30)
8.	DK	3	--
0.	No interest	13	--
		100%	(100%)

(Source: 1964, Q.17-17b, deck 4.)

ATTITUDE TOWARD GOVERNMENT GUARANTEE OF EMPLOYMENT

1. "The government in Washington ought to see to it that everybody who wants to work can find a job." Now would you have an opinion on this or not? (IF YES) Do you think the government <u>should</u> do this? (Do you agree that the government <u>should</u> do this or do you think the government should <u>not</u> do it?--1956)

		1956		1958		1960	
		% Total	(% with Opinion)	% Total	(% with Opinion)	% Total	(% with Opinion)
1.	Agree strongly	43%	(48%)	44%	(49%)	48%	(53%)
2.	Agree but not very strongly	13	(15)	13	(14)	11	(12)
3.	Not sure; it depends	7	(8)	7	(8)	8	(9)
4.	Disagree but not very strongly	10	(11)	9	(10)	8	(8)
5.	Disagree strongly	17	(18)	17	(19)	16	(18)
9.	DK	1	--	1	--	1	--
0.	No opinion	9	--	9	--	8	--
		100%	(100%)	100%	(100%)	100%	(100%)

(Source: 1956, Q.12b, deck 3; 1958 Q.12a, deck 3; 1960, Q.18-18a, deck 4.)

2. "In general, some people feel that the government in Washington should see to it that every person has a job and a good standard of living. Others think the government should just let each person get ahead on his own." Have you been interested enough in this to favor one side over the other? (IF YES) Do you think that the government:

		1964	
		% Total	(% with Opinion)
1.	(YES) Should see to it that every person has a job and a good standard of living	31%	(36%)
3.	(YES) Other. Depends. Both boxes checked	11	(13)
5.	(YES) Should let each person get ahead on his own	43	(51)
8.	DK	2	--
0.	No interest	13	--
		100%	(100%)

(Source: 1964, Q.18-18a, deck 4.)

RESPONSIBILITY OF GOVERNMENT FOR LIVING STANDARDS
RECODED TO INCORPORATE CERTAINTY OF POSITIONS

		1964	
		% Total	(% with Opinion)
1.	Favors government aid and mind made up	27%	(32%)
2.	Favors government aid and has some doubts or NA certainty of position	4	(4)
3.	Other. Depends. Both boxes checked on question of government aid	11	(13)
4.	Favors individual initiative and has some doubts or NA certainty of position	4	(5)
5.	Against medicare and mind made up	39	(46)
8.	DK	2	--
0.	No interest	13	--
		100%	(100%)

(Source: 1964, Q.18-18b, deck 4.)

ATTITUDE TOWARD GOVERNMENT PRODUCTION OF ELECTRICITY AND HOUSING

1. "The government should leave things like electric power and housing for private businessmen to handle." Do you have an opinion on this or not? (IF YES) Do you think the government should leave things like this to private business? (Do you agree that the government should do this or do you think the government should not do it?--1956)

		1956		1958		1960	
		% Total	(% with Opinion)	% Total	(% with Opinion)	% Total	(% with Opinion)
1.	Agree strongly	31%	(43%)	32%	(44%)	37%	(47%)
2.	Agree but not very strongly	11	(15)	12	(17)	12	(16)
3.	Not sure; it depends	7	(10)	6	(8)	6	(8)
4.	Disagree but not very strongly	7	(11)	8	(11)	7	(9)
5.	Disagree strongly	15	(21)	15	(20)	15	(20)
9.	DK	2	--	1	--	2	--
0.	No opinion	27	--	26	--	21	--
		100%	(100%)	100%	(100%)	100%	(100%)

(Source: 1956, Q.12k, deck 3; 1958, Q.11a, deck 3; 1960, Q.17-17a, deck 4)

2. "Some people think it's all right for the government to own some power plants while others think the production of electricity should be left to private business." Have you been interested enough in this to favor one side over the other? (IF YES) Which position is more like yours, having the:

			1964	
			% Total	(% with Opinion)
1.	(YES)	Government own power plants	19%	(31%)
3.	(YES)	Other. Depends. Both boxes checked	4	(6)
5.	(YES)	Leaving this to private business	39	(63)
8.	DK		2	--
0.	No interest		36	--
			100%	(100%)

(Source: 1964 post, Q.37-37a, deck 12.)

GOVERNMENT OWNERSHIP OF POWER PLANTS
RECODED TO INCORPORATE CERTAINTY OF POSITION

		1964	
		% Total	(% with Opinion)
1.	Favors government ownership of power plants and mind made up	16%	(26%)
2.	Favors government ownership or power plants and has some doubts or NA certainty of position	3	(5)
3.	Other. Depends. Both boxes checked on question of government ownership of power plants	4	(6)
4.	Opposes government ownership of power plants and has some doubts or NA certainty of position	5	(8)
5.	Opposes government ownership of power plants and mind made up	34	(55)
8.	DK	2	--
0.	No opinion	36	--
		100%	(100%)

(Source: 1964 post, Q.37-37b, deck 12.)

LABOR UNION INFLUENCE

1. "The government ought to see to it that labor unions don't have much say about how the government is run." Now, would you say you have an opinion on this or not? (IF YES) Do you agree that the government should do this or do you think the government should not do it?

	1956 % Total	(% with Opinion)
1. Agree strongly	38%	(51%)
2. Agree but not very strongly	12	(16)
3. Not sure; it depends	5	(7)
4. Disagree but not very strongly	9	(12)
5. Disagree strongly	11	(14)
9. DK	2	--
0. No opinion	23	--
	100%	(100%)

(Source: 1956, Q.12ℓ, deck 3.)

2. In 1960, the above statement was prefaced by: "How do you feel about this statement," and followed by: "Do you agree that the government ought to see to it that labor unions don't have much say about how the government is run, or do you disagree? (Do you agree-disagree strongly, or not very strongly?)"

	1960 % Total	(% with Opinion)
1. Agree strongly	38%	(50%)
2. Agree	16	(22)
3. Not sure; it depends	*	(*)
4. Disagree	14	(18)
5. Disagree strongly	7	(10)
0. No opinion; DK	25	--
	100%	(100%)

(Source: 1956 post, Q.35-35a, deck 9)

* = Less than 1%

BIG BUSINESS

"The government ought to see to it that big business corporations don't have much
say about how the government is run." Now, would you say you have an opinion on
this or not? (IF YES) Do you agree that the government should do this or do you
think the government should not do it?

		1956	
		% Total	(% with Opinion)
1.	Agree strongly	38%	(53%)
2.	Agree but not very strongly	13	(17)
3.	Not sure; it depends	6	(8)
4.	Disagree but not very strongly	8	(11)
5.	Disagree strongly	8	(11)
9.	DK	2	--
0.	No opinion	25	--
		100%	(100%)

(Source: 1956, Q.12g, deck 3.)

CUT TAXES

"The government ought to cut taxes even if it means putting off some important things that need to be done." Now, would you say you have an opinion on this or not? (IF YES) Do you agree that the government should do this or do you think the government should not do it?

		1956	
		% Total	(% with Opinion)
1.	Agree strongly	15%	(19%)
2.	Agree but not very strongly	11	(13)
3.	Not sure; it depends	11	(13)
4.	Disagree but not very strongly	16	(19)
5.	Disagree strongly	29	(36)
9.	DK	1	--
0.	No opinion	17	--
		100%	(100%)

(Source: 1956, Q.12a, deck 3.)

FEDERAL AID TO PAROCHIAL SCHOOLS

1. Respondents asked this question were those who on a prior question were in favor of federal aid to education.

    "Many schools around the country are maintained by various religious groups." Do you think the government should provide aid to these schools as well as to public schools?

		1962	
		% Total	(% with Opinion)
1.	Yes, all schools should be helped whether public or private (unqualified support of aid to private schools)	29%	(50%)
2.	Yes, qualified -- Catholic schools should not be helped; doubt because of Catholic schools	*	(*)
3.	Yes, qualified; other	3	(5)
4.	Yes, transportation can be provided; buses to private religious schools	--	--
5.	No, schools	26	(44)
6.	No, but might change mind if Catholic schools exempted from such aid; "No, we can't help those Catholics"; specific mention of Catholic schools as reason for opposition	*	(*)
7.	No, but other qualification	*	(1)
8.	DK	4	--
0.	Inap., coded 5, 8, 9, or 0 in col. 33, no opinion on federal aid to education or against it	38	--
		100%	(100%)

(Source: 1962, Q.45b, deck 14.)

2. Respondents asked this question were those who on a prior question indicated an interest in the general subject of "federal aid to education".

    Many grade schools and high schools around the country are run by various churches and religious groups of all faiths--Protestants, Catholics, Jews. Do you think the government should provide help to these schools or not?

2. (Cont'd)

	1964	
	% Total	(% with Opinion)
1. Yes	33%	(44%)
3. Other. Depends. Both boxes checked	*	(*)
5. No	41	(56)
8. DK	8	--
0. Inap., no interest in federal aid to education question	18	--
	100%	(100%)

(Source: 1964, Q.15d, deck 4.)

GOVERNMENT POWER

"Some people are afraid the government in Washington is getting too powerful for the good of the country and the individual person. Others feel that the government in Washington has not gotten too strong for the good of the country." Have you been interested enough in this to favor one side over the other? (IF YES) What is your feeling, do you think:

		1964		1966	
		% Total	(% with Opinion)	% Total	(% with Opinion)
1.	(YES) The government is getting too powerful	30%	(44%)	39%	(56%)
3.	(YES) Other. Depends. Both boxes checked	3	(4)	4	(5)
5.	(YES) The government has not gotten too strong	36	(52)	27	(39)
8.	DK	3	--	2	--
0.	No interest	28	--	28	--
		100%	(100%)	100%	(100%)

(Source: 1964, Q.16-16a, deck 4; 1966, Q.A2-A2a, deck 1.)

POWER OF FEDERAL GOVERNMENT RECODED TO INCORPORATE CERTAINTY OF POSITION

		1964	
		% Total	(% with Opinion)
1.	Feels government too powerful and mind made up	25%	(37%)
2.	Feels government too powerful and has some doubts or NA certainty of position	5	(7)
3.	Other. Depends. Both boxes checked on question of power of government	3	(4)
4.	Feels government not too strong and has some doubts or NA certainty of position	7	(10)
5.	Feels government not too strong and mind made up	29	(42)
8.	DK	3	--
0.	No interest	28	--
		100%	(100%)

(Source: 1964, Q.16-16b, deck 4)

GENERAL GOVERNMENT INVOLVEMENT

Some people think the national government should do more in trying to deal with such problems as unemployment, education, housing, and so on. Others think that the government is already doing too much. On the whole, would you say that what the improvement has done has been about right, too much, or not enough?

		1952	
		% Total	(% with Opinion)
1.	Definitely should do more	1%	(1%)
2.	Should do more	17	(18)
3.	About right, OK	48	(51)
4.	Should do less	14	(15)
5.	Definitely should do less	2	(2)
6.	Should do more or same, DK or same or others	7	(8)
7.	Should do more or same, less or others	2	(2)
8.	Should do less or same, DK or same or others	3	(3)
9.	DK	6	--
		100%	(100%)

(Source: 1952, Q.21, deck 3)

OTHER DOMESTIC POLICY QUESTIONS

1. Have you heard anything about the Taft-Hartley Law? (IF HAS HEARD) How do you
    feel about it? Do you think it's all right as it is, do you think it should be
    changed in any way, or don't you have any feelings about it? (IF SHOULD BE
    CHANGED) Do you think the law should be changed just a little, changed quite a
    bit, or do you think it should be completely repealed? How is that?

		1952	
		%	(% with
		Total	Opinion)
1.	Completely repealed	11%	(23%)
2.	Changed quite a bit -- in favor of labor	1	(3)
3.	" " " " -- in favor of management	*	(1)
4.	" " " " -- NA in whose favor	3	(6)
5.	Changed a little -- in favor of labor	3	(6)
6.	" " " -- in favor of management	1	(3)
7.	" " " -- NA in whose favor	8	(18)
8.	Changed, NA how much	6	(12)
+.	All right as it is	12	(28)
9.	DK	25	--
0.	Inap., haven't heard about Taft-Hartley Law	30	--
		100%	(100%)

(Source: 1952, Q. 23-23a(1), deck 3.)

2. Over the years most Democrats have said that the government in Washington ought
    to see to it that everybody who wants to work can find a job. Many Republicans
    do not agree that the government should do this. How about you--would you
    agree with these Democrats that the government ought to see to it that everybody
    who wants work can find a job? (IF AGREE OR DISAGREE) Would you say you agree
    (disagree) strongly or not very strongly?

		1960	
		%	(% with
		Total	Opinion)
1.	Agree strongly	40%	(41%)
2.	Agree	17	(18)
3.	Not sure; it depends	11	(11)
4.	Disagree	12	(12)
5.	Disagree strongly	17	(18)
0.	No opinion; DK	3	--
		100%	(100%)

(Source: 1960 post Q. 33-33a, deck 9.)

CIVIL RIGHTS AND RACIAL ATTITUDES

Civil rights is currently one of the most important and most emphasized issue areas in politics. As a result, the 1964 and 1966 election studies devoted considerably more time to the probing of attitudes in this area than did earlier studies--probably reflecting that the issue has not always been a central one to the electorate. This earlier lack of emphasis prevents an extensive analysis of racial attitude trends on certain subjects. However, for those questions repeated in most studies (as in the areas of school desegregation and job equality), some analysis of trends can be undertaken, but even here the analyst must be cautious in his interpretations since the questions, though on the same subjects, are often worded differently in different studies.

Some items central to the early civil rights struggle concerned the role of government in education, employment, and housing. Negroes wanted integration of public schools, equality in job opportunities, and decent housing at a moderate cost. The issue of education was probably the most publicized of the three and also, perhaps, the most important. Despite varied wordings of this question in the election studies, the data showed a fairly constant public approval of governmental intervention in this sphere, the support level ranging from 44 to 51 percent in all election years except 1962. In that latter year, enthusiasm rose even higher, with 61 percent of the sample sponsoring a federal role in school integration.

On the subjects of jobs and housing, the different wording of the questions appear to have severely hindered comparability and, hence, confounded interpretation of the data trendlines observed. The 1956, 1958, and 1960 studies included both "job equality" and "housing" subjects in a single question. This seemed to force the respondent to evaluate both subjects as a package rather than separately. On the other hand, the 1952 and 1964 studies only included the "job equality" aspect of the questions, deleting any reference to the "housing" element. In addition, the questions from even these two studies were worded quite differently. The trends that can be meaningfully discerned from such questions seem to indicate growing support for job equality and decent housing for the Negro through 1960, with a dip in the pattern occurring in 1964. The support levels for job equality ranged from 54 percent in 1952 to 72 percent in 1960, with a decline of 45 percent being witnessed in 1964. The area of housing had a more restricted time range, but seemed to indicate over 70 percent advocating open housing between the years 1956 and 1960.

Attitudes toward these issues of education, employment, and housing for Negroes intercorrelated quite strongly and also correlated well with six other civil rights questions included in the 1964 study. As might be expected, the correlation of these questions with background variables revealed that Negroes were more oriented toward integration than whites and that middle and upper class people were more likely to be liberal on this question than those of lower socio-economic status, although the correlation was much more pronounced for the question on job equality than it was for the school integration issue. Older people and rural residents--a disproportionate number of whom were southern--were likely to be segregationists, while more women than men were in favor of school integration. Outside of the segregationist vote for Goldwater in 1964, racial attitudes have not been strongly related to party affiliation or to actual vote. Only in 1952 were party differences visible and here Republicans were more likely than Democrats to say that government should stay out of the job discrimination area.

TABLE 1: CORRELATION OF CIVIL RIGHTS QUESTIONS WITH BACKGROUND VARIABLES

	Sex	Race	Education	Income	Age	Community Size	Party Identification	Actual Vote
1952 Job Discrimination	-.06	-.13	.05	.10	.04	.11	.09	.13
1956 Fair Treatment	-.06	-.15	.15	.15	-.04	.02	.03	.04
1956 School Desegregation	.06	.09	.04	.02	-.15	-.16	.03	.00
*1956 Negro Identification	.02	*	-.12	.14	.05	-.07	.03	.09
*1956 Care about Negroes	-.01	*	-.19	-.01	.09	.16	.03	.04
1960 Fair Treatment	-.05	-.21	.15	.15	-.04	.09	.03	.04
1960 School Desegregation	.09	.16	.07	-.01	-.15	-.18	.06	-.05
*1960 Negro Identification	-.15	*	.09	.20	.11	-.23	.28	.27
*1960 Care about Negroes	-.04	*	-.19	-.24	.32	.21	-.02	.05
1962 School Desegregation	.01	-.11	-.07	-.06	.01	NA	-.08	NA
1964 Fair Employment								
1964 School Desegregation								
1964 Segregationist								
1964 Open Housing ⎫ 1964 Civil Rights Index	-.05	-.22	-.11	-.03	.13	.02	.08	.32
1964 Open Accommodations								
1964 Kids in Mixed Schools (W)								
1964 Kids in Mixed Schools (N) ⎭								
1964 Busing	.00	-.10	-.05	-.05	.02	.10	.07	.05
1964 Change in Position	.06	.25	-.02	-.11	-.04	-.15	-.13	-.20
1964 Too Fast or Slow	-.04	.15	.19	.10	-.06	-.20	-.03	-.11
1964 Negroes Violent	.01	-.23	-.11	-.01	.08	.15	.09	.18
1964 Negroes Help Cause								

* Asked only of Negroes

Note: Values in the table are Pearson product-moment correlation coefficients. Correlations were performed on standard SRC code systems for these variables unless otherwise noted in the text.

TABLE 2: INTERCORRELATION OF CIVIL RIGHTS QUESTIONS

	FT	SD	NI	CN
1956 Fair Treatment	X			
1956 School Desegregation	-.33	X		
1956 Negro Identification	.20	-.01	X	
1956 Care about Negroes	.19	.01	.28	X
1960 Fair Treatment	X			
1960 School Desegregation	-.40	X		
1960 Negro Identification	.26	.10	X	
1960 Care about Negroes	.40	-.33	-.02	X

	FE	SD	SEG	OH	OA	KS(W)	KS(N)	B
1964 Fair Employment	X							
1964 School Desegregation	.47	X						
1964 Segregationist	.31	.43	X					
1964 Open Housing	-.32	-.41	-.56	X				
1964 Open Accommodations	.44	.51	.46	-.49	X			
1964 Kid in Mixed School (Whites)	.11	.31	.37	-.36	.30	X		
1964 Kid in Mixed School (Negroes)	-.01	.54	.49	-.10	.22	X	X	
1964 Busing	.18	.17	.14	-.12	.18	.10	.20	X

	CP	TFS	NV	NH	SEG
1964 Change in Position	X				
1964 Too Fast or Slow	-.07	X			
1964 Negroes Violent	-.12	.44	X		
1964 Negroes Help Cause	.21	-.46	-.63	X	
1964 Segregationist	.10	-.40	-.40	.34	X

Note: Values in the table are Pearson product-moment correlation coefficients (except in 1964 where tau-beta is used). Correlations were performed on standard SRC code systems for these variables unless otherwise noted in the text.

The strongest background correlate of integrationist views was the respondent's region of residence, a variable which was excluded from the table of correlation coefficients since region does not constitute an ordinal scale. The table below shows some of the explanatory power of the "region" variable. Average scores of the respondents on a civil rights index, constructed from the 1964 election study, vary considerably according to the person's region of residence. (The civil rights index on which these scores are based will be described in more detail below.)

	All Respondents	Negro Respondents
Northeast	3.7	3.2
West	4.3	3.8
North Central	4.5	3.6
Southern Border States	5.1	3.1
Solid South	5.7	3.4

The higher scores on this index indicate more segregationist views and the lower scores indicate support for integration. As can be readily seen, the solid South and the border states are least tolerant of civil rights; the Northeast is by far the most tolerant. Among Negroes, index scores are lower than or hover around the Northeast figures for all respondents. Separate further analyses of these data reveal that the better educated person is more likely to be integrationist, except in the South, where just the opposite trend holds.

The civil rights index[*] referred to above was constructed from the following items: a straightforward query on segregation, the above-mentioned

---

[*] A separate index generated from five of these eight items was also constructed and results with this five-item index were reported in Angus Campbell, "Civil Rights and the Vote for President," Psychology Today, Feb., 1968, p.26ff.

questions on governmental intervention in fair employment and school integration areas, similar questions on open housing and public accommodations,
an item on school busing, and two questions, one asked only of whites and the
other only of Negroes, on personal response to a newly-integrated school. A
person's score on the index was determined by adding the code values of the
seven responses he gave. According to the code systems, the most pro-
integrationist response for a given question was scored as a "1" and the most
pro-segregationist reply as a "5," making the possible scores for the sample
range from 7 to 35. This measure was then converted to a nine point index
according to the following table with the resulting distribution of responses
shown.

Index Score	Original Score Interval	% of Sample
1 (Integration)	7-10	9%
2	11-13	15
3	14-16	12
4	17-19	14
5	20-22	13
6	23-25	12
7	26-28	11
8	29-31	8
9 (Segregation)	32-35	6
		100%

The attitude distribution of the index shows a fairly even division
between conservative and liberal replies to the civil rights issue; the
average score is 4.6, slightly on the integrationist side of the scale.
Percentage breakdowns of the individual questions further reveal this greater
tendency for people to favor the liberal side of the question. For example,

the straight question about feelings toward segregation showed more people favoring the Negro position than not favoring it, although many people took an intermediate or undecided stance. This pattern of support for the Negro cause was roughly followed for most of the other questions--especially in the areas of residential integration, school integration, reaction to integration in one's community, and integration of public accommodations. Only in one area--school busing, perhaps the one of greatest inconvenience--was there shown a definite and strong opposition to the prevailing civil rights sentiment.

Other perceptions of the civil rights movement were also collected in the 1964 and 1966 studies. These questions were not focused on any specific area of social or economic life but rather on the civil rights movement in general. Examining the first two questions, one sees that the percent of the total sample who thought that the Negro position in this country had changed and that civil rights leaders were pushing too fast in their crusade remained fairly constant between the two years, with about 40 percent saying that the position of the Negroes had changed "a lot" and about two-thirds saying that civil rights leaders were pushing "too fast." In answering two further questions (included only in 1964, after some civil disorder had occurred but a year before the first large scale urban riot in Watts),58 percent of the citizens said that Negroes' actions were hurting their cause. Obviously, although a large part of the public had come to accept the role of government in helping the Negro with his socio-economic plight, people felt at the same time a definite "uneasiness" about the temper and tempo of the Negroes' own movement. This "uneasiness" might also be one factor behind the declining public support in 1964 for the Negro position in such areas as job equality in relation to support in previous years. Even with these declines, on most questions people still gave strong support to civil rights, but it would appear that increasing support for governmental policy in this area will be dependent on the public's reactions to the actions of the various civil rights groups.

These four questions on the general nature of the civil rights movement show high intercorrelations, especially the three dealing with Negro leaders pushing too fast, Negro leaders being too violent, and Negroes hurting their own cause. All four items correlated quite well with the segregation-desegregation question, which formed an integral part of the civil rights index described above. It is not surprising, therefore, to find the four civil rights questions relating to many of the same background variables as the index. Comparing the association of background variables to the four civil rights questions (and the index) in the correlation table reveals that Negroes, the better educated, the young, and the more affluent are more sympathetic to the nature and tempo of the civil rights movement than those with the opposite socio-economic characteristics. Exactly the opposite viewpoint was taken by Goldwater supporters, Republican party identifiers (to a lesser extent), and rural and small-town residents, especially in the South. In some cases, the correlations are not striking, but most are significant (at the .05 significance level) and do indicate distinct attitude preferences of these differing classes of people.

Civil rights seemed to be very much on the public mind in 1964. For one thing, the sample showed amazing knowledge of the stands of the two presidential candidates on the civil rights bill and, presumably, on the general civil rights movement as well. Ninety-nine percent of the people accurately identified President Johnson's position, and 96 percent knew how Senator Goldwater voted on the bill. Rarely does the public identify issues with the two candidates as accurately as this. When asked how white people in their areas felt about the integration question, the respondents also identified approximately the same type of attitude distribution found at the national level.

In the 1964 election campaign, the three requirements of true public opinion on an issue seemed to be fulfilled--people were aware of the question, took a position on it, and correctly identified the positions of the two presidential nominees as a basis for rational decision-making at the polls.

The crux of the civil rights movement rests in many respects on the loyalty and unity of the Negroes to their race and its cause. To assess these psychological feelings of identification, two questions were asked of Negro respondents in the 1956, 1958, and 1960 studies. The response patterns to both questions were quite positive in terms of the civil rights movement. The proportion of Negroes feeling "close" to other Negroes was around the 80 percent level in all three years. The percent of respondents who said they cared "a great deal" how Negroes as a whole were getting along in the country jumped from 67 percent in 1956 to 85 percent in 1960, indicating a substantial increase in the salience of identification with other Negroes during this period. The two questions showed a fairly strong positive correlation in 1956, although this was not the case in 1960. The demographic distribution of Negro identifiers was located in the better educated and lower income Negro groups in 1956 (although not at a statistically significant level) and among less educated and lower income respondents in 1960. Also, strong Negro identification was found among Negro Democratic Party supporters, Negroes in smaller towns, Negro women, and older Negroes; however, none of these correlations were significant in 1956. On the other hand, concern with how Negroes were doing was greatest among the younger, urban, and better educated Negroes in 1956; these relations were even stronger in 1960.

It is well to remember that the number of Negroes in these studies was very small (under 200) and highly clustered as well and these two factors could account for the unstable correlation patterns in the preceding paragraph.

ATTITUDE TOWARD GOVERNMENT ACTION ON SCHOOL DESEGREGATION

1. "The government in Washington should stay out of the question of whether white and colored children go to the same school." Do you have an opinion on this or not? (IF YES) Do you think the government should stay out of this question? (Do you agree that the government should do this or do you think the government should not do it?--1956)

		1956		1958		1960	
		% Total	(% with Opinion)	% Total	(% with Opinion)	% Total	(% with Opinion)
1.	Agree strongly	35%	(40%)	36%	(40%)	33%	(38%)
2.	Agree but not very strongly	8	(9)	8	(9)	6	(7)
3.	Not sure; it depends	6	(7)	5	(6)	7	(8)
4.	Disagree but not very strongly	10	(11)	7	(7)	8	(9)
5.	Disagree strongly	30	(33)	34	(38)	33	(38)
9.	DK	1	--	2	--	3	--
0.	No opinion	10	--	8	--	10	--
		100%	(100%)	100%	(100%)	100%	(100%)

(Source: 1956, Q.12p, deck 3; 1958, Q.18a, deck 3; 1960, Q.25-25a, deck 4.)

2. "The government in Washington should see to it that white and colored children are allowed to go to the same schools." Do you have an opinion on this or not? (IF YES) Do you agree that the government should do this or do you think the government should not do it?

		1962	
		% Total	(% with Opinion)
1.	Yes	47%	(55%)
2.	Yes, qualified	3	(3)
3.	Yes, but there should be no force; moderate; gradual	2	(3)
4.	No, qualified	1	(1)
5.	No	32	(38)
8.	DK	1	--
0.	Inap. (No, DK, or NA to interest)	14	--
		100%	(100%)

(Source: 1962, Q.47-47a, deck 14.)

3. "Some people say that the government in Washington should see to it that white and colored children are allowed to go to the same schools. Others claim that this is not the government's business." Have you been concerned enough about this question to favor one side over the other? (IF YES) Do you think that the government in Washington should:

	1964		1966	
	% Total	(% with Opinion)	% Total	(% with Opinion)
1. (YES) See to it that white and Negro (colored) children go to the same schools	41%	(48%)	46%	(51%)
3. (YES) Other. Depends. Both boxes checked	7	(8)	7	(8)
5. (YES) Stay out of this area as it is none of its business	39	(44)	34	(38)
8. DK	3	--	3	(3)
0. No interest	10	--	10	--
	100%	(100%)	100%	(100%)

(Source: 1964, Q.23-23a, deck 5; 1966, Q.A3-A3a, deck 1.)

SCHOOL INTEGRATION RECODED TO INCORPORATE CERTAINTY OF POSITION

	1964	
	% Total	(% with Opinion)
1. Favors school integration and mind made up	37%	(43%)
2. Favors school integration and has some doubts or NA certainty of position	4	(5)
3. Other. Depends. Both boxes checked on question of school integration	7	(8)
4. Against school integration and has some doubts or NA certainty of position	3	(3)
5. Against school integration and mind made up	36	(41)
8. DK	3	--
0. No opinion	10	--
	100%	(100%)

(Source: 1964, Q.23-23b, deck 5.)

ATTITUDE TOWARD GOVERNMENT ACTION ON JOB DISCRIMINATION

There is a lot of talk these days about discrimination, that is, people having trouble getting jobs because of their race. Do you think the government ought to take an interest in whether Negroes have trouble getting jobs or should it stay out of this problem?

(IF GOVERNMENT SHOULD TAKE AN INTEREST) Do you think we need laws to deal with this problem or are there other ways that will handle it better?

(IF "OTHER WAYS" to 22a) What do you have in mind?

(IF "LAWS" to 22a) Do you think the national government should handle this or do you think it should be left for each state to handle in its own way?

(IF GOVERNMENT SHOULD STAY OUT) Do you think the state governments should do something about this problem or should they stay out of it also?

		1952	
		% Total	(% with Opinion)
1.	National government should pass laws <u>and</u> do other things too	1%	(1%)
2.	National government should pass laws or NA national or state	23	(24)
3.	State government should pass laws <u>and</u> do other things too	1	(1)
4.	State government should pass laws	14	(15)
5.	Government should do other things <u>only</u>	8	(8)
6.	Government should take an interest, NA how	6	(7)
7.	National government should stay out, <u>but</u> state government should take action	16	(17)
8.	Government (national and state) should stay out entirely	20	(21)
+.	R favors restrictive legislation (include here clear anti-Negro statements) PRIORITY	5	(6)
9.	DK	6	--
		100%	(100%)

(Source: 1952, Q.22-22d, deck 3.)

ATTITUDE TOWARD SOCIAL EQUALITY IN JOBS AND HOUSING

"If Negroes are not getting fair treatment in jobs and housing, the government should see to it that they do." Do you have an opinion on this or not? (IF YES) Do you think the government <u>should</u> **do** this? (Do you agree that the government <u>should</u> do this or do you think the government should <u>not</u> do it?---1956)

		1956		1958		1960	
		% <u>Total</u>	(% with <u>Opinion</u>)	% <u>Total</u>	(% with <u>Opinion</u>)	% <u>Total</u>	(% with <u>Opinion</u>)
1.	Agree strongly	43%	(49%)	48%	(54%)	50%	(52%)
2.	Agree but **not** very strongly	18	(21)	16	(18)	19	(20)
3.	Not sure; it depends	6	(8)	6	(7)	8	(8)
4.	Disagree but not very strongly	6	(7)	5	(6)	5	(5)
5.	Disagree strongly	13	(15)	13	(15)	14	(15)
9.	DK	2	--	1	--	2	--
0.	No opinion	12	--	11	--	2	--
		100%	(100%)	100%	(100%)	100%	(100%)

(Source: 1956, Q.12f, deck 5; 1958, Q.16a, deck 3; 1960, Q.22-22a, deck 4.)

ATTITUDE TOWARD EQUAL JOB OPPORTUNITIES

The item below is not comparable to the above questions since it omits any reference to housing. It is included here for general interest.

"Some people feel that if colored people are not getting fair treatment in jobs the government in Washington ought to see to it that they do. Others feel that this is not the federal government's business." Have you had enough interest in this question to favor one side over the other? (IF YES) How do you feel? Should the government in Washington:

	1964	
	% Total	(% with Opinion)
1. (YES) See to it that Negroes (colored people) get fair treatment in jobs	39%	(45%)
3. (YES) Other. Depends. Both boxes checked	7	(9)
5. (YES) Leave these matters to the states and local communities	40	(46)
8. DK	4	--
0. No interest	10	--
	100%	(100%)

(Source: 1964, Q. 22-22a, deck 5.)

EQUAL JOB OPPORTUNITIES RECODED TO INCORPORATE CERTAINTY OF POSITION

	1964	
	% Total	(% with Opinion)
1. Favors FEPC and mind is made up	36%	(41%)
2. Favors FEPC and has some doubts or NA certainty of position	3	(4)
3. Other. Depends. Both boxes checked on question of federal intervention	7	(9)
4. Opposes federal intervention and has some doubts or NA certainty of position	4	(4)
5. Opposes federal intervention and mind is made up	36	(42)
8. DK	4	--
0. No opinion	10	--
	100%	(100%)

(Source: 1964, Q.22-22b, deck 5.)

ATTITUDE TOWARD SEGREGATION

What about you? Are you in favor of desegregation, strict segregation, or something in between?

		1964
1.	Desegregation	32%
3.	In between	44
5.	Segregation	23
8.	DK	1
		100%

(Source: 1964, Q.41, deck 5.)

ATTITUDE TOWARD RESIDENTIAL INTEGRATION

Which of these statements would you agree with:

		1964
1.	White people have a right to keep Negroes (colored people) out of their neighborhoods if they want to	26%
5.	Negroes (colored people) have a right to live wherever they can afford to, just like white people	57
8.	DK. Depends. Can't decide. Both boxes checked	17
		100%

(Source: 1964, Q.31, deck 5.)

RESIDENTIAL INTEGRATION RECODED TO INCORPORATE DEGREE OF FEELING

		1964
		% Total
1.	White people have a right to keep colored people out of their neighborhoods. Feel strongly	21%
2.	White people have a right to keep colored people out of their neighborhoods. Feel not too strongly	5
4.	Colored people have a right to live wherever they can afford to. Feel not too strongly	20
5.	Colored people have a right to live wherever they can afford to. Feel strongly	37
8.	Don't know; depends	17
		100%

(Source: 1964, Q. 31-31a, deck 5.)

ATTITUDE TOWARD INTEGRATED PUBLIC ACCOMMODATIONS

Congress passed a bill that says that Negroes should have the right to go to any hotel or restaurant they can afford, just like white people. Some people feel that this is something the government in Washington should support. Others feel that the government should stay out of this matter. Have you been interested enough in this to favor one side over another? (IF YES) Should the government support the right of Negroes:

		1964	
		% Total	(% with Opinion)
1.	To go to any hotel or restuarant they can afford	46%	(53%)
5.	Stay out of this matter	38	(43)
3.	Other. Depends. Both boxes checked	4	(4)
8.	DK	2	--
0.	No interest	10	--
		100%	(100%)

(Source: 1964 post, Q.68-68a, deck 13.)

INTEGRATED PUBLIC ACCOMMODATIONS RECODED TO INCORPORATE CERTAINTY OF POSITION

		1964	
		% Total	(% with Opinion)
1.	Favors integrated public accommodations and mind made up	42%	(49%)
2.	Favors integrated public accommodations and has some doubts or NA certainty of position	4	(4)
3.	Other. Depends. Both boxes checked on question of integrated public accommodations	4	(4)
4.	Opposes federal intervention and has some doubts or NA certainty of position	4	(4)
5.	Opposes federal integration and mind made up	34	(39)
8.	DK	2	--
9.	No opinion	10	--
		100%	(100%)

(Source: 1964 post, Q.68-68b, deck 13.)

BUSING

What if you had children the school board said must be taken a little farther from home by bus like this. Do you feel you should go along with the decision, try to have it changed, or what?

		1964
1.	Go along	23%
2.	Depends on distance, all right if not too far away	*
3.	Depends on educational standards of school	1
4.	Too expensive (will raise taxes)	*
5.	Try to change decision	64
6.	Children should go to neighborhood, nearest school	*
7.	Other	1
8.	DK. No response because R has no children (of school age)	11
		100%

(Source: 1964, Q. 30, deck 5.)

PERSONAL RESPONSE TO NEW INTEGRATION

1. (ASK ONLY OF WHITES) What if you had children going to a white school and the court ruled the school had to admit a few colored children. Would you have your children keep going to school there, would you try to get them into a different school, or what?

	1964
1. Keep them there	84%
2. Send to different school	11
3. Depends on proportion of whites and Negroes	1
4. Depends on age of children	*
5. Depends on behavior, condition of Negro children	*
6. Only if they live in same neighborhood	*
7. Other	*
8. DK	4
0. Inap. Negro R (% of total sample)	(10)
	100%

(Source: 1964, Q. 26, deck 5.)

2. (ASK ONLY OF NEGROES) What if you felt that a white school near where you lived was much better than a colored school. Would you want your children to go to the white school even if they were among the first few colored people to attend it, or would you rather have them stay in the colored school? (IF NECESSARY: Can you tell me more about how you feel on this?)

	1964
1. Would send to white school	62%
3. Other. Depends. Both boxes checked	3
5. Would keep in Negro school	22
8. DK	13
0. Inap., white R (% of total sample)	(90)
	100%

(Source: 1964, Q. 28, deck 5)

554

3. In some places school boards trying to have both white and colored children in the same school are taking some children out of their closest neighborhood schools and are sending them by bus to other schools farther away. Has anything like this happened around here?

		1964
1.	Yes	7%
5.	No	82
8.	DK	11
		100%

(Source: 1964, Q.29, deck 5.)

ATTITUDE TOWARD THE CIVIL RIGHTS MOVEMENT

1. In the past few years we have heard a lot about civil rights groups working to improve the position of the colored people in this country. How much real change do you think there has been in the position of the colored people in the past few years: a lot, some, or not much at all?

		1964	1966
1.	A lot	41%	39%
3.	Some	38	39
5.	Not much at all	19	18
7.	Depends	--	*
8.	DK	2	4
		100%	100%

(Source: 1964, Q.24a, deck 5; 1966, Q.A8, deck 1.)

2. Some say that the civil rights people have been trying to push too fast. Others feel they haven't pushed fast enough. How about you: do you think that civil rights leaders are trying to push too fast, are going too slowly, or are they moving about the right speed?

		1964	1966
1.	Too fast	63%	64%
2.	Mostly about right but some going too fast	--	1
3.	About right, pro-con	25	19
4.	Mostly about right, but some going too slowly	--	*
5.	Too slowly	6	4
7.	Depends; other	--	1
8.	DK	6	11
		100%	100%

(Source: 1964, Q.24b, deck 5; 1966, Q.A9, deck 1.)

3. During the past year or so, would you say that most of the actions colored people have taken to get the things they want have been violent, or have most of these actions been peaceful?

		1964
1.	Most been violent	58%
2.	More violent than peaceful	0
3.	Some violent, some peaceful (both boxes checked)	4
4.	More peaceful than violent	*
5.	Most been peaceful	27

556

3. (Cont'd)

   8. DK $\frac{11}{100\%}$

   (Source: 1964, Q.25a, deck 5.)

4. Do you think the actions colored people have taken have, on the whole, <u>helped</u>
    their cause, or on the whole have <u>hurt</u> their cause?

                                                          <u>1964</u>

    1. Helped   27%

    2. Helped more than hurt   *

    3. Some help, some hurt. Both boxes checked   4

    4. Hurt more than helped   0

    5. Hurt   58

    8. DK $\frac{11}{100\%}$

    (Source: 1964, Q. 25b, deck 5.)

NEGRO IDENTIFICATION

1. (ASK ONLY OF NEGROES) Would you say you feel <u>pretty close</u> to Negroes in general or that you <u>don't feel much closer</u> to them than you do to other <u>kinds</u> of[*] people?

(% of Negro sample)	1956	1958	1960
1. Feel pretty close	77%	82%	78%
3. Can't decide; it depends; feel both ways	--	--	--
5. Not closer than to others	23	18	22
9. DK	--	--	--
	100%	100%	100%
(Percent of Negroes in total sample)	8%	9%	10%

(Source: 1956 post, Q.46, deck 8; 1958, Q. post 22, deck 9; 1960, Q. post 23, deck 7)

2. How much interest would you say you have in how Negroes as a whole are getting along in this country? Do you have a <u>good deal</u> of interest in it, <u>some interest</u>, or <u>not much interest</u> at all?

	1956	1958	1960
1. Good deal	67%	79%	85%
3. Some	25	15	12
5. Not much at all	8	6	3
9. DK	--	--	--
	100%	100%	100%

(Source: 1956 post, Q.47, deck 8; 1958, Q. post 22a, deck 7; 1960, Q. post 24, deck 7)

[*]In 1958 and 1960 the words "kinds of" were omitted.

KNOWLEDGE OF CIVIL RIGHTS LEGISLATION

1. Have you heard whether Congress did anything this year in the way of civil rights (what did they do?) (IF MENTIONS CIVIL RIGHTS BILL) Do you remember whether or not President Johnson favored the civil rights bill? (Did he favor it?)

		1964	
		% Total	(% with Opinion)
1.	Yes (President Johnson did favor it)	74%	(99%)
5.	No (President Johnson did not favor it)	*	(1)
8.	DK	3	--
0.	Inap., No mention of Civil Rights Bill	23	--
		100%	(100%)

1a. (IF MENTIONS CIVIL RIGHTS BILL) Do you remember whether Senator Goldwater voted for or against the civil rights bill? (For or against?)

		1964	
		% Total	(% with Opinion)
1.	For	3%	(4%)
5.	Against	65	(96)
8.	DK	9	--
0.	Inap., No mention of Civil Rights Bill	23	--
		100%	(100%)

(Source: 1964 post, Q. 67-67b, deck 13.)

OTHER CIVIL RIGHTS QUESTIONS

1. In general, how many of the colored people in this area would you say are in favor of desegregation--<u>all</u> of them, <u>most</u> of them, <u>about half</u>, <u>less than half</u> of them, or <u>none</u> of them?

		1964	
		% Total	(% with Opinion)
1.	All	14%	(30%)
2.	Most	15	(34)
3.	About half	7	(15)
4.	Less than half	7	(16)
5.	None	2	(5)
8.	DK	30	--
0.	Inap., coded 1 in Q.32 to Q.38. No responses in this area	25	--
		100%	(100%)

(Source: 1964, Q.39, deck 5.)

2. How about white people in this area? How many would you say are in favor of strict segregation of the races--<u>all</u> of them, <u>most</u> of them, <u>about half</u>, <u>less than half</u> of them or <u>none</u> of them?

		1964	
		% Total	(% with Opinion)
1.	All	14%	(18%)
2.	Most	27	(37)
3.	About half	14	(19)
4.	Less than half	15	(20)
5.	None	4	(6)
8.	DK	25	--
0.	Inap.; coded 5 in Q.32 to Q.38. No whites in this area	1	--
		100%	(100%)

(Source: 1964, Q.40, deck 5.)

INTERNATIONAL ATTITUDES

Included in this section are four aspects of international attitudes--
isolationism, foreign aid, relations with foreign countries in general, and
relations with Communist nations in particular. Correlations of these questions with various background variables and with each other are presented in
the tables on the following pages.

Turning first to the subject of isolationism, one notices steadily
declining support for this view in the 1952-1960 period. In 1952, 57 percent
of the sample supported a "stay-at-home" attitude, but a revised question
asked in the next three election studies elicited much lower rates of approval--
28 percent in 1956, 27 percent in 1958, and 20 percent in 1960. In comparing
such distributions from year to year, the reader is reminded of the changes
in item format and the possible influence they could have on responses.
However, the steep decline evidenced is probably attributable in large part,
if not wholly, to a real change in attitude position.

Over the years, isolationist attitudes have been most prevalent among
the lower socio-economic groups, the elderly, rural inhabitants, and Negroes.
The relation between isolationism and party affiliation showed a dramatic
shift between 1952 and 1960, Democrats being more isolationist in 1952 and
Republicans more isolationist in 1956 and 1960. (An index of isolationism
to be discussed below also shows the Republicans to be less internationalist-
oriented in 1964.) The second table of correlations suggests that the people
who preferred the isolationist position also tended to oppose foreign aid,
and, in 1960, seemed to think that the United States had not done well in its
foreign relations and that its position in the world had become weaker.

TABLE 1: CORRELATION OF INTERNATIONAL ATTITUDE QUESTIONS WITH BACKGROUND VARIABLES

	Sex	Race	Education	Income	Age	Community Size	Party Identification	Actual Vote
1952 Isolationism	-.02	.00	.16	.12	-.11	-.11	-.16	-.20
1956 Foreign Aid	.00	-.03	-.04	-.04	-.03	.09	.01	.03
1956 Isolationism	-.04	-.09	.33	.28	-.20	-.10	.06	.01
1956 Aid to Neutrals	.06	-.06	-.18	-.13	.11	.04	-.04	.04
1956 Friendliness	.07	.05	-.09	-.08	-.05	.07	-.04	.04
1960 Foreign Aid	.04	.01	-.09	-.09	-.01	.07	-.05	.00
1960 Isolationism	-.10	-.06	.30	.32	-.14	-.11	.08	.06
1960 U.S. Done Well	.04	-.03	.18	.18	-.10	-.03	-.32	-.37
1960 U.S. Stronger	.05	-.07	.19	.13	-.05	.02	-.25	-.29
1964 Foreign Aid / U.S. Done Well / U.S. Stronger / Trade with Communists / China into UN / Talk with Communists } 1964 International Relations Index	.04	-.03	.01	-.02	.11	.07	.44	.27

Note: Values in the table are Pearson product-moment correlation coefficients. Correlations were performed on standard SRC code systems for these variables unless otherwise noted in the text.

562

TABLE 2:   INTERCORRELATION OF INTERNATIONAL ATTITUDE QUESTIONS

	FA	IS	AN	FR
1956 Foreign Aid	X			
1956 Isolationism	-.19	X		
1956 Aid to Neutrals	.33	-.22	X	
1956 Friendliness	.18	-.14	.23	X

	FA	IS	DW	ST
1960 Foreign Aid	X			
1960 Isolationism	-.28	X		
1960 U.S. Done Well	.03	.07	X	
1960 U.S. Stronger	-.03	.09	.54	X

	FA	DW	ST	TR	CH	TK
1964 Foreign Aid	X					
1964 U.S. Done Well	.04	X				
1964 U.S. Stronger	.05	.50	X			
1964 Trade with Communists	.15	.08	.09	X		
1964 China into UN	.11	.10	.08	.28	X	
1964 Talk with Communists	.18	.16	.15	.13	.25	X

Note: Values in the table are Pearson product-moment correlation coefficients (except in 1964 where tau-beta is used). Correlations were computed from the standard SRC code systems for these variables unless otherwise noted in the text.

The trend away from an isolationist position was also evident in the response to questions about foreign aid in the 1956-1964 period. A greater percentage of people favored aid to foreign nations in 1958, 1960, and 1964 than in 1956. The percentage increase was only moderate--from 52 percent to roughly 59 percent, but showed a definite trendline of support that remained steady in the last three election years. If one contrasts the 1956 question on "aid to neutral countries" with the 1958, 1960, and 1964 questions, the percentage difference would be even larger--from 40 percent to 59 percent. Apparently, the tendency to oppose foreign aid in 1956 was strengthened when the countries involved would not necessarily support the U.S. position of being unfriendly to Communist countries or curtailing the spread of Communism.

The demographic correlates of foreign aid policy were generally weaker in value than the comparable figures for the isolationist-internationalist dimension. This held despite the association between people's attitudes in the two issue areas. For instance, there was little correlation between education, income, or age and foreign aid attitudes, but noticeable correlations prevailed when isolationism was the dependent variable. On the other hand, the customary correlates of isolationism were in evidence on the 1956 question concerning "aid to neutral countries." For some reason, the same types of people reacted in similar fashion to the factors of isolationism and "aid to neutral countries" but in a different manner to the more general question on foreign aid policy. An additional observation in the table is the often noted phenomenon of party identification and current vote not being related to one's opinions on foreign aid.

America's relations with foreign countries have not generally earned public praise. Samples in 1958, 1960, and 1964 were not very satisfied with our dealings with other countries and with our position of strength in the

world. On neither question did the American public give majority support to
U.S. endeavors with foreign countries. Some people hedged their opinions by
saying that the U.S. was doing well in some ways but not well in other ways.
Nevertheless, a quarter to a third criticized the activities and strength of
the U.S. in this sphere with no equivocation.

In 1956, a third question on foreign relations was asked which corroborated
the increasing trend toward internationalism--50 percent of the people thought
the U.S. should be willing to go more than halfway in being friendly with the
other countries of the world. Perhaps some of the criticisms of American
foreign policy were based on the belief that the U.S. was not as friendly as
it should be with other countries. Increasing acceptance of foreign aid,
as noted above, would be another indication of this belief.

In contrast to the demographic analysis of the foreign aid question,
assessment of the foreign relations and relative world position of the United
States was highly dependent on party affiliation. In 1960, Democrats felt
that their country was not doing well in this area; in 1964, Republicans took
this position. (Note, however, that the correlations in 1964 were obtained
with an index on foreign relations composed of many questions and not just
the two of concern here.) Other familiar correlates were observed--the
younger, better-educated, and higher income individuals were quite critical
of this nation's foreign relations as one might expect. The correlations were
more pronounced in 1960 than in 1964.

Specific questions on this nation's relations with Communist states
were asked in 1964. The first item probed the isolationist-internationalist
dimension in our relations with these countries. Not surprisingly, as the
above-mentioned trend toward internationalist sentiment would indicate, an
overwhelming percentage of people (84 percent) wanted our government to "sit

down and talk to the leaders of the Communist countries and try to settle our differences." Very few took the opposite position. A second item revealed a more isolationist bent. It concerned one's reactions to trading with Communist countries. Fifty-seven percent of the respondents disagreed with this liberal position and almost all of them were completely certain of their attitude on this question.

Two other items centered on specific Communist countries, China and Cuba, and prompted somewhat different responses. Concerning Cuba, approximately half of the sample did not want to intervene in their affairs in an attempt to remove the Communists from government; however, on the Red China question, an overwhelming 75 percent thought the U.S. should not consent to China being admitted to the United Nations. On one subject, the sample took a noticeably "soft" stance toward Communism, and, on the other, a "hard-line" reactionary position. A long history by American administrations of denial of Red Chinese membership to the U.N. could partly explain the latter attitude distribution.

In the 1964 study, an index on foreign relations was created which consisted of the following six items: foreign aid, foreign trade with Communists, foreign position of the U.S., foreign dealings of the U.S., negotiations with Communist states, and China's admission to the U.N. These items appeared to intercorrelate at an adequate, if not high, level of significance. Each of the six questions was scored from 1 to 5 in the index according to how isolationist the reply was, with summed scores thus ranging from 6 to 30. Low scores represent fairly consistent internationalist replies to the six items, and high scores reflect the isolationist stance.

Index scores, their corresponding intervals on the original scale scores, and the percentage distribution of the 1964 sample are as follows:

Index Score	Original Scores	% of Sample
1 (Internationalist)	6-10	14%
2	11-13	20
3	14-15	18
4	16-17	14
5	18	10
6	19-20	11
7	21-22	6
8	23-25	5
9 (Isolationist)	26-30	2
		100%

The preponderance of scores fit on the internationalist end of the continuum as one would expect from the attitude distributions of the single questions composing the index. The background correlates are also not much different from what has earlier been noted. Republicans, older people, rural inhabitants, and, to a lesser extent, Goldwater supporters were far more likely to be typed as "isolationists" than as "internationalists." The correlations with the education and income variables, however, fail to follow the pattern of the earlier election studies in that they provide no explanatory power in 1964.

ISOLATIONISM

1. Some people think that since the end of the last world war this country has gone too far in concerning itself with problems in other parts of the world. How do you feel about this?

		<u>1952</u>
1.	Agree	48%
2.	Agree, with qualifications	9
3.	Pro-con, depends	2
4.	Disagree, with qualifications	7
5.	Disagree	26
9.	DK	<u>8</u>
		100%

(Source: 1952, Q. 24, deck 3.)

2. "This country would be better off if we just stayed home and did not concern ourselves with problems in other parts of the world." Do you have an opinion on this or not? (IF YES) Do you think our country <u>should</u> stay home? (Do you agree that the government <u>should</u> do this or do you think the government should <u>not</u> do it - 1956.)

		1956		1958		1960	
		% Total	(% with Opinion)	% Total	(% with Opinion)	% Total	(% with Opinion)
1.	Agree strongly	15%	(17%)	15%	(18%)	13%	(14%)
2.	Agree, but not very strongly	10	(11)	8	(9)	6	(6)
3.	Not sure, it depends	5	(6)	8	(9)	6	(7)
4.	Disagree, but not very strongly	14	(16)	14	(16)	12	(13)
5.	Disagree strongly	43	(50)	42	(48)	54	(60)
9.	DK	1	--	1	--	1	--
0.	No opinion	12	--	12	--	8	--
		100%	(100%)	100%	(100%)	100%	(100%)

(Source: 1956, Q. 12c, deck 3; 1958, Q. 13a, deck 3; 1960, Q. 19-19a, deck 4.)

ATTITUDE TOWARD FOREIGN ECONOMIC AID

1. "The United States should give economic help to the poorer countries of the world even if they** can't pay for it." Do you have an opinion on this or not? (IF YES) Do you think the government should do this? (Do you agree or do you think the government should not do it?--1956)

	1956		1958		1960	
	% Total	(% with Opinion)	% Total	(% with Opinion)	% Total	(% with Opinion)
1. Agree strongly	21%	(26%)	26%	(32%)	33%	(34%)
2. Agree, but not very strongly	22	(26)	25	(30)	24	(25)
3. Not agree, it depends	15	(18)	13	(15)	16	(17)
4. Disagree, but not very strongly	10	(11)	7	(8)	7	(7)
5. Disagree strongly	16	(19)	12	(15)	16	(17)
9. DK	1	--	2	--	2	--
0. No opinion	15	--	15	--	2	--
	100%	(100%)	100%	(100%)	100%	(100%)

(Source: 1956, Q. 12e, deck 3; 1958, Q. 15a, deck 3; 1960, Q. 21-21a, deck 4.)

2. We now come to a few questions about our country's dealing with other countries. "How about aid to foreign countries? Some say that we should give aid to other countries if they need help, while others think each country should make its own way as best it can." Have you been interested enough in this to favor one side over the other? (IF YES) Which opinion is most like yours? Should we:

	1964	
	% Total	(% with Opinion)
1. (YES) Give aid to other countries	52%	(59%)
3. (YES) Other. Depends. Both boxes checked	18	(20)
5. (YES) Each country make its own way	19	(21)
8. DK	2	--
0. No Interest	9	--
	100%	(100%)

(Source: 1964, Q. 20-20a, deck 4.)

** In 1960, "they" was replaced by "those countries"

FOREIGN AID RECODED TO INCORPORATE CERTAINTY OF POSITION

		1964	
		% Total	(% with Opinion)
1.	Favors giving aid and mind made up	46%	(51%)
2.	Favors giving aid and has some doubts or NA certainty of position	6	(8)
3.	Other. Depends. Both boxes checked on question of foreign aid	18	(20)
4.	Against giving aid and has some doubts or NA certainty of position	3	(4)
5.	Against giving aid and mind made up	16	(17)
8.	DK	2	--
0.	No interest	9	--
		100%	(100%)

(Source: 1964, Q. 20-20b, deck 4.)

3. Recently many Republicans have felt that the United States should give economic help to the poorer countries of the world even if they can't pay for it. Many Democrats disagree. How about you - would you agree with these Republicans that the United States should give economic help to the poorer countries of the world even if they can't pay for it? Would you say you agree (disagree) strongly or not very strongly?

		1960	
		% Total	(% with Opinion)
1.	Agree strongly	21%	(23%)
2.	Agree	25	(28)
3.	Not sure; it depends	18	(20)
4.	Disagree	10	(11)
5.	Disagree strongly	17	(18)
0.	No opinion; DK	9	--
		100%	(100%)

(Source: 1960 post, Q. 34-34a, deck 9.)

570

AID TO NEUTRAL COUNTRIES

"The United States should give help to foreign countries even if they are not as much against Communism as we are." Now, would you say you have an opinion on this or not? (IF YES) Do you agree that the government should do this or do you think the government should not do it?

	1956	
	% Total	(% with Opinion)
1. Agree strongly	12%	(17%)
2. Agree, but not very strongly	17	(23)
3. Not sure; it depends	12	(17)
4. Disagree, but not very strongly	10	(14)
5. Disagree strongly	21	(29)
9. DK	2	--
0. No opinion	26	--
	100%	(100%)

(Source: 1956, Q. 12o, deck 3.)

GENERAL STATE OF U.S. FOREIGN POSITION

1. Would you say that in the past year or so the United States has done pretty
   well in dealing with foreign countries, or would you say that we haven't
   been doing as well as we should?

		1958	1960	1964
1.	Pretty well	42%	37%	46%
3.	Well in some ways, not well in others	11	10	8
5.	Not too well	28	41	31
8.	DK	19	12	15
		100%	100%	100%

(Source: 1958, Q. 25, deck 3; 1960, Q. 30, deck 5, 1964, Q. 46, deck 5.)

2. Would you say that in the past year or so our position in the world has
   become stronger, less strong, or has it stayed about the same?

		1958	1960	1964
1.	Stronger	23%	22%	28%
3.	About the same	38	31	36
5.	Less strong	23	32	20
8.	DK	16	15	16
		100%	100%	100%

(Source: 1958, Q. 26, deck 3; 1960, Q. 31, deck 5; 1964, Q. 47, deck 5.)

INTERNATIONAL FRIENDLINESS

"The United States should be willing to go more than half-way in being friendly with the other countries of the world."   1) Now, would you say you have an opinion on this or not? (IF YES) Do you agree that the government should do this or do you think the government should not do it?

		1956	
		% Total	(% with Opinion)
1.	Agree strongly	44%	(50%)
2.	Agree, but not very strongly	19	(21)
3.	Not sure; it depends	7	(8)
4.	Disagree, but not very strongly	12	(13)
5.	Disagree strongly	7	(8)
9.	DK	1	--
0.	No opinion	10	--
		100%	(100%)

(Source: 1956, Q. 12m, deck 3.)

RELATIONS WITH COMMUNIST COUNTRIES

1. Some people think our government should sit down and talk to the leaders of the Communist countries and try to settle our differences, while others think we should refuse to have anything to do with them." Have you been interested enough in this to favor one side over the other? (IF YES) What do you think? Should we:

		1964	
		% Total	(% with Opinion)
1.	(YES) Try to discuss and settle our differences	72%	(84%)
3.	(YES) Other. Depends. Both boxes checked	4	(4)
5.	(YES) Refuse to have anything to do with leaders of Communist countries	10	(12)
8.	DK	3	--
0.	No Interest	1	--
		100%	(100%)

(Source: 1964, Q. 21-21a, deck 4.)

TALK WITH COMMUNISTS RECODED TO INCORPORATE CERTAINTY OF POSITION

		1964	
		% Total	(% with Opinion)
1.	Favors talking and mind made up	66%	(78%)
2.	Favors talking and has some doubts or NA certainty of position	6	(6)
3.	Other. Depends. Both boxes checked on question of talking with Communists	4	(4)
4.	Against talking and has some doubts or NA certainty of position	1	(2)
5.	Against talking and mind made up	9	(10)
8.	DK	3	--
0.	No interest	11	--
		100%	(100%)

(Source: 1964, Q. 21-21b, deck 4.)

2. "Some people say that our farmers and businessmen should be able to go ahead and do business with Communist countries as long as the goods are not used for military purposes. Others say that our government should not allow Americans to trade with the Communist countries." Have you been interested enough in this to favor one side over the other? (IF YES) How do you feel? Should farmers and businessmen be:

		1964	
		% Total	(% with Opinion)
1.	(YES) Allowed to do business with Communist countries	28%	(37%)
3.	(YES) Other. Depends. Both boxes checked	5	(6)
5.	(YES) Forbidden to do business with Communist countries	43	(57)
8.	DK	3	--
0.	No Interest	21	--
		100%	(100%)

(Source: 1964 post, Q. 38-38a, deck 12.)

TRADE WITH COMMUNIST COUNTRIES RECODED TO INCORPORATE CERTAINTY OF POSITION

		1964	
		% Total	(% with Opinion)
1.	Favors trade with Communist countries and mind made up	21%	(28%)
2.	Favors trade with Communist countries and has some doubts or NA certainty of position	7	(9)
3.	Other. Depends. Both boxes checked on question of trade with Communist countries	5	(6)
4.	Opposes trade with Communist countries and has some doubts or NA certainty of position	4	(6)
5.	Opposes trade with Communist countries and mind made up	39	(51)
8.	DK	3	--
0.	No opinion	21	--
		100%	(100%)

(Source: 1964 post, Q. 38-38b, deck 12.)

3. Some people feel that we must do something to get the Communist government out of Cuba; others feel that it is up to the Cuban people to handle their own affairs. Have you been interested enough in this to favor one side over the other? (IF YES) What is your feeling, that we should get:

		1964	
		% Total	(% with Opinion)
1. (YES) Communist government out of Cuba		25%	(39%)
3. (YES) Other. Depends. Both boxes checked		8	(12)
5. (YES) Cuban people handle their own affairs		32	(49)
8. DK		3	--
0. No interest		32	--
		100%	(100%)

(Source: 1964 post, Q. 41b-41c, deck 12.)

4. Do you think Communist China should be admitted to the United Nations, or do you think it should not? (SHOULD NOT) If Communist China were admitted to the United Nations, should we:

	1964	
	% Total	(% with Opinion)
1. Communist China should be admitted to United Nations	15%	(25%)
2. (SHOULD NOT) If admitted, United States should stay in	33	(55)
3. (SHOULD NOT) If admitted, DK if U.S. should stay in; other; depends; both boxes checked	5	(8)
5. (SHOULD NOT) If admitted, U.S. should get out of United Nations	7	(12)
8. DK if Communist China should be admitted to the United Nations	10	--
0. Inap. (coded 1, 8, 9 or 0 in Q. 40 - ignorance on China in UN)	30	--
	100%	(100%)

(Source: 1964 post, Q. 40b-40c, deck 12.)

WAR-RELATED ATTITUDES

The SRC attitude questions in this area can be grouped under four headings: general expectations of war, specific opinions on the Korean and Vietnam wars, attitudes toward specific policies concerning Communist countries, and general knowledge about the governments of Communist countries.

General expectations of war and worries about war were more prevalent in 1960 than in either 1956 or 1964. In 1956 and 1960, people also reported that the Republicans were more likely to keep the country out of war than the Democrats. Such a belief obviously has some basis in the experience of Democratic administrations being in office during the conduct of both major world wars and the Korean and Vietnam conflicts. However, in 1964, the tables were turned-- Goldwater's Republican image came across as too bellicose, and the Democrats, for one time, were viewed as "the party of peace."

The following correlation tables reveal that these several items on the public's war perceptions and their political backgrounds are interrelated. People expecting that a war was more likely to occur were sure that there was a definite difference in which party would get us into war. Those who were worried about the imminence of war also saw definite differences in the parties' attitudes on this issue. Responses to these "fear of war" questions, however, appeared to be generally unrelated to the other attitudes discussed in this section.

Several background correlates of these attitudes on war appear in the analysis. Women, for instance, were found to worry more about war than men did and, especially in 1960, tended to feel that it was more likely to occur. A similar pattern of responses was noticed among younger people. Party identification and actual vote were also related to one's estimate of the

TABLE 1:   CORRELATION OF WAR-RELATED ATTITUDES WITH BACKGROUND VARIABLES

	Sex	Race	Education	Income	Age	Community Size	Party Identification	Actual Vote
1952 Right thing in Korea	.14	.03	-.17	-.17	.15	.07	.16	.18
1952 Korean policy	-.12	-.12	.12	.12	-.03	.02	.02	.09
1956 Worried about war	.08	.00	.03	.03	-.12	.03	-.11	-.10
1956 Chance for war	.02	.07	-.09	-.06	-.08	-.01	-.30	-.34
1956 War party	.01	-.10	.11	.10	.01	.05	.55	.58
1956 Soldiers vs. Communism	.03	.01	.00	-.01	-.09	.07	.01	.00
1956 China-Russia policy	.08	-.02	.14	.01	-.03	.04	.01	.01
1960 Worried about war	.21	-.02	.00	.00	-.09	.06	-.07	-.06
1960 Chance for war	.14	-.02	-.04	.03	-.10	.04	-.27	-.28
1960 War party	-.06	-.04	-.03	-.03	.12	.05	.51	.61
1960 Soldiers vs. Communism	.05	.00	.02	-.03	.01	.03	.00	-.02
1964 Worried about war	.11	.04	.01	.00	-.07	.04	.01	-.02
1964 Chance for war	.06	-.01	.04	.02	-.05	.07	.14	.18
1964 War party	-.05	-.09	.04	.05	.12	.09	.48	.52
1964 Right thing in Vietnam	.11	.06	-.15	-.21	.16	.06	.07	.13
1964 Vietnam policy	-.16	-.08	.18	.17	-.12	.02	.09	.15
1964 Communists out of Cuba	.05	.01	-.03	-.07	.00	-.02	-.15	-.20

Note: Values in the table are Pearson product-moment correlation coefficients.   Correlations were performed on standard SRC code systems for these variables unless otherwise noted in the text.

TABLE 2: INTERCORRELATION OF WAR ATTITUDE QUESTIONS

	RK	KP
1952 Right thing in Korea	X	
1952 Korean policy	-.16	X

	WW	CW	WP	SC	CR
1956 Worried about war	X				
1956 Chance for war	.34	X			
1956 War party	-.12	-.40	X		
1956 Soldiers vs. Communism	-.04	.04	-.01	X	
1956 China-Russia policy	-.02	-.03	.03	.15	X

	WW	CW	WP	SC
1960 Worried about war	X			
1960 Chance for war	.43	X		
1960 War party	-.09	-.29	X	
1960 Soldiers vs. Communism	.04	.02	.00	X

	WW	CW	WP	RV	VP	CC
1964 Worried about war	X					
1964 Chance for war	.29	X				
1964 War party	.00	.22	X			
1964 Right thing in Vietnam	.04	.09	.11	X		
1964 Vietnam policy	-.04	.08	.12	-.36	X	
1964 Communists out of Cuba	*	.03	*	.09	-.18	X

Note: Values in the table are Pearson product-moment correlation coefficients. Correlations were computed from the standard SRC code systems for these variables unless otherwise noted in the text.

* Not calculated

chances of war, but the relationships were less pronounced with regard to one's worries about war. In 1956 and 1960, Republican identifiers and voters thought the chances for avoiding war were greater than the Democrats believed, but the Democrats were more optimistic on this point in 1964. Another strong correlation existed between party preference and feelings about which party was best suited to keep the United States out of war. This is hardly an unexpected finding since few voters would consciously view their party as one likely to get us involved in a war. The relationship was somewhat less in 1964 than in either 1956 or 1960.

The questions on United States policy in Korea and Vietnam have elicited quite similar attitude distributions,[*] despite obvious differences between the two wars. The percentages in each attitude category are shown below:

	Korea 1952	Vietnam 1964	Vietnam 1966
Pull out	10%	9%	9%
Stay but try for peace	46	24	36
Take stronger stand	38	31	36
Other	--	--	2
Don't know	6	36	17
	100%	100%	100%

The main difference between the three sets of figures is in the "don't know" category. If these "don't know" responses are allocated mainly into the "middle-of-the-road" policy alternative, the distributions match even more closely.

On the question of whether we should have become involved with these

---

[*]A further discussion of these attitude distributions compared with other poll data about Vietnam is given in John Robinson and Solomon Jacobson, "American Public Opinion about Vietnam," Papers of the Peace Research Society, Volume VIII, 1968 (Available from the Wharton School of the University of Pennsylvania in Philadelphia).

countries in the first place, it is interesting to note that the "right thing to do/wrong thing to do" ratio was higher for the Vietnam War (1964: 38 percent/ 24 percent; 1966: 44 percent/29 percent) than it was for the Korean conflict (1952: 41 percent/43 percent). The questions on involvement and policy intercorrelate at a higher level for the Vietnam War as well, although the relation was not as large as one might initially expect. In general, those who agreed to our involvement in Vietnam (or Korea) took a stronger stand on the war and the policies needed to achieve a military victory in that war.

A demographic analysis of war attitudes reveals that similar types of people took similar positions with regard to the two military conflicts. The better-educated, higher income, and Republican-oriented groups tended to favor U.S. entry into the Korean and Vietnam wars and the policies associated with this commitment. In fact, these people wanted the U.S. to take a more aggressive stand in both wars. Women, on the other hand, believed that getting involved in the two wars was a mistake and favored troop withdrawals. Negroes also tended to take anti-war positions in both time periods, as did younger people.

A few questions have been asked by the SRC regarding the policy of this country toward Communism and relations with Communist countries. Only one of these questions was asked in more than one survey. It dealt with the issue of whether the U.S. should keep its soldiers overseas as a protection against Communism and its spread. Of those respondents with an opinion, 73 percent supported this view in 1956, 79 percent in 1958, and 81 percent in 1960. No background variables showed any relation to this question, with the possible exception of a weak correlation with age in 1956.

Other questions were asked in single studies about the U.S.'s relations with specific Communist countries such as Russia, China, and Cuba. In 1956, the reaction to a question on U.S. policy toward Russia and China was decidedly to get tougher with them, "to act just as tough as they do." The better-educated and female sectors of the sample were most likely to disagree with this view. In 1964, as mentioned in an earlier section, almost 40 percent of those with an opinion favored getting the Communists out of Cuba. Only those with a Republican preference backed this view significantly more than any other sample grouping. A final question attempted to find out which of three countries--Vietnam, Cuba, or China--respondents were most worried about in 1964. (Russia was not included in this comparative question.) The answers pointed to Red China as the chief source of worry, with Vietnam close behind, and Cuba running third in the rankings. If the question had been asked in 1966, one would expect the distribution of replies to have changed, with Vietnam dominating the top spot in the rankings.

Respondents were quizzed in 1964 on their knowledge of various Communist governments. At that time (as is the case in 1968), these governments figured prominently in the news and would be classified in U.S. foreign policy as potential or actual enemies of this country. About 78 percent of the national sample identified the Chinese government as communistic and 75 percent believed the Cuban government could be similarly characterized. Other questions on Russia and North Vietnam would undoubtedly elicit similar response patterns. If one probed for further knowledge of the countries and their governments, undoubtedly fewer correct responses would be expected. There is considerable difference between a few pieces of information by which to describe or "stereotype" a country and the appropriate "fill-in" or auxiliary material needed to understand why a particular stereotype exists. The latter type of knowledge is probably well beyond the knowledge confines of most of the public.

KOREA

1. Do you think we did the right thing in getting into the fighting in Korea two years ago or should we have stayed out?

	1952
1. Yes, did the right thing	41%
3. Pro-con	5
5. No, should have stayed out	43
9. DK	11
	100%

(Source: 1952, Q. 26, deck 3.)

2. Which of the following things do you think it would be best for us to do now in Korea?

	1952
1. Pull out of Korea entirely	10%
2. Keep on trying to get a peaceful settlement	46
3. Take a stronger stand and bomb Manchuria and China	38
4. Either 1 or 3 (but R refuses to or does not make a choice)	1
9. DK	5
	100%

(Source: 1952, Q. 27, deck 3.)

VIETNAM

1. (In 66)   "Earlier you mentioned Vietnam was an important problem" or (IF R DID NOT MENTION VIETNAM IN A1)

Have you been paying any attention to what is going on in Vietnam?

(IF YES) Do you think we did the right thing in getting into the fighting in Vietnam or should we have stayed out?

		1964		1966	
		% Total	(% with Opinion)	% Total	(% with Opinion)
1.	(YES) Yes, did right thing	38%	(60%)	44%	(60%)
3.	(YES) Other. Depends. Both boxes checked.	1	(2)	1	(1)
5.	(YES) No, should have stayed out	24	(38)	29	(39)
8.	DK	17	--	19	--
0.	No interest	20	--	7	--
		100%	(100%)	100%	(100%)

(Source: 1964 post, Q. 39-39a, deck 12; 1966, Q. A5-A5a, deck 1.)

2. Which of the following do you think we should do now in Vietnam?

		1964		1966	
		% Total	(% with Opinion)	% Total	(% with Opinion)
1.	Pull out of Vietnam entirely	9%	(13%)	9%	(11%)
2.	Keep our soldiers in Vietnam, but try to end the fighting	24	(38)	36	(43)
3.	Take a stronger stand even if it means invading North Vietnam	31	(49)	36	(43)
7.	Other	*	(*)	2	(3)
8.	DK	16	--	10	--
0.	Inap., coded 9 or 0 in previous question	20	--	7	--
		100%	(100%)	100%	(100%)

(Source: 1964 post, Q. 39b, deck 12; 1966, Q. A5b, deck 1.)

584

KEEP SOLDIERS OVERSEAS AGAINST COMMUNISM

1. "The United States should keep soldiers overseas where they can help countries that are against Communism." Do you have an opinion on this or not? (IF YES) Do you think the government <u>should</u> do this? (Do you agree that the government <u>should</u> do this or do you think the government <u>should not</u> do it. --1956)

	1956		1958		1960	
	% Total	(% with Opinion)	% Total	(% with Opinion)	% Total	(% with Opinion)
1. Agree strongly	39%	(49%)	45%	(55%)	53%	(63%)
2. Agree, but not very strongly	19	(24)	20	(24)	15	(18)
3. Not sure; it depends	9	(11)	6	(8)	6	(7)
4. Disagree, but not very strongly	5	(6)	4	(5)	3	(4)
5. Disagree strongly	8	(10)	7	(8)	7	(8)
9. DK	2	--	1	--	3	--
0. No opinion	18	--	17	--	13	--
	100%	(100%)	100%	(100%)	100%	(100%)

(Source: 1956, Q. 12j, deck 3; 1958, Q. 17a, deck 3; 1960, Q. 23-23a, deck 4.)

POLICY TOWARD CHINA, RUSSIA, AND CUBA

1. "The best way for this country to deal with Russia and Communist China is to act just as tough as they do." Now, would you say you have an opinion on this or not? (IF YES) Do you agree that the government should do this or do you think the government should not do it?

		1956	
		% Total	(% with Opinion)
1.	Agree strongly	51%	(62%)
2.	Agree, but not very strongly	11	(14)
3.	Not sure; it depends	6	(7)
4.	Disagree, but not very strongly	6	(7)
5.	Disagree strongly	8	(10)
9.	DK	1	--
0.	No opinion	17	--
		100%	(100%)

(Source: 1956, Q. 12h, deck 3.)

2. Some people feel that it was our government's fault that China went Communist, others say there was nothing that we could do to stop it. How do you feel about this?

		1952
1.	It was our fault	17%
2.	It was our fault, with qualifications (partially our fault)	8
5.	Nothing we could do to stop it	50
9.	DK	25
		100%

(Source: 1952, Q. 25, deck 3.)

3. Some people feel that we must do something to get the Communist government out of Cuba; others feel that it is up to the Cuban people to handle their own affairs. Have you been interested enough in this to favor one side over the other? (IF YES) What is your feeling, that we should get:

			1964	
			% Total	(% with Opinion)
1.	(YES)	Communist government out of Cuba	25%	(39%)
3.	(YES)	Other. Depends. Both boxes checked	8	(12)
5.	(YES)	Cuban people handle their own affairs	32	(49)
8.	DK		3	--
0.	No interest		32	--
			100%	(100%)

(Source: 1964 post, Q. 41b-41c, deck 12.)

VIETNAM, CUBA, AND CHINA

We have been talking about our troubles with Vietnam, Cuba and Communist China. Which of these would you say you are <u>most</u> worried about? Which are you least worried about?

		1964	
		% Total	(% with Opinion)
1.	Cuba (most), Vietnam (moderate), China (least)	11%	(12%)
2.	Cuba (most), China (moderate), Vietnam (least)	8	(9)
3.	Vietnam (most), Cuba (moderate), China (least)	9	(10)
4.	Vietnam (most), China (moderate), Cuba (least)	19	(21)
5.	China (most), Cuba (moderate), Vietnam (least)	10	(12)
6.	China (most), Vietnam (moderate), Cuba (least)	27	(30)
7.	Worried about all three. Other	6	(6)
8.	DK	6	--
0.	Not worried about any	4	--
		100%	(100%)

(Source: 1964 post, Q. 42a-42b, deck 12.)

KNOWLEDGE OF FOREIGN COUNTRIES

1. Have you paid any attention to what kind of government most of China has
    right now, that is, do you remember whether it is democratic, communist,
    or something else? (IF NECESSARY) Which kind? (IF COMMUNIST RESPONSE)
    As far as you know, is Communist China a member of the United Nations?

		1964 % Total	(% with Opinion)
1.	China is Communist and United Nations member	4%	(6%)
5.	China is Communist, but not United Nations member	71	(90)
8.	China is Communist, DK if United Nations member	3	(4)
9.	China is Communist, NA if United Nations member	*	*
0.	China not known to be Communist	22	---
		100%	(100%)

(Source: 1964 post, Q. 40, deck 12.)

2. How about the situation in Cuba? Have you been watching it closely enough to
    notice what kind of government it has? (IF YES) Is it:

		1964 % Total	(% with Opinion)
1.	(YES) Communist	75%	(97%)
5.	(YES) Democratic or something else	2	(3)
8.	DK	*	--
0.	No interest	23	--
		100%	(100%)

(Source: 1964 post, Q. 41-41a, deck 12.)

FEAR OF WAR

1. Now I'd like to ask you some questions about the chances of our country getting into war. Would you say that at the present time you are <u>pretty</u> worried about this country getting into another war, <u>somewhat</u> worried, or <u>not worried</u> at all?

		1956	1960	1964
1.	Not at all worried	44%	32%	44%
3.	Somewhat worried	44	46	45
5.	Pretty worried	11	21	10
9.	DK	1	1	1
		100%	100%	100%

(Source: 1956, Q. 19, deck 3; 1960, Q. 32, deck 5; 1964, Q. 45, deck 5.)

2. During the (last) past few years do you think our chances of staying out of war have been getting better, getting worse, or stayed the same?

		1956	1960	1964
1.	Getting better	42%	19%	31%
3.	Stayed the same	41	41	48
5.	Getting worse	13	36	18
9.	DK	4	4	3
		100%	100%	100%

(Source: 1956, Q. 20, deck 3; 1960, Q. 33, deck 5; 1964, Q. 49, deck 5.)

3. Now looking ahead, do you think the problem of keeping out of war would be handled better in the next four years by the <u>Republicans</u>, or by the <u>Democrats</u>, or about the same by both?

		1956	1960	1964
1.	Better by Democrats	7%	15%	38%
3.	Same by both	45	47	46
5.	Better by Republicans	41	30	12
9.	DK	7	8	4
		100%	100%	100%

(Source: 1956, Q. 21, deck 3; 1960, Q. 34, deck 5; 1964, Q. 50, deck 5.)

4. How about the chances of our country getting into a bigger war? Compared to a few years ago, do you think we are <u>more likely</u>, <u>less likely</u>, or have <u>about the same</u> chances to get into a bigger war?

		<u>1966</u>
1.	Less likely	21%
3.	About same chances	33
5.	More likely	34
7.	Depends	2
8.	DK	10
		100%

(Source: 1966, Q. A6, deck 1.)

5. Looking ahead, do you think the problem of keeping out of a bigger war would be handled better in the next two years by the <u>Democrats</u>, by the <u>Republicans</u>, or <u>about the same</u> by both?

		<u>1966</u>
1.	Better by Democrats	11%
3.	Same by both	57
5.	Better by Republicans	15
8.	DK	17
		100%

(Source: 1966, Q. A7, deck 1.)

POLITICAL ACTIVITY

Of all the areas in which questions have been asked by the Political Behavior Program over the last sixteen years, the area of political activity reveals the greatest comparability of questions for delineating trends and for ascertaining the consistency of relationships over time. Seven of the political activity questions have been asked in all but one of the election studies since 1952. Percentage distributions of respondents' replies to these questions are given below for presidential election years:

Activity	1952	1956	1960	1964
Belong to club	2%	3%	3%	4%
Work for parties	3	3	6	5
Go to meetings	7	10	8	9
Give money	4	10	12	11
Use sticker or button	Not asked	16	21	16
Give opinions	27	28	33	31
Vote in election	73	73	74	78

In general, the percentage figures point to a rise over the years in most forms of political participation. For the two most prevalent activities-- voting and opinion-giving--a fairly consistent increase in participation has occurred across the span of presidential election years. A similar increasing trend appears in the off-year elections--58 percent reporting voting in 1958, 60 percent in 1962, and 62 percent in 1966, while 17 percent mention opinion-giving as an activity in 1958, 18 percent in 1962, and 22 percent in 1966. Considering each activity separately, voting turnout seems to be most prevalent in the 1964 election period and opinion-giving in the Kennedy-Nixon contest of 1960.

Of the remaining five activities, using a political sticker or wearing a campaign button was most common in the electorate, followed closely by acts of giving money and going to political meetings. There was some variability in the popularity of each item considered by itself over the years, although the trend has been generally one of increased participation in all activities. The table shows that more people participated in political meetings in 1956 than in any other year; working for the parties, giving money, and using a sticker or button were most frequently reported in the Kennedy-Nixon contest of 1960; and belonging to a political club or organization was most prevalent in 1964. Generally though, the 1960 election contest seemed to generate the most enthusiasm for participation in these activities. This contest also prompted large amounts of opinion-influencing among the electorate and encouraged as well a large voting turnout, as noted above.

A person's rate of political activity is known to be linked, in part, to his socio-economic background. Table 1 shows the correlation of some of these background characteristics to the various forms of political activity mentioned above. Although the correlations are moderate in value, they tend to show a general increase in size over the years. The most significant and most consistent background correlate of activity is education; another strong correlate is income. Political activity as a preoccupation is most likely found among the wealthy and well-educated. Party identification also has some explanatory impact. For the most part, Republicans tend to be more active than Democrats. The 1964 election data showed Republicans and Goldwater supporters to have been far more active than Democrats and Johnson backers. The large increase in opinion-giving by Republicans and Goldwater supporters in 1964 over previous years was especially striking. In the area of sex roles and their implications for political participation, men were shown to be more

TABLE 1: CORRELATION OF POLITICAL ACTIVITY WITH BACKGROUND VARIABLES

	Sex	Race	Education	Income	Age	Community Size	Party Identification	Actual Vote
1952 Opinion giving	.12	-.11	-.23	-.18	.05	.08	-.10	-.07
1952 Give money	.09	.06	-.19	-.16	-.01	.11	-.05	-.06
1952 Go to meetings	.02	.04	-.11	-.10	.00	.10	-.09	-.04
1952 Work for parties	.05	.06	-.12	-.05	.01	.04	-.09	-.05
1952 Belong to club	.01	.04	-.07	-.06	-.02	.09	-.06	.00
1956 Opinion giving	.15	.01	-.16	-.15	.03	.05	-.06	.03
1956 Give money	.05	.03	-.17	-.21	-.02	.07	-.04	.04
1956 Go to meetings	.05	.04	-.14	-.11	-.01	.02	.01	.04
1956 Work for parties	.01	.03	-.12	-.11	-.04	-.02	-.07	-.03
1956 Belong to club	.04	.02	-.08	-.08	-.03	.05	-.04	-.02
1956 Button or sticker	.08	.06	-.11	-.15	.05	.05	-.11	-.02
1960 Opinion giving	.16	.06	-.15	-.14	.07	.01	-.04	-.03
1960 Give money	-.01	.02	-.19	-.24	-.01	.05	-.16	-.13
1960 Go to meetings	-.04	-.06	-.05	-.06	.00	.04	-.10	-.05
1960 Work for parties	.06	.02	-.07	-.08	-.02	-.05	-.10	-.05
1960 Belong to club	.00	.01	-.10	-.05	-.02	.07	-.12	-.08
1960 Button or sticker	-.02	.09	-.13	-.16	.13	-.03	-.08	-.03
1962 Opinion giving	.14	.00	-.14	-.17	.03	NA	-.02	NA
1962 Give money	.03	.04	-.19	-.17	-.04	NA	-.06	NA
1962 Go to meetings	.05	.02	-.15	-.14	-.02	NA	-.02	NA
1962 Work for parties	.00	.03	-.10	-.13	.00	NA	-.01	NA
1962 Belong to club	.01	.01	-.06	-.04	-.07	NA	-.03	NA
1962 Button or sticker	.09	-.03	-.04	-.11	.01	NA	-.04	NA
1964 Opinion giving	.17	.04	-.27	-.18	.10	-.09	-.14	-.21
1964 Index *	-.05	-.06	.32	.22	-.05	.06	.18	.20

* Index is built so that larger numbers are equivalent to more participation, whereas the opposite relation obtains for the individual participation items in previous years.

Note: Values in the table are Pearson product-moment correlation coefficients. Correlations were computed from the standard SRC code systems for these variables unless otherwise noted in the text.

NA--data not available

active than women, especially in the sphere of opinion-giving.

Items on political activity have a strong tendency to be intercorrelated for election respondents. This tendency shows evidence of strength throughout all presidential years, especially so in recent elections as Table 2 points out. The strength of these intercorrelations could justify treating the political activity items as more unidimensional in nature than political attitude items. Respondents in the 1964 election study were scored along such an activity dimension according to their political activity on the following items:

1) Attendance at political meetings or rallies
2) Work in behalf of a party or candidate
3) Membership in a political club or organization
4) Use of a political button or campaign sticker
5) Communication (via letter) with a public official
6) Communication (via letter) with an editor of a newspaper or magazine
7) Influence on others to contribute money to a party
8) Contribution by self to a party or candidate

(The intercorrelations of items 5, 6, 7, and 8 are not presented in the table but are all significant at the .01 level.)

A scoring system was constructed for this index which gave one point for each activity in which the respondent participated. The resulting distribution of the national sample is presented below.

No activities	63%
One activity	22
Two activities	8
Three activities	3
Four activities	2
Five activities	1
Six or more activities	1
	100%

TABLE 2: INTERCORRELATION OF POLITICAL ACTIVITY ITEMS

	OG	GM	ME	WP	BC	BS
1952 Opinion giving	X					
1952 Give money	.21	X				
1952 Go to meetings	.25	.29	X			
1952 Work for parties	.23	.25	.32	X		
1952 Belong to club	.14	.22	.33	.30	X	

	OG	GM	ME	WP	BC	BS
1956 Opinion giving	X					
1956 Give money	.24	X				
1956 Go to meetings	.20	.33	X			
1956 Work for parties	.22	.25	.40	X		
1956 Belong to club	.13	.24	.34	.44	X	
1956 Button or sticker	.30	.27	.23	.22	.17	X

	OG	GM	ME	WP	BC	BS
1960 Opinion giving	X					
1960 Give money	.20	X				
1960 Go to meetings	.27	.34	X			
1960 Work for parties	.25	.32	.37	X		
1960 Belong to club	.18	.33	.41	.36	X	
1960 Button or sticker	.31	.29	.24	.29	.21	X

	OG	GM	ME	WP	BC	BS
1962 Opinion giving	X					
1962 Give money	.24	X				
1962 Go to meetings	.33	.41	X			
1962 Work for parties	.25	.31	.37	X		
1962 Belong to club	.14	.35	.37	.39	X	
1962 Button or sticker	.35	.24	.29	.28	.23	X

Note: Values in the table are Pearson product-moment correlation coefficients. Correlations were computed from the standard SRC code systems for these variables unless otherwise noted in the text.

The activity index reveals uneven rates of participation among the
citizenry in 1964. Sixty-three percent of the sample did not engage in even
one form of political activity among the eight items cited. The picture is
one of little active involvement with the political system, except among a
few "elite" members of the population. For the rest, as our earlier figures
indicated, voting--and, to a much lesser extent, opinion-giving--seem to be
the basic and most popular forms of overt political activity. Voting, in
particular, is seen to be quite prevalent--over 70 percent of the SRC respondents reporting this activity in each of the presidential election years. Even
with a slight overreporting of this item as compared with national figures,
voting still seems to stand virtually alone as the element of democracy that
the citizen believes in and uses. Needless to say, our political activity
index was correlated with the vote--people showing more activity in politics being
more likely to vote. But the crucial point is that people who have low scores
on the index are often voting too, though the probability of voting decreases
with lessened activity.

Because of the importance of the voting act and the prevalence of it
compared to other activities, the SRC studies have attempted to collect a
complete picture of the voting record of each respondent. This involves
asking him questions on present voting activity, past activity, and participation in primary elections as well. In the pre-election interview,
SRC collects information on whether the respondent is eligible to vote (i.e.,
if he or she is registered or intends to register) and if he intends to vote,
if eligible. Comparison of these responses with the respondent's reported
voting activity on the post-election schedules usually reveals an overreport
of vote eligibility and vote intentions. Those reporting such intentions
usually comprise just over 80 percent of those interviewed, but the actual

percent voting is 5 to 9 percent less than this in presidential election years.

Two questions are usually asked about the respondent's past voting record. One question is directed toward finding out if he voted in the preceding presidential election. The other taps his frequency of voting in those presidential elections occurring after he had become legally old enough to vote. Responses to the first question indicate, as a general rule, that people were more likely to have voted in the present presidential election than in the one four years previous to it. The differences are not great, ranging from 4 to 9 percent, but probably reflect some small increase in voting activity over the four year period. However, some respondents might have underreported their voting activity in the earlier election simply because of memory problems. The other question also has recall problems more severe than the first one. Granting this source of bias, one can see that 60 to 70 percent of the samples thought they had voted in all or most of the presidential elections since they were eligible to vote. This level of activity is fairly high and almost on a par with the levels of voting reported by these respondents in the presidential election years in which they were interviewed.

Levels of voting in primary elections vary considerably according to how the question is worded and the election year in which it is asked. In 1958, only 28 percent reported voting in a primary election for congressman. In 1964, the question was changed to a more general form of whether the respondent had ever voted in a primary election and the level answering "yes" correspondingly rose to 63 percent. The figure fell back to 41 percent when the question was worded to find out if the respondent had voted in a primary in 1966 (for any office). Absence of question comparability here makes it difficult to pinpoint the general level of primary voting over the years but upwards of 30 percent participating in this fashion seems apparent. One cannot easily ascertain the exact difference in voting turnout between primary and general elections since some states do not hold primary contests for presidential and other offices in given election years.

Voting and the other acts mentioned above are quite overt forms of political participation. However, there is another form of political activity which has a completely different orientation and probably a completely different motivational pattern as well. This is being exposed to, or exposing oneself to, information about politics from the various mass media sources. Whether the situation is one of consciously searching out this information, or more or less being bombarded by it regardless of preference, is difficult to tell since the SRC questions do not directly probe this area. Probably, it is a combination of the two, with the more passive elements dominating the mixture. This combination of elements would, of course, vary for people with different socio-economic backgrounds.

The percentage of the samples following campaign and other political news on the various mass media is given below for presidential election years.

Mass Media Source	1952	1956	1960	1964
Television	51%	74%	87%	89%
Newspapers	79	69	80	79
Radio	70	45	42	48
Magazines	40	31	41	39

Generally, one can see that the public is more attentive to the media than to the more overt, direct forms of political activity. Nowhere before has the reader witnessed percentages on this level for any form of activity except voting. The trends in the data also seem obvious--television is by far the most popular medium of political information today and has shown a monotonic increase in importance over the years, severely eclipsing the prior

dominance of radio as a conveyor of political news. Newspapers are also very

important sources of information, second only to television in every presi-

dential year except 1952. While magazines are last in the ratings, a steady

30 to 40 percent read campaign news in them; given the nature of this medium,

this is a definite sign of some conscious motivation to seek such information.

Overall, the greatest concern with these media centered on the 1960 election,

probably, in part, because of the particular personality and background

characteristics of the two presidential candidates and the added feature of

a nationally televised debate between them.

The trends in the data across election years may reflect something about

the motivational background involved in receiving information from these sources.

The increase in television exposure over time might well be partly deliberate

to the extent that non-purposive viewing eventually inculcates a subsequent

attitude of purposive viewing. Auxiliary questions on frequency of television

viewing also suggest this idea. About half of those watching the campaign

on television did so regularly in each election year, the trend increasing

across election years through 1960, although not in 1964. However, these

findings are probably confounded with the increase in sales of television

sets within this general period. More purposively oriented sources of infor-

mation, magazines and newspapers, show a much smaller popularity gain over the

years. The frequency of reading these sources also has not gained appreciably

over time. Particular elections and the political stimulation they generate

undoubtedly increase the number engaged in conscious seeking of news, but the

increase, whatever it may be, is not large. Hence, one could tentatively

conclude that an increase in media exposure is probably paralleled by a much smaller increase in the purposive use of such media, but the exact figures of the increase are by no means clear.

Another possible indication of conscious and purposive exposure to the political news of the media would be the amount and type of information the citizen has about the campaign and subsequent election results. Obviously, being exposed to information about the election, whether one chooses to or not, will lead to some new information intake. But watching television or reading a magazine does not in and of itself constitute (or ensure) learning. A more conscious and active use of the news media would enable the person to better learn and understand the information at hand--and the motivation is present to learn. The SRC has asked a few basic questions about the distribution of power in Congress before and after the election, along with questions about the names of the local congressional candidates, to ascertain if these rather basic pieces of information have been assimilated by the citizen. The percentage of correct answers to these questions varies considerably from one election to the next--with the overall range extending from 44 to 79 percent. Usually at least half of the samples answered these simple questions correctly. However, the extent to which this was "known" or "learned" information or just a "good guess" between two alternatives is unclear. Certainly, if the guessing factor were controlled for, the electorate would not appear to be too well informed on even these basic pieces of information. In some future study it would be interesting to ask from what source these facts were learned and under what circumstances.

As a final effort in this area, the SRC customarily asks questions about a person's interest in politics in general and in that year's election campaign in particular. While there are definite shortcomings to asking such direct questions, the distribution of responses does not seem at variance from what one would expect. The samples divided roughly into thirds on being "very interested," "somewhat interested," or "not much interested" in the current campaigns, while the number replying in a positive vein to the more general question on political interest was only slightly greater. Probably both questions, because of the way in which they were asked, slightly inflated the percentages of those interested in politics and the campaigns.

Obviously, political interest cannot be equated strictly with political activity, at least not in the overt sense of "activity." Interest, too, must be seen as a more passive means of participation (of essentially viewing the political game and getting information in the process) or as a precursor to active involvement in politics. But more people seem to have, or report to have, this general interest than those who engage in more direct forms of activity (outside of the act of voting itself). To the extent that such figures are representative of the national electorate, it seems that the minority of individuals who are interested in politics, possess some basic information on it, and use the media regularly to get political news are not pushing on to the next logical step in political activity--to more overt forms of helping the campaigns of the party and candidates of their choice.

Needless to say, self-reported rates of participation in any socially-approved activity are always subject to the likelihood that respondents will report themselves as more active than they really are. In the 1964 SRC election study, respondents' self-reports of whether they had voted or not were validated against actual registration rolls. The results of this validation study are planned to be published in the near future.

POLITICAL ACTIVITY ITEMS

I have a list of some of the things that people do that help a party or a candidate win an election. I wonder if you could tell me whether you did any of these things during the last election campaign. ** 1) Did you talk to any people and try to show them why they should vote for one of the parties or candidates?

		1952	1956	1958	1960	1962	1964	1966
1.	Yes	27%	28%	17%	33%	18%	31%	22%
5.	No	73	72	82	67	82	67	78
9.	DK	0	0	1	*	0	0	0
		100%	100%	100%	100%	100%	100%	100%

1a. (IF YES) Was this somebody in your family, some one of your friends, or some one where you work?

		1960	1962	1964
1.	Yes, family	3%	-	3%
2.	Yes, friends	11	-	8
3.	Yes, someone at work	5	-	5
4.	Yes, NA whom	*	-	0
5.	No	67	-	69
6.	Yes, family and friends	6	-	6
7.	Yes, family and fellow-workers	1	-	1
8.	Yes, friends and fellow-workers	3	-	2
9.	DK	*	-	0
0.	Other combination, other	4	-	6
		100%		100%

	1966
0. No (to: did you talk)	78%
1. Yes, family	3
2. Yes, friend (and/or neighbors)	8
3. Yes, someone at work	4
4. Yes, family and friend	3
5. Yes, family and fellow-worker	*
6. Yes, friend and fellow worker	1
7. Yes, family, friend and fellow worker	3
Yes, other person or combination or NA who	-
8. DK	-
	100%

(Source: 1952 post, Q. 22a, deck 7; 1956 post, Q. 17a, deck 7; 1958, Q. 37, deck 4; 1960 post, Q. 24a, 24b, deck 9; 1962, Q. 44a, deck 14; 1964 post, Q. 24a, 24b, deck 11; 1966, Q. C5, C5a, deck 2.)

2. Did you give any money or buy tickets or anything to help the campaign for one of the parties or candidates? (During this last year were you or any member of your household asked to give money or buy tickets to help pay the campaign expenses of a political party or candidate? IF YES - Did you give any money or buy any tickets? - 1966)

	1952	1956	1958	1960	1962	1964	1966 % Total	% of Those asked
1. Yes	4%	10%	-	12%	9%	11%	8%	46%
5. No	96	90	-	88	91	89	10	54
9. DK	0	0	-	0	*	0	0	0
0. Inap. was not asked by party	-	-	-	-	-	-	82	-
	100%	100%	100%	100%	100%	100%	100%	100%

(Source: 1952 post, Q. 22b, deck 7; 1956 post, Q. 17b, deck 7; 1960 post, Q. 24c, deck 9; 1962, Q. 44b, deck 14; 1964 post, Q. 33, deck 11; 1966, Q. C7, C7b, deck 2.)

604

2a. (IF NO - Did not give money in 1964 or was not asked by party or candidates to do so in 1966) Would you yourself have given money or bought tickets if you had been asked by a worker for your favorite party or a candidate you liked?

		1964	1966
1.	Yes	29%	20%
3.	Maybe; under some circumstances; depends	-	1
5.	No	67	67
8.	DK	4	12
		100%	100%

(Source: 1964 post, Q. 33f, deck 11; 1966, Q. C7d, deck 2.)

3. Did you go to any political meetings, rallies, dinners or things like that?

		1952	1956	1960	1962	1964
1.	Yes	7%	10%	8%	8%	9%
5.	No	93	90	92	92	91
9.	DK	0	0	*	0	0
		100%	100%	100%	100%	100%

3a. (IF YES) How many would you say you went to?

		1960	1964
0.	No, attended none	92%	91%
1.	1 meeting	5	5
2.	2 meetings	2	2
3.	3 meetings	1	1
4.	4 meetings	*	*
5.	5 meetings	*	*
6.	6 meetings	*	*
7.	7-10 meetings	*	*
8.	11 or more meetings	*	1
9.	DK (1964, yes, DK how many)	*	*
0.	Yes, NA how many	*	*
		100%	100%

(Source: 1952 post, Q. 22c, deck 7; 1956 post, Q. 17c, deck 7; 1960 post, Q. 24d, 24e, deck 9; 1962, Q. 44c, deck 14; 1964 post, Q. 24c, 24d, deck 11.)

4. Did you do any other work for one of the parties or candidates?

		1952	1956	1960	1962	1964
1.	Yes	3%	3%	6%	4%	5%
5.	No	97	97	94	96	95
9.	DK	0	0	0	0	0
		100%	100%	100%	100%	100%

(Source: 1952 post, Q. 22d, deck 7; 1956 post, Q. 17d, deck 7; 1960 post, Q. 24f, deck 9; 1962, Q. 44d, deck 14; 1964 post, Q. 24e, deck 11.)

5. Do you belong to any political clubs or organizations?

		1952	1956	1960	1962	1964
1.	Yes	2%	3%	3%	4%	4%
5.	No	98	97	97	96	96
9.	DK	0	0	0	0	0
		100%	100%	100%	100%	100%

(Source: 1952 post, Q. 22e, deck 7; 1956 post, Q. 17e, deck 7; 1960 post, Q. 24g, deck 9; 1962, Q. 44e, deck 14; 1964 post Q. 24f, deck 11.)

6. Did you wear a campaign button or put a campaign sticker on your car?

		1952	1956	1960	1962	1964
1.	Yes	-	16%	21%	10%	16%
5.	No	-	84	79	90	84
9.	DK	-	0	0	0	0
			100%	100%	100%	100%

(Source: 1956 post, Q. 17f, deck 7; 1960 post, Q. 24h, deck 9; 1962, Q. 44f, deck 14; 1964 post, Q. 24g, deck 11.)

7. Have you ever written to any public officials giving them your opinion about
    something that should be done?

                                                 1964

    1. Yes   17%

    5. No, never   83

                                                100%

    (Source: 1964 post, Q. 25, deck 11.)

8. Have you ever written a letter to the editor of a newspaper or magazine giving
    any political opinions?

                                                 1964

    1. Yes   3%

    5. No, never   97

                                                100%

    (Source: 1964 post, Q. 26, deck 11.)

9. Did you yourself ask anyone else to give money to help pay the costs of the
    campaign of a candidate or a political party this year?

                                                 1964

    1. Yes   2%

    5. No   98

                                                100%

    (Source: 1964 post, Q. 31, deck 11.)

CITIZEN COMPETENCE

1. If you had some trouble with the police - a traffic violation maybe, or being accused of a minor offense - do you think that most likely you would be given a <u>harder time</u> than other people, would be treated about <u>the same</u> as anyone else, or would be treated a <u>little better</u> than most people?

		1966
1.	Better	3%
3.	Same	87
5.	Harder time	3
7.	Depends	2
8.	DK	5
		100%

(Source: 1966, Q. C56, deck 5.)

2. Do you think you would be better off in this situation if you went to an elected official and had him talk to the police for you, or wouldn't that make any difference, or would that make things worse? (IF BETTER OFF) How much good do you think that would do: <u>very much</u>, <u>some</u>, or <u>not very much</u>?

		1966
1.	Better off - very much good	6%
2.	Better off - some good	9
3.	Better off - not very much good	1
4.	Better off - depends; DK or NA good	1
5.	No difference	58
6.	Worse	10
7.	Depends	4
8.	DK	10
0.	Rejects Q.; "wouldn't do such a thing"	1
		100%

(Source: 1966, Q. C57-C57a, deck 5.)

3. Suppose there were some question that you had to take to government office - for example, a tax question or a housing regulation. Do you think that most likely you would be given a <u>harder time</u> than other people, would be treated about <u>the same</u> as anyone else, or would be treated <u>a little better</u> than most people?

	1966
1. Better	3%
3. Same	88
5. Harder time	2
7. Depends	2
8. DK	5
	100%

(Source: 1966, Q. C58, deck 5.)

4. Do you think you would be better off in this situation if you went to an elected official and had him talk to the people in the government office for you, or wouldn't that make any difference, or would that make things worse? (IF BETTER OFF) How much good do you think that would do: <u>very much</u>, <u>some</u>, or <u>not very much</u>?

	1966
1. Better off - very much good	6%
2. Better off - some good	17
3. Better off - not very much good	1
4. Better off - depends; DK or NA how much good	2
5. No difference	58
6. Worse	3
7. Depends	4
8. DK	9
0. Rejects Q.; "wouldn't do such a thing"	*
	100%

(Source: 1966, Q. C59-C59a, deck 5.)

5. Suppose a regulation were being considered by (SPECIFY MOST LOCAL GOVERNMENT UNIT: CITY, TOWN, VILLAGE, TOWNSHIP, ETC.) that you considered very unjust or harmful...
If you made an effort to change this regulation, how likely is it that you would succeed: <u>very likely</u>, <u>somewhat likely</u>, or <u>not very likely</u>?

		1966
1.	Very likely	8%
3.	Somewhat likely	30
5.	Not very likely	42
7.	Depends	11
8.	DK	9
		100%

(Source: 1966, Q. C60-C61, deck 5.)

6. If such a case arose, how likely is it that you would actually try to do something about it: <u>very likely</u>, <u>somewhat likely</u>, or <u>not very likely</u>?

		1966
1.	Very likely	26%
3.	Somewhat likely	28
5.	Not very likely	36
7.	Depends	6
8.	DK	4
		100%

(Source: 1966, Q. C62, deck 5.)

7. Have you ever done anything to try to influence a local decision? (IF NECES-
    SARY) What was that?

	1966		
	First	Second	Third
1. Yes, worked through informal groups; talked to neighbors, friends to get them to take action	8%	8%	2%
2. Yes, worked through political party or formal, organized groups	2	*	*
3. Yes, as an individual, contacted representatives, officials, mass media; used vote, legal means	8	2	*
4. Yes, took part in demonstrations, or other visible means of protest	*	*	*
5. No, never tried to influence a local decision	76	5	--
7. Yes, other; yes, NA what R did	6	*	--
8. DK	*	--	--

100%

(Source: 1966, Q. C63-C63a, deck 5.)

8. Now, suppose a law were being considered by Congress in Washington that you
    considered to be very unjust or harmful... If you made an effort to change
    this law, how likely is it that you would succeed: very likely, somewhat
    likely, or not very likely?

	1966
1. Very likely	3%
3. Somewhat likely	21
5. Not very likely	58
7. Depends	9
8. DK	9

100%

(Source: 1966, Q. C64-C65, deck 5.)

9. If such a case arose, how likely is it that you would actually try to do something about it: very likely, somewhat likely, or not very likely?

		1966
1.	Very likely	19%
3.	Somewhat likely	26
5.	Not very likely	45
7.	Depends	6
8.	DK	4
		100%

(Source: 1966, Q. C66, deck 5.)

10. Have you ever done anything to try to influence an act of Congress: (IF NECESSARY) What was that?

		1966		
		First	Second	Third
1.	Yes, worked through informal groups; talked to neighbors, friends to get them to take action	2%	*	*
2.	Yes, worked through political party or formal, organized groups	1	*	0
3.	Yes, as an individual, contacted representatives, officials, mass media; used vote, legal means	9	*	0
4.	Yes, took part in demonstrations, or other visible means of protest	*	*	0
5.	No, never tried to influence an act of Congress	84	94	0
7.	Yes, other; yes, NA what R did	2	*	0
8.	DK	*	--	0
		100%		

(Source: 1966, Q. C67-C67a, deck 5.)

VOTING ITEMS

1. In talking to people about the election we find that a lot of people weren't able to vote because they weren't registered or they were sick or they just didn't have time. How about you, did you vote this time? (or did something keep you from voting? - 1964, 1966)

		1952	1956	1958	1960	1962	1964	1966
1.	Voted	73%	73%	57%	74%	60%	78%	62%
5.	Did not vote	27	27	42	26	40	22	38
+.	Voted, but not for president	-	*	-	-	-	*	-
-.	DK, NA if voted	0	0	1	-	*	0	*
		100%	100%	100%	100%	100%	100%	100%

(Source: 1952 post, Q. 7, deck 7; 1956 post, Q. 7, deck 7; 1958, Q. 37, deck 4; 1960 post, Q. 12, deck 8; 1962, Q. 40, deck 14; 1964 post, Q. 6, deck 10; 1966, Q. C17, deck 3.)

** Recoded version of original variable

2. Now, how about the election this November? Do you know if you are (registered) (eligible to vote) so that you could vote in the November election if you wanted to? (if necessary) are you (registered) (eligible) to vote?

		1956	1960	1964
1.	Yes, definitely or without qualifications	75%	78%	82%
2.	Yes, qualified; I think so	2	2	2
3.	Not registered, but intend to register	5	3	3
4.	No, qualified; I don't think so	1	1	1
5.	No, definitely or without qualifications	16	15	12
9.	DK	1	1	*
		100%	100%	100%

	1952
1. Yes, registered or eligible to vote	76%
4. No, but R can still register in his state	7
5. No, and R can <u>no</u> longer register in his state	16
9. DK	1
	100%

(Source: 1952, Q. 34-34a, deck 4; 1956, Q. 28-28a, deck 4; 1960, Q. 41-41a, deck 5; 1964, Q. 60-60a, deck 6.)

3. So far as you know now, do you expect to vote in November or not?

	1952	1956	1960	1964
1. Yes, definitely	9%	10%	8%	8%
2. Yes	66	66	71	73
3. Yes, qualified (I guess so, think so, probably will)	3	4	4	3
4. Pro-con, depends (I may, I might)	1	1	1	1
5. No, qualified (probably not; I might but probably won't)	1	2	1	1
6. No	16	10	11	10
7. No, definitely	3	5	3	3
9. DK	1	2	1	1
	100%	100%	100%	100%

(Source: 1952, Q. 35, deck 4; 1956, Q. 29, deck 4; 1960 Q. 42, deck 5; 1964, Q. 61, deck 6.)

4. Now in (last presidential election year) you remember that (Democratic presidential candidate) ran on the Democratic ticket against (Republican presidential candidate) for the Republicans. Do you remember for sure whether or not you voted in that election?

		1952	1956	1958	1960	1962	1964	1966
1.	Voted	64%	70%	73%	74%	74%	73%	73%
5.	Did not vote	34	28	26	24	25	26	26
7.	Did not vote because not old enough to vote before or not a citizen before - resident of Washington, D.C.	-	-	-	-	-	-	-
8.	DK	2	2	1	2	1	1	1
9.	Refused to say	-	*	0	0	*	0	0
		100%	100%	100%	100%	100%	100%	100%

(Source: 1952, Q. 33, deck 4; 1956, Q. 26, deck 4; 1958, Q. 35, deck 4; **
1960, Q. 39, deck 5; 1962, Q. 37, deck 14; 1964, Q. 58, deck 6; 1966, Q. C10c, deck 2.)

** Recoded version of original variable

5. In the elections for president since you have been old enough to vote, would you say you have voted in all of them, most of them, some of them, or none of them?

		1952	1956	1958	1960	1962	1964	1966
1.	All of them	43%	42%	45%	46%	48%	50%	49%
2.	Most of them	19	22	22	24	21	18	21
3.	Some of them	16	16	17	15	16	14	16
5.	None of them	16	15	14	14	13	10	10
6.	Voted, NA how many	*	0	0	0	0	0	0
7.	None of them because not old enough to vote before or not a citizen before; resident of Washington, D.C.	6	5	2	1	2	8	4
9.	DK	*	0	0	0	*	0	0
		100%	100%	100%	100%	100%	100%	100%

(Source: 1952, Q. 30, deck 4; 1956, Q. 23, deck 4; 1958, Q. 33, deck 4; 1960, Q. 37, deck 5; 1962, Q. 35, deck 14; 1964, Q. 56, deck 6; 1966, Q. C10, deck 2.)

6. Some districts choose candidates for Congress in a primary election. Others do it different ways. Was there a primary election in this district earlier this year? (IF YES) We find that a lot of people don't pay much attention to primary elections. Do you remember whether or not you voted in the primary election for Congressman this year?

	1958
1. Yes, definitely	28%
3. Yes, think so	*
5. No, did not vote	70
9. DK, not sure	2
	100%

(Source: 1958, Q. 45-45a, deck 4.)

7. ** As you know, most candidates for Congress or governor or other offices are nominated in a party primary election. Have you ever voted in a primary election?

	1964
1. Yes, have voted	63%
5. No, have not voted	33
8. DK	4
	100%

(Source: 1964, Q. 64, deck 6.)

**Recoded version of original variable

**
8. How about the primary election this year? Did you vote in a primary election this past spring or summer?

	1966
1. Yes	41%
5. No	59
8. DK	*
	100%

(Source: 1966, Q. C11, deck 2.)

** Recoded version of original variable

MASS MEDIA ITEMS

1. We're interested in this interview in finding out whether people paid much
    attention to the election campaign this year. Take newspapers, for instance –
    did you read about the campaign in any newspaper?

		1952	1956	1960	1964
1.	Yes	79%	69%	80%	79%
5.	No	21	31	20	21
8.	DK	0	*	*	*
		100%	100%	100%	100%

1a. (IF YES) Would you say you read quite a lot, or not very much?

		1952
1.	Yes, quite a lot, pretty much	39%
2.	Yes, not very much	40
3.	Yes, NA how much	*
5.	No	21
9.	DK	0
		100%

(Source: 1952 post, Q. 2, 2a, deck 7; 1956 post, Q. 1, deck 7; 1960 post,
Q. 1, 6, deck 8; 1964 post, Q. 1, 1b, deck 10.)

1b. How much did you read newspaper articles about the election – regularly, often,
     from time to time, or just once in a great while?

		1960	1964
1.	Yes, regularly	43%	40%
2.	Yes, often	12	14
3.	Yes, from time to time	16	18
4.	Yes, once in a great while	7	6
5.	No, read no newspapers about the campaign	20	21
7.	Yes, NA frequency	2	1
8.	DK	*	*
		100%	100%

2. How about radio - did you listen to any speeches or discussions about the campaign on the radio?

		1952	1956	1960	1964
1.	Yes	70%	45%	42%	48%
5.	No	30	55	58	52
8.	DK	0	*	*	*
		100%	100%	100%	100%

2a. (IF YES) Would you say you listened quite a lot, or not very much?

		1952
1.	Yes, quite a lot, pretty much	35%
2.	Yes, not very much	35
3.	Yes, NA how much	*
5.	No	30
9.	DK	0
		100%

2b. (IF YES) How many programs about the campaign did you listen to on the radio - a good many, several, or just one or two?

		1960	1964
1.	Yes, good many	14%	13%
2.	Yes, several	17	23
3.	Yes, just one or two	10	12
4.	Yes, NA frequency	1	*
5.	No	58	52
8.	DK	*	*
		100%	100%

(Source: 1952 post, Q. 3, 3a, deck 7; 1956 post, Q. 2, deck 7; 1960 post, Q. 2, 7, deck 8; 1964 post, Q. 2, 2a, deck 10.)

3. How about magazines - did you read about the campaign in any magazines?

		1952	1956	1960	1964
1.	Yes	40%	31%	41%	39%
5.	No	60	69	59	61
8.	DK	0	*	*	*
		100%	100%	100%	100%

3a. (IF YES) Would you say you read quite a lot, or not very much?

		1952
1.	Yes, quite a lot, pretty much	14%
2.	Yes, not very much	26
3.	Yes, NA how much	*
5.	No	60
9.	DK	0
		100%

3b. (IF YES) How many magazine articles about the campaign would you say you read - a good many, several, or just one or two?

		1960	1964
1.	Yes, a good many	12%	10%
2.	Yes, several	15	16
3.	Yes, just one or two	13	13
4.	Yes, NA frequency	1	*
5.	No	59	61
8.	DK	*	*
		100%	100%

(Source: 1952 post, Q. 5, 5a, deck 7; 1956 post, Q. 4, deck 7; 1960 post, Q. 4, 8, deck 8; 1964 post, Q. 3, 3a, deck 10.)

4. How about television - did you watch any programs about the campaign on television?

		1952	1956	1960	1964
1.	Yes	51%	74%	87%	89%
5.	No	49	26	13	11
8.	DK	0	*	*	*
		100%	100%	100%	100%

4a. (IF YES) Would you say you watched quite a lot, or not very much?

		1952
1.	Yes, quite a lot, pretty much	32%
2.	Yes, not very much	19
3.	Yes, NA how much	*
5.	No	49
9.	DK	0
		100%

4b. (IF YES) How many television programs about the campaign would you say you watched - a good many, several, or just one or two?

		1960	1964
1.	Yes, a good many	47%	42%
2.	Yes, several	29	34
3.	Yes, just one or two	11	13
4.	Yes, NA frequency	*	*
5.	No	13	11
8.	DK	*	*
		100%	100%

(Source: 1952 post, Q. 4, 4a, deck 7; 1956 post, Q. 3, deck 7; 1960 post Q. 3, 9, deck 8; 1964 post, Q. 4, 4a, deck 10.)

5. (IF YES to two or more of questions 10-13) Of all these ways of following the campaign, which one would you say you got the most information from - newspapers, radio, television or magazines?

		1952	1956	1960	1964
1.	Newspapers	23%	24%	23%	25%
2.	Radio	28	11	5	4
3.	Television	32	49	60	58
4.	Magazines	5	5	4	7
5.	Newspapers and Radio	2	1	*	*
6.	Newspapers and Television	1	1	2	2
7.	Radio and Television	1	*	*	*
8.	Magazines and Newspapers or Radio or Television	1	*	1	1
+.	Any other combination	*	*	*	*
9.	DK	*	0	*	*
0.	Inap., R did not follow campaign on any medium	7	9	5	3
		100%	100%	100%	100%

(Source: 1952 post, Q. 6, deck 7; 1956 post, Q. 5, deck 7; 1960 post, Q. 5, deck 8; 1964 post, Q. 5, deck 10.)

5a. We're also interested in finding out how people got information about the election campaign this year. Would you say you got most of your information from newspapers, radio, television, or magazines?

		1966
10.	Newspapers	28%
20.	Radio	8
30.	Television	44
40.	Magazines	3
51.	Newspapers and Radio	1
52.	Newspapers and Television	8
54.	Radio and television	1

			1966
5a.	59.	Magazines and any other medium, NA which	0
	--.	Any other combination	3
	98.	DK	2
	91.	(And 80) Inap., R did not follow campaign on any medium	2
			100%

(Source: 1966, Q. C3, deck 2.)

622

POLITICAL INFORMATION ITEMS

1. Do you happen to know which party had the most Congressmen in Washington before the election (this) (last) month? (IF YES) Which one?

	1958 % total	1958 (% with opinion)	1960 % total	1960 (% with opinion)	1964 % total	1964 (% with opinion)	1966 % total	1966 (% with opinion)
1. Yes, Democrats	47%	72%	64%	92%	64%	90%	69%	96%
2. Yes, Republicans	19	28	5	8	7	10	3	4
5. Inap., No DK	34	--	31	--	29	--	28	--
	100%	100%	100%	100%	100%	100%	100%	100%

(Source: 1960 post, Q. 28-28a, deck 9; 1964 post, Q. 19-19a, deck 11; 1966, Q. C15, deck 3.)

2. Do you happen to know which party elected the most Congressmen in the elections (this) (past) month? (IF YES) Which one?

	1958 % total	1958 (% with opinion)	1960 % total	1960 (% with opinion)	1964 % total	1964 (% with opinion)	1966 % total	1966 (% with opinion)
1. Yes, Democrats	78%	98%	55%	88%	79%	99%	21%	32%
2. Yes, Republicans	1	2	8	12	1	1	44	68
5. Inap., No, DK	21	--	37	--	20	--	35	--
	100%	100%	100%	100%	100%	100%	100%	100%

(Source: 1958, Q. 10-10a, deck ; 1960 post, Q. 29-29a, deck 9; 1964 post, Q. 20-20a, deck 11; 1966, Q. C16, deck 3.)

3. Do you happen to remember the name(s) of the candidate(s) for Congress that ran in this district this November?

	1964	1966
1. No correct mentions	47%	62%
2. One correct mention	26	18
3. Two correct mentions	25	20
4. Three correct mentions**	1	*
5. Four correct mentions**	1	*
	100%	100%

3. (Source: 1964 post, Q. 21, deck 11; 1966, Q. C13, deck 2.)

   ** Concerns states having more than one congressional race in the district (at-large contests, etc.)

4. Do you happen to know (if either one of these candidates) (if he) is already in Congress? (R has previously been told the name of the (D) and (R) congressional candidates if he did not know their names in response to an earlier question.)

		1964	1966
1.	Yes - correct candidate	63%	55%
2.	Yes - incorrect candidate	2	4
3.	Yes - NA which	*	3
5.	Neither - correct answer	3	3
6.	Neither - incorrect answer	1	1
7.	Other	1	--
8.	DK	30	34
		100%	100%

(Source: 1964 post, Q. 23, deck 11; 1966, Q. C14, deck 3.)

POLITICAL INTEREST ITEMS

1. We'd also like to know how much attention you pay to what's going on in politics generally. I mean from day to day, when there isn't any big election campaign going on. Would you say you follow politics very closely, fairly closely, or not much at all?

		1960	1962
1.	Very closely	21%	16%
3.	Fairly closely	42	42
5.	Not much at all	37	42
9.	DK	0	0
		100%	100%

(Source: 1960 post, Q. 27, deck 9; 1962, Q. 39, deck 14.)

2. Some people seem to think about what's going on in government all the time, whether there's an election going on or not. Others aren't that interested. Would you say you follow what's going on in government: **

	1964			1966	
1. All the time	30%		1. Most of the time	35%
2. Some of the time	42		2. Some of the time	30
3. Only now and then	17		3. Only now and then	18
4. Hardly at all	11		4. Hardly at all	17
5. Never	0		8. DK	0
	100%			100%

(Source: 1964 post, Q. 28, deck 11; 1966, Q. C2, deck 2.)

** Slightly reworded question used in 1966.

3. Some people don't pay much attention to the political campaigns. How about you? Would you say that you have been very much interested, somewhat interested, or not very much interested in following the political campaigns so far this year?**

		1952	1956	1958	1960	1962	1964	1966
1.	Very much interested	37%	30%	26%	38%	36%	38%	30%
3.	Somewhat interested	34	39	33	37	38	37	40
5.	Not much interested	29	31	41	25	26	25	30
8.	DK	*	*	0	0	0	*	0
		100%	100%	100%	100%	100%	100%	100%

(Source: 1952, Q. 20, deck 3; 1956, Q. 27, deck 4; 1958, Q. 36, deck 4; 1960, Q. 40, deck 5; 1962, Q. 38, deck 14; 1964, Q. 59, deck 6; 1966, Q. C12, deck 2.)

** Question slightly reworded to reflect the past tense in the post-election schedules of congressional year studies.

4. Some people don't pay too much attention to election campaigns. How about you - were you very interested in this campaign, fairly interested, just slightly interested, or not interested at all in it?

		1960	1964
1.	Very interested	60%	41%
2.	Fairly interested	25	36
4.	Slightly interested	10	18
5.	Not at all interested	5	5
9.	DK	0	0
		100%	100%

(Source: 1960 post, Q. 26, deck 9; 1964 post, Q. 27, deck 11.)

ATTITUDES TOWARD THE POLITICAL SYSTEM

This section deals with the citizen's feelings of efficacy, competence, and duty in the political system and the corresponding responsiveness he sees government displaying toward his and others' actions. In short, SRC is studying some of the basic elements of democratic theory as seen through the eyes of the respondent--the extent to which the voter feels that his political actions are effective and important in making government consider "the will of the people."

In each presidential election study, four items on political efficacy have been asked which meet the common criteria of a Guttman scale. A "disagree" response to each item*is coded as "politically efficacious." (See Chapter 12 for a more complete description of this scale as well as some of the others we shall be discussing in this section.) As one can readily observe, two items reveal such "efficacious" feelings on the part of the electorate and two do not. The first and fourth items belong in the former category--people obviously believe that they have some say about what the government does and that public officials do care about what they think. Agreement with the middle two items reflects the reverse of efficacy--people do not feel that there are other ways besides voting that can influence governmental policy nor do they regard politics as simple enough to be easily understood. The belief behind the responses to the voting item is especially important--it indicates that for a large number of people the meaning of political democracy starts and ends at the polling booth, certainly a very restricted meaning for this term.

A survey of responses to these questions over time reveals that there was some increase in the proportion of people who felt effective in politics

---

*This item format, open to distortion due to agreement response set, was not changed in 1964.

from 1952 through 1960, but that this trend was reversed, as a general rule, in 1964 and 1966. The political efficacy items in 1966 especially showed declines from the scores of earlier years. The changing of response categories in 1966 to a more Likert-type format, however, should not affect the trend in the data to any real extent, indicating that the distributions observed were the result of real attitude changes among the samples being studied.

The fact that the political efficacy items form a satisfactory Guttman scale suggests that they generally have substantial intercorrelation values. Such is the case in each election study, although the correlation figures for comparable items across election years have by no means been uniform in value. For instance, the item stating that "voting is the only way people like me can have a say in how the government is run" shows low intercorrelations with the other items in the early studies but has produced stronger correlations in the more recent ones. The items when formed into a scale also correlate fairly well with expected political behavior patterns. In 1964, for example, there was a correlation of .25 between this scale and the index of political participation, suggesting that psychological feelings of effectiveness and competence help to determine whether a citizen participates in the democratic process and, in effect, whether the process can claim to be democratic at all.

The political efficacy scale shows a pattern of correlations with background variables which is similar to that exhibited by the SRC's measure of reported political activity. This should be the case since the efficacy and activity measures are themselves related. Persons with higher education and income have higher scores on both measures, whereas Negroes, rural residents, older people, and Democratic Party identifiers do not. On the efficacy scale, women tend to give less efficacious responses than men, especially to the item dealing with the complexity of politics, as might be expected. In contrast,

TABLE 1: CORRELATION OF POLITICAL SYSTEM ATTITUDES WITH BACKGROUND VARIABLES

	Sex	Race	Education	Income	Age	Community Size	Party Identification	Actual Vote
1952 No Say	-.08	-.11	.25	.20	-.09	-.07	.08	.09
1952 Voting only way	-.03	.00	.20	.14	-.08	.00	.05	.06
1952 Politics complicated	-.17	-.05	.29	.26	-.04	-.09	.12	.01
1952 Officials don't care	-.05	-.09	.29	.23	-.13	-.10	.07	.04
1956 No say	-.09	-.15	.36	.27	-.10	.01	.15	.04
1956 Voting only way	-.08	-.07	.30	.22	-.12	-.03	.07	.06
1956 Politics complicated	-.14	-.09	.33	.26	-.03	-.08	.08	.01
1956 Officials don't care	.00	-.12	.34	.27	-.12	-.02	.15	.07
1958 Government waste ⎫ Trust in Gov. scale	-.01	-.02	.06	.03	-.06	-.04	.06	NA
1958 Trust government								
1958 Government crooked								
1958 Government smart ⎭								
1960 No say ⎫ Pol. Effi-cacy Scale	-.02	-.08	.28	.18	-.11	.01	.14	.17
1960 Voting only way	-.03	-.09	.24	.16	-.12	-.02	.12	.14
1960 Politics complicated	-.12	-.04	.23	.19	.01	-.07	.11	.10
1960 Officials don't care ⎭	-.05	-.08	.26	.20	-.11	-.06	.11	.08
1964 No say ⎫ Pol. Effi-cacy Scale	-.07	-.08	.43	.31	-.16	-.07	.09	-.01
1964 Voting only way								
1964 Politics complicated								
1964 Officials don't care ⎭								
1964 Government waste ⎫ Trust in Gov. Scale								
1964 Trust government								
1964 Government crooked	-.01	-.06	.01	.02	-.11	.01	.20	.30
1964 Government smart								
1964 Government for the big ⎭								
1964 Government att'n to people ⎫ Gov. Respon-siveness Scale								
1964 Government att'n to parties	-.01	.04	.18	.17	-.12	.02	-.10	-.17
1964 Government att'n to election								
1964 Government att'n to electors ⎭								

Note: Values in the table are Pearson product-moment correlation coefficients. Correlations were computed from the standard SRC code systems for these variables unless otherwise noted in the text.

NA--no data available

TABLE 2: INTERCORRELATION OF ATTITUDES TOWARD THE POLITICAL SYSTEM

	NS	VO	PC	OD
1952 No say	X			
1952 Voting only way	.01	X		
1952 Politics complicated	.26	.13	X	
1952 Officials don't care	.41	.06	.25	X

	NS	VO	PC	GS
1956 No say	X			
1956 Voting only way	.20	X		
1956 Politics complicated	.34	.15	X	
1956 Government smart	.28	.30	.27	X

	GW	TG	GC	GS
1958 Government waste	X			
1958 Trust government	.29	X		
1958 Government crooked	.36	.30	X	
1958 Government smart	.28	.30	.27	X

	NS	VO	PC	OD
1960 No say	X			
1960 Voting only way	.19	X		
1960 Politics complicated	.27	.15	X	
1960 Officials don't care	.43	.03	.28	X

	NS	VO	PC	OD
1964 No say	X			
1964 Voting only way	.20	X		
1964 Politics complicated	.26	.23	X	
1964 Officials don't care	.44	.19	.25	X

Table 2 (continued)

	GW	TG	GC	GS	GB
1964 Government waste	X				
1964 Trust government	.30	X			
1964 Government crooked	.39	.34	X		
1964 Government smart	.28	.32	.26	X	
1964 Government for the big	.34	.41	.35	.40	X

	PE	PA	EL	EL
1964 Government att'n to people	X			
1964 Government att'n to parties	.46	X		
1964 Government att'n to elections	.36	.47	X	
1964 Government att'n to electors	.37	.37	.35	X

Note: Values in the table are Pearson product-moment correlation coefficients (except in 1964 where tau-beta is used). Correlations were computed from the standard SRC code systems for these variables unless otherwise noted in the text.

this same item apparently was the only one on which Negroes and the elderly did not express less efficacy than their counterparts, the whites and younger people.

Another belief or feeling which (according to many political theorists) is necessary for a stable democratic polity is one of "citizen duty," "citizen-mindedness," or the like--a feeling that it is one's responsibility to participate in the political process, regardless of whether such activity is seen as efficacious or not. Four items on the subject of civic obligation were asked in the 1952, 1956, and 1960 studies, the items fulfilling the common criteria of a Guttman scale. A "disagree" response to any item was coded as expressing sentiments of citizen duty and civic obligation (as noted in Chapter 12 where a complete description of this scale is presented).

The distribution of opinions on the four items revealed a clear and consistent pattern. The first three items indicated an overwhelming feeling of citizen obligation, with the fourth showing at least majority support for this position. Furthermore, feelings of citizen duty appeared to monotonically increase over the years (even if this increase was slight due to the percentage ceiling imposed by the initial responses to these items in 1952). Undoubtedly, some distortion of "true opinion" underlies responses to these items since many people would want to give the "right" or "proper" answer (to cast themselves in a favorable light). However, there are many indications that the scale was tapping a real dimension of meaning for many people--the customary socio-economic correlates are evident (as will be seen below) and the scale is related to the SRC measure of political activity.

The socio-economic correlates, though not shown in the accompanying correlation table, follow lines substantially similar to those found with the political efficacy scale. Education, income, occupation, and race are related

to sense of civic obligation. Region and type of community relationships
are also evident. The associations of the scale with the sex and age variables, however, are much lower; they virtually disappear in some cases.

Important criteria for a democratic system are feelings of civic duty
and political efficacy among the electorate. But another important element
is needed--the feeling that the government must be responsive to the needs
and demands of the people (or at least appear to be so). In 1964, SRC
attempted to find out if this was indeed the feeling of the people. Four
separate questions were asked, and all revealed basic optimism of respondents
on this item. Government was seen as responsive "a good deal" or "somewhat"
to the people and to the presumed instruments of their will--political parties
and the electoral process. The number of people taking the optimistic position
on these questions ranged from 70 to 90 percent. This finding corresponds
fairly well with the 1964 data on political efficacy, although there was some
decline in the positive response to this latter measure in that particular
year.

The four items on "government responsiveness" were strongly enough
intercorrelated in 1964 to indicate their basic unidimensionality. Party
differences related well to the scale developed from these items, casting
the Republicans in the role of seeing government as less responsive to the
people than the Democrats. Obviously, the fact that Republicans were not in
power affects this relation as well as the differing images of the two parties
with regard to the extent of governmental intervention into socio-economic
life they support. However, the scale showed many people with a high education
and income level believing the government to be responsive to the populace.
The people most likely to react against this belief in government responsiveness
were the older generations.

Other questions have been asked about the respondent's feelings toward his government. In 1958, 1964, and 1966, selected questions probed for deeper feelings than those of governmental responsiveness and responsibility--ones concerned with the worth, integrity, and honesty of the government. The attitude distributions of these questions within each year pointed to a general, though moderate, support of the government and its ethics (with a few exceptions). Comparing the distributions across time reveals that more people were trustful of government in 1958 than in 1964 and in 1964 than in 1966, although the differences are negligible in many cases. This pattern coincides with that of the political efficacy items. To the extent that the differences observed are meaningful, common conditions or events could be said to be causing people to be less trustful of the government (and how it is run) and also less sure of their own effectiveness in influencing the course of governmental actions.

Some of the questions in the 1958 and 1964 studies were used to construct a "trust in government" (or "cynicism") scale. As one can note from the correlation table, the inter-item correlation values seem to justify treating the questions as essentially unidimensional in nature. There were few background correlates to this scale. Republicans were less trusting of government than Democrats in 1964, and the reverse was true in 1958. It would appear that trust in government is related to whether or not one's party candidate is in office. The only other demographic factor which related consistently to trust in government was age, with older people being less trusting in this respect than younger people.

Significant intercorrelations were also observed among three of the measures considered in this section. The measures of political efficacy, governmental responsiveness, and trust in government were related among the 1964 electorate in the direction one would suspect. It was found that politically efficacious respondents tended to have a higher trust in government and were more likely to feel that the government was responsive to the needs and opinions of the people. One of the criteria of democracy would be that there be a large proportion of such people with respect to those who placed low on these scales. A large segment of cynical people who did not feel that their demands were being considered by government could either withdraw from the political system entirely or revolt against it. In either case, democracy would be the loser.

POLITICAL EFFICACY ITEMS

Now I'd like to read some of the kinds of things people tell us when we interview them and ask you whether you agree or disagree with them. I'll read them one at a time and you just tell me whether you agree or disagree.

1. People like me don't have any say about what the government does.

	1952	1956	1960	1964
1. Agree	31%	28%	27%	29%
5. Disagree	68	71	72	70
9. DK (depends)	1	1	1	1
	100%	100%	100%	100%

(Source: 1952, Q. 47g, deck 5; 1956, Q. 32a, deck 4; 1960, Q. 45a, deck 5; 1964, Q. 65a, deck 6.)

2. Voting is the only way that people like me can have a say about how the government runs things.

	1952	1956	1960	1964
1. Agree	81%	73%	73%	73%
5. Disagree	17	25	25	26
9. DK (depends)	2	2	2	1
	100%	100%	100%	100%

(Source: 1952, Q. 47d, deck 5; 1956, Q. 32b, deck 4; 1960, Q. 45b, deck 5; 1964, Q. 65b, deck 6.)

3. Sometimes politics and government seem so complicated that a person like me can't really understand what's going on.

	1952	1956	1960	1964
1. Agree	71%	64%	59%	67%
5. Disagree	28	36	41	32
9. DK (depends)	1	*	*	1
	100%	100%	100%	100%

(Source: 1952, Q. 47i, deck 5; 1956, Q. 32e, deck 4; 1960, Q. 45e, deck 5; 1964, Q. 65c, deck 6.)

4. I don't think public officials care much what people like me think.

	1952	1956	1960	1964
1. Agree	35%	27%	25%	37%
5. Disagree	63	71	73	61
9. DK (depends)	2	2	2	2
	100%	100%	100%	100%

(Source: 1952, Q. 47b, deck 5; 1956, Q. 32h, deck 4; 1960, Q. 45h, deck 5; 1964, Q. 65d, deck 6.)

In the 1966 questionnaire, the responses to these items were captured on a five-point Likert-type scale.

Now I'd like to read some of the kinds of things people tell us when we interview them and ask you whether you agree or disagree with them. I'll read them one at a time and you tell me whether you strongly agree, agree, disagree, or strongly disagree.

5. People like me don't have any say about what the government does.

	1966
1. Strongly agree	8%
2. Agree	26
3. Not sure, it depends	5
4. Disagree	48
5. Strongly disagree	12
8. DK	1
	100%

(Source: 1966, Q. C22, deck 3.)

6. Voting is the only way that people like me can have any say about how the government runs things.

		1966
1.	Strongly agree	16%
2.	Agree	53
3.	Not sure, it depends	4
4.	Disagree	23
5.	Strongly disagree	3
8.	DK	1
		100%

(Source: 1966, C23, deck 3.)

7. Sometimes politics and government seem so complicated that a person like me can't really understand what's going on.

		1966
1.	Strongly agree	19%
2.	Agree	51
3.	Not sure, it depends	4
4.	Disagree	22
5.	Strongly disagree	4
8.	DK	*
		100%

(Source: 1966, Q. C24, deck 3.)

638

8. I don't think public officials care much what people like me think.

	1966
1. Strongly agree	9%
2. Agree	26
3. Not sure, it depends	8
4. Disagree	48
5. Strongly disagree	8
8. DK	1
	100%

(Source: 1966, Q. C25, deck 3.)

CITIZEN DUTY ITEMS

Now I'd like to read some of the kinds of things people tell me when I interview them and ask you whether you agree or disagree with them. I'll read them one at a time and you just tell me whether you agree or disagree.

1. It isn't so important to vote when you know your party doesn't have any chance to win.

	1952	1956	1960
1. Agree	11%	9%	7%
5. Disagree	88	90	92
9. DK	1	1	1
	100%	100%	100%

    (Source: 1952, Q. 47a, deck 5; 1956, Q. 32c, deck 4; 1960, Q. 45c, deck 5.)

2. A good many local elections aren't important enough to bother with.

	1952	1956	1960
1. Agree	18%	14%	12%
5. Disagree	81	85	87
9. DK	1	1	1
	100%	100%	100%

    (Source: 1952, Q. 47e, deck 5; 1956, Q. 32g, deck 4; 1960, Q. 45g, deck 5.)

3. So many other people vote in the national elections that it doesn't matter much to me whether I vote or not.

	1952	1956	1960
1. Agree	12%	10%	8%
5. Disagree	87	89	91
9. DK	1	1	1
	100%	100%	100%

    (Source: 1952, Q. 47f, deck 5; 1956, Q. 32d, deck 4; 1960, Q. 45d, deck 5.)

4. If a person doesn't care how an election comes out he shouldn't vote in it.

		1952	1956	1960
1.	Agree	53%	46%	44%
5.	Disagree	46	53	55
9.	DK	1	1	1
		100%	100%	100%

(Source: 1952, Q. 47h, deck 5; 1956, Q. 32f, deck 4; 1960, Q. 45f, deck 5.)

GOVERNMENT RESPONSIVENESS

1. Over the years, how much attention do you feel the government pays to what
    the people think when it decides what to do, a:

	1964
1. Good deal	32%
3. Some	38
5. Not much	24
8. DK	6
	100%

    (Source: 1964 post, Q. 51, deck 13.)

2. How much do you feel that political parties help to make the government pay
    attention to what the people think, a:

	1964
1. Good deal	41%
3. Some	39
5. Not much	13
8. DK	7
	100%

    (Source: 1964 post, Q. 52, deck 13.)

3. And how much do you feel that having elections makes the government pay atten-
    tion to what the people think, a:

	1964
1. Good deal	65%
3. Some	25
5. Not much	6
8. DK	4
	100%

    (Source: 1964 post, Q. 53, deck 13.)

4. How much attention do you think most Congressmen pay to the people who elect
    them, when they decide what to do in Congress, a:

	1964
1. Good deal	42%
3. Some	38
5. Not much	15
8. DK	5
	100%

    (Source: 1964 post, Q. 54, deck 13.)

ATTITUDE TOWARD GOVERNMENT ITEMS

Now I'd like to talk about some of the different ideas people have about the government in Washington and see how you feel about them. These opinions don't refer to ** any single branch of government such as Congress or the President or the Courts, ** but just to the government in general. For example:

1. How much (of the time - 1958, 1964) do you think we can trust the government in Washington to do what is right - just about always, most of the time, or only some of the time? (just about always, most of the time, some of the time, or almost never? - 1966)

		1958	1964			1966
1.	Always	57%	14%	1.	Just about always	17%
3.	Most of the time	16	63	2.	Most of the time	48
5.	Some of the time	23	22	4.	Some of the time	28
7.	None of the time	--	*	5.	Almost never	3
8.	DK	4	1	7.	It depends	1
		100%	100%	8.	DK	3
						100%

(Source: 1958, Q. 72.3, deck 6; 1964 post, Q. 64, deck 13; 1966, Q. C50, deck 5.)

2. How much difference do you think it makes to people like you what the government in Washington does: a good deal, some, or not much?

		1966
1.	Good deal	65%
3.	Some	19
5.	Not much	12
7.	Depends	1
8.	DK	3
		100%

(Source: 1966, Q. C51, deck 5.)

3. Do you think that people like you have <u>too little</u> political power, or just <u>about the right amount</u>?

	<u>1966</u>
1. About the right amount	53%
5. Too little power	33
6. No power at all; none	*
7. Depends	4
8. DK	<u>10</u>
	100%

(Source: 1966, Q. C52, deck 5.)

4. Would you say the government is pretty much run by a few big interests looking out for themselves or that it is run for the benefit of all the people?

	<u>1964</u>			<u>1966</u>
1. For benefit of all	64%	1. For benefit of all		53%
3. Other. Depends. Both boxes checked	4	5. Few big interests		34
		7. Depends		6
5. Few big interests	29	8. DK		<u>7</u>
8. DK	<u>3</u>			100%
	100%			

(Source: 1964 post, Q. 66, deck 13,; 1966, Q. C53, deck 5.)

5. Do you think that the high up people in government give <u>everyone</u> a fair break whether they are big shots or just ordinary people, or do you think some of them pay more attention to what the big interests want?

	<u>1958</u>
1. Give everyone a fair break	18%
3. Pro-con; it depends	1
5. Pay attention to big shots	76
9. DK	<u>5</u>
	100%

(Source: 1958, Q. 72.4, deck 6.)

6. How much do you feel that having elections makes the government pay attention to what the people think, a:

	1964			1966
1. Good deal	65%	1.	Good deal	62%
3. Some	25	3.	Some	25
5. Not much	6	5.	Not very much	9
8. DK	4	7.	Depends	1
	100%	8.	DK	3
				100%

(Source: 1964 post, Q. 53, deck 13; 1966, Q. C54, deck 5.)

7. Do you feel that almost all of the people running the government are smart people who usually know what they are doing, or do you think that quite a few of them don't seem to know what they are doing?

	1958	1964
1. Know what they are doing	57%	69%
3. Other. Depends. Both boxes checked	1	2
5. Don't know what they are doing	37	27
8. DK	5	2
	100%	100%

(Source: 1958, Q. 72.5, deck 6; 1964 post, Q. 65, deck 13.)

8. Do you think that people in the government waste a lot of the money we pay in taxes, waste some of it, or don't waste very much of it?

	1958	1964
1. Not much	10%	7%
3. Some	43	44
5. A lot	43	47
8. DK	4	2
	100%	100%

(Source: 1958, Q. 72.2, deck 6; 1964 post, Q. 63, deck 13.)

9. Do you think that <u>quite a few</u> of the people running the government are a little crooked, <u>not very many</u> are, or do you think <u>hardly any</u> of them are crooked at all?

		<u>1958</u>	<u>1964</u>
1.	Hardly any	26%	18%
3.	Not many	44	49
5.	Quite a lot	24	29
9.	DK	6	4
		100%	100%

(Source: 1958, Q. 72.1, deck 6; 1964 post, Q. 62, deck 13.)

Items 1, 7, 8, 9 and 1, 4, 7, 8, 9 comprise the 1958 and 1964 Trust in Government (Cynicism) Scales, respectively.

**Between double asterisks, this phrase read in 1964 "Democrats or Republicans in particular"

PARTY CONTROL

Over the years, do you think that control of the government should pass from one party to the other every so often, or do you think that it's all right for one party to have control for a long time?

		<u>1964</u>
1.	Control should change	71%
3.	Other. Depends. Both boxes checked	3
5.	One party all right	24
8.	DK	<u>2</u>
		100%

(Source: 1964 post, Q. 55, deck 13.)

POLITICAL POWER

How much political power do you think people like you have: a <u>great deal</u>, <u>some</u>, <u>not very much</u>, or <u>none</u>?

		<u>1966</u>
1.	Great deal	6%
2.	Some	35
3.	Pro-con; depends; other	*
4.	Not very much	38
5.	None	18
8.	DK	3
		100%

(Source: 1966, Q. C33, deck 4.)

PERSONALITY VARIABLES

Measures of five personality variables[*] have been included in various
SRC election studies. Three variables were used only once--a measure of
authoritarianism in 1956, an index of trust in people in 1964, and an index
of nostalgia in 1964. A measure of "strong-mindedness" was included in both
the 1960 and 1964 studies. For the remaining variable, personal competence,
items were used in the last three presidential election studies and in the 1958
study as well. Since this last measure has produced the strongest correlations
with background variables, a report will be given of the personal competence
items for each of the election studies.

One should note at the outset that the measures of personal competence
in the different elections studied did not employ a uniform response mode:
the 1958, 1960, and 1964 items were in forced-choice mode, but the 1956 questions
were in a Likert-type format.

In 1956, the opinions on the various items generally depicted a group
of respondents who felt personally competent. The range of people replying
in the personally competent direction to items ranged from 40 to 88 percent,
with all but one item showing a 50 percent positive response rate or better.
Some of the items were worded in a positive and some in a negative vein with
respect to personal competence.   Subsequent analysis revealed that the
negatively-worded items correlated with some of the background variables, but
this was not the case with the positively-worded items. With the negative
group of items, it was found that people with higher education and income were
far more likely to express feelings of personal competence than those with

---

[*]Items measuring personal conservatism (as defined by McClosky) were
used in the 1956 and 1958 studies and are reviewed in Chapter 3.

less education and income, especially on the item dealing with planning ahead for the future. Also, the personally competent were more likely to be white, male, and Republican in background.

In the 1958, 1960, and 1964 studies, the general pattern of people expressing personal competence was demonstrated again. However, two questions did not reflect a majority of the sample having such attitudes--some people were not sure that their life was working out the way they wanted it to and were also uncertain of their attitude positions when others disagreed with them. Background variables related to these and the other items in 1960 and 1964 in much the same way they did to the negatively-worded items in 1956. Again, the better educated and higher income segments of the population, the Republicans, and the whites viewed themselves as having more confidence in their personal lives, actions, and decisions. In 1964, personal competence was only slightly higher among Goldwater than among Johnson supporters and was much higher among males than among females, the latter finding not occurring in the 1960 study.

A trend analysis of those competence questions asked in each of the three election studies reveals a mild tendency for more people to feel competent over the years from 1958 to 1964. The differences are in no case very large, but do seem to indicate that more people are having good luck than bad luck in their lives and that their future plans are more or less working out as expected.

The measure of strong-mindedness used in 1960 and 1964 was constructed from three general questions on the respondent's opinion flexibility, opinion strength, and changeability in arguments. The responses to the three questions varied considerably, with the third item showing the greatest proportion of people being strong-minded and the second and first items progressively less

TABLE 1: CORRELATION OF PERSONALITY QUESTIONS WITH BACKGROUND VARIABLES

	Sex	Race	Education	Income	Age	Community Size	Party Identification	Actual Vote
1956 Decide things	-.18	-.10	.21	.18	-.11	.03	.02	.03
1956 Bad luck	-.01	-.10	.29	.29	.00	-.05	.12	.12
1956 Plan ahead	-.15	-.15	.31	.26	-.03	.01	.12	.09
1956 Sure about life	.03	-.02	.02	-.01	.03	.03	.03	.01
1956 Trouble with decisions	.05	-.08	.10	.10	-.13	-.01	-.02	.01
1956 Sure of oneself	.12	-.07	.02	.05	-.04	.03	.05	.09
1956 No use trying	--	--	--	--	--	--	--	--
1960 Carry out plans	.10	.12	-.24	-.26	.06	.02	-.17	-.13
1960 Sure about life	.02	.09	-.21	-.23	.04	.00	-.09	-.12
1960 Bad luck	.01	.07	-.19	-.20	.02	.04	-.10	-.09
1960 Get own way	.11	.02	-.08	-.06	.08	.01	-.04	.01
1960 Strong opinions	.04	.00	-.15	-.12	.10	.00	-.03	-.02
1960 Change mind	.11	-.01	-.11	-.10	.05	-.03	-.02	-.04
1964 Carry out plans } 1964 Sure about life } Personal Competence Scale 1964 Bad luck }	-.09	-.09	.22	.21	.00	.10	.15	.04
1964 Get own way } 1964 Strong opinions } Strong-mindedness Scale 1964 Change mind }	.11	.03	-.15	-.07	.05	-.03	-.03	-.06
1964 People trusted } 1964 People helpful } Trust in People Scale 1964 Take advantage }	.03	-.12	.28	.22	-.04	.08	.10	.00
1964 Life better today } 1964 Life satisfying today } Nostalgia Scale 1964 More moral today }	.09	-.08	-.02	-.08	.10	.05	.13	.13

Note: Values in the table are Pearson product-moment correlation coefficients. Correlations were computed from the standard SRC code systems for these variables unless otherwise noted in the text.

TABLE 2: INTERCORRELATION OF PERSONALITY QUESTIONS

	DT	BL	PA	SL	TD	SO
1956 Decide things	X					
1956 Bad luck	.21	X				
1956 Plan ahead	.45	.42				
1956 Sure about life	.12	-.14	X	-.06		
1956 Trouble with decision	.15	-.04	.10	.33	X	
1956 Sure of oneself	.09	-.03	.06	.36	.32	X

	CP	SL	BL	GO	SO	CM
1960 Carry out plans	X					
1960 Sure about life	.38	X				
1960 Bad luck	.30	.26	X			
1960 Get own way	.09	.11	-.04	X		
1960 Strong opinions	.12	.10	.01	.24	X	
1960 Change mind	.14	.07	.00	.26	.38	X

	CP	SL	BL	GO	SO	CM
1964 Carry out plans	X					
1964 Sure about life	.32	X				
1964 Bad luck	.30	.27	X			
1964 Get own way	.15	.08	.06	X		
1964 Strong opinions	.08	.08	.08	.24	X	
1964 Change mind	.11	.07	.07	.19	.32	X

	PT	PH	TA
1964 People trusted	X		
1964 People helpful	.48	X	
1964 Take advantage	.50	.54	X

	LB	LS	MM
1964 Life better today	X		
1964 Life satisfying today	.44	X	
1964 More moral today	.10	.16	X

Note: Values in the table are Pearson product-moment correlation coefficients (except in 1964 where tau-beta is used). Correlations were computed from the standard SRC code systems for these variables unless other-wise noted in the text.

so. More people seemed unwilling to change their mind about something once
it was made up, than thought themselves having strong opinions on most
matters, or than believed they usually got their own way in an argument. Distribution of responses to these questions varied little between 1960 and 1964.

In some ways, the measure of strong-mindedness met with only limited
analytic success. Although there was a significant, if quite modest, positive
relation between the measures of personal competence and strong-mindedness,
the latter definitely produced weaker correlations with background variables.
However, in both the 1960 and 1964 studies, the correlations ran in the same
direction as those dealing with the personal competence variable. High scores
on strong-mindedness also tended to be found among the better educated, higher
income, male, and younger segments of the sample.

Two other personality measures were used in the 1964 study. The first
was a "trust in people" scale consisting of items which tap a respondent's
tendency to see other people as basically trustworthy or basically untrust-
worthy. The sample was fairly evenly divided in their responses to the first
two items of the scale but more respondents showed trusting feelings toward
people on the third question.

The second instrument was a nostalgia scale. The first two items of
this measure revealed an absence of feeling for the past as compared with
the present, but such was not the case with the third item. (Unfortunately,
the third item does not seem as related to a "nostalgia" dimension in the same
substantive sense as the other items.) The sample generally tended to think
that life was better today than fifty years ago and that more satisfaction
can be gained from life in the present period.

The trust in people scale showed stronger relations with background
variables than did the nostalgia scale. As was found with the personal
competence scale (to which it was substantively related), high scores on

the trust in people scale were found among those who were white, better educated, wealthy, and Republican-oriented. Feelings of nostalgia, on the other hand, were high not only among those who supported Goldwater and identified with the Republican Party, but also among women, whites, the elderly, and the poor.

The results from the authoritarian items proved disappointing. An attempt was made to control for agreement response set by including one set of items which were worded in the positive direction and another set worded in the negative direction. It was found that the two sets intercorrelated negatively-- that is respondents rating more authoritarian on the positive items were likely to rate less authoritarian on the negative items. Furthermore, neither set of items showed any appreciable relation to political attitudes or behavior. (For further details see Campbell et al. The American Voter, Wiley, 1960, p.512ff.)

PERSONAL COMPETENCE

1. I would rather decide things when they come up than always try to plan ahead.

		1956
1.	Agree, lot	22%
2.	Agree, little	21
4.	Disagree, little	30
5.	Disagree, lot	26
9.	DK; pro-con	1
		100%

(Source: 1956 post, Q. C17, deck 9.)

2. When you make plans ahead do you usually get to carry out things the way you expected, or do things usually come up to make you change your plans?

		1958	1960	1964
1.	Things work out as expected	54%	59%	59%
3.	Depends. Both boxes checked. Other	1	3	5
5.	Have to change plans	44	38	36
8.	DK	1	*	*
		100%	100%	100%

(Source: 1958, Q.73.5, deck 6; 1960 post, Q.38, deck 9; 1964 post, Q.46, deck 12.)

3. I have always felt pretty sure my life would work out the way I wanted it to.

		1956
1.	Agree, lot	20%
2.	Agree, little	29
4.	Disagree, little	31
5.	Disagree, lot	18
9.	DK; pro-con	2
		100%

(Source: 1956 post, Q. C18, deck 9.)

4. Have you usually felt pretty sure your life would work out the way you want it to, or have there been times when you haven't been very sure about it?

		1958	1960	1964
1.	Pretty sure	46%	47%	47%
3.	Depends. Both boxes checked. Other	*	1	*
5.	Sometimes not very sure	53	52	52
8.	DK	1	*	1
		100%	100%	100%

(Source: 1958, Q.73.1, deck 6; 1960 post, Q.36, deck 9; 1964 post, Q.44, deck 12.)

5. I seem to be the kind of person that has more bad luck than good luck.

		1956
1.	Agree, lot	9%
2.	Agree, little	11
4.	Disagree, little	35
5.	Disagree, lot	44
9.	DK; pro-con	1
		100%

(Source: 1956 post, Q. C19, deck 9.)

6. Do you feel that you are the kind of person who gets his share of bad luck, or do you feel that you have mostly good luck?

		1958	1960	1964
1.	Mostly good luck	65%	65%	76%
3.	Depends. Both boxes checked. Other	5	8	10
5.	Bad luck	29	27	14
8.	DK	1	*	*
		100%	100%	100%

(Source: 1958, Q.73.3, deck 6; 1960 post, Q.37, deck 9; 1964 post, Q.45, deck 12.)

7. I never have any trouble making up my mind about important decisions.

		1956
1.	Agree, lot	20%
2.	Agree, little	20
4.	Disagree, little	38
5.	Disagree, lot	21
9.	DK; pro-con	1
		100%

(Source: 1956 post, Q. C20, deck 9.)

8. Would you say that <u>quite often</u> you have trouble making up your mind about important decisions, or don't you feel you ever have much trouble making up your mind on important decisions?

		1958
1.	Not much trouble	58%
3.	Pro-con; it depends	1
5.	Quite often	41
9.	DK	*
		100%

(Source: 1958, Q.73.4, deck 6.)

9. I nearly always feel pretty sure of myself even when people disagree with me.

		1956
1.	Agree, lot	30%
2.	Agree, little	36
4.	Disagree, little	25
5.	Disagree, lot	7
9.	DK; pro-con	2
		100%

(Source: 1956 post, Q. C23, deck 9.)

10. When people disagree with you, do you sometimes start to wonder whether you're right, or do you nearly always feel sure of yourself even when people disagree with you?

		1958
1.	Feel sure	36%
3.	Pro-con; it depends	1
5.	Wonder	62
9.	DK	1
		100%

(Source: 1958, Q.73.2, deck 6.)

11.   There's not much use for me to plan ahead because there's usually something
      that makes me change my plans.

	1956
1. Agree, lot	19%
2. Agree, little	23
4. Disagree, little	33
5. Disagree, lot	24
9. DK; pro-con	1
	100%

(Source: 1956 post, Q. C22, deck 9.)

12.   I have often had the feeling that it's no use to try to get anywhere in this
      life.

	1956
1. Agree, lot	4%
2. Agree, little	8
4. Disagree, little	21
5. Disagree, lot	67
9. DK; pro-con	*
	100%

(Source: 1956 post, Q.C24, deck 9.)

OTHER PERSONAL COMPETENCE ITEMS

1. Are you the kind of person that plans his life ahead all the time or do you live more from day to day?

		1960
1.	Plans ahead	52%
3.	Depends, both boxes checked	1
5.	Live from day to day	47
9.	DK	--
		100%

(Source: 1960 post, Q. 42, deck 9)

2. Some people feel like other people push them around a good bit. Others feel that they run their lives pretty much the way they want to. How is it with you?

		1960
1.	Run own lives	89%
3.	Depends. Both boxes checked	2
5.	Get pushed around	9
9.	DK	*
		100%

(Source: 1960 post, Q. 43, deck 9)

3. Would you say you nearly always finish things once you start them or do you sometimes have to give up before they are finished?

		1960
1.	Always finish	70%
3.	Depends. Both boxes checked	*
5.	Sometimes give up	30
9.	Dk	--
		100%

(Source: 1960 post, Q. 44, deck 9)

4. If you had your choice, would you rather have a job where you gave the orders or a job where somebody else told you what to do?

		1960
1.	Rather give orders	53%
3.	Depends. Both boxes checked	2
5.	Rather be told what to do	44
9.	DK	1
		100%

(Source: 1960 post, Q.45, deck 9)

5. I have always felt that I have more will power than most people have.

		1956
1.	Agree, lot	15%
2.	Agree, little	24
4.	Disagree, little	38
5.	Disagree, lot	22
9.	DK; pro-con	1
		100%

(Source: 1956 post, Q. C21, deck 9)

STRONG-MINDEDNESS SCALE

1. When you get into an argument do you usually get your own way or do you often give in?

	1960	1964
1. Always get own way	20%	23%
3. Depends. Both boxes checked. Other	10	16
5. Often give in	70	60
8. DK	*	1
	100%	100%

(Source: 1960 post, Q. 39, deck 9; 1964 post, Q. 47, deck 12.)

2. Some people have strong opinions about a good many things. Other people are more in the middle of the road. Which kind of person are you?

	1960	1964
1. Strong opinions	48%	44%
3. Depends. Both boxes checked. Other	*	2
5. Middle of the road	52	53
8. DK	*	1
	100%	100%

(Source: 1960 post, Q. 40, deck 9; 1964 post, Q. 48, deck 12.)

3. When you make up your mind about something is it pretty hard to argue you out of it or do you change your mind pretty easily?

	1960	1964
1. Hard to change	73%	70%
3. Depends. Both boxes checked. Other	2	4
5. Change mind easily	25	26
8. DK	*	*
	100%	100%

(Source: 1960 post, Q. 41, deck 9; 1964 post, Q. 49, deck 12.)

TRUST IN PEOPLE ITEMS

1. Generally speaking, would you say that most people can be trusted or that you can't be too careful in dealing with people?

		1964	1966
1.	Most people can be trusted	53%	53%
3.	Other. Depends. Both boxes checked	1	1
5.	Can't be too careful	45	46
8.	DK	1	*
		100%	100%

(Source: 1964 post, Q.59, deck 13; 1966, Q. C31, deck 3)

2. Would you say that most of the time, people try to be helpful, or that they are mostly just looking out for themselves?

		1964	1966
1.	Try to be helpful	54%	52%
3.	Other. Depends. Both boxes checked	4	2
5.	Just look out for themselves	41	46
8.	DK	1	*
		100%	100%

(Source: 1964 post, Q.60, deck 13; 1966, Q. C32, deck 4.)

3. Do you think most people would try to take advantage of you if they got a chance or would they try to be fair?

		1964
1.	Would try to be fair	67%
3.	Other. Depends. Both boxes checked	3
5.	Would take advantage of you	29
8.	DK	1
		100%

(Source: 1964 post, Q.61, deck 13.)

NOSTALGIA ITEMS

1. Some people say that, considering everything life in this country was better 50 years ago than it is now. Others think this is a better time to live than those days were. How do you feel about it?

		1964
1.	This is a better time to live	76%
3.	Other. Depends. Both boxes checked	2
5.	Life better 50 years ago	19
8.	DK	3
		100%

    (Source: 1964 post, Q. 56, deck 13)

2. Do you think the average man gets more satisfaction out of life these days or do you think he got more out of life 50 years ago?

		1964
1.	More satisfaction these days	59%
3.	Other. Depends. Both boxes checked	3
5.	More out of life 50 years ago	34
8.	DK	4
		100%

    (Source: 1964 post, Q. 57, deck 13.)

3. Would you say it is harder for the average man to lead a good moral life today or was it harder to lead a good life 50 years ago?

		1964
1.	Harder 50 years ago	13%
3.	Other. Depends. Both boxes checked	15
5.	Harder to lead a good life now	67
8.	DK	5
		100%

    (Source: 1964 post, Q. 58, deck 13.)

AUTHORITARIANISM ITEMS

Now, for the last question, here is something different. I have some statements which I will read to you and I would like you to tell me whether you agree or disagree with them. I will read them one at a time and you just tell me whether you agree or disagree and whether you agree or disagree a little or quite a bit.

1. The artist and the professor are probably more important to society than the businessman and the manufacturer.

		1956
1.	Agree, lot	6%
2.	Agree, little	10
4.	Disagree, little	37
5.	Disagree, lot	41
9.	DK; pro-con	6
		100%

(Source: 1956 post, Q. C7, deck 9)

2. The findings of science may someday show that many of our most deeply and held beliefs are wrong.

		1956
1.	Agree, lot	26%
2.	Agree, little	33
4.	Disagree, little	22
5.	Disagree, lot	14
9.	DK; pro-con	5
		100%

(Source: 1956 post, Q. C8, deck 9)

3. Human nature being what it is, there must always be war and conflict.

		1956
1.	Agree, lot	34%
2.	Agree, little	29
4.	Disagree, little	19
5.	Disagree, lot	17
9.	DK; pro-con	1
		100%

(Source: 1956 post, Q. C8, deck 9.)

4. People ought to pay more attention to new ideas, even if they seem to go against the American way of life.

		1956
1.	Agree, lot	15%
2.	Agree, little	29
4.	Disagree, little	27
5.	Disagree, lot	25
9.	DK; pro-con	4
		100%

(Source: 1956 post, Q. C10, deck 9)

5. What young people need most of all is strict discipline by their parents.

		1956
1.	Agree, lot	51%
2.	Agree, little	24
4.	Disagree, little	15
5.	Disagree, lot	9
9.	DK; pro-con	1
		100%

(Source: 1956 post, Q. C11, deck 9)

6. Most people who don't get ahead just don't have enough will power.

		1956
1.	Agree, lot	32%
2.	Agree, little	27
4.	Disagree, little	26
5.	Disagree, lot	14
9.	DK; pro-con	1
		100%

(Source: 1956 post, Q. C12, deck 9)

666

7. It is highly unlikely that astrology will ever be able to explain anything.

		1956
1.	Agree, lot	18%
2.	Agree, little	19
4.	Disagree, little	32
5.	Disagree, lot	14
9.	DK, pro-con	17
		100%

(Source: 1956 post, Q. C13, deck 9)

8. Sex criminals deserve more than prison; they should be whipped in public or worse

		1956
1.	Agree, lot	25%
2.	Agree, little	15
4.	Disagree, little	22
5.	Disagree, lot	34
9.	DK; pro-con	4
		100%

(Source: 1956 post, Q. C14, deck 9.)

9. An urge to jump from high places is probably the result of unhappy personal experiences rather than something inborn.

		1956
1.	Agree, lot	31%
2.	Agree, little	31
4.	Disagree, little	16
5.	Disagree, lot	8
9.	DK; pro-con	14
		100%

(Source: 1956 post, Q. C15, deck 9.)

10. Bosses should say just what is to be done and exactly how to do it if they expect us to do a good job.

		1956
1.	Agree, lot	45%
2.	Agree, little	21
4.	Disagree, little	18
5.	Disagree, lot	15
9.	DK; pro-con	1
		100%

(Source: 1956 post, Q. C16, deck 9)

GENERAL VIEWS OF PEOPLE AND LIFE

Now here is something a little different. It helps us know what kinds of people
we have talked to if we find out how they feel about other things besides politics.
For example:

1. Which of these types of people would you generally prefer--the practical man or
the man of ideas?

		1958
1.	Man of ideas	28%
3.	Pro-con; it depends	4
5.	Practical man	65
9.	DK	3
		100%

(Source: 1958, Q. 74.1, deck 6)

2. If something grows up over a long time do you think there is certain to be much
wisdom in it, or do you think sometimes it may get pretty old-fashioned?

		1958
1.	Is old-fashioned	46%
3.	Pro-con; it depends	3
5.	Much wisdom	44
9.	DK	7
		100%

(Source: 1958, Q. 74.2, deck 6)

3. Do you think it's always a good idea to look for new ways of doing things, or
do you think in some cases it's better to stick by what you have than to be
trying new things you don't really know about?

		1958
1.	Look for the new	63%
3.	Pro-con; it depends	3
5.	Stick by what you have	33
9.	DK	1
		100%

(Source: 1958, Q. 74.3, deck 6)

4. Do you think we usually should respect the work of our forefathers and not think that we know better than they did, or do you think that we must figure out our problems for ourselves?

		1958
1.	Figure out for selves	80%
3.	Pro-con; it depends	4
5.	Respect forefathers	15
9.	DK	1
		100%

(Source: 1958, Q. 74.4, deck 6)

5. Do you think that a person has many worthwhile ideas whatever his age, or do you feel that usually a man doesn't get to have much wisdom until he's well along in years?

		1958
1.	Ideas whatever age	76%
3.	Pro-con; it depends	1
5.	Wisdom comes late	21
9.	DK	2
		100%

(Source: 1958, Q. 74.5, deck 6)

CHAPTER 14: CONTENTS OF APPENDICES TO THIS VOLUME

Two further volumes will be produced as appendices to this attitude handbook. Appendix A treats measures of occupational attitudes and occupational characteristics. This first appendix, very near completion, is outlined in detail in the Table of Contents which appears on the following pages.

Appendix A contains an introductory chapter followed by three chapters reviewing the history, findings, and problems of research into job satisfaction. A large chapter is then devoted to measures of general job satisfaction, with the four succeeding chapters dealing with specific aspects of job satisfaction. The next four chapters deal with occupational values (such as inner-other directedness and work measures akin to the local-cosmopolitan distinction discussed in Chapter 9 of this volume), leadership styles, other work-related attitudes (such as union-management attitudes and attitudes toward working for the government), and vocational interest measures.

The final five chapters deal with more objective occupational characteristics, rather than subjective attitudes. The first of these chapters reviews and contrasts the various measures of occupational characteristics, including all 500 or so Bureau of the Census job categories. A review of the literature on the interesting analytic variables of status incongruency, occupational status, and social mobility follow in the next three chapters. Finally some new research evidence is analyzed on the interesting topic of job similarity which prompts consideration of new code systems in survey research for a respondents "occupation".

Appendix B cannot currently be described in such detail. In general, the measures in this appendix are more purely psychological in nature. The first chapters of this appendix deal with the very familiar and often misused terms--alienation and anomie (or, more properly, anomy or anomia). Measures of the related variables of life satisfaction and happiness are discussed in the next chapter. These variables in turn have been found to be related to the measures covered in a further chapter--those dealing with self-esteem (or alternately ego-strength or personal efficacy). Measures of general attitudes toward other people (trust-in-people, Machiavellianism, etc.) and authoritarianism (plus rigidity and dogmatism) comprise the topics of the next two chapters. Three final chapters are planned which will generally cover personality scales (namely those in famous batteries like the MMPI or the CPI and personality variables not covered above), scales of religious attitudes, and scales dealing with various topics not covered in any of the preceding categories.

We plan to make these appendices available at moderate cost through the Publications Department of the Institute for Social Research. In their current condition, the appendices are considered as useful drafts for research purposes. Shortage of time, personnel, and funds preclude publication of these volumes on a more polished and highly sophisticated professional level.

TABLE OF CONTENTS OF APPENDIX A:
MEASURES OF OCCUPATIONAL ATTITUDES AND OCCUPATIONAL CHARACTERISTICS

Page

WHAT IS CONTAINED IN THIS VOLUME   i

CHAPTER

1. INTRODUCTION   1

2. RESEARCH ON WORK AND WORKER IN THE UNITED STATES (Kimmel). 17

3. OCCUPATIONAL NORMS AND DIFFERENCES IN JOB SATISFACTION: A SUMMARY
    OF SURVEY RESEARCH EVIDENCE (Robinson) 25

        Blauner's Review 27
        Gurin, Veroff and Feld Mental Health Study 29
        Kilpatrick, Cummings and Jennings Study. 34
        Wilensky's Labor-Leisure Study of Detroit. 43
        Converse and Robinson Meaning-of-Time Study. 47
        Some Further Data on Related Issues. 58
        Summary and Conclusions. 65

4. JOB ATTITUDES AND OCCUPATIONAL PERFORMANCE: A REVIEW OF SOME
    IMPORTANT LITERATURE (Athanasiou). 79

        Relation between Attitudes and Performance 79
        Previous Literature Reviews. 81
        Effects of Specific Factors on Satisfaction as a Dependent Variable. 86
        Organizational Structure Variables 88
        Satisfaction as an Independent Variable. 91
        The Use of Occupational Interest Inventories 93
        Conclusions. 95

5. GENERAL JOB SATISFACTION SCALES. 99

        1. Job Description Index (Smith, et al. 1963) 105
        2. Index of Job Satisfaction (Kornhauser 1965). 108
        3. Factors for Job Satisfaction and Job Dissatisfaction
            (Dunnette, et al. 1966). 112
        4. SRA (Employee) Attitude Scales (Carlson, et al. 1962). 116
        5. IRC Employee Attitude Survey (1951 and 1966) 117
        6. Index of Employee Satisfaction (Morse 1953). 120
        7. Job Satisfaction Scale (Johnson 1955). 122
        8. Job Dimensions Blank (Schletzer 1965). 126
        9. Job Satisfaction Index (Brayfield and Rothe 1957). 129
       10. Job Satisfaction (Hoppock 1935). 132
       11. Tear Ballot (Kerr 1948). 136
       12. Employee Morale Scale (Woods 1944) 138
       13. How Do you Like Your Job? (Handyside 1953) 142
       14. Work Information Inventory (Bernberg 1958) 143

Page

6. JOB SATISFACTION FOR PARTICULAR OCCUPATIONS 145

    1. Need Fulfillment Questionnaire for Management (Porter 1962) . .148
    2. Managerial Job Attitudes (Harrison 1960). 152
    3. Job Attitudes and Job Satisfaction of Scientists
        (Hinrichs 1962) 154
    4. Attitudes of Scientists in Organizations
        (Pelz and Andrews 1966) .160
    5. Job Satisfaction Inventory (Twery, et al. 1958) 162

7. SATISFACTION WITH SPECIFIC JOB FEATURES 165

    1. Supervisory Behavior Description (Fleishman 1957) 167
    2. Attitude toward the Supervisor (Nagle 1953) 169
    3. Satisfaction with Supervisor (Draper 1955). 171
    4. Attitudes toward the Supervisor (Schmid, et al. 1957) 173
    5. Employee Opinion Survey (Bolda 1958). 175
    6. Need Satisfaction in Work (Schaffer 1953) 179
    7. About Your Company (King 1960). 181
    8. Group Morale Scale (Goldman 1958) 184

8. FACTORS FROM SOME MULTIDIMENSIONAL ANALYSES OF JOB SATISFACTION
    (Peay and Wernander). 187

9. CONCEPTS RELATED TO JOB SATISFACTION. 197

    1. Indices of Alienation (Aitkin and Hage 1966) 200
    2. Alienation from Work (Pearlin 1962) 204
    3. Job-Related Tension (Kahn, et al. 1964) 206
    4. Job Motivation Index (Patchen 1965) 209
    5. Identification with the Work Organization (Patchen 1965). . . .212
    6. Defining Dimensions of Occupation (Pearlin and Kohn 1966) . . .217
    7. Meaning of Work Scales (Guion 1965) 219

10. OCCUPATIONAL VALUES 223

    1. Occupational Values Scales (Kilpatrick, et al. 1964). 229
    2. Occupational Values (Rosenberg 1957). 233
    3. Faith-in-People Scale (Rosenberg 1957). 236
    4. Scale of Inner-and Other-Directedness (Bowers 1966) 238
    5. Inner-Other Social Preference Scale (Kassarjian 1962) 240
    6. Career-Oriented Occupational Values (Marvick 1954). 244
    7. Career Orientation in the Federal Service (Slesinger 1961). . .247

11. LEADERSHIP STYLES 249

    1. Leadership Opinion Questionnaire (Stogdill and Coons 1957). . .254
    2. The SRA Supervisory Index (Schwartz 1956) 258
    3. Leadership Practices Inventory (Nelson 1955). 261
    4. How Supervise? (File and Remmers 1948). 263
    5. A Proverbs Test for Supervisor Selection (Reveal 1960). 267
    6. A Managerial Key for the CPI (Goodstein and Schrader 1963). . .272
    7. Managerial Scale for Enterprise Improvement 274
    8. Organizational Control Graph (Tannenbaum 1966). 275
    9. Profile of Organizational Characteristics (Likert 1967) 276

12. OTHER WORK-RELEVANT ATTITUDES 281

    1. Union and Management Attitudes toward Each Other
       (Stagner, et al. 1958). 284
    2. IRC Union Attitude Scale (Uphoff and Dunnette 1956) . . . , . . . 287
    3. Index of Pro-Labor Orientation (Kornhauser 1965). 289
    4. Pro-Labor Attitude Error-Choice Tests (Hammond 1948). 293
    5. Attitudes toward Labor and Management (Weschler 1950) 295
    6. Attitude toward Working for the Government (Aalto 1956) . . . 298
    7. Attitudes toward Working for the Government
       (Kilpatrick, et al. 1964) 302
    8. Attitude toward Automation (Rosenberg 1962) 304
    9. Attitude toward Employment of Older Persons
       (Kirchner 1954) 307
   10. Opinions about Work of the Mentally Ill
       (Streuning and Efron 1965). 310

13. VOCATIONAL INTEREST MEASURES. 313

    1. Selective Word Memory Test (Edel and Tiflin 1965) 321
    2. Job Analysis and Interest Measure (Walther 1961). 324
    3. Sales Attitude Check List (Taylor 1960) 328
    4. Work Attitude Key for the MMPI (Tydlaska and Mengel 1953) . . 331

14. OCCUPATIONAL STATUS MEASURES. 313

    1. Socio-Economic Status Scale (Duncan 1961) 342
    2. Socio-Economic Status Scores (Bureau of Census 1963). 357
    3. Occupational Ratings (North and Hatt 1947, 1965). 359
    4. Index of Status Characteristics (Warner, et al 1963). 362
    5. Index of Social Position (Hollingshead and Redlich 1958). . . 367
    6. Index of Class Position (Ellis, et al. 1963). 369
    7. Class Identification (Centers and others 1949-1966) 371
    8. Facets for Job Evaluation (Guttman 1965). 375

15. STATUS INCONSISTENCY: SOME CONCEPTUAL AND METHODOLOGICAL
    CONSIDERATIONS (Kasl) 335

    Types of Status Inconsistency 377
    Theoretical Considerations. 378
    Some Empirical Findings 379
    Methodological Considerations 380
    Methods of Statistical Analysis 383
    Conclusions 385
    Some Measures of Status Inconsistency 391

16. OCCUPATIONAL SITUS. 397

    1. Situs Categories (Morris and Murphy 1959) 399
    2. Occupational Groups (Roe 1956). 400
    3. Occupational Classification (Super 1957). 401
    4. Census Bureau Industry Groupings (1960) 403
    5. Data, People, Things (Dictionary of Occupational Titles
       1965) 404

676

17. SOCIAL MOBILITY 407

Steps for Measuring Occupational Mobility
(Tumin and Feldman) 410

18. OCCUPATIONAL SIMILARITY 413

  1. Sociological Evidence of Occupational Similarity. 418
  2. Mappings of Occupational Similarity Underlying the Strong,
     Kuder, and Minnesota Vocational Interest Measures 422
  3. Some Similarity Assessments Implicit in the Dictionary of
     Occupational Titles 433
  4. A Tentative Revised Occupation Code for Survey Research . . . 436

TABLE OF CONTENTS OF APPENDIX B:
MEASURES OF SOCIAL PSYCHOLOGICAL ATTITUDES

Chapter

1. Introduction

2. Alienation (Olsen)

3. Alienation Scales

4. Life Satisfaction and Happiness

5. Self-Esteem

6. Attitudes toward Other People

7. Authoritarianism and Related Scales

8. Other Personality Scales

9. Religious Attitude Scales

10. Miscellaneous Social Attitude Scales

CHAPTER 15: CONTENTS OF RELATED VOLUMES

There are at least three other separate publications which have the same aim as this volume. Unfortunately, we were unaware of these publications before this particular research project began. Had we known of them beforehand, the orientation of this volume would have changed noticeably to complement, rather than overlap, the contents of these other volumes.

Nevertheless, we hope that this volume does make some unique contributions. For example, it is the only handbook which attempts some evaluation and integration of measures in a comparative context. Thus, in Chapter 3, we hope to have provided the reader with some practical guidelines for the use of liberal-conservative scales--guidelines based on sound research experience. By arranging the scales in estimated order of merit, we hope to have drawn the reader's attention to the most promising measures available and to the reasons why they are preferable to other measures. (Again we caution the reader against taking these orderings too seriously; we want the reader to draw his own conclusions.)

Examining these three related works, we find more basic similarities than differences in rationale and procedure, both among our work and theirs, and among their own works. Taking these three works in order of most recent publication, their contents are briefly as follows:

1) Sociological Measurement by Charles Bonjean, Richard Hill, and Dale McLemore was published in 1967 by Chandler Publishing in San Francisco (price $12.00). For the most part, this book is a comprehensively-organized bibliography of 78 categories, into which references to some 2,080 scales and indices are placed. Every issue of four major sociological journals (American Journal of Sociology, American Sociological Review, Social Forces, and Sociometry) was thoroughly reviewed between 1954 and 1965 for relevant scales. Only those 50 scales which were cited six or more times in this literature were described

and discussed further than a basic reference; the scale items themselves were made available for only a limited subset. This book then is a most comprehensive and useful collection of references, but it is unlikely to contain the basic information about a scale in which a potential user might be interested. Nevertheless, the scope of measures listed goes well beyond those covered in this volume.

2) Scales for the Measurement of Attitudes by Marvin Shaw and Jack Wright was published in 1967 by McGraw-Hill in New York (price $14.50). This work is more oriented towards the psychologist and most of the 176 scales contained are drawn from the psychological literature. While the Shaw-Wright volume does contain very detailed descriptions of scales--including the items themselves and relevant criticisms--many of the scales are either out-of-date, of very specialized intent, or of very limited theoretical import . Of the three volumes, this one is most similar structurally to ours. The chapters in our volume deal with much more limited topics, however. (Thus, we have seven chapters dealing with aspects of political attitudes, while the Shaw-Wright volume has only one chapter on "Political and Religious Attitudes," and we deal with racial attitudes in one separate chapter while it is covered with other "Social Issues and Problems" by Shaw and Wright.)

3) Handbook of Research Design and Social Measurement by Delbert Miller was published in 1964 by the David McKay Company in New York (price $3.50). A little over half of this book is devoted to measures, the remainder dealing with general research procedures. This book is mainly sociologically oriented, and in addition to the 37 scales which are presented and described in detail, Miller has appended a 20-page inventory of measures used in the American Sociological Review between 1951 and 1960. The 37 selectively-chosen scales in Miller's more modest volume tend to be of higher overall quality and more prominent than the measures in the Shaw-Wright volume or our volume. A revised and updated edition of the volume is expected shortly.

The lists of contents of these three books are given on the following pages: the 78 content categories and 50 scale discussions of the Bonjean et al. volume, the 176 scales appearing in the Shaw-Wright volume, and the 37 scales appearing in the Miller book.

There are two other projects of similar nature now in progress:

1) a compilation of measures relevant to an educational context under the direction of Matthew Miles at Teacher's College of Columbia University;

2) a compilation of organizationally-relevant measures undertaken by Bernard Indik at Rutgers University.

CONTENT CATEGORIES FOR MEASURES REFERRED
IN BONJEAN, HILL, AND MCLEMORE'S <u>SOCIOLOGICAL MEASUREMENT</u>

(Titles in small type refer to scales for which extended discussion is given beyond the reference.)

1. ACHIEVEMENT
2. ACHIEVEMENT MOTIVATION
    Achievement Motivation (Murray, McClelland, Atkinson)
    Achievement Training (Winterbottom)
3. ANOMIA AND ALIENATION
    Alienation, Powerlessness (Liverant, Rotter, Seeman, Neal)
    Alienation (Nettler)
    Anomia (Srole)
4. ASPIRATIONS
5. ASSIMILATION
6. AUTHORITARIANISM
    California F Scale
7. AUTHORITY: ATTITUDES TOWARD AND CHARACTERISTICS OF
8. CLASS CONSCIOUSNESS
9. COHESION
10. COMMUNITY: ATTITUDES TOWARD AND CHARACTERISTICS OF
11. COMPLEX ORGANIZATIONS: ATTITUDES TOWARD AND PERCEPTIONS OF
12. COMPLEX ORGANIZATIONS: CHARACTERISTICS OF
    Administrative Rationality (Udy)
13. COMPLEX ORGANIZATIONS: INFORMAL RELATIONS
14. CONFORMITY AND DEVIANCE
15. CONSENSUS
16. CRIME AND DELINQUENCY
    Delinquency Proneness, Social Responsibility (Gough)
    Delinquent Behavior Checklist (Nye, Short)
17. EDUCATION: ATTITUDE TOWARD AND PERCEPTIONS OF
18. EDUCATION: BEHAVIOR IN AND CHARACTERISTICS OF
19. FAMILY: INTERPERSONAL RELATIONS AND AUTHORITY
20. FAMILY: PERCEPTIONS OF AND ATTITUDES TOWARD
21. FAMILY: COHESION
22. HEALTH: INDIVIDUAL
23. INNOVATION AND DIFFUSION
24. INTERESTS
25. INTERGROUP RELATIONS: ETHNOCENTRISM
    Ethnocentrism (California E Scale)
26. INTERGROUP RELATIONS: NONRACIAL AND NONETHNIC
27. INTERGROUP RELATIONS, RACIAL AND ETHNIC: CHARACTERISTICS OF
28. INTERGROUP RELATIONS, RACIAL AND ETHNIC: DISCRIMINATION
29. INTERGROUP RELATIONS, RACIAL AND ETHNIC: GROUP BELONGINGNESS
30. INTERGROUP RELATIONS, RACIAL AND ETHNIC: PREJUDICE AND SOCIAL DISTANCE
    Social Distance (Bogardus)
    Social Distance, Summated Differences (Westie)

31. INTERGROUP RELATIONS, RACIAL AND ETHNIC: STEREOTYPES
        Stereotype Check List (Katz, Braly)
32. INTERPERSONAL RELATIONS: ATTITUDES TOWARD
33. INTERPERSONAL RELATIONS: CHARACTERISTICS OF
34. JOB SATISFACTION, MORALE, AND RELATED MEASURES
35. LEADERSHIP, COMMUNITY AND ORGANIZATIONAL: BEHAVIOR AND CHARACTERISTICS
    OF
        Consideration (Ohio State Leader Behavior Description
          Questionnaire and Related Measures)
        Initiating Structure (Ohio State Leader Behavior Description
          Questionnaire and Related Measures)
36. LEADERSHIP, COMMUNITY AND ORGANIZATIONAL: IDENTIFICATION OF REPUTATIONAL
    APPROACH
37. LEADERSHIP, SMALL GROUP: BEHAVIOR AND CHARACTERISTICS OF
38. LEADERSHIP, SMALL GROUP: IDENTIFICATION OF
39. MARITAL ADJUSTMENT AND COURTSHIP
        Marital Adjustment (Burgess, Cottrell, Locke, Wallace)
        Marital Satisfaction (Burgess, Wallin)
40. MARITAL AND FAMILY ROLES
41. MEDICINE AND HEALTH: ATTITUDES TOWARD
42. MEDICINE AND HEALTH: BEHAVIOR IN AND CHARACTERISTICS OF
43. MENTAL ABILITY
        American Council on Education Psychological Examination
44. MISCELLANEOUS CATEGORIES
45. NEIGHBORHOOD: ATTITUDES TOWARD AND CHARACTERISTICS OF
46. NORMS
47. OCCUPATIONAL ROLES
48. PERSONAL ADJUSTMENT
        California Test of Personality
49. PERSONALITY: GENERAL
50. PERSONALITY TRAITS: CREATIVITY
51. PERSONALITY TRAITS: DOMINANCE
52. PERSONALITY TRAITS: MASCULINITY-FEMININITY
53. PERSONALITY TRAITS: MOTIVES AND NEEDS
        Personal Preference Schedule (Edwards)
54. PERSONALITY TRAITS: SOCIABILITY-WITHDRAWAL
55. PERSONALITY TRAITS: VARIOUS CATEGORIES
        Dogmatism (Rokeach)
56. POLITICAL ATTITUDES
        Conservatism (McClosky)
57. POLITICAL BEHAVIOR
58. RELIGION: ATTITUDE TOWARD, PARTICIPATION IN, AND CHARACTERISTICS OF
        Religious Orthodoxy (Putney, Middleton)
59. SELF-IMAGE, SELF-CONCEPT, AND RELATED MEASURES
60. SMALL GROUPS: ATTITUDES TOWARD, IDENTIFICATION WITH, AND PERCEPTIONS OF
        Social-Emotional Reactions (Bales)
61. SMALL GROUPS: BEHAVIOR AND INTERACTION IN
62. SMALL GROUPS: STATUS AND STATUS RELATIONS IN
        Sociometric Status and Structure (Popularity, Liking or Disliking
        Another, Rejection, Personal Preference, Personal Choice, and
        the Like)

63. SOCIAL MOBILITY AND RELATED MEASURES
        Occupational Mobility, Intergenerational (Census, Edwards
        Related)
64. SOCIAL PARTICIPATION
        Social Participation (Chapin)
65. SOCIETAL CHARACTERISTICS
        Urbanization (Davis)
66. SOCIOECONOMIC STATUS: COMPOSITE, OBJECTIVE
        Indexes of Social Position (Hollingshead)
        Index of Status Characteristics (Warner)
        Socioeconomic Status (Sewell)
67. SOCIOECONOMIC STATUS: COMPOSITE, SUBJECTIVE AND OBJECTIVE
68. SOCIOECONOMIC STATUS: OCCUPATIONAL
        Occupational Prestige (North, Hatt)
        Occupational Status (Census)
        Occupational Status (Duncan)
        Occupational Status (Hollingshead)
        Occupational Status (Warner)
69. SOCIOECONOMIC STATUS: REPUTATIONAL
        Social Class: Judges or Informants
70. STATUS CONCERN
        Status Concern (Kaufman)
71. STATUS CONSISTENCY AND RELATED MEASURES
        Status Crystallization (Lenski)
72. URBAN AREAS: METROPOLITAN AREAS AND DOMINANCE
73. URBAN AREAS: SEGREGATION
        Segregation (Cowgill, Cowgill)
        Segregation (Duncan, Duncan)
        Segregation (Jahn, Schmid, Schrag)
        Segregation (Shevky, Williams, Bell)
74. URBAN AREAS: SOCIOECONOMIC STATUS
        Social Rank (Shevky, Williams, Bell)
75. URBAN AREAS: URBANIZATION (FAMILY STATUS)
        Urbanization (Family Status) (Shevky, Williams, Bell)
76. URBAN AREAS: VARIOUS CATEGORIES
        Centralization (Duncan)
77. VALUES
        Values (Allport, Vernon, Lindzey)
78. WORK-VALUE ORIENTATIONS

LIST OF SCALES AND SCALE DESCRIPTIONS
IN SHAW AND WRIGHT'S <u>SCALES FOR THE MEASUREMENT OF ATTITUDES</u>

(The scales are organized into eight sections according to the prefixed number.
The number 3 refers to the section on social practices, the number 4 to social
issues and problems, the number 5 to international issues, the number 6 to
abstract concepts, the number 7 to political and religious attitudes, the
number to ethnic and national groups, the number 9 to significant others, and
the number 10 to social institutions.)

Social Practices

3-1 A survey of Opinions Regarding the Bringing Up of
Children (Itkin, 1952)

3-2 A Survey of Opinions Regarding the Discipline of
Children (Itkin, 1952)

3-3 Attitude toward Discipline Exercised by Parents (Itkin,
1952)

3-4 Attitude toward the Freedom of Children (Koch, Dentler,
Dysart, and Streit, 1934)

3-5 Attitude toward Parental Control of Children's Activities
(Stott, 1940)

3-6 Attitude toward Self-reliance (Ojemann, 1934)

3-7 Attitude toward the Use of Fear as a Means of Controlling
the Behavior of Children (Ackerley, 1934)

3-8 Attitude toward Parents Giving Sex Information to
Children Between the Ages of Six and Twelve (Ackerley,
1934)

3-9 Attitude toward Older Children Telling Lies (Ackerley,
1934)

3-10 The Traditional Family Ideology (TFI) Scale (Levinson
and Huffman, 1955)

3-11 Attitude toward Teaching (F. D. Miller, 1934)

3-12 Attitude toward Teaching as a Career (Merwin and Di
Vesta, 1960)

3-13 Attitude toward Physical Education as a Career for
Women (Drinkwater, 1960)

3-14 Attitude toward Education (Mitchell, 1941)

Social Practices   3-15 Opinionnaire on Attitudes toward Education (Lindgren
(continued)   and Patton, 1958)

3-16 Education Scale (Kerlinger and Kaya, 1959a)

3-17 Attitude toward Intensive Competition in Team Games
    (McCue, 1953)

3-18 Attitude toward Intensive Competition for High School
    Girls (McGee, 1956)

3-19 The Competitive Attitude (Ca) Scale (Lakie, 1964)

3-20 Attitude toward Sunday Observance (Thurstone, 1929-1934)

3-21 An Attitude Scale toward Church and Religious Practices
    (Dynes, 1955)

3-22 A Dating Scale (Bardis, 1962)

3-23 An Intimacy Permissiveness Scale (Christensen and
    Carpenter, 1962)

3-24 Attitude toward Divorce (Thurstone, 1929-1934)

3-25 A Divorce Opinionnaire (Hardy, 1957)

3-26 The Custodial Mental Illness Ideology (CMI) Scale
    (Gilbert and Levinson, 1956)

3-27 The Psychotherapy-Sociotherapy Ideology (PSI) Scale
    (Sharif and Levinson, 1957)

3-28 Medication Attitudes (Gorham and Sherman, 1961)

3-29 Attitude toward Earning a Living (Hinckley and Hinckley,
    1939)

3-30 Attitude toward Work Relief as a Solution to the Financial
    Depression (Hinckley and Hinckley, 1939)

3-31 Attitude toward Farming (Myster, 1944)

3-32 Attitude toward Any Practice (Bues, 1934)

3-33 Attitude toward Any Home-making Activity (Kellar, 1934)

3-34 Attitude toward Any Occupation (H.E. Miller, 1934)

Social Issues   4-1 Attitude toward Birth Control (Wang and Thurstone, 1931)
and Problems
    4-2 Birth Control (Scale BC) Scale (Wilke, 1934)

Social Issues
and Problems
(continued)

4-3　Attitude toward Menstruation (McHugh and Wasser, 1959)

4-4　Attitude toward Movies (Thurstone, 1930)

4-5　Attitudes toward Safe Driving:　Siebrecht Attitude Scale (Siebrecht, 1941)

4-6　The Academic Freedom Survey (Academic Freedom Committee, American Civil Liberties Union, 1954)

4-7　Opinions about Mental Illness (Cohen and Struening, 1959)

4-8　The Socialized Medicine Attitude Scale (Mahler, 1953)

4-9　Attitude toward Censorship Scale (Rosander and Thurstone, 1931)

4-10 Attitude toward the　Constitution of the United States (Rosander and Thurstone, 1931)

4-11 Attitude toward Capital Punishment (Balogh and Mueller, 1960)

4-12 Attitude toward Capital Punishment (Thurstone, 1932)

4-13 Attitude toward Punishment of Criminals (Wang and Thurstone, 1931)

4-14 Attitude toward School Integration (IA) Scale:　Form 1 (Greenberg, Chase, and Cannon, 1957)

4-15 Attitude toward Segregation Scale (Rosenbaum and Zimmerman, 1959)

4-16 The Segregation Scale (Peak, Morrison, Spivak, and Zinnes, 1956)

4-17 The Desegregation Scale (Kelley, Ferson, and Holtzman, 1958)

4-18 Attitude toward Accepting Negro Students in College (Grafton, 1964)

4-19 Relation between Religion and Psychiatry Scale (Webb and Kobler, 1961)

4-20 The Vivisection Questionnaire (Molnar, 1955)

4-21 Attitude toward Employment of Older People (Kirchner, Lindbom, and Patterson, 1952)

4-22 The (Work Related) Change Scale (Trumbo, 1961)

688

Social Issues   4-23 Attitude toward Receiving Relief (Hinckley and Hinckley,
and Problems   1939)
(continued)
                    4-24 Distribution of the Wealth (DW) Scale (Wilke, 1934)

                    4-25 Attitude toward Any Proposed Social Action (Remmers, 1934)

International   5-1 Internationalism Scale (Likert, 1932)
Issues
                    5-2 Nationalism Scale: Scale III (Ferguson, 1942)

                    5-3 A Survey of Opinions and Beliefs about International
                         Relations (Helfant, 1952)

                    5-4 The Internationalism-Nationalism (IN) Scale (Levinson,
                         1957)

                    5-5 The Worldmindedness Scale (Sampson and Smith, 1957)

                    5-6 The Patriotism (NP) Scale (Christiansen, 1959)

                    5-7 Attitude toward Patriotism Scale (Thurstone, 1929-1934)

                    5-8 Attitude toward Communism Scale (Thurstone, 1929-1934)

                    5-9 The Peterson War Scale (Thurstone, 1929-1934)

                    5-10 A Scale of Militarism-Pacifism (Droba, 1931a)

                    5-11 Attitude toward Defensive, Cooperative, and Aggressive
                         War (Day and Quackenbush, 1942)

                    5-12 Attitude toward War (Scale W) (Wilke, 1934)

                    5-13 A Scale for Measuring Attitude toward War (Stagner, 1942)

                    5-14 The M-P Opinion Scale (Gristle, 1940)

                    5-15 Attitude toward the Tariff (Thurstone, 1929-1934)

Abstract Concepts   6-1 The Education Scale (Rundquist and Sletto, 1936)

                    6-2 Attitudes toward Education (Glassey, 1945)

                    6-3 Attitudes toward Mathematics (Gladstone, Deal, and
                         Drevdahl, 1960)

                    6-4 Revised Math Attitude Scale (Aiken and Dreger, 1961)

                    6-5 Physical Education Attitude Scale (Wear, 1955)

                    6-6 Attitudes toward Physical Fitness and Exercise (Richard-
                         son, 1960)

Abstract Concepts (Continued)

6-7   Attitude toward the Law (Katz and Thurstone, 1931)

6-8   The Law Scale (Rundquist and Sletto, 1936)

6-9   The Ideological and Law-abidingness Scales (Gregory, 1939)

6-10 Attitudes toward Law and Justice (Watt and Maher, 1958)

6-11 Attitudes toward Evolution (Thurstone, 1931)

6-12 Death Attitudes Scale (Kalish, 1963)

6-13 Problem-solving Attitude Scale (Carey, 1958)

6-14 The Existence of God Scale (Scale G) (Wilke, 1934)

6-15 Attitude toward God: The Reality of God (Chave and Thurstone, 1931)

6-16 Attitude toward God: Influence on Conduct (Chave and Thurstone, 1931)

6-17 Attitudes toward Feminism Belief Patterns Scale (Kirkpatrick, 1936)

6-18 Attitude toward Freedom of Information (Rogers, 1955)

6-19 Attitudes toward Dependability: Attitude Scale for Clerical Workers (Dudycha, 1941)

6-20 Attitude toward the Aesthetic Value (Cohen, 1941)

6-21 Attitude toward Any School Subject (Silance and Remmers, 1934)

6-22 A Scale to Study Attitudes toward College Courses (Hand, 1953)

Political and Religious Attitudes

7-1   The Conservatism-Radicalism (C-R) Opinionnaire (Lentz, 1935)

7-2   The Florida Scale of Civic Beliefs (Kimbrough and Hines, 1963)

7-3   The Economic Conservatism Scale (Rundquist and Sletto, 1936)

7-4   Questionnaire on Politico-economic Attitudes (Sanai, 1950)

7-5   Conservatism-Radicalism (C-R) Battery (Centers, 1949; Case, 1963)

7-6   Tulane Factors of Liberalism-Conservatism Attitude Values Profile (Kerr, 1946)

Political and
  Religious
  Attitudes
(continued)

7-7   The Social Attitudes Scale (Kerlinger, 1965)

7-8   Political and Economic Progressivism (PEP) Scale (Newcomb, 1943)

7-9   Public Opinion Questionnaire (Edwards, 1941)

7-10 Religionism Scale; Scale I (Ferguson, 1944)

7-11 Belief Pattern Scale; Attitude of Religiosity (Kirkpatrick, 1949)

7-12 Religious Ideology Scale (Putney and Middleton, 1961)

7-13 The Religious Attitude Inventory (Ausubel and Schpoont, 1957)

7-14 The Religion Scale (Bardis, 1961)

7-15 Religious Belief Scale (Martin and Nichols, 1962)

7-16 A Survey of Attitudes toward Religion and Philosophy of Life (Funk, 1958)

7-17 Humanitarianism Scale: Scale II (Ferguson, 1944)

7-18 Belief Pattern Scale; Attitude of Humanitarianism (Kirkpatrick, 1949)

Ethnic and
  National Groups

8-1   Attitude toward the Negro (Hinckley, 1932)

8-2   Attitude toward Negroes (Thurstone, 1931)

8-3   Attitude toward the Negro Scale (Likert, 1932)

8-4   The Anti-Negro Scale (Steckler, 1957)

8-5   Negro Behavior Attitude Scale (Rosander, 1937)

8-6   Experiences with Negroes (Ford, 1941)

8-7   The Social Situations Questionnaire (Kogan and Downey, 1956)

8-8   The Anti-Semitism (A-S) Scale (Levinson and Sanford, 1944)

8-9   Attitude toward Jews Scale (Harlan, 1942)

8-10 Opinions on the Jews (Eysenck and Crown, 1949)

8-11 The Anti-white Scale (Steckler, 1957)

8-12 Attitude toward the German People (Thurstone, 1931)

Ethnic and
National Groups
(continued)

8-13 Attitude toward the Chinese (Thurstone, 1931)

8-14 A Survey of Opinions and Beliefs about Russia: The Soviet Union (Smith, 1946)

8-15 Ethnocentrism Scale (Levinson, 1949)

8-16 Intolerant-Tolerant (IT) Scale (Prentice, 1956)

8-17 The Social Distance Scale (Bogardus, 1925)

8-18 Scale to Measure Attitudes toward Defined Groups (Grice, 1935)

Significant
Others

9-1 Familism Scale (Bardis, 1959a)

9-2 The Family Scale (Rundquist and Sletto, 1936)

9-3 Attitudes toward Parents (Form F) (Itkin, 1952)

9-4 Parents' Judgment Regarding a Particular Child (Itkin, 1952)

9-5 The Self-Others Questionnaire (Phillips, 1951)

9-6 Acceptance of Self and Others (Berger, 1952)

9-7 People in General (Banta, 1961)

9-8 Attitude toward the Supervisor (AS) Scale (Schmid, Morsh, and Detter, 1956)

9-9 The Superior-Subordinate (SS) Scale (Chapman and Campbell, 1957)

9-10 Attitude toward the Supervisor (Nagle, 1953)

9-11 Attitude toward the Police (Chapman, 1953)

9-12 Attitude toward Probation Officers (Chapman, 1953)

9-13 Juvenile Delinquency Attitude (JDA) Scale (Alberts, 1962)

9-14 The "Value Inventory" (Jarrett and Sherriffs, 1953)

9-15 The Open Subordination of Women (OSW) Scale (Nadler and Morrow, 1959)

9-16 The Chivalry (C) Scale (Nadler and Morrow, 1959)

9-17 Attitudes toward Old People (Tuckman and Lorge, 1953a)

9-18 Older Workers Questionnaire (Tuckman and Lorge, 1952d)

Significant Others (continued)	9-19 Old People (OP) Scale (Kogan, 1961a)
	9-20 The "CI" Attitude Scale (Khanna, Pratt, and Gardiner, 1962)
	9-21 Attitudes toward Mentally Retarded People (Bartlett, Quay, and Wrightsman, 1960)
	9-22 Attitude to Blindness Scale (Cowen, Underberg, and Verrillo, 1958)
	9-23 Attitude toward Disabled People (ATDP) Scale (Yuker, Block, and Campbell, 1960)
	9-24 Medical Information Test (Perricone, 1964)
	9-25 Knowledge about Psychology (KAP) Test (Costin, 1963)
	9-26 An Attitude Scale for Measuring Attitude toward Any Teacher (Hoshaw, 1935)
Social Institutions	10-1 Semantic Distance Questionnaire (Weaver, 1959)
	10-2 Faculty Morale Scale for Institutional Improvement (AAUP, 1963)
	10-3 Attitude toward College Fraternities (Banta, 1961)
	10-4 Attitudes toward Mental Hospitals (Souelem, 1955)
	10-5 Attitudes Relating to the State Hospital (Pratt, Giannitrapani, and Khanna, 1960)
	10-6 Counseling Attitude Scale (Form, 1955)
	10-7 Attitude toward Legal Agencies (Chapman, 1953)
	10-8 Attitude toward Labor Scale (Newcomb, 1939)
	10-9 IRC (Industrial Relations Center) Union Attitude Questionnaire (Uphoff and Dunnette, 1956)
	10-10 Scale for Management Attitude toward Union (Stagner, Chalmers, and Derber, 1958)
	10-11 Scale for Union Attitude toward Management (Stagner, Chalmers, and Derber, 1958)
	10-12 About Your Company (Storey, 1955)
	10-13 Scales to Measure Attitudes toward the Company, Its Policies and Its Community Contributions (Riland, 1959)

Social
  Institutions
(continued)

10-14 Attitude toward Newspapers (Rogers, 1955)

10-15 Attitude toward the Church (Thurstone, 1931)

10-16 Attitudes and Beliefs of LDS Church Members toward their
      Church and Religion (Hardy, 1949)

10-17 Attitude toward Any Institution (Kelley, 1934)

10-18 High School Attitude Scale (Remmers, 1960)

694

SCALES DESCRIBED IN MILLER'S <u>HANDBOOK OF</u>
<u>RESEARCH DESIGN AND SOCIAL MEASUREMENT</u>

SECTION A. SOCIAL STATUS

1. Alba M. Edwards' Social-Economic Grouping of Occupations
2. Revised Occupational Rating Scale from W.L. Warner, M. Keeker, and
    K. Eells's Index of Status Characteristics
3. Hatt-North Occupational Prestige Ratings
4. Warner's Evaluated Participation Method of Social Class Measurement
5. Chapin's Social Status (Living Room) Scale, Revised 1952
6. Sewell's Short Form of the Farm Socioeconomic Status Scale

SECTION B. GROUP STRUCTURE AND DYNAMICS

1. Hemphill's Index of Group Dimensions
2. Bales's Interaction Process Analysis
3. Seashore's Group Cohesiveness Index
4. Sociometry Scales of Sociometric Choice and Sociometric Preference
5. Bogardus Social Distance Scale

SECTION C. MORALE AND JOB SATISFACTION

1. Short Form of the Minnesota Survey of Opinions (General Adjustment
    and Morale Scales)
2. The Science Research Associates Employee Inventory
3. Morse Indexes of Employee Satisfaction
4. Guttman Scales of Military Base Morale
5. Brayfield and Rothe's Index of Job Satisfaction

SECTION D. COMMUNITY

1. Community Attitude Scale
2. Community Solidarity Index
3. Community Rating Schedule
4. Scorecard for Community Services Activity

SECTION E. SOCIAL PARTICIPATION

1. Chapin's Social Participation Scale, 1952 Edition
2. Leisure Participation and Enjoyment
3. Bernard's Neighboring Practices Schedule
4. A Guttman Scale for Measuring Women's Neighborliness
5. Citizen Political Action Schedule

SECTION F.   LEADERSHIP IN THE WORK ORGANIZATION

1. Leadership Opinion Questionnaire
2. Supervisory Behavior Description
3. Work Patterns Profile

SECTION G.   IMPORTANT ATTITUDE SCALES

1. Wants and Satisfaction Scale
2. Social Insight Scale
3. Guttman-Type Scales for Union and Management Attitudes toward
    Each Other
4. Perception of Internal Communist Danger
5. Willingness to Tolerate Nonconformists
6. Semantic Differential

SECTION H.   FAMILY AND MARRIAGE

1. Marriage-Prediction Schedule and Marriage-Adjustment Schedule

SECTION I.   PERSONALITY MEASUREMENTS

1. Minnesota Multiphasic Personality Inventory (MMPI)
2. Authoritarian Personality (F) Scale, Forms 45 and 40

INDEX OF NAMES

A

Abelson, H. 426, 437
Adorno, T.W. 83, 105, 108, 116, 203, 245, 248, 303, 321, 322, 403, 404
Agger, R.E. 441. 445, 475, 476, 479
Alford, R. 163
Allport, G.W. 123, 124, 208, 209
Almond, G.A. 441. 442, 444, 446, 448, 471
American Psychological Association. 20, 22
Athanasiou, R. 190
Atkinson, T. 285, 286

B

Baerwaldt, I. 81, 87, 154
Banerjee, D. 187, 188, 202
Bell, W. 391
Berelson, B. 423, 426, 434, 438
Bettleheim, B. 208, 209
Biggar, J. 95
Blalock, H.M. 468, 469
Bogardus, E.S. 293, 295, 297, 298, 242, 243
Boldt, W.J. 81, 145
Bonjean, C. 8, 22, 268, 679, 682-684
Bosworth, C.A. 389, 392
Boudon, R. 468, 469
Brink, W. 203, 209
Buchanan, W. 242, 243

C

Campbell, A. 18, 22, 79, 90, 94, 95, 96, 187, 191, 192, 279, 296, 411, 419,
    423, 433, 441, 456, 459, 461, 463, 465, 466, 467, 475, 476, 479, 480, 487,
    539, 654
Cantril, H. 150, 242, 243, 263
Case, H. 102
Centers, R. 80, 82, 102, 103, 116, 412
Chave, E.J. 116
Christiansen, B. 6, 280, 288, 331, 332, 339, 351
Christie, R. 13, 22, 83, 90, 249, 479, 480
Converse, P. 1, 3, 79, 90, 95, 191, 192, 296, 419, 456, 495, 487
Cook, S. 203, 204, 206, 209, 240
Coombs, C. 390, 391, 401
Cronbach, L. 4, 20, 22

698

D

Day, D. 331, 334, 383
Dobriner, W.A. 389, 390, 403
Dombrose, L. 331, 332, 370
Doob, L. 80, 89, 90
Durlak, J. 80, 88, 90
Dye, T. 389, 397

E

Edwards, A. 13, 22, 86
Eels, K. 408
Erskine, H. 412
Eysenck, H.J. 80, 83, 113, 114, 116

F

Ferguson, L.W. 331, 333, 377
Fessler, P. 391
Fisher, B. 189, 190
Fiske, D. 18, 22
Ford, R.R. 208, 461
Frenkel-Brunswick, E. 108, 322, 404

G

Gallup International Incorporated. 338, 497
Garrison, K.C. 303
Gaudet, H. 423, 426, 434, 438
Getzels, J.W. 203, 207, 265, 266, 270
Gibbs, J. 391
Gleser, G. 4, 20, 22
Goldstein, M.S. 441, 445, 476, 479
Grace, H.A. 280, 288, 331, 332, 353
Grigg, C.M. 124, 161, 162, 179, 444, 475, 476
Gristle, M. 334, 338
Gullo, P. 322
Gurin, G. 192, 296, 433, 459, 461, 463, 466, 467, 476, 480

H

Haer, J.L. 389, 390, 408
Hammond, K.R. 279, 285, 329
Handy, U. 135
Harding, J. 5, 203, 204, 206, 210, 211, 223, 224, 241
Harper, M. 85, 145, 146
Harris, L. 203, 209
Harrison, A. 322
Hartley, E. 242, 243
Hartley, R. 242, 243

Hartmann, G. 80, 84, 126
Hartry, A. 279, 281, 309
Head, K.B. 190
Hefner, R. 279, 282, 283, 285, 286, 315, 317
Helfant, K. 331, 333, 374
Henry, A.F. 459, 461
Hero, A. 3, 4, 335, 338
Hetzler, S.A. 81, 86, 150
Hicks, J. 80, 84, 119
Hill, R. 8, 22, 268, 679, 682, 684
Hinckley, E.B. 203, 207, 208, 777
Hoffman, P. 453
Hovland, C.I. 207, 277
Hoyt, G.C. 351
Huffman, J. 80, 83, 116
Hyman, H. 108, 109, 205, 209, 249

I

Inkeles, A. 108, 109, 205, 209, 249

J

Jacobson, S. 579
Jahoda, M. 83, 90, 249
Janowitz, M. 208, 209, 406
Jennings, M. 389, 390, 400
Jonassen, C. 391

K

Katz, E. 423, 425, 436
Kaufman, W.C. 360, 361
Kaya, E. 99
Kerlinger, F. 82, 98, 99
Kerr, W.A. 80, 84, 123
Key, V.O. 296
Kilpatrick, F.P. 80, 151, 263
Kilpatrick, W.H. 127
Komorita, S. 208, 209
Kornhauser, A. 189, 190
Kubany, A.J. 187, 188, 200

L

Lane, R. 412
Lazarsfeld, P. 404, 423, 425, 426, 434, 436, 438
Lentz, R. 80, 81, 84, 134, 135, 141
Lerner, D. 80, 88, 90
Levinson, D.J. 108, 279, 281, 306, 322, 331, 333, 370, 404
Likert, R. 79, 90, 208, 321, 322, 397, 398
Lindauer, F. 13, 22
Litt, E. 441, 444, 475
Lutzker, D.R. 279, 285, 321

M

Marvick, D. 389
Maslow, A. 83, 117
Matthews, D.R. 95, 96, 143, 203, 296, 258, 260, 262, 411, 413, 423, 424, 427, 441, 444, 446, 447, 468, 469, 471, 473
McClintock, C.G. 321, 322
McClosky, H. 6, 49, 80, 81, 82, 94, 95, 124, 161, 170, 171, 279, 280, 293, 294, 441, 442. 453, 468
McLemore, S. 8, 22, 268, 679, 682, 684
McQuail, D. 85, 90
Meeker, M. 408
Menzel, H. 447
Merton, R. 389, 390, 391, 403, 404
Meyer, P. 258
Milbrath, L. 425, 426
Miller, D.C. 8, 22, 334, 338, 391, 680, 690-695
Miller, W.E. 191, 192, 296, 419, 433, 456, 459, 461, 463, 466, 467, 476, 480
Morgan, J. 81, 87, 154
Murphy, G. 79, 90, 321, 322, 398

N

National Opinion Research Corporation. 335, 338
Nettler, G. 80, 83, 116
Newcomb, T. 86
Noble, L. 161, 162, 184
Noble, R. 161, 162, 184

O

O'Hara, R. 453
Opinion Research Corporation. 87, 88, 90, 155, 159, 187, 193
Osgood, C.E. 3, 22, 331, 333, 380
Oskamp, S. 279, 281, 309

P

Pace, R. 81, 85, 142, 143
Pearl, S.A. 441, 445, 476, 479
Photiadis, J.D. 95
Pickard, P. 81, 85, 86, 148
Prothro, J.W. 95, 96, 124, 143, 161, 162, 178, 203, 206, 258, 260, 262, 411, 413, 423, 424, 427, 441, 444, 446, 447, 468, 469, 471, 473, 475, 476
Putney, S. 331, 332, 360, 361

Q

Quackenbush, O.F. 331, 334, 383

R

Riecken, H.Q. 303
Robinson, J. 189, 190, 279, 282, 283, 285, 286, 315, 317, 411, 412, 415, 417, 579
Robinson, W.S. 423, 425, 434
Rogers, E. 88, 90, 423, 425, 426, 436, 437, 438
Roper, E. 423, 424, 431
Rorer, L. 12, 22
Rosenau, J. 294
Rosenberg, M.V. 187, 188, 193
Rosenthal, I. 21, 22
Rugg, W. 426, 437
Rundquist, E. 84, 86, 143

S

Sampson, D.R. 279, 286, 302, 306
Sanai, M.S. 81, 85, 86, 148
Sanford, R.N. 108, 322, 404
Satinder, P.K. 303
Schonbar, R.A. 161, 162, 182
Schultze, O. 389, 390, 406
Schuman, H. 5, 203, 204, 206, 210, 211, 223, 224, 241
Schwartz, M. 203, 209
Scoble, H. 164
Scott, W.A. 6, 16, 22, 279, 287, 288, 335, 338
Sears, D. 412
Selznick, G. 80, 81, 91
Shaw, M. 8, 22, 86, 90, 98, 207, 208, 209, 277, 680, 685-693
Sheatsley, P. 108, 109, 203, 204, 205, 209, 236, 249
Sherif, M. 207, 277
Shevky, E. 391
Shimberg, B. 279, 285, 326
Singer, J.D. 307
Sirageldin, I. 81, 87, 154
Sletto, R.F. 86, 143
Smith, D. 13, 22, 80, 88
Smith, H.P. 279, 281, 302, 306
Snider, J. 3, 22
Stagner, R. 331, 333, 334, 377, 380, 385
Stanton, F.N. 404
State Citizens Council. 391
Steckler, G. 207, 209
Steinberg, S. 80, 81, 91
Stokes, D.E. 95, 191, 296, 419, 456, 474
Stouffer, S. 161, 162, 163, 167, 498
Strand, S. 322
Stroud, J.B. 81, 145

T

Thompson, G.A.   377
Thurstone, L.   116
Trenaman, J.   85, 90
Triandis, H.   205, 209, 242, 243
Triandis, L.   205, 209
Turner, J.   453, 454

V

Verba, S.   331, 332, 366, 423, 441, 442, 444, 446, 448, 471
Vernon, P.E.   123
Voor, J.J.   124

W

Waisenan, F.   80, 88, 90
Walsh, J.J.   203, 207, 265, 266, 270
Warner, W.L.   408
Warren, W.E.   95
Westie, F.   203, 207, 265, 266, 267, 268
Withey, S.   189, 190, 334, 335, 338
Woodmansee, J.   203, 204, 240
Woodward, J.L.   423, 424, 431
Wright, J.   8, 22, 80, 84, 86, 90, 98, 119, 207, 208, 209, 277, 680, 685-693
Wrightsman, L.S.   13, 22, 203, 206, 209, 265, 271, 279, 281, 298

ADDENDUM

The following two scales, the first by Milbrath and the second by Scheuch, came to our attention too late to be included in Chapter 11 of this volume.

The Milbrath scale of "inputs to the political system" consists of general participation in politics, making it more similar to the Woodward-Roper and Matthews-Prothro scale in Chapter 11 than to the scales of Campbell, et al. and Robinson which deal with activity during a specific campaign. Milbrath's scale is a promising start in the direction of a multidimensional measure of political participation. As yet, however, exact scoring instructions and norms on the instrument as a scaling device are not available. Milbrath does present some interesting data on the scale's reliability and relative freedom from agreement response set.

Scheuch's Opinion Leadership scale is based more on evidence of associated political activity than on actual opinion leadership. That is, the scale assumes that greater participation in associations and greater use of the mass media will result in an individual's being an opinion leader. There is sound research evidence to substantiate this assumption (and Scheuch himself presents data showing a fairly strong relationship between participation and political knowledge). However, evidence relating this measure to reported or observed opinion leadership is needed before a proper evaluation of this scale is possible.

INPUTS TO THE POLITICAL SYSTEM (Milbrath 1968)

Variable   This measure of general political participation is based
                on the premise that "beliefs are important determinants
                of the political behavior of ordinary citizens."

Description   There are a total of 21 inputs to the political system.
                In this investigation, each of these inputs was listed
                separately on a card and the respondent was told to place
                each statement into one of four piles headed:

                        Things you do regularly   (4)
                        Things you do fairly often   (3)
                        Things you seldom do   (2)
                        Things you never do at all   (1)

                The numbers in parentheses refer to the numerical value
                associated with each response.

                In addition to sorting the 21 cards under this "real"
                condition, respondents were also asked to place the
                statements under an "ideal" condition into one of the
                following four categories:

                        Things you feel it is essential to do   (4)
                        Things you have an important responsibility to do (3)
                        Things you have some responsibility to do   (2)
                        Things you feel you have no responsibility to do (1)

Sample   An unspecified sample of about 960 residents of the
                Buffalo, New York area were interviewed. Of these,
                about 260 were Negro and about 700 white.

Reliability/   The author reports the following factors emerging from a
  Homogeneity   factor analysis of the 21 items:

                1) Party and Campaign Participation (Items 1, 9, 10,
                   13, 14, and 19)
                2) Protest and Question (Items 4, 5, 6, and 17)
                3) Teach Children (Items 11, 15, and 18)

                The following inter-item correlation matrix is reported
                for five of the items in the first factor:

	1	9	10	14	19
1) Participate between elections	X	.60	.31	.44	.48
9) Take part in campaign		X	.39	.49	.46
10) Engage in discussions			X	.52	.27
14) Inform others				X	.35
19) Join political party					X

Validity   No data bearing directly on validity are reported. The
                    author presents the following findings which indirectly
                    relate to validity.

                        1) The substantial correlations (in the .30 to .60
                           range) between responses on the real and ideal
                           card sorts

                        2) A substantial correlation (tau-beta = .57) be-
                           tween the card sort and an open-ended question on
                           the same topic

                        3) Some laudible evidence on the lack of systematic
                           bias due to agreement response set.

Location   Milbrath, L. "The Nature of Political Beliefs and the
                    Relationship of the Individual to the Government."
                    Paper delivered at the Midwest Political Science As-
                    sociation, Chicago, Illinois, May 2-3, 1968. To appear
                    in the November, 1968 issue of The American Behavioral
                    Scientist.

Administration   The real and ideal sorts together take about 10 minutes
                    to administer. The author does not give any special
                    instructions for scoring the items as if they comprised
                    a scale. This is true both for all 21 items and those
                    subsets which comprise the factors discussed above un-
                    der Reliability/Homogeneity.

Results and   In addition to inputs, Milbrath has constructed a similar
Comments   set of 23 statements dealing with "outtakes from the
                    political system." Respondents also sort these statements
                    into four "real" piles and four "ideal" piles. The
                    statements and piles are listed below after the input
                    items.

                    Milbrath offers the following tentative generalizations
                    from this study:

                    Most people are plugged into the political system in at
                    least a minimal way; they pay taxes, they are loyal, they
                    try to keep informed, they try to vote, and they try to
                    teach their children to be good citizens. More than half
                    of the people feel that their duty as a citizen ends there.
                    Interestingly, people who take this minimal view of their
                    political inputs are somewhat more likely than others to
                    wish to confine governmental outputs (outtakes) to stan-
                    dard old-fashioned governmental duties such as keeping
                    public order (minimal inputs and minimal outtakes are
                    significantly correlated).

                    A minority of people feel some responsibility to take an
                    active role in politics and an even smaller percentage
                    actually do so. Conventional participation by this
                    minority seems to have kept the political system func-
                    tioning reasonably adequately up to now. For a very small

group, non-conventional participation (demonstrations
and riots) may be used, Negroes being somewhat more
willing to do this than Whites. In fact, our data show
that Negroes are somewhat more likely than Whites to
use both conventional and non-conventional means of
political participation. Negroes seem to be developing
a sense of racial identity and a sense of political
skill and effectiveness that they did not possess a few
years ago. At the same time one can see from the outtakes data that Negroes are much less happy with the
performance of the political system than are Whites
while also believing that the system has greater responsibility to do things for them than the Whites are
likely to request.

One could expect, then, in the near future of American
city politics that Negroes will act increasingly as a
tight bloc, using both conventional and un-conventional
tactics, trying to get the political system to do many
things that more conventional and traditional Whites
will think inappropriate for government to do. The conflict will be intense and emotional and may significantly
transform the nature of government and the way that
citizens relate to their government.

INPUTS TO THE POLITICAL SYSTEM

	MEAN SCORES				TOTAL SAMPLE REAL-IDEAL CORRELATIONS
	Negro		White		
	Real	(Ideal)	Real	(Ideal)	
1. Participate in a political party between elections as well as at election time	1.72	(2.21)	1.69	(2.06)	.47
2. Keep informed about politics	2.75	(2.96)	3.01	(3.14)	.50
3. Vote in elections	3.46	(3.59)	3.39	(3.68)	.41
4. Send messages of support to political leaders when they are doing well	1.62	(2.24)	1.64	(2.22)	.38
5. Send protest messages to political leaders when they are doing badly	1.52	(2.19)	1.50	(2.13)	.38
6. Protest both vigorously and publicly if the government does something that is morally wrong	1.83	(2.43)	1.88	(2.28)	.43
7. Join in public street demonstrations	1.39	(1.56)	1.12	(1.21)	.59
8. Riot if necessary to get public officials to correct political wrongs	1.23	(1.43)	1.10	(1.19)	.44
9. Take an active part in political campaigns	1.69	(2.20)	1.58	(1.99)	.48
10. Engage in political discussion	2.34	(2.52)	2.40	(2.26)	.50
11. Teach my children the importance of give and take in the democratic way of life	3.11	(3.24)	3.09	(3.38)	.52
12. Pay all taxes	3.72	(3.69)	3.81	(3.79)	.37
13. Be a candidate for public office	1.23	(1.44)	1.14	(1.42)	.33
14. Inform others in my community about politics	2.10	(2.30)	1.91	(2.13)	.52
15. Teach my children to participate in politics beyond voting	2.15	(2.59)	2.05	(2.65)	.49
16. Have undivided loyalty and love for my country	3.67	(3.59)	3.71	(3.70)	.48
17. Question the legitimacy of regulations issued by authorities before obeying them	2.12	(2.25)	2.19	(2.36)	.51
18. Personally see to it that my children understand and accept the responsibilities of citizenship	3.14	(3.36)	3.15	(3.49)	.47
19. Join and support a political party	2.33	(2.63)	2.17	(2.49)	.48
20. Be a calming and informing influence in my own community	2.48	(2.71)	2.30	(2.63)	.51
21. Actively support community organizations	2.64	(2.96)	2.52	(2.76)	.51

N = about 260   N = about 700

POLITICAL OUTTAKES

1. Being careful in using public money and trust

2. Taking actions that make me proud of my country

3. Taking actions that make me proud of my city

4. Trying to even out differences in wealth and prestige

5. Arranging things so it is easy for citizens to move from place to place, job to job, class to class

6. Providing a chance to make a good living

7. Seeing to it that every man who wants a job can have a job

8. Insuring equal opportunity for citizens to participate in making political decisions

9. Providing protection and security

10. Providing public order: for example, traffic regulations

11. Securing civil rights and liberties for all

12. Providing justice for all

13. Providing national system of health insurance for people of all ages

14. Making it possible for a person to be heard when he feels he has something to say

15. Competently handling foreign affairs

16. Providing welfare services

17. Provide courts for resolving conflicts between private parties

18. Providing strong leadership

19. Arranging things so that business is left alone

20. Providing free university education for all who can qualify

21. Intervening to stop an individual or group from persecuting another individual or group

22. Providing stability in society even if it means slowing down the role of progress

23. Make it possible for a person with the means to live where he wishes to live.

POLITICAL OUTTAKES (Continued)

Real Sort Piles

1. Things the government does a <u>very</u> effective job of providing
2. Things the government does a <u>moderately</u> effective job of providing
3. Things the government is <u>not</u> <u>very</u> effective in providing
4. Things the government does <u>ineffectively</u> or not at all

Ideal Sort Piles

1. Things you feel it is <u>essential</u> for the government to do
2. Things the government has an <u>important</u> responsibility to do
3. Things the government has <u>some</u> responsibility to do
4. Things you believe the government should <u>not</u> attempt to do <u>at</u> <u>all</u>

OPINION LEADERSHIP (Scheuch 1960)

Variable   This is a tentatively proposed index of opinion leader-
                  ship developed on a West German sample.

Description   The intention of the scale was "to separate a pre-
                  supposed proportion of roughly 10% of the adult popula-
                  tion who can be considered active in the sense of
                  opinion moulding." Two sets of criteria make up the
                  scale:

                       a) political and organizational participation
                          and

                       b) exposure to the mass media.

Sample   An unspecified sample of 1843 persons in West Germany
                  were interviewed for empirical data on the scale.

Reliability/   The following table shows the relation between the two
   Homogeneity   criteria used in the index:

                                           Participation

                  Media Used   Very Active   Active   Inactive

                       4   62   73   79
                       3   94   117   124
                       2   106   130   236
                       1   60   122   281
                       0   17   71   271

                  The correlation (Yule's Y) between these two criteria
                  is .45.

Validity   No data bearing directly on the validity of the scale
                  are reported, although a definite relation between par-
                  ticipation and amount of information was found. While
                  39% of those who were "very active" scored as very well
                  informed, only 5% of those qualifying as "inactive"
                  scored as very well informed.

Location   Scheuch, E. "Determination of Opinion Leadership." Un-
                  published paper available from the author who is at the
                  Department of Sociology, Köln University, West Germany.

Administration   The following scoring scheme for participation was em-
                  ployed, with the number of respondents in the sample
                  giving the response pattern in parentheses.

Functionaries	Classification
Association members-- attend meetings	Very active (61)
Association members-- do not attend meetings	Very active (24)
Non-members-- attend meetings	Very active (19)
Non-members-- do not attend meetings	Active (15)

Non-office holders

Association members-- attend meetings	Very active (235)
Association members-- do not attend meetings	Active (259)
Non-members-- attend meetings	Active (239)
Non-members-- do not attend meetings	Inactive (991)

This leads to a distribution of participation with 18% scored as very active, 28% active, and 54% inactive.

The following scoring scheme for opinion leadership was employed:

	Participation		
Media Used	Very Active	Active	Inactive
4	opinion leader	opinion leader	leader
3	opinion leader	leader	leader
2	leader	leader	apathetic
1	leader	apathetic	apathetic
0	apathetic	apathetic	apathetic

Under this scheme, 12% of the respondents scored as opinion leaders, 33% as leaders, and 55% as apathetic.

Section I

PARTICIPATION

1.) Do you perhaps pursue any other kind of activity or hold any other kind of office outside your job--such as listed on this card?

	(As councillor in rural areas,
	(city councillor, or county representative
	(In a refugee organization
	(In a professional or trade organization
	(As village or county selectman
6,7%	(As a representative on the shop committee
	(In a trade union
	(In a political party
	(In a youth organization
	(In a fraternity
	(In a business organization
6,8%	In a voluntary association or club
86,5%	None of this

1a.) (If "none of this") --or do you perhaps pursue some similar activity or office which is not listed here?

0,6%	Yes
85,9%	No

2.) About how often do you attend meetings or gatherings at which also economic or political questions are discussed?

3%)		Frequently
7%)	27%	Occasionally
17%)		Rarely
73%		Never

3.) Are you a member of a club, association, trade union or political party?

20%)		Member of voluntary association
12%)	35%	Member of trade union
3%)		Member of a political party
69%		No membership

Section II

MEDIA USAGE

(Exact questions are not reported)